Personality and Interpersonal Behavior

Personality and Interpersonal Behavior

Robert Freed Bales
Harvard University

HOLT, RINEHART AND WINSTON
New York   Chicago   San Francisco   Atlanta   Dallas
Montreal   Toronto   London   Sydney

To Dorothy, my wife,
with love and appreciation

Copyright © 1970 by Holt, Rinehart and Winston, Inc.
All rights reserved
Library of Congress Catalog Card Number: 71–84682
SBN: 03-080450-7
Printed in the United States of America
2 3 4 5 6 7 8 9

Preface

Almost twenty years ago I presented a method for the study of small groups called Interaction Process Analysis. Since that time a great deal of experience with the method has accumulated. Interaction process analysis is revised in this book and made part of a general approach to the understanding of personalities and groups in their natural settings. Other methods are coordinated with it which are less technical and more easily adapted to varied settings. The methods and concepts are embedded in a general interpretive and diagnostic theory for practical use not only by researchers, but also by group leaders, administrators, managers, teachers, and therapists, as well as informal leaders and group participants of all kinds.

In addition to the revision of interaction process analysis, which focuses upon overt interpersonal behavior, a method is presented for analyzing attitude and value statements that may form the basis and rationale for group norms, and a related method for recognizing and interpreting group fantasy themes. These approaches, once learned, become a part of one's intuitive mode of understanding. They need not be applied in technical form in order to be helpful. In intuitive form they may be used currently in the guidance of one's understanding as a participating member of a group. They also help to predict and understand the impressions group members form of each other. A method is presented for eliciting the interpersonal perceptions of group members after meetings, or for use by the participant observer.

From a systematic use of observations and impressions the interested observer or group member may obtain predictions as to how each individual in the group might score on a variety of standard personality tests. Research findings concerning personality tests are integrated with the general approach, but emphasis is laid upon first-hand observation in natural situations as the starting point for understanding personalities, rather than upon tests, questionnaires, or experimental situations.

The interpretive and diagnostic theory takes the form of a three-dimensional spatial model which may be used to visualize and describe the positions of the participants in a group, and to infer what their relations with each other are likely to be. The spatial model is based upon the statistical methods of factor analysis. An extensive body of new research findings and several new theories are integrated into the general framework. The research results, and the theories, however, are organized for practical application. They are presented as concrete descriptions of kinds of group members and personalities found in different parts of the group space and their typical relationships with each other. In this way, a great mass of facts is reduced to a compact form, more easily remembered and applied.

In line with the emphasis on practical application, this book also includes information about a type of group especially adapted to teaching and learning about personality and interpersonal behavior: academic self-analytic groups which deal with their own processes and internal problems rather than with external tasks. Hopefully, enough information is provided to encourage the formation of college courses involving group self-analysis.

It seems likely that in time self-analytic group methods will be applied in courses over a range of subject matters. One way to combine emphasis on a given subject matter with some analysis of what is going on psychologically and socially in the discussion group is to start the discussions with prepared written cases dealing with the given subject. The mixture of case-analysis with self-analysis is perfectly feasible. It remains to be seen how restricted group self-analytic methods may be with different ages, intellectual levels, occupational and socioeconomic levels, with different cultural groups and with different applied interests or allied subject matters. It is also true that even in the liberal arts college setting the self-analytic group organized as a regular course needs the support of a surrounding culture of students, professors, and administrators who accept the subject matter and the procedure as appropriate and legitimate. In many educational settings, case-analysis may be a helpful mode of entry into the use of groups more exclusively focused on self-analysis.

Much remains to be done to make more recognizable and generalizable the many unexpected and fascinating aspects of experience in self-analytic groups. Increased psychological insight is one of the goals participants seek, but their experience seems often to have artistic, aesthetic, and religious implications for them as well. That such groups meet some fundamental psychological and social needs is strongly suggested by the rapid spread of sensitivity training groups in applied settings over the past few years. They are only beginning to be known in college settings.

Varieties and adaptations of the self-analytic group probably have an important part to play in general humanistic education, as well as in many applied settings. It is hoped that this book may suggest how self-analytic groups can be introduced into the regular liberal arts curriculum, and how the raw experiences they provide may be transmuted into the more generalized kind of knowledge usually sought in psychology, sociology, and social anthropology.

R. F. B.

Cambridge, Mass.
September 1969

Acknowledgments

Many of my debts, both intellectual and practical, in the formation of the present book go very far back. I have been engaged in the empirical work upon which the book is based, one way or another, since about 1942, when I established contact with the local Alcoholics Anonymous group and was permitted to observe their meetings with the hope of getting some inkling of the astonishing motivational changes they seemed to be bringing about. Some method was needed by which one could study the structure and development of groups, particularly the relations between individual persons and the way in which their personalities and their relations might play a part in therapy, re-education, behavior and personality change. Eventually I turned to the laboratory and the experimental formation of groups as the setting in which methods for the study of these basic processes might most easily be developed.

Much stimulation and critically important help came from my assistants and students during the period in which we studied experimentally formed groups. Fred Strodtbeck collaborated in the early development and testing of interaction process analysis. John Evans and Sigmund Gruber were among the first to try it out on widely different kinds of groups outside the laboratory. Early assistants whose substantive contributions, as well as statistical help, are embedded in the present work, include Christophe Heinicke, Theodore Mills, and Philip Slater, followed a little later by Bernard Cohen, Joseph Berger, Michael Olmstead, Mary Roseborough Salisbury, Nathan Altshuler, Warren Bachelis, Robert Avery, and Richard Mann. Others of the latter part of the laboratory period when attention was shifting to the study of self-analytic groups include Lindsey Churchill, Paul Breer, Philip Bonacich, Philip Stone, Dexter Dunphy, and Daniel Ogilvie.

Two colleagues in the Laboratory of Social Relations, A. Paul Hare and Edgar F. Borgatta, played a very special role in helping to summarize and bring to publication the results of the preceding period of observational work, together with results of their work, and to clarify the relations of approaches based upon the observation of social interaction to the literature in the small group field. The results of this collaboration are represented in a series of joint papers and in a collection of readings. I am also indebted to both of them for helpful criticism on the manuscript of the present book.

My most extensive and substantial debt in the formation of the present work is to my colleague Arthur S. Couch, formerly a student and research assistant, who worked with me over a number of years in close and equal collaboration. Most of the ideas in this book owe something to him, some of them a great deal. He performed most of the factor analyses upon which the theoretical synthesis of the work is based. Without what I learned of factor analysis from him, without his original conception of the importance of dealing with the whole correlation space rather than just with selected factors, and without his incredible labors in coming to terms with two generations of constantly evolving and changing computers, I could never have arrived at the realization of the present model. His work, containing a great deal of the original data, exists as an unpublished dissertation at Harvard.

By degrees, the focus of my work shifted from the experimental formation of groups in the laboratory to the observation of more naturally formed groups in the classroom. Two of my former assistants, Theodore Mills and Philip Slater, introduced me to an exciting new venture in which they had become involved as teachers: an experimental course, then in the General Education program at Harvard, known as Human Relations, under the direction of Hugh Cabot. The forerunner of the course had been started in 1946 by Dean Donham of the Business School, and was then based upon the discussion of concrete cases in problems of business administration. As time went on students among others wrote cases, and emphasis changed to family problems, roommate situations at college, and other types of problems of interest and concern to undergraduates.

To Hugh Cabot I owe my introduction to case-analysis as a way of teaching about human behavior, and to him I also owe my first recognition of the tremendous variety of fascinating psychological events that occur in discussion groups engaged in case-analysis and make such groups so well worth studying. It was for this reason that I used discussion of human relations cases as the standard kind of group task in most of my studies of experimentally formed groups. In 1954 I began teaching in the Human Relations course, and later took administrative responsibility for the course. Case analysis of the earlier course gradually evolved into group self-analysis, the focus of the present course, the format for which is given in Appendix 6.

Charles Whitlock, Philip Slater, and Theodore Mills were my earliest colleagues, indeed my teachers, as instructors in the case-analysis course. These three, and Hugh Cabot, helped me to withstand the pressures one encounters in groups where structure is low and adventure is high. Out of our endless discussions of what was going on in our respective groups, I formed my first conceptions as to how to teach in such groups, what to expect, how to remain silent, how to listen, and how and when to interpret.

My conceptions of teaching in self-analytic groups were further developed by instruction in psychoanalytic theory and technique at the Boston Psychoanalytic Institute, where I was trained as an academic (nonmedical) candidate for purposes of research. I owe a great debt of gratitude to my teachers at the Institute, particularly to Grete Bibring, Edward Bibring, Alfred Valenstein, Helen Tartakoff, Elizabeth Zetzel, and Elvin Semrad. I regard myself as a psychoanalytic theorist in the personality area, although I admit I avoid psychoanalytic language for the most part in my writing since it seems to put so many academic psychologists into an unreceptive frame of mind. My conceptions of good technique in the conduct of self-analytic groups are more or less direct adaptations of the classical Freudian approach to psychoanalysis, applied to the group situation. There are, of course, many critical differences between individual analysis and the self-analytic group. I shall have occasion later, I hope, to write on problems of technique in the conduct of self-analytic groups.

My younger colleagues in the evolving course, especially Theodore Mills, Philip Slater, Richard Mann, and Dexter Dunphy, have written on various aspects of the course. Others who have taught in the course, Charles Whitlock, Daniel Ogilvie, Thomas Cottle, and Lane Conn, have made distinctive contributions to it. I have learned from all of these, as well as from our predecessors and visiting colleagues. One of our predecessors, William Perry, deserves special recognition for his formulation of the general humanistic and educational values of the course. Warren Bennis taught with us for one year, to our great benefit, and David Shapiro taught for several years. He brought to us, among other contributions, some of the influence of his mentor, Elvin Semrad. Our debt is great to Norman Zinberg, who especially helped shape the psychoanalytic aspects of the rationale of the course, and to Leo Berman, his colleague in a similar, though independent, educational venture.

The transition from the observation of laboratory task-oriented groups to participation in the unstructured, self-analytic group is a tremendous one, psychologically, for the academic social psychologist. Theodore Mills, perhaps more specifically than any of the group of colleagues engaged in making that transition, has faced up to these problems, formulated them, and made a determined effort to overcome them. He has recognized that there are problems, not only of personality and personal defenses of the researcher to be overcome, but also of philosophical and ethical orientation. I have benefitted much by his writing on these problems, recognition of which is so important in the training of teachers to work with self-analytic group methods.

To Philip Slater, I owe much inspiration in attempting to understand the cross-cultural, particularly the mythological overtones of events that occur in self-analytic groups. The self-analytic group is indeed a microcosm of societies and cultures. A given group is very limited, and like a jewel, reflects only tiny flashes, but the poetic observer will not miss the true and penetrating reflections that it gives. Not only the unusual situations studied in anthropology, but also certain aspects of our classical and literary past are sometimes astonishingly illuminated by experiences in self-analytic groups.

Students in the self-analytic group course have shaped its evolution through several college generations of magnificent effort, honesty, and insight in self-analysis. Their experiences and reflections have provided much of the groundwork for the present book. I am deeply grateful for their collaboration and for the satisfactions in teaching and learning they have given me. And I am equally grateful to the still earlier students who served as subjects in the many laboratory studies. I hope both students and subjects will find part of their labors preserved in this work and will experience some of the satisfaction in it that I feel in appreciation for their contribution.

In the preparation of the manuscript of the book I have been aided by Bertha I. Berry, Susan Swinburn, and Elizabeth Burnham, of the Center for the Behavioral Sciences at Harvard. I greatly appreciate their help, and also that of Stephen Cohen who read and criticised, to good effect, most of the manuscript, and helped to prepare part of the data for Chapter 3.

Finally, I should like to record my gratitude for the financial and organizational support for this research which has gone on for so many years. The Laboratory of Social Relations at Harvard University, now the Center for the Behavioral Sciences, has continuously provided physical facilities and logistic support. The Carnegie Foundation and the Rockefeller Foundation provided early financial support, as did the Ford Foundation at a later period. The RAND Corporation helped during one period. The Commonwealth Fund helped with my psychoanalytic education. Both the National Institutes of Health and the National Science Foundation have supported parts of the research. The John Hancock Life Insurance Company and both the M.I.T. and the Harvard Computing Centers deserve thanks for special services in the use of computers.

R. F. B.

Contents

PART III

APPENDICES

PART I

Methods
of Analyzing
Interpersonal Behavior

1

Introduction

The practical purpose of this book is to supplement a natural observational approach to the understanding of personalities and groups in everyday situations. When participating with other persons one cannot fall too far behind the natural flow of events to think things through, or else his participation in the group will suffer. Similarly one is not ordinarily in a position to ask his fellow group members to fill out psychological tests for his benefit in understanding—even if such a thing should occur to him. On the contrary, one must depend upon natural observation of himself and his fellow group members if he wishes to improve his understanding and effectiveness.

But if one really wishes to do so, nearly any group member can improve his understanding of what has just happened by thinking things over afterward. He can exercise his memory by systematic attempts to recall, and he can employ a technical inference-making model. One can train himself to observe and understand more effectively in natural interpersonal situations. This book is meant to help prolong one's thinking about periods of interaction just past, and to prepare for periods to come. It will ordinarily be used selectively, with a particular person or pair in a particular group as the focus of attention. In a typical case, perhaps, one will have just participated in a group or have been thinking about it. He may have a feeling of dissatisfaction. He may wonder why things have gone so badly—or on the other hand, he may be puzzled as to why they went so well. This book provides a way to begin to unravel the problem. Taking one person in the group (usually a person felt to figure prominently in the dilemma) as the beginning focus, this book then provides a set of questions that one may ask himself about that person. In the beginning of a process of analysis one depends, as best he can, upon his memory and his ill-defined feelings. Increased accuracy and refinement may be introduced in later stages, by application of more objective methods.

An illustrative list of questions, one short enough to be practical, is given in the Introductory Exercise below. Some of the questions may be unanswerable, because of a lack of information, or conflicting impressions, or perhaps because the question is simply not clear. A certain lack of clarity is inevitable at the beginning. Problems as to what the questions mean can be cleared up later, but even so, there will always be some questions for which a reasonably clear yes or no answer cannot be given. For the exercise, these questions are simply omitted.

Each question in the list, is built around some known facts from observation in previous studies. An easy way is provided to discover what these known facts are. Information from previous studies is arranged and compressed into a description of a set of types, found in Part II, called Types of Group Roles and their Value-Directions. Each type is given a name (such as type U, type P,) with a title suggesting the meaning or value-significance of the behavior of the individual for others in the group. For example, type U is said to be directed toward material success and power, type UN toward tough-minded assertiveness, type P toward equalitarianism, type F toward conservative group beliefs, and so on. The types are defined in terms of the way the acting person is perceived and evaluated by others in the group. These perceptions and evaluations depend upon his personality, his behavior, and his position in the group, as well as those of all the other members of the group. One might expect utter chaos with all this relativism of definition, but in many operating groups there is a surprising amount of consensus on the way in which most individual members are perceived and evaluated. The ratings an individual receives from others are usually related to his personality as well as his group role. If these basic generalizations are not true in some particular case, the present methods will not be feasible.

Each type is really an abstract theoretical construction, a factual compendium tied together with many inferences and a set of theories as to what things go together psychologically and sociologically, and why. The overall theory is based on facts, but it goes considerably beyond the facts. All the facts possible were included in the intellectual construction, but the gaps have been filled in with speculation where necessary, taking sufficient care to leave the interested reader a way to find out what the actual evidence is. Appendix 1 provides detailed information and evidence concerning each variable.

The type description is simply a way of saying that some given aspect of interpersonal behavior observable in a group is likely to be associated with something else not yet observed. One uses the type descriptions to guide further observation. After this rather dry and cautious statement it is perhaps worth assuring the reader that, in the process, he is likely to receive some satisfaction of his thirst to know "why." His understanding is likely to be improved about the particular situation, both about the personalities of the members involved, and the way they fit together or conflict. The answer to one's puzzled feeling is often given by the sudden insightful recognition of underlying connections he has neglected. He may be brought to wonder why he failed to recognize them in this particular instance. It may be because of his own position in the group, or his own personality, and he may recognize this also.

It is probably not possible to go so very far in the analysis of others in a group without undertaking some self-analysis as well. At any rate, self-analysis may be urged as an ethical responsibility. If knowledge of others to some extent gives power or potential power over them, then one should take care not to misuse such power. He should try to understand his own motives and evaluate them as carefully as he does those of others. Appendix 6 describes a format for an academic self-analytic group designed to create appropriate conditions for learning to analyze more effectively interpersonal behavior, including one's own, and to meet squarely the ethical problems involved in such an attempt (3;135). This book is addressed in the first instance to the members of such a self-analytic group, although it may be used appropriately, I hope, in many everyday contexts.

Since this book is meant to guide actual working efforts to understand particular persons in particular groups, it is most natural to address the reader directly in many places, as in the following exercise. The exercises throughout the book are designed to make the exposition more concrete and practically useful for the working reader. They need not be performed by the reader who is interested mainly in the intellectual content, though they may help. This book is actually a theoretical treatise in the form of a didactic handbook. It is hoped that it will serve both practical and theoretical purposes, and that the more theoretical reader will not be too much put off by the "how to do it" tone of the exposition.

INTRODUCTORY EXERCISE

For the purposes of the exercise attention should be focused on a person you hope to learn something more about, and the group within which you think it most relevant to describe him.

In order for the typological system to work optimally, select a group

INTERPERSONAL RATINGS, FORM A

1. Does he (or she) seem to *receive a lot of interaction* from others?
2. Does he seem *personally involved in the group*?
3. Does he seem *valuable for a logical task*?
4. Does he *assume responsibility for task leadership*?
5. Does he *speak like an autocratic authority*?
6. Does he seem *dominating*?
7. Does he seem to *demand pleasure and gratification*?
8. Does he seem to *think of himself as entertaining*?
9. Does he seem *warm and personal*?
10. Does he *arouse your admiration*?
11. Does he seem especially to be *addressed when others have serious opinions* about which they want confirmation?
12. Does he seem to stand for the most *conservative ideas and beliefs of the group*?
13. Does he always seem to try to speak *objectively*?
14. Does he seem to feel that his *individual independence* is very important?
15. Does he seem to *feel that others are generally too conforming* to conventional social expectations?
16. Does he seem to *reject religious belief generally*?
17. Do you feel *liking* for him or her?
18. Does he seem to *make others feel he admires them*?
19. Does he seem to believe that *equality and humanitarian concern* for others is important?
20. Does he seem very *introverted,* serious, shy, introspective?
21. Does he seem to believe that it is necessary to *sacrifice the self* for higher values?
22. Does he seem *resentful*?
23. Does he seem to accept *failure and withdrawal* for himself?
24. Does he seem to *withhold cooperation passively*?
25. Does he seem to *identify with some group of underprivileged persons*?
26. Does he tend to *devaluate himself*?

that spends some significant part of its time in trying to accomplish some task in conformity with expectations of an external authority. If a particular group has no such phases in its activities (such as a group of juvenile delinquents—a group which is negatively oriented in many important ways to external authority), some aspects of the system will probably not work well with it. Some of the questions (particularly those

KEY TO INTERPERSONAL RATING FORMS
(This key is used for Forms A, B, C.)

	No	Yes
1.	No = D	Yes = U
2.	No = DN	Yes = UP
3.	No = DNB	Yes = UPF
4.	No = DB	Yes = UF
5.	No = DPB	Yes = UNF
6.	No = DP	Yes = UN
7.	No = DPF	Yes = UNB
8.	No = DF	Yes = UB
9.	No = DNF	Yes = UPB
10.	No = N	Yes = P
11.	No = NB	Yes = PF
12.	No = B	Yes = F
13.	No = PB	Yes = NF
14.	No = P	Yes = N
15.	No = PF	Yes = NB
16.	No = F	Yes = B
17.	No = NF	Yes = PB
18.	No = UN	Yes = DP
19.	No = UNB	Yes = DPF
20.	No = UB	Yes = DF
21.	No = UPB	Yes = DNF
22.	No = UP	Yes = DN
23.	No = UPF	Yes = DNB
24.	No = UF	Yes = DB
25.	No = UNF	Yes = DPB
26.	No = U	Yes = D

related to the content of conservative group belief) will have to be given a special definition appropriate to that particular group, and this complicates matters. For best results in the initial exercise, pick a group that has some authority-oriented task as a part of its regular activity, and describe it in its task-oriented phase.

If a group in its task-oriented phase is selected, it will ordinarily be true that there is some pressure to use resources of the group constructively: time; money; the abilities and efforts of the members; things owned by the group and its members; and so on. Some evaluation will be expected from the external authority, depending upon the quality or success of the task-performance, some reward, or punishment, or exchange of goods, or help of some kind. There will be some pressure to conserve the reputation of the group in the eyes of those in authority, and to maintain the group beliefs that strengthen the group's reputation and acceptability. There will be some positive value given to thinking straight, to reasoning carefully, and to being reasonably careful and exact. Good ideas will be valued, and the attention of members to each other and to the task will be desired. There will ordinarily be some restraint upon emotionality, "goofing off," joking, and expressions of fantasy. The following diagnostic system is biased in this respect (because of the conditions under which the facts were obtained (see Appendix 1), and it works best where these kinds of statements tend to be true. If the conditions are different, appropriate modifications have to be made.

Preferably select a person you know well for this beginning exercise. All of the questions should be understood to ask about your reactions to the interpersonal behavior of that particular person. Another alternative for the exercise is to answer the questions with regard to yourself in a particular group. If you are rating another person, give your own personal reactions. You will later learn to take your own biases into account to a certain extent. If you are rating yourself, answer as you think others, on the average, would rate you.

Now, to begin, concentrate your attention on the person you are rating. Try to recall how he has behaved, what he has said, what his attitudes seem to be, and how you feel about him. When you have these memories activated, read the questions on the form above entitled Interpersonal Ratings, Form A. Try to answer each question "yes" or "no." If you are unable to give a clear answer, either because of a lack of information, or because of some conflict or ambiguity, put down a question mark, omit that question, and go on to the next question. Record your answers on a separate sheet of paper, a yes, no, or a question mark for each of the twenty-six questions.

Scoring Procedure for Interpersonal Ratings

Immediately following the questions on the Interpersonal Rating Form you will find a key. After either a "yes" or a "no" answer on each question you will find a code of one, two, or three letters that tell how you are to score the answer. The scoring is done on a form like that shown in Figure 1.1.

After you learn the procedure you will not need the full form. All you really need is a vertical list containing the code letters U, D, P, N, F, B. The procedure now follows in steps:

1. Go through your answers to all twenty-six questions and *enter tallies* according to the code shown on the key, making *one tally mark for each letter* in the code. For example, suppose a "yes" answer is followed

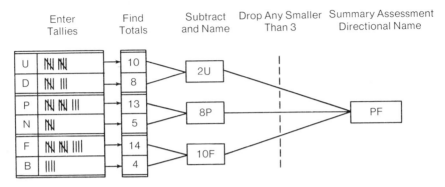

| Enter
Tallies | | Find
Totals | Subtract
and Name | Drop Any Smaller
Than 3 | Summary Assessment
Directional Name |

Figure 1.1 Scoring procedure for interpersonal ratings.

by the code UPF. Enter one tally mark after U, one after P, and one after F, on the form: three tally marks in all. Some codes call for only one tally, as in the case of question 1, coded yes = U. Others call for two, as in question 2, coded yes = UP. Still others call for three, as in question 3, coded yes = UPF. The separate letters stand for the names of "directions" in the system (explained in step 3), and a complete set of one, two, or three such component letters is called a "directional indicator."

    2. After you have entered all tallies, *count the number of tally marks after each code letter* and enter the totals in the boxes marked Find Totals.

    3. Next, *compare* the number entered for the direction U with the number entered for D. The letter U stands for the direction called "upward" in the spatial model of this system, and D stands for the one called "downward." It is understood that, as in ordinary three-dimensional physical space, movement upward is the opposite of movement downward. They are opposite directions; movement in either direction cancels movement in the other. The object of the comparison is to find which direction is indicated most frequently, and by how much. To record this result, note the larger total, subtract the smaller from the larger of the pair, and put down the number standing for the difference, followed by the name of the larger (U or D) in the first box titled Subtract and Name. Go through the same steps for P (positive) compared to N (negative) on the assumption that, as in algebraic addition, the directions positive and negative cancel each other. Then do the same for F (forward) compared to B (backward), with the rule that forward and backward cancel each other (see Figure 1.1).

    4. In order to avoid paying too much attention to slight evidence, an

arbitrary rule is adopted that *differences smaller than three* in the directional components just calculated *are dropped.* The illustration shows one directional name, U, dropped for this reason: U was greater than D by a difference smaller than three, and hence dropped.

5. Those *directional components remaining are combined* into a final directional name, which may have one, two, or three letters. The letters will be listed in the order they appear in the column Subtract and Name, reading from the top down. In the illustration the two letters P and F, in that order, are combined to form the final Summary Directional Name, PF, appearing in the column Summary Assessment.

Procedure in Interpretation

The scoring procedure, if properly carried through, will end with a classification of the person you are thinking about into one of the personality and group role types designated by a directional name, such as type PF, that is, positive-forward. The next step is to look up the description of that directional type in Part II of the book. The types are always listed in the order shown in the Table of Contents.

Remember that the descriptions apply in a statistical kind of way to the sorts of persons that have been found in the particular type of group role described. The descriptions are of interpersonal behavior in the first instance. From the behavior one hopes to infer something about personality, or group role, or both. What you have done is to answer certain questions about how the person in question seems to you—how you perceive and evaluate him from his behavior. But you have also described him in a specific group context; you have a description of his behavior *in that group, as seen by you.* You know that you have preferences and biases different from those of some others in the group, that your information differs to some extent, and that your perceptions are likely to be different in some respects. Nevertheless, your perceptions and evaluations are a *sample* of those aroused by the person in whom you are interested; with a readiness to go on with self-analysis, you are now in possession of some of the kind of information you need. Ideally, you would like to know how each of the other persons made their ratings and evaluations. If you did, you would then know in what respects you differ, and in what respects your own ratings are a good or representative sample of those given (or potentially given) by others.

The behavior of the person, including what he says and how he says it, in the particular group, as seen through the perceptions and evaluations of all members including himself, and the resulting expectations of him may be called his *group role.* His group role is not the same as his *personality.* His personality consists of his relatively enduring characteristics as a total being. You see only his interpersonal behavior which may reflect only one *side* of his personality, elicited by this particular group, its structure and his role in it, the expectations others have of him. There is no way, with the limited information we are assuming, to know whether what you see is representative of either the personality of the individual or his group role, or both. One possesses, by way of information, only his own perceptions, evaluations and expectations. He tries to use these as a sample of the perceptions, evaluations, and expectations of all group members, which, taken together, would define the *group role* of the individual. If the group role of the individual can be well assessed, one can then use statistical information about the kind of personality traits usually correlated to that group role type as a source of further ideas in the attempt to understand the particular *personality*. But as one perceives and evaluates the behavior of the person in a particular group, there is no way of knowing whether what one sees is more closely related to the group role of the person, or to his more permanent personality, or to one's own personality as a rater.

As you read the description of the type, supposed to apply to the particular person you have in mind, use the descriptive statements as hypotheses to stimulate and question your memory further. If your memory says the statement is true about the person you are trying to understand, it may give you some further refinement of insight or understanding, and lead you to new observations at the next opportunity. If your memory says the statement is false for the person you are actually considering, then reconsider your ratings of him. If they still seem valid, see if you can locate the respects in which the prediction may be wrong. Is it possibly wrong because the type description is wrong? It may be, since the evidence upon which the type description was based in the first place may have been poor, or the theory may be poor. The spatial model (described in Chapter 3) for making inferences underlying the types is a rather loose fit to the swarms of actual facts it represents.

In spite of all the opportunities for slippage, however, the general type description may seem surprisingly good in some cases. In other cases the type description may seem to fit well in general, but may involve some glaring exception or some paradox. For example, the person may make value-statements in favor of equalitarianism, but in his manner of interaction he may seem authoritarian. Or he may have a superficially positive manner and yet seem tense and anxious underneath. In these cases, see if you can locate and describe the discrepancies by specifying the two or more types which they seem to represent. Perhaps there are different *sides* to the personality, which may, to some degree, be in conflict with each other.

The tendency must be guarded against either to agree or to disagree, uncritically, with the hypotheses suggested by the typological descrip-

INTERPERSONAL RATINGS, FORM B

1. Is his (or her) *rate of participation* generally high?
2. Does he seem to assume he will be *successful and popular*?
3. Does he seem to *see himself as a good and kind parent*?
4. Is his rate of *giving suggestions on group tasks* high?
5. Is his rate of *receiving disagreement* generally high?
6. Does he seem to *make others feel he dislikes them*?
7. Does he *receive a lot of laughter*?
8. Does he seem very *extroverted*?
9. Does he seem *able to give a lot of affection*?
10. Does he *seem friendly* in his behavior?
11. Is his rate of *giving agreement* generally high?
12. Does he tend mostly to *give opinion or analysis* when he participates?
13. Does he seem to emphasize *moderation, value-determined restraint*?
14. Does he *seem unfriendly* in his behavior?
15. Does he seem *pessimistic about group ideals*?
16. Does he seem *preoccupied with wishful fantasies*?
17. Does he seem to *make others feel they are entertaining, warm*?
18. Does he seem calm, *understanding*?
19. Does he seem to be *submissively good*?
20. Does he seem often to *ask for suggestion* or for task-leadership?
21. Does he seem to feel *anxious, fearful of not conforming*?
22. Does he seem *only to participate when others ask him* for his opinion?
23. Does he seem *preoccupied with feelings of dislike* for others?
24. Does he show many *signs of tension and passive resistance*?
25. Does he seem *unlikely to arouse dislikes*?
26. Does he seem to confine his participation mostly to *only giving information* when asked?

tions. One tends to believe when one wants to believe, and to disbelieve when one wants to disbelieve. One should try to believe for a little while, in order to obtain the benefit of whatever associations may occur, but one should not take these associations too seriously. One should then try to disbelieve for a little while in order to ask oneself what one would have to know to really test the idea.

In any case one should eventually be led back to the study of the personality in the group to test one's new conceptions. As an illustration of this "predict-and-test" procedure, a second and third set of questions—Forms B and C—for interpersonal ratings are included. If actually em-

INTERPERSONAL RATINGS, FORM C

1. Does he (or she) tend to *address the group as a whole* rather than individuals?
2. Does he seem to *rate himself highly on all good or socially popular traits*?
3. Does he seem likely to be *rated highly on "leadership"*?
4. Does he seem to feel he represents some *impersonal higher plan* for the group?
5. Does he make *inhibitory demands and want to enforce discipline*?
6. Does he tend to *rate others low on self-confidence*?
7. Does he *guess that others will rate him high on domination*?
8. Does he *make many jokes or show many fantasies*?
9. Does he seem to be *able to make others feel less anxious*?
10. Is his rate of *asking others for their opinions* high?
11. Does he seem generally *prone to feel admiration* for others?
12. Is he generally very *strongly work-oriented*?
13. Does he *tend to arouse guilt* in others?
14. Is his *rate of disagreement* generally high?
15. Does he have a tendency to *feel others are dominating*?
16. Does he tend to *see others as too acceptant of authority*?
17. Do others tend to *address their jokes and fantasies to him*?
18. Does he seem to have a general *trust in the goodness of others*?
19. Does he tend to believe that aggression and sex can be replaced by *tender love*?
20. Does he seem to be very *acceptant of authority*?
21. Does he seem to *plow persistently ahead* with great inertia?
22. Does he tend to be somewhat *depressed*?
23. Does he tend to *believe that others dislike him*?
24. Is *laughter* his main or only mode of participation in the group?
25. Does he seem to be *appealing for understanding*?
26. Is his total *rate of participation generally very low*?

ployed, these forms should give results roughly comparable to Form A, since they are built on alternative sets of indicators for the same types. On the other hand, the lack of perfect match should have a salutary effect in increasing one's skepticism about any definitive classification. The use of all three sets of questions with the answers added together should give additional reliability in the approximation of the best type, if one has the stamina to make so many ratings.

Forms A, B, and C of the Interpersonal Rating questions are all arranged in the same order. There are twenty-six questions, one for each of the twenty-six types, and the questions are listed in the same order as the listing of the types in the Table of Contents of the book. The same key, included earlier, is used for all three forms. If one has arrived at a preliminary classification of the type from Form A and wishes to predict how the person's ratings should come out on each question on Form B, he may assume that the answer pattern on Form B will be just like that on Form A. A *preferable* procedure, however, is to look up the "type pattern" in Appendix 2. Under the type pattern for type UPF, for example, information is given as to how that direction correlates with each of the other directions. One finds in Appendix 2, that the correlation of direction UPF with direction U is "plus," that is, positive, and so on for each of the twenty-six directions. The list may be translated into an expected set of answers on the twenty-six questions of Forms A, B, and C. One simply substitutes "yes" for "plus," "no" for "minus," and "?" or no answer for "zero." Given the assumption that the person belongs to any one of the group role types, a prediction as to how he will come out on all questions of all three of the Interpersonal Rating Forms can be obtained.

The expected set of observations (ratings) predicted by the type pattern is especially useful in locating discrepancies or paradoxes in the person's behavior. The summary directional type will represent the preponderant direction of his behavior, against which more minor clusters may stick out as "uncharacteristic" traits *for him.* It seems to be a useful hypothesis that uncharacteristic traits for a given person are usually strongly motivated, are usually focal points of conflict within the personality, and may represent a part or side of the personality, perhaps an unconscious part, held apart from the present group role.

Sometimes the uncharacteristic traits appear in one modality of behavior only. For example, the person may have an ideology of radical social change, but everything else about his manner of behavior, the impression that he makes on others, and even his self-picture in most respects may be that of a conservative task-leader—UPF. The type pattern for UPF, shown in Appendix 2, would correctly predict how one rated him on most questions, but would be conspicuously wrong, let us say, on question 12 in Form A, "Does he seem to stand for the most conservative ideas and beliefs of the group?" It might predict correctly on the corresponding questions on Form B, "Does he tend mostly to give opinion or analysis when he participates?", and on Form C, "Is he generally very strongly work-oriented?" The point is that the type pattern prediction enables one to find an uncharacteristic ideological cluster of traits or items that fails to match the general summary direction of the group role. Such a paradoxical cluster is a natural place to concentrate in the attempt to understand the personality better. To give another simpler instance: the self-rating of a person might fail to recognize the negative elements in his personality and group role that appear in the ratings given to him.

The descriptions of the personality and group role types in Part II of this book are written as if the incumbent of the given role type were indeed just the kind of personality that would naturally seek and obtain such a role, and as if there were no "uncharacteristic" traits, due either to personality or to group role. This is an artificial simplification, of course. Actual personalities are more complex, perhaps even typically internally conflicted and so also are group roles. Properly understood, the directions represented by the personality and group role types may also be used to represent forces within the individual personality, or subparts of a group, different sides or parts of the personality, subselves, situationselves, or even quite highly developed subpersonalities. In coming to understand the individual personality better, what one often does is to become acquainted with these different sides of the same total personality; then one is able to represent the conflicts and accommodations between them. In Chapter 3 a spatial model of group structure is presented within which subparts of a group may be represented. There is no reason why such a model might not also be used to represent the relation of subparts within the same personality to each other.

According to current social-psychological theory, some of the subselves in a single total personality derive more or less directly from the internalization of parental figures, bad ones as well as good ones. Some subselves come from heroes, from rivals as well as friends; some come from fantasy preoccupations; some come from institutional roles—in the school, the church, the army, the office and the shop; and some come from males and some from females. The total personality can be conceptualized as a group of interacting tendencies, each approaching a subself in complication: subselves with different origins, different characters, associations, value implications, behavioral manifestations, and so on. From this set of assumptions it is a problem to understand how the actual individual ever manages to pull himself together, and one is not surprised to detect a lack of complete consistency.

Before taking the idea of a subpersonality too seriously in a given case, however, it is advisable to look for an actual person with whom the subject of one's analysis has been in concrete interaction, from whom or with whom he could have learned the group role that he now manifests. A knowledge of the person's parents, even the picture of them that he reports, is of value in understanding his personality. More generally, the more one knows of the person's life history, the better one can understand him. There are no psychological tests nearly as effective in understanding the personality of another as an extensive concrete knowledge of the experiences through which he has gone. But that quality of information requires a long-time relationship with the person, and a degree of intimacy which goes beyond that we ordinarily have.

In general, one supposes the critical and emotionally significant relations with others experienced in the person's life history are retained in his memory in a way that tends to leave his preferred picture of himself as strong, secure, and triumphant as possible. The weaklings and the villains in earlier episodes are retained in memory, and the person can enact their roles, but rather than do so, he seeks actual other persons on whom these roles can be foisted in present situations, so that he can make his accepted self picture move in the desired directions. It may be that roles of earlier origin so overdetermine the person's perceptions and feelings in the present group situation that they must be recognized, exposed, and dealt with in some constructive fashion by the other group members if damaging relations are to be avoided. This is part of the work of a self-analytic group.

SOME CONSIDERATIONS IN TRYING TO CHANGE OTHERS

For the purposes of understanding the behavior of an individual in a group, it is helpful to make a distinction between two broad classes of determinants: those pertaining to the more permanent features of the individual *personality* of the acting person; and those pertaining to his *group role,* or situation (4). When first witnessing the behavior of a person, one does not know whether one is seeing mostly the effects of one or the other of these. And yet, if one is interested in the behavior, either because of the desire to change it, or to retain it, he needs to understand the respects in which the characteristic behavior is correlated with the personality, and those in which it is correlated with his group role.

Each of these classes of determinants branches off in its own direction. The group role of a given person is determined in part by all the other group members, the way they behave, and the way they evaluate the acting person. Their evaluations, expectations, and behavior profoundly affect him, in most cases. To change a person's group role, one may need to change others in the group, not the personality of the acting person. On the other hand, if the behavior is importantly determined by special features of the personality of the acting individual, then one cannot expect it to change much without changes in his more basic personality. It is true that the individual may be forced into a certain kind of interpersonal behavior by the perceptions, evaluations, expectations, and behavior of other members, but they may be reacting mainly to special features of his personality. In this case, it may be easier to try to modify the personality of the individual than to change the evaluation of all group members. In other cases the evaluation of group members may be relatively easy to change. The important thing to recognize is that if one wishes to bring about behavior change most effectively, one cannot give a *generalized* priority to either one or the other class of determinants. One must look for the key determinants in the particular case.

As an alternative to the personality-oriented mode of understanding, if one wishes to understand a group and perhaps to change it, as participant, leader, teacher, or therapist, one must be able to take into account the way in which personalities, or selected sides of personalities, fit together and form larger group structures. A characteristic mode of behavior of an individual may be induced by his group role, which in turn, is related to the total constellation of roles in the group—the group structure that forms his situation. The group structure may leave gaps into which the individual is drawn; other parts of the group may form closed coalitions which exclude him; other persons as part of a group structure may unwittingly use him or coerce him in many subtle ways. An approach to these problems is taken up in Chapter 3, where a spatial model of group structure is presented that can be constructed from interpersonal ratings.

The persistence of a given structure of the group sometimes traces quite directly to a particularly strong attachment or antipathy of one person in a strategic position in relation to another particular person. The nature of the power structure in groups is such that this can often be the specific critical feature, which if changed, would change the whole nature of the group. Sometimes such a relationship is not manifested in overt action, and depends upon a consciously concealed relationship, or sometimes upon an unconscious interlocking of the partial sides of personalities in which each individual stands for a part, hidden or repressed, of the personality of the other. Though such pairs of persons may disapprove of each other, or openly conflict with each other, or have a curious joking relationship, they each obtain a forbidden satisfaction. There is a hidden gain for each.

The psychological gain for each in such a case is the satisfaction of his unconscious tendency, attributed to the other. This leads each to maintain the status quo, though the relationship may seem nonmeaningful or negative to observers. The maintainance of such a status quo for a pair of persons may be very costly to the group as a whole. It may throw the balance of power to the negative or backward side. It may prevent the unification of the group on any working constitution or set of values. It may victimize the weaker members. In the case of the family, a relationship of this unconscious, collusive kind between parents or older children may seriously affect the development of the younger child.

The leader, teacher, therapist, or anybody who tries to elicit a change in another person deals directly with the residues within that person of earlier family relationships. The person who tries to bring about the change takes a role similar to that of a parent and has the parental memories of the other focused upon him (83). The resources of a leader, teacher, or therapist, for dealing with this situation, will depend upon his own background, parents, teachers, and the residues of his own socialization. When one thinks of himself in such a position, and realizes that he must do his best through self-analysis to avoid hampering misperceptions and unfortunate forms of behavior on his own part, it is a sobering thought. He should realize that he may unconsciously try to arrange or change things so that he proves *he* was right in taking some earlier path in the solution of his own problems in dealing with his own parents and others. He should realize that he may try to foist his own unwanted subselves upon other members of the group, just as they will try to foist theirs upon him. In general he will be able to rise above his own early resources only with great effort. Most persons probably tend, in fact, to act in most respects as their parents did, but they see themselves in some imagined glory. In their mind's eye, they do not have the faults of their parents, but in the eyes of others who view them as parents, they often do. They may retain their parents' faults as well as virtues when they grow up to become leaders, teachers, therapists, and parents.

CONTINUED STUDY OF THE GROUP

To continue in the mode of the exercise, one may not be satisfied for long with the analysis of a single personality on the basis of the meager amount of information ordinarily available from behavior in a group setting. As one begins to find a plausible typological description for the person first taken as the beginning focus of analysis, one may find that the description refers often to the way in which that type interacts with particular other types. Perhaps there are persons in the actual group corresponding to the other mentioned types. One may want to study other personalities, perhaps each person in the group. One may begin to pick out particularly strategic pairs, trios, and larger coalitions within the group. One may see the way in which the values and beliefs of individual persons conflict with those of others in the group. In the descriptions of the types one will find references to the division of the group into factions, or coalitions, and one may want to place the person who is the focus of attention somewhere in the "structure" of the group, in which different people have different roles, represent different things, have different status and different degrees of power, and so on. You may want a way to think about the total structure of the particular group you are studying. Such a method, using the kind of ratings already employed, is presented in Chapter 3.

Chapter 5 explains how the observation of who-speaks-to-whom gives further desirable specificity about the relations of members to each other. From the results of this kind of observation it is possible to begin to think concretely about each individual member; to make a useful approximation of the power hierarchies and conflicts; to detect who supports whom; and to visualize the consequent division of the group into specialized roles, segments, cliques, or factions. The place of a given person in such a structure has much to do with the way he behaves, and whether the consequences of his actions are important or not to others in the group.

The presentation of a method of classifying the behavior of persons toward each other, a method called "Interaction Process Analysis," which will give information for the assessment of personality and group roles, is continued in Chapter 6.

The more general nature of a "space" within which the positions of people in a group can be described is discussed in Chapter 8. This space is defined by value-positions and the significance of what persons say and do in relation to these more abstractly defined values. A systematic method for analyzing and recording the content of value statements persons make in groups is presented in Chapter 8.

More General Gains in Knowledge and Understanding

All of the methods presented in Part I of this book describe more technical ways of observing, recording, and analyzing than one ordinarily employs in natural participant observation. It is *not* suggested that after studying these methods one should appear at the next meeting of his work group with a tape recorder and a pad of observation forms. Nevertheless, some persons will be in a position to make technical studies. The self-analytic group, in particular, is one in which natural participation merges into observation, and can pass on into technical research. Appendix 6 describes a type of academic self-analytic group which can provide the necessary conditions and ethical protections (3, 135) for training and the advance of knowledge in the analysis of interpersonal behavior. Appendix 7 describes some desirable features of an appropriate physical setting for such training and research. Finally, Appendix 8 describes a useful technical device one can use appropriately in such a setting. All of these adjuncts may be helpful; none is indispensable.

Nevertheless, I believe that the learning of a technical method and practice with it is valuable in sharpening one's conceptions of reality. An observational method makes one aware of concrete realities of the interaction of persons in group settings as nothing else can. Once having learned to observe for a given kind of behavior or type of content— having tried to capture it by a definition, having seen it in many variations, having had to decide definitely whether it is seen at a given point or not by putting down a score of some kind; after these experiences, one finds that he sees things differently. For better or for worse, he sees and hears things which were comfortably blurred before. If, having made the observations, one has had some success in drawing inferences he could not draw before, then so much the better. He may then be motivated to improve both the observations and the inferences.

The diagnostic and inferential system of the present book is built completely around measurable variables—all of these are listed in Appendix 1. The definitions of each of them can be explored, sharpened, and altered. Observations can be repeated by others, or applied in different settings. All the variables in the present system are connected with each other in an integrated system for making inferences. It is hoped that these features will help the observer to improve his abilities to observe, infer, and understand.

The pragmatic aim of observations and inferences is prediction and increased ability to control events. It is true that all the inferences that can be made still do not add up to "prediction" in any strong or certain sense, to say nothing of control. More than a hundred years ago John Stuart Mill, speculating upon the possibilities of the discipline of sociology, then in its infancy, stated a view which still seems to be sound and fundamental:

It is evident," [he says,] that Sociology, considered as a system of deductions a priori cannot be a science of positive predictions, but only of tendencies. We may be able to conclude, from the laws of human nature applied to the circumstances of a given state of society, that a particular cause will operate in a certain manner unless counteracted; but we can never be assured to what extent or amount it will so operate, or affirm with certainty that it will not be counteracted; because we can seldom know, even approximately; all the agencies which may coexist with it, and still less calculate the collective result of so many combined elements.[1]

Mill was not discouraged by these limitations, however, nor should we be. He rather emphasized what practical men of all kinds accept, that "knowledge insufficient for prediction may be most valuable for guidance." He goes on to say,

[1] John Stuart Mill, *A System of Logic, Ratiocinative and Inductive: Being a Connected View of the Principles of Evidence and the Methods of Scientific Investigation*, Book VI, *On the Logic of the Moral Sciences* (London: Longmans, Green & Co., Ltd., 1936).

It is not necessary for the wise conduct of the affairs of society, no more than of any one's private concerns, that we should be able to forsee infallibly the results of what we do. We must seek our objects by means which may perhaps be defeated, and take precautions against dangers which possibly may never be realized. The aim of practical politics is to surround any given society with the greatest possible number of circumstances of which the tendencies are beneficial, and to remove or counteract, as far as practicable, those of which the tendencies are injurious. A knowledge of the tendencies only, though without power of accurately predicting their conjunct result, gives us to a considerable extent this power.

The methods presented in this book are meant to give a way of observing real events and describing their tendencies (the directional indicators are the names of tendencies) and a way of adding them together (the scoring procedure of the Introductory Exercise) to predict their conjunct results. The group role types contain statements of predictions based upon previous findings. The known relations of the types (or directions) to each other enable one to extend his predictions greatly by inference. Though imperfect in many ways, I believe that the system does have some tangible predictive power.

2

The Use
of Subjective Impressions

This book is devoted to ways of making more systematic observations and of strengthening our powers of inference, but the starting point in all instances is a subjective impression made upon the observer. One can learn how to use his subjective impressions as a part of the information available to the more logical part of his mind. The well-trained observer "observes," as well as "has" his own feelings, and reasons upon them.

EXERCISE

Appendix 1 is offered as an extended list of questions which one might use to "debrief" himself with regard to whatever impressions have been gathered in experience with a specific group.[1] Retrospective impressions may be employed in the study of persons in any group, and depend upon no written records. These are the great virtues of the use of extended stimulated recall—its faults are those of all subjective procedures.

In first starting to study a group one may have only very subjective impressions from memory, perhaps, and if he uses questions from Appendix 1 he will have to imagine what the answers to the questions *might be* if he had been able to apply more objective or systematic procedures. Even so, the effort to imagine will sharpen his perception, and prepare

[1] The Interpersonal Rating Forms A, B, and C, in Chapter 1, were compiled from this list.

him to seek and find relevant information at the next opportunity. It may turn out, also, that he really has much more information at a given time than he had realized. He may be able to recall it under the stimulation of the specific questions.

The procedure is very simple—simply go through the list of questions looking for those which stir some memory, or about which one has some impression, omitting the others. Start with one of the most prominent persons in the group, and with him as the focus, start at question 1 in the list of variables in Appendix 1. Record the directional indicator for each answer, as in the Introductory Exercise. Answer the questions as well as you can, for as long as you can, guessing or imagining as much as you dare. As a precaution, you might wish to keep those scores separate where you feel you have little or no basis in fact, but are willing to guess or imagine.

No doubt you will find that a picture of the type of the person or his group role will begin to crystalize after you have been through a number of questions. The problem will then be the degree to which such a picture is simply a product of your imagination. Even if it is, crystallize it and subject it to examination, since it lurks in the background of your mind and probably affects your further perception. It is better to have it out and disprove it, or prove it, by specific facts. Look for inconsistences as well as consistencies in the directional indicators. The types are pure only in the imagination, and all actual personalities will be more complex in their behavior than suggested by the types. All that has been said about interpretation in the Introductory Exercise, of course, applies here. The more inconsistencies found the more you will build up an appetite for relevant information when it again becomes available. Repeat the process for other members.

As you are able, you may wish to move to more objective methods as described in further parts of this book. Certainly you may want to look at them before exhausting yourself with the present exercise of extended recall. But you will find that they are partial, and undependable, as well as the present more subjective method. Moreover, you will find that because each of them is selective, any one or more of them in a given case may call your attention to a distorted, defensive, or deceptive aspect of the personality, and thus be unrepresentative of the total personality. So long as you depend upon any one source of information or impressions, whether "subjective" or "objective," you may handicap yourself unnecessarily. It is better to be as empathic and imaginative as one can, through the full use of one's natural human abilities and sensitivities, and then to firm up and correct this picture as well as one can through the use of more formal and repeatable objective procedures. Having learned to use more formal procedures, one's ability to form and retain new subjective impressions is enhanced, and so, by mutually supporting steps, one gradually mounts to a more complex and complete understanding.

Understanding through Empathic Identification

To understand a personality or a group is to be able to reproduce in one's own mind relevant parts of what goes on in the minds of others. This is what the child ordinarily learns to do in relation to his parents, siblings, and playmates, in the process of growing up. But this requires a long time, close contact, strong motivations and the desire, in the optimum case, of the child to *be* like the other. In growing up and creating a personality, something like *empathic identification* is a primary and fundamental approach on the part of the child. The process is probably mostly nonverbal, it is applied by the very young and by the nonsophisticated, it grows out of motivation "turned full on," and it depends upon an almost hypnotic kind of observation—taking in as much information as possible by all possible means, and then turning it over in all possible ways. The motivation is to become *like* the object, or more simply, to *become the object.*

In a more sophisticated form, the approach of empathic identification is widely applied in the arts: in acting in the so-called Stanislawsky method and in the Zen-influenced Chinese and Japanese painting. Many religious disciplines stress this approach in some form, and it plays a part in the theory of psychotherapy, and of education. The growing human being in his natural, fully motivated attempt to become the other is unsurpassed in his ability to sense, to feel, to synthesize, and to reproduce selective aspects of the behavior of another person. The difficulty of empathic identification in unaided form is that it is really very selective, though it has the feeling of total receptivity, and it is also subjective; that is, about as likely to lead one to infuse his own characteristics unknowingly into the object, as to internalize the object correctly.

There is no simple way around these difficulties. One must both accept and supplement the process of empathic identification if one wishes to understand other persons. The self and the other constitute a group. The understanding of another personality, or a group, implies an understanding of the self to some extent, since the self is always implicated in some way vis-a-vis the other. Thus, even a study which concentrates on the personality of one other also involves the self and to some extent is the study of a group—the self and the other. When the object to be understood is a group, or a group-made world of beliefs, values, and fantasies, the mental stretch is very great, and the tendency is very strong to identify with one person or subgroup within it, and to employ the same defenses as he or they employ. Such an identification, if held exclusively, is an enemy of understanding. But if such an identification is part of a rapid alternation and comparison of the points of view of all the persons involved, it is a most important aid to understanding.

Detachment and Understanding

In the learning of any art, one may have to learn how to broaden his focus of attention, so that it takes more and more factors into account simultaneously. In the understanding of personalities and groups there are some important facts which can only be detected by a fine and rapid process of scanning and comparison across a number of persons and activities. Scanning and comparison require a kind of "detachment"—the ability to avoid getting stymied by a specific local fact when one has to be aware of what is going on in a whole changing system of events.

Is this kind of "detachment" compatible with "empathic identification"? I would say yes, the two can be parts of a more highly synthesized process. An intense involvement with a larger whole carries with it the ability to resist the temptation to narrow the focus, and to take pleasure in a local process only. Detachment at a local level can be attained by empathic identification with a larger whole. Moreover this can be done without losing empathic identification with the part, by a process of rapid alternation and comparison of part-to-part and part-to-whole. The self, and the process of understanding, are themselves local parts, and they should be held in broad focus in relation to all the rest. The actual accomplishment of this requires the investment and expenditure of energy and effort over a long period.

One of the results of a lack of sufficient detachment from one's own subjective interests and needs is the tendency to ignore or blot out things not understood. A person may say something we think quite odd, for example, which seems to have no relation to what we expect. Usually we do not grasp eagerly at such facts. After a short try, we usually give up, shrug our shoulders, decide that we must not have heard correctly, or that the other simply "made a mistake," or that he "has something else on his mind," and "didn't mean to say what he said." We decide that the best thing to do is ignore it and go on. Often, in retrospect, we recognize that if only we had frankly recognized that we were being presented with facts which demanded a rethinking of the situation, we could have foreseen what was in the making. Isolated, paradoxical facts we do not understand constitute our best point of entry into improved understanding.

Of course, more than laziness is usually involved in the decision to "let something go" that has not been understood. Often, to understand is to recognize the existence of something unpleasant, either about ourselves or some other person. An ability to stand unpleasant facts may be a great help to understanding. A broad feeling of sympathy extending to the self as well as the other is probably very helpful—one needs the feeling that not every imperfection and deviation will be punished, or justifies moralistic intervention. A fear of punishment or a harsh conscience is a great interference to understanding others, as well as the self.

But more than this, one needs a positive recognition that persons change, grow, and develop, that creativity is possible, and important. One does not gain an understanding of a person or a group once and for all. One must seek new information constantly, and examine it for its new implications. One needs the experience of gaining new insight from taking stray facts seriously, from making a constant search for indicators of impending change. One needs a knowledge of how to think and how to try to understand, especially when the object of understanding is at least as complicated as oneself is.

Prediction

One must look for repetitions of some kind in order to formulate generalizations. Once formulated, a generalization can serve as a starting point from which something new may be deduced. One should deduce as hard as one can from generalizations one may make about personalities and groups. But one should not suppose that this will succeed entirely. To suppose that one can work entirely deductively in understanding a personality or a group is to misunderstand both the nature of the knowing process and the objects to be known. On the other hand, to maintain that systematic methods are useless is to carry pessimism too far (26).

The human mind seems to be made to work and to play—to imagine, to deduce from premises and induce from instances. Change in behavior and change in the subjective world of the individual is the natural consequence of the activity of the mind. The mind always seeks new combinations, it has a hunger for information, it is basically a combining, synthesizing, creative set of processes. If there were no new problems the mind would create them, just to give itself some work to do—or some play. There is never a lack of problems, however, as the larger world changes around the individual. The processes of perception, of emotion, and of fantasy, ordinarily provide starting points for further operations of the mind. These processes, however, or the products given by them, are not simply or purely products of the mind. Typically some set of circumstances is taken as a starting point, given by both the world and the mind as they are at that time. The mind then works to extend its perception of these circumstances, to rationalize and recombine them, but will not as a rule completely reduce all of them to things more elementary, or dissolve them. It produces a higher-order "amalgam" of the elements with which it starts from its lower-order processes. The nature of this "amalgam" is discussed further in Chapter 7.

Many of the basic difficulties of studying personalities and groups center around the facts of (1) their openness to the environment, and (2) their extreme internal complication. Given these conditions, recognition of both uniqueness and the tendency to change seem primary in trying to understand them. If uniqueness and tendency to change are characteristic of them, there are implications for the methods one must depend upon in the attempt to understand. One can never have his method fully systematized for one thing; and for another, he can never finish the job.

The internal complication requires that one must have a large amount of information about the state of affairs in many critical parts of the personality or the group, and be able to trace the repercussions of local changes as they proceed through many paths of interconnection. Practically speaking, the observer and theorist can never know all that he might need to know. Some of what he needs to know is unique to the one case and is not likely to be picked up with his already established modes of classification. He must depend upon something like empathic identification to help fill the gap.

The openness of each personality and each group to the environment, along with their tendencies to evolve, mean that information about them tends to become rapidly outdated, and that new information must constantly be gathered. The processes of change in the personality or group must be "monitored" or "tracked" by the constant gathering of new information. The problem is logically very similar to that faced in weather forecasting. Some prediction or forecasting is possible, but the forecast requires constant correction, which depends upon new information.

My colleagues and I have observed many academic self-analytic groups (of the kind described in Appendix 6) through a year's development and change, in which the schedule was made as nonconstrictive as possible, with no close specification as to how interaction should go, and no day-to-day structuring of interpersonal activity. We have employed many different methods of gathering information about what is going on. In one group, for example, the members rated each other after each meeting on traits of personality, performance, and attitudes about each other. They heroically provided this information through some seventy meetings of the regular academic year. In other groups observers have kept careful observations of social interaction as described in Chapters 5 and 6, and followed the group carefully as to stability and change. In still other groups, members have written periodic descriptions, over the course of the year, of what is going on as they see it, and why.

These studies have produced evidences of developmental trends.

Mills (122), Mann (114), Dunphy (75, 76), and Slater (142) each present a number of valuable findings about time trends. Their findings are generally rather consistent and are a great help in forming the kind of expectations leaders and instructors need in such groups as an aid to their understanding of the group and its development. It is true, however, that the time periods one must use in order to find regularities are quite long—halves, thirds, or quarters of the year. It is also true that quite often the trends seem to be pegged to changes of conditions as imposed by the academic and seasonal calendar—vacations, examinations, the end of the year. It is also true that the general predictions one is able to make sometimes seem pretty weak as applied to the unique case. This must be true so long as the generalizations are simply hooked to the passage of time, the traversal of the academic calendar, or the life-cycle of the group, rather than to more detailed conditions that one can observe changing currently.

In spite of the insight and aid they give, then, the generalizations presently available are not completely satisfying. If one studies the interaction of individuals in such a group over time, there will be sudden drops and rises in rates for which past averages or gross known effects of certain times of the year or of the life-cycle of the group give no warning and no explanation. Sometimes the behavior of a given person changes drastically in the course of a year. Sometimes a member who is very active for the first two months suddenly drops his participation to a very low point where it remains for most of the rest of the year. Sometimes the opposite occurs—a member who has hardly been noticed for a part of the year suddenly comes into great prominence. Sometimes the group continues in the same old way on the same old topic in spite of obvious efforts to break the spell and change. Sometimes individuals or subparts of the group get "trapped" in roles they try unsuccessfully to escape. And yet change may come, sometimes a major change, with little to indicate what set it off or what took it so far. Sometimes a major change is evidently brought about by a single interpretation by an instructor, or a group member, that seems to "hit the spot."

And yet, in wishing for the power to understand, and perhaps to influence, one must recognize that the desire for omniscience is a complete fantasy. It is not very helpful to think that if one only knew *all* about the personalities of the members in advance he would be able to predict them. Whether this is so or not, we shall presumably never know. It is clear that a great deal would have to be known about each subprocess, to a degree of fine detail, along with an ability to combine the predictions from all of the subprocesses, with an exactness that seems completely fantastic, and surely too expensive. For practical purposes we shall always work with a fraction of the probably-relevant information about each person, and with highly oversimplified conceptions of how long subprocesses take to come to completion, when they will reach critical points, and what else will be around for them to combine or collide with when they do. Much of the time we shall have to be content with "understanding" events either after, or as they take place, instead of "predicting" them far in advance.

Our objects of study—personalities and groups—are highly complex, highly synthesized, active entities. We study the accessible evidences of subprocesses that can not be seen, processes we often do not know about until they show up in overt behavior. They are not only concealed, but they are also unthinkably multiplex and variously determined. We would be swamped with more information than could ever put together if we were somehow to come into possession of a direct "wiretap" to every relevant subprocess. The behavior we make the object of our study is quite as complex as the behavior with which we try to understand it. Behavior is a process involving information gathering, compromising, and synthesizing, in which many factors come to bear. The complex result is what we are interested in. Reduction to constituent elements is not enough. We need to know how constituent elements will be put together, their effects on each other, and must somehow be able to accomplish the calculation required (23, 32). There is ultimately no getting around the conclusion that we must have a good *theory,* or rather, a good *theoretical system,* which requires only a moderate, practical, amount of information, which reduces the complexity to a limited number of selected variables and enables us to accomplish the calculation required for inferences.

On the other hand, in every practical application we do in fact consider many elements and forces and try with some success to synthesize them in our minds by a partly logical, partly intuitive process. Our present task can be thought of as simply learning how to do this better. In my view the most relevant practical tasks in this endeavor, and the most relevant scientific tasks tend strongly to coincide, in a binocular view. If there is a problem for the scientific student of behavior in this point of view, it is simply that this kind of activity has usually been called "artistic" and has sometimes been thought unnecessary or even inimical to scientific attempts to study behavior. It is my belief that we should first be as artistic and empathic as we can, and then add as much scientific aid in analysis and synthesis as we are able. The next chapter is a step toward synthesis.

3

A Spatial Model
of Group Structure

The aim of this chapter is to show how the information obtained by any of the methods of observation and analysis described in this book may be used to make inferences about group structure and thus to highlight important problems of the group.

The Introductory Exercise gave one the experience of combining a number of directional indicators based on one's own observation and subjective impressions to arrive at a classification of the personality and group role type of individual group members. One may also have had some practice in visualizing the three-dimensional spatial model. It is now possible to put these skills together into a higher synthesis which will enable one to recognize some important aspects of group structure, and to raise a new order of questions.

BASIC OBSERVATIONS REQUIRED

An example based upon an actual group will be presented in this chapter, and if you are engaged in the study of a particular group you may parallel the steps. The members of the illustrative group evaluated each other on the Interpersonal Rating Form, approximately the same as the one presented as Form A in Chapter One. They were members of an academic self-analytic group as described in Appendix 6. The results of the ratings were a classification by each member of himself and each of the other members of the group into one of the twenty-seven directional types. All the ratings each person received were then added, by directional components, so that it was possible to specify how many members had classified each given member in a direction which contained the component upward, how many in a direction which contained the component downward, and so on. A summary position was obtained by finding the balance upward or downward (by algebraic addition), and

**Table 3.1   List of Group Members
with Positions in the Evaluative Space**

Member Identification	Number of Times Classified in Types Involving Each Direction							Summary Position			Summary Type*
RFB	13U,	1D,	11P,	3N,	14F,	2B,	=	(12U,	8P,	12F)	= (UPF)
IB	4U,	14D,	14P,	5N,	7F,	4B,	=	(10D,	9P,	3F)	= (DP)
RWB	3U,	16D,	8P,	8N,	11F,	3B,	=	(13D,	00,	8F)	= (DF)
LD	23U,	0D,	11P,	4N,	3F,	14B,	=	(23U,	7P,	11B)	= (UPB)
CE	17U,	1D,	5P,	9N,	17F,	1B,	=	(16U,	4N,	16F)	= (UF)
JF	11U,	7D,	17P,	3N,	4F,	9B,	=	(4U,	14P,	5B)	= (PB)
DG	10U,	9D,	19P,	1N,	12F,	1B,	=	(1U,	18P,	11F)	= (PF)
JG	2U,	10D,	25P,	0N,	8F,	5B,	=	(8D,	25P,	3F)	= (DP)
JH	3U,	10D,	12P,	2N,	2F,	20B,	=	(7D,	10P,	18B)	= (DPB)
DH	5U,	10D,	9P,	7N,	19F,	3B,	=	(5D,	2P,	16F)	= (DF)
DL	2U,	16D,	19P,	1N,	1F,	14B,	=	(14D,	18P,	13B)	= (DPB)
JL	3U,	14D,	11P,	3N,	2F,	22B,	=	(11D,	8P,	20B)	= (DPB)
MM	5U,	10D,	22P,	1N,	21F,	0B,	=	(5D,	21P,	21F)	= (DPF)
EM	18U,	1D,	11P,	5N,	5F,	12B,	=	(17U,	6P,	7B)	= (UPB)
SP	26U,	0D,	14P,	6N,	10F,	7B,	=	(26U,	8P,	3F)	= (UP)
JR	10U,	9D,	5P,	16N,	0F,	20B,	=	(1U,	11N,	20B)	= (NB)
AR	8U,	6D,	24P,	1N,	16F,	1B,	=	(2U,	23P,	15F)	= (PF)
MS	1U,	21D,	9P,	4N,	8F,	4B,	=	(20D,	5P,	4F)	= (DP)
JS	9U,	9D,	10P,	4N,	15F,	3B,	=	(00,	6P,	12F)	= (PF)
LLT	3U,	16D,	6P,	4N,	3F,	12B,	=	(13D,	2P,	9B)	= (DB)
LWT	22U,	0D,	20P,	1N,	3F,	10B,	=	(22U,	19P,	7B)	= (UPB)
CT	3U,	9D,	24P,	0N,	9F,	8B,	=	(6D,	24P,	1F)	= (DP)
GV	15U,	6D,	8P,	7N,	10F,	3B,	=	(9U,	1P,	7F)	= (UF)
JV	4U,	12D,	0P,	20N,	6F,	8B,	=	(8D,	20N,	2B)	= (DN)
ADW	10U,	8D,	15P,	5N,	12F,	4B,	=	(2U,	10P,	8F)	= (PF)
ABW	15U,	4D,	22P,	2N,	21F,	1B,	=	(11U,	20P,	20F)	= (UPF)
HZ	2U,	13D,	12P,	0N,	8F,	3B,	=	(11D,	12P,	5F)	= (DPF)

*Number of persons rating, twenty-six, number of group members, twenty-seven (RFB did not rate). Summary position indicators smaller than 5 were dropped in the statement of the Summary Type. Experience indicates that when the position is determined on the basis of the number of persons in the group assigning a given indicator in their final ratings, as in the present case, a useful rule of thumb can be stated for determining this cutting point: Divide the total number of members rating into thirds (8-2/3 in the present case), rounding upward (9). Divide that number by two (4-1/2), again rounding upward (5). Require at least that number on either side of the zero point before retaining the directional indicator.

the same type of algebraic addition was performed for each of the other two dimensions. These computations are shown above as Table 3.1 The final result can be said to represent the position of the individual in the interpersonal rating space. The position of member SP, for example, plotted in Figures 3.1, 3.2, and 3.3 was (26U, 8P, 3F). In detail, one can see from Table 3.1 that he had actually received twenty-six ratings of U, and not a single one of D; he had received fourteen ratings containing the component P, counterbalanced with six of N, leaving a balance of 8P; finally he had received ten Fs counterbalanced with seven Bs, leaving a balance of 3F. The amount of agreement or disagreement in the ratings on a given dimension is of course important for some purposes, but is neglected as a first approximation.

If you are analyzing a group you may not have such ratings, but you can at least arrive at a summary position for each person in the group (as in Table 3.1) based upon your own ratings and observations. It is all the better to use forms A, B, and C added together. You may use the number of times you have assigned a given directional component and its opposite, based on individual questions, as the means of giving a quantitative description of how far in each direction the individual's location lies. The descriptions of personality and group role types in Part II drop all quantifiers, but this is only for tolerable simplicity. For the present exercise you will want the best quantification you can get, although you can still do something with the type designations alone.

PLOTTING THE POINTS

Figure 3.1 shows the positions of all members of the illustrative group plotted on a two-dimensional graph of the interpersonal rating space as seen *from the backward* position looking forward. This perspective enables one to see the relations of members in the dimensions upward-downward and positive-negative. Figure 3.2 shows the space seen *from the positive* position, and Figure 3.3 *from the upward* position. The three perspectives are assumed to be of equal importance, and one should try, in looking at any one of them, to imagine the missing dimension at the same time—in other words to visualize an actual three-dimensional structure. As an aid to this, the information about the location of the point in the missing dimension is included to the left of the point. For example, member SP, mentioned earlier, is shown at the top of Figure 3.1 (with his initials, SP, to the right of the plotted point, for identification). The missing information about his position, in this case that it is 3F, is shown to the left of the point. In Figure 3.2 the missing information about the same point is that it is 8P, and so on. This information is important. On

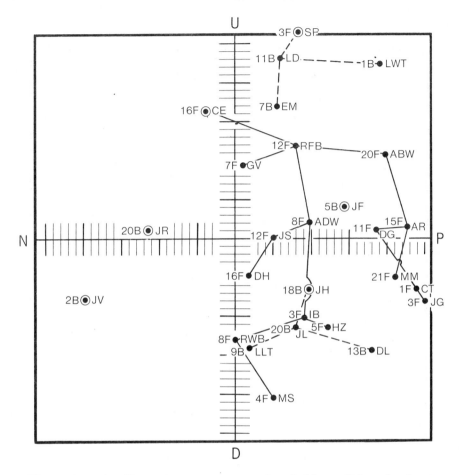

Figure 3.1   An illustrative group, map of probable coalitions (evaluative space seen from the *backward* position). (Points = locations of individual group members; solid lines = networks located forward; dotted lines = networks located backward; circled points = isolates or terminal upper members of networks.)

Figure 3.2, for example, member JV (8D, 20N, 2B) seems to be quite close to member CT (6D, 24P, 1F), but in fact they are very far apart on the positive-negative dimension; and in the group, they seemed as different as two people could be. They are widely separated on Figure 3.1.

The plotting of the members in all three dimensions is an illustrative device, and may not be necessary for your purposes, if you can visualize the positions from the numerical description. But the next step

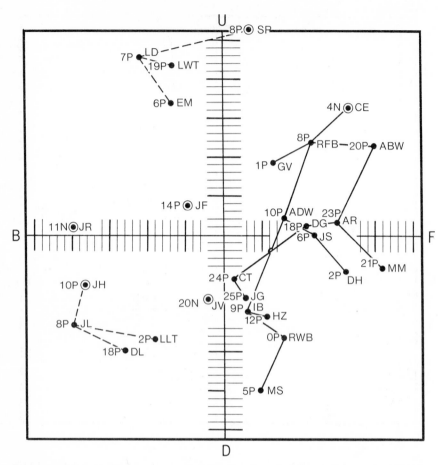

Figure 3.2   An illustrative group, map of probable coalitions (evaluative space seen from the *positive* position). (Points = locations of individual group members; solid lines = networks located forward; dotted lines = networks located backward; circled points = isolates or terminal upper members of networks.)

in the synthesis of the data requires the ability to determine the distances of points from each other. This can be determined numerically, by subtracting one location from another, as will be illustrated below, but a plot from at least one perspective, perhaps that of Figure 3.1, is a great help. The aims of this procedure are (1) to obtain a conception of the most probable coalitions among subgroups of members; (2) to locate potential leaders and strategically-placed persons in these coalitions; (3) to

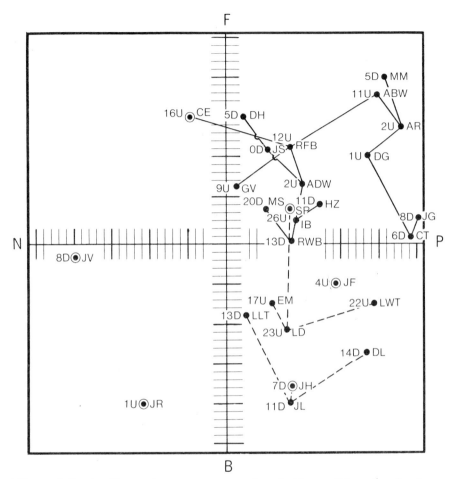

Figure 3.3 An illustrative group, map of probable coalitions (evaluative space seen from the *upward* position.) (Points = locations of individual group members; solid lines = networks located forward; dotted lines = networks located backward; circled dots = isolates or terminal upper members of networks.)

locate probable isolates; (4) to form estimates of the likelihood that the coalitions will link up with each other to form more powerful subgroups; (5) to locate who are the strategically-placed persons to make these linkages, and so on for many similar problems.

There are many ways in which one might go about connecting the points in the space into larger structures. I advance a theory below which is largely untried, but for which indirect evidence exists. Some of this evidence is presented in the next chapter, where it is shown that there is a strong pervasive tendency for most members in groups to direct their communications upward, as if they were seeking status for their ideas and values, if not for themselves. The theory explained below is represented in Figures 3.1, 3.2, and 3.3, by the lines drawn connecting the points.

A Theory of Probable Coalitions

Each person may be thought of as wishing to maintain his movement, and indeed the movement of all members of the group so far as possible, in his own characteristic value-direction. He would like others to perceive, feel, think, act, and evaluate as he himself does. In fact, he can seldom realize his wish to any high degree since, if there is a normal variation of individual personalities in his group, and if each individual wishes to go in his own particular direction, they will wish to go in different directions. There may be other members more or less close to the given person, whose similarity he will recognize, at least in part, and who he will hope to count on for cooperation. Sometimes cooperation will be in the nature of a "vote" on which he can count. Sometimes he will want the other to speak for his value-position, to take the leadership in the realization of his values. These are reciprocal expectations in an actual coalition. The person who wishes to remain more passive or who is, for any reason, less powerful, wants the other to take the leadership, to "represent" him, to further his cause. The person who wishes to take leadership in a given value-direction wants to be able to count on the other to follow, to "vote" for him, or support him, in return.

The realization of one's values in a group depends to a certain extent upon one's power in the group. If one has power in the group, that is, a position in the upward portion of the space, one can use it in the realization of one own and others' values. If one does not have power himself, then he may gain power to some extent, perhaps, by attaching himself to someone more powerful whose direction coincides in part with his own. In some way, possibly quite indirect, he offers his support, or perhaps unconsciously identifies himself with some more powerful other member who wishes to go more or less in the same direction. Some two or more members of the group who thus form an alliance, who coalesce in their motivation into a partial unity for the sake of exerting additional power in a given value-direction may be said to form, or to constitute, a *coalition*. Each of the members of the coalition gains in power. A coalition may also be called a subgroup, or a subnetwork.

It is assumed that in order to alter one's value-direction as little as possible one will tend to form a coalition with one or more others as close to his position as possible. But in the ordinary case members of a group differ from each other in power. Let us assume that there is a tendency for *each* person to form a coalition with a person *more* powerful than himself, in order that the other may better "represent" one's value-direction (or some direction close to it) to the rest of the group. That person, in turn, may be willing to form the relationship, but he may be more concerned to form a coalition with a person still higher in the power structure than himself.

If this is the case, each person will face a conflict. He will give a high priority to some other person further up in the power structure than himself. But he will also wish to form a coalition with someone lower than himself in the power structure who offers him support. If that person, in turn, has still others who offer their support to *him,* it becomes all the more important to form a coalition with him. In this way one may become the leader of a subgroup or faction.

Various networks of such coalitions are shown as interconnected series of points on Figures 3.1, 3.2, 3.3. Each person higher in the U-D dimension of a given particular network is supposed to be a kind of representative of those below him. Each person lower in the network receives some additional probability of movement in his own direction of value-realization through the connection. He is thus "represented." The network of coalitions permits those below to obtain the feeling (possibly also the fact) of partial value-realization, and gives to those above the feeling (possibly also factual) that they are supported by followers.

The networks probable in a given group depend in part upon the value-directions of the persons at the time they enter the group. It may be that one or more members are so different from the others in their value-position that they remain isolated. Other individuals may be surrounded by so many persons of a similar value-direction that they hardly need even think who might be their closest ally. For the sake of simplicity of the model to be used here, however, we shall make the following definite assumptions: Each person in the group will try to form an alliance, or will identify himself in a psychological sense with the one other person who is closest to his position, provided that person is further upward in the power structure, *unless* there is no person close enough, in which case the given person will remain either an individual isolate, or will remain the terminating upper member of a network of those further downward linked to him.

The application of this set of assumptions will result in one or more networks for the group, as shown in Figures 3.1, 3.2, and 3.3. The same set of networks is shown in all three figures, although they appear quite different at first, when viewed from each of the three perspectives. The theoretical map of probable coalitions produced in this way may now be used to focus attention on particular aspects of group structure and the positions of particular individuals. One naturally looks for a leader of the whole group, if any, or if not, the division of the group into factions, the direction and extent of separation, the top members of factions, or others who are at the junction of a number of lower branches or networks, and the probabilities that they will combine or compete. One looks for pairs of members in different factions who may, nevertheless, be close enough together that some change in their orientation might enable the two networks to become tied together. One looks for isolates, who may be in any position in the space.

Quantification and Scale of the Graphs

If you are making such maps for a group a few suggestions may be useful. For one thing, there is the problem of the scale of the graph. A reasonable solution as to the number of steps is to show the highest number that could have been attained by an individual in a given direction using the method of quantification you have adopted. In Figures 3.1, 3.2 and 3.3, twenty-six steps in each direction from the zero point are shown, since twenty-six was the number of persons rating in the group, and each person's summary classification of another was taken as the basis for counting one unit in each direction contained in the component letters of the type name. If you are using Interpersonal Rating Form A, for example, from Chapter 1, answered by yourself alone, then a group member cannot attain a score higher than eighteen in any direction, hence this may be taken as the number of steps on each side of the zero point. If you are using the additional forms B and C, as well as A, then you would have three times that number, or fifty-four. You will want to base your point locations on as much information as you possibly can, for greater reliability, but you can still apply the general idea even though you do not have much data.

As a result of your assessment procedure, however sketchy or careful it may be, you will need to end up with a list of the members and a tabulation of the ratings received by each, with summary positions as shown in Table 3.1. When you recognize, as this list shows, that the summary position of the individual on each dimension is obtained by balancing the two opposing directions against each other, you will be reminded of the desirability of having the same number of questions in each of the two opposing directions, although it is true that the "yes"-"no" answer form will produce scores in both directions. The Interpersonal Rating Forms A, B, and C, are balanced in this respect on all three dimensions. You will remember that each form is made up of one question for each of the twenty-six directions, each of which may be answered "no" as well as "yes," thereby tending to equate the opportunities for each opposing direction to make itself felt.

Once you have a list of all members and the quantified summary position for each, you are ready to plot the points. The easiest procedure is to start with the perspective of Figure 3.1, and plot the positions of all members with the identification of each member on the right of the point, and the location of the point in the missing dimension on the left of the point. You may not need to make additional plots to help determine the networks.

DETERMINING THE NETWORK OF COALITIONS

You are now ready to locate the theoretical networks of coalitions. It is convenient to start with the lowest point, corresponding to that of member MS as in Figure 3.1. The problem is to connect that point to the *nearest point upward* from it. Point RWB seems by inspection to be a good candidate, though it is a little further upward than point DL.

At any time you are uncertain which of two points may be closer, or whether any other point is close enough to connect (see below), you may check the distance numerically. This may be done easily as follows: List the locations of the first two points, one below the other, and perform the operations indicated:

Your point of reference:	MS	(20D,	5P,	4F)
The other point:	RWB	(13D,	0,	8F)
Subtract algebraically:		7,	5,	4
Square each difference:		49,	25,	16
Sum these squared differences:		49 +	25 +	16 = 90

The subtraction is performed algebraically so that, for example, if the first subtraction had been 20D minus 13U (instead of 13D), the difference would have been 33 instead of 7. The actual distance is finally found by taking the square root of the sum of the squared differences on the three dimensions. The computation is simply the three-dimensional version of the computation required to determine the hypotenuse of a right-angle triangle. The actual distance between MS and RWB in the present case is about $9\frac{1}{2}$ (the square root of 90). However, it is not necessary to compute the actual distance in order to compare how far various pairs of points are from each other. The sum of the squared differences does quite as well for comparisons, and it avoids the burden of extracting square roots.

To continue with the example, the distance between MS and DL is next determined in the same way:

Point of reference:	MS	(20D,	5P,	4F)
The other point:	DL	(14D,	18P,	13B)

Subtract algebraically:	6,	13,	17
Square each difference:	36,	169,	289
Sum these squared differences:	36 +	169 +	289 = 494

The sum of the squared differences between MS and DL (494) is thus seen to be much greater than that between MS and RWB (90), and since there are no other plausible candidates the line may be drawn from MS to RWB.

A solid line is used in this case. In order to help keep the networks distinguishable in the plots, those that lie mostly in the forward part of the space are connected with solid lines, and those that lie mostly in the backward part of the space are connected with dotted lines. This separation is seen most clearly in Figure 3.2.

Before a line is actually drawn, however, one must determine that the nearest point upward is not "too far" away. How far is "too far"? Three of the members in the present group, members JV, JR, and JF, are shown as isolates, with no line connecting them to any other member. There is no way to establish from experience, at present, exactly what the cutoff distance should be. And yet it seems reasonable that there must be such a distance if the theory is any good. Theoretically one might define it as a distance so great that the individual can not receive any help or support in the value-direction he wishes to go by forming a coalition.

In the present case the distance was chosen by judgment. Any distance beyond 15 was judged to be "too far." This was the distance that seemed, in this particular group, to do the best job of leaving in the same network those individuals who actually cooperated to some degree, and of separating those who did not. Since, in comparing the distances between points, it is more convenient to work with the sum of the squared differences, as indicated above, it is also convenient to state the cutoff point in terms of the square of the actual distance. In the present case, this index is 225, $(15^2 = 225)$. All of the connections shown as lines between points on the graphs of the group represent actual distances of not more than 15, or indexes of not more than 225.

There is not much deductive justification for the particular cutting point chosen in this case. Empirically, it is about 58 percent of the radius (15 is about 58 percent of 26). The empirical procedure of taking 58 percent of the radius may serve as a rule of thumb for other applications until a better rule can be found. In finding a better rule there is a problem of choosing a distance (perhaps a variable one rather than a fixed one), which takes into account the fact that some pairs of points are close to the center, whereas others are far out. From the distributions of points studied in actual groups so far it appears that a single fixed distance chosen by the above empirical rule may not be a bad compromise. In the groups studied, two points at about the median distance out from the center on a typical two-dimensional plot, separated from each other by this distance, will ordinarily subtend an angle of about 90 degrees. Two such points will be far enough out from the center to receive a typological classification, and the typological directions so determined are uncorrelated with each other.

Intuitively this degree of separation of points seems to meet the criterion that two individuals in such a relation to each other would not receive help *directly* from each other in the value-directions they each wish to go, although they might *indirectly* help each other. The result of their cooperation, if they did form a coalition, would theoretically be a direction of movement between them, about 45 degrees removed from each. (This is the same angle which, on the average, separates one type from another in the typology.) This much of a gain might be worth while, especially if the two were cooperating vis-à-vis some person or network with a directional tendency opposite to both of them, but without such an opponent common to both, neither would appear to the other to be of much help—or so it seems intuitively. On the other hand, since their directions are simply uncorrelated, not opposite, there would seem to be no bar to cooperation between the two if there were some advantage vis-à-vis others in the group. Perhaps rational or political arguments for cooperation might make a critical difference in such cases, and might benefit a number of other persons in the group by bringing two or more networks into effective integration.

We seem to be close to a mathematical model of potential or actual coalitions at this point, and one may hope for development in this direction. It is important to realize, however, that what has been presented so far is only heuristic. The substantive assumptions are not really clear, nor is it clear what they should be. Consequently the mathematical model one would want to represent the assumptions most closely cannot be clear. Nor is it clear just what empirical predictions one would most like to make, and how this might affect the assumptions and the model. Nevertheless, the heuristic model as presented may be of some help.

Isolates in the Illustrative Group

The three members, JV, JR, and JF, who are identified as isolates by the heuristic procedure did indeed seem isolated in that they rejected the group. Member JV, classified as type DN, tried early in the life of the group to get the members to follow a set discussion procedure, to choose a topic, and then stick to it. When he received no support he served notice that he was going to keep quiet from then on, and for the most part did so, although there were numerous attempts to bring him back into participation. He answered questions, usually with a single sentence, and the rest of the time kept a sardonic silence.

Member JR, classified as type NB, was apparently in the midst of adolescent alienation troubles. He said the other members of the group seemed like "turnips" to him, but when they asked him what they could do to improve matters he said "Nothing." He indicated that he felt this way in general, however, and his reaction was not specific to the group.

Member JF, classified as type PB, made a dramatic gesture at the very beginning of the group as a means of announcing his name, and on various occasions drew pictures on the board, but he had a very low rate of verbal interaction, and toward the end said that the group had not meant much to him.

All three of these members, with the partial exception of JF, seemed to match quite well the impressions given by their type descriptions, and this was generally true for most members. It is worth noting that the isolates identified by the present heuristic procedure fall in quite different locations in the space. An isolate as defined here is not a particular type of personality or group role, but a person of any type who has no other members sufficiently close to him in his group to give him help or support in his value-direction, whatever it may be.

Terminal Upper Members of Networks

A member may be at the top of a network and so connected with members below him, but still be isolated in the sense that he and the other members of his network are too far from any members further upward to establish a connection. Such a person may or may not be an effective leader of his subnetwork.

In Figure 3.2, three networks are shown, headed by terminal upper members SP, CE, and JH. Member SP, at the very top of Figure 3.2 might be considered as a candidate for the leader of the total group—he certainly tried hard and openly to obtain the title of leader—and yet there may be some question of his success as one looks at the map. He is connected to a network of only three other members, all of them further backward than he. A defender of SP, who wanted him to have the title of leader, might reply that the very top member of a group, by definition, cannot be connected to any person further upward (at least in the group). How could one ask more of a leader under the present descriptive system?

Perhaps one could not ask more of the person, and yet one might hope that he had a better position, or perhaps a lieutenant in a better position to help him. There is no formal reason why a member in the position of SP could not head up more than one subnetwork. He might have done so in this group, for example, if member CE had been close enough to him, or if SP and CE had somehow managed to form an alliance in spite of the distance between them. This did not happen. These two members were openly hostile to each other, though CE was more hostile than SP.

Member CE is at the top of a network and so is connected with members below him, but he is too far from any members further upward in the group structure to establish a connection. A member in this position may be in an important sense isolated in spite of his connection with those below him. This seemed to be true of CE. He was not an effective leader of those below him and seemed quite frustrated though active throughout most of the year. He did not realize until the group made ratings of its members that he was seen as somewhat negative. When he asked to be told why, others told him that he was too moralistic and dominant. He reduced his participation, but his sense of moralistic frustration seemed to increase.

Members at Junctions of Networks

The position of member RFB in the network below CE calls attention to another important opportunity for leadership. A member may hold a strategic position, not because he is the furthest upward in a network, but because his position is at the juncture of two or more subnetworks. This kind of position is held in other networks; by member LD in one, and by JL in another. Within the same network below RFB, members AR, ADW, and IB are also at junction points.

It is of interest that members LD, JL, and AR were all females. In observing the group one might have gotten the impression that they performed an integrative function within their networks for this reason. Perhaps this was important. On the other hand, their position at junction points may have given them a special opportunity to function this way. There is no reason why the present method of locating members should tend to put well-liked or attractive members at junction points. Whatever the combination of reasons, there was a visible alliance, and some joint planning outside of sessions between members LD (female) and SP (male) who fall in one network, and similarly a positive joking relationship between member LD and EM (male), and between LD and LWT (male). All four of the members in this network, terminated at the top of SP, were high participators and participated with each other frequently. They undoubtedly had a major influence on the topics introduced into discussion, and on the emotional tone of the group. Member SP was not only the member furthest upward in this network, but also the member furthest forward, and hence in the best position to make a junction with the large network in the forward part of the space, terminated at the top by member CE. As noted above, CE and SP were quite antagonistic to each other. Were the two networks antagonistic to each other? Was there in fact no connection?

In fact, though no connection is predicted by the model, there was a cooperative relationship between member SP in the one network and member RFB in the other. Member SP openly praised RFB and urged him to participate more. Member RFB was a relatively low participator (in spite of his moderately upward location) and did not respond to the urging of SP. On the other hand, he did not interfere with the strong leadership efforts of SP in any way, and he did not resist in any way the discussion of topics introduced by SP's network. In this sense, RFB cooperated by tacit acceptance. In effect the two networks were tied together through the relationship of SP and RFB.

Member CE, although tacitly accepted also by RFB, occupied a somewhat negative position in the evaluation of group members and remained almost isolated and in conflict with SP. The distance separating CE and SP was considerably greater than that between SP and RFB, which probably encouraged the coalition between SP and RFB. The more general point is that the latter two members were in a strategic position with regard to the possibility of linking the two networks, since they were closer together than any other representatives of the two networks. Political rationality, if nothing else, might have led SP to try hard to form the coalition.

Integration within the Same Network

The forward network in the present group is unusually large, theoretically linking together almost two-thirds of the members of the group over quite a range of positions. Was it in fact so well integrated as the model implies? Probably it was not, at any rate there were not always visible signs of cooperation between the members shown as linked. In particular, member CT, a female on the far-positive side of the group, hardly participated in the group, that is, she talked very little, and neither did member JG, another extremely popular female, shown near CT. The model implies that JG and CT cooperated, but in fact it was difficult to tell whether they did or not, since they talked so little in the group. It was similarly difficult to tell whether they were cooperating with other members in the forward network, or whether they were simply the passive recipients of liking on the part of others. However, it was reported that they both participated a great deal with others outside the formal sessions of the group. Why were they not more active and apparently cooperative in the group?

Although these two girls, CT and JG, were very positively evaluated by other members of the group, they remained notably locked in silence during the sessions. There were some evidences in their final communications to the instructor, that they had waited patiently, like good and loving children, for a return of acceptance and love from a leader who would take the role of a good parent and tell them what to do to receive his appreciation. Lacking this, they remained puzzled and hurt, more and more secretly angry, as the year wore on. Why did they not receive the active appreciation of the instructor? At this point I must confess that I was the course instructor, the member designated RFB above, who presumably could have obtained greater integration within the network by making an active effort to cooperate with members far removed but still within the network. Whether I should have made such efforts is perhaps debatable, in view of the structured neutral role of the course instructor (see Appendix 6). But the purpose of the neutral role is to highlight just such emotional needs and demands on the part of course members in order that they may become visible and open to interpretation. In retrospect it seems to me that I failed to understand the condition sufficiently well and failed to make interpretations that might have resulted in a resolution of the feelings, and hence a more active coalition.

Integration of Networks by Outside Contacts

There is some implication, as indicated above, that members CT and JG performed integrative functions within their network through their contacts with members outside the group sessions. The same thing, perhaps, may occur to tie together networks that appear to be separate according to the model. Was the network in the downward-positive-backward area of the space actually separated from the forward network, as the model implies?

The members of the DPB network showed considerable internal cooperation. As remarked above, member JL, a female, was to some extent a central member of this network and was both consoled and ardently protected on various occasions by members DL (a male) and LLT (also a male). Member JH (male) a little further upward, did not have the same relation to JL, nor was he superficially much like the other three, but he did have probably the most active and original fantasy life in the group, and in this sense he resembled the others, particularly JL and DL, each of whom had aspirations in artistic directions. Artistic aspirations seemed to appear more frequently among those in the backward part of the space than in the forward, as the descriptions of the group role types predict.

The backward part of the space is more thinly populated than the forward part, however, and the network in the DPB region remained apparently rather isolated from the forward network. Although member LLT was notable for absences, and was much reproached for this, the members of the network did participate verbally and supplied a fair share of content, much of it in line with that suggested by the description of the type DPB. Whether a "long stretch" to clasp hands between some pair of members might have tied this network in with the forward network is debatable, but it seems not out of the question. Specifically, it was reported that member CT, one of the two very popular females in the forward network, discussed above, took quite a motherly role vis-à-vis member JL outside of sessions. If this relationship could have been examined and perhaps activated within the group, it might have had an integrative effect for the group as a whole. Knowledge of this potentiality, plus good interpretation, might have brought the relationship into play. It is hoped that the present heuristic model of potential coalitions and the overall structure of the group will help to highlight such opportunities.

Distribution of Members in the Group Space

Plots have been made of the networks in ten academic self-analytic groups (see Appendix 6), according to the method described for the group above. The rating form was approximately the same as Form A in Chapter One. (Forms B and C have not yet been used.) A few useful things may be said on the basis of this experience, perhaps, without the formal presentation of data.[1]

The instructors and the group members generally agree that the resulting model of their group is a reasonably good one, and that a study of the structure of their particular group is enlightening. The example used in this chapter seems quite characteristic. First, as in the example, the members are not typically distributed at random or equally throughout the space; more are found on the positive side of the space than on the negative side, and the tendency to be on the positive side is very marked for women as compared to men. More members are found in the forward part of the space than in the backward, and this tendency is more marked for men. On the average, women are further downward, considerably more positive, and slightly backward from the men. Men are

---

[1] I am indebted to Stephen Cohen for preliminary work in the tabulation and interpretation of these data.

about equally distributed between the upward and downward parts of the space, with a few more in the downward part, but women are definitely found more frequently in the lower part of the space. The differences between the positions of men and women are about what might be expected from the cultural stereotypes of the male and female adult sex roles, and the findings parallel those of Strodtbeck and Mann (152) in another kind of group.

The distribution of points representing the positions of all persons in all groups resembles a spiral with the lower end reaching around backward toward the DNB region. The main body of points curves positively forward and upward, reaching its largest concentration in the UPF region, then trails off thinly into the UNF region. The N, UN, and UNB regions are thinly populated, and even UB and UPB are rather low in number of points. The regions DN and DNF are very sparsely populated indeed, but with a few more males than females. Isolates are found more frequently in the negative and backward parts of the space.

The male instructors of the groups are most frequently found in the UF, UPF, and UP regions; the female coinstructors in the PF, P, and DP regions. These are the positions, roughly, that I have formerly called those of task and social leaders (21), although both male and female instructors are probably a little lower in the space and a little more positive than the task and social leaders in the all-male five-person problem-solving groups studied. The instructors and coinstructors are seldom isolated, and are often found in strategic positions within their networks.

No self-analytic group so far has shown a completely integrated network of all members. There are normally three or four networks in a group of about twenty-five members, the largest one in the group ranging from about seven to sixteen members, the second largest from five to ten members, the third from three to six members, and the fourth from two to four members. All groups have had some isolates, ranging in number from three to five per group. The isolates are more likely to appear on the thinly populated negative side of the space, but they may appear in any region.

The largest coalition is usually in the UPF region, and it may or may not connect with a second largest, further downward, more positive, and not so far forward, usually close to the PF and P regions. A third is often found in the PB region, and it may or may not connect across to a fourth in the DB or DNB region. This disposition of the separate networks is consistent with spiral shape of the distribution of all members described above.

The total distribution of member locations is quite similar to that which one usually imagines for a political spectrum—ranging from the far right in UNF, with a sprinkling of NF and DNF, around through the conservative center parties in UPF with a few members in PF and DPF, on through the center parties in P, with some UP and some DP; and on around to the left-of-center liberal parties, centering in PB and DPB, with a few in UPB; and finally around to the far left, centering in DB, B, and a few in DNB. As in the case of political entities, it is very difficult to obtain a coalition of the whole. Opportunities for changing the direction of the group as a whole appear to lie in bringing together two or more subcoalitions or networks. This can probably be done most easily by strategically placed members. Probably some implicit agreement for a better distribution of the resources and rewards available to the group is usually the basis for a more complete integration.

A Ladder of Role-Models

So far as individual members are concerned, the spectrum of networks can be seen as a kind of social ladder, a series of interconnected and more or less similar roles. The individual who is trying to change his personality or group role may identify with persons slightly higher than himself in the status structure. By emulation, he may climb step by step in the status structure of the group, or by degrees, overcome types of deficiencies and deviance which have heretofore kept him more downward, negative, and backward. Thus the ladder is not only a means of social climbing in the pejorative sense, but also a means of education, re-education, and therapy (5, 6, 8, 22). The normal process of socialization of the child presumably involves such a climb, perhaps a repeated series of climbs at each crisis in socialization (37). Perhaps some children fail to progress normally in socialization because in their family or situation no such ladder of easy stages exists; the same may be true of a self-analytic or a therapy group.

The social structure of complete societies has often been pictured as a kind of social pyramid. The structure seen in these self-analytic groups is more like a spiral than a pyramid—an irregular spiral web of interconnected group positions, with some breaks, mounting from DNB to UPF, by way of the spiral route through P. It is common to visualize three main social classes for societies. In small groups we are more likely to see about four subnetworks, which often do not quite connect, but which, with some breaks, do mount in social status in some generalized sense, with isolates off the ladder in every direction. In our groups, the apex of power is likely to be not at the point of greatest generalized social status, but somewhere past that optimal stage, specialized in the power direction, trailing off at the top through UNF, UN, and U. The point of greatest *generalized* social status is probably in the region of UPF, with U not too greatly emphasized (27).

Within each subnetwork, also, the terminating upper member is likely to be isolated because, although he is at the apex of *power* within his subnetwork, he is too specialized in the U direction, and so is located

off the main ladder by which his subgroup could most easily be connected with the next higher network. The price of his greater power is
isolation. It is thus probably true that the most strategic member for
connecting his subnetwork to the next higher subnetwork is a member
not so high in the power direction, but rather a secondary subleader,
who perhaps is more positive, more forward.

Possibly for each person the person most likely to be able to give him
"a hand up," is the person who is nearest to him in the upward-positive-
and forward direction from him, all three simultaneously, as an older
brother often is. Such a person is likely to arouse "status envy," as John
Whiting has called it (159). On the basis of his greater power to
reward he is able to arouse liking and affection, perhaps admiration,
which invites identification and emulation, and he has value-conceptions
and patterns of conduct which, if successfully internalized, are likely to
bring greater rewards from a larger portion of the group when put into
practice. The difference of that other person from the self is at the same
time, hopefully not too great, so that the "generation gap" can be
overcome. In the relation, or coalition, between two such members a
psychological and social quid pro quo is possible, that is, an exchange
profitable to both, as emphasized by George Homans (101) and others
who tend to think in terms of concepts derived from economics. The
rewards to the higher person consist of being the object of envy, affection, admiration, even emulation, and of being able to help another
similar to himself. To be able to help or teach in such a way presumably
helps one's normal defenses by providing in one's overt behavior a good
example for the more regressive inner self (6;8). The rewards to the
lower person consist in the gains in all of these same respects which he
may make by some minimal readjustment of his personality and behavior, subsequently the change of his group role and the rewards that go
with the new role. In such a relationship the leverage for change should
be at a maximum, and this is indeed the prototype, I believe, of most
normal and beneficial processes of attitude and personality change. If one
wishes to induce change, he should try to provide such a set of opportunities within a group setting. What we call "leadership" is simply the
most salient large-scale example within the group.

For the person lowest in the ladder, around DNB, affection and
acceptance may be the greatest need. For the person in the middle
position, around P, who has more affection and acceptance, the needs for
greater value control through idealization, and for more power, or at
least a better distribution of power within the group, are probably more
strategic. For the person at the optimum point in the spiral network,
around UPF, the needs for more power over the situation of the group
and for creative change, are probably crucial, but if these needs are
combined with a need for the expression of aggression, they are likely to

cause him to move toward UF, UNF, U, and so to overshoot the mark. For persons in such a position, a chastening fall from power, a status humiliation, a self-reappraisal, and a later recovery may be the only route back to an optimum balance.

EFFECTS OF INTER-MEMBER EVALUATIONS

The assessment of group roles and personalities by a public or semipublic procedure, such as the rating exercise used in these self-analytic groups tends to arouse tensions and to evoke change (45). When the summary positions resulting from the ratings are made known, a reaction is inevitable. Some members are pleased, some are surprised, a few are horrified, and a few are bitterly confirmed in their worst anticipations. A few are likely to denounce the procedure, the analytical system, and the group goal of self-analysis, with an attack on its nonhumanistic implications. Efforts to change personalities, group roles, the group structure, and the group goals usually begin with renewed vigor.

Some success is possible, and much success over a long term, but usually resistances and blocks to change appear, the reasons for which are not evident. These difficulties furnish much of the material for analysis— or should. The instructors, and the more knowing group members, must gently but persistently keep attention focused on such problems, and assist in their interpretation, or the group will stall and trail off in some eccentric direction. This is the fate of many naturally formed small groups without adequate leadership or interpretive help: they become persistently more self-enclosed, protective, cultlike, and are eventually turned under by the relentless plow of evolution.

A conception and realistic hope that constructive change is possible should be fostered among all members of the group—not only because it is the truth, but because it gives group members the basic rationale for their efforts, and in particular the courage for the somewhat abrasive process of intermember evaluation. Members' efforts to analyze each other, instructor's efforts to interpret, and especially the imposition of the more formal ratings and training in observation procedures are otherwise likely to be viewed as a kind of exploitation for research, as a kind of fortune telling, or as a dehumanization—all of which might best be avoided. In groups (self-analytic or otherwise) where it seems best not to ask the members to assess each other by any formal procedures, or to precipitate a process of change, the well-trained observer can arrive at a reasonable approximation of the group structure by his own ratings and observations, and can also trace changes by these means. This is the more naturalistic approach, and I believe that it too, can add much to knowledge.

4

Aids to
Inference

Ordinarily we do not reason very well in three dimensions, as one may feel in trying to visualize the spatial model described in the last chapter. Two dimensions are easily handled visually on a plane surface, as in each of the three perspectives of the space. In common-sense thinking, if there are no good visual aids we seem to have a strong tendency to reduce our problems to one dimension. We tend to think in terms of opposites, dichotomies, "is" and "is not."

Opposites are easily understood. But the relation of "no relation," (neither dependably the same nor dependably the opposite) is harder to think about. In the area of attitudes and values, for example, we typically have a very partial view of the complete range of possible values—the "total space"—and two attitudes are often thought of as opposite from each other when they are really unrelated in the minds of other persons. If research is actually done on the relation of two attitudes to each other over a large population of persons, we may discover that the two attitudes thought to be opposite to each other turn out to be neither compatible nor incompatible, when enough people are questioned. The two attitudes may be simply different from each other, and combinable in any way.

In order to understand how personality and group role types relate to each other, we must be able to visualize more than one or two dimensions within which they may differ from each other. The present system for describing and relating aspects of behavior to each other is built upon three dimensions. This does not mean that the world of variation we are studying "really" has exactly three dimensions, no more and no less. For example the factor analysis of values which is part of the basis of the present work showed four dimensions (see Appendix 5), of which only the first three are used for the present model. There are no doubt more ways than three or four in which values or value-statements can differ from each other, but still they may be compared on three. The restriction to three dimensions does not necessarily mean that some types of value-statements are completely disregarded. It means that they are less exactly defined and located than they might be. But the gain in exactness may not be worth the cost in complication. The restriction to three dimensions for the present system is a restriction for the sake of practical manageability.

Two dimensions, although simpler, are not enough for our purpose. Much of the work in the factor analysis of attitudes has been organized around a conception of two dimensions, as well described by Eysenck (78). It is desirable to go further than two dimensions when one is interested in the relation of values or attitudes to interpersonal behavior, since factor analytic studies in the interpersonal perception and behavior realm have repeatedly shown at least three dimensions, as first noted by Carter and Couch (53; 58; 59; 71; 72; 138). It is hoped that one of the contributions of the present work will be to bring the study of attitudes and interpersonal behavior more closely together. One of the basic hypotheses underlying the present system is that the factors often discovered in these two domains can be fitted together in a single three dimensional space.

In order to understand the meaning of this statement one must have the ability to visualize the relation of a two dimensional to a three dimensional space. Some of the work in the description of interaction and personality has assumed, or discovered, a two-dimensional space (87, 88). Perhaps the best example is the two-dimensional descriptive system of Leary (80, 109). In his terms the two dimensions are called dominance versus submissiveness, (upward versus downward in the present system), and love versus hate, (positive versus negative in the present system). The two dimensions usually recognized in attitude studies do not coincide with these. They are, in Eysenck's terms (78), conservative versus radical, (forward versus backward in the present system), and tough-minded versus tender-minded, (upward-negative in the present system, versus downward-positive). Although these polarities can all be easily related to each other in a three-dimensional space, as indicated, their relations can not be described in less than a three dimensional space. Neither two dimensions reduces to the other two, but they partly coincide. A three-dimensional space is necessary.

Actually at least a three dimensional space is necessary to deal properly with interpersonal behavior alone, even though one does not try to deal with values or attitudes explicitly. Such an interaction observation system has been developed by Borgatta and Crowther, based upon several careful factor analytic studies (55). The three factors of their system are directly related to the three factors of the present system, though the conceptualization is somewhat different for one factor.

There is good reason to believe that more than three factors will usually be found when one employs a large number of personality tests as well as direct observations of interpersonal behavior and ratings by group members. In Couch's study (71) of the personality domain, based upon written personality tests alone, he found five factors worth separate recognition, and reviews of factor analytic studies of personality indicate that there is some convergence on the nature and number of personality factors (112; 113 and 125). The space employed in the present work concentrates upon interpersonal behavior and its evaluation by others, rather than on the full range of personality traits, and it is confined to three dimensions for practical use in an observational approach. There is nothing sacred about the number three, nor about the particular rotation of the directions in the space, nor about any of the names used to refer to them.

The work of Osgood and his associates has repeatedly shown a three-dimensional space within which the meanings persons assign to objects, including other persons, can be represented (127). It seems highly likely that Osgood's space is related to the one used in the present system. I shall discuss the problem as to the more general reasons for the dimensionality of my space in Chapter 8. It is held there that the dimensions are the product of the tendencies of persons to "evaluate" each other. Osgood's space is concerned with something very similar, though he speaks more of "meaning." It seems to me that the spaces correspond in the following way: His good versus bad dimension is probably the same as my positive versus negative. My best guess is that his fast versus slow dimension passes from upward-backward to downward-forward in my space, and that his powerful versus weak dimension passes from upward-forward to downward-backward of my space. No actual work on this has been done, however.

Perhaps the time is already overdue for some practice in thinking in three dimensions. In order to make the above kind of discussion more easily understandable it may be helpful to pay some specific attention to the names of the directions, how to locate them, and how to tell their relation to each other.

EXERCISE: VISUALIZING DIRECTIONS IN THE SPATIAL MODEL

The basic conception of the spatial model is that of a three-dimensional space. To avoid resorting to mathematics or graphical presentations, the present system employs a common-sense visualization and a set of names.

The easiest common-sense visualization is to think of the three-dimensional physical space surrounding one. The self is taken as the central point of reference within an imagined sphere with indefinite outer boundaries. The space within the sphere has three reference dimensions, intersecting at the central point where one locates himself. The dimensions are named upward-downward, positive-negative, and forward-backward. Upward means the direction straight up from one's head, and downward means the direction toward one's feet. Positive is the direction horizontally to one's right, as one points outward with the right hand; negative is the opposite direction, as one points outward with the left hand. Forward is the direction one is facing, straight ahead of one's eyes, and backward is the direction straight from the back of one's head. One can easily keep three separate dimensions and their combinations straight using this common-sense model. Naming the directions and using the names consistently is a further aid.

The names of the directions are used as the titles of the types described in Part II of this book. A type is named by indicating its direction from the central point. In naming the type, its direction in the *upward-downward* dimension is always specified first, unless the type is at the middle in this dimension, in which case neither direction is named. The direction uniformly specified next is the location in the *positive-negative* dimension. The direction in the *forward-backward* dimension is specified last. The composite names so generated consist of one, two, or three names of directional components. The Table of Contents contains the complete list. There are twenty-six directions specified, plus one additional case of no direction in any of the three dimensions, which is called *direction zero*. The corresponding type is called type AVE, for "average."

The order of listing of the directions is always the same. The order starts with the central point of reference, direction zero, then goes to the upward direction, at the top of the sphere. It may help to visualize the sphere in the form of an earth globe. The upward direction starts from the center of the globe, and passes through the North Pole. There is a horizontal ring of directions halfway between the North Pole and the equator which follows the north temperate zone around the earth globe. The next horizontal ring of directions on the globe corresponds to the equatorial zone. The one below that is halfway from the equator toward the South Pole and corresponds to the south temperate zone. Below that is the position exactly at the bottom of the sphere—the South Pole, through which the downward direction passes.

In listing the types, or in reproducing the list from memory, one needs to remember the starting points and the order of passing from ring to ring. After mentioning direction zero, the point of origin, one starts at the North Pole with the direction upward. Then one passes to the ring of directions next below, beginning with the upward-positive type. One then proceeds around the ring counterclockwise as follows: upward-positive-forward; upward-forward; upward-negative-forward; upward-negative; upward-negative-backward; upward-backward; and upward-positive-backward; thus completing the ring of directions combined with the upward direction corresponding to the north temperate zone on the earth globe.

One then drops to the equatorial ring, next below, beginning with the direction positive. From here, proceed around the ring, counterclockwise, as before, thus: positive-forward; forward; negative-forward; negative; negative-backward; backward; and positive-backward. This completes the rings of directions which are independent of either the upward or the downward direction.

To continue, one drops to the ring below, corresponding to the south-temperate zone, each direction representing a combination with the downward direction. One begins at downward-positive, and continues counterclockwise around the ring, as before, thus: downward-positive-forward; downward-forward; downward-negative-forward; downward-negative; downward-negative-backward; downward-backward; and downward-positive-backward. This completes the ring, and leaves only the final direction to be specified—downward.

One needs to remember, for convenience, that the top ring begins with upward-positive, the equatorial ring begins with positive, and the bottom ring begins with downward-positive. These reference points and the listing order are, of course, arbitrary, but some such system is necessary as an aid to memory.

The ability to visualize the directions and their relations to each other will be greatly enhanced if one will simply practice naming the directions in order, actually pointing at the same time. Some practice is necessary to fix the system in the mind, as in learning to box the compass. Much of the text of this book depends upon the ability to visualize spatial directions rapidly from their names. Without this ability and some skill, it will be impossible to reason about the relations of the types to each other, or the variables. The spatial model of group structure described in the last chapter will have given some introductory practice.

The names and the common-sense pointing procedure help one in thinking of the physical-spatial model. The spatial model in turn represents a mathematical model, the model of factor analysis, of the relations between variables (156). The model, in its several forms, is used as a kind of computer, or inference-maker, which helps in reasoning about the relationships between variables, types, and persons. The basic spatial model *can* be used rigorously, as it is in factor analysis, but it need not be used rigorously for all purposes. For many practical problems in application, if one learns to visualize the directions explicitly, with the aid of the names and the pointing procedure, he will be able to draw most needed inferences intuitively.

The list of directions as shown in the Table of Contents is useful for practice since it also gives for each direction a short verbal title for the content or direction of the values associated with the type. This title is needed to help recall the type of person and the other variables associated with each direction. It is desirable to memorize the title of the value-direction at the same time as the spatial name of the direction, and at the same time to visualize its location in the physical space. The location in visualized physical space is the means by which one is able to use the mathematical model intuitively. The spatial model, standing for the mathematical model, is the logical structure that gives one a boost in his power to make inferences about relationships. On the other hand, the title of the value-content of the direction is the means by which one is enabled to remember the body of empirical findings and substantive theory about personality and interpersonal behavior. Without these intermediary links one can neither get *into* the spatial model from his observations, nor *out* of it back to its meaning for personality.

USING THE SPATIAL MODEL FOR MAKING INFERENCES

The position of any point in three-dimensional physical space can be described by stating where it is along each of the three reference dimensions. So described, one can determine by computation its location in relation to any other point in the space, or its direction and distance from the center. The direction and distance of each point from the center gives a highly useful means of describing the relation of each point to each other. Knowing this, one can tell whether any given two points: (1) are close enough together to be considered to be "the same" direction from the center; (2) are not exactly in the same direction from the center, but in a neighboring one; (3) are in directions which are at right angles to each other, such that if one travels from the center toward one he neither travels toward nor away from the other; (4) are in directions from the center that are somewhat, but not completely oppo-site to each other; or finally, (5) are in directions which are completely the opposite of each other.

This kind of grouping is of interest because in a verbal model one cannot stand the complication of recognizing an infinite number of directions. For the verbal model the indefinite number of possible direc-tions has been grouped into twenty-six (plus a region around the point of origin for points which are not far enough out from the center in any direction to be considered significantly directional.) All possible points in the space are thus grouped by the classification in such a way that they fall along the lines of the twenty-six directions or within the zero region, each point being brought to the directional line to which it is closest, or to the zero point. In spite of the grouping one may still describe the relation between any two points in terms of the way their directions are related to each other. We may say that their directions are (as indicated above): (1) the same; (2) positively correlated with each other; (3) uncorrelated with each other; (4) negatively correlated with each other; or finally, (5) opposite. The zero region is uncorrelated with any of the twenty-six directions.

In the common-sense visualization of the physical space these degrees and directions of correlation can be grasped, for the most part, easily and correctly. It is obvious that the physical direction upward is positively correlated with the physical direction upward-positive, for example. It is our intuitive grasp of the relations of directions in the physical model that makes that model so useful. Our intuition in the wordless pointing modality is not necessarily perfect, however, and when the directions are grouped into a limited number of classes as designated by names, rather than wordlessly pointed to, our intuitive grasp is to some extent disturbed, even impaired. For example, it may not be intuitively certain whether the direction upward-positive-forward, (UPF) is *unrelated* to the direction upward-negative, (UN), or *negatively* related to it.

In order to make up for this impairment of intuition, since we cannot dispense with the grouping of directions into a few manageable named classes, a logical chart has been prepared as Appendix 2, which shows the relation of each named direction to each other. One may look in this chart under the direction UPF and find that it is zero-correlated, that is, unrelated to the direction UN. The classifications given in the logical chart do some minor violence to the physical model and the mathematical model, in the interests of simplification, as explained in the preliminary note to the chart. This chart was, in fact, the inference-maker used for the construction of the personality and group role types used in this book.

The advantage of the spatial model, and its verbal version, when reasoning about the substantive areas to which the model applies, such as personality traits, types of behavior, types of values, and so forth, can hardly be realized until tried. For example, if one knows the position of a personality trait in the spatial model, or in the verbal typology of the present system, he can intuitively infer its relation to every other type in the system. Briefly stated, he can infer that the trait in question will be most strongly related to the type that lies in the direction identical to it. It will be somewhat positively correlated to all the adjacent types that lie topologically in a ring around the reference type. It will be most strongly negatively correlated to the type in the direction which is the direct opposite to the reference direction. It will be somewhat negatively correlated to the types which lie in the adjacent ring around that direct opposite; and finally, it will be zero correlated to all the types which lie in the belt between the positive and negative areas just specified. In imagination the whole space can be polarized into a positive, a negative, and a neutral zone with regard to any given trait or type. The intellectual gain of this visualization is very great, even though the conclusions from the verbal model are not very precise.

HOW THE TWENTY-SIX TYPES IN THIS BOOK WERE CONSTRUCTED

The inferences required for the description of the twenty-six types were actually made mechanically using the Logical Chart in Appendix 2. It is worthwhile to consider an example in detail. The example will indicate how the findings of the factor analyses were translated into the present set of types. At the same time it will indicate how new findings of other analyses can be incorporated into the present system, and inferences may be drawn from them.

One of the items in Appendix 1, the list of variables, is "self-confidence." In a large study which Arthur Couch and I conducted, both observers and members of laboratory groups answered a question after each meeting on a questionnaire entitled Interpersonal Perceptions which read as follows:

1. To what extent do you feel that each member was self-confident and self-assured?"
    0 = "He seems very unsure of himself and lacks confidence."
    7 = "He seems very self-confident and self-assured."
    (The prior instructions read ". . . make your ratings using numerical scale (0, 1, 2, 3, 4, 5, 6, 7.) where the extreme ends (0) and (7) are defined under each question.")

Member Number	How do you rate him? (include yourself)	How do you guess he will rate you? (omit yourself)
1.	_____	_____
2.	_____	_____
3.	_____	_____

The main factor analysis of these data included measures of many different kinds, such as: kinds of overt interaction initiated and received; kinds of interpersonal perceptions given, guessed, and received; personality measures, including self-described traits; dreams and fantasies; attitudes and values endorsed; and remembered perceptions of parents. Because this factor analysis was intended to establish relationships between these different domains of behavior, Couch called it the Interdomain Analysis (71). It is this factor analysis that forms the backbone, though not the total content, of the information concerning location of specific items or types of measures in the three-dimensional space of the present system. His analysis showed six factors, of which the first three, the three most important in accounting for variance, are taken as the three reference directions of the present system. I have named his factor I upward-downward in the present system, his factor II is called positive-negative and his factor III is called forward-backward.[1] The factors are listed in the order of their importance in accounting for variance, an order which is reflected in the present naming system, where the most important factor is specified first.

In Appendix 1, under the name of the variable "Self-Confidence" is the specifying question, "Do observers rate him high on self-confidence? If yes, then expect U." As the source of evidence for this generalization one finds the notation: "Couch Interdomain Factor Analysis, I (U) = .67, II (P) = .03, III (F) = .13, summary direction U." The Roman numerals are Couch's factors, and the corresponding letters are directional names in the present system. The numbers are factor loadings from Couch's analysis, and they indicate the correlation of the item with the factor.

In the language of our model factor loadings indicate how far out the point representing the location of the item is in each of the reference directions. The factor loadings, like correlations, read from $+1.00$ through zero to -1.00. By rough judgment, then, it is easy to see that in the present case the location of the item is pretty far upward (.67), but hardly out at all in the positive direction (.03) or in the forward direction (.13). In order to incorporate this information in the verbal system one must make a classification of the item into *one* of the named directions of the present spatial model which will indicate to which one of them it is closest. In the present case the answer is clear; it is upward, and the classification judgment is indicated by the choice of the directional indicator, U.

This then, is the kind of research evidence underlying each of the

---

[1] I have actually reversed the polarity of his factor III (changed plus to minus), and have mentally (though not actually) rotated the forward end of the factor toward one of his orthogonal factors, factor VI, in order to obtain the desired conceptual fit. See Appendix 1, Preliminary Note.

items on the Interpersonal Rating Forms, and in Appendix 1. The directional indicator is a summary classification of a large amount of actual fine-grained information. In a few cases, I have made a guess at the location of an item. A seemingly simple guess may conceal a large amount of speculation. But if the location is well established and reliable, one is then in a position to infer the relation of the item or variable to all other directions in the space. In the present case, one may infer that the trait "self-confidence" as judged by the observer, although most likely to be characteristic of persons who are classified as upward, is also likely hold to some degree for the whole ring of types surrounding the upward direction, namely, UP, UPF, UF, UNF, UN, UNB, UB, and UPB. It is unlikely to characterize the downward type, since this is the opposite direction from upward, but it is also somewhat unlikely for the ring of types surrounding the downward direction, namely DP, DPF, DF, DNF, DN, DNB, DB, and DPB. Finally, for the ring of types around the equatorial belt (P, PF, F, NF, N, NB, B, and PB), one can infer that over a large number of individuals, there will be no dependable relation. Knowing that an individual is well classified in one of these latter types, the observer concludes that he had best make no prediction about whether that person will be rated "self-confident."

The types described in Part II of this book were constructed by the above procedure. Every measure used was located in the space, either from direct evidence, or indirect evidence, or in a few cases by speculation. A few variables, which were needed to fill holes in the space, were "invented" without being based on actual questionnaire responses, or observation. These invented variables may be said to be located where they are by definition, and the later research job is to construct a measure that will answer the definition properly. These distinctions are not always preserved in the text descriptions, but they are always indicated in Appendix 1 where the source of evidence for the location of each variable is given. (See for example the discussion of the variable optimistic idealism in Appendix 1.)

Once the variable was located in the space by assignment to a given direction, the Logical Chart in Appendix 2 was used to infer the relation of the test or measure to each of the other directions, or types. The spatial model was thus used to characterize each of the types not only directly, by the tests or measures which were found clustered close to that location, but also indirectly by inference, that is, by projection of the information existing in all other parts of the space into the location of the type. Proceeding in this way, one can sometimes fill in hypotheses about a given type by looking at its opposite, and inferring that the given type will somehow reverse those traits. At other times one gets valuable clues by looking at all of the neighboring types that ring the given type, projecting into it traits that are known to be characteristic of the encircling types. At still other times the information that a given type or direction is zero-correlated with another dimension helps one to clarify his conception of it by seeing to it that his conception is logically independent of traits in the orthogonal dimension. These are some of the main ways in which the spatial model may be, and was, used as an aid to inference.

The real gain in inferential power is still not appreciated, however, until one realizes that each of these steps supports the other, and any gain in knowledge may have secondary, tertiary, and further implications all around the space. The theory has a strong tendency to complete itself and articulate its details by inviting inference and this, of course, is one of the things most desired in a theory.

By the process of reflecting and rereflecting the information around the space, a full collection of items of real information as well as inferences about each type was prepared. It was then assumed that insofar as the facts or inferences about a given type were sound, it should be possible to understand the various traits and characteristics dynamically. They should fit together in terms of a conceivably existent personality, they should make sense in terms of a life history that could be visualized to result in such a personality. They should help make clear why the individual acts in the way he does and why he has the effect on others that he does. The writing of the description of the type was thus an attempt at psychological and sociological interpretation. In this process still further speculations were required, which also entered in many subtle ways into the conception of the space and colored the description of other types. Although the wording of the descriptions may sometimes sound reassuringly firm, their speculative, indeed tenuous nature should not be forgotten. It is hoped that they can be improved by experience and application. The way in which they can be improved by further research is, I hope, also clear.

5

Observing
Who Speaks to Whom

Useful inferences concerning the relative power of persons in a group can often be made by observing who speaks to whom. These cues are given in other ways also, of course: in tone of voice; terms of respect in address; and the like. It is true that the amount of speaking is not a completely reliable cue to status—the overt behavior of certain persons or subgroups sometimes seems markedly out of conformity with what one would expect if amounts of participation followed the conventional status order. Nevertheless, paying attention to who speaks how much and to whom can be unexpectedly enlightening, even though one may feel that he already has a pretty good picture of the status structure of the group.

The present chapter describes, in the form of an exercise, a simple method by which one can train himself to pay attention to the quantity and direction of interaction, apart from its content, and shows how this method may be helpful in analyzing the relations of persons in a particular group. The method described is, in addition, a basic operation necessary for the classifying of interaction according to its manner or quality. It might be helpful to look briefly at the interaction-process categories in Chapter 6, Figure 6.1, since the conception of what constitutes an act to be recorded depends to some extent on the categories one has in mind. The present method presupposes the later use of the categories defined in Chapter 6.

CHOOSING A GROUP FOR THE EXERCISE

The only equipment necessary for recording is paper and pencil. But whether the activity of recording is sufficiently unobtrusive to be acceptable to the members of the group is another matter. Some group situations will certainly permit it. Groups devoted to training may easily hold special sessions. Groups may be assembled for the purpose. Movies and television performances of plays may be useful, although there are some differences from natural interaction. Sound recordings alone, without vision, are not very suitable, although they are very satisfactory for practice in the recognition of "units"—that is, for the division of the total flow of talk into single acts, each of which is to be scored.

All difficulties considered, it is probably best to find some natural group which will permit you to observe and score. The group may be, but need not be, one of great psychological interest to you. It should have at least three members, and had best have not more than about seven, or you will have too much trouble remembering who is whom. You need at least three members in order that the idea of speaking "to the group as a whole" as distinct from speaking to a specific member will be appropriate. If you wish to score from some group larger than seven, you might choose the five members or so who generally speak most often, and concentrate on these, lumping all others together by a single symbol, say *x*. This is only necessary, of course, if, as we are assuming, you do not know the members already.

Naming the Members

A symbol should be chosen in advance to stand for each group member you intend to concentrate on. If the members are seated in a circle an easy procedure is to start at some given person whose position is easy to locate, perhaps yourself, or the person at the head of the table. Call that person number "1," and then assign a number in order to each of the others, clockwise from that person: 2, 3, 4, 5, and so on, back to the starting point. With this system you can easily reconstruct the proper number for a given person, and so train yourself to associate the number to the person.

If it seems easier to use another kind of symbol, say a single letter standing for the name of the person, this may be preferable. If you do not know the names of the persons, or if their spatial location is not fixed, then it may be easier to pick some unique characteristic for each, and use the name for that as the source of the symbol. For example, you might note that one person has a red tie, and decide to name him "R" for the red tie. Another might be the only one wearing glasses, so you might decide to name him "G" for glasses. The reason for choosing the symbol may be completely trivial, but it is crucial to have a symbol. The symbol should be short, a number or letter, and it should be possible for you to reconstruct, and hence recall, from something always visible or memorable about the person or his position.

Before you start to score the interaction you will need a period of memorizing the symbols that stand for the members. Choosing a memorable characteristic of the person is a great help, but do not depend upon that alone—repetition and rote learning are also necessary. Silently go through the list of symbols, such as: 1, 2, 3, 4, 5, or R, G, x, and find each person with your eyes as you silently repeat the symbol. If you are using numbers you do not need a list, since you already know the list of numbers in order. In the case of letters standing for words you will need to make a list of the words. It is best to draw a diagram of spatial positions, if these are fixed enough to be of any help. Practice repeating the list or redrawing the diagram, if necessary. You must be able to come up without hesitation with the symbol for a member when he speaks or acts.

Having worked out a way of producing the list of symbols from memory, and having practiced going from the symbols to the persons, now reverse the process. Find the persons with your eyes in a random order, one by one, recall the salient characteristic, such as the red tie, and produce the symbol from memory. Go over each person in turn, and produce the symbol which is his "name" for the purposes of scoring. Repeat this process until you can easily go from person to name, or from name to person, and finally through the list of names in order.

In scoring interaction from life you will go from the person (whom you observe speaking) to his "name" (which you will write down). In preparing your data for interpretation you will re-order the list of names. Finally, in applying your findings back to the persons in the group, you will go from the names to the persons. Since you will be using the memory system in various ways you will not be wasting your time to get it well set up and practiced in your mind. Commonplace though it may seem, it is nevertheless true that one of the reasons we have trouble thinking about groups is that we are often not clear about the individual members. Having failed to learn their names, or to fix the individual members in memory by some device, we are unable to visualize member-to-member relationships in the mind, and hence fall back on some vague, amorphous conception of a team, a hoard, a gang, a crowd, or that thinnest of all such abstractions, a "group."

This plea for recognition of individual members is not to be understood as a denial of the importance of the concept of "the group as a whole." Each individual member presumably has such a concept, and needs it. When he thinks of his group in relation to other groups, or of his group as having a place and a function to perform in a larger organization, he presumably uses such a concept to refer to himself and other group members collectively. There are ways in which the group as a whole can "act," as seen from such a perspective, outside the group. But when one is thinking of the process of interaction among the members, as they try to come to a group decision for example, the "group as a whole" is *not* one more actor among other actors. In the present system of recording interaction, it is defined as impossible for the "group as a whole" to *act*—only individual members act. But it is possible for individual members to *address* their acts to the "group as a whole"—that is, to whomever in the group may care to answer.

If a group member wishes to address the group as a whole in this fashion he may let his eyes rove over all the other members of the group as he speaks; he may raise the level of his voice as if to reach everybody including the member farthest away; he may speak in a slightly more elevated style and vocabulary; he may take care to make his voice sound more impersonal—more neutral than he would for his friends, less hostile than he would for his enemies. Or he may indicate that he is presenting a story or dramatization which is not to be taken literally, but savored and reacted to by appreciation or laughter. If the observer is to record the addressee of communications of this sort he needs a symbol to stand for the group as a whole. The symbol zero, 0, is used to stand for this target of communication. It may be thought of as referring to "everybody in general" in the group, or sometimes (as in the case of showing tension), the symbol zero may be understood to refer to "nobody in particular."

The symbol zero is never used to stand for an initiator of interaction, but only for the group as a whole as a target to which an individual member may address communications. There is one occasion (a general laugh) during which the symbol zero is *temporarily* used as an indication that each person has initiated an act—a laugh—to another person, usually the teller of a joke. The temporary zero, used to save time, is replaced by a score for each of the members before tabulation. This is a minor exception which should not be allowed to obscure the substantive rule: the present system permits the group as a whole to be recorded as the target of interactions or communications, but not as the initiator of them.

Before the observer can record an interaction he must be able not only to recognize the participants by name, but also to recognize what constitutes an act to be scored. How this may be done is discussed below. Assuming this problem to be solved for the moment, the process of recording is simple. The observer watches and listens constantly and very carefully. When an act occurs, he puts down on the paper the number of the person speaking, or initiating the act, followed by the number of the person spoken to, or intended as the recipient of the communication. The latter symbol may be the zero standing for the group as a whole rather than a specific member. The two symbols may be separated by a dash if there is any danger of confusion by running them together. The pair of symbols records the fact that the person designated by the first symbol directed an act to the person or group as a whole designated by the second symbol.

The next score may be written following horizontally, if a space is left, or vertically under the preceding score, if it is desired to keep the scores in time order. The scores are later to be tabulated and analyzed. Such a series of scores conveys the kind of information indicated in Table 5.1.

**Table 5.1. Interaction Scores
in Vertical Sequence and Implied Meaning**

Scores	Implied Meaning
1-0	Person 1 speaks to the group as a whole.
1-0	Person 1 speaks (again) to the group as a whole.
1-0	Person 1 speaks (again) to the group as a whole.
2-1	Person 2 speaks (replies) to person 1.
1-2	Person 1 speaks (replies) to person 2.
1-2	Person 1 continues speaking to person 2.
3-1	Person 3 speaks (replies) to person 1.
3-1	Person 3 continues his reply to person 1.
4-0	Person 4 speaks (let us say, jokes) to all.
0-4*	Each person speaks (for example, laughs) to person 4.

*The notation 0-4 is temporary, and "illegal" as it stands. Before tabulation it is replaced as follows, (assuming the number of persons in the group to be five): 1-4, person 1 laughs to person 4; 2-4, person 2 laughs to person 4; 3-4, person 3 laughs to person 4; 5-4, person 5 laughs to person 4. Note that person 4 is not credited with an additional act.

Determining Who Is Addressed

If one has the mechanics of scoring well in hand and keeps his eyes on the group almost constantly, the determination of who is speaking creates little difficulty. Deciding who the act is addressed to is often harder. The content itself, of course, gives many clues; for example, agreeing and disagreeing are nearly always addressed to the person who just spoke. These cues should be used to the fullest extent, but only to form expectations. Often expectations are disappointed. Questions, for example, may be addressed to a particular individual, and answered by another, or not answered at all. The observer should use ordinary expectations of social interaction to tell him what to look for next, then he should score according to what actually does happen.

In directing remarks to specific other members, the speaker ordinarily gives some clues as to whom he is addressing. He may use the name of the other. He may "catch the attention" of the other by some means before he gives his message. He may often look toward the other to note his response and adjust the pitch of his voice to reach the other comfortably, not short of him, nor beyond him. If the two are in free movement, standing or walking, the speaker will ordinarily approach to a standard distance (which differs somewhat by individuals as well as by social class and culture). If seated, he will ordinarily turn toward the other, and place himself so as to be seen. In attacking another member a person will sometimes ostentatiously avoid addressing him directly, but instead will pretend to make remarks to third persons. In such cases the person attacked rather than the person physically addressed is taken as the receiver, on the reasoning that the emotional point of the attack is meant for him. Such cases are rare, however, and the physical cues as to who is addressed may be taken as adequate most of the time. In a more exact definitional sense the person addressed is the person required to complete the interaction category description; that is: Seems friendly to ———— (whom) ? Gives information to ———— (whom) ? Seems unfriendly to ———— (whom) ? In small groups most communications are *heard* by all persons in the group, in the literal sense, but acts (as described by the interaction categories) are *addressed* more specifically.

Addressing the group as a whole is to some degree an assertion of dominance. Group leaders ordinarily do it more often than other group members, or members may do so as a bid for leadership. Usually such a person does not wait until he has the silent attention of all, but at some moment sufficiently quiet he raises his voice to the pitch necessary for all to hear. He may use a term of address that indicates he is speaking to the group as a whole: "Members of the . . ."; "Hey, you guys . . ."; or "The group . . . ." He maintains his voice at a level of elevation sufficient to discourage interruption. He lets his eyes rove over all members as he speaks, being careful not to pause on any one person long enough to encourage the belief that he speaks to that particular one. He may look away from all members if he pauses to think a moment, in order that no one may politely gain his attention and so legitimately bid to interrupt. He may employ some speech mannerism that fills such pauses, such as a prolonged ". . . uh . . .," or give other signs that he desires to keep the floor. He often speaks longer than others, even though the situation is not defined as one in which he is expected to give a lecture.

In observing persons who speak a great deal to the group as a whole, the observer should be on the alert to catch acts in which the speaker addresses particular individuals, since in spite of apparent self-confidence, the speaker does need specific supporters. Ordinarily when a speaker is confronted with a disagreement, he speaks to the specific person disagreeing while he makes his argument, or at least starts with him. However, when there is agreement, he continues to address the group as a whole.

The Unit To Be Scored

The unit to be scored is the single "act." An "act" is a communication or an indication, either verbal or nonverbal, which in its context may be understood by another member as equivalent to a single simple sentence. In grammatical definitions as to what constitutes a simple sentence, a variety of types are recognized. Sentences may be declarative, interrogative, imperative, or exclamatory. The simple sentence contains, or at least implies, a subject (that which is spoken of) and a predicate (what is said about the subject), thus presenting a complete thought to which the person addressed may make a reasonable reply or reaction. An act may be defined as a communication or indication sufficiently complete to permit the other person to interpret it, and so react in relation to its content and to the speaker. This is a definition in terms of interpersonal relations rather than of grammar, and though vaguer, is probably preferable for our purposes, because it is broader. Unfortunately it is also more dependent upon the interpretation of the observer. The grammatical conception of the simple sentence will help the observer, but should not be taken as the final criterion.

Ordinarily the observer can transform fragmentary communications or indications into a form complete enough to permit classification according to the set of categories used. If a member says "What?" the observer might translate, according to context, "What was that?" or "I do not understand you," or "I disbelieve you," or "Would you repeat that?" in such a way as to represent the interpersonal meaning in the interactive context. He thus fills out both subject and predicate, and so interprets the meaning more fully. These remarks are not meant to indicate that the observer literally phrases all fragmentary communication into complete sentences, but rather that in the normal process of categorizing he makes interpretations that could be represented in this way. One does not always have to resolve such dilemmas when simply scoring who is speaking and to whom.

A single word, "yes" would ordinarily be classified as Agrees. A nod of the head, without words, satisfies the definition of Agrees; just as a turning-away of the head might be classified as Disagrees. A smile would usually be classified as Seems Friendly, a frown as Seems Unfriendly. These examples make it clear that nonverbal acts are to be recorded, as well as verbal ones. They also indicate that, even if the act is verbal, it is not necessary that the words include literally both subject and predicate, provided they convey the meaning of the single simple sentence.

Since the present exercise is meant to simplify the actual procedure of scoring interaction one need not make a systematic attempt to classify acts into the qualitative categories defined in the next chapter. But it must be noted that the definition of what constitutes an act is not independent of the qualitative categories one assumes in the background. Isolating the unit to be scored definitely assumes the set of categories. Having the set of categories in mind, the observer listens and watches for the smallest items or segments of behavior that will enable him to make a score in one of his categories. He cuts the process up into the smallest classifiable pieces. The nature of the categories determines how small the pieces may be. The set of categories used with the present system, known in its complete form as Interaction Process Analysis, is geared to complete units of meaningful communication of the size best exemplified by the single simple sentence. There are marginal cases, for example, the unintentional signifying to others of one's feelings (as in Shows Tension), but these may be treated as complete acts within the meaning of the category in which they fall. Because of the dependence of the unit upon the set of categories the reader is urged again to become generally familiar with the set and their definitions contained in the next chapter.

Complex sentences (as distinguished from simple sentences) always involve more than one score. Each dependent clause may receive a separate score if it expresses an additional complete thought. If a series of predicates are asserted of a single subject, a separate score may be given for each additional predicate on the reasoning that each one constitutes a new item of information or opinion which might provoke a new or different reaction from the listener. Compound sentences joined by "and," "but," and so forth, are broken down into their component simple parts, each of which is given a score. As an example, the following sentence would be analyzed into four units (the end of each unit is indicated by a diagonal): "This problem which we talked about for three hours yesterday/ impresses me as very complicated/, difficult/, and perhaps beyond our power to solve./" It is debatable whether each of the last two units really adds a new item of information, but the dilemma is resolved in favor of additional units anyway. The observer maintains a bias in favor of more rather than fewer units. His scores thus may come a little closer to approximating the time consumed, and will appropriately reflect the emphasis desired by the speaker if he does repeat.

In addition to speech centered around the issue being discussed, interaction includes facial expressions, gestures, bodily attitudes, emotional signs, or nonverbal acts of various kinds, either expressive and nonfocal or more definitely directed toward other people. These expressions and gestures can be detected by the observer, given an interpretation in terms of the categories, and recorded. The observer should remain as alert as possible; keeping his eyes on the group constantly. He should canvass the separate members for nonobstrusive expressive reactions at every opportunity—any slight pause may give an opportunity—but the search should be as nearly constant as he can make it. Silent indications of attitudes and feelings, such as boredom, withdrawal, and disapproval, may not break up naturally into units. A score should be put down as soon as the observer notes the attitude. Thereafter, each time there is any increase in its intensity, or any new or renewed sign of it, another score should be entered. If close attention is paid the observer will probably obtain a sufficient number of scores, since in many instances there is a hidden intention to communicate the feeling, and the member will keep finding new ways to place his feeling in evidence.

Training in Scoring

In order for an observer to record without missing units he must have a high degree of training along with a full understanding of the rationale which underlies the categories. If he later actually uses the categories, he will develop position habits—expectations as to where each category is on the list—so that he can find them easily. Rote-memory training should also be employed to develop these position habits. The observer must have the members well identified with their names or symbols, so that he does not have to fumble. Such an observer will find that he can get "on top of his job." He will have time to look around the group as he goes along, scoring many things more or less automatically. When sudden bursts of interaction occur he can fall four or five scores behind without becoming confused. If a mistake is irretrievable, he should forget it and go on. Needless to say, the observer should take care not to permit himself to "fall asleep" or to skip over little things which he might think are out of context or unimportant. This judgment may be made later in the interpretation of the scores. The expected frequencies are premised on the assumption that nothing is trivial, and that literally all interaction that can be scored should be.

Inexperienced observers typically fail to look up from their scoring pad, and so miss many scores they should obtain. The experienced observer may obtain more than twice as many scores as the inexperienced. When two learners score together it is probable that the observer with fewer scores is missing units he should be scoring. Nonverbal or fleeting acts are likely to be missed. Agreement often occurs so fast as to be missed. In practice it appears that a properly trained observer, on the leisurely interaction of six or seven adults engaged in group discussion, may obtain from fifteen to twenty scores per minute.

Reliability of scoring depends very heavily on the training of the observer (51; 67; 158). It is a good plan, if possible, for scorers in training to work together on the same interaction. A sound recording of a group discussion is excellent at the very beginning, simply for identifying units. Observers all listen together, and each taps with his pencil at the time he thinks a score should be put down. Discrepancies are thus immediately apparent, and can be discussed. It should be recognized that even though observers are trying to obtain agreement only on units for the later purpose of scoring who speaks to whom, they must still think in terms of the categories of observation. Discussion of differences is a great teacher. But too much discussion too soon can paralyze practice, hence discussion should be only periodic, not constant. Such a training group will tend to converge on a set of practices that adapt the general method of observation to their particular situation. They should always remember the purposes for which they later wish to use their scores in making their decisions. Discussion in the light of the purposes of the scoring and in the light of the general system will tend to bring about convergence in scoring procedures among observers.

The observer working alone at his own training will miss some of the advantages of the group discussion method of training, but he can nevertheless learn satisfactorily. When he begins to use his scores for actual improvement of his understanding of the group, he will naturally amend his scoring in a way that improves his ability to understand and predict.

Tabulation of the Results

Let us assume that you have recorded who speaks to whom in a group of some interest to you for the period of an hour or so, or a single meeting. One hour of interaction at a rate of 20 scores per minute or so might give you something over 1000 scores. How can these scores be used to increase your understanding? The first step is to make a tabulation form like that shown in Fig. 5.1.

Along the vertical axis, under the caption "From" arrange the symbols referring to the group members, in whatever order you have memorized them. Then arrange the symbols in the same order along the horizontal axis. In Fig. 5.1 the numbers one to five have been assumed to be the names you have assigned to group members according to their spatial order around a table. Any other symbols or order would do as well.

The next step is to tabulate the scores and record the appropriate

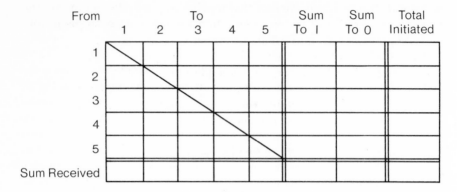

Figure 5.1   General form of the interaction matrix.

totals in the cells of this matrix. An easy way to do this is to work one cell of the matrix at a time; for example, the cell recording person 1 speaking to person 2. Person 1 as an initiator of acts is located on the vertical under the caption "From." Person 2 as a receiver of acts is located on the horizontal under the caption "To." The intersection of row 1 and column 2 gives the cell that may be called 1-2. Now go through your list of recorded acts, counting as you go, and checking off lightly each original score 1-2 as you count it. At the end of the vertical list of 1000 acts, you will have the total which should be entered in the cell 1-2. It might be fifty acts or so.

Repeat this operation for each cell in the matrix corresponding to a pair of persons in your group. This portion of the matrix is sometimes called the set of "internal cells" of the matrix, and appears on Figure 5.1 as the portion crossed by the diagonal. The diagonal removes all cells from consideration that would indicate the identical person as both initiator and receiver of the same act. (Although we sometimes speak of a person as "talking to himself" this happens so seldom as to make it not worth retaining in the general system.) Note that each pair of specific persons appears twice in the matrix, once for each of the persons as initiator. A single cell represents a single one of the two possible directions between two individuals. The two cells may be said to describe the relationship, and if one wishes to refer to the acts proceeding in one direction only, the term "direction from 1 to 2" (for example) may be used, or "the cell 1-2."

The next step is to tabulate, from your original record, the number of acts each person has initiated to the group as a whole, recording these totals in the cells under the caption SUM TO 0. When this is complete all of the acts recorded on your original sheets should have been counted and checked off. This is a good place to make sure that any bursts of laughter, or the like, which you have temporarily recorded with "0" as the initiator, have been properly recorded as one act for each of the individuals in the group (other than the joker).

All of the remaining cells shown in Figure 5.1, along the marginals, and in the column SUM TO I, are obtained by additions of the cells already recorded. The caption SUM TO I means the sum of acts addressed by a particular person to all other persons as *individuals,* and the sum is found by addition of the cells in the row preceding it. For person 1, for example, the SUM TO I would be found by adding the totals in the cells 1-2, 1-3, 1-4, and 1-5. The SUM TO I for each person is now found by similar addition.

The caption TOTAL INIT means the total of all acts initiated by a given individual, whether to specific individuals, or to the group as a whole. It is found, of course, by addition of the numbers in the two cells SUM TO I and SUM TO 0. This total is closely related both to the amount of time consumed by the person, and to the amount of power he has tried to exercise in the given session.

Finally, the caption SUM REC means the total of all acts addressed to a given member by all other members. It is found by adding the cells in the column above it. For person 1, for example, the sum received (SUM REC) is obtained by adding the amounts in cells 2-1, 3-1, 4-1, and 5-1. The Total of all SUMS REC is the same, of course, as the total of all SUMS TO I, that is, all acts addressed to an individual are assumed to be received by him. Finally, the total of all SUMS TO I added to the total of all SUMS TO 0 is the grand total of all acts initiated in the group.

Samples of matrices which may clarify any points of confusion in the foregoing description can be found in Appendix 3. Average interaction matrices for groups of each size, two to eight persons, are found there. They may be used for comparison with your own results. First, however, two additional steps are necessary: a rank order transposition; and a conversion of the raw amounts to percentages.

In order to compare matrices it is necessary to rearrange the members into a comparable order. For comparison with the average matrices in Appendix 3 the members of your group should be ordered according to their TOTAL INITIATED. The member with the highest number of acts initiated may be renamed *rank* 1, the member with the next highest number renamed rank 2, and so on. The identification numbers on the matrices in Appendix 3 are the names of ranks. First rearrange the rows of your matrix, which read horizontally, so that rank 1 on TOTAL INITIATED is at the top, followed by rank 2, and so on. Then rearrange the columns, which read vertically, so that they follow the same order; that is, the first man listed as a receiver, named rank 1, is the same person who was so-named because he was rank 1 on TOTAL INITIATED (not necessarily rank 1 on SUM REC). A matrix so arranged is called a *rank ordered matrix,* and the rank order so represented tends in fact to be approximately that of the relative power of the members, or their position on the upward-downward dimension of the spatial model. The matrix is now ready for inspection, and the various comparisons to be described below.

A further step which facilitates comparison of your rank ordered matrix with those found by other investigators is the conversion of the raw amounts in each cell into percentages of the raw amount in the grand total initiated. The matrices in Appendix 3 are shown in such percentages. You may compare the rank ordered percentage matrix for your group with the average matrix shown for groups of the same size as your own group. You should remember that the matrices shown are actual summary results for some number of groups under diverse conditions, and so are not completely regular. If your matrix differs in some substantial respect from the one shown it is possible that your matrix better represents the average characteristics of groups of that size than the matrix shown.

On the other hand, careful study of the average matrices will show quite a number of regularities, which if understood, will help you evaluate any departures your own matrix may show—(13; 14; 15; 41; 105; 145; 146). The following sections will point out some of the most important of the regularities, and show how adherence to them in your group, or departures from them, may be used to throw light upon the interpersonal relationships. Some of the main items of interest may be highlighted by very simple comparisons of cells in the matrix, and for this purpose you need not have the matrix reduced to percentage form, but can compare raw numbers directly.

THE RANK ORDER OF THE TOTAL INITIATED (TOT INIT)

No doubt the feature of most immediate interest in the matrix is the rank order of the members on total interaction initiated. This rank order is intuitively understood to have some relation to status, or power, or both. The question is: what is the relationship in your particular group? The first generalization you may want to test is the simple one that the amount an individual speaks in the group is based upon, or regulated by, the outside status he brings into the group. The question may be stated as follows:

1. *Does the position of the individual in the rank order of total amounts of interaction initiated (TOT INIT) agree with the rank you would expect him to have based upon "outside" status criteria?*

(There is usually some relation, but with interesting exceptions.)

If *no,* you may wish to speculate as to why, and whether any of the members (such as a person not talking as much as expected) may later make his status evident.

A member enters a group with a presumed status in the eyes of other members based upon whatever is known about him "outside" the group. His age, sex, color, ethnic background, religion, family, family role, friends, education, occupation, amount and source of income, and an indefinite number of other characteristics are taken by members of the present group as a basis for granting him (or denying him) a certain importance or deference in the group (150; 151; 152). Since the feeling of what is appropriate for him is based, not upon his behavior or performance within the group, but upon his general characteristics and outside connections, the status he is granted is called his "ascribed" status. (The status he earns, gains, or loses, by his performance in the group may be called his "achieved" status.)

Each person in the group may be imagined to make an overall subjective evaluation of the relative importance or deference due to each other person in the group, and to himself as well. In the beginning of a new group there may not be much consensus in these subjective appraisals. The interaction is often given over to a half-concealed process of comparing these appraisals, arguing over legitimate criteria of status, and attempting to arrive at a consensus as to relative status of each member (98). Many of the overt struggles, which appear to be about abstract values or situations far removed from the group, are in fact struggles over whether such and such a criterion of status in the larger society shall also pertain in the particular small group, and hence whether some person shall be given the status he desires, usually to the detriment of some other. Each member tries to give both direct and indirect information about himself that will lead others to ascribe to him the status that he wants.

Not all members want a high status in the particular group however. Some may prefer a lower status to avoid too much obligation or responsibility in the group. There are some also who will accept a high status, but will refuse to engage in what they feel is a vulgar competition. The descriptions of the directional types indicate that personalities are very different from each other in the way they react to the status dimension. But each person presumably does have a preferred self-picture and a preferred place in a status-order, and tries to act in such a way that others will give him the position he wants. Some members, but not all, compete for top positions.

As the group develops the members may arrive at a working consensus as to the status order in the group. The order may be full of conflicts and potential conflicts. It may not be exactly the order that would be expected from the outside status characteristics of the members, but it is probably close in many respects. Even a group like a delinquent boys' gang will often grant importance to age, probably to sex, ethnic background, friends, and money, as criteria for ascribed status. The number of status criteria of the larger society that are rejected is a measure of the deviance of the group, but if the group holds together one can expect that there will be *some* orthodoxy, some conservatism, some authority, relative to which the legitimate status of members in each others' eyes, may be measured. Every small group is partly orthodox with regard to the larger society, partly variant, probably usually partly deviant from the larger culture in certain ways (106; 107). The variant and deviant features enable it to perform special social and psychological functions for its members. As these features become crystallized they become orthodox for that particular group.

The observer can expect, then, that in spite of certain unique properties, variations, or deviations, many of the criteria of status in the larger society will carry over to the particular small group. From his knowledge of status criteria in the larger society, plus his knowledge of the ways in which the particular small group is variant and deviant, the observer now makes up a rank order of the members of the group based on their outside status. He may have too little information about the members for this, but on the other hand the members will probably have given much information or dropped many hints in the course of a first or early meeting. A comparison of this rank order from the outside, with the rank order of total initiated will probably show a noticeable similarity. But it may also show some notable exceptions, and this is really more interesting, since it raises the question of "power" as distinct from "legitimate status" based on outside criteria.

The rank order of actual participation in the current interaction of the group stands in potential contrast to any established rank order of status expectations. Who speaks how much to whom in the group is a "brute fact" characterizing the actual present situation. Speaking takes up time. When one member speaks it takes time and attention from all other members of the group, some of whom may want to speak themselves. To take up time speaking in a small group is to exercise power over the other members for at least the duration of the time taken, regardless of the content (119; 120). It is an exercise of power that may not coincide at all with the status position of the individual based on outside criteria, or even on special criteria developed within the group.

Power is often exercised in groups in a way contrary to any conventional order of status. It is best not to think of "status" and "power" as two words for the same thing, but rather to ask whether power is being exercised in reinforcement of some conventional status order, in a way relatively unpredictable in relation to it, or in opposition to it. If one is a conventional member of the group he may sometimes wish to overlook the degree to which power is actually being preempted by unconventional, deviant, alienated, or supposedly "lower status" members of the group. Conversely, if one is a nonconventional or lower-status member by conventional standards within the group he may well recognize that although he cannot gain legitimate status, he can nevertheless determine the actual outcome of current group efforts by the exercise of power. The actual observation of who speaks how much and to whom can help the observer clarify the difference between a conventional or wishful picture of what the status order "should be," and the current factual challenge to it. Although amounts of participation generally follow some established order of status, they are very sensitive to current challenges and tendencies to change.

Within the small group the time taken by a given member in a given session is practically a direct index of the amount of power he has attempted to exercise in that period. The person who talks most does not always win in terms of victory for his ideas, but he can prevent a full consideration of any other kind of content. And he is at least sure of exposing the content he wishes to present.

In terms of the spatial model described in Chapter 3, the person who possesses a high legitimate status may be thought of as occupying a position in the upward *and forward* region of the space. The forward direction represents the element of legitimacy, conformity, orthodoxy attributed to him. A conventional attempt to obtain legitimate status involves performance in conformity with the conventional norms of the group. These norms are often to a considerable degree in conformity with the requirements of the external authority, which controls the rewards and punishments of the group as a whole. In return for excellence in achievement as so defined, one may receive higher status as a reward—the right to expect deference and to be thought important. One is thus given power and legitimacy at the same time. Unconventional attempts to obtain legitimate status usually involve the obtaining of power as a preliminary step.

The possession of power, as distinguished from legitimate status, may be thought of in terms of the spatial model as location in the upward region of the space. The possession of power is the possession of the actual ability, whether legitimate or illegitimate, to control or dominate the actions of others. Movement toward this position and the exercise of power may be called movement upward. Legitimacy may be thought of as located forward in the space, and so is logically and statistically independent of power. One may try to gain both, either one without the other, or neither. To possess legitimate higher status is to possess both legitimacy and power at the same time. To talk a lot in a group is to exercise, or attempt to exercise, power. It does not necessarily bring legitimate status.

For assessment of the individual and his position in the group, it is often desirable to be able to represent the amount he talks in the group as compared to others. A handy form of the question is as follows:

2. *Does the total amount of interaction initiated by the individual (TOT INIT) fall within the upper, middle, or lower third (approximately) of the rank order?*

> (If the number of members in the group does not divide into equal thirds, let the "middle third" be the unequal one.

> If *upper*, then directional indicator   = upward

> If *lower*, then directional indicator   = downward

ACTS ADDRESSED TO THE GROUP AS A WHOLE (SUM TO 0)

Most participators spend most of their interaction time in pair-discussions, speaking directly to another participant, responding directly to him. This pattern tends to keep the gains in participation of each member of the pair about equal to the gains of the other, since each provides a stimulus or opportunity for the other to speak. On the contrary, however, those persons who reach the highest amounts of participation in a group typically do so by relatively long "speeches," uninterrupted by others, in which they address the group as a whole (15; 18; 19; 20; 21). It is simply a matter of observation that only a few individuals in a given group, perhaps only one, will far surpass in this way the amount of interaction he receives from others. The diagnostic question may be phrased:

3. *Is the total number of acts initiated by the individual to the group as a whole (SUM TO 0) greater than the total number of acts he receives (SUM REC)?*

> (The answer for most group participants is no, but a usual exception is the highest participator.)

> If *yes*, then one may say that the person makes an unusual number of attempts to influence the group as a whole.

> directional indicator   = upward

> If *no*, directional indicator   = downward

When a man speaks in a group he speaks to, and is heard by more than one person (except in a two person group). He speaks "in the first person" and he addresses a "second person or persons." Although he addresses a second person (from whom he expects an interactive response), he also speaks in the presence of one or more "third persons." A "third person" in the most relevant sense, is a present nonparticipant, who nevertheless knows what is said, what is agreed to, and will remember it later. The third person is symbolically the judge of the first two and what they have done (28; 36).

In a two person group there is no literal third person, hence there is no impartial or impersonal judge. If a two-person group cannot run on the assumption of "love" it cannot run, since neither norms nor coalitions have their usual representation in actual third persons. Individuals in two person groups tend to adjust to their problem of having no third person, or judge, to appeal to, by being very careful to maintain the appearance, at least, of solidarity. They tend to have high rates of agreeing, and low rates of disagreeing, but they also have high rates of showing tension—all indications that they tend to suppress disagreement and negative feeling (28).

The amount of interaction an individual addresses to the group as a whole (SUM TO 0) is useful in telling how much the individual addresses his attention and effort to third persons—impersonally—as the embodiments of judges, group members generally, supporters of the group norms, and followers taken for granted. The more the individual feels the need for explicit support from others, the more he is apt to address specific second persons—either those who address him, or those whom he wishes to influence. The more he addresses third persons, or speaks impersonally; that is, speaks to the group as a whole, the less he recognizes specific second persons whom he considers it important to win over to his side or to silence. To speak a lot to the group as a whole, and little to specific members, is the earmark of the person who thinks of himself (even though mistakenly in some cases) as the embodiment of the whole group and the group norms. In the extreme, such a person may not even feel the need to elicit overt agreement or comments from others at all—he assumes the role of invited and respected lecturer; failing to remember the names of specific members is also symptomatic of this attitude.

If other persons in the group *do* in fact generally agree, the first person does not need to reply to their agreement specifically in order to continue with his argument, nor does he need to seek the support of second persons specifically, and so he may continue to speak to the group as a whole. He is in "high gear" when he can talk mostly to the group as a whole, is mostly agreed with, and need not take the time to deal with individuals specifically. In this set of conditions the amount in his cell (SUM TO 0) is usually greater than the amount in his cell (SUM REC), which in turn, is greater than the amount in his cell (SUM TO I). The comparison of these three cells for each individual is thus instructive.

There is a certain ambiguity about the meaning of a high amount in the cell (SUM REC). There are findings which indicate that when the ratio of receiving to total interaction initiated for top participants is high, it predicts liking for the person initiating. If agreement is being received at a high rate this is understandable. It is also true, however, that if an individual takes a deviant or unpopular position, other persons in the group are likely to converge upon him in the attempt to persuade him to change, and thus the amount he receives will go up markedly, at least for a limited period until he either changes, or is rejected (137). Thus a high rate of receiving is ambiguous. If one notes it in the inspection of a matrix, he must look to other measures to make the meaning clear.

What one can generally say is that if the individual addresses a high rate of interaction to the group as a whole he is *trying* to exercise power and influence in the group. If he is addressed at a high rate he is engaged with second persons, attempting to forestall disagreement or defending himself from it, and either receiving support, or attack, or perhaps both.

ACTS RECEIVED FROM OTHER MEMBERS OF THE GROUP (SUM REC)

A good way of forming an idea of the magnitude and the meaning of the number of acts the individual receives is to compare that sum to the total that he gives out to specific other individuals. The question may be asked more exactly as follows:

4. *Is the total number of acts received by the individual (SUM REC) greater than the total number he initiates to particular other individuals (SUM TO I)?*

(The answer for most group participants is *no*, but a usual exception is the highest participator.)

If *yes*, then one may say that the person arouses an unusual number of reactions from others, and that he is probably exercising power, either in the form of accepted leadership or of domination. The reactions may be either positive or negative, and must be separately checked. In either case,

directional indicator for the individual   = upward

If *no*, directional indicator for the individual   = downward

The usefulness of comparing these two cells in the matrix (SUM REC with SUM TO I) depends upon certain facts or empirical generalizations about interaction which have been observed, but not as yet very well explained (41).

Two generalizations may be crudely stated and illustrated by inspection of the matrices given in Appendix 3: (1) with the exception of top participators, the number of acts a person receives from all other persons in the group (his SUM REC) tends to *almost, but not quite, equal* the number that he initiates to specific other persons (his SUM TO I); (2) above groups of size two the *top participator* typically receives more interaction from all other persons in the group (SUM REC), than he addresses to specific individuals (SUM TO I). There seems to be something unique about the typical top participator. We have noted earlier that he typically addresses more communication to the group as a whole than he receives. Let us try to understand better these generalizations.

The first generalization really has two parts which need to be understood separately. The first part is an assertion of relative equality in the amount a group member gives to specific individuals, and the amount he receives from them. This similarity can be seen in comparing the interchange between specific individual rank positions (the amount from individual 1 specifically to individual 2, compared with the amount from individual 2 specifically to individual 1) (14; 105). It is true that one gets the impression that the departures from equality are not random (and this will be discussed as another generalization below), but meanwhile one should not lose sight of a really impressive generalization: *The number of acts a person receives from a given other person in the group tends to equal the number that he gives to that other person.* This generalization may seem plausible, and it is certainly repeatedly illustrated by the matrices in Appendix 3, but it is not transparently true by definition, nor is it true in every instance, nor is it hardly ever exactly true. Moreover, it leaves out something very important—namely the influence of rank—as we shall see. But insofar as it is true, what does it mean—that is, how is one to understand the reasons for it?

One can get an intuitive idea of the reasons by considerations of the following sort. Persons in interaction apparently tend to maintain a logical and interpersonal congruity in interaction sequences. Acts do not occur in isolation, but in sequences in which actions are made in anticipation of reactions, and reactions are made in reference back to preceding actions. In terms of the kinds of distinctions made by the categories of the present system, questions tend to elicit answers, at least most of the time. Answers or task attempts (giving information, opinion, suggestion) tend to elicit agreement or disagreement as a closure of the sequence. Unfriendly acts tend to elicit unfriendly acts, unless people exercise special restraint. Jokes tend to elicit laughs, at least about half or more of the time. Friendly acts tend to elicit friendly acts, unless people are unusually negativistic as personalities. There is a normal or highly frequent reaction for every type of action (128 Ch. IV). Interaction consists of typical action-and-reaction sequences. The action and reaction of a typical sequence are tied together as the two halves of a social process of evaluation or norm making.

For the same reasons, persons in interaction tend to maintain continuity in who communicates with whom. Answers tend to be addressed to the person who asked the question. Agreement and disagreement, logically, tend to be addressed to the person who gave the task attempt. Unfriendly acts tend to be addressed to the persons who have given unfriendly acts; laughs tend to be addressed to the person who made the joke; and friendly acts tend to be addressed to persons who have given friendly acts. One would surely feel that something unreasonable or disorganized were going on if reactions were not addressed to the authors of the provoking actions. The result of these tendencies is an overall tendency toward equality in the number of acts an individual initiates to a given other, and the number he receives in turn from him. When he addresses the other, he receives an answer. And when the other addresses him, he gives an answer. But this is *not* so true of the top participator in the group, to whom we now turn.

It has been noted above that the top participator typically receives more interaction than he addresses to specific individuals. It was also noted that he typically addresses more communication to the group as a whole than he receives. There seems to be a kind of "directional current" in the way interaction is directed, when one looks at the total network of possibilities—the matrix. It is as if the members of the group arrange themselves into a kind of semirestricted network, such that one person, the top participator, tends toward a monopoly on the right to address the group as a whole. Others tend to address him in disproportional amount, as if he were their spokesman to the group as a whole. But he does not return their specific communications. He is disproportionately low in returning communication to the specific individuals who address him. He continues to speak to the group as a whole. It is as if he and the others understood the arrangement as a dialogue between the top participator, or leader, on the one side, who initiates the actions, and the rest of the group, followers, on the other side, who reply in chorus. The elements of this pattern are increasingly evident as the size of the group increases, especially from about size five upward, (see the matrices in Appendix 3).

When the amount received by the individual (SUM REC) is greater than the amount he initiates to specific individuals (SUM TO I), it is a signal to the observer to examine whether the other signs of this pattern are present. Such a relationship of rates is characteristic of "leadership." But it is also characteristic of "domination," and more generally of precedence of status or power. It has the primitive meaning of "upward," but one has to determine its significance—particularly whether the individual who is receiving more than expected is seen positively or negatively.

ACTS RECEIVED FROM OTHERS LOWER IN RANK

The pattern just described for the top participator of the group is not in fact confined to him. The tendency to receive more from a person lower in participation (TOTAL INIT) than one addresses to him is characteristic to some degree of all rank positions. The general tendency and its converse may be stated as follows: *At each rank position (on TOTAL INITIATED) there is a tendency to address more to any person in a higher rank position than one receives from him, and conversely, to address less to any person in a lower rank position than one receives from him.* Inspection of the matrices in Appendix 3 will illustrate this generalization, with some exceptions. (A common exception is that the rank 2 man or the rank 3 man fails to receive as much as expected, the surplus being directed to the rank 1 man instead.) A theory which makes the general tendency seem reasonable assumes that the differences in participation rank reflect felt status differences among members, and that members generally have a tendency to pay attention to, and try to influence those of higher status than themselves, as well as to neglect or ignore those of lower status. The unifying concept is, perhaps, that most members have some status aspiration, or at least some instrumental realism in the way they direct their communications. The political realism of such a tendency will be commented upon below.

The top participator is probably only apparently an exception in this tendency to address communications "upward." We may suppose that he assumes an entity with status higher than that of any individual member—namely, the group as a whole, and addresses himself to that. Others do this to a lesser degree. Apparently they tend to accept the top participator as the representative or gatekeeper, of the group as a whole. In most of the matrices shown in Appendix 3, member rank 2 and those of lower rank address the top ranking member more often than they do the group as a whole. But this is regularly more true for the groups above size 5, and it is also more regularly true of the rank 2 member specifically than of other members of lower rank. With increasing size there is not only a tendency for the top man to address acts disproportionately to the group as a whole, but also for the second man to address disproportionately the *top man rather than* the group as a whole. These are signs, we may suppose, of a primitive division of labor in the group, between a preeminent "initiator" of action, and a preeminent "reactor" to him (16; 38). The former has the higher rank. The latter is somewhat neglected, both by the former, and by the other members.

Between any two members, in a group above size two, the sign of such a status differential and division of labor is that the upper participates more, but addresses the lower specifically less than the lower addresses him. This is not possible, of course, in a two-person group. There, the top participator can not sensibly address a "concept" of the group as a whole, apart from the specific other, and the other person, although lower in participation, is in a much stronger position than lower status members in small groups of sizes other than two.

A slight surplus directed upward in the rank order is a general phenomenon for members of all ranks, but the surplus directed upward by the top member (to the group as a whole) is not recorded as received by any specific person. For this reason it happens that members of all except the top rank usually receive less (SUM REC) than they initiate to other members (SUM TO I), but the top ranking man is an exception. This may be stated as a generalization that stands as an exception to the general tendency toward equality of acts given and received by pairs of persons: *For the top participator in a group, or for persons tending successfully upward, the (SUM REC) is likely to be greater than the (SUM TO I).* The top man is the culminating point of the pervasive tendency to address a *little more* to a person of higher rank position than one ordinarily receives from him, even though there is a more powerful tendency toward equality.

The tendency to address a little more to the person of higher rank may hold even though one is in conflict with him. We should avoid the assumption, of course, that a status order or a given order of power is always accepted in the group, and that members always dutifully present their petitions upward in the status order. Communication directed upward will often be in disagreement, and may represent a status struggle with the person addressed.

But it should also be recognized, when we look at the tabulation for a complete meeting, or an extended period, that the numbers are likely to reflect the way things finally came out as well as the acts of contention or challenge. In looking at the matrix one may generally suspect that if there is disagreement or conflict in the relationship (either active or passive on the part of the lower-ranking member), the balancè of numbers in the matrix will end up with the higher-ranking member addressing the lower-ranking one much more than expected, in an attempt to forestall his opposition, to persuade him, or to put him down and silence him. A higher-ranking member who depends upon this method of defending his status is likely to be seen by lower-ranking members as dominating, hence negative as well as upward (20).

On the other hand, if, in looking at the matrix one finds that a higher-ranking member receives the expected small surplus over what he gives to the lower-ranking member, one may usually assume that the higher-ranking member is seen as positive, or at least, as neutrally important. These generalizations are given from intuitive experience, and require further test. Although the basic ideas are simple, the formalities of the questions one must ask in looking at the matrix tend to get a little complicated.

The following question should be asked only in relation to those other group members who are lower than the individual in question as to total participation initiated (**TOTAL INITIATED**). The question should be asked in relation to *each* such lower-ranking member:

5. *Is the amount the individual receives from a lower ranking member greater than the amount the individual addresses to that lower-ranking member?*

   (The answer in most cases is *yes.*)

   If *yes,* then one may usually assume that the lower-ranking member is in agreement with the individual, accepts his leadership, and tries to influence the group as a whole by agreeing with him and addressing his opinions to him. The directional indicator for the individual is thus: = positive

   If *no,* then one may usually assume that the lower-ranking member is in disagreement with the higher. The lower may be passively disagreeing, or actively, but his disagreement is being countered by unusual attempts on the part of the higher-ranking individual to influence him. Such a relationship will often turn out to be a focus of conflict not only between the two individuals, but between two subgroups or coalitions within the total group. The directional indicator for the individual is thus: = negative

Now let us turn the perspective around and look at the relationship of the individual (our point of reference) to those who are higher in rank than himself.

ACTS ADDRESSED TO OTHERS HIGHER IN RANK

Since other persons, by their assent, legitimize one's status, one generally addresses his remarks to those he hopes will agree with him, and who are at the same time more powerful or of higher status than himself. If opposition appears within the group, one concentrates on the opposing person and tries either to win him over, or to win over him. Opposition removed, interaction is once more addressed to the most likely higher-status source of agreement. This is the view to which we have been led by the analysis so far.

One not only tries to gain a desired status for himself in the group as a person, he also tries to gain acceptance for the content of his ideas, beliefs, fantasies, and values. Often these are not clearly distinguished from the self, but they can be, and in the group process it sometimes happens that a man is stopped in his tracks so far as his own status is concerned, while his idea "goes marching on." It is useful to regard the process of gaining acceptance for an idea as similar to a legislative process. The content of an idea, a value-statement, a fantasy, is like a bill that is presented to a legislative body for enactment. In the small group, assent by enough others, or by strategic others, is equivalent to "enactment." The accepted content of the statement then becomes the basis for further overt action in the group.

In a legislative body a bill on its way to passage may be sent back and forth through several committees, and if it survives, may finally be presented on "the floor," where it is argued to a final vote. Let us assume that for an idea to become an effective determinant of action in a small group, it must somehow pass from its point of origin, a particular member, wherever he may be in the status order, through the assent of some series of persons, in an order of ascending rank, to the point where it commands the assent of the person who holds the strategic position in the group at that time. Anybody may have an idea, but only certain persons apparently can get them accepted. To gain acceptance for an idea one must direct it to the right person or persons in the right order.

According to this conception, ideas gain acceptance in a group through a series of interpersonal communications in which one person expresses or somehow presents the idea, and another assents. The status of an idea is affected by the status of the person who asserts it, but it is also affected by the status of the person who assents to it. Ideas may originate in the lower ranks of the status structure, and be carried upward by a series of steps, in which a person higher in the status structure assents (sometimes not overtly) to the idea, and re-expresses it, thereby increasing its status to the point where another higher-status person will assent to it, and so on, until the person who holds the strategic position asserts it and addresses it to the group as a whole. The idea may then be certified for the group as a whole by agreement from the rank 2 member to the rank 1 member, or it may be left to stand without dissent, at which point it is generally conceded to have been decided upon.

Such a process is like a legislative process—in a primitive form it is a legislative process. It is also like the process known as "social climbing," except that in this case an *idea* climbs in status rather than a person. Sometimes, of course, a person may be carried along. In fantasy, no doubt, the person who expresses an idea or a value generally hopes for this, and when he directs his communication upward, it is not only an act of political realism, but it also expresses his fantasy of status mobility.

One's status position, or that of his ideas, can only be legitimized by the assent of others—preferably all others in the group, but if not all of them, then of some. It is more legitimizing, of course, if these others themselves have legitimate high status. But failing that, it is better to have *somebody* assent rather than nobody. The need for assent, I believe, is more primitive and less discriminating than the need for higher status. The assent of some others, even though not of the highest status, at least reinforces one's power, and may even begin to create some new source of legitimacy—a dissident subgroup. Failing to receive assent, one may still persist completely alone. But trying to win one's way alone by sheer force of talk, without the assent of *any* others, is a last resort, and hardly ever wins for long. Such an attempt may attract participation from others for a short time—particularly from the higher-status persons threatened—but such conflicts are quite limited in time, ordinarily. Either the challenger carries others with him, and wins out over the former higher-status person, or he remains as the leader of a deviant subgroup with their support, or he loses, and is isolated as an impossible deviant by all or most of the group members (137).

This is a dismal descent in a man's status, and seldom does one see it pursued to the very bottom. The descent can be arrested and the position stabilized, usually, by simply ceasing to push one's ideas so hard. In any case, the persons above one in the power hierarchy are typically gatekeepers of the resources of the group, and remain important persons to influence for the sake of one's own status. They are usually the recipients of more communication than they give. The attitude of the individual toward them can often be inferred from the amount of inter-action he addresses to them.

The following question should be asked *only* in relation to those other group members who are *higher* in rank than the individual as to total participation initiated (TOTAL INITIATED). The question should be asked in relation to *each* such higher member.

6. *Is the amount the individual addresses to the higher-ranking member greater than the amount the higher-ranking member addresses to him?*

   (The answer in most such cases is *yes*.)

   If *yes*, then one may usually assume that the individual agrees with the higher-ranking member, and is trying to make his influence felt on the group as a whole by showing his agreement to that particular higher-ranking member, and addressing his opinions to him. The directional indicator for the individual (in this case the lower-ranking member), is thus: = positive

   If *no*, then one may usually assume that the individual disagrees, perhaps passively, but nevertheless enough to be seen, with the higher-ranking member, who in turn, is making unusual attempts to influence him. The directional indicator for the individual (in this case, the lower-ranking member), is thus: = negative

THE EXCESSIVE ABSTRACTNESS OF THE MATRIX

One sees, in summary, that a surprising number of inferences about the social position of the individual can be made by careful comparison of the sheer quantities of acts recorded in the cells of the matrix. The questions numbered one through six in this chapter are meant to capture this information in compact form, so that one can assign directional indicators to the probable group role of the individual on the basis of them. Indicators of the individual's position in the upward-downward dimensions, and in the positive-negative dimension, can be obtained, but none in the forward-backward dimension, hence not enough to arrive at a classification of the individual's probable group role type.

The seeming regularity of the gradients, and other features of the matrices shown in Appendix 3, may be tempting to those who wish to build mathematical models. This problem has received a certain amount of attention in the literature (14; 105; 145; 146); a large amount of work with the matrices has in fact been done both by me and by collaborators, and some others that has ended in discouragement, with no publication. Perhaps, as one who has puzzled on the matrix for a long time, though admittedly not with much mathematical skill, I may nevertheless be permitted to express an opinion. It is my belief that concentration on the exact expression of the numerical gradients of the marginal cells of the matrix is a useless procedure in itself, even though one may reach modest success under some fixed conditions of observation. It has been my experience that it is not until one translates the numbers in the cells of the matrix back into the *categories and category sequences* they represent that one finds himself able to penetrate their social-psychological meaning.

Recording only who speaks and to whom is an excessively abstract procedure, and the addition of the scores into a matrix can create an attractive nuisance—a numerical puzzle-box that one can never penetrate again if he ignores the qualitative sequences of the social behavior he has first categorized, and then counted. Observing who speaks to whom is a useful exercise, and can be done without much training because it is so formal and abstract, but it is best regarded as a preliminary step to the classification of interaction which is treated in the next chapter.

In spite of these warnings, I believe that the naturalistic study of the matrices we have pursued in the foregoing sections has made it possible to extract several generalizations of considerable theoretical importance. Of these perhaps the least obvious and the most important is the existence of the small surplus generally directed to the person of higher rank, which in turn supports the more interpretive generalization that persons try to advance their ideas and realize their values by seeking acceptance for them from persons higher in the power hierarchy. If this is generally true, it provides support for the theory as to how coalitions and subgroups form within the larger group, as described in the spatial model of group structure found in Chapter 3.

The Most Important Indexes Summarized

Since the scoring of who speaks to whom is ordinarily done in conjunction with the simultaneous classification of the quality of acts, the observer will usually want to combine the directional indicators from both aspects of the method. For this purpose it may be useful to repeat here, by way of summary, the three most important questions that may be answered from the interaction matrix which yield directional indicators for the individual that may best be combined with the other indicators to be obtained from the individual's interaction profiles, given and received, as described in the next chapter (see page 99).

Does the total amount of interaction initiated by the individual (TOT INIT) fall within the upper, middle, or lower third, (approximately) of the rank order?

(If the number of members in the group does not divide into equal thirds, let the "middle third" be the unequal one.)

If *upper,* then the directional indicator = upward

If *lower,* then the directional indicator = downward

Is the total number of acts initiated by the individual to the group as a whole (SUM to 0) greater than the total number of acts he receives (SUM REC)?

If *yes,* then the directional indicator = upward

If *no,* then the directional indicator = downward

Is the total number of acts received by the individual (SUM REC) greater than the total number he initiated to particular other individuals (SUM to I)?

If *yes,* then the directional indicator = upward

If *no,* then the directional indicator = downward

6

Classifying Interaction

If you have learned how to record who is speaking to whom for each act you will already have learned most of what you need to know to go ahead with simultaneous classification of the interaction. A scoring pad may be arranged with the list of categories shown in Fig. 6.1. Figure 6.2 shows a convenient form for scoring that will help you keep your place both horizontally and vertically on the pad, but you may start with more crude forms. The categories should be on the left margin, as shown, with space to the right of each one. It may help to have the categories separated by lines to help you keep your place. It is also helpful to have the set of twelve categories divided by heavier lines into the four sections shown, and into the two halves by a still heavier line. These divisions are important conceptually, but they also help you build up the position-habits necessary for sufficiently rapid scoring. It is definitely worthwhile to drill yourself to go from the name of the category to the proper spatial position on the scoring pad. Similarly you should learn to go from the category number to the category name, and from the number to the spatial position.

To record an act you simply put down the two numbers standing for who-speaks-to-whom in the space following the category into which you decide to classify the act. The problem with paper forms is that the spaces following the most frequently used categories soon tend to fill up (even though you may put two or three scores in each box). It becomes increasingly difficult to keep track of the spatial position, although the lines help, and the time order of acts tends to get lost. The time order

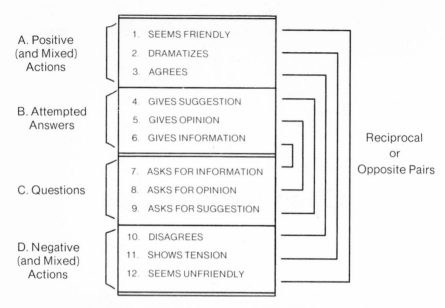

Figure 6.1   Categories for Interaction Process Analysis.

may not be important if you are mainly interested in the summary frequencies at the end, but for some research purposes one may need to keep the time order straight. In Appendix 8 a machine called an *interaction recorder* is shown, which supplies a paper tape moving under the list of categories at a constant speed. The interaction recorder makes it easy to keep the time order straight, and gets around the spatial problems of paper forms.

The method of simultaneously classifying the quality of the act, who performs it, in relation to whom, as described in this book is called *Interaction Process Analysis* (11; 12). The term "process-analysis" is meant to distinguish the method from various modes of "content-analysis." The interaction categories do not classify *what* is said, that is the content of the message, but rather *how* the persons communicate, that is, *who does what to whom in the process* (*time order*) *of their interaction.* The time order, and the back-and-forth character of the inter-action, are conceptually central to the understanding of the categories, although one may be mainly interested in summary frequencies over the period of a meeting.

Perhaps these points are more clearly implied by the titles of the categories, and their reciprocal references to each other, as indicated in Figure 6.1. To say that a person "gives information" (category 6), for example, does not tell what is the *content* of the information; or to say

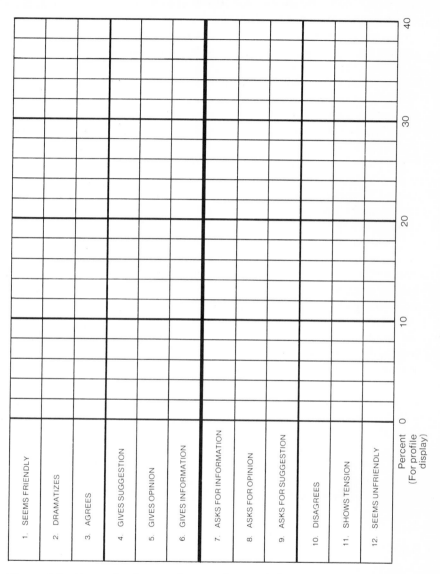

Figure 6.2 Form for interaction scoring pad (and for later display of profile).

that a person "agrees" (category 3) is not to say *what* he agrees with in terms of the idea content. This general distinction holds true of all twelve categories of the system. They are all concerned with the form, the manner, or the mode of interpersonal communication, and they all abstract from its specific content. A few qualifications should be added to this statement to forestall problems that may arise in classification discussions. First one must acknowledge that since the categories deal with communications there is a sense in which they all "give information" to other participants and to observers. But category 6 (Gives Information) is more narrowly defined, as one may see by checking the definitions later in this chapter. Second, one may remark that not all the acts classified in the system, particularly nonverbal signs such as those included in category 11 (Shows Tension, Laughs) are necessarily intended by the acting person as interpersonal communications, though they may indeed give information, in the broad sense, to others. Third, it should be recognized that some acts, verbal or nonverbal, for example acts in category 1 (Seems Friendly) or category 12 (Seems Unfriendly) may not have much idea content beyond the message that the person feels a certain way about the other.

The main reason for making the distinction between the interaction category and the content of the message as clear as possible is that it removes much of the ambiguity of classification to realize that one is letting content slip through as he scores. Otherwise one might fear that he is losing so much of the meaning that the scoring will be useless. This is far from the case. As one uses the category frequencies in the context of the personality and group role types, he soon sees that the rather formal abstraction he makes as he classifies the interaction really retains extremely important information, from which many inferences may be made. In the next two chapters two types of content-analysis will be presented that will surely tap some of the content one intuitively feels he wants to retain. When the time comes to consider those tasks it will become clear that they have been made much easier and less ambiguous by the interaction scoring. One of these, the classification of the value-content of statements, depends mostly upon statements classified as giving opinion and giving suggestion. The other, the description of fantasy themes, depends mostly upon acts of dramatizing, joking (category 2), and giving information (category 6), as classified by their interaction form.

INTERACTION SEQUENCES

The categories are defined verbally in great detail later in this chapter, and those learning to score interaction should study the definitions carefully, but in fact, much of the operation of scoring is intuitive and very close to common-sense. The twelve categories shown in Figure 6.1 will be seen to have a basic simplicity of conception—they seem to suggest the back-and-forth character of action and reaction that we all know in normal conversation and social behavior. For convenience in conception, the total set of twelve may be grouped mentally into four subsets, as shown in the figure. Categories 7, 8, and 9, asking for information, opinion, and suggestion, respectively, may be called *questions,* whereas the corresponding set: 6, 5, and 4, may be called *attempted answers.* The other two sets may be named simply also. Categories 1, 2, and 3 may be called *positive (and mixed) reactions,* whereas the corresponding set of 12, 11, and 10 may be called *negative (and mixed) reactions.*

Leaving aside some complications for the moment, it can be said that one observes just about the simple sequences implied by these titles (128: Chapter IV). When a person asks a question, he tends to receive an answer by somebody else, and when one attempts to give an answer, he receives a reaction, either positive or negative. Some people attempt answers to the problems represented in the communications without having been asked questions—in fact attempted answers are provoked by explicit questions rather rarely. On the other hand, questions are usually followed by attempted answers. Some persons seldom attempt answers to group problems, but seem rather to specialize in listening and giving positive reactions, whereas others seem to specialize in negative reactions and counter-arguments. Every so often a joke appears—a mixed action, neither clearly positive nor negative, but some of both, and it is followed by a laugh. The group then often goes into a short period of joking and laughing, before they get back to the serious business represented by giving opinion. In nontask periods there is often a good deal of information and friendly behavior, interspersed with dramatizations, jokes, and laughs. This often happens both before and after the more serious task-oriented part of the session (40).

Interaction process analysis is built on a very simple common-sense base, and much that one intuitively believes about everyday conversation can be confirmed by it. The surprising thing, perhaps, is that it goes much further than one would suspect in revealing basic attitudes of people, their personalities, and their positions in a group, if one employs the method systematically. People often do not pay much attention to the form of their interaction, or do not have much control over it. They are usually more attentive to the content of what they are saying. But they unintentionally convey much in their manner, and this is intuitively understood by most of their listeners. A language of manner, or form of interaction, in fact exists along with the more explicit language, and is regularly employed in interpersonal communication, but at a low level of awareness by some, and with quite imperfect understanding. Although the basic sequences are easy to grasp, the quantitative balances and relations of rates to each other are quite subtle, and soon reach a level of

Table 6.1 Interaction Process Analysis, Profile; Acts Initiated, Estimated Norms*in Percentage Rates. Directional Indicators to be Inferred from Interaction Initiated

Category of Acts Initiated	If Low:	Medium Range**	If High:
1. Seems Friendly	N	2.6 – 4.8	P
2. Dramatizes	DF	5.4 – 7.4	UB
3. Agrees	NB	8.0 – 13.6	PF
4. Gives Suggestion	DB	3.0 – 7.0	UF
5. Gives Opinion	B	15.0-22.7	F
6. Gives Information	U	20.7-31.2	D
7. Asks for Information	DN	4.0 – 7.2	UP
8. Asks for Opinion	N	2.0 – 3.9	P
9. Asks for Suggestion	UB	.6 – 1.4	DF
10. Disagrees	P	3.1 – 5.3	N
11. Shows Tension	UF	3.4 – 6.0	DB
12. Seems Unfriendly	P	2.4 – 4.4	N

*These norms are estimated by a long process of inference, described in Appendix 4.
**Rates lower than the Medium Range shown are classed Low; rates higher than the Medium Range shown are classed High.

complication beyond easy conscious control. This is especially true when one takes into account the nature of activity *received* by the individual as well as the nature of what he initiates. The diagnostic power of interaction process analysis depends upon the quantitative relations of rates (13; 27; 35). The indicators are built upon the significance of minor quantitative departures from the general normal rates.

The general normal rates for a variety of different sorts of groups in different sorts of situations are estimated in Tables 6.1 and 6.2. The basis of these estimates may be examined more carefully in Appendix 4. One should not take the numbers too seriously, but on the other hand they should enable one to arrive at an assessment of the individual's personality or group role type that is comparable to, and probably as good in its way, as the rating procedure described in Chapter 1. Knowing the quality of the person's interaction, one should be able to predict to the result of the rating procedure, and vice versa, with a reasonable degree of success. The estimate of the personality or group role type from overt interaction probably has greater objectivity than an estimate made by ratings, though it may be more unreliable when the data come from unrepresentative periods of group interaction. Ideally, one would wish to employ both modes of estimation, but the scoring of the interaction must be done at the time of its occurrence (or from a sound recording), whereas the rating may be done afterward.

Table 6.1 shows a profile of rates for interaction initiated by the individual, whereas Table 6.2 shows the profile of rates for interaction received. The assessment procedure we are concerned with utilizes such profiles, and is applied to each individual in the group separately.

Table 6.2 Interaction Process Analysis, Profile, Acts Received, Estimated Norms* in Percentage Rates. Directional Indicators to be Inferred from Interaction Received

Category of Acts Received	If Low	Medium Range**	If High
1. Seems Friendly	N	2.6 – 4.8	P
2. Dramatizes	NF	7.5–12.2	PB
3. Agrees	B	12.7–19.4	F
4. Gives Suggestion	DN	2.9 – 5.2	UP
5. Gives Opinion	NB	15.0–22.7	PF
6. Gives Information	N	15.0–22.8	P
7. Asks for Information	UF	4.0 – 7.2	DB
8. Asks for Opinion	UP	1.4 – 2.8	DN
9. Asks for Suggestion	B	.5 – 1.2	F
10. Disagrees	DPB	3.6 – 6.3	UNF
11. Shows Tension	DPF	4.4 – 7.5	UNB
12. Seems Unfriendly	DPB	2.4 – 4.4	UNF

*These norms are estimated by a long process of inference, described in Appendix 4.
**Rates lower than the Medium Range shown are classed Low; rates higher than the Medium Range shown are classed High.

ASSESSMENT OF THE INTERACTION PROFILE

As a result of scoring who-speaks-to-whom in what category of interaction for the period of a meeting or longer, one will have a record from which to make the required tabulations. For present purposes the specific order or sequence of acts is ignored, with one exception. As explained earlier (p. 65-66), a shorthand convention is used in the original scoring which consists of using the symbol 0 as the initiator of acts when a general laugh is recorded. The laugh will typically be received by the person who has told a joke. Before the tabulations are made it is necessary to expand the symbol 0 by a series of scores which attribute a laugh to each person in the group addressed to the person who made the joke, except that he himself is not given credit for laughing, at least not automatically.

Two tabulation forms for the given individual are then set up: one for his acts initiated; and the other for acts addressed to him. His raw scores in each of the twelve categories are then tabulated in the order shown in Tables 6.1 and 6.2. In tabulating acts initiated, the person to whom they are addressed is ignored (acts addressed to the group as a whole are included as well as acts addressed to specific individuals). In tabulating acts received, the person from whom they are received is ignored.

The total number of acts *initiated* is then determined by addition of the raw scores in the twelve categories. The next step is to convert the profile of raw scores in each category to percentage rates based upon the total. One should be careful not to take rates based upon small numbers very seriously. A percentage profile based on less than a hundred total scores is probably not worth much, but still one may do what he can. The profile of acts *received* is next converted to percentage rates by an exactly parallel procedure, using as the base its *own* total, the total of acts received.

The two profiles are now ready for comparison with the profiles shown in Tables 6.1 and 6.2. Table 6.1 shows a range of rates for category 1, acts of seeming friendly, initiated, which extends from 2.6 to 4.8. This range is labeled the *medium range,* and it represents the range that included approximately the middle third of all rates available in the comparison or normative population (35). If the rate obtained falls within the range, then record no diagnostic inference, or directional indicator. If the rate obtained is higher than 4.8, however, record the directional indicator P, as shown; and in case your rate is lower than the 2.6 shown, you record the directional indicator N. The directional indicators are recorded on a form exactly like that used for recording the results of answering rating questions, as shown in Figure 1.1 of Chapter 1. The tally marks partial out the components of the directional indicators into a tabulation of how many times each direction (U, D, P, N, F, B,) is mentioned.

The profile of acts initiated will provide a maximum of twelve directional indicators, and so also will the profile of acts received. When separated into their components the two profiles taken together give a maximum of opportunities for each of the directions to be indicated as follows:

U maximum 12
D maximum 12
P maximum 15
N maximum 15
F maximum 14
B maximum 14

If the cutting points are well set in Tables 6.1 and 6.2 (which cannot be guaranteed), there is a fair chance for each direction to be represented in the final assessment of the personality or group role type of the individual. The balance of the three dimensions in relation to each other can be improved by including the three additional indicators of directions U and D that can be obtained by a comparison of the total amounts of acts initiated, to specific individuals, to the group as a whole, and received, as described in the previous chapter (questions 2, 3, and 4 summarized on pp. 89-90. These indexes are logically independent of those obtained from the profiles, but complement them in a desirable way. The addition of these three possible indicators of the directions U and D would give a maximum of fifteen in each instead of the twelve shown above—a desirable addition. The procedure for adding the directional indicators to obtain a final summary assessment of personality or group role type is exactly the same as that shown in Figure 1.1 of Chapter 1.

DEFINITIONS OF THE INTERACTION CATEGORIES

In the sections that follow, each of the twelve interaction categories is defined and discussed in detail, including more detailed scoring conventions wherever necessary. One may be able to begin immediately to classify the interaction if one can already score who speaks to whom easily, and one can probably do fairly well with only a passing knowledge of the detailed definitions. It is hoped that the categories are close enough to common sense to make this possible, or almost possible. But you will find that the adherence to common sense in the definitions is not quite complete, and if you wish to get the most out of the quantitative use of your scores, you should try to obtain a fundamental understanding of each of the categories, its subvarieties, and its relation to the other categories in the complete set. Operationally, each category is defined by more concrete forms and examples, but theoretically, each is defined by relation to the total space of group roles. In specific cases, you may have to develop adaptations of the more concrete forms.

How to Score Interaction Category 1, Seems Friendly

The interaction category Seems Friendly is used to classify all overt acts which seem to the observer to be anywhere on the positive side of the space except for acts in category 3 or category 8. There are theoretically nine subtypes, one applying to each combination of friendliness with the upward-downward positions, and the forward-backward positions. Not all of these are equally well defined by words and phrases, nor are the subtypes used in the scoring. For convenience in conceptualization, however, they are separately discussed.

Subtype UP. Of the nine types, acts that are specifically definitive of the UP direction have the combination of a socially extroverted ascendant quality with a socially positive attitude shown toward the other. For example, hailing the other, waving, drawing near him or her in order to speak, greeting him in a friendly manner or by saying "hello," approaching him, touching, shaking hands, placing a hand on his shoulder, clapping him on the back, putting an arm around him, linking arms, welcoming, extending an invitation to him to be a member of the group, treating him to food or drink, offering him a cigarette—these are all acts extroverted in character and symbolic of solidarity and acceptance.

Other examples of this subtype are taking the initiative in befriending the other person, or any act of showing him hospitality, of being neighborly, or comradely. An expression of sympathy or similarity of feeling—"I can see how you feel"—would be included. An indication that a relationship is becoming more intimate or familiar, as when one begins to use the other's first name, or a nickname, or the term "we" where it has not been used before would be included. Friendly and pleasant leave-takings are included, such as accompanying or escorting the other a part of the way, saying or waving "goodbye."

Indications that one is attracted to the other, demonstrations of affection, love, as well as sexuality, acts of courting, flirting, coquetry, embracing, fondling, petting, carressing, kissing, are included.

In situations where an action is friendly to one person and either inadvertently or intentionally unfriendly to another, it may be scored twice: one score is entered for seeming friendly to the one person; and an additional score for seeming unfriendly to another person, or perhaps to the group as a whole. A pair of persons whispering together in a group, ignoring others or shutting them out, sometimes give reason for this kind of double score.

Subtype UPF. A part of the total category of acts in which the member may seem friendly are definitive of the UPF direction. These are acts in which the promotion of the solidarity of the group as a whole is the object, when these acts at the same time convey the assumption that the person acting is taking an ascendant position, and is concerned for the progress of the group in the task direction. For example, interceding or mediating, conciliating or moderating in a difficulty between two or more others might have these three qualities simultaneously. Acts of pacification, attempts to mollify two or more others, to allay opposition, to be discreet, tactful, diplomatic, to avoid wounding the other may be included, provided the ascendant position is maintained. The urging of unity or harmony, agreement, cooperation, mutual obligation, and the expression of other values of solidarity will usually be included, though if they are lacking in friendly feeling they may better be classified simply as Giving Suggestion.

So long as the ascendant position is maintained, offering assistance to another, volunteering or assuming a task or duty, offering to undertake a job on behalf of others because one has the power or resources to do it, and in this paternalistic manner, offering services, assistance, time, energy, money or any other resource, would seem to have the UPF direction. The same kinds of acts, with the implication of downward movement instead of ascendance, would be included under the subtype DPF, or if neither ascendant nor submissive, under the subtype PF. Since all friendly acts, however, of whatever direction, so long as they have the positive component are scored under the same category, Seems Friendly, the distinction is not necessary for scoring. It is theoretically important in interpreting and understanding results, however, to know that the subtypes may seem rather different from each other when they are different on the two remaining dimensions. These distinctions are mostly recaptured in the assessment which takes all the other categories into account. It is not feasible to try to interpret a high rate in category 1 alone, without taking the other dimensions into account. The diagnostic system takes all three dimensions into account automatically.

Subtype UPB. Acts characteristic of the UPB direction are not only positive and ascendant in attitude toward the other, but also show a protective and nurturing attitude, even though the other may be deviant in some way. They are acts of "unconditional love." A declaration that one considers himself to be on the same side in an argument as the other, or considers himself to be a partisan in his behalf, could be examples. Taking the initiative in praising, rewarding, boosting the other, giving him approval or encouragement belong in this category. A statement, question, or comment in which the intent is to sustain, reassure, or bolster the status of the other when he is having some difficulty in performing adequately will usually have the UPB quality, since it represents a reward not conditional upon his conformity to some expected pattern. Such remarks might take the form: "That's fine;" "You've done a good job;" "You've made a good try;" "You've covered a lot of ground today;" "Swell," "You're making progress." Such acts are particularly definitive if they seem to be given whether or not the performance has been good in an absolute or socially conventional sense.

Any behavior in which the member defends another, protects him, acts as a guardian for him, represents or advances his interests, vouches for him, certifies his integrity, speaks for him, advocates his cause, or assists him when he is in need is included. Giving support, reassurance, comfort, consolation, encouragement; the showing of sympathy, pity, compassion, tenderness, expressing condolence and commiseration are included. Attempts to calm the other or assuage some hurt, by feeding him, nursing, healing, gratifying needs of any kind are included. The manifestation of any attitude which the observer interprets as nurturant, gentle, maternal, paternal, benevolent, humanitarian, merciful, or charitable, is included.

Subtype P. Remarks that seem friendly may come from persons in positions anywhere on the positive side of the space—ascendant, submissive, forward or backward, or, as in the present subtype, from the equalitarian center. The member who assumes equality between himself and the other may seem congenial, sociable, affiliative, cordial, or informal. He may complement the other as an equal, congratulate him, give credit to him, show enthusiasm for his views, applaud him, cheer him, and even give him approval, provided the status implications are those of equality. Most of these kinds of acts can also be performed from other status positions, however. Most of the acts classified above under subtype UP might also be listed in the present subtype, the difference being only in the degree of implied ascendance. When one takes the initiative in being friendly, the quality of ascendance is implied. When friendliness is being exchanged freely from both sides, equality is implied.

Subtype PF. An act, verbal or nonverbal, in which one chooses to be a contracting fellow-member with the other, an act of making a covenant on the basis of equality, or of forming an alliance, or of adhering to an alliance with another may be said to have a positive-forward direction. Nonverbal acts which have a contractual, but noncompetitive, flavor suggest the direction PF, such as exchanges of objects, trading, paying, loaning. Verbal acts of agreement, which have the same direction, PF, however, are placed in category 3, Agrees, unless they are explicitly marked as sealing a contract, meant to be unusually binding.

Subtype PB. Acts that seem friendly, which set aside or have no relevance to group task-norms, and which imply neither ascendance nor submission, are defined as positive-backward in direction. It is sometimes difficult to tell what is implied about relative status in friendly remarks, but this is not critical, since all such acts are classed together as seeming friendly, provided the element of friendly feeling or emotion is felt to be present. Responsive encouragement of another's joke or story by signs indicating a readiness to laugh or be entertained answer the definition. Nonpaternalistic indications of a permissive attitude, where the other is led to understand that he is accepted and liked, as an equal, "as he is," so that any failure in the quality of his performance does not adversely affect his status are included. A permissive grin or shrug, sometimes a wink or a knowing look, or a wag of the head are good examples. Attempts to make sure that the other is supplied with what he needs, invitations to him to participate in some satisfaction or reward available to all members—that is, to "come on into the group" are included. The implication of ascendance may be avoided if it is not implied that the giver has some exclusive possession of the reward, which he distributes, but is simply "one of the boys"—a peer. In this context acts of sharing, of giving, or distributing materials, goods, resources, may also be included.

Subtype DP. Acts in which there are signs of positive feeling or emotion, and which at the same time are somewhat submissive, and without clear reference forward (conservative) or backward (deviant) are definitive of the direction DP. Acts in return to a friendly gesture of another person, such as accepting a treat, accepting an offer of help or assistance, thanking the other, may be included, provided they have a somewhat submissive tone. Indications in manner that the person identifies himself with a more ascendant other, or confides in him, or entrusts himself to the other are included. Where the other is viewed as superior, acts which express gratitude or appreciation, show admiration, esteem, respect, wonder, awe, or reverence may be included. Acts which indicate that the person is attempting to imitate or emulate an admired superior are included, as are acts of praising, honoring, eulogizing a superior; lauding, acclaiming, extolling, idealizing him, paying him homage, tending to adore, deify, or worship him.

Sometimes the positive feeling may appear primarily in contrast to the other, as, when in response to aggression directed toward him, the person is submissive, acquiescent, pliant, or meek. Allowing one's self to be talked down, surrendering, giving in, acknowledging defeat, renouncing a goal or object in favor of the other who demands it; standing aside and letting the other aggressively push by may be included. Similarly, the direction is downward positive when one submits passively without withdrawing, allows himself to be bullied, dispossessed of objects; or when he accepts coercion, domination, injury, blame, criticism, censure, punishment, without retaliation, rebuttal, rebellion or complaint. The ability to do this is often called the ability "to take it."

The subtype DP may also include more minor signs of the friendly passive attitude, for example, introductory phrases which anticipate disagreement of the other and attempt to forestall it by admitting the disagreement in advance, such as "This is not an important point, perhaps . . .", or "Maybe you won't think so, but. . . ." Expressions of a lack of knowledge or lack of clarity may be included if they have a friendly feeling, such as: "I don't know about this, but . . ."; "It isn't clear to me, but . . ."; or "It may be true or it may not be, but. . . ." The idea conveyed in these examples is that the person is turning to the other in a submissive yet positive way. The task direction, if any, is weak or not clear.

Subtype DPF. The feeling conveyed by acts in the **DPF** direction is respect for group norms as well as positive feeling and respect for the other. Acts in which one verbally or overtly complies with a request or suggestion, does something to oblige, follows an order, and does as he has been requested are included; these acts are scored as Seems Friendly in preference to Agrees, unless the attitude is not friendly. Agreement is thought of as a more routine act, with less submissive implication. Yielding, obeying, following, or desisting from some activity when requested are scored as Seems Friendly.

Other similar acts are included, such as admitting an error or oversight, admitting that some objection or disapproval of the other is valid, conceding a point to the other on the basis of a logical proof or a value-based argument, asking the other's pardon when shown wrong—all of these indicate respect for norms as well as for the other as a person. So also do responses to accusations in which one acknowledges, confesses, admits responsibility for some act of his which has been inconvenient, unjust, or unfair to another, or which has violated a norm. Confessions of ignorance or incapacity, acts of apology, contrition, penitence, or the like, may be included, unless they are so marked or extreme as to indicate that one has the underlying expectation that the other is bad and punishing, in which case they may be scored for negative content, direction DNF, and placed in category 12, Seems Unfriendly. Submissive friendliness overdone begins to seem unfriendly. However, acts which the observer interprets as genuinely altruistic, or even to some extent self-denying and self-sacrificing may be included, provided the positive feeling or emotion is apparent. The same may be said for indications that the person is modest, humble, respectful, unassertive, and retiring. When genuine and not overdone, these kinds of acts may seem friendly. If overdone they begin to seem unfriendly.

Subtype DPB. Submissive friendly responses, which at the same time are not task- or value-oriented define the DPB direction. One sees such responses to a compliment sometimes: smiling, giggling, grinning with pleasure, appearing to be charmed, beaming. A laugh which seems sufficiently suffused with intimacy, pleasure in the other's company, or filled with good will, may be scored as Seeming Friendly rather than as category 11, where most laughs are scored.

How to Score Interaction Category 2, Dramatizes
Directionally in the theoretical space, this category is defined as UB—ascendant, nontask-oriented, or perhaps deviant. As to positive and negative elements, it is ambiguous or mixed. The common element of acts scored in this category is that they present images or potential emotional symbols to the listener, to which he may respond without explicit attention or conscious knowledge. The emotional implications of the images or symbols may be very diverse. A joke which is a "story" or an "anecdote" about persons or personified beings is one type of case in which diverse acts and diverse feelings are portrayed. The element of dramatization may not be so clear in the case of "one-line" jokes, that is single humorous remarks, but anything that is ordinarily called a joke, even though the element of dramatization is not very clear, is included. There are many cases of dramatization that are not jokes—indeed some may be far from humorous in intent or effect.

The performance of symbolic actions which involve no words is included, particularly when the enactment is spontaneous or original, without conventional ritual form. If the act arouses the fantasy of the observer it should be scored in this category.

To dramatize is to portray fantasy in the form of action. The imaginary actions of the dramatization thus not only mean what they seem on the surface to mean, but they also portray and express underlying emotions giving rise to the fantasies. More than one level of symbolic meaning or emotional connotation is always present in a dramatization. But further than this, reports of acts of other persons or personified beings are very likely to have indirect levels of symbolic meaning, though the report or account may appear quite factual, as in telling what one has read in a newspaper or magazine. We all tend to perceive selectively and to color emotionally most of the things we talk about, but a story or fact remembered in the midst of interaction with other persons is especially likely to be emotionally colored and have double meanings. It is likely to be remembered *because* it is somehow emotionally related to the present situation, and because it offers appropriate symbols for some of the emotions felt. By presenting symbols for these emotions the teller to some extent promotes a mobilization of sentiment or feeling in the other. Aspects of the story provide action models, or channels into which feelings may flow, feelings that might never otherwise have had the force, the time, or the form for expression. The dramatized story not only reflects the problems of the teller and the audience, but to some extent molds and influences their feelings in new ways.

The presenter of a dramatized image may be said to give *indirect* suggestion, as compared to the action of direct suggestion, classified in category 4. The present category, Dramatizes, is thus the nonserious or nonliteral counterpart of serious and literal direct suggestions. Often, however, the person who gives indirect suggestions in the form of dramatization and joking does not fully realize that he is giving suggestions—he may deceive himself as well as his listener. He may do so in the service of a need to enhance his self-picture, to feel more attractive and powerful, to discharge aggression or dispel anxiety, and yet be quite unconscious of these motives or of the extent to which dramatization is being employed. Listeners also, partially trapped in the interplay of emotions and images may not be able to sort out what is going on or successfully counter it. They may be entertained or even enthralled by the images that are being presented. They may be conscious that their feelings are very mixed, and be resentful at being pulled along indirectly, and yet be unable to change the modality or emotional tone of the interaction.

Since fantasy underlies the effects of dramatization, the analysis of dramatic images, personages, and their acts, presented in conversation, gives a way of approaching underlying emotional problems of the individual and the group. Chapter 7 is devoted to a method of analyzing fantasy themes presented in interpersonal situations. It would be desirable to scan this chapter in order to form a better idea of the acts to be classified in the present category, since many of these acts will receive a fantasy-content scoring. In order to be scored for fantasy, the act must consist of a sentence or set of words that describes, as if in the past or in another place, a kind of person, or personalized being (such as an animal), or the act of such a person toward another. The set of categories for classifying such images of persons or acts are essentially the set of group role types used throughout this book, but in this case adapted to a special purpose, and interpreted liberally, since they must cover such a wide assemblage of products of the human imagination. Thus, if a person presents an image of Jupiter sending down a thunderbolt upon some hapless mortal, a score will be entered in the category UN of the scoring system for fantasy themes. Similar scores may be given for images which purport to be everyday and factual. When a person reports in a conversation for example (let us say quite factually) that the government has removed another draft deferment, and 20,000 men will be taken, a score may be entered in the same category.

The important point for definitional purposes is that the expected later use for fantasy-content scoring gives a criterion for scoring acts in the present category: *whenever the action of a person or imaginary being is reported, even though the group member reporting it may feel he is "giving information," the interaction observer should place the act in category 2, Dramatizes if it is amenable to a score in the scheme for content analysis of fantasy.*

Sometimes observance of the above rule will cause one to feel that he is unjustifiably attributing a dramatization or a symbolization to the act, and if this sense is too strong, the act may be kept in category 6. This may be the case, for example, if the reporting individual is simply responding to a question, perhaps a question about his past history. But in many other cases the rule will keep one alert to emotional meanings that he would otherwise miss. There are certain cues which should always alert one to look for hidden fantasy meanings—when the teller seems suddenly to think of the story and volunteers it on little pretext; when he seems to be caught up in the emotion of it; when he shades or tones his voice for effect; when he uses metaphor or any poetic or literary device; when he exaggerates; when he uses colorful words; when he acts a part physically as well as vocally, and so on. If he is plainly telling a story or a joke, there is no doubt that the acts should be scored in the present category, but if he is describing events outside the group which have, presumably, a factual base, then one hesitates, but the manner of telling may indicate dramatization. The rule given above will allow one to separate out those parts of a report which are dramatic in form, and he may depend upon later analysis to decide how much, if any, fantasy or double meaning may be involved. Those parts dramatic in form, that is, reporting the actions of persons, or of *personae* as in a drama, are scored in the present category. It should not be concluded that all fantasy consists in the actions of persons, imagined or remembered, but a large amount probably does.

If the element of fantasy is present, category 2 is preferred over any other classification that could be given. Many jokes contain both friendly and unfriendly elements mixed in some way and so clearly belong in the present category. If one or the other of these elements is too strongly preponderate, then a classification in category 1 or 12 may be more appropriate, but ordinarily category 2 is preferable since it earmarks the act for later analysis of the fantasy content. Many anecdotes have the form of giving information (category 6), and some arguments have the form of giving opinion (category 5), but if they contain appreciable elements of dramatization or signs of fantasy, they should be classified in category 2. Where a joke or an anecdote is extended, each sentence (not merely the "punch line") is scored in the present category, so long as the "as if" attitude is maintained. Thus, much that might otherwise be scored as "gives information" (particularly if the anecdote is about the teller) is scored as dramatizing or joking if the observer feels the "as if" mood of the teller, the intent to entertain, or the "loaded" significance of the words, symbols, persons, places, or acts.

The joke is a very common form of dramatization in group interaction. The joker expects, though perhaps not always too clearly, to produce a shock of recognition of the hidden meaning, to provoke a laugh, a sudden release or display of tension. The content he offers is loaded, but by the time the explosion is over he cannot be held guilty alone, since whoever laughs has also admitted the hidden truth. In addition to jokes which aim for a quick sudden explosion, there are those which are meant to light a delayed-action fuse. Many stories and anecdotes are not meant to produce a sudden outburst, but to amuse and entertain, to elicit interest and enjoyment, to deal playfully and at length with a theme, or to prolong a pleasurable state. There are realms on realms of poetic and artistic fantasy and free exercise of the creative faculties. All these, as disparate as they may be, are meant to be included in the present category. In terms of psychological services performed, and general importance in group as well as individual life, these activities are not task-oriented, but they are nevertheless serious psychological business.

The attitude may of course be light-hearted. Any jovial, jocular, humorous, funny, frivolous, silly or nonsensical remark may be included. Clowning, bantering, "kidding," "horseplay," and "rough-housing" are included as well as high art. Expressions of feeling better after a period of tension, any manifestation of cheerfulness, buoyance, satisfaction, gratification, contentment, enjoyment, relish, zest, enthusiasm, pleasure, delight, joy, or happiness; any indication that the member is thrilled, elated, ecstatic, euphoric, or the like, may act as a tension-releaser for others, and so may properly be classed in this category. Such acts can be classed as Seems Friendly provided they seem to be in response to the other as a person, but often such acts appear in relation to some change in the nonpersonal situation, or simply by a welling-up of good spirits. They may lay the groundwork for a friendly response but in themselves be mostly responsive to a diffuse state of feeling of the person acting. In this case they are best classified in the present category.

How to Score Interaction Category 3, Agrees

The directional significance of category 3 is usually PF, but the interaction form of agreement is easier to recognize than the direction. There are preliminary and minor forms of agreement as well as binding and substantial forms. Preliminary forms include giving any sign of recognition as the other gets ready or starts to speak; showing interest, receptiveness, readiness, responsiveness, such as looking at the speaker, sitting erect, or getting in a position where one can see or hear the other better. The minor forms include giving specific signs of attention to what the other is saying as he goes along, as a means of encouraging him to say what he wishes, by nodding the head, saying "I see," "Yes," "M-hmn"; completing what the other is trying to say by adding a word he searches for or is hesitant to say, or otherwise aiding and facilitating communication. Other minor forms include showing comprehension, understanding, or insight, after a period of puzzlement. Examples: "Oh!"; "I see."; "Yes."; "Sure, now I get it." (The latter example would receive two scores, one for "Sure" and one for the following phrase.)

The more substantial forms of agreement have a more binding or contractual implication—they are given as if meant to commit the agreeing member to the substantial content of what has been said, and as if they might be relied upon later. An expression of content followed by a substantial agreement is the nucleus of a social norm. It is this norm-forming significance which gives the category Agrees its forward directional significance. The agreement may be about information, opinion, or suggestion. It may express belief, confirmation, conviction, accord, concurrence, assent about facts, inferences, hypotheses. Examples: "That's the way I see it too."; "I think you are right about that."; "Yes, that's true."; "Precisely." Similarly, the category includes approval or endorsement of expressions of value, feeling, or sentiment; for example: "I feel the same way you do."; "I hope so too."; "Those are my sentiments exactly."; "That's right." Some of these latter examples might better be scored as Seems Friendly. The degree of friendly emotional tone in the actual case is the deciding element.

How to Score Interaction Category 4, Gives Suggestion

To give suggestion is to take the lead in the task direction—a combination of ascendance and movement forward, UF. The category is meant to include routine control of communication and direction of the attention of the group to task problems as well as substantive suggestions. Thus, mentioning a problem to be discussed, calling attention to what one is going to say, or pointing out the relevance of what one is saying or doing are instances. For example: "Watch closely now."; "Next I want to call your attention to. . . ." Calling a meeting to order, reference back to an agenda, the giving of any routine signal that one is beginning a new phase of activity or a new focus of effort, signifying the end of a phase of activity or pronouncing the meeting adjourned, these are clear instances of procedural (rather than substantive) suggestions. Signals that are meant to control attention include even such apparently trivial signs as clearing the throat, saying "Ah . . . uh . . . uh . . .", engaging the eyes of the other or holding up the hand, when the aim seems to be to hold the floor or to call attention. Speaking the other's name is a common example, "Say John. . . ." These are ways of suggesting "Please be quiet and listen, I am going to speak." References to prior events and divisions of content can be treated as giving procedural suggestions: "There are two points I'd like to make,"; "In the first place . . ."; "Now with regard to our problem of . . ."; "Going back for a moment. . . ."

Acts in the category Gives Suggestion may occur when a new person arrives in the middle of a group discussion: "I might bring you up to date on what we've been doing. . . ." There are many instances in professional relationships where suggestive orientation is given to the other, as when a student comes to see a teacher, a patient comes to see a doctor, a client comes to see a lawyer. In these cases the nonprofessional person comes to receive suggestions of a substantive sort, and he also receives many minor procedural suggestions as the interview is initiated and conducted to a conclusion.

In group situations instruction or briefing preliminary to cooperative activity may better be treated as giving suggestion than as giving information. In setting up a hypothetical example or situation for exploration or demonstration, suggestions are given as to how the situation is to be defined, the purpose and nature of the roles to be taken, how the task is to be done, where, when, and why. For example: "Suppose we set up an industrial situation . . ."; "The foreman in this situation approaches one of the men in the shop . . ."; "John, will you take the role of the foreman?"; "Go right ahead."; "Consider for a moment what would happen if . . ."; "We will have to stop at the end of the hour."

The classic instance of hypnotic suggestion falls plainly into the present classification. The suggestions are generally very direct and repeated a number of times, the general consent of the other being taken for granted by previous agreement to receive the suggestion: "You are feeling very sleepy."; "Your eyes are very tired."; "You are slowly falling asleep."; "Just concentrate on that bright spot."

In general, direct attempts to guide or counsel, or prepare the other for some activity, to prevail upon him, to persuade him, exhort him, urge, enjoin, or inspire him to some action, by dependence upon authority or ascendance rather than by logical inference are called *giving suggestion.* In the present system, however, suggestions must be neutral, that is, neither negative nor positive in feeling, in order to be classified in the category Gives Suggestion. *A suggestion should be scored in the category Seems Unfriendly if any negative feeling is detectable. Similarly, it should be scored under Seems Friendly if any appreciable positive feeling is present.* This scoring rule is meant to make categories 1 and 12 more sensitive, and to leave in the present category only those suggestions that maintain a strictly neutral feeling.

The category Gives Suggestion is supposed to maintain the ascendant implication, however, even though neutral. Thus, some acts which might otherwise be scored under Gives Opinion, or even Gives Information, may be scored as Gives Suggestion when the implication is present that they are expected to control the behavior of the other for some legitimate reason. Forcefully stated opinions should be categorized as Gives Suggestion, in order to recognize the component of ascendance, however, if negative feeling is present, they should be classified as Seems Unfriendly. These scoring conventions imply that the classifications of giving information, opinion, and suggestion, are not based upon formal characteristics alone, such as grammatical form, or problem-solving function. A judgment must also be made of the presence of positive or negative feeling and of the degree of ascendance. Any problem-solving attempt (information or opinion) as well as suggestion, is classified as Gives Suggestion if it has an ascendant implication, but is still neutral.

The exercise of routine-accepted control is generally felt as neutral (rather than negative) when the control is exercised in such a way that it is clear that the right to make the suggestion or the request rests ultimately on the free consent of the other, who retains the residual right to protest or modify the request so that his own autonomy is not threatened. Thus, acts in which a recognized leader requests the other (s) so do things as a part of the routine mechanics of group management, or as administrative shortcuts to group-determined goals, are ordinary cases of giving suggestion. The leader's requests may be unsolicited by the other and yet anticipate conformity provided it is felt that the leader is acting as a legitimate agent or instrument of the group. Such cases may include the assignment of tasks, the appointment of persons to committees, where the chairman or leader has been given the authority to do so, the giving or assigning of a role to another, that is, a request by the leader to another individual to play a certain role in a group discussion, such as acting as a recorder or observer, or selecting the other for some activity on the basis of the other's interest or consent. The delegation of authority or initiative is included.

Substantive suggestions are those which propose concrete ways of attaining a desired goal by attacking or modifying the outer situation, the group, the individual members, the group norms, or by adapting to any of these. Such actions propose a solution to something that has been recognized as a group problem or task, indicating or suggesting where to start, what to do, how to cope with the problem in terms of action in the near future time-perspective. If the time-perspective is too vague or extends indefinitely far into the future, the suggestion loses potential binding power over the concrete actions of others, even if they agree, and hence the implication of ascendance or control of the other tends to be moderated or lost. Such statements are sometimes called "pious hopes," and if they lack the quality of ascendance should be classified not as suggestions, but as opinions. Giving Opinion is so defined as to retain only problem-solving attempts that have no discernable implication of either ascendance or submission, and neither a positive nor a negative attitude toward the other. Substantive suggestions that are sufficiently specific to have binding power if agreed to are the building blocks of group norms. They do have some implication of ascendance, and are properly classified under Gives Suggestion.

Sometimes substantive suggestions are followed by an announcement of agreement which indicates that the suggestion has just been "enacted into law," and henceforth binds action, as in the case of an announcement by a parliamentary chairman after a vote: "It is so ordered." Whoever gives such a signal, as if to speak for the group as a whole, may be viewed as giving a suggestion. But one may notice acts of a less formal kind which seem similar in intent and function: a kind of final confirmation by repetition or affirmation, which comes at the end of a difficult process of thinking or discussion, when the speaker appears to come to a decision, to make up his mind, to crystalize his intention, or to adopt a plan of action or resolution, and then accepts a responsibility to carry it on into overt action. For example: "Yes, that's it." "That's what we should do." "Then I guess we're all agreed on that." The announcement of an agreement as if it should be final for the group as a whole may be best classified as Gives Suggestion.

Finally, there are some requests where the implication of ascendance is minimal, but the request is nevertheless sufficiently specific and binding to seem better classified as a suggestion than any other of the categories of action. For example: "Would you hand me the ash tray please?" There are in fact some persons so sensitive to the implications of ascendance in even so simple a request that they will adopt any circumlocution or do without rather than make such a request.

How to Score Interaction Category 5, Gives Opinion

Category 5 is the workhorse of all the interaction categories. It is the category most frequently used in many observation situations, and it includes many of those types of acts by which the group gets its "work" done—its problem solving, decision making, and legislative and administrative work. The observer must take care not to score acts in this category when he can detect either ascendant or submissive elements, either positive or negative elements, or elements of showing tension or fantasy. The present category is intended to include only acts which have strictly neutral, serious, objective implications of forward instrumental movement. As seen by someone in a backward part of the space these kinds of acts are "sincere" and "square." Concrete scoring rules to help place all acts not "squarely forward" in their appropriate categories will be discussed below. Even as strictly defined and scored, however, Gives Opinion is a category that includes a lot of subtypes.

The types of action that seem most congruent with the name of the value-direction, "toward conservative group beliefs," direction F, are statements of moral obligation, affirmations of major beliefs or values, statements of policy, intention, guiding principle, or law, reference to a broad and indefinite future time perspective, as yet unimplemented as to ways and means. Examples: "I wish we could fix it so that . . ."; "I think we ought to be fair about this . . ."; "I hope we can do something about that . . ."; "It seems right to me that . . ."; "Of course, we have always adhered to a policy of . . ."; "It has always been my belief that . . ."; "In this group we . . . ." Any expression on the part of a member of the group of the need to realize certain values, any expression of normatively approved ambition or aspiration, of determination or courage, is included. Manifestations of attitudes which would be called earnest, grave, reverent, serious, or prayerful are included insofar as they involve expression of a major value or intention. Certain parts of prayer or performance of ceremonial or ritual acts may be included—when they are expressions and intensifications of intention, dedication, or desire to realize values, to conform to norms, or to achieve socially approved goals.

Whether used deductively or inductively the category Gives Opinion includes all indications or verbalizations of the processes of thought leading to an understanding or dawning insight, such as introspection, reasoning, reckoning, calculating, thinking, musing, cogitating, or concentration.[1] Giving Opinion includes actual statements of hypotheses or expressions of understanding and insight, as well as verbalizations of the processes of arriving at them. Further logical elaborations, explorations, or tests of the hypothesis are included, whether by example, analogy, analysis of cause and effect relations, categorical labeling, or any other sort of logical, intuitive, or conjectural process. For example: "I think it might be . . ."; "Maybe it could be . . ."; "If we add two and two we

---

[1] The inferential and evaluative elements distinguish acts of Giving Opinion from acts of Giving Information. Information consists of descriptive factual statements about observable objects.

get . . ."; "Hmmnnn . . ."; If that's true then we can guess that . . .";
"Now let me see . . ."; "Therefore . . ."; "From that it follows
that. . . ."

Processes of reasoning are applied to various aspects of the situation
in which the group works on its task-problems. Most obvious among
these perhaps is the "outer situation" facing the group as a whole. Many
groups are primarily concerned with tasks that require them to pay
attention to the outer situation. Work groups, teams, and decision-
making committees are examples. In such groups giving opinion may
consist of remarks such as these: "I think we will have to have a rope to
get over that wall."; "They probably won't expect us to try this
move . . ."; "If we choose this alternative they will probably have to
give up the other one . . ." These are opinions since they are not bare
statements of observable fact, but have been arrived at by a process of
reasoning, analysis, conjecture, or interpretation. They may be said to be
opinions about the "outer" situation simply because they are about
objects and affairs which are not a regular part of the personalities of the
members, their group roles and relations to each other, or the beliefs and
values of the group. These latter elements may be thought of as internal
to the group—aspects of its processes.

There are many groups that pay a good deal of attention to their
internal processes. Legislative groups and judicial groups are examples.
Class-conscious social groups pay attention to who is a member and who
knows what about whom. Therapy groups and self-analytic learning or
training groups have as a specific formal task the analysis of the characteristics of the group, the members' actions and motivations. These
groups have a "task" also, though it may not be primarily concerned with
the outer situation. The formation of soundly-based opinions and the
reaching of consensus is a problem to groups that concentrate on their
inner processes as well as to those that concentrate on the outer situation.

Thus giving opinion also includes activity in which a member
attempts, by inference or reasoning, in a primarily objective way, to
understand, diagnose, assess, or interpret the motivation or activity of
another member, or any feature of the group, its structure, dynamics, or
past action. In counseling or educational situations, statements in which
the counselor or instructor makes inferences, interpretations, or diag-
noses, or points out patterns and relationships in the material presented,
of which the other has not yet expressed awareness, are included as
Giving Opinion. For example: "Perhaps this situation is like the one you
told me about yesterday."; Or in a group: "Maybe we got off the track
because we are really trying to decide who should be leader."

Activity in the category Gives Opinion is distinguished from that in
Gives Information in that the former involves inference or interpretation

rather than simple reporting, reflecting, or rephrasing. What is usually thought of as an ideal response for the "nondirective" therapist or counselor is one which stays so close to a simple "reflection" of what the patient or client has said that it must be classed as giving information rather than as giving opinion.

In group activity, giving opinion about internal processes may occur in a "nonpsychological" way, as well as in the ways discussed just above. In a practical problem situation, any assessment or evaluation of the effectiveness or efficiency of one's past action may be included, as when one reflectively examines a plan he has just tried out, or when he examines his own rehearsal of future action. For example: "I guess I failed to take account of . . . ." "That seemed to work out well. . . ."

In self-analytic groups, interpretations may, of course, be made about the self as well as of the other. In such groups, any statement or indication that the student, trainee, client, patient, or member sees patterns and relationships in his own motivation, conduct, or verbal production is included under giving opinion so long as it indicates to the observer an attempt at a logical and reasoned explanation rather than a self-defensive rationalization of conduct with a negative or backward direction. The observer need not agree with the interpretation in order to class it as an opinion. For example: "I must have been so mad at him that I didn't see he was trying to help me." "Probably I don't realize how nervous I am in situations like that." "It looks like I might have been thinking of. . . ."

Acts scored in category 5 are intended to exclude all those which have any appreciable positive or negative feeling, any ascendant or submissive feeling, or any appreciable backward component, that is, any appreciable showing of tension, laughing, joking, or dramatizing. The intention is to confine category 5, Gives Opinion, to those acts which imply only serious worklike forward movement, with no other direction involved. In fact, a considerable number of acts which could logically be scored as Gives Opinion also involve some hostility, some affection, some ascendance or submission, some tension, some joking, double-meaning, symbolism, metaphor, or the like. In such cases of fusion of elements it is more important for the observer to recognize the *additional* element than to retain the information that the act was also one of giving opinion. The "way" in which the opinion is given is considered more important than the fact that an opinion was given. Hence, the simple, but very crucial scoring rule: *Do not score an act in category 5, Gives Opinion, if you can reasonably score it in any other category.*

Acts which would otherwise be called Gives Opinion, but which have any negative feeling are scored in category 12, Seems Unfriendly, instead. Thus a statement or argument in support of a disagreement one has just made may often fall in category 12 rather than in category 5. Similarly, acts that would otherwise be called giving opinion but which have a positive feeling, for example, an additional argument or statement in support of an agreement with another person, may be scored in category 1, Seems Friendly. Acts otherwise called giving opinion which have an ascendant feeling, but avoid either positive or negative feeling are scored in category 4, Gives Suggestion. Finally, acts otherwise called giving opinion which have a noticeable submissive feeling are scored in category 9, Asks for Suggestion (assuming, of course, that they have avoided either positive or negative feeling). In the latter case, they would be scored in either category 1 or 12.

Since each act is scored in one and only one category, there must be a set of priority rules to indicate what to do if there is a conflict over several of the additional meanings. In addition to the rule above (*Do not score an act in category 5, Gives Opinion, if you can reasonably score it in any other category*), the following simple rules take care of most of the problems:

First, any fantasy content or sign of tension is considered to be the most important aspect of the act to be recognized. Hence, *always give priority to a scoring in category 2, Dramatizes, or category 11, Shows Tension, over a scoring in any other category,* including category 5.

Second, any negative or positive feeling is considered to be the next most important information to be recorded. Hence, *always give priority to a scoring in category 1, Seems Friendly, or category 12, Seems Unfriendly, (except of course, acts in category 2, Dramatizes, or category 11, Shows Tension).* The application of this rule is likely to take an appreciable number of acts that would otherwise be scored as Gives Opinion, and classify them as seeming negative.

Third, the next most important information is any implication of ascendant or submissive attitude. Hence, *always give priority to a scoring in category 4, Gives Suggestion; or category 9, Asks for Suggestion, over a scoring in category 5, Gives Opinion.*

These four scoring rules should be applied in the order listed. If followed, the acts that are finally recorded in category 5 will be residual, and relatively neutral or objective in tone. Even so, the number of acts classified here is likely to be high, hence it is desirable for the observer to have a general predisposition to classify elsewhere, if possible.

How to Score Interaction Category 6, Gives Information

Giving information is potentially a very broad category, since anything that a person may be aware of or deal with, including his own feelings, actions, and those of others, as well as the outer situation, may be a subject about which factual remarks are made. Even saying "Yes," which is ordinarily classed as agreeing, could if one wished, be regarded as giving information about one's reaction. Not all statements that logically or grammatically could be treated as giving information are in fact so scored in the present system, however. The meaning of the category within the observational system is very close to the common-sense conception. Information is defined as neutral, factual in form (though not necessarily true), based on perception or direct experience of potentially public events or objects, and hence testable. Any statement too vague in principle to be tested is not classified as giving information, but, usually, as giving opinion.

Giving information has a downward direction, by definition. In order to answer the requirements of classification as giving information the act must be nonascendant, neutral, (that is, neither seeming friendly nor seeming unfriendly), noninferential (not forward), and nonself-revealing through dramatization, joking, or showing tension (not backward). If any of these other directions are fused with the act, the act should be classed in the proper category expressing that other direction. The priority system described above is applied to giving information as well as giving opinion. As explained in the discussion of category 2, *acts that might otherwise be classified as giving information are classed as dramatizations whenever they report the action of a person not present in the group, or an imaginary being,* since reports of acts are such apt carriers of images that may support fantasy.

Probably the clearest cases of giving information are statements about the supposed factual nature of the outer situation facing the group, statements which are recognized as generally established or easily confirmed by observation. "They usually have coffee for us just down the hall." "The phone is out of operation." "The number is 868-7600." "It would take three days to reach him by mail." "They pick up the mail at 5:30." "We only have two days left." These statements are essentially objective, noninferential, not much emotionally toned, not vague, and are in principle, testable.

Information is often given gratuitously, and at length, as in a lecture, or in the process of conveying knowledge in a context where the implication is that the other wants to know something the speaker can tell him. The expectation is that the information given will be accepted, if understood. It is not offered as if it were problematic, or a matter of decision, though in fact many acts of giving information are disagreed with. In giving opinion the expectation is usually less optimistic—a greater amount of disagreement is expected than in the case of giving information, and the expectation is usually justified.

Giving information about the self is only partly included in the present category. Only giving facts about the more public aspect of the self, colorless and drained of present emotion are included—that is, nondramatic reports. "My name is John Smith." "I am twenty-one years old." "I have lived here all my life." "I have a headache." On the other hand, information about one's present or past emotional life, which is dramatic and possibly revealing as symbolic material is preferably classed in category 2, Dramatizes. For example: "In this dream I was standing there, and this tiger . . ."; "It was the biggest, fattest, juiciest ice cream cone I have ever seen. . . ." Remarks which stir the observer's imagination should be classed in category 2. Much quasi-factual anecdotal material reported in conversation is better classified as dramatizing than as giving information.

Repeating what the other has said back to him, restating, reflecting the content or feeling back to him, may be classed as giving information. This type of activity used in counseling is often called "nondirective," since it aims to be essentially nonascendant, emotionally neutral, noninferential; it also aims to follow whatever direction the person being counseled takes, for the time being (84). The "reflection of feeling" as it is also called, should rephrase, or report the essential content of what the other has said back to him without much inference or interpretation, otherwise it may be better classified as giving opinion. "Interpretations" in therapy, on the other hand, are meant to cut somewhat below the surface, and to go somewhat beyond what the other has said— interpretations are clearly giving opinion. In practice, "reflections of feeling" may include putting ideas or feelings in somewhat clearer or more recognizable form, with the intent of aiding the other in the formulation or reformulation of his problem, but the intent is to keep the element of inference minimal. The ratio of giving information to giving opinion is very different in different types of therapy.

In problem-solving or self-analytic groups a similar kind of action with primarily informational intent is sometimes called "feedback." Certain observations about the characteristics of the group by observers, or group members, are reported to the group without interpretation, in order to make it possible for the members to make an analysis of their own personalities, organization, and procedure. "Three of the members indicate dissatisfaction with the meetings." "In the interpersonal ratings John received a classification of UPF." "The rate of disagreeing in the last meeting was higher than it has ever been." Any reflective looking back on past activity of the group may be classified as giving information. Most groups, though not self-analytic, do a certain amount of looking back. Reading the minutes of the last meeting is the most familiar example.

Finally, there are certain minor forms of giving information which consist of immediate and current efforts to prevent or repair breaks in the flow of communication, such as repeating when somebody says "What?", clarifying confusion about something said, explaining, enlarging, summarizing, restating, not with the purpose of convincing or carrying the argument further, but simply with the purpose of making the communication more adequate. Attention to the mechanics may also be used, of course, to avoid getting down to brass tacks, that is, to avoid dealing with the important content. Nevertheless, the scores are important, partly for that reason. The observer is as careful to score the time spent on minor repairs of the communication as the acts he considers important in themselves.

How to Score Interaction Category 7, Asks for Information

Acts of asking for information, that is, high rates in this category in the individual's profile, tend to be associated with movement in the UP direction. But this is a matter of empirical findings in the groups actually studied, rather than of definition, and may not be characteristic of other situations. One can imagine group structures in which the functions of gathering and checking information had been assigned to lower ranks in the status structure. In this case the directional implication of a high rate might be different. However, the stability of diagnostic meanings over different groups and settings is a general problem for all categories. The correlations and the factor analysis taken as the basis of the descriptions in this book were all obtained in a particular kind of group structure (sometimes called leaderless group discussion), and with a particular type of problem (case-analysis of human relations situations, with some group self-analysis). Where the structure of the group and task are different, some differences in diagnostic meanings of high and low rates of interaction in given categories may be expected. But in leaderless group discussions on case-analysis and self-analysis, high rates of asking for information seem to be associated with an aspect of leadership that elicits positive regard. This may not be unusual, but characteristic of many types of groups and situations.

Asking for information refers to questions requesting a factual, descriptive, objective type of answer, an answer based upon experience, observation, or empirical research. If such a kind of answer is impossible, in that it requires guessing, supposing, looking forward in time to events that have not yet occurred, or the like, then the question should be classified as asking for opinion rather than information. The questions can be about the outer situation or task facing the group, about the group itself, its structure or organization, about the other person, about the self, or about what has been said or done in the process of communi-cation currently going on. The question may be direct or indirect. For example, "What day of the month is it?" is a direct question about the outer situation. If, in the course of a description a person says, "I'm not sure of the exact date," this may be considered an indirect or implied question, and also classified as asking for information. "Who is in charge of the arrangements for the next meeting?" is a direct question about the structure of the group. The remark, "I have forgotten whom we appoint-ed," is an indirect question. "How long have you lived here?" is a direct question about the other. "What did you say?" is a direct question about the current process of communication, as are the shorter forms, "What?" or "Huh?" The statement "I didn't hear you," may be regarded as an indirect question about the current process of communication. Any routine request for repetition is properly classified as asking for informa-tion.

Questions designed to cause the other person to redefine, clarify, or redescribe a feeling, as in nondirective counseling, are sometimes more properly classified as giving opinion. For example: "You mean you don't really like him?" If the mode of statement seems to be a disguised interpretation, meant to bring an unadmitted feeling of the other to his consciousness, it should be classified as giving opinion.

Asking for information as a category is meant to include primarily those questions that require the giving of a rather simple factual answer, rather than an evaluation, or an inference, or the expression of a feeling. To ask for information is to ask for an answer which can be judged as true or false on the basis of simple observation (though not necessarily possible at the moment), or an answer which is generally regarded as an empirical fact, and is likely to be accepted as nonproblematic, once given and understood.

How to Score Interaction Category 8, Asks for Opinion

Asking for opinion includes any kind of question which attempts to encourage a statement or a reaction on the part of the other without limiting the nature of the response except in a very general way, with the implication that the other has freedom to express interest or disinterest, where he is not put under pressure to agree or disagree, or to come out with any predetermined answer, type of answer, or attitude. The direc-tional implication is thus simply positive—the person who asks the question indicates a friendly interest or attitude, he avoids taking an ascendant attitude, and he does not ask for conformity to any pattern. For example, "What do you think?" "I wonder how you feel about that?"

One common phrase, "Don't you think so?" fails to qualify on the above criteria. It is an attempt to elicit a particular answer—an agreement about something already said. Similar phrases are "You know?" "Do you know what I mean?" "Right?" "See?" These are usually rather strong persuasive attempts, and as such are classified as giving suggestion, or if too insistent, as seeming unfriendly.

In neutral group problem-solving situations, questions which seek an inferential interpretation, a hypothesis, diagnosis, or further analysis of some idea from another member, which ask for his definition of the situation or his attitude on some topic in a nonthreatening or objective manner, are included. The wish may be to get the other's interpretation or opinion as an aid where there is no known answer and only conjecture is possible, such as "I wonder what that would involve?" Or in a more therapeutic context the intent may be to help the other to see implications of something he has said, or to explore his motivation, for example: "I wonder why you feel that way?"

There are cases in which the asking is more implicit than explicit. For example: "I can't figure out what that might mean." "I don't know how I really feel." These are cases of a more indefinite expression of inability to make satisfactory inferences or to resolve emotional conflict or ambivalence. They are scored as asking for opinion unless there is a tone of distress, in which case they should be scored as showing tension.

When the person asking for opinion is in an ascendant position, as in the case of therapeutic or counseling situations, it may be difficult to tell whether he is asking for opinion or giving suggestion. For example, the questions "How is it going?" or "How do you feel today?" seem like asking for opinion, whereas "Tell me more about it," and "Talk about anything you like," seem more like giving suggestion. It would be a mistake, probably, to assume that it is impossible for a person in a professional ascendant role to ask for opinion, but it is perhaps especially difficult for him to avoid giving suggestion. If he uses the verbal form of suggestion, the remark, even though kindly, should be classified as giving suggestion. Elected chairmen or group leaders are in a similar position. The remarks "Could we have an expression of feeling on this point?" is probably best classified as a suggestion, so would be the question "What is the sense of the meeting?"

How to Score Interaction Category 9, Asks for Suggestion

The category asking for suggestion is meant to define acts in the DF direction—that is, neutral task-oriented acts which at the same time are submissive, or which aim to turn the initiative over to the other. Often such acts will also indicate a feeling of confusion or uncertainty about the position of the group with regard to its goals, the course of discussion to the present point, or about what has been said or is going on. For example: "Where are we?"; "Where do we stand now?"; "I don't know what to do." Asking for suggestion may also include more deliberate attempts to get the group to assess and clarify its position in the problem-solving process, whether or not the person asking is actually confused or disoriented himself, so long as he maintains a submissive position and acts to turn the initiative over to some other person. For example: "I wonder what we can do about this?" "What shall we do?" "What shall our policy be?" "What do you think we ought to aim at?"

However, it is difficult to raise questions about forward movement, especially to the group as a whole, without assuming ascendance. For example, the question "I wonder if there are any other possibilities?" tends to imply that there are. "What shall we talk about today?" may imply the power to decide after the other has made his suggestion. The question, "Is there a motion on this point?" definitely seems to assume that the asker is putting himself in a leadership position. Acts which do in fact imply ascendant task-leadership, even though they ask for substantive suggestions from others, should be classified as giving suggestion. The criterion for the classification of an act is not the exact wording, but a prediction as to how the act will be evaluated by others in the group.

Appeals for suggestion which have an emotional tone of distress may be classified as showing tension. Indications of a resentful dependence, an inability to take responsibility for direction, rather than a sharing of the right to determine direction, may be classified as seeming unfriendly. An irritated retort, such as "Well, what do you suggest then?" should be classified as seeming unfriendly. On the other hand, one can imagine acts of asking for suggestion that should be classified as seeming friendly, for example: "What would you like for dinner tonight?"

There are certain attitudes of task-oriented or value-oriented readiness which may not take the verbal form of asking for suggestion, but which may nevertheless be scored in this category. Acts which logically could be scored as giving opinion, for example, may be given in a tone tentative enough to be scored as asking for suggestion—a preferable scoring according to the priority rules.

Acts which seem to be over-careful, over-cautious, over-prudent, vigilant, tense, and inhibited because of fear of possible blame, should be classified as asking for suggestion, since their directional implication seems well expressed by the DF direction. These acts indicate that the person is sensitive about or concerned with the good opinion of others, that he is over-scrupulous, conforming, conscientious, conventional, dutiful, because of fear of breaking group norms and thus experiencing disapproval and guilt. Acts in this category include a part, but not all, of what is usually called submissiveness. If the person is proceeding in a task-oriented way, in spite of uncertainty or fear of blame, his act may be scored as asking for suggestion. If he is hanging back from task-oriented activity, because of conflict, he should be scored as showing tension.

How to Score Interaction Category 10, Disagrees

Disagreement is an act with negative implications—it implies direction N, but not all acts with negative implications are classed as disagreement. Disagreement is defined more specifically in terms of where it comes in interaction sequences. Disagreement is the *initial* act of conveying the information to the other that the content of his proposition (his statement of information, opinion, or suggestion) is not acceptable, at least not immediately. For example: "No." "I don't think so." "I disagree." "I don't agree." "I can't accept that." "Well. . . ." "But. . . ." Sometimes the information is repeated by a combination of two or three of these kinds of reactions. In this case a separate score is given for each act. Disagreement is a *re*action to the others action. The negative feeling conveyed is attached to the content of what the other has said, not to him as a person. And the negative feeling must not be so very strong, or the act will seem unfriendly.

Mild degrees of disagreement are included, such as showing surprise, temporary disbelief, astonishment, amazement, or incredulity. For example: "What!"; "You don't say!" "That can't be!"; "Would you believe it!" One may also disagree by omission, failing to pay attention when the other is speaking, failing to give a requested repetition, or the like. Either verbal or nonverbal indications that the member is skeptical, dubious, cautious about accepting the proposal, hesitant, or critical, may be included as disagreement, provided the implications of ascendance or of hostility are absent. When these indications are present, the act should be scored as seeming unfriendly.

Unless there is repetition of disagreement as described above, only the *initial* act after the other speaks is marked as disagrees. The propositions which follow in making the argument, in the form of information about the situation, analysis of the facts, opinions, alternative suggestions, and the like, are scored in their regular category, *unless* the tone of voice, the facial expression or bodily attitude conveys negative feeling. Whenever the observer sees or hears any actual signs of negative feeling or emotion directed at the other person, the act should be scored as seeming unfriendly.

But the simple fact that an argument stands in logical opposition to the content of the other's argument does not require that the argument be scored as Disagrees. For example, suppose that one person gives some information to another. Then the other reacts by saying, "I don't think so. It seems to me that there were more than that. In fact, I remember seeing at least five." The first reaction would be scored as disagrees, assuming there were no signs of negative feeling toward the other as a person. The second act would *not* be scored as disagrees, but as giving opinion, since it is neutral, and a conjecture. The third act would be scored as giving information, on the assumption that it is also neutral, since it reports a concrete observation. The thing to note is that *after the initial act of disagreement, the scoring reverts to the neutral categories based upon the interaction form of the acts.* After an initial act of disagreement, "the slate is wiped clean," so far as relations of logical contradiction are concerned. If the slate were not wiped clean, one would have to continue to follow logical contradictions in an argument indefinitely. Finally, it might happen that everything said would be in logical contradiction to something said earlier. The category Disagrees would have become a "sink" into which all interaction would be drawn.

The frame of reference within which disagreement is judged is thus short in time, consisting of one or more acts during which a logical position is taken, and the initial act only of the rejoinder. The frame of reference for judging agreement is similar. If the reaction is an agreement, after the initial act of agreement, the scoring reverts to the neutral categories based upon the interaction form of the acts. Unless, that is, there is an emotional tone of seeming friendly.

Assume that another person's act of giving information is followed by these three acts: "I don't think so. It seems to me we should be more careful! You have no right to go around saying things like that!" The first act might be scored as disagrees, although in the context that follows one might also have felt some negative feeling in the phrase "I don't think so," in which case it might be scored as seeming unfriendly. The next two remarks, in any case, seem clearly to imply some negative feeling toward the other, and so should be scored as seeming unfriendly.

How to Score Interaction Category 11, Shows Tension

The directional implication of acts in this category is DB, submissive and nonconforming, yet not clearly negative in feeling about the other as a person. Several varieties of acts are scored in this category, not all of which seem similar on a superficial level. Laughter, in particular, may seem quite different from signs of anxious emotionality.

Signs of anxious emotionality indicate a conflict between acting and withholding action. Minor outbreaks of reactive anxiety may first be mentioned, such as appearing startled, disconcerted, alarmed, dismayed, perturbed, or concerned. Hesitation, speechlessness, flurry, fluster, confusion, trembling, blushing, flushing, stammering, sweating, blocking-up, gulping, swallowing, or wetting the lips persistently may also be included.

Anxiety may be aroused by unpreparedness, but it is often reinforced by the image of punishing other persons similar to parents. Conflict is of various kinds. Sometimes fear of disapproval conflicts with instinctual or impulsive desires. Sometimes the tendency to conform to one set of values or authoritative demands conflicts with another set of values or authoritative demands. The person in conflict may suppress, conceal, hide, or fail to mention something which is considered discreditable, such as ineptitude, ignorance, a defect, a misdeed, or a humiliating trait or event. Indications of holding back in this way are scored as showing tension.

More passive forms of hanging back from task demands are also included, such as evading the actual content of requests, shrinking from what is felt to be dangerous, or refraining from action because of failure. Reactions to disapproval, either actual or fantasied, may be included also, such as appearing to be embarrassed, fussed, sheepish, chagrined, dejected, crestfallen, chastened, at a loss, or mortified. Showing tension more generally includes any verbal or motor expressions of fear, apprehension, worry, dread, fright, terror, or panic.

Laughter seems to be a sudden escape into motor discharge of conflicted emotional states that can no longer be contained. The emotions may be anxiety, aggression, affection, or any other. So long as the person contains the emotion and passively "hangs back" from forward movement, that is, from conformity, he is said to show tension. Laughter is a momentary breaking of a state of tension, and if continued may help to reduce the general state of tension, but it is equally appropriate to treat it as a *sign* of tension. It is so classified, as a sign of tension, in the present set of categories. Since this may run counter to common sense, to a certain degree, it is well to indicate the reasons for it. The first reason is empirical: laughter, which was scored separately from other modes of showing tension in the original set of interaction categories, turned out to fall in the same position in the space as other modes of showing tension—DB. Laughter is more dependably a sign of tension, apparently, than a reducer of it. The second reason is more arbitrary. For practical reasons it is desirable to keep the number of interaction categories small, and it does not seem worth the cost to include a separate category for laughter. Furthermore, many laughs do seem well described as showing tension. Laughing alone, giggling nervously or apologetically, for example seem perfectly well represented by a classification as showing tension.

If one wishes a measure of laughter alone, a good approximation may be obtained by noting only acts in category 11 that follow jokes. In many instances a break-over into laughter by the group as a whole is precipitated by a joke, or an unconscious slip which dramatizes some fantasy, or by a sudden event or change in the situation which has symbolic relation to the motives or feelings held in tension. In such cases one does not conclude that the underlying tension is necessarily severe, although it may be. Prolonged laughter, or hysterical laughter, or laughter that appears to be close to tears, crying, or moaning, is generally indicative of severe tension. It is important to listen to the quality of laughter in estimating its significance. I am convinced from the observation of groups that the element of distress in laughter is more prominent than is usually recognized.

In scoring interaction it is very important to watch and listen for signs of tension, since these signs appear around emotionally loaded topics and give clues as to the severity of the conflict. The observer who wishes to understand personalities and groups better must always give a high priority to detecting the hidden meanings disclosed in jokes and dramatizations, and the hidden conflicts disclosed in showing tension. The scoring rules give these two categories the highest priority of all categories in the system. *If an act can reasonably be scored as dramatizing or showing tension, it should be scored in category 2 or 11 in preference to any other category.* In order to apply this rule, the observer must remain constantly alert to hidden meanings.

Careful attention to the above priority rule provides two categories that can be used in later content analysis as markers of probably significant, but suppressed, emotions. Their possible use in this way should help the observer decide what should go into the categories. Every remark or action which the observer thinks might repay a later content-analysis for double meanings should go into the category of dramatizing, and every sign which indicates that the preceding content was loaded with emotion for a given member should be recognized by a score in the category of showing tension.

In cases where the group as a whole engages in a general laugh, the score is entered by using a zero to stand, temporarily, for everybody. Thus, if member 1 makes a joke, and if everybody laughs, the score for the laughter is entered as 0-1 (all to one) in category 11. Later, when scores are tabulated, the zero is replaced by a series of scores: 2-1, 3-1, 4-1, and so forth, for as many persons as there are in the group (except for the joker). It will happen, under this system, that a person who speaks hardly at all in the group will still be counted as contributing one act each time the group as a whole laughs. In general, this does no harm, since it will tend to represent his position correctly as DB. However, scores which indicate that everybody in the group laughed (using the zero), when in fact not everybody did laugh, will fail to distinguish between persons who are more, and those who are less conflicted. Hence one should use the zero-shorthand sparingly, and should preferably identify the specific persons who laugh, and who keep laughing the longest, as the general period of laughter subsides. Scores for individuals alone will be more helpful than scores attributed loosely to the group as a whole.

An arbitrary convention is adopted to deal with occasions where laughing continues without the intervention of further jokes. Each new "wave of laughter" is given a new score. Essentially each time the person or the group seems to "take a new breath" and starts laughing again, a new score is entered. If the person who originally made the joke still seems to be the recipient, he may be scored as receiving the laughs. If, on the other hand, the glances of communication seem to pass around among the members, then the score may be entered 0-0, and in later tabulation, each person will be credited with having initiated a laugh, and each with having received one.

It is expected, as a matter of experience, that when joking and laughing set in, they tend to continue in alternation for some period during which a number of variations on the loaded theme are "rung in." This presents no particular difficulty to the scorer, except that it may tax his speed. He should try to get every joke and every laugh, and not assume, as members of the group tend to do, that a moratorium has been declared during which nothing really significant can happen. Nor should the observer be perturbed if joking and laughing, anecdotes and stories go on almost uninterruptedly for long periods. He should recognize that a kind of hidden work is being done, and that the construction of symbolic forms to which emotions are associated is a vital necessity in all groups.

How to Score Interaction Category 12, Seems Unfriendly

The category of seeming unfriendly is used to classify all overt acts which seem to the observer to be anywhere on the negative side of the space, except for those in category 10, Disagrees. There are theoretically nine subtypes, one applying to each combination of unfriendliness with the upward-downward dimension and the forward-backward dimension. The scope of the category, and the number of subtypes, is cognate with the category of seeming friendly, which similarly refers to all parts on the positive side of the space.

The name of the category is chosen so as to require only very slight signs of negative feeling in order to justify a classification of seeming unfriendly. The word "seems" is meant to put the matter on a subjective basis, and the word "unfriendly" is meant to sound very weak and unemotional compared with some of the acts that are scored in the category. Thus the signs may be very minimal, and the negative feeling very slight. The cutting point for admission of an act to the category is deliberately placed very low, because in most interaction the rate in the category will be low anyway, and it seems best to err on the side of inclusion when in doubt. The nine subtypes follow, discussed separately for conceptual clarity, but in practice the distinctions do not have to be made at the time of scoring. All nine subtypes are given the same scoring, Seems Unfriendly.

Subtype UNF. Acts characteristic of the UNF direction are those in which there is a fusion of ascendant attitude, moralistic orientation, and negative feeling toward the other. These include acts in which there is an attempt to control, regulate, govern, direct, or supervise, in a manner which seems arbitrary and in which the freedom of choice or consent of the other person is either greatly limited or nonexistent, with the implication that he has no right to protest or modify the demand, but is expected to follow the directive immediately without argument. The category includes arbitrarily assigning a role, locating or relocating the other, defining or restricting his powers by fiat, making demands or giving commands such as "Come here!" "Stop that!" "Hurry up!" "Get out!" Any act in which the person peremptorily beckons, points, pushes, pulls, or otherwise directly controls, or attempts to control the activity of the other may be included (unless, of course, it is routine and thus neutral).

Intervention in an argument or conflict with arbitrary attempts to judge or settle it or to render a decision are included. The moralistic-legalistic aspects of the relevant behavior are also shown in disapproval, including acts ranging from mild forms, such as reprimanding the other, blaming him, scolding him, admonishing or reminding him of his duty, on to more extreme forms, such as indications that one is shocked, indignant, appalled, scandalized at something the other has done, and shows horror or disgust. Indications that one is indignant, offended, or insulted about a personal affront are included. Indications of a more generalized moral indignation, such as a grim expression, appearing incensed, irate, outraged, or infuriated by some deviance of the other are included. Finally, indications of satisfaction based upon identification of the self with the "highest and best" moral authority are included, such as appearing pompous, pontifical, ceremonious, self-opinionated, self-important, self-righteous, self-satisfied, self-complacent, or smug.

Subtype UN. Acts particularly characteristic of the UN direction are simultaneously ascendant and negative, but neither moralistic (forward), nor anti-conventional (backward). Conspicuous attempts to override the other in conversation, interrupting the other, interfering with his speaking, gratuitously finishing his sentence for him when he does not want help, insisting on finishing, or warding off interruption are all comparatively mild examples.

There are a number of varieties of attacks or deflation of the other's status, ranging from mild to violent. Any implication of inferiority or incompetence on the part of the other is included. Appraising the other contemptuously, belittling him, depreciating, disparaging, ridiculing, or minimizing the other, reducing his remarks to absurdity, and making fun of him, are included. More extreme acts that could be described as maliciously sarcastic, satirical, or ironical, in which the person lampoons, caricatures, burlesques the other, or becomes unduly and insultingly familiar are included. Teasing, taunting, heckling, gloating, crowing, jeering, scoffing, mocking, sneering, bedeviling, goading, baiting, or provoking the other to say something indiscreet or damaging are included. Damning the other, finding fault with him, complaining, criticizing; any act that is abusive, accusatory, or acrimonious is included. Making charges against the other, imputing unworthy motives to him, blaming him, denouncing him, excoriating, berating, prosecuting, ill-treating, or browbeating him are all, of course, included. The category includes any act of gossip, libel, slander; smirching of the other's character, branding him with undesirable characteristics, demeaning him, exposing him, or undermining his position; maligning or discrediting him, placing him at a disadvantage or oppugning his motives. Other similar acts include tricking, hoaxing, duping, deceiving, fleecing, hazing, humiliating the other, or rendering him conspicuous.

Acts of asserting one's claims strongly, trying to outdo the other, showing rivalry, and the like are also included, although they may occur in a context where the actor does not seem to be (at least yet) in a superior position of power. The manifestation of any attitude that seems aggressive, combative, belligerent, pugnacious, quarrelsome, or argumentative should be scored in the present category. Some acts of aggression are less focused than others. Less focused forms are included also such as appearing to be provoked, showing annoyance, irritation, heat, anger, or rage. Diffuse indications of intolerance or malevolence, such as glaring, frowning, cursing, fuming, hissing, jostling, pushing, screaming, kicking, or scratching are included. Moving or speaking in a threatening manner, challenging, defying, attacking, assailing, assaulting, hitting, striking, beating, or fighting are included. The manifestation of a destructive, cruel, or ruthless attitude, or any resentful, vengeful, vindictive, or retaliative act is included. The category includes any indication of envy, jealousy, covetousness, cupidity, avarice, acquisitiveness at the expense of the other, or attempt to take something away from the other.

From the perspective of a status of superior power over the other, the present category includes attempts to force, compel, coerce, subdue, subject, tame, master, or dominate the other; acts in which the stronger member prohibits the other from doing something, represses him, proscribes some activity, or gives warnings or threats. The category includes showing any overbearing, dogmatic, assertive, imperious, inconsiderate, or severe attitude. Acts of rejection, dismissal, or expulsion are included, such as rebuffing advances of the other, repulsing, jilting, or excluding him—dropping, deserting, abandoning, evicting, discharging, or banishing him.

Attitudinal indicators of a self-picture exalted at the other's expense are included, such as acts that would be regarded as haughty, proud, vain, arrogant, snobbish, self-admiring, self-conceited, presumptuous, condescending, or disdainful.

Subtype UNB.   Acts in the UNB direction show a fusion of ascendance, anti-conformity, and antipathy to other persons. A good many acts in which the person works against authority or persons in authority are included: showing nonsubmissiveness in the face of authority; nonconformity or excessive independence; acts which from the point of view of the person in authority are seen as disobedient, insubordinate, rebellious, irresponsible, willful, obstreperous, unrestrained, disorderly, carping, harping, griping, nagging, badgering, harrassing, annoying, perturbing, disturbing, or pestering. In the same category are acts that seem disrespectful, discourteous, impudent, bold, saucy, flippant, and attitudes that seem impervious, unashamed, or unrepentant.

In a context where conventional norms require that personal status and attention received should be based upon merit demonstrated by achievement, attempts to obtain status by other means have the implications of direction UNB. In such a context, attempts to attract attention by mannerisms, expressive gestures, emphatic or extravagant speech, posturing, posing for effect, displaying the self, seeking the limelight, bragging, boasting, strutting, blustering, are included, as are other modes of praising the self, glorifying, exalting, applauding, approving, or advertising the self.

In addition to acts that seem deviant from conventional norms of merit through achievement, there are actions which are also deviant from expectations that group members should be frank, open, affectionate, trusting—in short, positive. Inconsiderate or exploitive attempts to excite, amaze, fascinate, entertain, shock, intrigue, or amuse others as a means of raising one's own status may be included. "Acting," showing off, seeking applause or approbation, playing the clown, making jokes which fall flat, trying to impress the other with one's importance, trying to be seen and heard, and pushing one's self forward may be included in this category. Behavior in which the person seems exhibitionistic, spectacular, or conspicuous, or poses as unique, mysterious, or incalculable may be included, provided the negative element is felt to be present. On the other hand, some of these acts may have a substantial element of underlying symbolic meaning, and if so, should be scored as dramatizing rather than seeming unfriendly. The classification in category 2, dramatizing, takes precedence over classification in the present category, in case of doubt.

Subtype NF. Movement in the NF direction is task-oriented and negative, but not ascendant. It is difficult to find single verbs or adjectives describing acts of this direction. One sees relevant cases sometimes in the argument given in support of a disagreement. The member amends or corrects another's opinion about the situation, his interpretation, or diagnosis, in a distant impersonal way. He may avoid giving the impression that he is ascendant, he appears mainly value-oriented or task oriented, persistent in spite of resistance from others. The disapproval shown is of the "idea" or the value-position expressed by the other, and appears to be not meant to detract from his status, or to extend to him as a person, or to raise the status of the speaker. The terms "conscientious," or "principled" are sometimes applied to action of this kind.

Subtype N. In action which has the direction N, there is negative feeling or emotion directed to the other, but there is no clear implication of either ascendance or submission, or of forward or backward movement. It is not always easy to tell whether these directions are implied, but this is not critical during scoring, since all acts with any negative component, except disagreement, are classified under the category Seems Unfriendly. Perhaps the best cases are those in which the person seems psychically detached, isolated, indifferent, impersonal, formal, distant, unsocial, reserved, secluded, unapproachable, exclusive, or forbidding, especially in responding to an approach of the other.

Passive refusals to act which frustrate the other may be included; acts in which one thwarts, balks, blocks, obstructs, or puts barriers in the way of the other, confines, constrains, or stands in his way, or renders his efforts vain, upsets his plans, forestalls, contravenes, foils, or checkmates him. This category also includes acts of withholding resources from the other, the manifestation of possessive, retentive, retractive, or secretive attitudes. Any act in which the other is denied something requested, in which the person disappoints the other, refuses to let the other participate in some satisfaction or have access to some resource may be included here. Acts of disagreeing are fundamentally of this general kind, but are given the more specific classification of disagreeing unless the element of negative feeling becomes perceptible.

Acts of "defensiveness" often fit into the present category, in which the person manifests an attitude of being on his guard, of having a chip on his shoulder, such as interpreting a harmless remark as a slur, bristling when criticised; protesting, defending or protecting the self, or one's sentiments or theories in an ego-involved way. The category includes any act of self-vindication or exculpation, such as explaining, excusing, justifying, offering extenuations or rationalizations of inferiority, guilt, or failure.

Subtype NB. The key to the conception of the NB direction is that it involves a negative attitude both toward the other or others as persons, and toward the values or group norms for which they stand; but the negative attitude does not reach the point of ascendant acts of defiance, rather it appears mostly reactively. Acts in the NB direction include responses to attempts of the other to control, in which the reacting person shows autonomy, is noncompliant, unwilling, or disobliging, where he resists some effort or imagined effort of a superior other person in authority to take some satisfaction from him. The category includes acts in which the person rejects, refuses, or purposefully ignores directions, commands, demands, or authoritative requests, where he defies authority, is negativistic, stubborn, resistant, obstinate, refractory, contrary, sulky, or sullen. Shrugging the shoulders, avoiding or quitting activities prescribed by authority, resisting coercion and restriction, or trying in any manner to shake off restraint or get free of physical or moral restraint is included. Acts of disavowal, disclaiming, denial, refusal to admit responsibility, guilt, inferiority, or weakness may be included. In all of the acts classified in this category it is assumed that at least minimal signs of negative feeling or emotion are seen or heard by the observers.

Subtype DNF. Some acts of self-sacrifice, or apparent self-sacrifice, seem unfriendly because, although submissive and value-oriented, they imply an excessively harsh picture of the other. Attempts to shame the other into some kind of desired behavior by acting as if injured, hurt, martyred, or put-upon may be included. Acts which attempt to place the responsibility for the solution of one's own problems on the other or on the group are included when they imply that the other has not given the aid, advice, or support he should have given. In this context, appealing to the other's good nature, mercy, or forbearance may have a negative feeling. This is also true of acts in which the person flatters the other, cajoles, or attempts to appease him, where he insincerely abases himself, cowers, curries favor, fawns, foot-licks, or is servile with ulterior purposes.

Acts of atonement, in which the person humiliates himself to expiate guilt, or indicates that he expects punishment from the other who is thus defined as bad and punishing, may be placed in the present category.

Moaning or cringing, covering the face with the hands, acts which indicate consciousness of guilt, indications that the person is furtive, ashamed, morose, depressed, or remorseful are included. More extreme forms of blaming, belittling, and mutilating the self are included. Acts which are markedly self-dissatisfied, self-critical, self-depreciating, self-accusing, self-exposing, self-convicting, self-condemning, self-dispraising, self-disparaging, self-reproving, self-reproachful, self-upbraiding, self-scornful, self-degrading, self-humiliating, self-contemptuous, or self-destroying are included.

Subtype DN. Acts in the DN direction are at the same time relatively passive and yet expressive of negative feeling toward others, particularly, perhaps, toward popular members of the group. Conformity to group norms is not an issue—rather the expression of feeling or attitude toward the self and one's membership in the group is the focus. Indications of an attitude which seem over-cool, frigid, inexpansive, or unsmiling may be included. Any situation in which an emotional response would be expected, where the person refuses to give applause, or is unappreciative, unacknowledging, ungrateful, unallured, "hard to please," or "hard to get" is included. Many passive forms of rejection are included, such as remaining immobile, rigid, restrained, silent, close-mouthed, uncommunicative, inexpressive, impassive, imperturbable, reticent, or responseless in the face of approaches of the other, any passive withholding of love or friendship. Also included is any manifestation of a partially repressed negative reaction to the other which seems cranky, uncongenial, touchy, tiffish, testy, surly, irritable, ill-tempered, or irascible.

Not only anger held in, as in the cases above, but also anxiety about exposing the self to social evaluation, notice, or even to praise, may lie behind action in the DN direction. Social timidity, shyness, a tendency to appear abashed, self-conscious, to shrink from social notice—signs of all these may be classed in this category.

Subtype DNB. Acts in the DNB direction are those in which the acting person seems submissive, alienated from other persons, and deviant from group norms. Indications that one feels his efforts have failed, that some problems confronting him in his earlier efforts to conform still remain, expressions of feeling frustrated, thwarted, or deprived may be included in this category. Expressions of unhappiness, indications that the person is dissatisfied, discontented, disappointed, discouraged, disheartened, disconsolate, downcast, downhearted, resigned, desolate, despairing, or miserable may all be included here, but the feeling must be one of rejection of both the affection of other persons and the demands of group norms.

Paying attention to something other than the activity with which the group is concerned, when there is an expectation that all members will be attending or actively participating, is included. Speaking or paying attention to outsiders, such as observers, when the group as a whole is working on another problem is included. All undetermined member-to-member contacts, that is, asides, whispering, winks, and so on, while the main discussion is going on between others may indicate rejections by both participants of the rest of the group. Each of these contacts may be given one or more scores in the present category, directed to the group as a whole.

Actions or the display of attitudes which indicate that the person is unattentive, bored, or psychologically withdrawn from others and from the problem at hand are included, for example: slouching; yawning; closing the eyes; daydreaming; looking away from the others in the group; looking away from the work; and letting the eyes wander. Attitudes that seem listless, languid, bemused, absorbed, abstracted, or oblivious to others are scored in the present category. More definite and overt acts of withdrawal, such as retiring, leaving, quitting, resigning, deserting, or retreating from humiliation are also included. More extreme forms of autistic, subjective, or socially irrelevant behavior which indicate a lack of contact with what is going on may be included, such as talking to oneself, or mumbling. Refusing to talk loud enough to be heard is also scored in the present category. Any indication of excessive inaction or nonresponsiveness may be included, or signs that the person is psychologically shut-in, indisposed, apathetic, resigned, despondent, numbed, stunned, stupefied, or inarticulate.

SUMMARY OF PRIORITY RULES FOR SCORING

By way of summary it may be helpful to collect and present here in a single place the various rules for deciding which category is to have priority in cases of conflict as to where an act should be scored. With only minor exceptions, a given act is to be placed in one and only one category.

1. *Give priority to a scoring in category 2, Dramatizes, or category 11, Shows Tension, over a scoring in any other category.* This rule is particularly relevant to acts that would otherwise be placed in category 6, Gives Information. Whenever the action of a person or imaginary being is reported, even though the group member reporting it may feel he is giving information, the interaction observer should place the act in category 2.

2. *Give priority to a scoring in category 1, Seems Friendly, or in category 12, Seems Unfriendly, if an element of interpersonal feeling*

is present. This rule is particularly relevant to acts that would otherwise be categorized as giving opinion and giving suggestion. Simple acts of agreement and disagreement are exempt from this rule.

3. *Give priority to a scoring in category 4, Gives Suggestion, or category 9, Asks for Suggestion, over a scoring in category 5, Gives Opinion.* Do not score an act in category 5, Gives Opinion, if you can reasonably score it in any other category; try to prevent category 5 from being a residual category.

4. *After an initial act of disagreement, or of agreement, the scoring reverts to the neutral categories based upon the interaction form of the act.* This rule is necessary to prevent category 10 or 3 from being a "sink."

The general effect of these rules is to divert the classification of acts that tend to be most frequent, in the form of giving opinion and information, into less frequently-used categories which depend upon more subtle cues and are of greater diagnostic interest.

7

Describing
Fantasy Themes

The purpose of this chapter is to present a method of content analysis of imagery and metaphor, of verbal or acted-out presentations as they appear in natural groups. Imagery has the quality of catching the attention and imagination of others, and of influencing their behavior by indirect suggestion. Indirect suggestion is often given by individuals without conscious intent, and the response is often not consciously controlled (132; 142).

The daydreams or reveries of the individual may preoccupy his attention, and at times carry his rational action away. In groups there is a corresponding phenomenon that might be called a "group fantasy." There are many varieties in society at large: public ceremonies; plays; artistic productions; rituals; as well as the more volatile forms one finds in the riot; the mob-scene; a lynching; a panic. There are also forms much more diffuse in their spread over a large population and development over time—the fashion, the fad, the craze. Social movements and revolutions are still larger in scale and more serious in import. We shall not be concerned with the large-scale forms, except to draw what we can from our general knowledge of them. Similar processes take place in interpersonal situations, and, when they occur, may be powerful determinants of behavior. We cannot satisfactorily understand what is going on in many interpersonal situations without being aware of the symbolic undercurrents of fantasy in individuals, their spread into verbal form among members of the group, and sometimes into physical enactment.

RELATION OF FANTASY TO OVERT BEHAVIOR

The last chapter described overt behavior in groups. In order to simplify the description we abstracted from the content: that which the individuals in a group talk *about*. We are now concerned with the *content* of what they talk about. It turns out, of course, that, among other things, they talk about behavior. Descriptions of behavior are choice kinds of symbols in which to portray fantasies. Fantasy is not overt behavior, but it is a mode of psychological action that has many similar properties. It can be a model for behavior, for example, or a mirror of it.

Fantasy is a mode of psychological action not subject to the same restraints as more consciously controlled forms of thought; certainly it is more free than overt behavior. It is often thought that fantasy precedes overt behavior and forecasts it, so that knowing the content of an individual's fantasy, one can predict how he is likely to behave when certain restraints are removed. Surely this conception is too simple. I suggest that we should not expect any definitive relation to hold generally over many cases. We should regard fantasy as a mode of psychological action that may have any one of a number of different relations to overt behavior. Sometimes fantasy precedes overt action and forecasts it. Sometimes fantasy perseveres after the action and preserves it as a model. Sometimes fantasy mirrors behavior as a direct model. Sometimes it inverts it or substitutes the opposite for the overt form. Sometimes fantasy creates new possibilities or enriches the mental life in ways that have no correspondence to overt behavior. Knowing only fantasy we cannot predict behavior. Knowing only behavior we cannot predict fantasy. Each is a creative realm in itself. We shall assume that neither can be predicted from the other but that we may be able to unravel the connection in a given instance. Fantasy is connected with overt behavior as the unconscious aspects of the mind are with the conscious aspects, that is, through many distorting and concealing defenses (81).

In self-analytic groups one listens carefully for the fantasies that are presented, and attempts to understand the relations between fantasy and behavior of the particular individual at the particular point in time. Individual fantasies do not always lead to group fantasies, but sometimes they do. One watches for such instances as an opportunity to learn more about the group structure, and the relations of persons in the group to each other.

GROUP FANTASIES ARE CHAIN REACTIONS

In group interaction, symbols (words, metaphors, images), which have the power to stimulate fantasies, are presented by persons to each other in their communication and action. Each or most of the persons communicating harbors individual fantasies that contain many similar or related elements. A group fantasy derives its compelling power from elements which have unconscious meanings for each or most of the active participants. The unconscious meanings may be different to some extent for different individuals; the desired fantasy outcomes may also be different. A chain reaction of fantasy in the group is set up when one or some of the participants presents in his communication symbols which have unconscious meanings for one or some of the other participants. Each tries to control the symbols presented by the other in the way he tries to control his own unconscious fantasies. The control often fails, and the chain reaction begins.

Once such a process is set in motion, others tend to get drawn in because of their own unconscious associations to the things being said and done. Once a common fantasy theme is aroused by a certain number of images and emotionally charged interactions, other individuals tend to "fill in" additional elements from their own associations. A confusion sets in between the images talked about and the persons talking about them. The chain reaction of associations is *enacted* by the persons. The chain of fantasy begins to develop a certain coercive power over the participants. People are forced into the roles portrayed by the fantasy, by projection, seduction, or manipulation. Emotions are further channeled and aroused. The fantasy then tends to be played out in a more and more complete way, unless interrupted by the incursion of sufficiently powerful new conditions.

Such occasions in groups seem to have a mysterious power to drag the interaction of the group into some extreme form, perhaps not consciously desired by any of the participants, nor understood by them (142). There is nothing "outside of persons," however, that compels the chain of fantasy. The chaining or joining by free association from one person to another is caused by the associations that people already have in their minds, aroused by some features of the present situation. The feeling of some kind of mysterious drag is due to the fact that the fantasies aroused are partly unconscious, because they are repressed. It is also partly due to the fact that the precipitating features of the present situation are also repressed, thus not recognized. The interpretations of leaders or members of self-analytic groups are centrally concerned with establishing these repressed connections. The problem is much the same as in the interpretation of dreams.

HOW TO RECOGNIZE A CHAIN OF FANTASY

A chain of fantasy involves more than one person. It usually involves more than two or three in groups of any size, but not always all the members participate. Interest in some image or topic of conversation seems to "catch on" and to bring new people rapidly into the conversation. Interaction usually speeds up, a pitch of excitement is heard in the voices; often there is some conflict or an edge of hostility. The volume of sound often goes up as the group begins the chain association. Many signs of interest are seen among those who do not participate verbally. Restless and agitated movements increase as people try to find a way to get into the conversation. New images and reported events may be rapidly injected, but apparently somehow on the same theme, psychologically. Throat-clearing, hand movements, and other attempts to catch attention increase. Whispered conversations may begin among pairs, smothered laughter or sometimes groans or hisses may be heard. Conversation builds up around a more or less similar set of images or concerns—usually a dramatic event of some kind or several similar ones—and continues with the same selected set of participators for some period—a minute or two, sometimes much longer.

Suddenly the chain is broken. Perhaps something embarrassing has been said. Perhaps somebody shows too much hostility, or reveals himself too far. A silence falls. Somebody says, "I'm bored," or "Who cares?" Or perhaps, without warning, another dramatic image will be injected, and the conversation then veers off at another angle, with a somewhat different topic, a somewhat different set of participators, and a different pace or emotional tone. If one can manage to recognize and isolate such episodes, he will find they often yield to understanding by much the same procedure as the analysis of dreams.

ANALYSIS OF FANTASY CHAINS

The theory of analysis and interpretation of dreams is highly developed in the psychoanalytic literature. There is no point in trying to repeat here, in only slightly adapted form, the principles of dream interpretation. They are applicable, with only minor modifications, to chains of group fantasy. For those who have had no previous introduction, there is no better way to start than by reading Freud's *Interpretation of Dreams*, (81), and then to emulate him in the analysis of one's own dreams and fantasies.

For self-analytic groups the interpretation of group fantasy chains is probably the single most important means of increasing insight, once the basic essentials are understood. It is difficult to make the method objective, but it is not difficult to begin to understand it and apply it. As a method, it is almost dangerously sharp. It can cut deeper than any other, hence it should be employed with care and respect (83). At the same time, the defensive mechanisms in group processes are usually quite strong and provide built-in protections against interpretations that cut too deep. One need not fear an honest and respectful approach. There is reason to avoid over-eager attempts to press too hard, to approach difficult matters too soon, to concentrate too much on particular members, or to put normal defenses under too much strain. Personal defenses must be respected—they are of great importance—the person can be helped to relax them and analyze them, but he should never be forced. One should rightly fear the employment of "wild" or forceful methods of weakening defenses such as over-activity, over-excitement, fatigue through prolonged interaction, drugs, fasting, or other similar methods, which group members and their leaders can always be depended upon to invent (83). Once the power of fantasy is realized there is a great temptation to put it to work in the invention of new methods for circumventing the defenses. There are dangers in this, and group members or leaders who employ dangerous pressures for excitement, adventure, or for emotional or monetary exploitation, are to be condemned (3).

There is no use obscuring the fact that there have always been sophisticated seducers who have understood how to manipulate fantasies through indirect suggestion, and who have employed their abilities in the exploitation of others. If one has reason to believe that he has somehow become involved in a wild group with such a person or persons, he should ask the opinion of a responsible psychologist as to whether dangerous pressures are being brought to bear and, if necessary, break contact with the group (3). It is dismal to sound such a warning about such a naturally healthy and available approach to insight in groups, but the use of group methods for all sorts of applied purposes has already reached the proportions of a social movement in this country, and it is bound to continue. The appearance of fads and cults with some dangers is probably unavoidable. After all, the employment of group interaction to heighten emotional tone, religious feeling, aggressive frenzy, sexual excitement, guilt, repentance, conversion, attitude change, even change in social identity and social commitment is as old as man. The arousal of group fantasy is the sovereign social medicine, and the proper dosage has often been exceeded. But perhaps increased understanding will have moderating effects.

In the usual case, a group fantasy chain is multiply motivated, as is a dream. There is a psychological *overlap* of three symbolic and emotional domains:

First, there is the domain of the manifest content: the situation and persons being talked about, usually "outside the group," the personages and events of a piece of news, of the distant public, a war or political struggle, a play, a piece of gossip, a joke, or a reported episode from some other time and place.

Second, there is the domain of the "here-and-now"—the interacting group with its present members, their relations to each other, the problems of the group, the hidden attitudes; the dislikes, fears, jealousies, envies, loves, despairs, confusions, and anxieties; the things going on between some of the members which are concealed from some of the other members, and so on. The chain of fantasy starts to build, usually, because the manifest topic of the conversation somehow mirrors or sets into resonant vibration the problems of the group here-and-now. The topic threatens to "run away," because it is in fact being used to express motives relevant to the here-and-now.

Third there is the domain of past experience of the members, particularly their common childhood experiences in relation to families in which their personalities were formed: relations to mother, father, and siblings. The here-and-now interacting group is always haunted by memories and anticipations of family life and its problems: the status of family members; authority; the exercise of coercive power; attitudes toward the physical body; sex differences; appetites, habits, and disciplines; love and hate; admiration and identification; the establishment of individual self-identity; giving up the things of infancy and childhood; of growing up and breaking family ties; of establishing independence; of marriage, children, loneliness, and death. The chain of fantasy in the here-and-now often resonates with common problems of infancy and childhood, as well as with related anticipations and fears of the future.

The concordance of these three domains of symbolism in group interaction results in a reinforcement of similar associations among members that leads toward involuntary completion, since the forces toward expression are strong and reinforced, whereas the defenses of the members are uncoordinated and hence weakened. Since individual members defend themselves psychologically in different ways and repress different aspects of the same themes, they circumvent and undo each other's defenses. The unconscious tendencies are not controlled as they are in a single well-integrated personality, but rather come tumbling out. The chain reaction builds up to unexpected strength, but then may break off suddenly. If the emerging content threatens enough people, they may suddenly agree implicitly on the need to suppress at any cost. So the chain breaks.

Each of the symbolic domains has unique features—but they are recognizable as similar at a certain level of abstraction. The major way in which they are similar is that they all involve images of the interaction of persons or symbolic beings vis-à-vis each other. They can all be described in *psychodramatic* terms. It is this similarity that brings about the overlap, the confusion, and the reinforcement that one sees in a chain of fantasy.

Fantasy contains many elements, only some of which are psychodramatic, but these are the most important elements one needs to understand in order to be able to translate the manifest content of a discussion into the here-and-now significance for the group, and to relate both of these domains to unconscious infantile and childhood associations. The psychodramatic elements of content are those which present an image of a person, or some kind of being that has personal qualities, behaving in a certain way toward a situation or some other personage.

In group interaction the kinds of acts which will be scored for their psychodramatic content will often fall in category 2, Dramatizes. Indeed it is the central element of the definition of this category that the observer senses that the act has a psychodramatic fantasy content and wishes to earmark it for later analysis with the present method. Relevant acts will also often occur in category 6, Gives Information, presented as factual reports of one's past experience, or of something one has read or heard. If factual reports present images of behavior or interaction of persons or personalized beings, then the relevant part of the content may be categorized in the present system. The system itself is relatively simple, once the other parts of this book are well understood. The process may be described in the form of an exercise.

EXERCISE

For this exercise it is necessary to have a written transcript of some period of verbal discussion or interaction in a group that is not concentrating exclusively on a narrowly defined task. A group that does some "joking around," or which spends some time in apparently aimless social conversation is desirable. On the other hand, cocktail conversation, as it really occurs in the superficial social contacts of an actual cocktail party, may be too stylized and transient to be of much interest. The members of the group should know each other well and should be able to maintain a single focus of conversation in their playful interaction as well as their work. Interaction within a self-analytic group is ideal for the purpose at hand, since all these conditions pertain, and the members know, even while they play, that they are producing material they may later analyze.

The transcript need not be long, providing it contains some portion that seems to have the characteristics of a "chain reaction of group fantasy" as described above. It is helpful to have been present, of course, and it is necessary to know a good deal about the relationships of the members and the problems of the group. It is probably best to make the written transcript from the sound tape oneself, as one needs to consider the sounds, the tones of voice, the volume level, the tempo of the interaction, as well as the verbal text. In making the transcript one should omit literally nothing. Include all hems and haws, sighs, incomplete words, false starts, slips of the tongue, and so on. Identify all speakers and all those who make inarticulate sounds, so far as possible. If observations of the interaction were made at the original occurrence of the interaction it is still better, since you will then have better indications of who is being addressed as well as who is speaking.

The first problem is to decide where your episode, or chain reaction, begins and where it ends. There is no absolute criterion for this decision. Do the best you can. An episode usually begins with a remark which presents some tangible psychodramatic imagery, after which the conversation "picks up" and elaborates on the image presented. The elaboration may continue for any number of acts until some point where "the chain breaks." Sometimes there is a remark which signals that a defensive reaction is setting in—indications of disinterest, of boredom, of desire to change the topic, of desire to get on with the task, sometimes with direct requests to one or more of the participants to stop talking, or to "forget it." Sometimes a new topic is simply introduced, and the old one is dropped without a single further reference. Often a new subset of participants takes over. Some combination of these signs may be used to give boundaries to the portion chosen as an episode. It may not be crucial just where the line is drawn, since if another episode follows, it is likely to be dynamically related to the one preceding—it may be another version of it, or perhaps a defensive reaction to it. You must be prepared to find repressed tendencies and the defenses to them in the same episode in any case, and this means you must be prepared to deal with apparent contradictions.

The next step is to score the interaction of the section of the meeting you have chosen, according to the method described in Chapter 6. The purpose of this scoring is to isolate portions of it for the present type of analysis. These portions are generally acts in category 6 or 2, or perhaps 11, which contain words representing *psychodramatic acts* of some kind. For example if person 1 in the group says, "You know a funny thing happened to me last night (2). I was walking along a dark street (2) when all of a sudden a very large guy stepped out of a doorway (2) and stopped directly in front of me (2)." Person 2 says "Wow! (11)" The remarks of person 1 are in the grammatical form of giving information, category 6, but the information given is a description of another person behaving in a certain way. The *described behavior* is what we are calling the *psychodramatic act*. A description of a psychodramatic act is scored in category 2, indicated above by (2).

The term *psychodramatic act,* or action, refers to the content of the *presented image.* Images of all kinds of behavior are included, not only overt behavior (as in the example), but also mental or psychological actions, such as thinking, feeling, wishing, imagining, or dreaming and imaginary portrayals meant to represent psychological states and actions, as they do in drama, literature, poetry, in painting or sculpture, in ritual, or the like. Nearly all the psychodramatic acts we shall be concerned with are presented in verbal descriptions, and it is possible to locate the words which contribute to the imagery. In the previous example, the words "night," "dark," and "all of a sudden" suggest a state of apprehension. The words "a very large guy" suggest a threatening person. The words "stepped out of a doorway" present the image of a psychodramatic act and, in the context prepared, the act seems a threatening or ominous one. This impression is reinforced by the image of the act described in the words "stopped directly in front of me." The response of person 2 "Wow!" in its interaction classification is an act of showing tension. It is perhaps debatable as to whether it also presents an image of a psychodramatic act—probably it is semidramatic, and hence could also be scored for its psychodramatic content. The example might thus be said to contain three or four psychodramatic acts: two of threatening acts (a very large guy stepped out of a doorway) and (stopped directly in front of me); and two of showing apprehension (walking along a dark street) and (wow!)

For purposes of this exercise it is not necessary to make a decision as to just how many acts are represented. The method of analysis we shall use records only the *presence* of images of a certain kind within the selected episode. A more quantitative method might be desirable for some purposes, but is not necessary here. The simplest possible conception is desirable for employment in the course of natural interaction, where one will usually want to apply his skills of analysis. In natural interaction, one must be able to perform the analysis mentally, without any kind of external aid, if he intends to use it as the background for interpretations he makes verbally in the group. The method I shall now describe is actually more explicit and detailed than the analysis one performs intuitively.

Table 7.1 at the end of this chapter presents a series of twenty-six questions, one pertaining to each of the group role types used in this book. The complete conception of the role type should be present in your mind as you try to answer the question. The descriptions of each of the twenty-six subtypes of interaction in Chapter 6 give a more complete idea of the kind of action as it appears in overt interaction, and the fuller context of each kind of interaction is given in the main descriptions of the role types. One should not try to perform the present exercise until he has become quite familiar with the full set of types, and understands them conceptually as well as descriptively. The conception of the full set of role types, and their relations to each other is the *associative space,* which the observer uses to amplify his own *free associations* to the images presented. His ability to understand and interpret the imagery of others depends directly on the number, relevance, and typicality of the associations he is able to make. He can interpret for others only insofar as his associations are more complete, typical, and accessible to him than the unconscious associations of others are to them.

With the typescript of the episode in front of him, and with the interaction analysis of it, the observer now goes through each of the twenty-six questions and tries to answer each one "yes" or "no." The procedure is the same as that used on the interpersonal rating form except that the answers "no" or "?" are simply ignored. Failing to answer a question "yes" may drop helpful information, but on the other hand, answering questions "yes" on the basis of too-slender evidence introduces unreliability. You must make your own compromise. If a given kind of image is presented once, that is enough for a "yes" answer. If it is presented several times, that makes one more sure of the imagery, but the answer is still simply "yes." The formal description of the single episode is the profile of "yes" versus blank answers that one obtains by answering each of the twenty-six questions. Episodes may be said to be similar to each other on the basis of the similarity of their profiles.

For quantitative study of trends, individual or group, rates for a given direction can be obtained by counting the number of episodes containing a reference to that direction per unit of time. But for interpretation at time of occurrence in the group, pay primary attention to the internal structure of the episode, which will contain references to several directions in dynamic relation to each other.

In interpretation, one pays attention to those questions answered "yes." The psychological structure of the episode can be represented by noting those positions in the space, or those role types, which have been made salient by the yes answers. Usually there will be several of these, and they will represent the interaction of two or more imaginary figures or role types, over some period of time. The representation made in one's head can be a three-dimensional model, in general nature just like that of the spatial representation of a group given in Chapter 3, except that the number of persons or role types represented will ordinarily be much smaller—perhaps two or three, or four.

By this procedure, the images of psychological action in the group fantasy are made into the *mental image of a group*—a set of several people in interaction with each other. This is a desirable mode of representation because, on the one hand, it is simple enough to hold in mind, and on the other, it is a suitable framework for selecting from a very large space of associations, representing actual typical relationships of persons in many kinds of small groups. Finally, it is a representation in terms of which one can compare: (1) the manifest content of the imagery used in the group fantasy chain; (2) the actual here-and-now structure of the group; and (3) the group structure (mother, father, child, and so forth), within which important early experiences of the child may have occurred. The psychoanalytic conception of the Oedipal situation—the relations of mother, child, and father—which is crucial to many psychoanalytic inferences, is easily represented in this imaginary spatial way. The spatial model has the advantage, moreover, of representing, more exactly than usual, the many different types of actual group roles that the mother, father, and child may assume, and their likely psychological reactions within those positions.

The actual procedure in searching for interpretation is to *superimpose mentally these three imaginary group models upon each other and look for similarities.* The assumption is made that corresponding positions in these three spaces may substitute for each other in fantasy. For example, the image of an authoritarian autocratic type of person, say General deGaulle (represented in position UNF) may be used, by substitution, or displacement of feeling, to stand for a person not enough talked about in the here-and-now group—an over-dominant group member or leader, who in turn may arouse, by transference of earlier feelings to the present, infantile memories in some members of their own autocratic fathers. Thus a group fantasy consisting of gossip about the latest news of a political figure, may represent the negative feelings aroused by one of the persons in the group who is behaving in a dominant, hostile, or moralistic way. The negative feelings toward him, in turn, may actually stem as much from the memories of a parent, or perhaps an older brother or teacher, as from the situation in the here-and-now group. One usually finds many other symbolic similarities between the domains in addition to the psychodramatic actions, but the latter are usually prominent and central.

The process of interpretation in the self-analytic group, for which both instructors and members are responsible, consists in calling attention to the actual evidences of similarity across the domains. The most effective interpretations are those which occur at just that point in time when the group fantasy has developed, and past evidence from one or both of the other two domains is obvious to most of the participants.

Timing, clarity, and actual weight of evidence are of the essence in successful interpretation within the group. It is of little use to suggest to group members that there *may be* similarities of some vague kind. If one actually has no evidence, or if the evidence is so slight that it is not recognizable to others, there is no point in attempting an interpretation. If the interpretation, in a few words, does not result in an immediate flash of insight, it is quite useless. The interpretation has in some way failed to grasp the truth. At the very least, it has failed to appreciate the nature and strength of the present defenses.

Effective interpretation must, above all, give insight into present defenses and help to resolve them (83). If the interpretation does not deal with present defenses, as well as with underlying motivation, if it is too deep, too wild, too speculative, or too abstract, it will not only fail, but it may strengthen present defenses and reduce the confidence of group members in psychological interpretations. In particular, the temptation to interpret speculatively in the group about the childhood or infancy of other persons, without evidence, should be resisted.

Your own private speculations about the past experiences of other members, their infancy, childhood, and relations to parents, may be of very great value in helping you to look for certain kinds of evidence, but a successful interpretation *to the other* must be based upon obvious present evidence and actual reported facts.

It should be recognized that in self-analytic groups, as contrasted to an individual therapy situation, one seldom has evidence about the infancy, childhood, or parents of the other members, although sometimes it is available. The most effective interpretations in groups will deal with similarities between group fantasy chains and the situation in the here-and-now group. Interpretations will draw upon things that group members have said and done in the past history of the group and will also include facts that members have given about themselves, but one will seldom be able to tie together all three domains in a single interpretation. It is ideal, however, if one is actually able to do so.

Avoidance of Over-Interpretation

One needs to recognize that there are limits to the successful interpretation of fantasy images as related to the here-and-now group, or even to the personality of the individual. Not everything has a double meaning or a triple meaning in any practically interpretable sense. To assume that *everything* in a group fantasy has a here-and-now relevance is to yield to a kind of superstitious attitude that does little for real insight, but rather leads to a cult that repels all but the true believers. A group fantasy chain should be regarded as an "amalgam," or a mixture of different elements, only *some* of which can be regarded as products of unconscious motivation, displacement, and other psychological processes of practical interest in understanding the group.

It is useful to recognize at least three different kinds of elements in the mixture that we see as a group fantasy chain. First, there are what might be called the original facts; then there are elaborations of the original facts; finally, there are accidents of combination. Basically, one can understand, in motivational terms, *only* the *selection* of particular original facts, and the *way in which they are elaborated*. The original facts must be accepted as such, and are not amenable to interpretation. The accidents of their combination in the original situation must be accepted as given. There are also accidents of combination during the process of elaboration, particularly in the combination of different images during the overt interaction in which the group fantasy chain is developed.

Fantasies are formed in the midst of environments naturally given. The subjective world of the individual is full of images which should be regarded, not as originated by his mind, but as produced in his mind by objects in his environment likely to be perceived in roughly similar ways by all normal human perceivers. It does little for understanding to overemphasize subjective aspects of perception, the effects of individual differences, language, cultural differences, and so on (26). It is more helpful to recognize substantial similarities and to assume that the objects and events of fantasy, group myth, religion, and various forms of art are not formed from nothing, nor yet entirely "out of the mind," but are traceable to *some* "original facts." Objects and events of the "real world" are selected, re-made, smoothed out, and bent to some semblance of consistency with the existing mental world of the particular individual or group. It is important to recognize that there are some original facts that one can not account for on psychological or motivational grounds. Otherwise one will simply confuse himself and others with a kind of pretentious occult nonsense.

In every actual group fantasy chain, there are certain particular facts of nature that are originally given, which are "worked in" somehow by the persons in the group and made the occasion of further elaboration. In the group observation room at Harvard, for example, there is a very large set of three mirrors, a large oval table with a substantial open space in the middle, and a red rug. Many fantasy chains of groups that meet in this room contain allusions to, or associations to, these somewhat unusual features. So far as the particular group is concerned, these features are like original facts of nature or of the culture. They are not explained by anything about that group. They were there "in the beginning." Their *selection* and *elaboration* in particular group fantasy chains at particular times may be understood in terms of members' motivations, but not their presence, of course.

The fragments of a dream that one can trace to experiences of the previous day are similar. Those experiences, from which fragments are taken, were "given" or made available by some accidental combination of circumstances beyond the control of the prospective dreamer. He in turn, selected certain fragments rather than others, fastened upon them, remembered them, and elaborated upon them in his unconscious. The dream is an amalgam or mixture of what was given, plus the selection and elaboration by the dreamer. In analysis of a dream, the selection and the elaboration may be recognized to be motivated, but a residue of the original given remains. This cannot be deduced from the motivational logic of that or other dreams (81).

There is a kind of logic about dreams which can be understood, however, even though the original facts must be taken as given. A knowledge of the kind of logic generally used by the unconscious mind helps greatly in the understanding of particular unique dreams of particular unique persons, as well as more common types of group fantasy chains. The logic of the unconscious helps to understand the selection and elaboration—the parts of the mixture that are directly accessible to understanding. It is true that the elaboration may contain unique and creative elements which could not have been anticipated, but such elements can to an important degree be "re-created" by empathic identification. The accomplishment of this is close to what we mean by understanding.

Finally, there is an element of chance: the accidents by which elements happen to come together in such a way at such a time. It does not dispose of chance as an independent element in one's theory to assume, as many scientists do, that nothing is *really* due to chance—that if we only knew enough we would see the reason for everything. The practical point is that we will never be in a position to know enough about the particular personalities, groups, and situations we deal with currently to dispense with the recognition of chance elements. To replace the last element of chance in one's theory by positive knowledge, one would require a theory and an information-gathering apparatus more complicated, very likely, than the object with which it deals. When personalities and groups are the objects one theorizes about, those objects are at least as complicated as the theorist himself. Complete determinism may not be an impossibility so far as nature is concerned, but it is an impossibly expensive theory for an observer to have about human behavior. In practice, the assumption of complete determinism *within the terms of one's theory* is simply one more type of superstitious cultism.

The chance properties of the mixture of elements in a group fantasy chain cannot be predicted or understood from a knowledge of the original facts, nor can they be deduced from the logic of motivation or any other system of meaningful elaboration. Practically speaking, they can only be recognized as elements due to accident within the terms of one's theory, accepted as given, and thereafter taken into account. Only the selection and elaboration of original facts and the selection and elaboration of accidental combinations can be untangled and understood in terms of psychological and group processes. It is of prime importance to accept this distinction in searching for acceptable interpretations. Otherwise one may tend piously to assume that *all* elements of fantasies presented in the group are psychologically created in relation to the group and, therefore, will give insight about the group. This leads away from insight rather than toward it. An interpretation should always be regarded as an hypothesis for further testing, in even the best supported case.

The presumption of the relevance of a group fantasy chain to the here-and-now group is based upon the following facts: (1) elements are *selected* for more extended discussion; (2) accidents are *taken advantage of* for the creation of symbolic meaning; (3) the selected elements and chance combinations are *elaborated*; (4) the elaboration is performed *cooperatively* as an interpersonal process; and (5) the group process has the qualities of a *"chain reaction"*—a process which reinforces itself increasingly in an accelerated growth curve of interest, excitement, and involvement. Unless these elements are present, one should not try to interpret presented images either in terms of relevance to the here-and-now group, or in terms of relevance to typical childhood memories of many group members.

The kind of reasoning one uses in the analysis of group fantasy chains is really very similar to that used in what is called "functional analysis" in sociology and social anthropology. A sound functional argument in sociology may generally be reduced to something like the following form: "If a *pattern* of behavior *survives* in a culture, in spite of ample opportunities for it to have dropped out (that is, to have been *extinguished* for lack of reward from others), then one may suspect that its positive consequences outweigh its negative consequences for *some* persons *other* than those who perform the particular acts. The performance of the behavior must have a *positive function* for persons *other than those who perform the pattern of acts,* and in fact *the pattern is in some way being maintained by reward from those other persons,* though perhaps it is not clear just who is doing the rewarding, and what the nature of the reward may be. The problem is to determine *who* is doing the rewarding, and *what* the reward is.

This is a very complicated set of conditions—indeed it may seem so complicated as to be of little use. Nevertheless, it is sometimes helpful. The purpose of such a formulation of the problem is to isolate those instances where functional analysis in terms of the larger culture is really applicable, and where research may reveal the hidden types and channels of reward. If the conditions described above are *not* met, and they seldom are, then functional analysis is not appropriate. One must concentrate then on the situation and the motivations of the persons who perform the acts.

The parallel formulation applicable to the present case might go something like this: "If a psychodramatic image presented by one person is picked up and elaborated by others, in spite of ample opportunity for other images to have been presented instead (and for the first image to have dropped out of attention), then one may suspect that there is some motivational incentive in the selection and elaboration that is not confined to the original presenter of the image, and that those persons who continue to elaborate the fantasy theme are somehow reinforcing each other; though perhaps the nature of the reinforcement may not be clear, and it may in some cases not be reinforcement in the sense of external reward of unconscious tendencies, at all, but rather the progressive stirring-up of unconscious fantasies allowed to continue because of the unintended contravention of member's uncoordinated ordinary defenses. The later kind of phenomenon is more like an accidental explosion (a chain reaction) than like the cultivated reinforcement of behavior by repeated rewards. The purpose of this formulation is to isolate those instances where it is relevant to suppose that images in the manifest content are being reinforced by some problems of the here-and-now group, or by residues of similar earlier experiences of group members.

It should be emphasized that there are many cases where individual members present images, which do not "catch on" with elaboration from other members. In these cases, the images may still be aroused in the individual by his reaction to the group situation, but interpretation must concentrate upon his own situation, perception, personality, and motivation. The fact that he has had a particular fantasy may or may not throw much light on the general problems of the here-and-now group.

FROM GROUP FANTASIES TO GROUP CULTURES

As the individual person creates and maintains a system of symbols with other persons in a group, he enters a realm of reality, which he knows does or can surpass him, survive him; which may inspire or organize him, and which may threaten to dominate him as well. He "comes alive" in the specifically human sense as a person in communication with others, in the symbolic reality which they create together, in the drama of their action. It is presumably this feeling that is referred to when people talk about "becoming a group," or "the time we became a group (132). A group in this sense is not the only kind of group dealt with by the sociologist—it is an interacting group in the midst of a group fantasy chain-reaction. It is a group in which the individuals have become emotionally involved and have begun to develop a culture of their own. The culture of the interacting group stimulates in each of its members a feeling that he has entered a new realm of reality—a world of heroes, villains, saints, and enemies—a drama, a work of art. The culture of a group is a fantasy established from the past, which is acted upon in the present. In such moments, which occur not only in groups, but also in individual responses to works of art, one is "transported" to a world which seems somehow even more real than the everyday world. One may feel exalted, fascinated, perhaps horrified or threatened, or powerfully impelled to action, but in any case, involved. One's feelings fuse with the symbols and images which carry the feeling in communication and sustain it over time. One is psychologically taken into a psychodramatic fantasy world, in which others in the group are also involved. Then one is attached also to those other members (132).

In the fantasy of a group culture, as in a work of art, things are closer to the heart's desire than in the everyday world. The fantasy world, though it has its origins in some original facts, is mentally formed; it tends to seem consistent, continuous, self-sufficient, and complete. It contains images of men and women, elders and children, gods and devils, animals, plants, and minerals. Images of time unfold, the seasons change, and the great adversaries of destiny loom and clash. The world of a group culture is big enough to hold a complete individual life, and yet it is completely existent within the perspective of the mind's eye. It can be traversed from the portal of heaven to the mouth of hell by mental means alone. Men fly in it more naturally than they walk. No wonder groups create and maintain fantasies, and individuals can hardly live without incorporation in one or more such groups.

Individuals in interaction create subjective worlds of culture. For most individuals, largely enclosed by ignorance, with relatively little command over the energies of the physical world, it is easier to make moonshine than to move mountains. But preference is quite as important as necessity. Human beings *prefer* a world they make themselves because it is filled with elements from their own minds and emotions. Their feelings adhere to every mental object in their subjective world. Feelings make the objects emotionally real, though some are hated, some are loved. The vast world of nature, the microscopic as well as the astronomic, mindless in disregard of man, is abhorrent to most individuals when actually confronted with it. The man of normal human sensibility, when suddenly confronted with some aspect of naked nature that breaks through his little world of meaning, immediately interposes a flood of integrating fantasy, a current of feeling that is normalizing, reassuring, often inspiring and memorable, and sometimes deeply religious in its significance. In this psychological defense of himself, the culture of a group is tremendously helpful to the individual, perhaps indispensable. The individual needs it and contributes to it.

In the face of society at large, as well as of nature, most individuals must surely feel limited, to some extent insecure and deprived. The larger society that surrounds the lone human being in both space and time shows more exalted instances in every direction of qualitative excellence than he can possibly equal. The culture of a society is a vast evolutionary residue, with the high-water marks of achievement in every direction of human endeavor preserved. Variability among persons and groups is rampant, even in conservative cultures. Natural growth and creativity builds the total culture out in thousands and millions of small cultural worlds, each developed in its given unique way. Individuals who happen to be at some critical place in some critical time, and who have some critical traits reach new high-water marks of achievement —or perhaps new lows. The particular individual may sacrifice everything to reach his achievement. But his mark is left, and all others who see it sense a deficiency in themselves.

With this kind of thing happening in all departments of the larger society, a vast world of excellences and exalted personages is created—a world in which each individual must feel small and to some extent insecure. Psychologically, he feels as if cast loose in a sea, the shores of which are impossibly far from each other, in the middle of which is a vortex. He must try desperately for some shore or other, and once having found some fringe of land, he is likely to hang on to it as if there were no other. Some people hang on to a geographic place, others to a job, or money; some make an adult life-work of a boyhood sport. Some feel that they must reach ultimate power, others that they must find God. And some, finding no shore, are drawn into the vortex.

Small face-to-face groups are among the means that individuals find to protect themselves from the vastness of nature, society, and the culture as a whole. Such groups are like rafts in a sea, holding together a few individuals in a similar plight. Most small groups, if they persist, develop a subculture that is protective for their members, and is allergic, in some respects, to the culture as a whole. The members are usually against something outside as well as for something inside. They draw a boundary around themselves and resist intrusion. Some things that are valued in the larger society are devalued in the small group; especially some conventional status characteristics are usually rejected.

A special point is made of these reversed values in the particular small group. Achievement becomes possible for the members in directions that are the reverse of those in the main society, or irrelevant to it: the group develops its own orthodoxy as well as its own mythology. However, a group will likely still depend upon some other groups for some of its rewards, and will likely be responsive to *some* overhead organization or to *some* authority, even though for some deviant groups the overhead organization may be that of an underworld. In time, however, for the same reasons that brought the small group into being in the first place, individuals and subgroups within it will require change; they will create other and newly-deviant subjective worlds and cultures. Thus either orthodoxy-versus-deviance or conservatism-versus-radicalism is a direction of polar-strain in all groups, large or small. Whenever an orthodoxy develops out of previous fantasies, more fantasy is at least an alternative to conformity, often it is used to defend deviance, sometimes it is also creative. Thus, although fantasy at any given time provides a relief from reality, in the longer run it turns into a new social reality and constrains where it formerly liberated. New fantasies are indispensable.

QUESTIONS FOR THE DESCRIPTION
OF PSYCHODRAMATIC IMAGERY

Though fantasy may be indispensible in groups, as I believe, perhaps no other aspect of group functioning is subject to so much skepticism as to its reality and importance. Partly this is due to resistance, understandable within the general theory of fantasy and its defensive nature. Partly it is due to the subtlety of the phenomenon, and especially the difficulty of any standardized approach to it. Partly it is due, I am afraid, to poor interpretation—the intrusion of the fantasies and egocentric needs of the interpreter into his attempts to interpret. There is no radical cure to any of these difficulties. But it is desirable to work toward more specification of methods by which one may train himself to do good work, if he aspires to interpret group fantasies, or to do research in this area.

Table 7.1 presents a series of questions one may ask himself about any given segment of group discussion content he may choose to consider a group fantasy chain. The questions are derived directly from the twenty-six personality and group role types described in detail in Part II of this book. A "yes" answer to a given question may be based upon intuition, but it is also true that it often depends upon the presence of specific words in the verbal text used to describe persons and acts in the fantasy. For research use, many such words can be specified in advance, if one wishes, and assembled into a dictionary, which, in turn, can be used for closer control of scoring. The definitions of the interaction categories (Chapter 6) contain many such words. It is only a few steps from the use of such a prepared dictionary to the utilization of machine methods for content analysis as described by Stone, Dunphy, Smith, and Ogilvie (148). The method they describe was first developed for content analysis of group discussion, and then has been used effectively for this purpose in a pioneering study by Dunphy (75; 76).

**Table 7.1   Questions for the Description of
Psychodramatic Imagery**

---

1. Does the episode contain any imagery in which the acting person seems dominant and powerful, but not clearly either friendly or unfriendly, and not clearly either task-oriented or expressively oriented against the task?   If *yes* = U

2. Does the episode contain any imagery in which the acting person seems socially and sexually extroverted, ascendant, and at the same time friendly, encouraging the other to interact and express himself and his opinion, but is not clearly either for the group task or against it?   If *yes* = UP

3. Does the episode contain any imagery in which the acting person seems ascendant and friendly, taking the initiative and leading in the task- or value-oriented direction, indicating concern for the solidarity and progress of the group as a whole?   If *yes* = UPF

4. Does the episode contain any imagery in which the acting person seems to take the initiative or leadership in giving suggestion to the other, or to the group, seems ascendant, value- and task-oriented, but at the same time is strictly impersonal, or affectively neutral, neither consistently friendly nor unfriendly?   If *yes* = UF

5. Does the episode contain any imagery in which the acting person seems dominating and unfriendly, taking the initiative in the value- or task-direction, assuming moral superiority over the other or the group, regarding himself as the authority, or the guardian of the moral and legal order?   If *yes* = UNF

6. Does the episode contain any imagery in which the acting person seems dominating, self-confident, aggressive, hostile, and unfriendly, ready to apply force to show his own power and superiority, unconcerned about morality or values, neither justifying himself in terms of values nor revolting against them, but taking pleasure in his own power over others?   If *yes* = UN

7. Does the episode contain any imagery in which the acting person seems dominating, self-confident, and hostile to other persons, as well as rebellious toward authority, self-centered, deviant, exhibitionistic, and exploitative?   If *yes* = UNB

8. Does the episode contain any imagery in which the acting person seems ascendant and expressive, nontask oriented, perhaps deviant or unconventional, neither clearly friendly nor unfriendly, but rather entertaining, joking, dramatic, relativistic, free in his associations, taking pleasure in play, activity, novelty, and creativity?   If *yes* = UB

9. Does the episode contain, any imagery in which the acting person seems ascendant and expressive, open, warm, friendly, affectionate, nurturant, permissive and rewarding to others, free to give unconditional love and praise?   If *yes* = UPB

10. Does the episode contain any imagery in which the acting person seems to approach others in a friendly, sociable, informal way, as equals, neither ascendant nor submissive, interested in them as persons, neither concerned with conventionality nor deviance, not concerned with either their task-relevance or their status?   If *yes* = P

11. Does the episode contain any imagery in which the acting person seems agreeable and friendly, task-and value-oriented, but not taking the initiative, neither ascendant nor submissive, but equalitarian, serious, and responsible about group agreements? If *yes* = PF

12. Does the episode contain any imagery in which the acting person seems primarily task- and value-oriented, neither ascendant nor submissive, but instrumental, analytical, problem-solving, concerned with the work of the group, as well as its serious beliefs, opinions, and assumptions; strictly impersonal or affectively neutral, neither friendly nor unfriendly, but tentative and searching?   If *yes* = F

13. Does the episode contain any imagery in which the acting person seems conscientious, principled, and persistent, value- and task-oriented, neither ascendant nor submissive, but trying always to be "objective" to the point of seeming unfriendly and inhibiting?   If *yes* = NF

14. Does the episode contain any imagery in which the acting person seems unfriendly and disagreeable, but neither ascendant nor submissive, neither value- and task-oriented nor against authority as such, but rather, self-concerned and isolated, detached, unsocial, defensively secluded, and negativistic?   If *yes* = N

15. Does the episode contain any imagery in which the acting person seems autonomous and resistant to authority, and also unfriendly to others in general, neither ascendant and actively rebellious nor submissive and passively withdrawing, but evasive, stubborn, obstinate, cynical, and radically nonconforming?   If *yes* = NB

16. Does the episode contain any imagery in which the acting person seems heretical and disbelieving, refusing to admit the validity of group beliefs and values, neither clearly unfriendly nor yet friendly,

Table 7.1 Continued

---

but ambivalent, neither ascendant and expressive, nor submissive and completely inhibited, but poised, lost in fantasy, and unable to decide anything?   If *yes* = B

17. Does the episode contain any imagery in which the acting person seems friendly and receptive to jokes and stories, neither ascendant nor submissive, but equalitarian, not task-oriented, but responsive to the other as a person, appreciative and likable, ready to share and enjoy sociability?   If *yes* = PB

18. Does the episode contain any imagery in which the acting person seems friendly and nonassertive, calm and ready to admire, neither task-oriented nor expression-oriented, but responsive to the other as a person, trusting and identifying with him, tending to emulate and imitate him?   If *yes* = DP

19. Does the episode contain any imagery in which the acting person seems friendly and submissive and, at the same time, task- and value-oriented, ready to follow and obey, ready to confess wrongs and conform, respectful, loving, gentle, idealistic, and altruistic?   If *yes,* = DPF

20. Does the episode contain any imagery in which the acting person seems submissive, dutiful, and conventional, wishing to follow a value- and task-oriented leader, neither friendly nor unfriendly, but strictly impersonal, affectively neutral, inhibited, cautious, persistently hard-working, fearful of disapproval and guilt, and introverted?   If *yes* = DF

21. Does the episode contain any imagery in which the acting person seems submissive, conventional, and dutiful to the point of self-sacrifice, but also self-pitying and resentful of self-sacrifice, expecting punishment and ready to martyr himself, but also wishing to blame the other and shame him, thus seeming unfriendly and passively accusing, making himself the object of aggression?   If *yes* = DNF

22. Does the episode contain any imagery in which the acting person seems self-conscious and unresponsive, unfriendly and resentful, passively rejecting overtures of friendship, wishing to be left alone, isolated and self-sufficient, indifferent to conventional value-and task-orientation of the group?   If *yes* = DN

23. Does the episode contain any imagery in which the acting person seems passively alienated and unfriendly, rejecting both the persons in the group and the conventional value- and task-orientation of

the group, discouraged and dejected, ready to resign and quit, wishing to withdraw from the group and all its concerns? If *yes* = DNB

24. Does the episode contain any imagery in which the acting person seems passively anxious, tense, and negative to the demands of authority, withholding cooperation, but neither clearly friendly nor unfriendly toward others, neutral or ambivalent in this respect, primarily oriented to repression of negative feelings about the requirements of convention, authority, or the value- and task-demands of the group? If *yes* = DB

25. Does the episode contain any imagery in which the acting person seems friendly and nonassertive, quite passive but perhaps in need of help, wishing to receive acceptance, intimacy, and pleasure in the other's company; not at all value- or task-oriented, but responsive to the help, nurturance, and stimulation of the other, and expectant of receiving what he needs without achievement? If *yes* = DPB

26. Does the episode contain any imagery in which the acting person seems self-effacing and completely nonself-assertive, passive, and powerless; accepts the other and the nature of things as they are without requesting anything, neither friendly nor unfriendly, neither dutiful nor resistant to value- and task-demands, but simply inactive and inert in his adaptation to all influences? If *yes* = D

8

Analyzing
Value-Statements

Sooner or later one begins to wonder why the three-dimensional space we have been using to predict the relationships of variables to each other should work—assuming that it does work to some useful degree. To what does it correspond in nature? Of course the three-dimensional physical space is only an analogy, providing a convenient language and set of mental pictures. But the variables referred to as having similar positions in the space are really related to each other in some kind of real interdependence. When one variable changes at some point in time, we can expect that the other has also changed, or will change, or will tend to change unless prevented. The space is one of empirical correlations of real phenomena with each other—at the very least the space is a chart of the way the variables *have been* connected with each other in the data studied, though we can never be sure just on what basis they will continue to be connected in some new situation.

Could it be that something like the spatial model has some substantial existence in the minds of individual group members? Could it be that the space describes something about the way individuals think as they interact with each other? Could it describe something they feel about the way persons affect each other in action and reaction? There are, of course, many reasons why variables might be related to each other quite independently of their interconnection in the minds of group members. But I think it is reasonable to suppose that some, perhaps many, of the variables we have been dealing with are interconnected with each other because of mental and social processes I shall here call "social evaluation."

SOCIAL EVALUATION

By social evaluation I mean those processes in the minds of individual persons, as they interact with each other, in which they look back to actions that have occurred, assess their consequences, and attempt to formulate or classify the actions more abstractly in such a way that rules for reacting to them in the future may be formulated. Social evaluation thus involves the application of abstract concepts, rules, attitudes, feelings, and values to ongoing behavior.

All human beings presumably evaluate, to some extent, their own and other persons' behavior and attempt to control or change it. No doubt it is true that some persons do not evaluate at a very high level of abstraction, or do not have a very large base of experience, or do not have much integration or internal consistency in the values or rules they apply. Some are probably not much guided by consciously abstract values. Others are guided by values that are deviant with regard to those of most of their associates. But all persons evaluate to some extent, both with and without conscious effort or forethought. Evaluative processes, I believe, are part of the economizing tendencies of mental life. The evaluative processes of the individual person; at any given stage in his life, potentially can be much more highly developed than they actually are: by experience, learning, imitation, deliberate thought, creative effort, and even scientific research. Values based upon these developmental processes may come to guide the behavior of some persons to a very high degree.

The more abstract processes of evaluation are "higher-order mental processes." They depend, of course, upon the more primitive mental processes that men share with animals. They also depend upon the human mental processes that young children share with adults, but they go beyond the experience and capability of the child in that they involve a more complete symbolization or representation to the self of all aspects of behavior and experience by more applied intelligence. They depend totally upon learned symbols and language. Through symbolization, man can represent to himself all aspects of his behavior, their causes and consequences. He can develop values, ideas of "the good," with regard to anything he can symbolize, and he can then apply the values to new cases. He can also develop more abstract symbolic representations of the lower-order values he is applying, and he can develop theories which regulate his mode of applying them.

In this chapter we shall be concerned with strong opinions expressed verbally in interaction that we shall call "value-statements." Value-statements, made in language, are symbolic representations of more abstract and general mental entities we call "values." The pyramiding of symbolic representations of values and value-statements to more abstract and highly integrated levels has no known upper limit, although for a given individual, changes in the nature and height of the pyramid probably take place relatively slowly and may reach a plateau, or in some cases may go downhill and disintegrate.

We may suppose that, at least *after* an action, if not before, or during the action, some conceptions of the determinants and consequences of the action are "associated" with each other in the mind of the individual. His memory will typically include the accompanying and resultant actions of other group members as he perceives and interprets them, and the effects of all these events on his self-picture will be especially salient to him. The memory processes of the normal human being, though selective and imperfect, are nevertheless astonishingly complete. All of the elements mentioned, coexisting in the memory of the individual, constitute a "set of associations," a dynamic psychological system of symbols and representations, a set of memories *potentially* connected with all other memories of the individual. The interconnection of any given memory with other memories is accomplished by mental work, much of it unconscious. The mental processes of "association" require time and are never complete. The mental processes of the individual presumably continue to work whether he is awake or asleep, sorting and reshaping the elements of a particular memory, resorting and reshaping other elements, also, in the "associational space," classifying things together, making distinctions, strengthening some associations and weakening others, working and changing the whole system or structure in many ways, both consciously and unconsciously.

The probability that an act (or really a new instance of a *type* of action) will occur again in the behavior of the individual depends upon the place that the memory of that type of action has at the given time in the associational space of his mind *after mental reworking*. Every concrete individual act tends to be classified or assimilated in the mind of the individual to a type of action, and every type of action is subject to continued evaluation and reevaluation. The evaluative processes include the association of the type of action, by mental work, with other memories, values, desires, and motives of the individual. It is by some such processes that values, those very abstract mental entities that result from the processes of evaluation, have their effect on future behavior along with many other determinants of behavior. In this view, the *consequences* of a type of behavior, as eventually seen by the individual, enter into the *determination* of whether or not new instances of that act will occur again. In this sense, consequences play a causative role in the continuation of the *type* of behavior. Of course, no concrete individual act is caused by its own concrete consequences, since those consequences occur later in time. But the *continued performance* of a type of action may be influenced by a *conception* of its consequences resulting from processes of reevaluation. This is the basis of normative or evaluative control of behavior as it occurs in social interaction.

The perspective of behavior then given by a value-formulation is, or can be, a perspective which can represent or symbolize all other perspectives. Just as a value-formulation gives the acting individual a more abstract and general platform to stand on as he tries to make decisions and guide his behavior, so also it may give the observer a more abstract, more general, and more all-inclusive standpoint for viewing behavior. The observer may describe an act, if he finds it useful to do so, by describing its *value-direction*. The value-direction of the act is given by its *presumed consequences* upon some more abstract value. *The value that an act most enhances is its primary value-direction.* Judgment of the consequences is made not only in anticipation of the act by the acting individual, but also retrospectively by the group members with whom the individual is interacting. His own reevaluation takes into account the way others have evaluated the act, so far as he has received information as to what their evaluations are. The processes of evaluation in normal group interaction are thus social as well as individual. It should be emphasized that all of these processes require time, effort, symbolic processing and reclassifying of information; all of these processes are costly. The processes are *uncertain* and *incomplete.* They are all imperfect. And they all depend upon *modes of classification* already established in the minds of the members. Classification and symbolization can introduce great economies in mental effort, but they are costly. Poor and confused classification systems in the minds of individuals can be decisive in limiting the effectiveness of all of the evaluative processes.

Certain of the social aspects of evaluation are quite accessible to observation, since the evaluations are conveyed in communications. Other group members attempt to persuade each individual to evaluate each object as they do. But they also try to persuade him on a more abstract level: they attempt to bring the more abstract values and modes of evaluation of the acting individual into line with their own. They try to obtain assent and consensus on verbal statements that they can then regard as something like "laws" on the statute books. These are sometimes stated explicitly in value-statements, aphorisms, sayings, dramatic or poetic lines. But most important of all, group members evaluate each other as persons, and then each evaluates himself. The individual's self-picture, his evaluation of himself, is the most vulnerable "object" of all with which he is concerned. It must be protected at all costs. If we regard most value-statements as indirect attempts to protect the individual's self-picture, I think we shall not go far wrong. This assumption is, I believe, the key to the understanding of value-statements as we hear them in natural interaction between persons.

EXERCISE

Before going further with abstract theorizing, it may be helpful to get down to concrete cases. How do we spot value-statements in the natural processes of interaction? And how do we use them to increase our understanding? If you have practiced classifying interaction, you will have learned how to recognize acts of giving opinion and giving suggestion. And you will have learned that when an opinion or suggestion has some negative or positive implication it will be classified as seeming unfriendly or as seeming friendly. If a value is stated in dramatic or picturesque form, it may be classified in category 2. What we are calling value-statements will usually fall into one of the following categories: 1, 2, 4, 5, or 12. Value-statements that can be analyzed are relatively rare, probably not more than 2 or 3 percent of all acts, but they are very important to spot when they do occur, and they do have a relative distinctness, which you will learn to recognize. They often sound like "quotations" from some moral tract. They are often rather strong in language; they often have a note of urgency and concern; they are often stated with some heat and conviction. The individual who makes a value-statement is usually trying in some way to "lay down the law."

It may be helpful at this point to read some examples. Table 8.1 at the end of this chapter gives a large collection of value-statements, representing many positions and directions in the abstract value space, which is our frame of reference. Many of these are paraphrases of statements actually heard in group discussions or arguments, but many are culled from literary and philosophical sources as well as from psychological test materials, as explained in Appendix 5. These statements will serve as our collection of specimens. The statements shown are selected from a much larger number (around 800), and they represent a choice selection in that they are the statements most likely to elicit agreement from one part of the test population, and disagreement from another part. They are maximally varied and maximally controversial, although they do not reach into all the nooks and crannies of the abstract value-space; I have had to invent or choose some in addition to complete the description of all the group role types.

Our purpose in this exercise is to learn to recognize value-statements, how to classify them and use them to further understanding. Actually all of these statements, plus additional ones, are distributed among the twenty-six personality and group role types included as Part II of this book, so that you will find extended discussions of the kinds of persons who make such statements and the positions in the group which they typify. But for the most part, these positions and types of persons may be inferred directly from the items by the following procedure. Once you learn to deal with the written items, you will be able, by degrees, to transfer your abilities to natural situations and to sense the value-direction of statements by intuitive understanding.

Imagine that you are a participant in a group, and that some person in the midst of the discussion makes a value-statement in the words (approximately) of one of the written items. For example, suppose somebody makes the statement in the midst of an argument: "Disobeying an order is one thing you cannot excuse—if one can get away with disobedience, why cannot everybody?" (This is item 30 in Table 8.1.)

Now put yourself in the position of a member of the group who is expected to agree or disagree, and ask yourself the following question: "What kind of position in the group is the person who makes this statement asking for himself?" In order to locate his value-position it may be helpful to approach the analysis of the statement one dimension at a time. This may be done by asking the following three questions:

1. Is it your impression that the person making the statement wants to be in a dominant position in the group?
   If *yes,* then = U
   If *don't know,* then = 0
   If *no,* then = D
2. Do you feel that the person making the statement likes most people in the group?
   If *yes,* then = P
   If *don't know,* then = 0
   If *no,* then = N
3. Do you feel that the person making the statement feels himself to be allied with conventional legitimate authority?
   If *yes,* then = F
   If *don't know,* then = 0
   If *no,* then = B

In case of the item taken as an example, you may very likely feel that the answer to the first question is "yes," since the speaker seems to assume that he himself is in a position to punish, or to excuse disobedience, hence is dominant. This answer will yield the directional indicator U. The second question, as to whether the person making the statement likes most people in the group is likely to be answered "no," since he sounds threatening and seems to be including everybody. This answer would yield a directional indicator N. Finally, the third question as to whether the person making the statement feels himself to be allied with conventional legitimate authority, seems readily answered "yes," since obedience is paid to authority, and the speaker seems to identify himself with authority and to insist on obedience.

The next step is to add the directional indicators, to obtain one summary directional indicator, in this case UNF. This is the indicated value-position. One then tests its appropriateness by looking at the description of the *value-direction of the type*. This is given in Part II as part of the title of the type. Type UNF is said to have a value-direction "toward autocratic authority." If this description seems to fit, the statement may be classified as this type. In the present case it does seem to fit. The item is thus classified UNF, and one may check to see that this item is included as a part of the description of type UNF in Part II.

The chart indicates after each item the way in which I have classified this item. The list of statements and their classifications may be used to continue the exercise. It is not too much to go over all the 143 items with this judging process. It may not always be clear to you why the item, a particular value-statement has been classified as shown. For example, it is not self-evident that item 130, the statement: "It is useless to quarrel with destiny" should be classified UNF. Why not *D*NF, on the assumption that the speaker is justifying or placing a positive value on submission, likely because he himself has submitted? There is no *logical* objection to this. The fact is that the speaker does not specify who is who in his generalization. Without further information one cannot tell whether he means "It is useless (for me) to quarrel with destiny." or, "It is useless (for you) to quarrel with destiny (me)." This kind of ambiguity is characteristic of value-statements. They are *general* statements, and just how they bind specific persons, *who* is supposed to act in the way described toward *whom* is often not clear. In context it is sometimes, but not always, more clear. If you find items that seem wrongly placed to you, try to imagine how another implication might be possible with another context. The items were actually classified where they are on an empirical basis (although a tenuous one, see Note, Appendix 1), and not primarily by the judging process outlined above. I believe that the judging process will give approximately the same results, however, and in any case, one wants a procedure he can apply in natural situations.

A value-statement may be thought of as composed of several elements: (1) It is a statement which is something like a *contract* in that it has a proposed binding power over future action. This may be only vaguely implied, but without some future implication the statement does not have the degree of generality required to bind the action of members. Sometimes the generality is not only evident but sweeping. There are statements which in their mode of declaration seem to apply to *all men,* in *all places,* at *all times,* and seem to be backed with a threat of force. These elements make the statement very general indeed. (2) A value-statement implies a proposed value-position or change in value position for the self (the speaker). (3) The proposed response of *the other,* the value-position he should have or take, is stated or implied. Thus the formal elements of a given statement might be represented something like this: "I propose that in the future I take position UNF and you take position DPF." A statement in the value profile which answers this formula is "Obedience and respect for authority are the most important virtues children should learn." A statement with quite a different formula is the following: "The solution to almost any human problem should be based on the situation at the time, not on some general moral rule." The paraphrase for this might be, "I propose that in the future I take a position UB and you take the same position."

For the items on the chart you may check your sense of the value-content of the item by looking at the directional classification following each item. The classification I have made is based upon a rather tenuous process of inference from rather slender findings. One of my collaborators, Gene Kassebaum (103) made observations in the main group study of who initiated value-statements of each sort, using a four-factor set of dimensions based upon the factor analysis described in Appendix 5. However, the study described in Appendix 5 was based upon a written questionnaire. I made the assumption that the *factor structure* (not the rotation) of the whole set of items would be similar, whether as applied to the initiators in overt interaction of such statements, or as applied to the responders on written forms of such written statements.

This assumption is certainly open to question. I assumed that what was required to make the findings of the questionnaire study appropriate for prediction of kinds of statements made by initiators was a rotation. Such a rotation, intuitively made, fitted Kassebaum's findings based upon overt verbal discussions reasonably well. Using Kassebaum's findings to give markers then, I mapped, by intuitive or artistic means, the structure of the value-items in the questionnaire study into the three dimensional space of the present conceptual scheme.

The grouping of the items in each of the twenty-six types was certainly done upon inadequate evidence. The naming of the types was completed artistically, both by induction from the content of the items in each position and by deduction from the content of items in surrounding areas of the space. The total structure has not yet been adequately tested by straightforward application, and of course, this needs to be done.

The critical step in arriving at the present model was thus a risky and artistic leap. But if I had not made it, I would not have been able to produce the synthesis of data and theory represented by this book. It was from the value items that I first fully grasped the nature of the space used for the model.

INTERDEPENDENCE OF ALL ASPECTS OF BEHAVIOR

All aspects of motivation and behavior in the actual processes of interaction in a group, I believe, tend over time to be brought by the members themselves into an interdependent system by the processes of social evaluation. This means that, over time, as the group continues, there will be a tendency toward the intercorrelation of certain variables, so that there are certain probable relations between, for example, the motivations of an individual, his behavior, the evaluation others make of him, his self-picture, and the self-picture he wants or needs from his past experience and his outside status. It is not possible to state all these relationships simply, however. The descriptive typology of the present system is an attempt to spell out and rationalize the many actual empirical relationships in detail. Various theories from psychology and sociology and perhaps some economics and political science as well are required for the rationalization of the actual findings. Some of the relationships could have been predicted, others have just been observed and rationalized after the fact.

But insofar as the processes of evaluation do bring about interdependence of various aspects of behavior, *those things are classed together which have like consequences.* Why is a certain perceived trait, like dominance, associated with a kind of behavior, such as talking a lot? Is it because "dominance" as an aspect of the talker's personality tends to cause talking? Perhaps in some sense, but I would say that it is just as important to note that both the personality trait (as perceived by the others) and the behavior are alike in that they affect others in the group in such a way as to make them feel that their power is reduced. To take another example, anger and sexual desire as motives are quite different from each other in their motivational origins, but they are similar in that they affect others in the group in such a way as to reduce their power, hence they are both evaluated as upward—one upward-negative, the other upward-positive. Acts of giving suggestion and acts of dramatizing may be different from each other in motive and mechanism, but they are similar kinds of acts in that they affect others in the group in such a way as to reduce their power. All of these traits, motivational states, types of activity, and perceptions are related to the upward direction. The reason they are associated with each other in the minds of members is that they have a common *consequence* for those persons in the group subjected to them. The traits and objects found in the upward part of the space are associated with each other, not necessarily because they have a common *cause*, like an underlying motive or a need of the actor, but *because they are evaluated in a similar way by other group members based on their consequences.* This evaluation, in turn, is adopted to some extent by the acting person, so that he also sees them as associated with each other. Evaluation of the consequences, I believe, is an important way in which aspects of behavior tend to become interdependent with other aspects. It is not the only way, of course. The other main way is through common causes.

In particular, the self-picture of the individual is relative to the picture others have of him. One seeks the realization of certain values as he seeks reward, primarily because the realization of one's values affects his self-picture. The reward comes (mostly) because, if one realizes the values, he is awarded a certain kind of group role or group position by others. This, in turn, appeals to his self-picture. The self-picture, in turn, has been developed historically for defense, security, gratification, and for many other reasons, none of which are simple. When the person gets the position he wants, so that he can maintain his desired self-picture, he tends to act so as to maintain that position. The rewards, so far as they exist, are mainly a product of maintaining that group position. It is typically, I suppose, a role or position that represents the best one was able to obtain, all things considered, in his family group or in later primary groups. What position one wants in a group reflects *how* or *how well* socialized he has been. If socialization has partially failed, if one has learned that in *his* family he is safest in, say, a negative-backward group role, he will tend to try to perpetuate this role for himself in new groups.

It remains to be seen how many of the relationships between variables are made understandable by assuming that the processes of social evaluation tend to bring the consequences of all actions together and to make them relevant to the acting individual by affecting his self picture. Certainly one would not expect *all* correlations between variables to arise in this manner. But if one wishes to make any of the processes studied a set of starting points for looking at the relations among all parts, the processes of social evaluation have many advantages.

For these reasons of perspective the spatial model in the present system is said to be a model of value-directions and locations. The substantive measures associated with each of the twenty-six types have been summarized and designated by a verbal description of their *value-direction.* The social-psychological nature of the type is most easily brought to mind by the name of its value-direction. The personality of an individual, as well as his interpersonal behavior in a given situation, may be said to have a *value-direction*. When an individual has been evaluated by others, he may be said to have been given a *value-position* in their evaluative spaces. More generally, any item of behavior, or any personal characteristic, when evaluated by some person may be said to have been given a value-position by that person in his own evaluative space.

Perhaps it should be emphasized that a judgment of value-direction, or the assignment of a value-position is always an act of evaluation by a *particular* person or persons—an observer, an acting individual who judges himself, another group member, all other group members, or some combination of these. To say, as one may, that a certain item, say a rating of "self-confidence" by observers, has a certain location in the value space, say UN, is not to state something eternally or unconditionally true. It is simply a summary statement about the evaluation of certain observers or persons in certain groups, and it remains to be seen how general a prediction based upon such particular observations may be.

CHANGES IN EVALUATION AS AN AIM OF NORMAL PROCESS

It is probably meaningful to think of an individual's "associative space"—that is, his memory, also as an "evaluative space." Mental conceptions of objects have a location in the space. It is possible to change the position of specific memories or conceptions of objects, such as the self-picture, in the associative and evaluative space. I assume it is appropriate to think of an individual going through a process of evaluation of some object, and as a result, changing the object's position, or *putting it somewhere* in his own evaluative space. He may put it forward or backward, positive or negative, upward or downward, or any combination of these in any degree. Similarly, insofar as there is a consensual or a conceived group space, we can think of the overt actions of group members as attempts to establish or maintain the position of conceived objects in the group space. This is the aim of a good deal of social interaction.

To put something forward in a group context means to offer it for explicit group acceptance, and hence to seek to place it under the protection of the authority in the group, or to invest it with authority. If the group rejects some outside authority, or even if it rejects the concept of authority, it will typically, nevertheless, have some accepted way of legitimizing actions and objects within the group. If the group has no procedure or persons in authority in this sense, it is without norms; that is, in a state of chaos or anomie. Such a state of affairs is comparatively rare and temporary. We find it in assortments of persons drawn together by chance for the first time, or in panics or in fatal group quarrels. But persons who interact together for any length of time tend to "get organized." This means, among other things, that they tend to set up an accepted process by which persons, objects, and actions may be put forward and invested with authority. They develop group norms and consensual values, to some extent.

To put something backward means to dissociate it from authority, so that it is not under the control of the legitimizing process. If something is put backward, the legitimizing process and its results cannot be blamed, or changed because of objectionable characteristics, qualities, or consequences of that thing. Things are sometimes put backward in order to protect the legitimizing process. Sometimes those things are in fact simply unrelated to authoritative things, sometimes they are actively opposed. But insofar as they are not dependable in support of the legitimizing process and the things already legitimized, they are regarded as potentially against it, and hence tend to be put backward in time of stress. From the point of view of a given individual, those things which the group puts backward may be very necessary or desirable, and hence are given a value of their own and are not abandoned; but from the sociological point of view of *that same person,* they may be considered dangerous to the legitimizing process, and hence not claimed to be legitimate. The value the individual places on them may be concealed from others, or even from his own conscious awareness.

To put something upward means to give it *power* or to recognize that it *has* that power for whatever reason, whether by authority, or desire, or hostility to authority, or love, freedom, or simply by the inability to prevent that thing from assuming dominance. Some things are powerful by nature, and hence are seen as upward from the first awareness of them. Others are put upward by complex psychological and social processes.

To put something downward means to reduce its power to dominate, to hold it in check, to harness it, or to make it submit or wait. Some things are weak as given by nature and are seen as downward; others are put downward by a process of binding and harnessing them by various kinds of psychological and social processes.

To make something negative is to associate it with other negative things, emotions, actions, persons, objects, perhaps particularly to attach anxiety or fear to it, or to endow it with hostility. Similarly to make something positive is to associate it with other positive things, especially positive feelings of love or gratification, or to endow it with these feelings in such a way that it promises to arouse the same positive feelings in the self.

According to this theory, each individual should be thought of as having and maintaining a psychological space with dimensions of this kind, containing conceptualized objects of all kinds, some with established and fixed positions, others persistently wayward or out of place, others as yet largely undefined. The self as visualized by the person is also a kind of "object"—a mental conception—and like other conceived objects has a place or movement within the space. Whatever can be conceived can become an object in the evaluative space of the individual. Thus values, and the processes of evaluation themselves, can also become objects within the evaluative space, since they can be, and are, mentally conceived.

Each individual constructs some picture, also, of the position of objects in the psychological space of other individuals. This picture is usually not very accurate, or complete, since it depends on what comes to the individual by way of information, and what he does with the information. The degree of detail is limited by the mental complication of maintaining separate and distinct pictures of the inner world of each of the other individuals with whom one is in contact. There is a powerful tendency toward simplification and a necessity to "make do" with limited information. The usual result of this is a kind of averaging simplification. In many groups, each member probably constructs a single picture of the "group world," which he then attributes to each of the other individuals, making only those exceptions he has been forced to make by information that the inner world of some members is somewhat different. The "group world" as seen by each individual is based primarily on events that have occurred in the group—events that have had the consequences of establishing certain actions, persons, and objects in salient places in the average group world.

Evaluation and Satisfaction

The question may arise as to the degree to which group members can find satisfaction in the same thing if they evaluate differently. The answer to this is not clear. It is clear that individuals differ from each other in values, and that realization of one's values is one, although only one, source of satisfaction. Insofar as it is an important source of satisfaction, however, one infers that no single direction of movement will bring satisfaction to everybody. There is probably some truth in this. But it overlooks two things, at least: (1) individuals typically have multiple values, and often conflicting ones, so that single individuals are not single-hearted in their desires; (2) even though the average movement of interaction in the group may be in a given direction, say forward, this does not mean that all individuals move forward, and some, indeed, (provided they remain a minority) can even move backward. Thus, they may paradoxically receive more (perverse) satisfaction out of a direction of majority group movement they disapprove of, than if the majority of the group were actually to move in the direction they themselves recommend. These are subtle questions. There is no clear criterion of "the greatest good" for even the single individual, to say nothing of "the greatest good for the greatest number."

Although it may not be possible to calculate the final impact of any given move on the satisfaction of all individuals, it is still possible to say something useful about the implication for satisfaction: of various types of interaction; of value-statements made and agreed, or disagreed with; the way the task is defined; success or lack of success in dealing with it; and so on. The basic assumptions, though neither complete nor adequate, are simple: (1) all behavior of all persons is evaluated by all persons in terms of their values; (2) behavior in conformity to, or conducive to values gives satisfaction, whereas that which is counter to values gives dissatisfaction. It follows from these assumptions that there must be dimensions of satisfaction that correspond in some way with the dimensions of the evaluative space. An unpublished analysis of satisfaction items, which Arthur Couch and I made, tends to confirm this and shows what kinds of behavior are related to which dimensions of satisfaction (29; 30; 70). Questions about satisfaction can be used to give another empirical approach to measurement of the general tendencies summarized in the evaluative space. I have included predictions about various dimensions of satisfaction in the descriptions of the group role types, along with the best items for measuring them.

The formation of a coalition of members in a group may be considered to give additional impetus to movement of the group in some weighted average direction of the coalition. The movement is presumably in some way proportionate to the number of persons in the coalition and to their relative power. If a coalition is formed, all persons included are joined in some sharing of the consequences of their movement. If there is more than one coalition, then the directions of the two coalitions are added algebraically, and may tend to cancel each other out. Value-realization of members in groups is obtained to some extent by coalition-formation, but it must also depend on the later distribution of rewards or movement to the members of the coalition.

Value-realization, of course, is not the only source of satisfaction, or perhaps it would be as true to say that values are not homogeneous. Some are very simple concrete formulations of satisfactions not very closely linked to any of the more abstract values, like the satisfactions of physical health, good food, and sleep. As a rule, people do not disagree very much about the desirability of these things for themselves. Presumably, there is some final process of pooling and weighing satisfactions that goes on in the individual, but presumably this process is only very partially carried on by symbolic abstractions or highly rationalistic means. The state of satisfaction of the individual, one might suppose, seldom corresponds exactly with the degree of realization of his major values. But we may also suppose there must be some correlation.

If the above assumptions are true, there is a lesson for theories in social psychology and sociology: although one must assume that total final satisfaction of the individual is a real variable, it is one that we shall probably never be able to calculate with much precision, since it has so many and such varied components. If this is the case, then one does not do well to found theories of behavior on statements about satisfaction, since he will never be able to measure his central variable. This is a problem with theories founded on the concept of "reward," "punishment," "self-interest," "pleasure," "gratification," "utility," "exchange of utilities," or the like. Such theories nearly always sound good—indeed one feels that they surely *must* be true, but on analysis, they are generally found to be true only by definition, and to be semantically and empirically almost empty. One should not allow himself to be deceived or consoled by such substitutes for empirically based theory. To be of any practical use a theory has to *start* with something you can observe, and it must enable you to predict something else you can observe. If it starts with an unmeasureable state of mind, of the behaving person, one which is a final summary of all influences acting upon him, it is very hard to extract practical predictions from the theory.

HOW SHOULD THE OBSERVER DEAL WITH HIS VALUE-BIASES?

The term *value-direction* is appropriate when one wishes to describe behavior of any kind, either of motivation or overt action, in terms of its significance for the realization of a given value. The term *value-position* is appropriate when one wishes to imply the occupancy of a given location in a range or spectrum, or space of values. The phrase *direction of interpersonal behavior* is appropriate as a broad summary description of the interaction of an individual within a group. Insofar as features of the personality, of motivation, of behavior, or the like are described in terms of their value-directions or their value-positions, the space is appropriately referred to as an *evaluative space*. For clarity, it is always necessary to specify "whose" evaluative space.

It is important to recognize that in order to judge the value-direction of an act, a value-statement, or the like, one need not himself hold the value in high regard. Observers of human behavior are often cautioned not to make value-judgments, which means, approximately, that they should not express their own prejudices. But it is possible to "judge the value-direction" of behavior for some other individual or group of them whether or not one approves of the value involved.

Indeed this kind of judging is a fundamental constitutent of understanding and the ability to predict. One cannot in fact avoid judging the value-direction of what one observes from the point of view of his own values, at least. If one's aim is understanding, he should attempt to attain a higher platform than simply his own set of preferred values, a platform from which he can see and understand a more complete range or space of values, so that the value-direction of given acts may be located in relation to the many other values of other persons who are also affected. One hopes by this vicarious process to foresee more and more consequences of given acts. A higher and more complete understanding of value-implications should be the ideal. The ideal is surely not the simple avoidance of value-judgments.

If one tries to avoid dealing with the value realm, as some behavioral scientists aspire to do, I believe one simply cuts oneself off from the most powerful means of understanding and prediction, namely the ability to estimate the social evaluation a mode of action is likely to receive (depending upon other group members and their relative power), and hence the probability of survival of the mode of action. It may be that one of the reasons this avenue to better understanding and prediction has been so persistently detoured is that there has been no adequate map or model of value-directions and positions. Contact with many other cultures has perhaps encouraged the hopeless idea that there is no order and no end to differences in values. Perhaps cultural relativism has been carried too far as Homans has also suggested (100; 101).

HOW GENERAL OR REPRESENTATIVE
IS THE VALUE-SPACE DESCRIBED IN THIS BOOK?

In some sense, value-relativism always accompanies wider knowledge of other persons and cultures, and also if one believes human beings are really creative, one then expects values to continue to change and develop. But variety and creativity do not exclude the possibility of some very general tendencies to uniformity, especially in the values which grow out of face-to-face interpersonal behavior. In many groups, notably in the family, certain important conditions prevail: the consequences of actions are immediate and very relevant to basic biological, psychological, and social needs of members. It is probably the value-implications of behavior that arise in these kinds of conditions, so well described years ago by Cooley (69) in his concept of "primary groups," which are expressed in the relations of values in the evaluative space as described in this book.

There may be a characteristic place and moment of expression for all the value-directions in the process of teaching the child, with its episodes of both successful and unsuccessful socializaton, as there are phases in group problem solving (40). The variety of value-positions represented in the space may correspond to a variety of outcomes in the processes of interaction between parents and children. This book assumes that the way values and group roles are associated with each other is indeed the outcome of the socialization of the child in group settings, and that similar conditions prevail in many primary groups. The theory may be found spelled out in detail by simply reading the sections on how the parents are seen, through the complete set of twenty-six types.

The value-space is probably the precipitate of developmental cycles in the socialization of the child, both complete and incomplete, successful and unsuccessful (37; 128). Each direction of value may be activated for parent or child, or both, at some point in a normal developmental cycle, or at least in the average of all cycles. The direction of value may fail to change as it does in normal development because of various kinds of blocks. With some imagination, one can understand most major neurotic and psychotic symptoms, as well as major types of deviant orientation of individuals and social movements as the result of failures of the group and its culture to pass through a normal series of developmental cycles.

In accounting for successes and failures in this respect, one must take into account the relation of the group and its products to the larger social environment, the rewards and resources it is able to secure from the environment, and the way in which these are distributed to the members, thus giving them or denying them the resources for further cycles of normal development. One must consider whether the outcome of a particular cycle is a renewed or enhanced capacity for normal development or an impairment of this capacity. Certain arrangements and features of personalities and groups may rightly be understood in terms of the value of their contributions to normal development. But others may be understood as the results of failures of normal development, and the disintegration of the group or personality or both into multiple, smaller, more self-contained systems. There is a normal cycle of value-activation and a normal cycle of *change in value-emphasis*. There are also deviant and regressive cycles, which may prevent change toward resumption of the normal developmental cycle.

The concept of a normal developmental cycle seems to be a critical one for the present theory. As everyone knows, hardly anything is harder to define than normal healthy growth. But I believe that one must try unless he is to avoid even worse pitfalls. I hope that the present conception of the evaluative space may be of some help in this endeavor.

Table 8.1 The Value Profile
Questionnaire

(List of value-statements used by Bales and Couch in their factor analysis of the value domain; see Appendix 5)

Item Number	Directional Significance Assigned[1]
1. It is the man who stands alone who excites our admiration.	N
2. Tenderness is more important than passion in love.	DPF
3. The ultimate and true reality is above the senses; immaterial, spiritual, unchanging, and everlasting.	NF
4. An insult to our honor should always be punished.	UNF
5. Contemplation is the highest form of human activity.	DF
6. In the ultimate test, truth only comes from inner experience—from inspiration, mystical union, revelation, or pure meditation.	NF
7. The individualist is the man who is most likely to discover the best road to a new future.	NB
8. In most groups it is better to choose somebody to take charge and run things, and then hold him responsible, even if he does some things the members do not like.	UNF
9. In general, full economic security is bad; most men would not work if they did not need the money for eating and living.	UNF
10. The most rewarding object of study any man can find is his own inner life.	DF
11. Divorce should be subject to fewer old-fashioned restrictions and become more a matter of mutual consent.	PB
12. Leaders of lynchings should be given the same cruel treatment they give their victims.	UNF
13. There should be equality for everyone—because we are all human beings.	P
14. Good group members should accept criticisms of their	

[1] The directional significance is assigned by the author, on the basis of rather uncertain inferences. It is the directional significance assigned to the person making such a statement in a group, and is *not* the same as the significance assigned to the person agreeing to such a statement on a written questionnaire, which was the case in the study on which the analysis was made. See Appendices 1 and 5.

Table 8.1 Continued

Item Number	Directional Significance Assigned[1]
points of view without argument, in order to preserve a harmonious group.	UF
15. Many events in human history took place only because a supreme being stepped in to make them happen.	F
16. Every normal man must be tempted, at times, to spit on his hands, hoist the black flag, and begin slitting throats.	UNB
17. What mankind needs most is dedication to moral values— values which are absolute, imperative, everlasting, and unchangeable.	DNF
18. The past is no more, the future may never be, the present is all that we can be sure of.	UNB
19. The immigration of foreigners to this country should be kept down so that we can provide for our own citizens first.	UNF
20. A group of equals will work a lot better than a group with a rigid hierarchy.	P
21. Each one should get what he needs—the things we have belong to all of us.	P
22. Love action, and care little that others may think you rash.	UNB
23. One should hold high ideals, purify himself, and restrain his desires for pleasure.	NF
24. Not to attain happiness, but to be worthy of it, is the purpose of our existence.	NF
25. Man's future depends primarily upon what he does, not upon what he feels or what he thinks.	UN
26. Familiarity breeds contempt.	UNF
27. He has achieved success who has lived well, laughed often, and loved much.	U
28. A well-raised child is one who does not have to be told twice to do something.	UNF
29. Man can solve all his important problems without the help from a supreme being.	B
30. Disobeying an order is one thing you cannot excuse—if one can get away with disobedience, why cannot everybody?	UNF
31. The facts on crime and sexual immorality show that we	

Item Number	Directional Significance Assigned[1]
will have to crack down harder on young people if we are going to save our moral standards.	UNF
32. When you make a threat you should be prepared to carry it out, and you should not make an exception because it applies to your friends.	UNF
33. There are no human problems that love cannot solve.	DPF
34. Racial discrimination should be made a criminal offense, which is punishable by a stiff jail sentence.	UF
35. All the evidence that has been impartially accumulated goes to show that the universe has evolved in accordance with natural principles, so there is no necessity to assume a first cause, cosmic purpose, or God behind it.	B
36. There has been too much talk and not enough real action in doing away with racial discrimination.	P
37. Heaven and hell are products of man's imagination and do not actually exist.	B
38. Man's future depends primarily upon the technical advances made by scientific knowledge.	UN
39. Let us eat, drink, and be merry, for tomorrow we die.	UNB
40. There is no worthy purpose but the resolution to do right.	DNF
41. A rich life requires constant activity, the use of muscles, and openness to adventure.	UN
42. No sane, normal, decent person could ever think of hurting a close friend or relative.	UNF
43. No weakness or difficulty can hold us back if we have enough will power.	UNF
44. One should aim to simplify one's external life and to moderate those desires whose satisfaction is dependent upon physical or social forces outside of oneself.	NF
45. A teen-ager should be allowed to decide most things for himself.	DPB
46. Character and honesty will tell in the long run; most people get pretty much what they deserve.	UNF
47. It is the duty of every good citizen to correct anti-minority remarks made in his presence.	P

Table 8.1 Continued

Item Number	Directional Significance Assigned[1]
48. The greatest fortunes are for those who leave the common path and blaze a new trail for themselves.	UNB
49. Morals must vary according to circumstances and situations—there are no sacred, unalterable, eternal rules which must always be obeyed.	B
50. A person who has bad manners, bad habits, and bad breeding can hardly expect to get along with decent people.	UNF
51. There is hardly anything lower than a person who does not feel great love, gratitude, and respect for his parents.	UNF
52. The most important function of modern leaders is to bring about the accomplishment of practical goals.	UN
53. In life an individual should for the most part "go it alone," assuring himself of privacy, having much time to himself, attempting to control his own life.	N
54. The solution to almost any human problem should be based on the situation at the time, not on some general moral rule.	UB
55. Human nature being what it is, there will always be war and conflict.	UNF
56. Friendship should go just so far in working relationships.	UNF
57. Labor unions in large corporations should be given a major part in deciding company policy.	DPB
58. What youth needs most is strict discipline, rugged determination, and the will to work and fight for family and country.	UNF
59. To starve is a small matter, to lose one's virtue is a great one.	DNF
60. There should be a definite hierarchy in an organization, with definite duties for everybody.	UNF
61. No time is better spent than that devoted to thinking about the ultimate purposes of life.	DF
62. In any organization if you lay down a rule it must be obeyed and enforced.	UNF
63. Society should be quicker to adopt new customs and to throw aside mere traditions and old-fashioned habits.	UB

Item Number	Directional Significance Assigned[1]
64. It is up to the government to make sure that everyone has a secure job and a good standard of living.	DPB
65. No scheme for living proposed by various religions and moralities is entirely suitable for every purpose, yet each scheme can offer something for everyone, one should use all of them, and no one alone.	UB
66. Depressions are like occasional headaches and stomach aches, it is natural for even the healthiest society to have them once in a while.	UNF
67. In any group, it is more important to keep a friendly atmosphere than to be efficient.	P
68. Life is something to be enjoyed to the full, sensuously enjoyed with relish and enthusiasm.	UNB
69. One's life should be directed completely by intelligence and rationality.	N
70. Most people do not realize how much our lives are controlled by plots hatched in secret places.	UNF
71. Patriotism and loyalty are the first and the most important requirements of a good citizen.	UNF
72. Whoever would be a man, must be a nonconformist.	UNB
73. There is nothing the body suffers that the soul may not profit by.	DNF
74. Art ought to show the world of nature in a natural realistic way, not in some distorted imaginary way.	UNF
75. A person should always be the master of his own fate.	UNB
76. What this country needs most, more than laws and political programs, is a few courageous, tireless, devoted leaders in whom the people can put their faith.	UNF
77. Life would hardly be worth living without the promise of immortality and life after death.	F
78. A man can learn better by striking out boldly on his own than he can by following the advice of others.	UNB
79. A man must make his own decisions, uninfluenced by the opinions of others.	UNF
80. In addition to faith we need help from God in order to resist temptation.	F

Table 8.1 Continued

Item Number	Directional Significance Assigned[1]
81. It is only right for a person to feel that his country or religion is better than any other.	UNF
82. Any red-blooded American will fight to defend his property.	UNF
83. An individual finds himself in merging with a social group, joining with others in resolute and determined activity for the realization of social goals.	UF
84. Obedience and respect for authority are the most important virtues children should learn.	UNF
85. The real appeal of love is in its sense of challenge, danger, and adventure.	UN
86. Groups with a real purpose should accomplish things and disregard hurt feelings and factions.	UN
87. The higher type of man makes a sense of duty the groundwork of his character.	UNF
88. Young people sometimes get rebellious ideas, but as they grow up they ought to get over them and settle down.	UNF
89. In choosing a husband, a woman will do well to put ambition at the top of her list of desirable qualities.	UNF
90. In a small group there should be no real leaders—everybody should have an equal say.	P
91. Every person has a set time to live and when his time comes to die, there is nothing he can do about it.	UNF
92. To lay down your life for a friend—this is the summit of a good life.	DNF
93. Not in cautious foresight nor in relaxed ease does life attain completion, but in outward energetic action, the excitement of power in the tangible present.	UN
94. The only true prosperity of the nation as a whole must be based on the prosperity of the working class.	P
95. Poverty could be almost entirely done away with if we made certain basic changes in our social and economic system.	P
96. You have to respect authority and when you stop respecting authority, your situation is not worth much.	UNF

Item Number	Directional Significance Assigned[1]
97. Man should control his bodily senses, his emotions, feelings, and wishes.	NF
98. When a person has a problem or worry, it is best for him not to think about it, but to keep busy with more cheerful things.	UNF
99. Only the desire to achieve great things will bring a man's mind into full activity.	UNF
100. The rich internal world of ideals, of sensitive feelings, of reverie, and of self-knowledge is man's true home.	DF
101. The most important function of education is its preparation for practical achievement and financial reward.	UN
102. There is a plan to life, which works to keep all living things moving together, and a man should learn to live his whole life in harmony with that plan.	UF
103. To be superior a man must stand alone.	UNB
104. We are all born to love—it is the principle of existence and its only true end.	PF
105. When we live in the proper way—stay in harmony with the forces of nature and keep all that we have in good condition, then all will go along well in the world.	UF
106. It is sympathetic love among persons which alone gives significance to life.	PF
107. Most of our social problems would be solved if we could somehow get rid of the immoral, crooked, and feebleminded people.	UNF
108. He that loses his conscience has nothing left that is worth keeping.	NF
109. Misfortune is to be conquered by bearing it.	NF
110. A good group has to limit the participation of critics who hamper action.	UNF
111. Excessive desires should be avoided and moderation in all things be sought.	DF
112. In art, music, and literature there is too much eccentric, exotic, Bohemian stuff being produced at the present time.	UNF

Table 8.1 Continued

Item Number	Directional Significance Assigned[1]
113. A child should not be allowed to talk back to his parents, or else he will lose respect for them.	UNF
114. Since there are no values which can be eternal, the only real values are those which meet the needs of the given moment.	UNB
115. A good group is democratic—the members should talk things over and decide unanimously what should be done.	UPF
116. Our modern industrial and scientific developments are signs of a greater degree of success than that attained by any previous society.	U
117. There is no better guide to success than the lives of the great men of history.	UNF
118. Nothing is static, nothing is everlasting; at any moment one must be ready to meet the change in environment by a necessary change in one's moral views.	UNB
119. If people would talk less and work more, everybody would be better off.	UNF
120. The worst danger to real Americanism during the past fifty years has come from foreign ideas and agitators.	UNF
121. The past is dead, there are new worlds to conquer, the world belongs to the future.	U
122. Life is more a festival than a workshop or a school for moral discipline.	UB
123. One must avoid dependence upon persons or things, the center of life should be found within oneself.	N
124. Science has its place, but there are more important things that can never possibly be understood by the human mind.	NF
125. There is no human desire so mean that it does not deserve expression and gratification.	UB
126. Everybody should have an equal chance and an equal say.	P
127. Every person should have complete faith in some supernatural power whose decisions he obeys without question.	F
128. The Bible contains many magical and superstitious beliefs.	B
129. A group cannot get their job done without voluntary cooperation from everybody.	UF
130. It is useless to quarrel with destiny.	UNF

Item Number	Directional Significance Assigned[1]
131. No man ever improved his impulses by refusing to express them.	UB
132. The most important qualities of a real man are determination and driving ambition.	UN
133. A person should let himself be molded by the great objective purposes in the universe which silently and irresistibly achieve their goal.	UNF
134. Inherited racial characteristics have more real importance in shaping the individual and nation than most people are ready to admit.	UNF
135. There is no satisfaction in any good without a companion.	UF
136. Christianity and all other religions are, at best, only partly true.	B
137. He, who knows that lusts have a short life and cause pain, is wise.	NF
138. The chief end of man is nothing other than eternal salvation.	F
139. The most important aim of the churches at the present time should be to encourage spiritual worship and a sense of communion with the highest.	F
140. Theology will ultimately prove more important for mankind than the sciences.	F
141. The greatest satisfaction in life is a feeling of the actuality of the present, of tireless activity, movement, and doing.	UN
142. No matter what the circumstances, one should never arbitrarily tell people what they have to do.	P
143. Every explanation of man and the world is incomplete unless it takes into account God's will.	F
144. Total F-score[2] (See the variable "Autocratic Authority," Appendix 1).	PF

[2] The total F-score is based on the sum of seventeen items selected from the original 30-item F-scale. This item is relevant only to the factor-analytic study, not to the present exercise.

PART II

Types
of Group Roles
and Their
Value-Directions

9

Type Ave: Toward a Balanced Average in All Directions

Unfortunately, not much can be said from the present research about the implications of receiving an evaluation of "average" from other group members. Such a group member has not been consistently far enough out in any one of the twenty-six directions to be classified in any of the definitive types. The average type is a residual type. The generalizations about the types made in this book rest upon the covariation of traits from the various domains of measures. If there are some definitive traits which are characteristic of the average type, it is not known what they are. If there are such traits, they do not consistently covary with any of those we have used to define the various types.

It would be possible to make a search for definitive traits by selecting all those group members who have received an evaluation of average, and giving them different psychological tests or making new observations. It seems likely, however, that this population of persons is heterogeneous, and one would conclude what can already be inferred, namely, that there are various ways in which a person may finally arrive in such a classification.

One way of arriving in an AVE position is by the possession of traits which are extreme, but in opposite directions. Since each type is a constellation of many traits in various domains, an individual might end up with an evaluation of average, let us say, because, although his interaction might indicate forward, with many opinions and suggestions, his values might indicate backward, with many radical and nonconventional features. On personality tests he might show many negative traits, evidence of neurotic problems, let us say, and yet on interpersonal evaluations from others he might be much admired, liked, and seem very equalitarian. The total interaction he initiated might fluctuate from some times of heavy participation to times during which he remained silent, and in spite of high interaction on given days he might seem to lack self-confidence. Such a person might be very salient in the group, and yet end up, by any of the various methods of assessment, in an average position.

For such a person the typological description AVE would be a very poor description indeed, since it drops all the interesting information. One would do much better in such a case to describe the conflicts and paradoxes in the evaluation than to end up with the noninformative designation, AVE. On the other hand, the types would still be highly useful in representing the conflicting tendencies. The concepts of the three-dimensional space, the directions, and the characteristic type patterns shown in Appendix 2 give a set of base lines for detecting and describing potential personality and role conflicts.

Another way in which a person may end up with an evaluation AVE is by unusual flexibility and mobility over time, with moderate excursions at various times in many directions, each appropriate to the situation and to the need. Such a type of personality, mode of conduct, and group role might even be construed as a desirable ideal by a certain set of values. Such an ideal might come close to the Greek ideal of the "golden mean." My own ideal as an instructor in a self-analytic group is something of this nature. If the instructor wishes to see that the implicit conflicts in the group are represented, he will find his interpretations often bring out the opposite side of a concerted group movement. On the other hand, the direction of the group, and its needs, change in time. The position taken in interpretation is thus likely to change. On the one hand, the instructor sometimes represents a missing role in the group, and on the other, he avoids occupying any role in such a way that a group member is prevented from taking it. The result of all this is a changeability and a surface inconsistency, which forces him toward the average. It is true that instructors of self-analytic groups tend to be evaluated somewhere in the vicinity of UPF, rather than AVE, but this is also partly due, perhaps, to wishful projection on the part of group members.

I believe it is impossible in the last analysis to capture in words or to fix in verbally-stated values what is really optimal for the good instructor by way of behavior and ideals over all the infinite variety of conditions faced by members of self-analytic groups. No more than any other group member do I, as an instructor, want to be immobilized by a fixed classification in the minds of others, and I search for ways of transcending the opposites and contrarities of everyday evaluation. The opposites of social evaluation represented by the three dimensions of the theoretical scheme all seem to be temporary and relative, not fixed by some immutable feature of nature. The felt necessity for giving an evaluation, a final single one, somewhere either toward one end or the other of a dimension, seems to be due, usually, to insufficient resources, insufficient time, insufficient strength, insufficient understanding, or the like. I would like to believe that these necessities can be alleviated or transcended, at least by some persons, and on some occasions (39; 54). Particularly I feel that some such counterbalancing, by the leader or leaders of self-analytic groups, is necessary to the progress of other members. The personality of the leader should supply the needed additional resources, strength, and understanding to allow other members of the group to loosen and change their evaluations, and to examine the insufficiencies which have forced them to some extreme or other.

Finally, in accounting for the ways in which one may reach the apparently inglorious position of AVE, one may need to recognize a more or less stable, nonflexible, and nonmobile type which really is near the middle on most variables. It is inevitable, by the process of comparison, that some persons will end up in an average position on any given variable. By chance, some of the persons will be in the average position on many of the variables and on all three of the dimensions. I have the impression, however, that as one adds more variables to the assessment procedure, he ends up with fewer and fewer persons classified as AVE, since small directional tendencies may be picked up by many of the variables and many of the raters. Thus even mildly variant personalities and group roles, providing they are more or less consistently so, will tend to be pushed toward one or another of the twenty-six types.

There is no necessary harm in this tendency of the assessment system to slight the average, since some definitive conception is better than none; but one should always remember not to take any assessment too seriously, nor to form too extreme a conception of the typological differences. The real persons classified in a given type may be extreme, but more often they are not. As persons, they are mixed, changeable and, to some degree, creative. They can to some extent change themselves and their group role, if they can form a conception of a higher ideal. It is, I think, the supreme function of leadership, and of education, to help in the crystalization of such higher ideals. If there are differences between persons, and continuities in the development of the individual person, the modes of leadership and of education must be multiform if they are to be successful. And if education is successful, personalities become ever more complex, inclusive, and unique. The descriptions of "types" of personality and their typical group roles in the following chapters should plainly be recognized as artificially accentuated and simplified caricatures of "directions" within more inclusive personalities.

10

Type U: Toward Material Success and Power

The member located in the upward part of the group space by his fellow members seems active, talkative, and powerful, but not clearly either friendly or unfriendly. He is neither clearly value- or task-oriented, nor is he expressively oriented against the task. In the realization of his own values he seems to be trying to move toward material success and power. "Our modern industrial and scientific developments are signs of a greater degree of success than that attained by any previous society." "There are no limits to what science may eventually discover." "Let no one say that money is of secondary value—it is the measuring stick of scientific, artistic, moral, and all other values in a society." [1]

How He Sees Himself and How Others See Him

The U type of person, or the person in that group role seems to identify his self-picture with a feeling of power in the possession of material things. He perceives himself correctly as talkative and self-confident, and guesses that others see him as self-confident. They do, but they see the UN type as even more self-confident. The U type overestimates himself and his powers, in that he is the member most likely to see himself as valuable for a logical task, whereas this evaluation is only partially confirmed by the judgments of other members and observers.

[1] This statement and the preceding one are probable value-statements of the U member. There is no footnote to the value-statements when they have been included in the original analysis described in Appendix 5.

193

Not only does the person in the U group role overestimate his task value, but he takes the lion's share of the group's time by his talking and makes no contribution to positive feeling in the group. Others feel resentful in relation to him, or at least they guess that he rates *them* high on resentfulness. He, on the contrary, tends to overrate others as to how warm and personal they are, which may indicate that he tends to ignore or blot out the negative reactions to him. It may be that he prefers the picture of himself he receives from the positive types of fellow group members (who try to compensate for their resentfulness by an effort to put on a pleasant front), while he tends to ignore the negative reactions he provokes.

His Place in the Interaction Network

The most salient feature of the overt behavior of the person in the U group role is his markedly high rate of total interaction initiated. He will probably rank high on the sum of interaction received also, but not so markedly high as if he were receiving in an amount proportionate to the amount he initiates to the group as a whole. Compared to the amount he receives, he tends to "overtalk" to the group as a whole. He is markedly low on the tendency to address specific individuals, since he concentrates on the group as a whole. He tends to ignore specific individuals and to receive more from each of them than he addresses to any *one* of them.

What Ideas and Values Will He Express?

The ideas and values the person assessed as a U type is likely to propose have the common feature of allowing him to express and satisfy his basic drives of aggression and sexuality. He thrives on competition. Material success is the value most squarely in the middle of the cluster he may advocate, but he may speak in favor of social success as a worthy goal, and he is also in favor of tough-minded assertiveness as a means to social and material success. Power is important as a goal in itself and also is desirable because it contributes to the satisfaction of many drives. The U type is in favor of social solidarity and progress for the group as a whole, but he sees no conflict between this and the pursuit of rugged individualism and individual gratification. He assumes that what is good for him is good for the group as a whole. Since his world is egocentric, he constructs the group in his own image. He may believe in loyalty to the group, but this means essentially loyalty *to him*. He also believes in cooperation, but this really means he assumes that others should cooperate with him. He believes in relativism of values and expression of drives, because he does not want to be bound by others.

As he tends to discount other persons, he also tends to discount the past: "The past is dead, there are new worlds to conquer, the world belongs to the future." His belief in science seems to be an identification of himself with the power and material success of technology, not with the intellectual structure of science. He may speak in favor of autocratic authority when he assumes that he and those he identifies with are in control, but he does not visualize himself as subjected to authority. Similarly, he may speak in favor of emotional supportiveness and warmth, but again this seems to be on the assumption that he is the person in the position to grant favors. The sexual drives, in his case, approximately balance the aggressive ones, and neither type of drive is much sublimated: "He has achieved success who has lived well, laughed often, and loved much."

The Quality of His Interaction

There is no one particular category of interaction on which the person in the upward group role is uniquely high, although his total quantity is high. He is uniquely low on the relative rate of giving information, however, probably because he does not have the restraint and caution characteristic of those who observe carefully and confine themselves closely to facts. His rates of agreement and seeming friendly and unfriendly are all about average. His movement forward and backward from realization of group norms is approximately balanced also. Although he may be high on giving suggestions, he is also likely to be high on dramatizing or joking. These categories of action are congruent with a tendency to let drives pass on into overt action. Since his emotions and needs for action typically find adequate outlet more directly, he does not often show tension or laugh, nor does he often ask others for suggestion. These activities are all associated with a restraint about imposing on others, which he does not have. He may be above average on asking for information, which has the effect of drawing others into the discussion who otherwise might remain silent. He may possibly be bothered by a felt lack of spontaneous response from others.

The quality of interaction that the U type of person provokes from others is on the negative side. Others are low in asking him for information and opinion, which is natural enough, in that he himself tends to keep on talking, whether or not he receives encouragement. Others are apt to be high on seeming unfriendly and showing disagreement toward him. But he receives about an average rate of agreement. Others have some tendency to show tension toward him and to laugh (as he provides opportunity through jokes), indicating perhaps that feelings toward him are tending to show through in spite of attempts to suppress. On the other hand, the rate at which others address suggestions to him indicates that he tends to provoke some efforts in the direction of task achievement and maintenance of group norms. It appears, however, that his own suggestions are often disagreed with, and other suggestions are presented to him instead. He is a force to contend with, since he holds a powerful position in the group. In general, the reaction of others to him is one of some resistance, with attempts on their part to remove the difficulty by suggestions different from his own.

Conflicts and Coalitions with Others

All eight of the other upward group role types tend to address their ideas and value-judgments to the upward type. The person in a U group role is central in the power structure, though not necessarily the most powerful, and his support is likely to be needed for the enactment of ideas put forth by other powerful members of the group. Since he himself is prone to make the same kinds of arguments as each of the surrounding types, he is not so very likely to get into arguments with them based on differences in values. There are two partial exceptions. He shows no special tendency to agree with arguments of group loyalty or autocratic authority, although he may initiate such statements.

The person in the U role is likely to be appealed to by those in middling power positions on both the positive and negative sides, but he is not likely to agree with both sides equally. When arguments in favor of equalitarianism and altruistic love are made to him from the positive side, he is likely to disagree with them. But when arguments are made from the negative and backward side in favor of individualistic isolationism, rejection of social conformity, and rejection of conservative group beliefs, he is likely to agree. From this it may be inferred that he is vulnerable to temptations or hidden appeals from the negative and backward side of his own personality, and holds his upward group role in spite of some tendency to regress to the negative and backward side. He may form a partially hidden coalition with a person representing the negative and backward side. In this case his increase in power may be considerable, though its source may not be apparent, since he himself is more in the public eye than the person forming the coalition with him.

Personality Traits

The persistently upward-moving person is likely to test high on written personality tests which measure adventurous, thick-skinned, and active and dominant traits (Thurstone's dominance). He may also test high on other traits which involve a major tendency to convert drives into overt action. For example, his adjacent type UP shows the traits of seemingly high social status, dominance (MMPI dominance), social participation, sociability and leadership. He may also have these traits to some extent.[2] The U type may, to some extent, share traits of the UPF type: sociable and persistent, as well as the UF trait sophisticated. Certain traits of the UN type are also possible, though they have a rather different feeling. These are the tendencies called neurotic, psychopathic, and manic. Normal persons may have these tendencies—they are not necessarily so extreme as they sound. In spite of the different feeling of the latter traits, they are not the opposites of the positive ones mentioned, but simply unpredictably related to them. The U type may combine them or not and may combine any of them without major strain because they all provide means for the conversion of sexual and aggressive drives. The prejudice of the related UNF type presumably allows for the conversion of aggressive drives into expression and overt action. Possibly related traits of the UNB type are the showing of nervous tension, seeming dominant, aggressive, eccentric, unconcerned, paranoid, impulsive and self centered. The UPB adjacent type is enthusiastic, talkative, and extroverted; and he shows poise, spontaneity, and confidence.

The traits of the types surrounding U are quite different in feeling as they range from positive to negative and forward to backward. It requires a deliberate effort of abstraction to understand how any or all of them may be combined (in a moderate measure) with the U type. The common element seems to be the tendency to convert drives into overt action. Conversely, the traits most apt to be missing are those related to downward movement, which all involve inhibition or control of some kind. It may be, as Eysenck believes (79) that there is a general temperamental factor operating, which is manifested as a resistance to learning by conditioning. It is also plausible to believe that there are inborn differences in the strength and demanding character of the instincts. If these hypotheses are all correct, the persistently upward-moving person is likely to be one who has unusually strong sexual and aggressive drives, perhaps by temperament, both about evenly matched, and is unusually impervious, also by temperament, to the learning of inhibition.

How He Sees His Parents

The person who persistently moves in an upward direction may, surprisingly, report that his father was high on inhibitory demands and discipline and, at the same time, high on emotional supportiveness and warmth. The father was presumably also a notably high interactor with

[2] It is worth noting at this point that tests called by the same name but by different authors may have significantly different implications. In this case, Thurstone's test *dominant* seems to measure more or less directly U, whereas Cattell's test of the same name measures UNB, and the MMPI test called *dominance* measures UP, see Appendix 1.

strong tendencies to move in the upward direction. How is it possible for a child to be so dominant when subjected to very dominant parents? In a single group meeting, with time constrictions, the persons who talk most tend to crowd other members out. But in the long process of socialization the same limitations of time do not hold. Socialization takes place over many years, with many periods of no interaction. There are normally many opportunities for a child to initiate interaction with the parents or to prolong it. In this long process, with little time constraint, the child tends to become *like* the parent in interaction. Children involved with highly interacting parents, according to the theory advanced in this book, tend to become high interactors. Children left much to themselves by nonverbal parents probably tend to become, or remain, low interactors like their parents. (Compare the description of Type D.)

Not only with regard to total interaction or the tendency to move upward or downward, but also with regard to the other directions, I shall assume that *the average tendency is for subjects to describe their parents in much the same way that they themselves are described by other group members.* The present set of data, upon which I base the general hypothesis, indicates that the old saying is true: "like father, like son," or more generally, "like parent, like child." Later I shall suggest a hypothetical dimension of parental roles which might be called "optimistic idealism" versus "cynical pessimism," a dimension extending from PF to NB. On this dimension I should expect the parent of the upward-moving child to be about average—not leaning to either extreme. If the parent were too far off center in either the PF or the NB directions, the child himself would be drawn off center and would turn out as one of the other upward types, either UPF or UNB.

The upward-moving person reports that his mother, like his father, tended to be high on inhibitory demands and discipline and, at the same time, high on emotional supportiveness and warmth. We infer that she would be average on optimistic idealism versus cynical pessimism. Like the father, the mother is presumably a high interactor and tends to move upward. For subjects on the positive side, there is a considerable tendency for father and mother to be described similarly. Subjects on the negative side tend to report the greatest discrepancies between the father and mother. In the present case, type U, the discrepancy is likely to be about average.

Effect on Group Satisfaction

The person moving in the Upward direction notably tends to move the group away from satisfaction with interpersonal relations. He is too egocentric, too inconsiderate; he tends to take up too much time and reinforces ideas and values on the negative and backward side.

His net effect on group satisfaction with goal attainment, however, is neither toward nor away, but average. Since his tendency is neither strongly forward nor strongly backward, and since he can cooperate in either direction, presumably whether the group as a whole moves forward or backward will depend upon the direction of action of other upward types in the group and the actual coalitions formed.

11

Type UP: Toward Social Success

The member located in the upward-positive part of the group space by his fellow members seems to be socially and sexually extroverted, ascendant but at the same time open and friendly. He encourages others to interact to express themselves and give their opinions, but he is neither clearly for the group task nor against it. In the realization of his own values he seems to be trying to move toward social success and popularity. "The most important thing in any group is to maintain a happy, friendly atmosphere, and let efficiency take care of itself." "Cooperation is far more enjoyable and more desirable than competition." "There are always plenty of people who are eager to extend a helping hand." [1]

How He Sees Himself and How Others See Him

The UP member, in spite of deserved popularity, seems to have an over-expanded image of himself and his social success and importance in the group. He appears to others as personally involved. Observers and group members rate him highly on personal involvement, and he correctly guesses that they do. His feeling of involvement seems to be expansive—he rates himself high on interest in the task, guesses that others will rate him high, and that they will see him as valuable for a logical task. His involvement expands in the backward direction as well as the forward: he is the member most likely to rate himself highly as warm and

---

[1] These are probable value-statements of the UP member.

personal. Expanding in the DP direction as well, he sees himself as understanding and, at the same time, he is the person most likely to rate others highly on understanding.

In all of these expansions of his self-picture except one, he tends to judge the ratings of other group members and observers incorrectly. Their ratings do not confirm his self-ratings. In one respect he seems to carry the group members, though not the observers with him—he is the person group members are most likely to rate highly as valuable for a logical task. If social success is the most central goal of the person moving in the UP direction, it appears that the effect of its achievement is to produce an expansion or extension of his self-picture and positive self-feeling to include many of the important features of the persons and events on the whole positive side of the social-psychological space.

His Place in the Interaction Network

The person moving in the UP direction is likely to be high in total interaction initiated. But he is likely to be relatively higher than expected on total interaction received; he may even receive more acts than the highest participator, since his response is generally of a more rewarding quality than that of the highest participator. His tendency to speak to the group as a whole rather than to particular persons is high, but not markedly so. Each individual in the group is apt to address him as an individual more often than he addresses them in that manner. His total proportion addressed to specific individuals is thus somewhat low, but not markedly so. In brief, he tends to take a position of *receptive leadership* vis-à-vis others in the group; individuals frequently respond to him and address their ideas to him, and he does not try to "talk them down."

What Ideas and Values Will He Express?

Social success appears to be the central value of the UP type. He may also speak in favor of other values with an upward component, except for those on the negative side. Thus he is likely to be in favor of material success as well as social success, and in favor of social solidarity and progress, group loyalty and cooperation, value relativism and expression, and emotional supportiveness and warmth. But he is not likely to speak for autocratic authority, tough-minded assertiveness, or rugged individualism and gratification. These values are too negative for him—he is pro-people. He may speak for equalitarianism, altruistic love, and permissive liberalism. He will not speak for their negative opposites, and particularly not for rejection of social success in the DN direction, since it is the direct opposite of his central value. He is highly identified with the group, his place in it is powerful and rewarding, which expands his self-picture—his outlook is benign.

The Quality of His Interaction

One category of interaction is highly characteristic of the person in the UP role—he is markedly high on asking for information (see page 119). He seems to be concerned about eliciting communication from others, probably partly as a way of bringing them into participation. He is also high on asking for opinion. Not only does he take the initiative in drawing others out, but he rewards them for responding. He is high on agreement as well as on seeming friendly (see page 100), and is low on disagreement and on seeming unfriendly. All these aspects of overt behavior seem consistent with the impression that the UP member is more concerned about positive social relationships than about either the realization of group norms or of specific task-accomplishment.

The UP member is relatively high on dramatizing and joking and low on showing tension and laughing. He apparently feels free to relax and is not rigidly held by task requirements. At the same time, however, he is also moderately high on giving suggestion, which indicates that he takes the lead at least part of the time in bringing the group back to its task-problems, even though he is only average on giving opinion; that is, performing the actual work of analysis, and is low on giving information.

Other group members in responding to the UP member are high on seeming friendly, and, in response to him, are also high on dramatizing and joking. He is probably often regarded as the leader of an equalitarian kind of subgroup within the total group, and he relates this subgroup or coalition to those in more authoritative positions. He may be what is sometimes called a "popular leader" (as distinct from a "task-leader"). The most interesting thing about him in this respect is that others are markedly likely to address suggestions to him. Others are also high on giving information and opinion to him, and he is high, it will be recalled, in asking for these activities. Thus, others seem to be led by the UP type to take responsibility for the task even though he is not fundamentally oriented to it. He is the receiver of high and unconflicted activity addressed to the realization of group norms and accomplishment of group tasks, even though his direction is not forward. Others seem to find him a source of stimulus and reward complementary to their task efforts. As we have seen above, group members on the average rate the member in the UP role more highly than any other type as valuable for a logical task. It may be that the less ascendant members on the positive side usually identify with him in such a way that they do not recognize the degree to which task work is coming from others, still further forward in the group, who simply address him for confirmation. As for the more ascendant leaders on the forward side, he may well seem valuable and even logical, since he pretty consistently agrees with them; he himself seems ascendant and powerful. In one category other members are low in addressing the UP type—they tend not to ask him for information. He himself specializes in drawing others into participation by asking for information, and apparently does not himself require to be drawn into the group in this way.

Conflicts and Coalitions with Others

The person most likely to address his ideas and values to the UP type is the UN type, who urges tough-minded assertiveness upon him. In addition, he is likely to receive recommendations and arguments for material success, group loyalty and cooperation, autocratic authority, rugged individualism and gratification, and value relativism and expression. Since he is on the positive side, we might expect him to disagree with ideas and values advanced from the negative side. This is not in fact what seems to happen. Actually he neither agrees nor disagrees with the advocates of tough-minded assertiveness or of rugged individualism and expression. It is not surprising that he agrees with the advocates of group loyalty and cooperation since the moral rectitude involved in that value position is impersonal—it is not yet really negative in tone. But one may be surprised, to learn that apparently the UP type will agree to the advocacy of autocratic authority. And he will also agree to statements urging value-determined restraint, which is associated with the NF type movement. The UP type, in other words, will not *initiate* statements in the UNF or the NF directions, *but he will agree to them when somebody else initiates them.*

This line of interpretation rests on little actual evidence; however, a number of known but poorly understood facts are relevant. Studies of my own with Slater have shown that the persons best liked in some small groups, particularly in early meetings, may have a relatively high "F" score—they may tend to have what has been called an "authoritarian personality" (38; 141). But these best liked persons do *not* dependably act as most people expect authoritarians to act. Other experimentors who have used the F-scale to pick authoritarian leaders have sometimes been frustrated and perplexed when the persons they select with the F-scale seem like "nice guys" rather than like the Prussian stereotype (95; 96, 97). The more usual stereotype of the "authoritarian personality" (1) among psychologists, I believe, is the UNF type. The UNF type meets these expectations so far as the tendency to *initiate* authoritarian statements is concerned. But in responding to written items on the F-scale, which measures authoritarianism (1), the UNF type is not so enthusiastic about agreeing, perhaps because he perceives the statements on a written questionnaire as made *to* him by somebody else. The person who measures high on the F-scale also tends to be high on the tendency to agree. The tendency to agree in overt interaction is associated with the PF type, whereas the tendency to agree with written text items, more or less regardless of content, is characteristic of the UP type. Perhaps this has some relation to the over-expanded concept of the self.

From these findings one may infer that *there are probably critically important discrepancies between the value-statements that a member will initiate in group discussion, and those that he will agree to on written tests and probably also in group discussion.* It can only prolong the confusion to speak of the "values of a person" without specifying whether one means the kind of value-statements he is likely to *initiate,* or the kind he is likely to *agree with.* There may also be critical systematic differences between the kind of value-statements a person will agree to on a written test, like the F-scale, and the kind he will agree to in group discussion. The studies on which this book is based do not provide information on the kinds of value-statements persons agree to in group discussion (Appendix 1). It is assumed for purposes of all the descriptions in this book that the kinds of value-statements people will agree to on written tests are also the kinds they will verbally agree to in group discussions, but this needs testing. It is possible, in fact, that the tendency to agree will be greater in group discussion than in written tests, since the motive of social acceptance is more salient.

The differences between the value statements a person will initiate and those to which he will agree are probably motivated by a need to protect his self-picture. Actions performed by the self presumably are associated with the self-picture most closely. Actions performed or suggested by other persons may be dissociated from the self-picture, and thus may be allowed, or agreed to, or even performed by the self, providing the other will *take the responsibility* for having taken the initiative. Milgram's experiments on "obedience" demonstrate this point with frightening clarity (116). The person may also encourage things to "happen" which he would not permit himself to do, and so obtain satisfaction for repressed or disowned parts of his own personality without having to abandon his idealized self-picture. This is presumably an important basis for "unconscious collusion" in groups; it develops between particular pairs of members within or between coalitions and sometimes explains both stubborn resistances to change and sudden unexpected social movements.

In the present case, the agreement of the UP type with statements advocating autocratic authority probably indicates that a negative side of the personality ordinarily exists, but tends to be repressed. The person seems to view himself as a good and benign father (or mother). Such a self-picture is typically modeled on an idealized parental figure, with whom the self is identified, and so the person becomes (subjectively) the idealized parent. One infers, then, that there is a need in the UP type to repress the negative side of the parent, as well as that of the self. If this is true it may be more understandable that other persons who advocate autocratic authority and value-determined restraint should tend to be "made over" or "transformed" psychologically by the UP type, into good and positive parental figures, with their negative aspects screened out and repressed. Value-determined restraint and autocratic authority perhaps seem useful, or even necessary, to keep other negative and more backward tendencies in check.

Personality Traits

The person with a marked tendency to move toward a UP group role is likely to test very high on the following traits: social status; dominance; social participation; sociability; and leadership. He is also likely to be very high on agreement response set, that is, the tendency to agree with all kinds of written statements on personality tests, more or less regardless of content.

He may also be high on traits characteristic of his most closely similar types. He may share the following U traits: adventurousness; thick-skinnedness; activeness; and dominance. He may share traits of the UPF type such as sociability and persistence, or the UF trait of sophistication. With his PF neighbor he may share the trait of conservatism, and show role-playing ability. He may be high on traits more characteristic of his less ascendant neighbor, P, such as positiveness, trustfulness, accessibility, along with intellectual efficiency and ego strength. He may be high on traits characteristic of the UPB type; he may be enthusiastic, talkative, extrovertive, and may show poise, spontaneity, and confidence.

Varied as these test traits may seem, they may all be combined in moderate measure in the UP type. In considering the meaning of any one of them, the presence of the others in moderate measure should also be assumed. The conception which may help one understand the present particular combination of traits is that they are all compatible with, or indicative of, a process of socialization that has produced a personality basically acceptant of, and identified with other people, and at the same time a personality that accepts a large measure of expression of basic drives, particularly the sexual drives in sublimated forms; a personality neither strongly rejecting of, nor strongly accepting of, the realization of social norms, or the achievement of group goals.

How He Sees His Parents

The father and mother are described similarly by the UP type, and the discrepancy between them is low. They are both described as high on emotional supportiveness and warmth and as average on inhibitory demands and discipline. Emotional supportiveness and warmth is presumably one of the most important traits in making identification with the parents easy. Emotional supportiveness and warmth brings the child regularly back to the positive side after the strains of meeting parental demands for discipline. The fact that the parents do not make demands that are too high presumably helps to prevent negative feelings that are too strong for the child to overcome.

A general assumption made throughout this book is that *very high demands on the part of the parent for inhibition and discipline on the part of the child are equivalent to movement of the parent toward the UNF role and tend to force the child, as an immediate reaction, in a negative and backward direction.* If there is to be successful socialization, the child must overcome and control these negative and backward reactions, *in addition to the original tendencies* about which the inhibitory demands are being made. The essential emotional resources of a parent, or any other socializing agent, are presumably the ability to give tension release through dramatizing, joking, or some other distancing of perspective; to evoke positive feelings by emotional supportiveness and warmth; to present a model of traits and behavior on the positive side which may be imitated, leading to identification and finally to the internalization of the new values. According to the theory advanced here, a hypothetical parental trait, optimistic idealism, corresponding to a PF direction, is a positive resource in socialization and is inferred to be high, on the average, for the parents of the child who develops in the UP direction.

According to this view, not only does the parent *evoke* in the child the emotional drives involved in the motivation of his socialization, but he also *provides a model* for the child and illustrates the techniques and psychological mechanisms by which the resemblance to himself may be attained. The UP parent, in the present case, presumably passes on to his child the ability to blot out or transform negative feelings and negative objects—the ability which enabled the parent himself to accept authority and value-determined restraint.

To examine the way in which the person, as a child, views his parents is to examine the way in which others are likely to view the person himself, when he is in a persuasive or socializing role. We might thus infer that the UP member will tend to provide, for other members of groups in which he participates, certain abilities in the overcoming or transmutation of negative feeling as the group works toward the development of its norms and realization of its values. He may provide, not only a counterbalance to the UNF, UN, and UNB types, but also a modus vivendi between them and other group members. The result of his efforts, and his reward, is his own social success.

His Effect on Group Satisfaction

It might be thought from the probability of his coalition with forward-moving types that the UP type would tend to move the group toward satisfaction with goal attainment. It is doubtful that this is the case in the final net effect. Although it is true that he is the type most likely to be rated highly by other group members as valuable for a logical task, it is also true that he is not rated most highly on interest in the task. In fact he elicits as much friendly, dramatizing and joking behavior as task behavior. It is also true that he fails to discourage some negative and backward types. His subgroup will likely contain a number of backward members, though most of them may be positive. Satisfaction with goal attainment appears to be associated with directly forward movement. The UP member's own direction is simply unrelated to, or balanced with regard to, forward and backward movement.

Again, it might be expected that the UP member would tend to move the group toward satisfaction with interpersonal relations, since there is a positive component to his behavior. But the direction of movement actually most highly associated with contribution to interpersonal satisfaction *of other members* is DP—a direction with a submissive component instead of the ascendant component UP has. The ascendant component appears to cancel the effect of the positive aspects of his behavior, but at the same time the effect is not negative. The direction associated with provoking dissatisfaction in others is UN. This seems intuitively plausible, since the most unpleasant and the most powerful aspects of domination are combined in that direction. The UP direction is not at all the same—it is simply unrelated to, or balanced, with regard to the UN direction. The UP type neither tends to move the group toward, nor away from satisfaction with interpersonal relations.

Curiously enough then, the UP member is the one type who tends to have the most balanced effect on the two major aspects of group satisfaction. The increments of satisfaction which one intuitively feels should be associated with the upward and positive movement toward social success are apparently felt in the satisfaction of the UP member himself, in his pleasure with his somewhat inflated self-picture, and are not associated with the satisfaction of other members. Presumably the UP member has no inkling of this.

12

Type UPF: Toward Social Solidarity and Progress

The member located in the upward-positive-forward part of the group space by his fellow members seems ascendant and friendly, but he also takes the initiative in leading the group as a whole in the task- or value-oriented direction. In the realization of his own values he seems to be trying to move toward social solidarity and progress at the same time. "A good group is democratic—the members should talk things over and decide unanimously what should be done."

How He Sees Himself and How Others See Him

The UPF member seems to identify himself with a good image of authority and to depend upon the power of over-idealized positive feelings to submerge, deny, or transform negative feelings and dislikes within the group. In a group where the task is given by an authority figure, the UPF member is most likely to show a high interest in the task. Observers and other group members see him as the highest type on this trait, and he also sees himself as high. (However, his UP neighbor, with his over-expansive self-picture, is apt to rate himself even more highly.) Similarly, observers rate the UPF member highest in the group on being valuable for a logical task, and he also sees himself as high. Other group members rate him highly, but they rate the UP member even more highly. It seems probable that observers may have a higher opinion of the UPF type than the other group members because the UPF type identifies himself with the giver of the task, as a good authority figure. The observers (in the present study) also tend to identify with the person who gives the task. By contrast, the UP type identifies himself a little more with the group members as the source of his rewards.

Of all the directional types, the UPF member is the most generally prone to say that he likes others, and to deny disliking them. This does not make what he feels true, of course, from the point of view of other group members. In fact, the member they are most apt to think likes them is the PB type—a type less ascendant, and one with a backward tendency rather than a forward identification with authority and the task. It may be that the interest of the UPF type in the task is partly determined by an attempt to deny or deal with negative feelings toward others and to stay on the positive side. When group members are asked to rate each other on "leadership," a UPF member is generally chosen.

His Place in the Interaction Network

The person assessed in the UPF position is likely to be high in total interaction initiated. His tendency to address the group as a whole rather than particular group members is high, but in return, his total rate of receiving is also high. Each member is likely to address him more frequently than he addresses that member, but the discrepancy is not marked. Each member is likely to be high in addressing him, and he is apt to be somewhat, but not markedly, low in addressing each of them specifically. He tends to be in a powerful, but not necessarily the most powerful position in the group, and he generally elicits acceptance, but not so markedly as his UP neighbor.

What Ideas and Values Will He Express?

The values for which the UPF member speaks combine an idealization of social solidarity of the group as a whole and movement toward group goals—making progress. The quotation at the head of the chapter seems to iron out one possible contradiction in this combination: "A good group is democratic—the members should talk things over and decide *unanimously* what should be done." Democracy to this type of member seems to imply either no dissent or a silencing of dissent at the time of decision. Apparently, it is unconsciously felt that negative and backward movement should be abandoned once a choice has been made, and progress begins. The UPF member will also initiate value-statements in favor of social success, material success and power, as well as group loyalty and cooperation, but he voices no negative or backward sentiments. He will speak for equalitarianism (as he understands it), for altruistic love, and for conservative group beliefs.

The items on which conservative group beliefs were measured in the basic studies for this book were (as it turned out, not by design) items asserting a fundamentalist religious belief in the existence of God, heaven, the afterlife, and a literal interpretation of the Bible. Conservative group beliefs as a variable within the present system should be understood as a much more general constellation of values than religious fundamentalism, however, and in some cases unrelated or opposed to it. One can probably find a cluster of values constituting a core of literal and fundamentalist orthodoxy in most established groups, even though that orthodoxy may be quite different from or even opposed to Christian fundamentalism. There is an orthodox communist position in any communist cell, for example, though it is opposed to Christian fundamentalism. The content of *what* it is that is religiously believed and taken in a literalistic orthodox way is likely to differ markedly from group to group, especially across religions, classes, or cultures. But whatever it is, if it exists in the common ideas and values of a particular group, it is the source of authority or legitimacy in that group. And it is this source of authority in the general sense with which the UPF person is identified, and toward which he moves in the forward direction.

The Quality of His Interaction

The person moving persistently in the UPF direction is likely to be high on several categories of interaction, but not uniquely or markedly high on any one or two. He is high on giving suggestions and giving opinions, which is consistent with his interest in the task. He is also high on asking for information and opinion and on seeming friendly, consistent with his generally positive attitude. He tends to be high on agreement and low on disagreement and on seeming unfriendly, which means that he tends to be rewarding to those who address their remarks to him. He is low on showing tension and laughing, since he is generally active and well motivated to work on group tasks. He is low on giving information as well—concentration on information requires a caution and a restraint which he does not have, and it also implies an *inductive* approach to task problems (facts first), whereas he employs a *deductive* approach (values first).

The UPF member, often the recognized leader of the group, is high on receiving suggestions and high, as well, on receiving opinions and information. He is also high on receiving requests for suggestion. Efforts to realize group values and to build new group norms center easily upon him, since he is usually in a powerful position, shows a strong interest in the task, and is encouraging to others who address task-oriented efforts toward him because of his high rate of agreement and low rate of disagreement. In return for his encouragement he receives a high rate of acts in which others seem friendly to him and a high rate of agreement for his own task efforts. The picture of his interaction with others is thus one of high cooperative concentration on tasks, accompanied by positive attitudes and actions on both sides. He is low on being asked for information and opinion. It is not necessary to bring him into the group by these cautious and solicitous means. He spontaneously provides a high rate of giving opinions and suggestions.

Conflicts and Coalitions with Others

It should not be assumed, from the generally positive and forward interaction of the UPF member, that he has some magical power of doing away with all opposition. He does receive opposition depending upon the personalities and positions of others in the group, particularly from any UNB members. An outlaw UNB leader, if one happens to be present in the group, is likely to advocate rugged individualism and gratification to the UPF leader. Advocates of tough-minded assertiveness, value relativism and expression, material success, and rejection of conservative group beliefs are also likely to address him. Of all these, he will probably agree with the arguments in favor of material success, but not with the others. On the other hand, he is not likely to disagree clearly with them. Like the UP leader he is tolerant on these negative and even backward values. And similarly, like the UP leader, he will probably actually agree with the advocates of autocratic authority and value determined restraint, though he will not initiate statements of these value-positions. It is possible for him to cooperate, especially in the task-oriented direction, with more negative types without serious reservation, and to tolerate even the most negative and backward types. This is consistent with his generally high ability to transform these directions and their advocates into something acceptable to him by idealization. Such an ability may be crucial in providing cooperative links between otherwise separated or conflicting networks, and this is most relevant to successful leadership of the group as a whole.

Personality Traits

The person who tends to move strongly in the UPF direction is likely to test very high on the traits of sociability and persistence. He may also show some of the U traits—activeness and dominance and the UF trait of sophistication. With his PF neighboring type he may have the trait of conservatism and show role-playing ability. He may share some of the traits of his neighboring type P—trustfulness and accessibility, and may show intellectual efficiency and ego strength. Finally, like his UP neighboring type, he may test relatively high on the traits of seemingly high social status, dominance, social participation, sociability, and leadership.

The traits characteristic of this type and the surrounding types seem consistent with each other when viewed in terms of the concept one may abstract by considering the total cluster. They suggest a personality resulting from a successful process of socialization, one which has ended in an identification with an idealized parent or parents, an acceptance of the appropriate sex role (whether male or female), an acceptance of the traditional social order and source of authority, while still maintaining an ability for active expression of impulses and drives, particularly the socialized forms of the sexual drive. Such a description may be made of either sex. There is an appropriate UPF feminine role as well as an appropriate UPF masculine role. This is true of all of the role types, though it is not always recognized in the descriptive language.

How He Sees His Parents

The discrepancy between the role of the mother and the role of the father toward the UPF member, as seen by him, or her, is moderately low—a condition which probably favors identification and internalization of their roles. Both parents are described as average on inhibitory demands and discipline, and average on emotional supportiveness and warmth. One infers that they would probably be described by the subject as moderately high on optimistic idealism, if we had such a test. The parents themselves are UPF types and, of all the types, seem most evidently to have the ability to produce an acceptance of traditional social norms and values by the idealization which they inspire and the values for which they stand. The UPF type is an inspirational leader, but on behalf of existing authority. This, apparently is what most people mean by "leadership," and many people look for it. The "great white father," and the "great good mother" are UPF stereotypes.

His Effects on Group Satisfaction

In other factor studies, the type of person judged high on leadership apparently tends to fall in the area corresponding to UPF in the present study, or on the margin between UPF and UF (58; 60; 72). The UPF member tends to move the group toward achievement of task-oriented goals. This is not surprising in view of his values, his position of relative power, and his ability to elicit and reward the efforts of other task-oriented types. Perhaps it is surprising, however, that he does not tend to move the group either toward or away from satisfaction with interpersonal relations. His attitudes toward other group members, though positive, tend to fuse them all together into a monolithic kind of group solidarity for the sake of progress, rather than for the sake of individuals, and he himself is ascendant and not overly sensitive to the actual feelings of others. His attitude is "paternalistic," with some of the bad, as well as some of the good implications that this term has to different types of members.

13

Type UF: Toward Group Loyalty and Cooperation

The member located in the upward-forward part of the group space by his fellow members takes the initiative or leadership in giving suggestions to the group. He seems ascendant, value- and task-oriented, but at the same time strictly impersonal, or affectively neutral, neither consistently friendly nor unfriendly. In the realization of his own values he seems to be trying to move toward group loyalty and cooperation. "An individual finds himself in merging with a social group, joining with others in resolute and determined activity for the realization of social goals." "A group cannot get their job done without voluntary cooperation from everybody."

How He Sees Himself and How Others See Him

The UF member seems to identify himself with a "larger plan," an impersonal plan, which is expected to elicit the loyalty of all members and reconcile any conflicts that they may have. The UF leader makes others feel that they should not be so individualistic—that is, he makes them feel he rates them high on this trait. His main concern is cooperation toward task achievement, and according to his conceptions, group unity is preserved through *loyalty,* rather than by more positive affectionate ties. His view of the world calls individual divergences to attention, and he tries to bring them into line. His method seems to be to point them out and then persuade by direct suggestion. The persuasion is not individually tailored to the motives of each divergent member. The method is rather simplistic, uniform, and impersonal—it is simply to

213

insist that cooperation is necessary, that there is and must be a larger plan, and that individualism of all varieties must be curbed in the interests of the larger plan and unity. Concentration on the outer requirements of the plan and the task is depended upon to compensate for any lack of inner harmony and congruence that may exist in his (UF) own or others' personalities.

His Place in the Interaction Network

The person in a UF group role is apt to be in a prominent place in the group. His total interaction initiated will probably be high, though not necessarily the highest in the group. His rate of initiating remarks to the group as a whole rather than to particular members is likely to be high, but his total rate of receiving interaction from others in turn will probably also be high. His rate of addressing specific other individuals is relatively low, and each individual is likely to be high in addressing him, whereas he is low on addressing that person in return. He thus pays relatively more attention to the group as a whole and tends to ignore specific individuals.

What Ideas and Values Will He Express?

As he addresses the group as a whole, the UF member takes the lead toward group loyalty and cooperation, which is his most central value, or the one he is most likely to voice. He tries to avoid seeming either positive or negative in feeling, as a father may try to avoid taking sides in quarrels among his children. The result is a kind of impersonality in his manner and in the formulation of his values. "There is a plan to life which works to keep all living things moving together, and a man should learn to live his whole life in harmony with that plan." "When we live in the proper way—stay in harmony with the forces of nature, and keep all that we have in good condition, then all will go along well in the world." The source of authority is impersonalized and projected above and outside the group. He believes in avoiding arguments and holding negative feelings, if any, in check. "Good group members should accept criticisms of their point of view without argument, in order to preserve a harmonious group." If anything provokes him it is the violation of fair and equal treatment among group members. "Racial discrimination should be made a criminal offence which is punishable by a stiff jail sentence." Sins against group loyalty and cooperation may provoke him to negative reactions. On the other hand, when he speaks in favor of anything more positive or warm in feeling than "loyalty," there is something cool in his conception. "There is no satisfaction in any good without a companion." Other value-statements which seem best to epitomize his position were quoted at the beginning of this chapter: From the second statement—"A group cannot get their job done without voluntary cooperation from everybody."—we see that "voluntary" really means "compulsory," and therein the iron hand is felt beneath the velvet glove.

Although he tries to maintain a strict balance between positive and negative feeling, the UF member will initiate value-statements on either side of neutrality in the service of his central value. He will speak for social solidarity and progress and social success on the positive side, and for autocratic authority and tough-minded assertiveness on the negative side, particularly when they are seen as instrumental to group loyalty and cooperation. Similarly, he may speak for material success and power. Of the less ascendant values, he is most likely to speak for conservative group beliefs, supported on the positive side by values of altruistic love, and on the other by value-determined restraint.

The Quality of His Interaction

The most characteristic category of interaction for the UF member is giving suggestion. This category contains not only substantive suggestions on the task, but also acts of taking the lead to bring the group to work on the task. Giving suggestions in this latter sense is the legitimate right and responsibility of an authorized group leader or manager. Whether he is actually authorized or not, this is the role that the UF member tends to assume. He may not present himself as the source of authority, but he feels he is at least the legitimate agent of authority. In addition to giving suggestions, he is high on giving opinions or on analyzing the task problems of the group. He tends to ask for information, however, rather than to give it. He is relatively low on giving information, perhaps because other less ascendant members, in attempting to avoid the role of "legitimate leader," concentrate on informational aspects of the problem. Giving information is often a preliminary phase in task-oriented work (40), but confining oneself to giving information generally avoids the connotation of ascendancy. Giving information can and often does help to build the groundwork for forward movement, but in itself it does not necessarily have a forward implication. Much giving of information is also part of every social conversation, and it may play a large part in dramatization and joking as well. The UF leader cooperates with those who build the groundwork of task information.

In his interaction, as well as in the content of his values, the UF leader is likely to be average both on seeming friendly and seeming unfriendly, consistent with his general attempt to hold a balance. He is markedly low on showing tension or laughing. He is in the vanguard of forward movement and shows ascendance in controlled form—both of these directions give satisfaction for his basic motivations. In a task-oriented group, at least, his motives are securely harnessed into action;

the conditions for showing tension and laughing are just the opposite: a lack of outlets for underlying motives.

In responding to the UF leader, other group members are markedly low on asking him for information and on asking him for his opinion. Cautious attempts like these to bring him into the group are unnecessary. He is already as "in" as he can be, by self-definition. Other members are moderately high in addressing opinion and suggestions to him, and they ask him for suggestion. For those who regard him as the legitimate agent of authority and the man in power, it seems appropriate to address value-statements and reasoned arguments to him for the stamp of approval, or in the absence of definite ideas, to ask him to take the lead in the task direction, or perhaps indirectly to ask him to endorse their own implied suggestions. To these task-oriented, or value-oriented efforts, the UF leader responds with a relatively high rate of agreement, on the average, and group members, on the average, respond to him with a relatively high rate of agreement. Thus far, the interchange seems a legalistic and cooperative one.

But in spite of "cooperation under the law of group loyalty" there are some signs of difficulty and resistance. Others are low in dramatizing or joking in relation to him. He is a serious figure. Unlike the leaders on the positive side, the UF leader tends to receive a relatively high rate of acts from others which indicate a reluctance to cooperate. Some others show tension or laugh, disagree, and seem unfriendly. One may suppose that the UF leader arouses ambivalence in some of the group members, and that the group begins to polarize, with some members cooperating, and some beginning to hang back and rebel. Or, it may be, as well, that in conditions where the group is already polarized, the UF leader arises in the attempt to bring cooperation out of the conflict by the moderating influence of a legalistic emphasis on group norms and common values. He asks for group loyalty and cooperation as a common value in the absence of a more complete consensus and group solidarity.

Conflicts and Coalitions with Others

As usual with the ascendant types, the vocal opposition tends to come, not from the diametrically opposite type, but from an opposed ascendant type. In the present case, the vocal opponent is most likely to be the UB type, who counters the argument for group loyalty and cooperation with an argument for, or a demonstration of, value relativism and expression. We may assume that the UB leader speaks implicitly on behalf of the less ascendant backward types, and the power of his jokes, demonstrations, and fantasies derives in part from their silent support, evidenced mainly by their laughs. But the UB leader does not typically lead the opposition alone. His two neighboring types may join him in opposing the movement toward values of group loyalty and cooperation. His UNB neighbor joins him with arguments or demonstrations in favor of rugged individualism and gratification, and his UPB neighbor sometimes joins him by arguments or demonstrations in favor of emotional supportiveness and warmth rather than task effort.

Furthermore, the N member may resist being drawn into enforced cooperation by insisting upon individualistic isolationism, whereas the NB member may voice outright rejection of social conformity. Either of these types can easily become scapegoats if the conflict develops too far. If the UF leader is unable to contain the conflict and obtain cooperation, he is likely either to turn in the UNF direction or to be replaced by a UNF leader who insists on autocratic authority. In this case, the selection of a scapegoat somewhere toward the backward side of the group is quite likely. The scapegoat may be chosen from the B direction—an advocate of the rejection of conservative group beliefs, or from the PB direction— an advocate of permissive liberalism, or he may be a DB member who advocates the withholding of cooperation. To students of large-scale social and political movements this will no doubt sound very familiar. The attack of the political right on the "atheistic communist," the draft resister, or the conscientious objector are such cases. The UN type frequently joins the coalition of the right.

Opposition to the UF leader arises from the positive side as well as the negative and backward. Especially in the problem of what to do about deviants, the leader in the UPB direction may urge emotional supportiveness and warmth as the proper treatment for deviants. The UPB type, together with the PB type, who urges permissive liberalism and the P type, who urges equalitarianism, form a possible coalition group in opposition to the UF leader. In large-scale political movements, coalitions around the UPB ideology are called parties of the left. It is especially interesting, in this context, to inquire whether the UF leader is completely impartial, as he seems to try to be. Indications are that the UF leader neither agrees nor disagrees with the arguments made to him for emotional supportiveness and warmth, but that he is likely to disagree with the arguments for equalitarianism. On the other hand, if urged, he is likely to agree with statements in favor of value determined restraint, and even with those in favor of individualistic isolationism. In spite of his attempt to be completely impartial, then, the UF leader is apt to lean toward the ideological right in his decisions.

Personality Traits

The UF type of person is likely to be high on the trait of sophistication. Like his U neighbor he tests moderately high on the adventurous, thick skinned, active, and dominant traits. On the UPF side he may show something of the traits of sociability and persistence. But the probable meaning of the UPF traits is somewhat undermined when we take into account that he is also moderately high on the UN traits of being neurotic, psychopathic, and manic. He may also show the UNF trait, prejudice. One must admit that such a personality does not seem very well put together, but it should be recalled that there are other hints that the UF type is internally conflicted, and that he specializes in the mediation of conflict in his social role. The trait of sophistication may be associated with smooth conventional control of a rather high level of aggression. The impression of conflict and its overcoming is further strengthened when it is noted that he may share some of the NF trait feminine masochism, but he may also be moderately high on the PF traits—role-playing ability and conservatism. Finally we may note the traits characteristic of the UP direction; social status; dominance; social participation; sociability; and leadership. When countered by the traits of the UN side noted above, the general impression is one of ascendance or relatively high tendency to move impulse into action.

How He Sees His Parents

Because of the mediating role of the UF leader, one might be led to wonder whether an attempt to mediate conflict between parents could have anything to do with the formation of the preferred social role. The indications are, however, that the discrepancy in role between father and mother is moderately low. Both are moderately high on inhibitory demands and discipline, and both are only average on emotional supportiveness and warmth. It would be consistent with our general assumptions to suppose that both were moderately high on optimistic idealism. The grounds for acceptance of traditional social norms and values can be seen in the parental traits, but there is something that begins to be missing—affection. Types described later will show this deficit in critical degree, and its results. In the present case the negative tendencies within the person are held in check, but the control of them begins to be precarious, and the personality is held together by a rather rigid and impersonal orientation. Affection from and for the parents seems not to have been strong enough to produce a decisive turn to the positive side after the strains imposed by the inhibitory demands and discipline the parents have imposed upon the child. The child is left, on reaching adulthood, with the same deficiency as his parents suffered. In groups that he attempts to lead, his ability to give and inspire affection are insufficient to prevent the polarization of the group into conflicting elements.

His Effect on Group Satisfaction

In the light of this discussion it will not seem puzzling that the UF leader tends to move the group away from satisfaction with interpersonal relations. He is not really in favor of equalitarianism and perhaps does not really have much appreciation of the importance of affection in human relations, nor of the importance of consideration for the feelings of others. Rather he seems inclined to a conception that people are something like billiard balls—they push each other around and need to be held together, but they do not generate much spontaneous attraction or solidarity. And indeed, that is the way other group members seem under his leadership. On the other hand, the UF leader does tend to move the group toward satisfaction with goal attainment, and that is his virtue. One wonders if it is impossible to produce both kinds of satisfaction at the same time, or if it is possible, what is the direction of movement that may do it? This question will be discussed further in relation to the PF, the DPF, and the DF types.

14

Type UNF:
Toward Autocratic Authority

The member located in the upward-negative-forward part of the group space by his fellow members seems dominating and unfriendly and takes the initiative in the value- or task-oriented direction. He assumes moral superiority over the others in the group and regards himself as the authority and the guardian of the moral and legal order. In the realization of his own values he seems to be trying to move toward autocratic authority. "In most groups it's better to choose somebody to take charge and run things and then hold him responsible, even if he does some things the members don't like." "Obedience and respect for authority are the most important virtues children should learn."

How He Sees Himself and How Others See Him

The UNF member seems to identify himself with the power of authority and to view himself, personally, as the legitimate source of authority. Of all types he is the most disliked by other group members. He is the active exponent of autocratic authority, inhibitory demands, and discipline. He is the type most likely to make others feel that he rates them low on understanding. His view of others is not generally flattering. He is concerned about the threats posed by what he regards as stupid, degenerate, and criminal types. He advocates a kind of human relations which indicates that he feels one must always be on his guard. He tends to view the world as a kind of jungle, with threats from outside the group that are urgently dangerous, and he fears that the outcome may be

220

catastrophic unless all the members of the group prepare themselves. In emergencies he tends to imagine that the most sweeping purge of inner weaknesses and the most draconic discipline are necessary and justified.

The UNF member is not especially likely to guess that others tend to dislike him. He offers himself as the leader in whom others can put their faith. As he sees it, he willingly undertakes the initiative and the responsibility for many unpleasant but absolutely necessary tasks of the group. He therefore tends to feel that all but the unfit, the feebleminded, and the traitorous should be grateful. He tends to project his own feared impulses into the external world and does not realize that some of the threats he feels come mostly from his own unconscious. He therefore emphasizes discipline and control of other people who, he feels, have deviant and aggressive tendencies. In actuality he distorts his perception of his own personality so as to put the bad and feared impulses into others and then often infuses his own aggression, fear, and even contempt for others into his actions toward them.

His Place in the Interaction Network

The person in the UNF role has a prominent place in the group. His total interaction initiated is high, though not necessarily the highest in the group. He tends, even so, to "overtalk." His tendency to talk to the group as a whole, rather than particular members, is high, but his total interaction received from others is only average. Either he tends to prevent replies, by overtalking, or others tend to withhold replies, or both. Each member addresses him only at an average level, he, in return, is low in addressing each of them. He addresses the group as a whole much more frequently than individual members.

What Ideas and Values Will He Express?

The ideological content likely to be expressed by the UNF member has been exhaustively explored in studies of the authoritarian personality (1; 95; 96; 97; 102; 111). It is important to note, however, that according to the results of the present study, the type of person who tends to agree most strongly with the characteristic value-statements on written tests is *not* the present one, UNF, but the F or PF types. The UNF member is rather the one who is most likely to *initiate* such statements. A characteristic statement: "A child should not be allowed to talk back to his parents, or else he will lose respect for them." The UNF member is most likely to *initiate* such statements, but the PF type is the one most likely to *agree*. It is an ironic and important fact, if indeed true, that the proponent of autocratic authority and the proponent of altruistic love tend to cooperate in this way. This strange cooperation suggests the persistence of memories of parent-child relationships within both members and a transference of unconscious feelings to present relationships. One imagines the UNF member as the parent, wishing to exercise autocratic authority, insisting that the child not talk back to him, fearing that the child may lose respect for him because of his unnecessary harshness; whereas the PF member as the good child, wishing not to lose respect for the parent, but to believe in the altruistic love of the parent for him, obediently represses whatever misgivings or negative reactions he may have and agrees with the parent. The would-be parent will initiate statements in favor of autocratic authority, though he is not eager to agree to them when they are presented to him, whereas the would-be good child *will agree to such statements when they are presented to him, although he will not initiate them.*

A large number of value-statements are available as specimens for the UNF type, not only from the studies of the authoritarian personality, but also from studies of social attitudes which have been made by many investigators following Thurstone. The questionnaires used by Eysenck and his associate, Melvin, have been most useful (78; 115). I was first able to coordinate the main factors in the social attitude domain with those of the present diagnostic space, using the factor analysis performed by Eysenck, who in turn has summarized the results of many other investigators.

Studies of the authoritarian personality have been particularly concerned with the relations of parents to children, and many of the test items associated with authoritarianism have a flavor which suggests parental admonitions: "Obedience and respect for authority are the most important virtues children should learn." "A well-raised child is one who doesn't have to be told twice to do something." "A person who has bad manners, habits, and breeding can hardly expect to get along with decent people." "Young people sometimes get rebellious ideas, but as they grow up they ought to get over them and settle down." "There is hardly anything lower than a person who does not feel a great love, gratitude, and respect for his parents." "The principle 'Spare the rod and spoil the child' has much truth in it, and should govern our methods of bringing up children."

The tendency to deal with disturbing feelings, fantasies, and negative reactions by forcing them out of consciousness as pointed out by Adorno and others (1) is reflected in the following sorts of statements: "No sane, normal, decent person could ever think of hurting a close friend or relative." "When a person has a problem or worry, it is best for him not to think about it, but keep busy with more cheerful things." "If people would talk less and work more, everybody would be better off." "In art, music, and literature there is too much eccentric, exotic, Bohemian stuff being produced at the present time." "Art ought to show the world of nature in a natural realistic way, not in some distorted imaginary way." "Depressions are like occasional headaches and stomach aches, it's natural for even the healthiest society to have them once in a while."

Another way of dealing with disturbing feelings, fantasies, and negative reactions is to "project" them or somehow fasten them onto outside objects, which are felt to be so different from the self or foreign to the self that they can safely be imagined to incarnate the repressed and disowned parts of the self. "Most people don't realize how much our lives are controlled by plots hatched in secret places." "The Japanese are by nature a cruel people." "The Jews have too much power and influence in this country." "Women are not the equals of men in intelligence, organizing ability, and so on." "Most of our social problems would be solved if we could somehow get rid of the immoral, crooked, and feebleminded people." "Inherited social characteristics have more real importance in shaping the individual and nation than most people are ready to admit." "Persons with serious hereditary defects and diseases should be compulsorily sterilized." "Colored people are innately inferior to white people." "Marriages between white and colored people should be strongly discouraged." "The facts on crime and sexual immorality show that we will have to crack down harder on young people if we are going to save our moral standards." "Crimes of violence should be punished by flogging." "Leaders of lynchings should be given the same cruel treatment they give their victims." "Character and honesty will tell in the long run; most people get pretty much what they deserve."

Heredity, nature, and foreigners are all likely to be feared and blamed for defects in hidden parts of the self, whereas the accepted parts of the self are identified with something large, strong, moral, and protective. Often this is law and order, strong leaders, the nation, religion, or God. The problem is to keep the good and get rid of the bad. "The worst danger to real Americanism during the past fifty years has come from foreign ideas and agitators." "The immigration of foreigners to this country should be kept down so that we can provide for our own citizens first." "Patriotism and loyalty are the first and the most important requirements of a good citizen." "It is only right for a person to feel that his country or religion is better than any other." "Any red-blooded American will fight to defend his property." "What youth needs most is strict discipline, rugged determination, and the will to work and fight for family and country." "Conscientious objectors are traitors to their country, and should be treated accordingly." "What this country needs most, more than laws and political programs, is a few courageous, tireless, devoted leaders in whom the people can put their faith."

There is often a note of hopelessness in the efforts of the UNF type to deal with his problems or those of the world. On the one hand he is strong in urging virtuous effort: "No weakness or difficulty can hold us back if we have enough will power." "The higher type of man makes a sense of duty the groundwork of his character." "In choosing a husband, a woman will do well to put ambition at the top of her list of desirable qualities." "Only the desire to achieve great things will bring a man's mind into full activity." "There is no better guide to success than the lives of the great men of history." But on the other hand the UNF type of person is pretty pessimistic about human nature, nonhuman nature, and the results of human effort: "In general, full economic security is bad; most men wouldn't work if they didn't need the money for eating and living." "Familiarity breeds contempt." "War is inherent in human nature." "Human nature being what it is, there will always be war and conflict." "There will be another war in twenty-five years." "It is useless to quarrel with destiny." "A person should let himself be molded by the great objective purposes of the universe which silently and irresistibly achieve their goal." "Every person has a set time to live, and when his time comes to die, there is nothing he can do about it."

With regard to the small group or organizational setting, as well as the family, the nation, and the great indefinite world of nature, the UNF type has a pessimistic and rather desperate philosophy. "In most groups it's better to choose somebody to take charge and run things and then hold him responsible, even if he does some things the members don't like." "A man must make his own decisions, uninfluenced by the opinions of others." "There should be a definite hierarchy in an organization, with definite duties for everybody." "In any organization if you lay down a rule it must be obeyed and enforced." "You have to respect authority and when you stop respecting authority, your situation isn't worth much." "An insult to our honor should always be punished." "Disobeying an order is one thing you can't excuse—if one can get away with disobedience, why can't everybody?" "When you make a threat you should be prepared to carry it out, and you should not make any exceptions because it applies to your friends." "Friendship should go just so far in working relationships." "A good group has to limit the participation of critics who hamper action."

In view of the ideas and values of the UNF type, as just described, it will probably not be surprising that he is also moderately likely to speak in favor of material success and power, group loyalty and cooperation, and tough-minded assertiveness. All of these values, like his most characteristic ones, involve a tendency to convert impulse into ascendant overt action. Other less ascendant values closely related, which he is moderately likely to recommend, are value-determined restraint, conservative group beliefs, and individualistic isolationism.

The Quality of His Interaction

There is no one category of interaction that is markedly characteristic of the UNF type. He is high on giving suggestion and giving opinion, consistent with his tendency to move forward, and he is high on disagreeing and seeming unfriendly. He tends not to ask others for opinion, not to seem friendly, and to be low on giving information. Others do not ask him for information, nor give it to him. He apparently has little interest in information and little patience for it, preferring to get more immediately into problems of values and action. This tendency is reminiscent of the anti-scientific and anti-intellectual aspects of authoritarianism.

His pattern of interaction, and probably the content of his values and suggestions, tend to divide the group and often to polarize it. There is some evidence he may often have a supporting subgroup in that others (probably from the positive and forward side) are moderately likely to agree and ask him for suggestion. But there is also evidence of strong resistance (probably from individuals or coalitions on the backward and negative sides). Others on the average are markedly likely to disagree with him and seem unfriendly. They are low on seeming friendly and on dramatizing and joking. His effects on the group, it appears, provide better diagnostic signs for recognizing him than the pattern of interaction he initiates. No other member is so likely to receive disagreement and unfriendly acts.

Conflicts and Coalitions with Others

The UNF member is typically the center of a value conflict within the group. He is typically opposed by the UPB leader, who urges emotional supportiveness and warmth, like the parent who intercedes on the child's behalf when the other parent insists on applying inhibitory demands and discipline. Also markedly likely to oppose the authoritarian autocrat is the defender of equalitarianism, with whom the autocrat is most likely to disagree, and the defender from the PB direction who urges permissive liberalism. In addition, there is some probability that a coalition of these types, which can be called, in political terms, a party of the left, will be joined in protest by the UB leader, who believes in value-relativism and expression, and the UP leader, who believes in social success, both of whom dislike the strongly moralistic tone of the UNF leader and his emphasis on value-determined restraint.

It is also probable that the upward type, U, who values material success and power, is moderately likely to interact frequently with the UNF leader, but not necessarily on the opposite side from him. One would suppose that the U type, along with the other upward types, according to their number, strength, and inclination will often play a critical role in the decision between the party of the left and the party of the right as to which one shall carry the day.

The party of the right is typically not well consolidated under the authoritarian autocrat, UNF, however, in the types of groups studied. The UNF leader appears to be at a critical point of internal division. He is markedly likely to be opposed from the NB direction both by the member who believes in the rejection of social conformity and by the negative member, N, who believes in individualistic isolationism. He is also moderately likely to be opposed by the backward member, B, who believes in the rejection of conventional group beliefs. One would think that hardly anybody likes inhibitory demands and discipline except the UNF leader. One might also wonder whether all these dissident elements might not form the basis of a successful opposition, since there are potentially so many. The problem appears to be, however, that they are too different from each other on the negative-to-positive dimension to cooperate with each other. It seems usual for the positive and backward types to form a coalition in opposition to the UNF leader.

The UNF type who tries to exert autocratic authority is not so far removed from the other negative types as might appear from their opposition to him. He struggles psychologically to contain his aggressive feelings, but he is very much in favor of violence in the form of punishment for deviants, traitors, and all kinds of outsiders. There is no evidence that the UN advocates of tough-minded assertiveness often press their point of view in opposition to the UNF leader, but rather, he himself often voices their values and is prepared to agree with them. And also it appears that although the less assertive N members may fear him and argue with him in protection of their own individualistic isolation, they do so only so long as they see him as an outside threat to their autonomy. He, as well as they, is afraid of all kinds of possible outside enemies and, in fact, tends to voice a philosophy of individualistic isolationism with regard to those enemies. He is prepared to agree with the isolationists at the levels of abstract statement and fantasy. All that is necessary for the N type of members to identify with him is to feel that he is *inside the same boundary with them* fighting the same enemies they fear. Feeling this, they can become part of a coalition with him and the UN type in a party of the right.

A critical thing to watch then, in attempting to predict whether a coalition of the right will form, is the way in which the boundary between the "in-group" and the "out-group" is drawn by the UNF leader. One would expect, from historical experience, that the UNF leader who wishes support will typically try to materialize one or more "outside" scapegoats and to find, or fabricate through fantasy, a basis for solidarity between himself and those on the negative side of the group: a scapegoat or enemy that will be convincing to them, and lead them to identify him as "inside" with them and regard him as their champion against dangerous "outside" enemies. Psychologically, the battle between the "in-group" and the "out-group" symbolizes for the authoritarian individual the battle between his "conscious self," identified with the "in-group," and the unconscious aspects of himself, projected onto the "out-group." The observer of such a psychological struggle can hardly fail to be impressed by its nightmarish quality or to be astonished by its emotional intensity.

In the light of these psychological considerations, then, if they are truly understood and properly generalized, it may be seen why a strong movement toward autocratic authority is so critical to a group, whether, for example, a parent-child group in a crisis of authority or a nation on the verge of Fascism. Such a movement both signals internal trouble, and sets into motion fears that in their acting-out may change the very boundaries and identity of the self or the group. Such a change in the definition of what constitutes the group, or the warring subgroups, may determine the direction of movement for long periods, even permanently. The attempts of a UNF leader if they are frightened attempts to prevent a threatened breakdown of repression, upon which the existing order has rested, may be followed by desperate measures toward retrenchment, restriction of the boundaries of the group, and restoration of internal consistency and safety. Failing that, the group may split.

Personality Traits

The one personality trait in the present study on which the UNF type is probably high is prejudice. The California F-scale, the so-called fascism scale constructed by the authors of *The Authoritarian Personality* (1) is usually thought to measure this trait. As pointed out above, although the UNF type fits the stereotype many people visualize when they read the items, the actual UNF type is much more likely to *say such things to others* than to agree with them himself. The F-scale used as a written questionnaire actually tends to be diagnostic of the PF type, at least in the present study, and if this is generally true it may account for some of the confusion in research on the authoritarian personality.

The UNF type tends to be moderately high on measures of ascendant movement. He is likely to share the traits of the U type, adventurousness, thick-skinnedness, and dominance. He may show the UF trait, sophistication, with conventional control of aggression. Similarly he may share such UN traits as being neurotic, psychopathic and manic. He may be moderately high on traits of the N type: suspecting and jealous;

and he may show some hypochondriasis, psychoasthenia, and dependency. Finally, he may be moderately high on the NF trait, feminine masochism.

Since we have perhaps only one test that directly characterizes the UNF type, it is worth remembering that a given type will tend to measure *low* on the tests which measure the *opposite* direction. The opposite direction to UNF, of course, is DPB. Unfortunately there are no tests that measure this direction either, but something is known about surrounding types. Tests from the P direction can give us some clues. The UNF type is likely to measure moderately low on the traits of trustfulness, accessibility, and on intellectual efficiency and ego strength. From the DP direction we infer that he will probably measure moderately low on the traits of maturity, calmness, stability, and will be low on probability of achievement. The authors of the authoritarian personality theories point out the frequency of a strong "masculine facade," of which more will be said later.

How He Sees His Parents

It is interesting to speculate as to how many of the authoritarian personality traits may be the outcome of growing up under the domination of autocratic and authoritarian parents. The UNF type reports his father as very high on inhibitory demands and discipline, but average on emotional supportiveness and warmth. The mother is reported as high on inhibitory demands and discipline and also average on emotional supportiveness and warmth. The discrepancy between the two is reported to be average. One infers that neither father nor mother is on either extreme end of the variable optimistic idealism versus pessimistic cynicism. One can imagine a picture with a worse prognosis, but the conditions for anything but a rather traumatic identification with the outward forms of authority seem to be lacking. There is probably not enough opportunity for well-timed tension release, associated with loving affection and a calm and thoughtful example. The child, in his desperation, may fall back upon the psychological maneuver known as "identification with the aggressor"—the psychological defense reported from concentration camps where some of the prisoners take the side of their tormenters in the persecution of other prisoners. Such a solution is crude in that the controls within the personality are not well associated with the impulses; the controls are not associated with anything attractive. The impulses are kept barely below the surface; they are given precipitous outlet in thinly-disguised forms, and they constantly threaten the barely-adequate ego. The conscious life is plagued by vague feelings of great forces, catastrophic dangers, and crumbling defenses. The authoritarian personality of the type UNF, it seems to me, is a personality type precipitated by an emergency in socialization. If so, it could be that, as a direction of movement in a group, the direction UNF is not dependent upon the presence of the particular UNF personality type. I would guess that such a reaction can be precipitated in almost any group by a severe emergency arising from the outer situation. The classic example is the realistic threat of war and invasion.

His Effect on Group Satisfaction

The UNF leader, as may well be understood, tends to move the group as a whole away from satisfaction with interpersonal relations, although there may be some gains of satisfaction by the members of a coalition of the right, if there is one. Assuming that the group does not polarize, with some radical re-organization of the goals on each side, the UNF leader tends to move the group toward satisfaction with goal attainment. But the UNF direction is precisely the one in which satisfaction with goal attainment is most sharply pitted against satisfaction with interpersonal relations, and the imponderable danger is that the resulting pressure will rupture the existing order of social or interpersonal relations, with a consequent breakdown in adherence to common goals and common tasks. Many parents, teachers, group leaders, and others in positions of authority know how thin the line is between the amount of pressure for achievement and task performance that succeeds, and the very little more it takes to precipitate alienation and deviance. I believe it is true that the amount of pressure that can be successfully exerted in a given relationship depends upon the strength of the prior attachment or positive affection between the person in authority and those in his charge. The existing affection is like "money in the bank," which is expended in meeting demands for achievement. And, as with money in the bank, when it is gone, the misery begins.

15

Type UN: Toward Tough-Minded Assertiveness

The member located in the upward-negative part of the group space by his fellow members seems dominating, self-confident, aggressive, hostile and unfriendly. He seems ready to apply force to show his own power and superiority. He is unconcerned about morality, values, or the group task. He neither justifies himself in terms of values, nor revolts against them, but takes pleasure in his own power over others. In the realization of his own values he seems to be trying to move toward tough-minded assertiveness. "The most important qualities of a real man are determination and driving ambition." "Groups with a real purpose should accomplish things, and disregard hurt feelings and factions." "It is just as well that the struggle of life tends to weed out those who cannot stand the pace."

How He Sees Himself and How Others See Him

The UN member seems to identify himself openly and proudly with the power of aggression. His fellow group members tend to see him as self-confident and dominating. Not only do group members and observers agree that he is dominating, but he also agrees gladly with their observation. He makes others feel he dislikes them, even though he is not the type who actually expresses most dislike. He tends to see others as resentful, as they often are. Other group members as well as observers see him as the least understanding of all types. They feel he rates them very low on value for a logical task, that he is the least likely of all types to feel admiration, which is to say, perhaps, the one most likely to feel contempt. He sees others as lacking in self-confidence. He rates himself as very low on acceptance of authority, and agrees with observers that he is the least equalitarian of all the types.

His Place in the Interaction Network

The UN member is likely to be high on total interaction initiated, but not necessarily the highest member in the group. He is high on speaking to the group as a whole rather than to particular members. He does not tend to receive a commensurate response from others. Other members speak to him specifically only at an average rate, but even so, they each pay more attention to him as an individual than he pays to each of them as an individual. His total addressed to specific individuals tends to be low as compared to his total addressed to the group as a whole. His orientation is more toward domination of the group as a whole than toward equalitarian interchange with each of the members.

What Ideas and Values Will He Express?

The value-statements likely to be initiated by the UN member convey a blend of ascendance and negative feeling that seems well described as tough-minded assertiveness. This attitude is exemplified by the three statements quoted at the beginning of this chapter: "The most important qualities of a real man are determination and driving ambition." "Groups with a real purpose should accomplish things and disregard hurt feelings and factions." "It is just as well that the struggle of life tends to weed out those who cannot stand the pace."

Other characteristic statements have less implication of aggression directed against persons and more emphasis on expression of energy through activity. "Man's future depends primarily upon what he *does*, not upon what he feels or what he thinks." "A rich life requires constant activity; the use of muscles and openness to adventure." "The real appeal of love is its sense of challenge, danger, and adventure." "The greatest satisfaction in life is a feeling of the actuality of the present, of tireless activity, movement, doing." "Not in cautious foresight, not in relaxed ease, does life attain completion, but in outward energetic action, the excitement of power in the tangible present."

Often, however, the disregard for others, the willingness to see violence done is explicit. "European refugees should be left to fend for themselves." "The so-called underdog deserves little sympathy or help from successful people." "It is just as well that the struggle for life tends to weed out those who cannot stand the pace." "People suffering from incurable diseases should have the choice of being put to death painlessly." "A person should be free to take his own life, if he wishes to do so, without any interference from society."

Values of this kind are not necessarily opposed to the goals of conservative or established social institutions, but when fused with them, they tend to emphasize selectively the overt, action-oriented, practical, and materialistic aspects of institutional goals. "The most important function of modern leaders is to bring about the accomplishment of practical goals." "The most important function of education is its preparation for practical achievement and financial reward." "Man's future depends primarily upon the technical advances made by scientific knowledge." "The maintenance of internal order within the nation is more important than ensuring that there is complete freedom for all." "Compulsory military training in peacetime is essential for the survival of this country."

The tendency to make statements in favor of tough-minded assertiveness does not necessarily imply an absence of all religious belief. But the more "tender-minded" aspects of religious belief tend to be rejected, those aspects which stress nonmateriality, salvation through love, and life after death. Thus Melvin (115) finds that tough-minded subjects tend to endorse the following assertions: "There is no survival of any kind after death." "The idea of God is an invention of the human mind." "Most religious people are hypocrites." "The average man can live a good enough life without religion." In spite of the tendency to agree with such items, however, the difference between the tendency to agree with such statements and the likelihood of initiating statements of the same kind should be recalled. Results of the studies upon which this book is based are most consistent with the assumption that tendencies to *initiate* statements rejecting conservative group belief, including religious fundamentalism, are characteristic of the B direction and are simply uncorrelated with the UN direction.

The similarity of the UN type to the UNF type is notable with regard to the tendency to be suspicious of persons or elements of the population felt to be foreign: "Nowadays, more and more people are prying into matters that do not concern them." "There may be a few exceptions, but in general, Jews are pretty much alike." But on the other hand, the *moralistic* emphasis of the UNF type tends to be missing and is replaced by a more egocentric, sometimes an anti-social feeling: "Life is so short that a man is justified in enjoying himself as much as he can." "There is no harm in traveling occasionally without a ticket if you can get away with it." "A white lie is often a good thing."

The range of values that may be advocated by the UN type, in addition to tough-minded assertiveness, is quite large, verging upon conflict, particularly with regard to the forward-backward dimension. On the one hand, the UN type may make statements in favor of autocratic authority, group loyalty and cooperation, and value-determined restraint. But on the other, he is equally likely to make statements in favor of rugged individualism and gratification, value-relativism and expression, and rejection of social conformity. One feels that the UN type has identified with group norms and authority figures only loosely and outwardly, if at all, and that he exempts himself, his actions, and his satisfactions, from all general rules and requirements of authority. His tendency to speak for material success, power, and individualistic isolationism are consistent with the emphasis on himself. One gets the impression that he has fought the strictures of arbitrary authority and, by his own definition, he has won! Henceforth, he can *use* a relationship to autocratic authority so long as the agent of that authority is subject to him. Authority is useful in holding the rest of the group in check. But the UN type can not submit to a person in authority over him. One expects, then, that the UN type will try to find a bad autocratic figure to attack, or that he will try to form a smaller local group within a closed boundary, in which he can either be the dictator or can control a figurehead of authority.

The Quality of His Interaction

The UN member is high on seeming unfriendly (see p. 128) on giving suggestions, and on dramatizing and joking. His adjacent types may consider him amusing, but not all members find him so. He responds to others' contributions with a high rate of disagreement. Conversely, he is low on agreement, low on showing tension and laughing, low on seeming friendly, and low on soliciting interaction from others by asking for opinion or suggestion. He is also low on giving information, as are all of the upward-tending types.

The reactions of others to the UN member are usually negative, although he may have a small clique for whom he vicariously expresses aggression. Negative interaction seems to elicit negative interaction from most others. They are likely to disagree, show tension, or laugh, and seem unfriendly. They are low in seeming friendly and dramatizing and joking. They address little information or opinion to him and expect to be rejected if they do.

Conflicts and Coalitions with Others

The type most likely to oppose the UN member is the UP member who believes in social success and generally feels that aggression is a sure way to alienate others. Although this opposition is likely, it is not likely to be the focus of much overt verbal conflict, since the tough-minded member does not actually tend to argue; he simply does not care. The UPF member is likely to urge social solidarity and progress upon him, and the UPB member urges emotional supportiveness and warmth;

and while the UN member does not agree with these values, he does not spend much time in disagreement. He tends to disagree with value-statements that put some restraint on his ascendance and autonomy. Apparently for this reason he may disagree with the UF member who urges group loyalty and cooperation upon him, and with the P member who advocates equalitarianism. The PF member tries to woo him with altruistic love, and the NF member urges value-determined restraint, but the UN member disagrees with both of them.

The UN member, although he opposes the P types mentioned, is not necessarily a member of the party of the right, though he may be. He not only opposes group loyalty and cooperation and value-determined restraint, but he also opposes arguments of autocratic authority if they are applied to him. If there is a coalition between the UNF leader and the UN type in a party of the right, this must somehow involve a suppression of the conflict that would occur if the moralism of the autocratic authority were turned against the advocate of tough-minded assertiveness.

There is, on the other hand, a potential coalition between the UN type and certain members of the party of the left. The UB type is likely to advocate value-relativism and expression to him, and he is likely to agree. The PB member, since he believes in permissive liberalism, is likely to be an advocate of social change also, which the UN member also sometimes wants. The N member may urge individualistic isolationism upon him, and he is markedly likely to agree. The NB member may advocate the rejection of social conformity, and he may agree. The point is that the UN member is not ideologically committed to any form of social order. He is primarily in favor of himself and the expression of his aggression, and he is a possible leader or at least a collaborator in a revolution headed toward anarchism or nihilism, based upon a coalition between elements of the party of the far right (the negative and forward side) and the party of the far left (the negative and backward side). Although the arguments are not very likely to be made to him overtly, he is prepared to agree to statements advocating rugged individualism and gratification, rejection of conservative group beliefs, the withholding of cooperation, and even identification with the underprivileged. He does not really care for the underprivileged, but he is in favor of aggression and possibly of revolution. Having fought with authority and won, he considers himself an experienced hand. His motto is "Have gun, will travel."

Personality Traits

The person who moves strongly and persistently in the UN direction is likely to test markedly high on neurotic, psychopathic, and manic traits. Traits of neighboring types, on which he may be moderately high include those of the U type: adventurousness, thick-skinnedness, activeness, and dominance. He may show the UF trait of sophistication. He may test moderately high on the UNF trait, prejudice, and on the UNB traits of nervous tension, dominance, aggressiveness, eccentricity, and unconcernedness, paranoia, impulsivity, and self-centeredness. The NB traits on which he may be moderately high include emotional sensitivity, seeming insecurity, radicalness, and criticalness. The near-by N traits include seeming suspecting, jealous, and having some symptoms of hypochondriasis, psychasthenia, and dependency. Finally, the UN type may be moderately high on the NF test, feminine masochism.

A tendency to overemphasize masculinity sometimes goes along with underlying feelings of confusion or failure in achieving what the person conceives to be the socially acceptable masculine role. An overemphasis to cover up or to keep these concerns from consciousness is sometimes called a "masculine facade" (1). If it is true that the kind of parental pressure and the model of the male role typically experienced by the male UN child is a father of the UN type, it may be understood why acceptance of positive or affectionate feelings might be experienced as feminine, and therefore rejected. At the same time, if affection is necessary to a secure and successful identification with the parent, it would seem that it would be particularly hard for the male child of the UN type to identify with the male role, without conflict, or for the female UN child to identify with the conventional female role. The male child is likely to identify, out of desperation and uncertainty, with an exaggerated stereotype of the male role, and he often tries to repress, out of shame and fear of failure, positive or affectionate feelings which suggest he might be feminine. The female child, also, may tend to be masculinized. But since affectionate and tender feelings can not really be disposed of altogether, but only repressed, they may make their way to disguised expression in various kinds of interests and preoccupations—or so one might suppose. A corollary of this line of theorizing would lead one to expect that the male of which this would be essentially true might be especially afraid of homosexuality; he might feel it as a threat and, in collaboration with the UNF type, might desperately attempt to seek it out and destroy it in others. In this case, particularly in the case of the male, the fear may be more specifically a fear of submitting passively, perhaps in a "feminine" way, to the threat posed by a demanding and negative parent.

How He Sees His Parents

The UN type tends to report his father as high on inhibitory demands and discipline and average on emotional supportiveness and warmth. The mother is described as very high on inhibitory demands and discipline—the highest described by any type, but still average on emotional supportiveness and warmth. According to inference, both the father and mother would be reported as moderately high on pessimistic cynicism (as opposed to optimistic idealism). Thus, although the parents may make high demands—demands that outweigh the affection they are able to give—they do not make the demands in the name of generalized values, but rather out of their own assertive autonomy and aggression. The message they convey as to the importance of values is that they are unimportant or hypocritical devices, which others use to cover their selfishness. The discrepancy between the roles of father and mother is reported as moderately high, and the messages they convey are thus likely to conflict with each other, still further increasing the difficulty of identification with a stable set of values or a stable social role. The tendency for values, self-picture, and adult sex role to be poorly developed, shifting, and hard for others to understand and count on, is basically what is meant by the trait description called "psychopathic." The tendency for the person to feel the demands of parents, others, and repressed parts of the self as harsh, intrusive, and threatening is reflected in the traits of suspicion and other negative feeling-tones relating to persecution, which sometimes reach extreme form, but often are well compensated and contained, or reach an exaggerated form only in one small area of the person's concern.

With the background of associated traits and behavior of the UN type in mind, it is not difficult to see that a parent of this type could produce a child who would grow up with similar tendencies, especially if the child begins with a strong set of aggressive and sexual drives, a good fund of physical energy, and perhaps a strong muscular physique. Lacking these traits, which presumably make for upward tendencies, such a child might well tend to one of the less ascendant types, still on the negative side. But it is hard to see how, without important outside influences, the child could develop far in the positive or forward directions.

As a parent, the UN type is not likely to socialize his child very far in the positive or forward direction, nor is the leader of this type likely to lead other members of a group in other than a negative and a backward direction. He will tend to find others in the group who personify his suspicions and fears. When the group is in a psychological state similar to his own—tending to move in the UN direction, from some stirring-up of aggression through internal conflict, or from some combination of aggressive tension with external conditions of threat—the UN member is likely to emerge into leadership. The ultimate effect on the group may be severe if he retains power and may differ greatly according to whether he is supported by a coalition from the right or from the left.

His Effect on Group Satisfaction

The effect of the UN leader on the forward or backward movement of the group depends upon the direction of the coalition he forms, which in turn affects how he contains and expresses his aggression. Since either direction may be acceptable to him, it is not possible to predict the effect of the UN leader on the satisfaction of the group with goal attainment— that will depend upon the presence and power of others who may form coalitions with him. But his effect on the satisfaction of the group with interpersonal relations is not ambiguous, rather it is likely to be markedly negative. More than any other type, he is likely to move the group away from the satisfactions that can be obtained from positive interpersonal relationships.

16

Type UNB: Toward Rugged
Individualism and Gratification

**The member located in the upward-negative-backward part of the
group space by his fellow members seems dominating, self-confident,
and rebellious toward authority as well as hostile to other persons. He
seems self-centered, deviant, exhibitionistic, and exploitative. In the
realization of his own values he seems to be trying to move toward
rugged individualism and gratification of himself alone. "Every normal
man must be tempted, at times, to spit on his hands, hoist the black
flag, and begin slitting throats."**

How He Sees Himself and How Others See Him

For the UNB personality, the self seems to be identified with the
power to defy authority and rise above and outside the law. He is seen by
observers and other group members as favoring expression and gratification. He rates himself as high on this, but not so high as does the B type.
Observers are apt to find him entertaining, and he arouses their curiosity. Group members, however, react differently; they find type UPB more
entertaining, and their curiosity is aroused by DN. It may be that UNB
presents too great a threat to group members (as compared to the less
exposed observers) to seem entertaining, although his significance as the
leading exponent of normally repressed tendencies is similar to both
observers and group members. He is the outlaw and apparently is
provocatively aware of it. He guesses that others will rate him high on
domination. He is in fact rated by group members as the lowest of all
types on equalitarianism, and he correctly guesses that he will be so

regarded. In his expectation that other members will rate him high on domination he is not far wrong—although the recipient of the highest ratings is his adjacent type, UN.

His Place in the Interaction Network

The UNB type is likely to be high on total interaction initiated, and like other upward types he has a tendency to speak to the group as a whole. In responding to him, others are not likely to give more than average amounts, and in responding to them individually, he is likely to be still lower. Each of them gives him only an average amount, and he in turn is likely to be low vis-à-vis each of them. Thus, he tends to over-talk to the group as a whole and to under-respond to each individual.

What Ideas and Values Will He Express?

The central values of the UNB type, as expressed vocally, favor rugged individualism and gratification. "Love action and care little that others may think you rash." "Let us eat, drink, and be merry, for tomorrow we die." The UNB position is one which fuses ascendance, both of social role and instinctual gratification, with a negative attitude toward social conventions, as well as toward others as a group. This kind of individualism seems aptly called "rugged." "Whoever would be a man must be a nonconformist." "To be superior a man must stand alone." "A man can learn better by striking out boldly on his own than he can by following the advice of others." "A person should always be the master of his own fate." "The greatest fortunes are for those who leave the common path and blaze a new trail for themselves."

There is not only a rejection of conventional social norms in the values of the UNB personality, but also a rejection of a longer time perspective in which rationality or morality might have some meaning or potential reward. "The past is no more, the future may never be, the present is all we can be certain of." "Nothing is static, nothing is everlasting, at any moment one must be ready to meet the change in environment by a necessary change in one's moral views." And from this set of assumptions the conclusion is drawn in favor of immediate gratification. "Since there are no values which can be eternal, the only real values are those which meet the needs of the given moment." "Life is something to be enjoyed to the full, sensuously enjoyed, with relish and enthusiasm."

Congruent with this position is the willingness or eagerness of the UNB member, to abolish customs, laws, or values which hamper the free gratification of individual drives. "Free love between men and women should be encouraged as a means toward mental and physical health." "Men and women have the right to find out whether they are sexually suited before marriage (by companionate marriage)." "The laws against abortion should be abolished." "Divorce laws should be altered to make divorce easier." With regard to restrictions on the sale of alcoholic beverages: "The present licensing laws should be altered, so as to remove restrictions on hours of opening." With regard to laws in general: "Present laws favor the rich as against the poor." With regard to customs: "Sunday observance is old-fashioned and should cease to govern our behavior." With regard to freedom of speech: "Unrestricted freedom of discussion on every topic is desirable in the press, in literature, on the stage, and so forth."

The value clusters immediately surrounding the central ones described above are also likely to be voiced by the UNB type. He may speak for tough-minded assertiveness, material success and power, and for value-relativism and expression, the values of his immediately adjacent upward types. He is also likely to voice the positions of his not quite so ascendant adjacent types: in favor of individualistic isolationism; rejection of social conformity; and rejection of conservative group beliefs.

The Quality of His Interaction

No one category of interaction is uniquely high for UNB, but his pattern of interaction initiated is distinguished by the large number of categories which are relatively low or neglected. Not one of the categories having to do with group problem-solving, preparation for the task, or eliciting problem-solving attempts from others is high.

Giving information and giving opinions are both low, as are asking for opinions and asking for suggestions. The UNB member is low on seeming friendly and on showing agreement. Showing disagreement, on the contrary, is high, and so is seeming unfriendly. Dramatizing and joking is high, and it is in this category that the UNB outlaw leader builds up his relatively high total of remarks to the group as a whole.

In response to his dramatizing and joking, others are likely to be markedly high on showing tension and laughing. Although laughter may bring some relief from tension, it does not necessarily do so and it may also be considered as indicative of tension that has been built up, as it is in the present scoring system. Group members are generally low on seeming friendly toward the UNB outlaw leader. They show little agreement with him, which is partly due to the fact that he offers little content for that kind of response. He tends not to carry on an argument by reasoning, but by provocative and suggestive words or actions that symbolize or demonstrate the triumph of drives over restraint. Others do not tend to reason with him; they address neither information nor opinion to him. They are understandably low in asking him for suggestions. His suggestions, if any, are meant to shock.

Conflicts and Coalitions with Others

The rugged individualist, UNB, is typically opposed from the positive and forward side. He is markedly likely to receive arguments for social solidarity and progress from the UPF leader. The UP leader reproaches him for his disregard of the appropriate ways to social success and popularity, and the UF leader urges him to show group loyalty and cooperation. In value-terms, the proponent of material success, type U, is not far from the UNB type, but in terms of who actually has the material success, there may be some argument between the two, in a kind of "rich man versus Robin Hood" conflict. The UNB type often poses as Robin Hood.

The value-position taken by the UNB outlaw leader is disturbing to those who have placed their trust in God, or some equivalent. The PF member is markedly likely to work for the reform of the outlaw, with words or deeds that recommend altruistic love. And from the NF direction, the member who believes in value-determined restraint is markedly likely to try to bring conscience to bear. Allied to these two, the proponent of conservative group beliefs is likely to urge his beliefs upon the UNB outlaw, even though the prospect of success is very small indeed. Of all the value-positions mentioned so far, there is one which is still more repugnant to the UNF outlaw: the submissive hope of salvation through love. This value-direction is contrary to everything the self-respecting outlaw stands for, and for him is a "slave's way out." The proponent of rugged individualism, like the proponent of tough-minded assertiveness, can hardly stand "good little boys" and "yes men." They are direct threats to his efforts to grow up and become a man. They are feminine boys as he sees it, the sissys who have submitted in the struggle against autocratic authority and conventionality, and have allowed themselves to be deprived of their masculinity in order to win favor in the eyes of tyrannical fathers. He rebels in the face of this threat: "Every normal man must be tempted, at times, to spit on his hands, hoist the black flag, and begin slitting throats."

The outlaw is a potential leader, or at least collaborator, in movements toward social change. Although he is not likely to initiate statements characteristic of his less ascendant neighboring types, he acts for them and partially releases their tensions. He is likely to agree with, though not to initiate, statements in favor of withholding cooperation, identification with the underprivileged, and permissive liberalism. It is in fact plausible that a UNB leader, or at least a movement in that direction by relevant members of the group, is an essential ingredient to revolution. A revolutionary party is a coalition of those on the B side, and it will typically combine members from the U as well as the D sides and members from both P and N sides. Defined and combined as it is, by opposition to forward directions, however, and lacking norms of its own, a revolutionary coalition is inherently unstable and is typically unable to survive its own triumph. To do so, it must establish a new orthodoxy, and its original leaders are usually unable to do this, for reasons of personality.

Personality Traits

The UNB leader is likely to measure high on the trait of nervous tension; and he seems aggressive, eccentric, and unconcerned. He is likely to seem paranoid, and to show impulsivity and self-centeredness. In addition to these traits, which are most characteristic, he may be moderately high on the traits of near-by directions. The U traits, for example, are adventurousness, callousness, activeness, and dominance. The UN traits are neurotic, psychopathic, and manic. Traits of the N traits are suspicion and jealousy, with symptoms of hypochondriasis, psychasthenia, and dependence. Or the UNB leader may show traits of his next-less ascendant type, NB; emotional sensitivity, seeming insecure, radical, and critical.

The picture seems reasonably consistent and understandable, though certainly "rugged." In the light of what has been said above concerning the apparent threat, to the outlaw, of the image of "the good boy," the DPF type, who has allowed himself to be deprived of his masculinity, and has submitted in a loving and feminine way to the demands of the autocratic father, it may be plausible to suppose that the UNB type is struggling against unconscious tendencies or temptations of this kind within his own personality. The eccentric and unconcerned traits represent the triumph of conscious elements of the personality over unconscious tendencies, whereas the paranoid and suspicious traits signal feelings of threat that the unconscious tendencies may break through. If so, the feared elements would be expected to include disowned tendencies toward autocratic authority, value-determined restraint, conservative group beliefs, as well as fears of feminine submission and a hope for salvation through love. For a female the feared elements presumably center around submission to either male or female authority, especially the acceptance of the position of a loving and submissive daughter.

How He Sees His Parents

The UNB type is apt to report that discrepancies between the personality and role of his father and mother were moderately high. The mother is apparently higher than the father on inhibitory demands and discipline, being moderately high, whereas the father is only average. Both parents are average on emotional supportiveness and warmth, but both are moderately high on pessimistic cynicism. It may seem that the parental picture is not so alienating as one might expect for a type so alienated as UNB. It should be recalled, however, that this type, though alienated, is not without resources. His ascendance is high as is his tendency to interact; the tendencies of parents to interact with each other and the child were presumably also high. Though opposed to conventional values and alienated from affectionate solidarity with other people, the outlaw is not alienated from his aggressive drives, his fantasy, nor from action, and these are some support for his ego. By pessimistic cynicism and by rather adventitious aggression on the part of his parents, not sufficiently offset by emotional support, he has been taught or forced to develop a pattern of reliance upon himself.

In his turn, when he is a parent or when he assumes a position of leadership in a group, he tends to talk and act in such a way as to teach others—his children or followers—that nothing is more dangerous than gullible faith, in God, religion, society, parents, in love or trust or tender mindedness. In order to prove that he is right he may deliberately mislead his followers and then punish them for faith and belief in him, if they naively fall for his deception. Thus, although he leads only on occasion, he has the best chance to lead when others are also hostile and alienated, or when he has a monopoly of physical force, or his followers are markedly more naive than he. His leadership lacks the stability that arises from affectionate idealization and legitimation by group norms. He tends to lead by manipulation, and he must profit by the confusions and passing opportunities of the situation.

His Effect on Group Satisfaction

The UNB leader tends to move the group away from satisfaction, either with interpersonal relations or with goal achievement. When a group has a UNB member various others tend to check the following statements after the meeting: "There was need for a leader to give everyone an equal chance for expression." "Some people in the group were unfortunately crowded out of the discussion."

Over-talking and lack of consideration for the less ascendant is one facet of the problem. The probability of conflict of leadership is another. "The members of this group spent too much of their energy jockeying for position as leader." "Some of the members had an intolerant spirit of no compromise." "There was too much antagonism between members." "Too many members allowed their personal feelings to override the group goal." The localization of a conflict between the UNB direction and the UNF direction is reflected in the comment: "Some of the members are too absolutistic in the way they think rules always have to be enforced." Whether in a conflicted deadlock, or a runaway coalition, dominant members tend to be a problem for others. "There was a tendency which I didn't like for group members to talk to one or two others instead of to the group as a whole." "Two members of this group seem to stick together and form a dominant pair."

Not only does the UNB leader tend to lower group satisfaction with interpersonal relations, but also their satisfaction with the completion of the job, or movement in the forward direction. "Some members were not able to control their emotions so that the group could get the job done." "Some members seem to lack perspective about the job—they tackle the problem from one angle and because a temporary solution is reached, they think the problem is solved." "A moderator should be appointed in the beginning so that there would be less time wasted discussing irrelevant or already discussed material." "Not enough people took up individual responsibility for keeping the discussion going." "I felt out of touch with some of the members during the discussion." "The meeting was disappointing because no unanimous recommendation was reached." "There was too much talk and not enough definite forward progress."

17

Type UB: Toward Value-Relativism and Expression

The member located in the upward-backward part of the group space by his fellow members seems ascendant and expressive, nontask oriented, perhaps unconventional or even deviant. He seems neither clearly friendly nor unfriendly, but entertaining, joking, dramatic, relativistic, free in his associations, taking pleasure in play, activity, novelty, and creativity. In the realization of his own values he seems to be trying to move toward value-relativism and expression of underlying emotions and feelings. "Life is more a festival than a workshop for moral discipline."

How He Sees Himself and How Others See Him

The UB member seems to identify himself with the power that comes from the ability to recognize and express unconscious tendencies in the self and in others and, thus, to escape from conflict. The UB member sees himself as extroverted and entertaining. Observers and other group members agree in seeing him as extroverted, but there is a division of feeling as to who is most entertaining. Observers tend to find UNB more entertaining, whereas group members give the rating for most entertaining to UPB. The UB type guesses correctly that others will find him extroverted, but that he will not necessarily be found most entertaining. He appears to feel a freedom from the constraint of authority. Of all the types, he is the least likely to be seen as acceptant of authority, either by observers or other group members, and he correctly guesses that he will be so seen. He rates himself as very low on psychological inertia, guesses that others will rate him low; he is essentially accurate. The observers see him as having least psychological inertia, however, group members give that rating to his adjacent type UPB. The UB type sees others as lower than himself on individualism, but he does not rate himself the highest on this. Although he feels a freedom from the constraints of authority and the group task, he is not alienated from the group, nor does hostility outweigh affection.

His Place in the Interaction Network

The UB member is high on acts addressed to the group as a whole, which seems congruent with his tendency to tell jokes, stories, and entertaining anecdotes. He is high on receiving responses from others, congruent with the number of laughs he is likely to receive. His tendency to speak to specific individuals is low, however, both in sum and with regard to each specific individual. He tends to receive at a high rate from each other individual in the group, and to address each other one at a low rate. Rather he concentrates on the group as a whole. His total interaction initiated is also high, though not necessarily the highest in the group.

What Ideas and Values Will He Express?

The central value of the UB type is a particular attitude about values themselves—namely that they should be relativistic rather than absolute and, going along with this, it is desirable that all conflicting values a person may have, as well as motivating drives, impulses, and tendencies, should at least be expressed so that their relations to each other may be seen. He is after a "sense of perspective," and his sense of perspective is given by a sense of humor. "There is no human desire so mean that it does not deserve expression and gratification." "No man ever improved his impulses by refusing to express them." "Life is more a festival than a workshop or a school for moral discipline." "No scheme for living proposed by various religions and moralities is entirely suitable for every purpose, yet each scheme can offer something for everyone; one should use all of them, and no one alone." "The solution to almost any human problem should be based on the situation at the time, and not on some general moral rule." "Society should be quicker to adopt new customs and throw aside mere traditions and old-fashioned habits."

Though the UB member as the proponent of value-relativism and expression tries to take a position above value-conflict, he cannot arrive at that position except by a rejection of more straightforward and literal forms of value-orthodoxy. Thus, he is likely, on occasion, to voice sentiments for rejection of social conformity, rejection of conventional group beliefs, and in favor of permissive liberalism. And, since he is in favor of expression, all of the ascendant value-positions are congenial to him, except the forward ones. On occasion he will speak for social success as a desirable goal, as well as material success and power, and tough-minded assertiveness. Similarly, he speaks for rugged individualism and gratification on the negative side, as well as emotional supportiveness and warmth on the positive side. In general his arguments are addressed to those on the upward and forward side, who, as he sees it, are trying too hard.

The Quality of His Interaction

The UB member is markedly high on dramatizing and joking (see page 105). This is his specialty, and it takes various forms, sometimes witty remarks, sometimes anecdotes and extended jokes, sometimes fantasies or enactments. He tends to express, usually by indirect and symbolic means, underlying tensions of his own, or possibly those of other members of the group—fears, anxieties, hostilities, affections, aspirations, and the like. He is markedly low on asking for suggestion, since this tends to turn the group back toward the feeling that it must work hard. He is low on giving information and opinion, probably for the same reason. He is moderately high in asking for information, however. This asking is probably not usually task-oriented preparation, but rather the preliminary to "making social conversation"—such as asking "Where are you from?" "Do you know Joe . . .?" and the like.

The response of others to the UB member is apt to be a profile of activity quite similar to his own. Dramatizing and joking are likely to be high as everybody joins in on the joke or fantasy, each taking his turn at it, in the familiar way. Showing tension or laughing is a frequent response, as expected in response to jokes. It is unexpected, however, that the UB member, of all people, should be relatively high on receiving suggestions. The prime recipient of suggestions is the UP type, nearby, and perhaps the explanation is related. The UB member may function part of the time as the leader of a potentially deviant part of the group, and he is being asked, in effect to say "yes" for them. It is interesting on this theory that he is *not* asked for his opinion.

The fact that other members show no particular tendency to seem friendly toward the UB leader may present a problem. Is it not reasonable to suppose that a joker or a dramatizer performs a useful function in integrating the group, and hence ought to be the recipient of friendly behavior? An important distinction must be made here. The direct effect of the personality must be distinguished from the "indirect" effect of the content the person presents. As may be seen by checking on the Logical Chart in Appendix 2, the direction of satisfaction with interpersonal relations (downward-positive) is negatively correlated to the present direction (upward-backward). The system of inference (the spatial model) leads us to infer that the UB member does not have an average effect of increasing interpersonal satisfaction. He is too ascendant and not positive enough. Is the joker not a useful member of the group after all?

There is an important parallel between the UB joker or dramatizer and the UF group manager. Whereas they may both feel that they are performing services for the group, they both tend to interfere with the satisfaction of other members with interpersonal relations. The reasons, in formal terms, are similar: in their personality, role, and manner, they are both too ascendant, and neither one gives any real friendly affection.

Both these types, however, present content to the group which may transcend the direct effect of their personal ascendance and lack of friendliness. The UF group manager presents suggested solutions to task problems, which, if found to be good solutions, may be of great value to the group. Similarly, the UB dramatizer presents symbols for the recognition and intellectual handling of tensions, emotional problems, and deviant tendencies which may be widespread among members of the group. If the symbols are really good in the relevant ways, they may be of great value to the group. But the value to the group depends upon the quality of the content, which in turn depends upon the degree of fit of the content to the characteristics of the real world to which it refers. This is the "indirect" effect mentioned above.

The degree of fit, the "goodness" of the suggestion, the joke or dramatization, is more or less unrelated to the personality or social role of the person who presents the content. The effect a member may have by excellence of content is somewhat less direct than the effect of the personality, role, and manner. The joker, or the group manager, has taken "the risk" as it were, for the group, and he may lose. A partial and more immediate test of his success is acceptance by the group. A suggestion which is answered by agreement(s) has partially succeeded, though it still remains to be tried. A joke answered by laughs has partially succeeded, though its insights remain to be exploited. Thus agreement and laughing are both positively related to satisfaction with interpersonal relations, whereas giving suggestion and joking are both negatively related to satisfaction with interpersonal relations. It is a melancholy inference, perhaps, that more than half of all suggestions, jokes, and dramatizations fail in that they have an ultimately negative effect on interpersonal relations. It is an even more melancholy fact that those who take the risks in these directions most frequently pay the price in ambivalent and negative reactions toward them. But their rewards come more directly—they have the pleasures of ascendance in their chosen directions.

It is important to make one more related point, though nothing will be done about it within this book. In recognizing that the "goodness" or "validity" of content must be treated as an independent variable, quite apart from the more direct effect of personality, role, and manner, we come to the outermost border of the inferential power of the present system. There is nothing in the present diagnostic system that at all deals with the cognitive truth, the empirical validity, the practical value, of ideas or dramatic symbolizations that group members communicate to each other, so far as these depend on the condition of the group, the outer situation in which the group has its setting, and on specific characteristics of the task. This is a huge gap! The variables contained within this gap may, in many situations, account for more of the variance in behavior, more of what develops in the group than the variables treated in the present system. This is not a discouraging fact, however. The variables which make for creative, innovative change, learning about the real outside world by experience, change of behavior by good interpretation of underlying motivation, by insight, reflection, and exercise of the higher mental functions, by evaluation and formation of new values and group norms, are simply unformulated and unaccounted for by the present system; they are not lost to sight nor thought to be ineffective.

Conflicts and Coalitions with Others

The joker or dramatizer is particularly likely to receive calls back to group loyalty and cooperation from the group manager, UF, whose business it is to "call the meeting to order." Others on the forward side also urge the UB member toward values which form the context of work rather than play: social solidarity and progress; autocratic authority; altruistic love; conventional group beliefs; and value-determined restraint. He also receives frequent communications from the proponents of social success, material success and power, and tough-minded assertiveness, but since he himself is likely both to initiate and to agree with these values, the interplay tends to be a joking one, in which the ascendance of all three types as well as himself is likely to be expressed and reinforced.

The UB joker or dramatizer argues with those on the forward side of the group space, or tends to work against them; and although he may not interact much with those on the backward side, it is for them and their tensions that he speaks, as well as for himself. He initiates statements in favor of rugged individualism and gratification, rejection of social conformity, rejection of conservative group beliefs, and in favor of permissive liberalism, emotional supportiveness and warmth, as indicated earlier. In addition, though he does not tend to initiate the more submissive backward values, he is prepared to agree with them. He is sympathetic toward feelings of failure and withdrawal, and he is in favor of withholding of cooperation. Toward the positive side, he is in favor of identification with the underprivileged. If there is to be a revolution, he will foreshadow it in symbolic terms, and he may enact it to light the fuse.

Personality Traits

There are no personality tests in the present study which seem to measure the direction UB directly. The UB type, however, may be relatively high on traits of the U type, adventurous, thick-skinned, active, and dominant although he must have at least an intuitive understanding of unconscious feelings. He may be high on the UP traits predicting social status, dominance, social participation, sociability, and leadership. He may have some traits of the UPB type, he may seem enthusiastic, talkative, extrovertive, and show poise, spontaneity, and confidence in his test scores. Toward the B side he may show the Thurstone trait, vigorous, which is something of a mystery in the present study, but which must somehow be connected with the tendency to reject conservative group belief, and may reflect some *fantasy* of vigorous ascendance and conquest, if not the reality.

There is a negative as well as a positive side to the UB personality. A more or less even balance between the positive and the negative tendencies is one of the defining characteristics of the type. UN traits include seeming neurotic, psychopathic, and manic. UNB traits are nervous tension, seeming dominant, aggressive, eccentric, unconcerned, paranoid, impulsive, and self centered. Finally, the UB type may show some of the traits of his less ascendant NB neighbor, emotional sensitivity, insecurity, and may seem radical and critical.

Persons in the near vicinity of the UB direction are somehow straddling the fence or maintaining a middle position on the positive-negative dimension. In view of all else we know, it does not seem likely that such a middle position is simply a result of the fact that no tendencies toward the negative or the positive side exist. We know rather that tendencies in these two directions are associated with basic drives toward love and hate, that they are of great social significance as well as psychological consequence, and that the conflict between the two is the very substance of many jokes, dramatizations, fantasies and anecdotes—all the specialty of the UB member. It is more in line with the general drift of the evidence to suppose that the middle position on this dimension is indicative of conflict, and the result of efforts to deal with conflict. (This may be true of the other dimensions as well). In such a struggle, one side may be uppermost, or the more conscious, but the other is likely strong also, and only uncertainly held down and regularly ventilated by the mechanisms of defense that the person has developed out of the struggle.

How He Sees His Parents

The UB type is likely to describe his parents as pretty much like himself, according to our general theory. His father and mother are both, we may suppose, likely to have been moderately high on pessimistic cynicism, with a rather negative attitude toward conservative social norms, unwilling to profess allegiance to any values or ideals, of whatever content, so long as the values have much feeling of generality. This does not prevent a moderately high insistence on inhibitory demands and discipline on the part of the mother; it only tends to take the generality and consistency out of the demands. The father is seen as only average on inhibitory demands and discipline. Both parents are moderately high on emotional supportiveness and warmth, however, and both, as we infer, tend to maintain a more or less middle position with regard to a preponderance of love over hate, or vice-versa. Ascendance is encouraged—love and hate find expression, in parents and in child, and conflicts tend to be solved by leaning toward nonconformity, humor, and fantasy. It is plausible to suppose that in many instances these mechanisms for dealing with conflict are taught, either directly or indirectly, in the relationship of parents to child. The child may be the only joker or dramatizer in the family, but may nevertheless be aided and abetted in developing his role by parents for whom he solves a conflict. He may himself represent "the joke" which reconciles father and mother, or he may develop his skills in an attempt to reconcile opposites. It is reported that the discrepancy between the roles of father and mother is moderately high.

His Effect on Group Satisfaction

The ironic fate of the dramatizer-joker has been discussed earlier. Although it is taken for granted that a good joker or spinner of fantasy is a serious necessity of social life, the success of candidates for the role is by no means assured. On the average, the joker or dramatizer tends to move the group away from satisfaction with interpersonal relations, as well as away from satisfaction with goal attainment. The latter he more or less intends and does not lament, but the former represents the kind of failure epitomized in the dual theatrical masks of comedy and tragedy: in the stereotype of the clown who outwardly jokes, but inwardly suffers.

18

Type UPB: Toward Emotional Supportiveness and Warmth

The member located in the upward-positive-backward part of the group space by his fellow members seems ascendant and expressive, open, warm, friendly, affectionate, nurturant, permissive, and rewarding to others. The UPB member seems free to give unconditional love and praise. In the realization of his own values he seems to be trying to move toward emotional supportiveness and warmth. "Everybody needs a little love all the time." "I never met a man I didn't like!" "There is no such thing as a bad boy!" [1]

How He Sees Himself and How Others See Him

For the person who tends to move strongly in the UPB direction, the self seems to be identified with the power to give and arouse affection. It is this power the UPB person counts on to solve his problems and those of the group. His feeling and his self-picture apparently get through. Observers and other group members typically see him as warm and personal. He correctly guesses that others will rate him high, and he rates himself high. The highest self-rating however, is given to the over-expansive UP member, who tends to identify himself with everything positive about all the members. The UPB member is the best-liked of all types by the observers, and is also well liked by group members. The group members give their very highest rating however, to his less ascendant neighbor, PB. Apparently group members tend to be put off a little

---

[1] These are probable value-statements of the UPB member.

252

by too much ascendance, even in the service of such a good thing as emotional supportiveness and warmth. Group members find the UPB member the most entertaining of all types, and he correctly guesses that they will rate him high. He does, however, make others feel he rates them low on self-confidence, which is probably part of the ascendance that detracts somewhat from his likeability for group members. Other members rate him very low on psychological inertia and on anxiety. He rates himself low on anxiety and correctly guesses that others will rate him low. It seems likely that he regards emotional supportiveness and warmth as almost a specific cure for anxiety, having received it himself; having learned to feel it and utilize it, and he passes it on to others in distress. Perhaps he tends to contrast himself with the UNF type, feeling himself to be a good parent who depends upon the power of love rather than a bad one who depends upon the power of aggression.

His Place in the Interaction Network

The UPB member has a prominent place in the interaction network. His total interaction initiated is high, though possibly not so high as the U type. He is high on addressing remarks to the group as a whole rather than to particular members and is high on receiving, in return. Each individual tends to address more interaction to him than he addresses to that one specifically in return, and so his total to individuals is relatively low. Like the other types on the upward side, he is likely to pay more attention to the group as a whole than to specific individuals. Although he is warm and personal in manner and content, he is still not so personal as he might be, if, for example, he showed a marked preference for addressing each individual specifically.

What Ideas and Values Will He Express?

In addition to his characteristic values in favor of emotional supportiveness and warmth, the UPB member is likely to speak for value-relativism and expression and for the rejection of conventional group beliefs, particularly, perhaps, religious beliefs. His values, taken together, somehow suggest the more liberal parent who tries to "temper the wind to the shorn lamb." When the question of punishment for the child arises, such a parent is likely to speak in favor of equalitarianism and permissive liberalism. His argument is that the child is a little older now than at the time of his last instruction, and that he should have more freedom; alternatively, the argument may be that the child is too young to be required to conform literally. The UPB member may speak in favor of social success as well as material success and power, but he sees himself as encouraging the young, allowing them to develop, and changing the hampering effects of tradition for the sake of growth.

The Quality of His Interaction

The UPB member entertains and makes social conversation by dramatizing and joking and by seeming friendly. His interest in others and his concern for them is shown in asking for information and asking for opinion, on both of which he tends to be high. On the other hand, he is low on activities that indicate work in the problem-solving direction. He is low on asking for suggestions, low on giving information and giving opinions. He apparently tends not to engage much in rational analysis or arguments. He is low on disagreeing and is not above average on agreeing. He is low on seeming unfriendly.

Possibly because he advances so few task-oriented statements, either information, or opinion, others are low in agreeing with him. Neither do they ask him for opinion or suggestion. However, they answer his requests for information by giving him information; they are likely to dramatize or joke and to seem friendly, as he does. One of the most interesting things, however, which does not fit the picture one gets so far, is the fact that the UPB member tends to be relatively high on receiving suggestions. We may suppose these most often come from the forward side of the space and consist of efforts to "check in" with him, or persuade him, as a leader of a potentially nonconventional or non-task-oriented faction, in the hope that he will help to bring others in that subgroup around.

Conflicts and Coalitions with Others

Arguments against the UPB proponent of emotional supportiveness and warmth come mostly from the UNF direction—from the proponent of autocratic authority. Arguments favoring group loyalty and cooperation and tough-minded assertiveness are also directed to him. The arguments are those parents might make about the proper course to take in the case of a disciplinary crisis with a child. The two positions that are taken, autocratic authority and emotional supportiveness and warmth, are sometimes felt on this basis to be naturally opposed directions. Actually, as their position in the diagnostic space implies, the proponents have one thing in common—the tendency toward ascendance. And so it comes about that the directions are partly similar, partly opposed, with the final result that they have no dependable relation to each other. They are essentially uncorrelated with each other as traits of individuals. Some individuals combine the two directions (the U type), some favor one but not the other, and some reject both (the D type). Thus we may recognize that when these two value-constellations are the focus of argument, as they typically are when either one is brought to prominence, the argument is partly one of two different proponents of ascendance. If the two are irreconcilable, it is partly because of the power struggle between the two proponents, not because the two directions of movement are completely opposite. The child is confronted with ascendance no matter which way the balance goes. Or perhaps it would be better to say, he is provided with ascendance as a model.

Personality Traits

The UPB member is likely to measure markedly high on the traits enthusiasm, talkativeness, extroversion, poise, spontaneity, and confidence. These traits suggest the easy passage into overt action of affectionate and sublimated sexual tendencies. The UPB member not only believes in emotional supportiveness and warmth, but apparently demonstrates it and plays it out directly. He may be high on the traits of his U neighbor; adventurous, thick-skinned, active, and dominant. Toward the UP side, he may show test traits predicting social status: dominance, social participation, sociability and leadership. Like the less ascendant P type, he may show the traits of trustfulness, accessibility, intellectual efficiency, and ego strength.

How He Sees His Parents

The distinguishing characteristic of the parental picture as reported by UPB members is that both parents are very high on emotional supportiveness and warmth, higher than for any other type. This seems appropriate and plausible, not only in terms of the general hypothesis that parents tend to produce their like, but in terms of the more specific hypothesis that affectionate feeling shown toward the child tends to reduce his anxiety, and vice versa, that if he does not receive affectionate feeling, then his anxiety tends to reduce his affectionate feeling. It may be true that affection is partly learned, but we also have reason to believe that it is a derivative of basic sexual drives, and hence we may suppose that it is partly *released,* and not just learned. It is a major hypothesis underlying much that is said in this book, that *anxiety is one of the most important determinants of whether the basic sexual drives are released into the derivative and sublimated forms of affectionate feeling, or whether they remain anchored in more primitive forms of expression.* If this is true, the power to feel affection, or love, is "passed on" as it were, from parent to child through the care of him that reduces his anxiety and makes his affectionate feeling available. The child is thus *given* the power to reduce anxiety—in himself as well as in others. This power to reduce anxiety is probably the most important general-purpose reward that may be applied in the socialization of the child. The child is not only socialized, but he is given the most important resource he may have in the socialization of others: the power to give affection and to elicit affection. This is the resource which makes it possible for the parent who has it to overcome the anxiety, the aggression, the negative and backward feelings that the child typically develops on the occasion of the inhibitory demands made of him in the process of socialization.

A movement of the parent in the forward direction, toward the maintenance or establishment of new group norms, is typically met by tendencies of the child to disagree and seem negative, as well as to move backward toward disobedience and deviance. In the successful episode of socialization the child is not left in the negative and backward part of the space. He is rather "brought around" by something like joking or dramatizing, which takes the literal character out of the values involved by allowing him an expression of deviant impulses through dramatization of fantasy or some other relativizing means of reducing tension, and finally by the arousal, or re-establishment of affectionate feeling.

The normal cycle of socialization is probably very much like the normal phase movements that my colleagues and I have described as characteristic of task-oriented small groups (18; 19; 40; 128). The power to elicit affectionate feeling by giving affectionate feeling is like "money in the bank." It must be drawn upon and partially expended during the phase of socialization that emphasizes inhibitory demands and discipline. In successful socialization the balance in the bank never falls so low that the alarm "insufficient funds" is sent out. But if "insufficient funds" is the constant condition, the child is never rescued from his own anxiety and hostility—he is left to struggle with overpowering and frightening feelings as best he may, and develops into one of the types on the negative side of the space. Such is the theory advanced here (see the last section of Chapter 8).

The UPB child is one whose parents have been especially well supplied with the power to give and elicit affection. They are, on the other hand, usually about average on inhibitory demands and discipline and are not under much temptation to make demands that go beyond their "ability to pay." They are also only about average on optimistic idealism versus pessimistic cynicism and so are not likely to inspire the more restrained, refined, and conventional forms of altruism in the child. They have the affectionate foundation, but not the forward direction. The discrepancy between parents is apt to be average. A consolidated and highly verbalized or abstract set of values is not very likely.

His Effect on Group Satisfaction

It may come as a surprise, but inference from the location of satisfaction with interpersonal relations in the diagnostic space indicates that the UPB type has no predictable relation to this aspect of satisfaction. From the point of view of the other group members, the UPB member is too ascendant, too talkative, and tends too much to crowd others out—this is a liability. On the other hand, he is positive in emotional feeling, and this is an advantage. Which effect will outweigh the other, or whether they will approximately cancel each other out, is anybody's guess.

As to satisfaction with task-accomplishment, the contribution of the UPB type is apt to be negative. It is interesting to return for a moment to the comments that pointed out that the UPB direction is not the opposite of the UNF direction, but simply is unpredictably related to it. However, the proponent of inhibitory demands and discipline *feels* he is speaking for movement in the forward direction, whereas the proponent of emotional supportiveness and warmth *feels* he is speaking for the protection of a backward-tending child or a similar type of group member; and the movements forward and backward are opposite. Insofar as the proponent of emotional supportiveness and warmth prevails, the child is brought toward the positive side, but task-accomplishment momentarily suffers. In the longer run, the foundation is being strengthened for possible later movements in the forward direction. Whether the child will move substantially forward, however, will depend upon forces that the UPB type is not likely to bring to bear. This also happens in groups of other kinds. The UPB type may perform a most important function, but by himself will not tend to bring the group closer to satisfaction with goal attainment. On the contrary, unless counteracted, he will tend to impair it. In fact, he often works in a leadership coalition with a more forward type and perhaps expects to be counteracted to some extent.

19

Type P:
Toward Equalitarianism

The member located in the positive part of the group space by his fellow members seems friendly, sociable, and informal. He approaches others as equals, neither ascendant nor submissive. He seems interested in them as individual persons with needs and motives of their own, as important as his own. He is not concerned about either their conventionality or their deviance, nor with either their task-relevance nor their status. In the realization of his own values he seems to move toward equalitarianism. "There should be equality for everyone—because we are all human beings."

How He Sees Himself and How Others See Him

The person moving in the P direction seems to be an appreciator of others. He tends to rate others high on their interest in the task and in their value for a logical task. He appreciates backward as well as forward movement, in that he also tends to rate others high on being entertaining. His aim seems to be to elicit positive reactions from others. He guesses that others will like him and feel admiration for him. He is liked and admired by the members, although not quite so much as his adjacent type, PB. He does, however, elicit the highest rating on admiration from the observers. Since the observers in the study from which the finding comes were identified with the task given to the group—with authority in this sense—it is understandable that they might tend to admire a type somewhat further forward than the group members.

There is some tendency for the P type to overlook or deny negative traits. He is least likely of all types to see others as anxious or as having psychological inertia. And he is least likely to make others feel he rates them high on either of these traits. His tendency to overlook or deny negative traits is thus understood by others. In a similar way the P type is least likely to make others feel he rates them high on domination. His self-picture seems positive but modest. He is modest in the sense that he is the least likely of all types to rate himself high on understanding, although he is in fact adjacent to the type that is actually given the highest rating (the DP type). The P type seems either to lack or to deny negative feelings in himself, being least likely of all types to guess that others may see him as resentful, and in this guess he is essentially accurate. (Type UP is actually seen as least resentful.) The P type is seen by group members as least individualistic, hence as highly identified with the group. He does not, however (in contrast to type UP), seem to confuse himself with the group as a whole. He perceives the group as made up of individuals separate from himself, but deals with these differences by wishing all to be equal. The ability to give appreciation is very important to him, and it seems to be this ability or power with which he most closely associates his self picture. He "accentuates the positive" to elicit affection and love from others.

His Place in the Interaction Network

The P type is neither an over- nor an under-participator. He is average on total interaction initiated. He is average or in the middle of the group in initiating remarks to the group as a whole rather than to particular individuals. This is not for lack of encouragement, since he is high on receiving acts from others. Apparently he prefers to be in the position of receiving. He generally tends to agree with information and suggestion from others. He tends to receive more from each individual than he addresses to that individual specifically in return, which is a general indication that he is supported, but he does not increase his participation even though thus encouraged. He is average on the sum addressed to specific individuals. His place in the middle ranks of total participation is congruent with his desire for equality among all members.

What Ideas and Values Will He Express?

The P type believes and says "There should be equality for everyone—because we are all human beings." "Everybody should have an equal chance and an equal say." Although he values work and forward movement of the group, he does not want to have to accept a hierarchy as a means to it, or as a result of it. "A group of equals will work a lot better than a group with a rigid hierarchy." Even leadership based directly on function he prefers to regard as temporary and partly fictional: "In a small group there should be no real leaders—everybody should have an equal say." And although forward movement may be desirable at times, the desire for efficiency should not be carried too far: "In any group it is more important to keep a friendly atmosphere than to be efficient." Desire to accomplish tasks or meet the demands of the environmental situation does not justify any arbitrary exercise of authority: "No matter what the circumstances, one should never arbitrarily tell people what they have to do."

Some of the values likely to be expressed by the P type lean toward emotional supportiveness and warmth. "Each one should get what he needs—the things we have belong to all of us." As he resists the tendency of those higher in the hierarchy to control others, so he tends to try to change the traditional system insofar as it leaves those lower in the hierarchy at a disadvantage. He will speak for permissive liberalism. "Poverty could be almost entirely done away with if we made certain basic changes in our social and economic system." "The only true prosperity of the nation as a whole must be based on the prosperity of the working class." He identifies with the underprivileged and is ready, upon occasion, to take action. "It is the duty of every good citizen to correct anti-minority remarks made in his presence." "There has been too much talk and not enough real action in doing away with racial discrimination."

In the later statement we may sense a certain tough-mindedness turned toward a more typically tender-minded goal. This should be no surprise, since every direction of movement in the value-space may function in part as a defense of the personality, which helps to counteract underlying, possibly repressed tendencies to move in some other, perhaps opposite, direction. Equalitarianism may be motivated in part by a need to counteract tendencies toward autocratic authority, in the self as well as in some other, and so may be expressed in a value on identification with the underprivileged. The more subtle point, which may be missed, is that not all equalitarianism is so motivated. A value placed on equalitarianism is equally compatible with a value on directly forward movement, the value expression of which is conservative group belief.

The value-positions which combine positive movement with forward movement are those in favor of social solidarity and progress, altruistic love, and salvation through love. The P type who speaks for equalitarianism may also on occasion speak for these values, and combine with those further forward than himself who believe in them. So long as the authority figure is positive he may be acceptable to the equalitarian. Similarly, the P member is not opposed to those who are somewhat higher in the hierarchy than himself, providing they are positive, and he will speak for social success on occasion, though he himself is less ascendant. He will also speak on occasion for trust in the goodness of others, though he is generally less submissive than the usual proponents of this value.

The Quality of His Interaction

The most characteristic acts of the P type are seeming friendly (see page 102) and asking for opinion (see page 120). In these categories of behavior, the P type is higher than any other directional type. This seems most congruent with the value he places upon equality of members. To ask for opinion is to indicate a respect for the other as a thinking and feeling individual. It does not beg the question as to whether the other will wish to respond in the forward or the backward direction, toward the ascendant or submissive side. It turns the initiative over to the other and leaves him free to take whatever direction he likes. Much the same can be said of asking for information, on which the P type is also high. He is markedly low on seeming unfriendly.

The most characteristic responses of others to the approach of the positive type are seeming friendly and giving information. These responses are markedly likely. Friendliness is a response the P type tends to value, and giving information is a logically appropriate response to his requests for information. He is likely, as well, to receive opinion, and suggestion, (the next steps forward and upward in a problem-solving process). Dramatizing and joking are also high in response to him.

On receiving information, suggestions, and friendly remarks, the P type is friendly in return, likely to agree, and markedly unlikely to disagree. His pattern of asking for opinion and avoiding disagreement is unlikely to arouse disagreement, laughing or showing tension, or unfriendly behavior from others. In a way, his pattern also tends to leave him with the unreciprocated role of asking for opinion and information, since on the average, others tend not to ask him for his opinion. But he does receive something in return. Not only does he elicit positive responses and avoid negative responses, but he also tends to receive suggestions to an unusual extent. It is probable that he is a potential representative of his peers—the equalitarians—vis-a-vis the forward leadership, and opinions and suggestions are addressed to him for his approval on behalf of his peer group.

Conflicts and Coalitions with Others

As we have seen, the interactive role taken by the P type tends to prevent rather than to provoke disagreement and argument. But holding a strong value on equality puts him implicitly, if not explicitly, in opposition to those who oppose equality, and exposes him to their opposition. If he receives opposition it is likely to come from those on the upward and negative side, the proponents of autocratic authority, of tough-minded assertiveness, and of rugged individualism and gratification. These types believe they are superior and tend to have a certain contempt for those who try to keep the general social tone friendly and moderate. They feel threatened by the softer sentiments of affection, and resent the threat that they may be dragged down from their position of superiority to one of mediocrity. The equalitarian disagrees with them, but he is handicapped and vulnerable. Since he wishes to avoid disagreement and overt conflict, he may accede to the values of autocratic authority unless he is needed to defend those persons weaker than himself. If the weaker group members are conspicuously wronged, and their defense is at stake, he will join them against the proponent of autocratic authority. But in the struggle between the ideological right and the ideological left, he is the pivotal member, since he is ambivalent and may switch his vote either way.

The equalitarian is not in favor of those who prefer a position at the bottom of the heap, or those who recommend lower status from a sense of alienation. He does not agree with those who advocate failure and withdrawal, rejection of social success, or even those who recommend self-sacrifice for values. There is some probability that these arguments will be made to him, since he takes the initiative in asking for information and opinion from those who are ordinarily silent. But if so, he joins with those on the positive side who recommend trust in the goodness of others and salvation through love.

Personality Traits

The person of type P is apt to test markedly high on the traits of intellectual efficiency and ego strength. In addition to these traits he may show those of adjacent types to a lesser degree. He may show some of the UP traits of predicted social status, dominance, social participation, sociability and leadership. But these are more ascendant traits than those which are most characteristic of him. On the UPF side he may show to some degree the traits of sociability and persistence. If he leans to the PF side he may seem conscientious, conservative, and high on role-playing ability. He may have some of the DPF traits, practicality, responsibility, submissiveness, with will-control and character stability. On the more submissive DP side he may seem high on responsibility and achievement and show the traits of stability and calmness. Finally if he tends to lean toward the UPB type, he may show to some degree the traits of enthusiasm, talkativeness, extroversion, and show poise, spontaneity, and confidence.

In general all of these traits can be construed to have a socially positive character, and a personality that centers in the cluster seems plausible. One would hardly expect to find a person who encompassed them all, who was both calm and enthusiastic, both dominant and submissive, but a flexibility that goes with high ego-strength might go far in uniting these otherwise opposite traits. There is a freedom from socially negative traits that suggests either a happy endowment or a successful process of growing up. Perhaps there are some "false positives" who maintain the position defensively, but most of the type P members must hold their position from a sense of strength.

How He Sees His Parents

Both father and mother are seen similarly by the equalitarian; the discrepancy between their roles is low. They are both high on optimistic idealism (versus pessimistic cynicism), both are high on emotional supportiveness and warmth, and both are low on inhibitory demands and discipline. This is, as usual, a description of the same type of person as the subject himself, seen as he appears in the role of parent. Whether it is wishful or accurate, is difficult to tell, but it is consistent with the type of socializing agent one would expect to be able to bring the child out of the negative phases of his socialization, to awaken in him feelings of affection and security, and to present him with a hopeful desire to perform more successfully in the future. Such parents might well convince the child that the arbitrary exercise of authority is never necessary, since they so seldom employ it, and leave him hopeful that affection and respect for the individual will always, or nearly always, bring the best results.

In his treatment of others in the group, the P child of P parents acts upon the conviction and hope that affection and respect will work, as it did with him. He takes the role toward others that his parents took toward him. If he could start as an adult with all the other group members as infants, his efforts might produce the desired result with higher frequency. Unfortunately, he deals with the infinite variety of nature. Some of his fellow members are tougher, more negative, more rigid, more anxious and neurotic, perhaps, than he. With these people he may not succeed, and he had best join forces with others on the positive side, as he does. The balance of power may help him accomplish what with affectionate equalitarian feeling alone, he cannot do.

His Effect on Group Satisfaction

The equalitarian P member tends to move the group toward satisfaction with interpersonal relations. He does not himself crowd others out by too high a rate of participation, and he turns the initiative for content and changes of direction over to others. He tends to moderate the tendencies of other members, toward too much dominance on the part of some, and too much submissiveness on the part of others. He supplies affectionate concern which is usually in short supply. He provides a worthy object of liking and admiration. There is some evidence that he is less subject to conflict than his fellow members on the negative side, though in the case of the "false positive" this might not be true.

On the other hand, the P member does not have any predictable effect on satisfaction with goal attainment. He tends to move the group neither forward nor backward. This is the reason why, in a task-oriented group, he can hardly function as the leader, even though he may be well-liked and admired. The requirements of a task-leader in a task-oriented group are given by the requirements of external authority or the impersonal external situation. There is no assurance that these will be congruent with the maintainance of internal solidarity and equality within the group—they may be or may not be—the two dimensions are orthogonal. Concerned, as he is, primarily with maintaining equality and affectionate solidarity within the group, the member who tries always to move in the P direction is sometimes unable to meet the reality requirements of the task. In this dilemma, he typically chooses to forego task leadership, as indeed he must.

20

Type PF:
Toward Altruistic Love

The member located in the positive-forward part of the group space by his fellow members seems agreeable and friendly, task- and value-oriented. He responds to task-oriented attempts of others, but does not take the initiative. He is not submissive, however, nor is he ascendant, but equalitarian. He seems serious and responsible about group agreements. In the realization of his own values, he seems to move toward a kind of dedicated, quiet, altruistic love. "We are all born to love—it is the principle of existence and its only true end."

How He Sees Himself and How Others See Him

The person who moves strongly in the PF direction seems to see himself as the good child of a good parent. He has experienced and believes in the power of goodness and idealization to make things right in the world. He sees the good in others rather than the bad and tends to raise their status. He is the most likely of all types to feel and express admiration, and the least likely to rate others as dominating, even those who are.

His Place in the Interaction Network

One might expect that a type of person who tends so strongly to raise the status of others and to reinforce them would himself be quite submissive, with a low rate of interaction, but in fact the PF type supplies something so much in demand—namely, agreement—that he is drawn into participation by the tendency of others to address remarks to him. In total interaction initiated he is average, and in remarks addressed to the group as a whole he is also average, but in the sum of acts received he is high. He tends to receive more from each individual than he gives to him. On remarks addressed to specific individuals, however, he is average. He has a strategic position in the interaction network in that he provides a way for others through the bottleneck of skepticism and resistance in the advancing of their ideas toward group acceptance.

What Ideas and Values Will He Express?

The PF member tends to specialize in agreeing with ideas and values, rather than enunciating them, but those most central to him and which he is most likely to initiate are those that express an attitude of devotional love. "We are all born to love—it is the principle of existence and its only true end." The love which is felt, presumably, and meant, is not erotic love nor the desire for sexual gratification, but rather altruistic love, "Christian love" or "agape." "Tenderness is more important than passion in love." So far as the love is sexual—and, developmentally, it is presumably a derivative of basic sexual drives—it is more like the love of parent for child than that between the sexes. It is closely related, one would think, to the Christian conception that all men are children of God, all needing care and affection, alike and equal as brothers and sisters are, bound to care for each other as the parent cares for them. "It is sympathetic love among persons which alone gives significance to life." The value-position implies a belief that if the familial ideal of love could only be extended to all men, then the motivation to do all the things necessary to solve men's practical problems would develop, and the main obstructions to their solution would be overcome. This belief is part of the optimistic idealism characteristic of the PF member.

The PF member is moderately likely to speak for equalitarianism. He is also moderately likely to speak for conservative group beliefs. For him there is presumably a psychological tie as well as a historical one between the experience of love and the feeling of faith. For those who have had the experience, it is the parent's love which gives the model and the experiential base for the child's love of the parent, and his identification with him. The parent is the child's first God, the omniscient and omnipotent law-giver, his first contact with tradition, his first idea of society. If the parent himself is identified with society, with its basic norms, with its impersonal or "higher" sources of authority, as expressed in the symbols of religion, the nation, the law, and the serious group beliefs, then the child naturally transfers his attitude toward the parent on to these more abstract symbols of higher authority. These conditions would be generally fulfilled if the parent himself were PF, idealistic, optimistic, and altruistic.

The PF member is moderately likely to speak also for the values of his less ascendant neighbors: for trust in the goodness of others; for salvation through love; and for self-knowledge and subjectivity. On the more ascendant side, he may speak for group loyalty and cooperation, for social solidarity and progress, and perhaps even for social success, though this does not seem characteristic, since a value on social success has a self-inflating rather than a modest altruistic quality.

The Quality of His Interaction

The most characteristic thing about the interaction of the PF member is his marked tendency to agree, (see p. 109) and thus to elicit opinion from others in turn. The PF member is high on seeming friendly and low on disagreement, low in showing tension or laughing, and low on seeming unfriendly. Not only does he seem to be an attractive person to talk to, but he is also high on soliciting interaction, that is, asking for information, asking for opinion, and asking for suggestion. He is also moderately high on giving opinion and giving suggestion himself, and is actively engaged in group tasks, not just a "yes" man.

Others are markedly likely to address opinions to him. They are moderately high on agreeing with him, seeming friendly, and on giving information and suggestion, as well as markedly high on giving him opinion. That they consider him as actively involved in developing the content and not simply as a "yes man" is indicated by the fact that they are moderately high in asking him for suggestion. However, they are low on asking him for information and opinion; he tends to ask them instead. Both he and his respondents are low on showing tension or laughing, neither do they dramatize or joke much.

The general impression given by the PF member and those he interacts with is one of strongly cooperative forward movement, unusually symmetrical or similar as between members, and unusually free of status conflicts or other obstructions. The main asymmetry is in the exchange of information and opinion. The PF member asks for these two types of activity, and others give them. Apparently he asks for information and opinion as a part of his general positive tendency, and they respond to his requests. It may be that he tends to draw downward members into the group, who prefer to confine themselves to information as the safest and most noncommital form of interaction.

Conflicts and Coalitions with Others

One might gain the impression from the description above that nobody would argue with the PF member, since he seems to present so little opposition. Yet he does stand for a value-position which is not acceptable to all types, and they do on occasion argue against him. The member most threatened by him, whether he actually voices the opposition or not, is probably the DNB type, who wishes to settle for failure and withdrawal. As a "down and outer" the DNB member finds altruistic love, with its inherent optimistic idealism, fatuous, unfounded, and objectionable. He does not believe in "pie in the sky by-and-by." He does not want to be cheered up, rescued, or made to feel better by false fantasies. He hates "do-gooders," and will tell them so on rare occasions, especially if cornered and smothered with talk of love. Love is just what he is sure he cannot have. Similarly, the member in the DN position, who maintains his self-respect by the rejection of social success, is sure he cannot have love either. The possibility of receiving altruistic love disturbs his defenses: it would obligate him, if he ever gave in to the temptation to receive it. The member in the B position, who believes in the rejection of conservative group beliefs is threatened by the tendency of the PF member to reinforce forward movement, group norms, and belief in the symbols of a "higher authority," particularly, of course, a literal or indeed any other kind of belief in God.

From the UN side, the proponent of tough-minded assertiveness tends to feel contempt for the PF member and to argue against him on occasion, as one who has "sold out" and become a "yes-man," because he tends to support those in authority. The UNB proponent of rugged individualism and gratification has essentially the same reaction, whereas the UB member, though not so hostile, feels and expresses joking resistance to the PF member because of his threat to value-relativism and expression.

There is a certain justification for the attitudes of the three ascendant types just mentioned, if we may believe the results of the study upon which this book is based. These members seem to understand what is not intuitively evident to all types, namely that the PF type is the most likely of all types to *agree* with statements upholding autocratic authority. The proponent of altruistic love, PF, is also most likely of all types to agree with statements in favor of group loyalty and cooperation, and with value-determined restraint. He does not himself *make* statements favoring autocratic authority and value-determined restraint, but he will accede to them when made by other more ascendant and more negative types. His optimistic idealism and his altruism is his vulnerability. He tends to overlook, deny, or beautify the negative and the ascendant when it is associated with parental figures, with group norms, and with symbols of higher authority. It is as if, in making his own identification with father and mother, he tended to overcome and forget whatever negative reactions he may have had. This is the "sell-out," the act of "treason," the "yellow-dog contract," the psychological bargain, for which the unredeemed rebels can not forgive him. If he were honest, they feel, he would be fighting autocratic authority and everything associated with it, as they are.

However one's own sentiments may go in this ever-regenerated conflict, one lesson should be remembered as an observer and theorizer— there is probably a *systematic discrepancy* between the value-statements people will initiate, and those to which they will accede. If this is indeed generally true, it may help us to understand many of the fascinating and bewildering alliances that people form, both in intimate interpersonal relations and in large-scale social movements. It is suggested that the enunciators of certain value-positions may not accept the value-statements as applied to themselves personally, but tend to look for and find other vulnerable persons who will accede, but who, left alone, would never enunciate the value. So the value-position is contractually stabilized as a norm, an ideology, a direction of social-psychological movement, a social movement. It takes two to make a contract, it may take at least two such reciprocal types to give an ideology a social existence. It is well-known that ideology makes strange bedfellows; perhaps some types of ideology can *only* be made by strange bedfellows. (See also the descriptions of coalitions of the UP type, and of the DPB type.)

Personality Traits

The PF type is likely to be markedly high on a set of traits which suggest an easy and successful process of identification of the child with the parent of the same sex. For the male, the traits may include masculinity; for the female there is presumably a corresponding conventional feminine set of traits. Persons in this role type of either sex are likely to be conscientious, conservative, and high on role-playing ability. The latter ability as measured, may either reflect some psychological means by which the role of the parent is assumed, or it may be an outcome of the psychological security given by a firm point of reference. In association with the other two traits, it certainly does seem congruent with the picture of a relatively unproblematic taking-over of that which the conservative part of the society expects—the masculine role by the male child and, by inference, the feminine role for the female child.

It should be recalled that the study upon which the personality findings are based included only male subjects, and if the interpretation suggested here is correct, it would imply that the corresponding process for females would be the taking over of the conservative version of the female role in the culture. It is perhaps true that an avowed value upon "altruistic love" and even upon optimistic idealism is more characteristic of females than males in our culture. It is probably true, in any case, that an avowed value upon "love" is regarded as "feminine" by those around the UNB position, which is the aggressively masculine, hostile, and anti-conservative position. It may well be true that the sex-role-rebels of both sexes tend to be found around the NB position, because of an inability to identify with more conservative and traditional definitions of their respective sex roles, whether feminine or masculine.

In addition to the most characteristic traits, just indicated, the PF member may show the traits of adjacent types to a moderate extent. The UPF type is sociable, and persistent; the UF type shows sophistication. Tests of the UP type predict social status, dominance, social participation, sociability and leadership. The P type of person tends to be trustful and accessible, with intellectual efficiency and ego strength. The DP types tend to be calm and stable. The DPF type is practical, responsible, has will control, character stability, and is submissive.

This constellation of traits seems consistent with the conception of the PF direction as essentially related to a successful process of identification through love with a parent felt to be good, and through him or her, with the conservative virtues of the traditional sex role. It is worth noting that the conventional sex-role identification of both sexes may be associated with either ascendance or submission, with either a comparatively free flow of basic instinctual drives, particularly those associated with sexuality, or a constriction of them. It is presumably a mistake to suppose that identification with the PF parent necessarily involves a strong repression of sexuality. What is more likely to be repressed is aggression, and the negative and backward tendencies that may be associated with it. These may include deviant or pre-adult forms of sex roles, of course, especially those which are held onto as defenses against the threat of conservative, adult sex roles.

How He Sees His Parents

The parents of the PF type are typically seen as similar to each other, the discrepancies between them low. It is worth noting that PF members, who test highest on conservatism, and who tend to agree with value-statements in favor of autocratic authority, in fact do not describe the father and mother in their families as taking the roles commonly associated with the traditional German authoritarian family. Both parents are presumably very high on optimistic idealism (versus pessimistic cynicism), and thus they present the content of idealistic values to the child directly. The father is described as average on inhibitory demands and discipline, and on emotional supportiveness and warmth. The mother is low on inhibitory demands and discipline (thus fitting the stereotyped expectation to a certain extent), and average on emotional supportiveness and warmth.

The action of the parent in bringing the powerful forces of affection and identification to the service of abstract ideals is probably critical in the formation of the type. If the parent is not himself identified with some of the more abstract symbols of higher authority such as those found clustered around conceptions of religion, the nation, the law, or the like, then the child who admires and loves the parent is not likely to emerge with an accepting attitude toward those symbols. On the other hand, if the child does not love and idealize the parent, then, even if the parent is himself identified with some of these symbols, the child will not identify with them. There seems to be no necessary connection between identification with the parent through love on the one hand, and conservative group beliefs, religious faith and the like on the other. The PF direction, in other words, is not in any particular sense "primary," rooted in some *one* basic drive, such as love (as the direction P may be), or some irreducible fact of the social condition, such as the tendency to form social norms (as the direction F may be), but instead is the result of a combination of two such elements by the personality and action of the parents. The combination is taught to the child.

The thing which is taught, in part, is the power or the ability to idealize. This ability, much needed in groups, and usually in short supply, is a part of what is ordinarily called leadership. This ability, along with sufficient ascendance, or sufficient help from others to win the power struggle, can provide a group with the power to overcome internal hostility, deviance, and passivity, and to harness its resources of liking and affection in the service of task achievement.

His Effect on Group Satisfaction

The PF member tends to perform a rare and improbable feat—he tends to move the group simultaneously toward satisfaction with interpersonal relations and toward satisfaction with goal attainment. This distinction he shares with only two other types: his less ascendant adjacent type, DPF, and with DF. Both of these latter types, however, presumably would need more help to emerge through the bottlenecks of the power structure than the PF type, and hence would less likely be effective. The UPF type, while he has many of the same characteristics, does not tend to move the group toward satisfaction with interpersonal relations. He is too ascendant.

Thus, either too much dominance or too much submissiveness may be critical in preventing the group simultaneously attaining both task satisfaction and satisfaction with interpersonal relations. The two types of satisfaction mentioned are group-oriented, whereas the kind of satisfaction involved in either extreme dominance, or extreme submissiveness, seem to be more egocentrically-oriented, a satisfaction of the acting member alone.

The balance maintained by the PF type is thus very precarious, but it can be successful. When the PF member is successful and leads the group in his preferred direction, various group members tend to check the following kinds of statements after the meeting: "This group was highly motivated to do a good job." "The reasoning in the discussion was clear and logical." "I liked the dispatch with which the problem was handled." A value on altruistic love seems to be good for the task, though it may not at first be obvious.

21

Type F: Toward Conservative Group Beliefs

The member located in the forward part of the group space by his fellow members seems primarily task- and value-oriented. He is neither ascendant nor submissive, but directly to the point, instrumental, analytical, and problem-solving. He is concerned with the work of the group as conservatively defined, or given to it by commitments of the past. He tries to implement the serious beliefs of the group, and to shape group opinion and precedent. He is strictly impersonal and affectively neutral, neither friendly nor unfriendly, but seriously searching for truth and the best solution, the best precedent. He does not try to impose his opinions or interpretations, but is tentative. In the realization of his own values he seems to move toward the conservation of the best in group beliefs and precedents. If religious he may say "The chief end of man is nothing other than eternal salvation." "In addition to faith we need help from God in order to resist temptation." If not religious, he will still feel that one should keep the faith with some form of ultimate truth.

How He Sees Himself and How Others See Him

The F member may depend importantly upon "the will to believe" for the security of his self-picture. His mode of adjustment is one of fastening and confining his conscious attention and will to the desired goals. It may be that he tends, more than usual, to lack understanding of repressed tendencies. Repressed tendencies do not, however, lose all their attraction. An inability to see clearly or to understand that which nevertheless attracts one seems to give rise to a feeling of curiosity. A feeling of curiosity is apparently typically aroused by that which is backward in relation to one's own position—in the realm of fantasy, freedom, humor, or expression—that which is denied or pushed toward the unconscious by one's sense of values.

For whatever reason, the person moving in the F direction is the type most likely to rate others as arousing his curiosity. His dedication to movement toward the realization of values, his need to maintain faith in the reality and worth of his values may require that he overlook or minimize his tendencies, perceptions, and interests in other directions. But other persons who epitomize these tendencies stimulate repressed parts of his personality and make him feel conflict. They are embodiments of temptation. Not only does the F type feel more curiosity than other types, but he also makes others feel that he holds them in this peculiar sort of double regard—he does not quite understand them, nor approve, but he is fascinated and preoccupied by their deviations. He rates himself low on favoring expression and gratification and he rates others low on acceptance of authority, but acknowledges a feeling of curiosity about others nevertheless.

His Place in the Interaction Network

The person moving directly forward in the value space, neither toward ascendance nor submission, is average in total participation initiated. He does not appear to have a critical place in the interaction network. He is neither a particular source of acts addressed to the group as a whole, nor is he a particularly sought-after target of acts. He is average on rate of acts received. He tends to address each particular member in about the same degree that he himself is addressed by that person; his sum of acts addressed to specific individuals is average. Perhaps this lack of distinguishing characteristics is made more understandable by pointing out that the quantitative interaction network reflects essentially a hierarchical power structure, with positive and negative gates or bottlenecks at each rank—the network reflects mostly the dimensions upward-downward and positive-negative. The F type, as such, is neutral or average on these dimensions, but distinguished on another: his identification with the compulsions and constraints placed on action by reason of the existence of common values or social norms. The F member chooses to exert his influence by working to increase the motivating and binding power of value-consensus.

What Ideas and Values Will He Express?

Conservative group beliefs are not necessarily related to Christian fundamentalism, but in many groups in our culture they probably are. Belief in God, a life after death, and a life on earth instrumentally oriented to salvation in the next world are common features of persons who tend strongly in the forward direction. "Every person should have complete faith in some supernatural power whose decisions he obeys without question." "Many events in human history took place only because a Supreme Being stepped in to make them happen." "Every explanation of man and the world is incomplete unless it takes into account God's will." "The chief end of man is nothing other than eternal salvation." "In addition to faith we need help from God in order to resist temptation." "Life would hardly be worth living without the promise of immortality and life after death."

A literal religious orthodoxy may involve a distrust of science: "Theology will ultimately prove more important for mankind than the sciences." "Scientists should take no part in politics." It may also involve an unquestioning acceptance of duly constituted religious authority: "We should believe without a question all that we are taught by the Church." However, orthodoxy need not be so literal and specific: "The most important aim of the churches at the present time should be to encourage a spiritual worship and a sense of communion with the highest."

The F direction is conservative also in the sense of economic, social, and political attitudes. The person who is identified with this position tends to resist changes that disturb traditional beliefs, traditional localism, traditional concentration of wealth, and traditional political arrangements. Science is distrusted not only because it tends to disturb traditional beliefs, but also because it is associated with technological change. Urbanism tends to disturb traditional rural or suburban localism: "Modern life is too much concentrated in cities; the government should take steps to encourage a 'return to the country.' " Strong national government, however, may also tend to threaten traditional localism and concentration of wealth: "The nationalization of the great industries is likely to lead to inefficiency, bureaucracy, and stagnation." "Production and trade should be free from government interference." The traditional class structure and stereotypes should remain undisturbed: "Only people with a definite minimum of intelligence and education should be allowed to vote."

The F member does not identify himself with mankind in general, nor does he trust people in general. But on the other hand, he does not regard himself individually as the source of authority. His is an impersonal orientation—God or the local representative of God is the source of authority, defined by the traditional interpreter, often the church or its equivalent. More specifically it is the locally-based church or its equivalent that is important—the interpreter of God that represents the F member's own social class, ethnic group, and economic position. There may seem to be some contradiction between a localism that distrusts a large national government, but trusts an even more powerful God. The contradiction is removed when it is realized that God, the afterlife, and the way to salvation are locally interpreted by the F type. The ultimate source of authority, God, can thus be made to judge in any way desired. The national government, however, and the legal regulation emanating from it is not interpreted by local judges, and has ultimate sanctions—the national government maintains a monopoly on physical force. Forward movement is movement toward traditional *local* social norms, attributed to the local God without much fear of contradiction.

The localistic attitudes *may* be extended to apply to the nation in times of war and with regard to foreign threats: "My country right or wrong" is a saying which expresses this expanding of identification. A more fleeting recognition of the national government is shown in the statement: "In taking part in any form of world organization, this country should make certain that none of its independence and power is lost." But these are extensions of localism made under the pressure of external threat. With regard to the distribution of wealth and power within the nation, the conservative retracts the boundaries of the territory, population, and government, with which he identifies, back to the local level where his own traditional social norms are maintained.

In addition to statements favoring conservative group beliefs the F member will on occasion voice all of the other value-positions on the forward side of the space. But always the localistic context within which the present group has its setting should be understood. Thus, the F member may speak for social solidarity and progress, but this assumes that the interacting group should also retain solidarity with the larger group which forms its local context, and that it should work toward the goals of that larger group. Similarly when the F member speaks in favor of autocratic authority, it is autonomy of the local source of authority that he has in mind. Similarly he may speak in favor of altruistic love within the local group, and value-determined restraint, but these values are for the sake of the local group. And finally, if the F member speaks of salvation through love, self-knowledge and subjectivity, and self-sacrifice for values, one should take into account his basic impersonality, the unspoken context of the local group or society, and the assumption of traditional social norms and goals.

The Quality of His Interaction

The F member in the interacting small group tends to think of the group as a task force, working instrumentally toward the goals given by a local organization of society, which is accepted as the more ultimate source of authority. The goals of the task group are not thought of as self-generated, but as received and accepted from the parent group. The guiding values and rules for accomplishing the task are essentially given from the outside also. The problem of the group is to work deductively, it is felt, from the given goals, values, and rules to a definition of their proper application to the specific problem at hand. Thus, there is a major emphasis on reasoning rationally from given premises, and on extending action instrumentally from conclusions so derived. The ultimate ideal is a completely worked-out program so detailed that every object to be dealt with is immediately recognizable as an instance covered by a general rule, which is immediately applicable to the specific situation. This approach emphasizes deduction and not induction. The most characteristic type of interaction in the small work group is giving opinion, which includes not only the giving of value-judgments, but also the main logical operations of classification, rational analysis, and impersonal inference.

In addition to giving opinion, on which the F member is likely to be markedly high (see page 112), he is also likely to be moderately high on giving suggestions and asking for them. In this he shows a balance between ascendance and submission, but he always shows concern for the task, a concentration which is further evident in his low rates of dramatizing and joking as well as low rates of showing tension and laughing. It is worth noting, however, that he is only average on asking for information and giving it. Information is the starting point in an *inductive* approach to problem solving, but the member in full forward movement is *deductively* rather than inductively inclined and is less concerned about information than about drawing inferences from general rules and values. Other members are also low in rates of asking him for information.

As the F member is markedly high in his rate of giving opinion, he is also high on receiving agreement. He and the PF member (who is the type markedly high on giving agreement) are thus the closest cooperators in enunciating, building, and applying the conservative norms of the group: those norms which provide the group its basis of approval from external authority and its rewards through successful accomplishment of assigned tasks. If the highest interchange of opinion and agreement is not found between the F and PF members or similar two types on the forward-to-positive side of the space, it is probable that the group is developing norms that make it deviant from the point of view of the immediately concerned external authority. It is also probable that the group is internally divided, with the more conservative faction losing, for the time being at least, to the more radical or deviant faction.

The F member is an important receiver as well as source of task-oriented efforts. Others are markedly high on asking him for suggestion and also high on giving him opinions. He, in turn, is high on agreement with them. Others tend not to address dramatizations or jokes to him. In all these respects one visualizes a strong, serious, cooperative current of task-oriented efforts and endorsements.

In fact, however, there is often a problem. The F member also tends to receive a relatively high rate of disagreement and other acts in which others seem unfriendly toward him. His efforts apparently tend to split the group into two parts—those who agree with him, as described above, and those who disagree. Or it may be that in a group which is already split between a positive-tending and a negative-tending faction, he takes the middle position. Since he specializes so strongly in problem-solving attempts, however, one must suppose that the content of his opinions and suggestions is such as to exert a splitting effect.

Conflicts and Coalitions with Others

The opposition to the F member comes primarily from the backward direction. The member most likely to protest is the B member, who argues for the rejection of conservative group beliefs. This member is generally against faith and belief in the symbols of local traditional authority, particularly the fundamentalist religious symbols. In a less specific sense, the B member resists the compelling and constraining power of all social norms, but most of all the existing traditional ones. In this he is joined by others on the backward side, for various reasons. The UNB member who argues for rugged individualism and gratification is against the F member because traditional social norms tend to interfere with his self-oriented satisfaction. The proponent of value relativism and expression (type UB) dislikes the literalism, localism, rigidity, and constraint of what he considers to be a partial and parochial set of values. He does not like to take verbal formulations and logical manipulations of them seriously. He plays with them as a means of avoiding their hold upon him. The proponent of emotional supportiveness and warmth (type UPB) feels that the approach of the F member is too cold, too calculating, that it is unfair to the young, the innocently deviant, and the underprivileged. The proponents of permissive liberalism (type PB) and identification with the underprivileged (type DPB) build their arguments on essentially the same basis. On the negative side, the proponents of the rejection of social conformity (type NB) and of failure and withdrawal (type DNB), unwilling or unable to conform, and alienated from the group as well as its norms, move toward a separation from the group altogether, or perhaps toward the formation of an isolated, deviant subgroup within the group. They do not wish to be drawn in. Similarly, the proponent of withholding of cooperation (type DB), though he may not be so alienated from the group, is unwilling to join in the tasks defined by an orientation to traditional social norms. These nonactive types of persons are not likely to engage in much verbal argument, but tend to use their passivity and alienation as weapons, and to cooperate tacitly with the more ascendant types near them who act as their representative in voicing opposition. The organization of the backward types is typically very haphazard and temporary, however.

In addition to the types on the backward side of the space, both the P and the N types tend to argue with the F type. The P type argues for equalitarianism. Although he may not disagree with all or even most aspects of the forward member's position, he objects to the implications of inequality that go with emphasis on localism. The equalitarian tends to include *all men* within his boundary of concern and positive feeling. The orthodox traditionalist tends to constrict the boundary to some *local community* with which he is identified. He thinks in terms of "we happy few." The N member carries this constriction one step further. He believes in individualistic isolationism—a *self-sufficiency* of each individual which leaves even the local moral community outside, although the unit that should be self-sufficient may be identified with a local community of some larger size under stress of war or outside threat. Thus, for the P member, the F member tends to exclude too many, whereas for the N member, the F member tends to include too many, especially if he (the N member) is among those included. The spectrum from P, through F, to N, then, is the spectrum of complete universalism to complete individualism. Type F, in the middle, is presumably "particularistic" in a social sense (128).

Some of the types have presented surprises with regard to the discrepancies between the value-statements they will initiate and those with which they will agree—not so the F type. There tends to be an exact match between what he professes and what he will agree to. Within the local moral community, he gives allegiance to the social norms—they have a reality and an objective existence for him. What these norms say, they mean, whether it is to his advantage or disadvantage, and rational arguments, if properly made, are compelling. He lives "by the rules" and will stand or fall by the rules. In this sense he is fair-minded and impartial, as well as impersonal. The undefined and vague element for him is the extent of the moral community, that is, who is "in" and who is "out," who is "saved" and who is "damned," who is "human" and who is "animal." Once people are classified, however, his course is clear and strictly deductive.

Personality Traits

None of the personality tests used in describing other types in this book provides a measure that is specifically characteristic of the F type. Consequently, it is necessary to do the best one can by inference from nearby measures. The PF member is conservative and shows role-playing ability. The NF type shows a kind of acceptance of adversity called feminine masochism. In the context of the personality of the F type, this might be interpreted as a willingness to sacrifice the self to some degree for the sake of social role definitions or social norms. A position midway between the PF and NF traits implies that which they have in common— conservatism, identification of the self with social roles defined by the relevant social norms. As we have seen, the PF type seems to identify with good parental figures on a basis of love and affection received and expected. On the other hand we may suppose that the NF type may identify with demanding or even bad parental figures on the basis of fear and anxiety. In the absence of any competing theory, one would expect that the basis for the F type, halfway between these two, is some balanced combination. Perhaps another way of saying this is to say that the F type has been taught, and has learned, by reward and punishment impartially meted out according to his degree of conformity with parental require- ments. Sometimes this is called conditional love—love on the condition of conformity; withdrawal of love on the condition of nonconformity. This is the ideal of "justice under the law." The belief in a just but terrible God and an equal emphasis on heaven and hell seem natural symbolic expressions of such a childhood socialization, as well as natural explana- tions to the child of the reasons for the treatment he receives.

On the DPF side the F type of person may measure reasonably high on tests predicting that he will be practical, responsible; that he will have high will-control and character stability. These traits seem quite congru- ent with what we would expect from the kind of training described. They are virtues in the conservative religious orthodoxy of all three of the major religions of the western tradition—Judaism, Catholicism, and Pro- testantism. Different as these three religions are in some respects, they are quite similar in these traits. Perhaps the F type does not exemplify these virtues to quite the extent that the more submissive and positive type (DPF) does, but these virtues are congruent with his direction.

The F type may also measure high to some extent on the traits of the UPF direction, sociability and persistence, although he is less ascendant and less positive than these traits imply. He may show the UF trait sophistication, or the UNF trait, prejudice. The element which seems most closely allied with the F direction is suggested by the fact that these traits imply a familiarity with a tradition of some aristocratic, or at least in-group flavor.

How He Sees His Parents

The father of the F type is seen as high on inhibitory demands and discipline, and also high on optimistic idealism, but low on emotional supportiveness and warmth. This is consistent with the hypothesis advanced above that the typical parent of the F type depends upon a balance between reward and punishment, but it suggests that the typical reward is not love and affection in the free sense of emotional support-iveness and warmth, but rather something more like approval; that is, the reward of letting the child know that he is measuring up to an ideal, and hence is worthy of love. It is doubtful if this assurance is capable of lowering anxiety and fear to the extent that emotional supportiveness and warmth will. Although approval in this sense acts as a reward, it leaves anxiety operating as a compelling motive in conduct.

The mother is seen as high on optimistic idealism, as the father is also, but she is only average on inhibitory demands and discipline and low on emotional supportiveness and warmth. The discrepancy between father and mother is low; they have similar effects upon the child.

The descriptions of the parents given by the F member are thus consistent with the general rule—that children tend to become like their parents. The child of F parents, like them, is capable of leading a group forward toward the development and realization of norms, but like them also, he is low on the resources for overcoming negativism and must depend upon others in the group for this.

His Effect on Group Satisfaction

Thus, the F member tends to move the group neither toward nor away from satisfaction with interpersonal relations. His singular feature is his marked effect in moving the group toward satisfaction with goal attainment. This is not to say that he has any particular immunity from power coalitions that lead in other directions, nor that he is unusually succesful in converting others to a belief in orthodox faith. But no other directional type has, to the same degree, the single-minded, persistent, undeviating devotion to the received tasks of the group. Insofar as instrumental success brings in rewards from outside the group, the F member may contribute to satisfaction, even of members who tend in other directions, since rewards to the group are usually shared in some degree.

22

Type NF: Toward
Value-Determined Restraint

The member located in the negative-forward part of the group
space by his fellow members seems conscientious, principled, and
persistent. He is value- and task-oriented, neither ascendant nor submissive, but tries always to be "objective," according to his own
conception of the objective truth. He is so persistent and grinding in his
insistence on always doing the right thing that he seems unfriendly and
inhibiting, in fact, guilt-inducing. In the realization of his own values
he seems to move toward the acceptance of all the restraints necessary
to realize values literally and maximally. "He that loses his conscience
has nothing left that is worth keeping."

How He Sees Himself and How Others See Him

The person moving strongly in the NF direction seems to find his
safety and his self-identification in the power of conscience to overcome
temptation. He emphasizes moderation and value-determined restraint.
He makes others feel he rates them high on favoring expression and
gratification. There is some tendency for others to feel curious about
him. He arouses guilt, by his manner and example, if not by direct
accusation; as a result, he is disliked. The observers rate him highest on
arousing their dislike, and although group members dislike the authoritarian autocrat even more, they express least liking and least admiration
for the NF member. The NF member, in turn, rates others low on
personal involvement and makes them feel he has little liking for them.
He finds them not at all entertaining or warm and personal. As a matter

of fact, his manner and perception seem defensive and oriented to the minimizing of involvement, personal warmth, expression, and gratification. All these feelings, perhaps, are too tempting to be tolerated. Perhaps he can hold the temptation in check only by turning negative and "trying very, very hard." If he tries hard enough, others turn negative toward him. He is willing to sacrifice positive feeling in order to move forward on the received tasks of the group.

His Place in the Interaction Network

The NF member, neither ascendant nor submissive, tends to be found in the middle ranks of the group as to total participation initiated. He is average in remarks addressed to the group as a whole, but it is significant of the relative lack of support from others that he is low in acts received from them. In the process of trying to persuade others to his point of view, he tends to address more remarks to each of them than they address to him. Each of them is low in addressing him, whereas he is average in addressing each of them, and is thus average on his total addressed to specific individuals.

The NF type does not have a powerful position in the interaction network in the first place, and although he plows ahead in his attempts to get the group to restrain itself and get its work done, he provokes negative reactions and ends in an even more disadvantaged position than that in which he started.

What Ideas and Values Will He Express?

The NF member who moves toward value-determined restraint believes the following: "One should hold high ideals, purify himself, and restrain his desires for pleasure." "Man should control his bodily senses, his emotions, feelings, wishes." Conscience is important to him, as a means of maintaining control: "He that loses his conscience has nothing left that is worth keeping." Pleasure and happiness are devalued and felt to be dangerous: "He who knows that lusts have a short life and cause pain, is wise." "Not to attain happiness, but to be worthy of it, is the purpose of our existence." Pain and unhappiness are accepted as inevitable: "Misfortune is to be conquered by bearing it." Part of the reason for devaluating pleasure is that it tends to tie one to other persons and to objects and circumstances over which one has no control. "One should aim to simplify one's external life, and moderate those desires whose satisfaction is dependent upon physical or social forces outside of oneself."

Not only are pleasure and happiness devalued, but in the extreme case the material and social world outside the self is denied ultimate reality: "The ultimate and true reality is above the senses, immaterial, spiritual, unchanging, and everlasting." "In the ultimate test, truth only comes from inner experience—from inspiration, mystical union, revelation, or pure meditation." "Science has its place, but there are more important things that can never possibly be understood by the human mind."

It may be seen then, that there are close ties between the ideas and values of the NF direction and those of adjacent directions. The NF member may speak for conservative group beliefs, for self-knowledge and subjectivity, and for self-sacrifice—all of these have a forward component. On the negative side, the devaluation of other persons is expressed in the preference for individualistic isolationism and for the rejection of social success.

Perhaps all of the ideas and values mentioned so far give a distorted impression of the degree of passivity involved. Actually the NF direction is neither markedly submissive nor markedly ascendant. There is also some tendency to express the ideas and values of more ascendant types with cognate direction; that is, the NF member may speak for autocratic authority on occasion, and for group loyalty and cooperation on the forward side, and tough-minded assertiveness on the negative side. Basically, the NF member seems to be a somewhat repressed and controlled authoritarian autocrat. His effect is more than that of one who simply exercises restraint upon himself. He tends to appear as one who tries to impose restraint upon others, and to present himself as the voice of their conscience. His position is one of a claim to moral superiority based upon special knowledge of values or the law, rather than one of ascendance in the more vulgar and material senses.

The Quality of His Interaction

The NF member is not markedly high on any of the twelve categories of interaction initiated or received. Concerned with forward movement toward the realization of values, he tends to be high on both asking for suggestion and giving suggestion. He is high on giving opinion, but low on asking for it, which seems consistent with an assumption that he feels himself an authority on the values and their implications which he thinks ought to govern the situation. Perhaps asking others for their opinion is to give them more than their due. He is also low on asking others for information and low on seeming friendly, consistent with his general devaluation of solidarity with others. Nor does he tend to dramatize or joke. He takes a serious view of life and especially of values. He does not show tension or laugh.

The reactions of others to the NF member seem to be ambivalent. Members of the group are markedly low on dramatizing and joking to him. He tends to split the group to some extent. Some members ask him for his opinions and suggestions, which he gives, and they tend to agree.

Others, however, tend to disagree and seem unfriendly to him. He, in turn, tends to disagree and often seems unfriendly toward them. He is the focus of a moralistic conflict over the restraint he urges. Others are low in seeming friendly toward him and they avoid giving suggestions to him, probably wanting not to give him additional chances to disapprove their proposals. They are low both on giving information to him and on asking him for information. He does not ask for information. The conflict revolves around values rather than facts, and neither side uses the approach of an exchange of information as a way of increasing positive feeling or of introducing an inductive approach to the problem. The NF type prefers to deduce conclusions from value-premises rather than arrive at them inductively through the careful consideration of many facts.

Conflicts and Coalitions with Others

Although the NF member is markedly likely to address his admonitions of value-determined restraint to the UNB type, being threatened by his display of rugged individualism and gratification, the verbal argument of values does not tend to center between these two. It may be that the UNB type is not severely threatened by the NF type. The UNB outlaw may feel that he has already fought the battle against constraining social norms and has won it against a more threatening and ascendant autocratic authority than the NF member himself is. As we infer from our general model, the UNB type tends to center his verbal argument on his more immediate rival for group leadership, the UPF type. He concentrates his scorn on the less ascendant "yes men" (types PF and DNF) who follow his UPF rival. For the UNB type the struggle for power is more important than the value-conflict pressed upon him by the NF type.

The main counter-arguments to the NF type tend rather to come from the positive-backward sector. The ascendant proponents of value-relativism and expression, emotional supportiveness and warmth, and of social success are likely to combine against him. His support of value-determined restraint is likely to be attacked by the rejectors of social conformity and conventional group beliefs. The negative orientation (of the NF type) toward persons is likely to bring arguments in favor of trust in the goodness of others and equalitarianism. His claim to moral superiority is resented and met either with arguments or with behavior which exemplifies withholding of cooperation, and he is a focus of attack from those who believe in permissive liberalism and identification with the underprivileged. With all of these positions the NF proponent of value-determined restraint is in disagreement, and the potentiality of a verbal struggle is always present.

From the negative type, the NF type is likely to receive arguments defending individualistic isolationism. But in this case the degree of conflict is probably more mild, or at least unpredictable. The NF type himself is likely to agree with value-statements in favor of individualistic isolationism, and these two types (NF and N) may well combine into a coalition against external threat, though the negative type is unlikely to agree to an emphasis on value-determined restraint as applied to *himself.* One would expect the relationship between these two types to be determined strongly by the external threats—in conditions of threat they will tend to combine, but when the threat eases, they return to their preferred condition of individualistic isolationism. Parties of the political right are apparently prone to this kind of internal splintering and, for cohesion, seem to need an external threat.

Personality Traits

There is only one personality test in the battery used on which the NF member tends to be markedly high. This is a test labeled feminine masochism. Presumably the relevant traits might also be described as a willingness to accept pain and unhappiness and to forgo ascendance and the gratification of instinctual desires, for the sake of safety to be obtained from the close association with a more ascendant autocratic authority. The fact that this is one of the common positions of women in the authoritarian family gives the traits their association with a feminine role, but presumably this association is a secondary one, and the primary meaning is more general.

Other traits of nearby types give some additional clues to the personality type associated with NF movement. The UF type shows a conventional control of aggression in the trait called sophistication. The nearby UN type seems neurotic, psychopathic, and manic. Since these traits are all ascendant they should be mentally corrected downward, and in this it may help to know that the traits of the nearby ND type, on which the present type is also moderately high, include depression and social introversion. The traits characteristic of the nearby N type, which, like the present type, is neither ascendant nor submissive, are suspecting and jealous, with signs of hypochondriasis and psychasthenia. All of these traits, being to the more negative side of the NF type, need to be mentally corrected forward.

One may put together a picture then, of an anxiety-driven personality, in which the expression of any impulse or fantasy, especially those involving either sexuality or aggression, is dangerous since it brings the anticipation of punishment from an autocratic authoritarian parent. The person tries to deal with the anxiety by controlling, repressing, and denying impulses; he succeeds to a certain extent, but the anxiety is not completely dispelled, and other objects are found to fasten anxiety upon, which then also seem dangerous. Like the UNF type, the NF type may be prejudiced, regarding other persons or groups as dangerous. The person tries to isolate and insulate himself from dangerous objects, and to crowd in closer under the wing of the authoritarian parent, even to the point of courting minor punishments, or punishing himself in advance, in order to assure himself of favor against the disaster of later discovery of things for which he might be punished. The effort required is considerable. More and more things must be given up, even aspects or activities and normal functions of the self, if the anxiety cannot be contained. The person tends to feel tired, sick, full of nagging symptoms. His appetite for life tends to be drained away, and he feels really rewarded for nothing. He is drawn more and more into concern with his own inner processes, of thinking, of willing, of trying to realize values, of building a rationale within which his self-denial will seem logical and worthwhile. He feels persecuted and alone, but also envious and jealous of those who feel pleasure freely, who are loved and rewarded for no good reason at all, and who expect to be cared for even though they do not work and do not deny themselves. One can hardly understand the disapproval and the smothered rage of this type of person against the parties of the far left in the political sense, without understanding that the NF type regards the leftists as wanting to receive for *nothing* the security and the rewards for which he has given *everything,* and is still unsuccessful.

How He Sees His Parents

Both the father and mother of the NF type are seen as high on inhibitory demands and discipline and low on emotional supportiveness and warmth. They are both average on optimistic idealism versus pessimistic cynicism. The discrepancies between the two parents as to exact place on these various dimensions are average. In general the parents are unable to give their child sufficient love to enable him to reduce his anxiety, to say nothing of rewarding him for the acceptance of their inhibitory demands. The demands are made in the name of values, but the values are not integrated with personal warmth or acceptance. The child is punished or frightened into compliance, or, if you like, "brainwashed." In some ways the child of UNF parents is more fortunate, in that, although the position of such a child is similar in certain ways, he is in fact more drawn into interaction with the parents, and learns (from them) more active and ascendant ways of fusing his impulses into his behavior. Such a child tends to be more objectionable to other people than the present type. Others actively *dislike* the UNF type more, but the NF type is less *liked* and less admired than the UNF type. As a parental characteristic, the lack of likability is most damaging in the socialization of the child, and this lack is passed on to the child.

It will readily be seen that any aspirations of the NF type for leadership in the group are severely handicapped. There are times when general feelings of guilt and depression may make him an appropriate symbolic leader, but his inability to inspire liking and admiration and his lack of an upward position in the power structure make it unlikely that he can hold leadership long. He probably holds on longest and is most effective in his given direction when he is under the protection of a more ascendant authoritarian autocrat, whose supporter he is likely to be. At other times, or in other conditions, especially when the general tendency of the group is in the backward direction, he is a likely scapegoat. He is the "little taxpayer," the "John Q. Public" of the political cartoons, who suffers to keep the "handout" programs of the political left supplied. He is the "greasy grind" of academic ill-repute, or the "rate buster" in the industrial setting, who draws unfavorable attention to the slack and deviant ways of others.

His Effect on Group Satisfaction

It is plain then, why the NF type tends to move the group away from satisfaction with interpersonal relations. He neither inspires positive feelings, nor gives them. He is unable to reward others, and he stands for the conscience within themselves that they live with uneasily, even without his prodding. On the other hand, he tends to move the group toward satisfaction with goal attainment—toward getting the job done. But he does so at considerable cost. He sacrifices satisfaction with interpersonal relations (which only make him nervous anyway), to satisfaction with task-achievement. In times of emergency the sacrifice may be necessary or worthwhile, but in general, others regard the costs imposed by the NF member as too high, and tend to depose and punish him at the first opportunity. This presumably seldom changes him, but only confirms him in his anxiety to do the right thing before he is punished again.

23

Type N: Toward
Individualistic Isolationism

The member located in the negative part of the group space by his fellow members seems unfriendly and disagreeable, but neither ascendant nor submissive, neither value- and task-oriented, nor against authority as such. He is rather self-concerned and isolated, detached, unsocial, defensively secluded and negativistic. In the realization of his own values he seems to be trying to move toward individualistic isolation. "In life an individual should for the most part 'go it alone,' assuring himself of privacy, having much time to himself, attempting to control his own life."

How He Sees Himself and How Others See Him

The person moving in the N direction is alienated from the group. He tends to feel himself alone and threatened and hence wants a protected, isolated position. He is rated by other members and also by observers as very high on individualism. He seems to feel any contact he has with others as a threat to his privacy, autonomy, and freedom of movement. He makes others feel he rates them high on domination, and guesses that others will see him as resentful, as they do in fact, although they see the DN type as even more resentful. He is more likely than any other type to rate other group members as anxious and high on psychological inertia; he also makes them feel he rates them high. Since he is clearly atypical in this perception, his high ratings of others may be an indication that he feels anxious and driven himself; he makes active efforts to disown these feelings in himself and attribute them to others.

At the same time, he maintains a falsely high opinion of his understanding, giving himself the highest rating on this as a trait, whereas both observers and other group members give their highest rating to a type almost opposite—to the DP type. It may be that the trait of "understanding" in the sense of acceptance of others is so foreign to the N member that he tends to construe the word as referring only to intellectual understanding of issues.

The N member is not deceived about his negativity, however. He guesses that he will be the least liked and least admired in the group. He is, in fact, least admired by the observers; other group members like and admire his adjacent type, NF, even less. The N member tends to rate others low both on interest in the task and on value for a logical task (himself high on "understanding"), and he is the least likely of all types to find any others entertaining. He "is not amused."

His Place in the Interaction Network

The N type is not likely to be high in total participation initiated. He is rather average. He does not wish to take the initiative of further involvement, perhaps. His role is more reactive than active. In remarks addressed to the group as a whole, he is only average, and he is similarly only average in his total addressed to specific other individuals. In return, others are low in speaking to him. He tends to receive less from each than he gives to them, an indication in part that he is not being supported by them, but also an indication that others are not spending much time trying to persuade or change him. Such points as he may attempt to make are made in the face of tacit opposition. This is no wonder, since he himself is the member in the group most likely to disagree when he does talk. He does not have a powerful position in the group in terms of his total participation, but he is a potential bottleneck or barrier to be avoided since he specializes in disagreement. His tacit support of a more ascendant negative type (UN, UNF, or UNB) may be strategic, though not always very visible, or salient.

What Ideas and Values Will He Express?

The N member is markedly likely to express sentiments in favor of individualistic isolationism. "One must avoid dependence upon persons or things; the center of life should be found within oneself." "In life an individual should for the most part 'go it alone,' assuring himself of privacy, having much time to himself, attempting to control his own life." One gathers that a prime reason for his high rate of disagreement is a fear of being drawn into the group, of being attached to it, of being made a member in the full sense. Another way of saying this is to point out that the direction is negative, not backward. It is anti-positive, rather than anti-forward. What is feared or rejected is inclusion in the group on a basis of equality, affection, and solidarity. Thus the content of any statement he may disagree with is secondary—he has a tendency to disagree regardless of content, since otherwise he fears he may be drawn into the group and may lose his protective individuality. "It is the man who stands alone who excites our admiration." One is reminded of the period of negativism through which many children go. In this period in the formation of his personality, the child seems to strive to realize the fact that he is different from the parent, separate from the mother, able to act independently, that he is not a slave to affection, reward, or seduction, that he has "ego strength."

The N member maintains "One's life should be directed completely by intelligence and rationality." One feels that there must be some rationalization in this attitude, however, since the tendency to disagree seems to be independent of content. Of all members, the N member tends to rate himself the highest on understanding—an accolade given to him by no others. He tells himself, perhaps, that he understands the situation better than others, and that he disagrees for rational reasons. If he feels others habitually misunderstand the situation, it tends to explain, perhaps, why he feels constantly obliged to disagree.

The N member may at various times express values anywhere on the negative side of the space, forward as well as backward, ascendant as well as submissive. At his level, neither ascendant nor submissive, he may at one time speak for value-determined restraint, at another for rejection of social conformity. In a more ascendant mood he may speak for autocratic authority at one time, for rugged individualism and gratification at another, and for tough-minded assertiveness in the service of either. In a more submissive mood, he may speak for self-sacrifice for values on the one hand, for rejection of social success, and for failure and withdrawal. It may be that there is a principle of "intelligence and rationality" which makes each of these appropriate under certain conditions, but it is also true that all of these values represent the negative side of the space, a constriction one would not expect if a flexible adjustment of values to situation were the only factor operating. Conflict and ambivalence rather than "intelligence and rationality" may be a part of the cause of the negativism of the N member. Finally, one should take account of the fact that the actual giving of opinion in overt interaction is not characteristic of the N type, as we shall see. All in all, the most helpful key to understanding the value-position of the N type is the conception that he avoids the values of the positive side—particularly those of equalitarianism. He does not wish to be classed with all others simply as an equal.

The Quality of His Interaction

Several qualities are very salient in the interaction of the N member. The first is that he has a markedly high rate of seeming unfriendly, second, he has a markedly high rate of disagreeing, third, he has a markedly low rate of asking for opinion, and fourth, he has a markedly low rate of seeming friendly. He is average or below on all task-oriented types of activities. He does not specialize in problem-solving activities of any kind, with the possible exception of disagreeing with the problem-solving attempts of others.

Others in return disagree with him and seem unfriendly. They are markedly low on seeming friendly and low on dramatizing and joking. Showing tension or laughing in relation to him and asking for opinion are high. Others apparently make some attempts to elicit positive attitudes from the N member, or to find out the reasons for his negativism. But he is not typically drawn into sustained problem-solving cooperation and makes essentially no attempt to elicit information or opinion in return. Others are markedly low both on giving information and on giving opinion and suggestion to him. The fact that others are low in remarks of these kinds addressed to him indicates that they tend to bypass him in the problem-solving or norm-enactment process and to avoid him as a bottleneck.

Conflicts and Coalitions with Others

So far as interaction is addressed to the N type of member it comes mostly from the positive side. Members from that side appear to feel that his negativism is more related to the problem of his inclusion in the group than to specific aspects of the task or task-values. The P member urges equalitarianism upon him, and all of the other values of the positive side are brought to bear. The UPB member urges, or tries to exemplify emotional supportiveness and warmth, the UP member tries to make the goals of social success salient and attractive to the N isolate, and the UPF member tries to make social solidarity and progress attractive. On the less ascendant positive and forward side, the values of trust in the goodness of others, altruistic love, and salvation through love may be presented.

On the less ascendant PB side, the values of permissive liberalism and identification with the underprivileged may be addressed to the N member. The other arguments from the positive side are attempts to convert the N member, to bring him into a unified group. But the arguments for permissive liberalism and for the underprivileged are attempts to solicit his support against a forward-moving faction—

attempts to enlist his negativism in the service of a change in group norms or a revolution. To these attempts he will probably agree, although he does not himself take the initiative of advocating change or revolution. He typically disagrees with all attempts to bring him into a unified group through positively oriented values, but he is vulnerable to arguments from a dissident or revolutionary movement, since it may give expression to his negativism.

As a potential member of a dissident movement he is also likely to receive arguments in favor of rejection of social conformity and in favor of his own position, individualistic isolation. He may also receive arguments in favor of value-determined restraint representing the forward faction. He typically agrees with the sentiments on rejection of social conformity and individualistic isolation, and disagrees with the forward faction. He is thus actually more in favor of the backward than the forward side in the value-statements he will permit to pass through the bottleneck he guards, although in the content he himself initiates, he appears to swing backward and forward equally often, or to be ambivalent.

As indicated in the discussion of the NF type, a coalition between NF and N is a possibility, especially if an external threat is present, but the N type does not want to be told that he must accede to value-determined restraint imposed upon him by others. His position is one of ambivalent and partially covered revolt. He is in conflict. On the more conscious or controlled level, he may appear to be in favor of forward-moving values, or he may form coalitions with persons representing these values. But on the more unconscious and uncontrolled level, he is revolting against authority figures and group norms. His appearance of sometimes supporting one side and sometimes the other is a result of the unresolved conflict within himself. He is at the exact location where tendencies toward social conformity and tendencies toward deviance tend to balance and fluctuate or cancel each other. The social fabric may part on either side of him—that is, he may be found in the coalition of the radical political right, or in that of the radical political left; he may be fought over as a prize potentially available to either. This may occasionally put him in a strategic position as keeper of a critical bottleneck, or holder of the balance of power. The result is that he does not have to be powerful in the usual ways that persons upward in the structure are powerful, in order to exercise a considerable influence over the outcome of certain power struggles. He may use this power to his advantage, but it is also a double-edged sword. To use it means to perpetuate the ambivalence, the operation of conflicting tendencies within the personality, and this in turn leads to manifold psychological or neurotic difficulties.

Personality Traits

The personality tests characteristic of type N generally indicate a proneness to neurotic problems. The person moving strongly in the N direction is likely to be markedly suspecting and jealous. He is likely to show hypochondriasis, a tendency to feel many vague and shifting illnesses, or psychasthenia, a tendency to feel indecisive, fearful, doubtful, and guilty. He is also likely to show dependency. It is believed that internal conflicts and the necessity of trying to stabilize aggressive impulses and anxiety may lead to the expenditure of a great deal of psychic energy. The N type has to work more or less consciously to suppress impulses which would be more automatically and unconsciously controlled by repression in a personality more successfully formed.

When parents and other controlling agents are loved and respected as they usually are for members on the positive side, a large portion of the motivational forces within the personality can be utilized to control aggression and anxiety. Emotional supportiveness and warmth from a loved parent is probably a generalized protector against anxiety and is the generalized source of reward which makes possible the idealization of the parent, and the acceptance of the norms he supports. The N type of person is one who, for whatever reason, feels he has been denied love and acceptance and has "decided," as it were, that what he cannot have, he will hate and destroy. His feelings of insecurity, worry and suspicion, and perhaps of jealousy can be understood as manifestations of his basic distrust. He feels he will not receive the rewards of love, no matter what he does, and he wants revenge. He becomes a "spoiler."

Where consistent rewards are lacking, and where large quantities of psychic energy must be devoted simply to holding the self together, the person may not be as effective intellectually as he might be were his ego stronger. It is probably best to think of general intelligence as an independent dimension with regard to the present typology. There are probably quite bright and quite dull persons within each of the twenty-seven directional types described in the three-dimensional evaluative space, and one should be prepared to find quite marked differences in the general "feeling" of personalities within the same type, according to the degree of intelligence. Nevertheless, in the N type one may expect some loss of intellectual efficiency on the basis of distraction with internal psychological problems.

The traits of surrounding types, properly corrected, may be helpful in understanding the personality of the N type. His more ascendant adjacent type, UN, seems neurotic, psychopathic, and manic. His UNF adjacent type shows prejudice. These traits seem to be consistent with poor control of aggressive drives. The N type may be thought of as struggling to suppress or conceal, to some extent, these more open or disorganized expressions of aggression.

The UNB type, adjacent to the N type, shows nervous tension, and seems dominant, aggressive, eccentric, unconcerned, paranoid, impulsive, and self-centered. At times the N type may show these traits in lesser measure, but persons showing these traits are more ascendant than he appears on the average, and they are more consistently nonconservative than he is. Ordinarily he works, with some success, to keep such tendencies within himself suppressed. He does continue to show allied traits, though, in less ascendant form. Like his NB neighbor, he may show emotional sensitivity and insecurity, and feel radical and critical. Part of the negativism of the NB type seems mobilized against conventional role requirements, and the traits probably reflect among other things difficulties in accepting conventional adult sex roles. The NF neighbor of the N type shows the trait feminine masochism, which I have interpreted as a willingness to accept pain and unhappiness, to forgo ascendance and the gratification of instinctual desires, for the sake of safety to be obtained from the close association with a more ascendant autocratic authority. Both the NF and the NB members seem to focus on the demands of an autocratic authoritarian parent. Presumably the boy is urged by the UNF type of parent to "become a man" and the girl to become a "real (conventional) wife and mother." The demand of the N type of parent is similar, at least part of the time. When the parent is the prototype of what it means to become a conventional adult in the conventional sex-role, and the parent is rejected and feared, the difficulty for the child can be imagined. The child in the N position is apparently neither able to accept nor to reject completely the parent, and neither able to accept nor reject the conception of the adult role that seems to be demanded.

The DN type shows the traits repression-denial, depression, and social introversion. Depression is sometimes believed to be a result of aggression turned against the self. The N type does have, in common with the UN type and the DN type, the trait of aggression as a major drive, and he neither controls it consistently nor finds a consistent target for it. Sometimes it is turned outward, sometimes inward. The tendencies toward depression are not completely consolidated. The N type may show some of the characteristics of the adjacent type, DNB: rough; simple; immature; independent; self-sufficient; and schizothymic, but these are not all marked nor consistent.

How He Sees His Parents

On the average, the discrepancies between the way the father and mother are described are moderately high. Some of the difficulties of assuming a conventional sex-role may result from parents who themselves present a confused and ambivalent picture of their own sex-role. They may exaggerate the differences between the male and female roles, or they may refuse to accept the role they feel is usually demanded of their sex and assume an exaggerated opposite. In spite of the discrepancies between them, however, both parents are presented as moderately high on inhibitory demands and discipline, and both are moderately low on emotional supportiveness and warmth. Both parents are moderately high on pessimistic cynicism.

The resources of the parents for bringing about a conventional socialization of the child are thus low. The parents do not agree well with each other, hence do not present consistent norms to the child; they are rather cynical about values in general, or ambivalent and conflicted about conventional values, and they have neither the power of rewarding and stabilizing the child through affection, nor of arousing his admiration. Hence the child is left on his own, to work out his psychological destiny as best he can, with no better resources than his parents have given him. That he should tend toward individualistic isolationism is to be expected. Isolationism is the factual pattern to which he has been exposed, and it may in fact be stabilizing for him in the short run, in that it tends to cut down the general level of stimulation. This may help, since he handles stimulation with difficulty.

His Effect on Group Satisfaction

The leadership potential of the N member is easily seen to be low, though he may hold an unexpected power through the exercise of disagreement, or through the support he may give to a dissident faction. He tends to move the group away from satisfaction with interpersonal relations, but his effect on satisfaction with goal attainment or task achievement is unpredictable. He may throw his weight in either direction, or neither.

24

Type NB: Toward Rejection
of Social Conformity

The member located in the negative-backward part of the group space by his fellow members seems autonomous and resistant to authority, and also unfriendly to others in general; neither ascendant and actively rebellious, nor submissive and passively withdrawing, at least neither one consistently. He seems evasive, stubborn, obstinate, cynical, and radically nonconforming. In the expression of his values, it is hard to discern a consistent positive philosophy—the key seems to be simply rejection of social conformity, particularly conformity with social roles expected of him—occupational, sexual, age roles, and those of social class and citizenship. "The individualist is the man who is most likely to discover the best road to a new future."

How He Sees Himself and How Others See Him

The NB member seems to base his self-picture on the power to be different and cynically defiant. He is cynical about conventional values and pessimistic about persons. He rejects not only conformity, but the proponents of conformity, positive though they may be by others' standards. He tends to deny feeling admiration for anybody and seems particularly sensitive to the threat of domination. He is the most likely of all types to rate others as dominating. There is some tendency for others to feel curious about him.

His Place in the Interaction Network

The NB member is not a high participator. He is average on total participation initiated and average on remarks addressed to the group as a whole. He is also average on remarks addressed to specific individuals, but is low on receiving acts from others. He tends to give more to each one than they give to him in return, an indication that he does not receive their support. To the extent that he does try to influence other group members, he proceeds against either opposition or lack of reaction. He is a possible collaborator in a far left revolutionary movement and, in this position as a supporter or silent partner, he may exert an unexpectedly great influence.

What Ideas and Values Will He Express?

The NB member is in favor of the rejection of social conformity. "The individualist is the man who is most likely to discover the best road to a new future." He is against both people and assigned group tasks, hence he is likely to speak in favor of individualistic isolationism and for rejection of conservative group beliefs. He does not wish to be constrained toward either positive or forward movement. On the upward-downward dimension he is not so sensitive. On occasion he may express the values of his more ascendant neighbors: tough-minded assertiveness; rugged individualism and gratification; and value relativism; but he is not in fact so consistently ascendant as these values imply. On the more submissive side, he may speak in favor of rejection of social success, withholding of cooperation, and failure and withdrawal, but he is more active in his protest than these imply.

The position of the NB member is defined primarily by a contrary reaction to what is expected for social conformity in the larger society and in task-oriented groups which receive their tasks from the larger society. Very often symbols of revolt will already have been developed by other groups, delinquent or otherwise alienated groups to which he belongs. In these groups the symbols of revolt are accepted more or less conventionally and are taken as the basis of a deviant orthodoxy. Styles of hair, styles of dress, cosmetics, ways of talking, ways of moving, gesturing, dancing, personal properties, vehicles, weapons, and territories—all are likely to be drawn into the symbolism of the deviant orthodoxy of the alienated group. Conventional age, sex, and occupational roles are very likely to be the target of attack. They may be exaggerated, ridiculed, reversed, or the differences obliterated. Since the attachment of delinquent or alienated subgroups to many of the conventional modes of status display is broken, the deviant group orthodoxy is likely to prescribe symbols which are more directly and personally associated with the individual: dress, speech, movement, and the like. The status display repertoire of the individual must be within his own control, and relatively portable.

In order to use the present system in a group with a deviant orthodoxy, the content of values associated with the various directions of movement may have to be recentered. The complications of this are too great to be undertaken within the present book. Instead, a point of view will be maintained in which such a group is treated as a subgroup within a larger group. The larger group is taken as the point of reference, within which a conventionality prevails that is being attacked. The present description is appropriate to an individual who may be a member of such an alienated subgroup, but it describes him as he interacts in the more conventionally oriented group with received tasks.

In such a task-oriented group, the NB member appears in many ways as a member of another culture, and his ideas and beliefs seem to clash deliberately, though perhaps sometimes subtly, with the conventional norms of the group. The values of the NB type may indeed have little internal coherence, though if they are a part of a deviant subculture, they may have developed toward some coherence in the way any orthodoxy does.

The Quality of His Interaction

The NB member is markedly low on agreement and is high on disagreeing and seeming unfriendly (see page 132). He is low on task-oriented activities, neither asking for suggestion nor giving suggestion or opinion. He is also low on the socially positive activities of asking for information, opinion, and seeming friendly. His backward tendencies are shown in moderately high rates of dramatizing, joking, showing tension, and laughing.

In responding to the NB type others are likely to show tension and to laugh, but all task-connected activities are directed elsewhere. Group members tend not to address information to him, nor opinion, nor suggestion. They markedly avoid giving opinion to him. He does seem to provoke some attempts to bring him into the group in the form of asking him for information and opinion, but these fail, essentially, as he continues to be evasive and cynical. It is true that he is not quite so low on giving information as on other task-connected activities, perhaps because he answers questions of information, but still he is out of the main current of the interaction. When he enters, it seems to be to display his alienation, and he does not even try, as a rule, to present a logical argument or defense of his position. His aim is not really to convert others, but to accuse them. Others are low on seeming friendly toward him and low on agreement.

Conflicts and Coalitions with Others

Those who try hardest to bring the NB member into the group and convert him are found on the positive and forward sides, although he is not the particularly chosen target of any of the types. He himself is most likely to address his rejection of social conformity to the autocratic authority, but the latter is attacked from so many directions that he does not always concentrate on the NB delinquent. The most active attacker of autocratic authority is the equalitarian (type P), and a secondary consequence of this is that the equalitarian spends little time trying to persuade the delinquent NB member to come into the group. One would otherwise expect the equalitarian, like the other positive types, to try to bring the delinquent in. The UP type, who may well be the one who addresses requests for information to the delinquent, tries to convert him to the goals of social success, whereas the DP type tries to persuade him to trust in the goodness of others.

Arguments for salvation of the delinquent through love, attempts to stir him to optimistic idealism and altruistic love, and to move him toward social solidarity and progress, in general, fail. Sterner arguments for value-determined restraint, self-knowledge and subjectivity, conventional group beliefs, and group loyalty and cooperation elicit disagreement from him. Insofar as he has anchored his security in another group, a delinquent subculture, and looks for his status and rewards from there, he tends to remain impervious to these appeals.

He and the other members of his subgroup are not unchangeable, however. They are in fact very vulnerable to a movement for social change that may claim them from the political far left. Though the delinquent is not likely to initiate value-statements in favor of either permissive liberalism or identification with the underprivileged, he is markedly likely to agree with such statements. He is also markedly likely to agree with statements in favor of withholding cooperation, and he himself may voice this position. He both voices and agrees with rejection of conventional group beliefs. Thus he may be brought into a coalition with a revolutionary group in a general attack on autocratic authority. And so, in spite of wide value differences, he may find himself on the same side of the battle as the equalitarian. This is a coalition of the far left, and these two types are indeed "strange bedfellows."

The delinquent NB member may voice as well as agree with sentiments calling for rejection of social success, failure and withdrawal, and individualistic isolationism. And also if there are more ascendant types within the group to take leadership in the direc-

tions of tough-minded assertiveness, rugged individualism and gratification, value-relativism and expression, he is ready to agree, as well
as to voice these values himself. He is ready for revolution "for the
fun of it," and cares little for the actual ideological cause.

Personality Traits

The NB member is likely to be markedly high on the traits of
insecurity, radicalism and criticalness. Inability or refusal to take
the conventional male or female sex role has been sufficiently
commented upon. If the theory is correct, however, one should not
expect any uniform reaction—it may take the form in some cases of a
tendency on the part of either sex to adopt the opposite sex-role
characteristics, and in other cases may take the form of an exaggerated, tough, sadistic sex-role. In still other cases, the revolt may
center upon the occupational or citizenship requirements of the
adult role. It will be noted that all of these dilemmas become
increasingly sharp as adolescence progresses, and the phenomena associated with the delinquent NB syndrome tend to assume their most
florid form at that time. In the life cycle, adolescence is the
bottleneck through which the poorly-socialized negative types of
personality may fail to pass.

The personality test traits of nearby types may give some
additional insight into the NB type. The more ascendant counterpart, UNB, is high on the traits of nervous tension, dominance,
aggression, eccentricity, and unconcernedness. He seems paranoid,
impulsive, and self-centered. These may be viewed as tendencies
which the somewhat less ascendant delinquent type holds in check
to some degree or expresses sporadically. The less ascendant type,
DNB, seems rough, simple, immature, schizothymic, independent, and
self-sufficient. There is some suggestion in these traits of a lack of
contact with the more sophisticated values and conventional social
norms of the parent culture—a lack of contact due to social
isolation of some kind, perhaps cultural deprivation or simple rural
or foreign origin. The NB delinquent shows more ascendance and
more aggression than these traits suggest, but still he may be
somewhat similar in lacking the effective inner controls and identification with conventional social norms to cope with his instinctual impulses. This is what one would expect if the parents are not
able to provide sufficient love and reward to produce an identification with themselves as positive exemplars of the main conventional
culture.

Essentially the same picture emerges from an examination of
the following traits of the nearby UN type: neurotic, psychopathic,

and manic. These are the accompaniments of a strong aggressive drive (ascendance) directed specifically toward other people (as distinct from norms). The adjacent N type shows the traits of suspicion and jealousy, with tendencies toward hypochondriasis, psychasthenia, and dependency. These traits in general suggest a degree of "neurotic" complication, with symptoms centering on psychological processes that are not so characteristic of the "delinquent" NB type. The opposition of the delinquent to social norms is more open and decided, less ambivalent and involved. In ordinary language, the N type seems, more "neurotically sick," the NB type seems more "delinquent."

The delinquent may not be so sick if he has started to deal with his problems of growing up by becoming more openly anti-conventional as well as anti-social, and may have joined or formed a delinquent group from which he gains some support. To take this path, however, is to depart increasingly from the possibility of integration with the main culture. Thus the delinquent personality, in its group context, is more "tough" and impervious to attempts at social control than the "sick" one.

The DN type, both more neurotically sick and less ascendant than the NB, shows the traits repression-denial, depression, and social introversion. These traits may be a result of low aggressive drive, or too-strong controls, which turn the aggression against the self. In the delinquent NB type, presumably, the aggression is turned mostly outward, against others in what is felt to be the repressive conventional culture.

How He Sees His Parents

The salient trait of both father and mother as seen by the NB member is that they are very high on pessimistic cynicism and low on optimistic idealism. No doubt there are many exceptions to this. In proverbial language there is simply no accounting for the fact that some children turn out negative and backward, or delinquent. In such cases, one looks for some critical gap in the means of transmitting the adult conventional culture to the child. In the case of all children, one may suppose adult status is achieved only against some negative and backward forces within the personality, and perhaps the first thing to be emphasized is that the transition to full adult responsibility is precarious at best. If there is even one seriously missing element, the organization fails to form.

In some cases, perhaps, the parents are admirable persons, but from another culture. Foreign-born parents, no matter how idealistic, may be rejected by the child as he becomes aware of their failure to fit the expectations of the group in which he is growing up. Thus the parents may have high ideals, but wrong ones so far as the adolescent and his friends are concerned. On the other hand, the parents may be estranged from the new culture to which they have come, and tend to be both cynical and pessimistic as to their own or their children's future in it. They fail to transmit the old culture to the child and are unable to help in the assimilation of the new.

In other cases where the child, seemingly in direct contrast to parents, turns out to be negative and backward, the answer may be found in a lack of interactive contact with the parents. Their physical absence during critical periods, their constant preoccupation with other matters, their interposition of third persons or agencies—nurses, schools—these and other preventions of affectionate interactive contact may leave the child cold and negative toward them and their values. Sometimes it may happen that the person interposed between parents and child is an older brother or sister, or several of them, who preempt various special places in the affections of the parents and leave the younger child with no role except a negative and backward one. It also happens that parents, brothers and sisters, or others, for unconscious reasons, may force a child into such a role, so that they may have a person within the family to express and act out the negative and backward elements in their own personalities, for which they are unable to accept responsibility. This is the "black sheep" pattern. The child may be cynical and defiant because he is in fact exploited and deprived. He may have good reason to connect conventional idealism with hypocrisy.

In many cases, however, one may see a more or less direct teaching process, by which cynical and pessimistic parents teach the child to be likewise. The father is seen as average on inhibitory demands and discipline and average on emotional supportiveness and warmth. The parent who himself takes the NB direction is not a stern disciplinarian, in other words, he is not a person who automatically provokes a revolt by too much insistence on a rigid code of values. He is rather a negative person who does not really believe in anything. He does on occasion give emotional supportiveness and warmth, but not in any clear relation to a set of values. Neither reward nor punishment from him bears any clear relationship to a set of values—either conventional or unconventional. What happens to the child seems adventitious, related to the egocentric mood of the parent rather than to a value-ideal. The lack of consistency tends to prevent the child's generalizing in any successful way.

The mother is seen as moderately high on inhibitory demands and discipline and average on emotional supportiveness and warmth. The discrepancy between father and mother is likely to be great in the mind of the child. They neither agree with the conventional culture nor with each other. The fact that in these data the mother turns out to be higher on inhibitory demands and discipline than the father may be a reflection of a tendency for the family to become mother-centered when the status base for the father breaks down, as it may in the case of immigrant families, or in other cases of economic deprivation.

His Effect on Group Satisfaction

The NB member has an adverse effect on satisfaction with goal attainment. With his cynicism and pessimism, he tends to break down all attempts at consensus upon which task activity could be based. Other group members are apt to complain, "There is no feeling of group solidarity—that is, the group working towards a common solution." Reactions to him and the lack of progress may differ. Some may defend him: "In the discussion, the members didn't show enough sensitiveness to the depth and complications of human motives." Others may attack his defenders: "This group couldn't solve the problem as it was supposed to, because some of the members believe in 'babying' trouble-makers in the case." (This remark in its original context was ostensibly about a case discussed in the group, but in fact the NB members of such groups tend to identify with, and defend, the similar NB persons described in the case.) Still other members merely complain about the lack of task-progress: "I disliked the indecisiveness of the solution." "I don't think our conclusions were detailed enough to be realistic." "This group didn't stay on the track so far as getting the job done is concerned."

The NB member himself is more likely to say, "Some of the suggestions seemed stupid to me." He may be right, but his negative attitude toward other group members is a part of the problem. He tends to move the group away from satisfaction with interpersonal relations as well as from goal attainment.

As a central figure in a group then, the NB member is more likely to be a "bad example" than a leader in any task-oriented sense. Nevertheless, on occasions when negative feeling is generally high in the group, and task progress difficult, he may exert a considerable influence through a kind of contagious spread of his tendencies toward deviance. He may become the chosen black sheep for simultaneous overt punishment and covert unconscious encouragement from others. He is generally incapable of holding to any consistent course, however, and is not likely to become more than the occasional leader of a deviant subgroup, so long as a general consensual value-base continues to hold the majority of the group together.

25

Type B: Toward Rejection
of Conservative Group Belief

The member located in the backward part of the group space by his fellow members seems heretical and disbelieving. He refuses to admit the validity of nearly all conservative group beliefs and values. He wishes to install another form of society, or perhaps a different mode of existence, a fantasy mode, in another place and time. He is neither clearly unfriendly nor friendly, but ambivalent. He is neither ascendant and expressive, nor submissive and completely inhibited, but tends to be poised, lost in the fantasy of wildly improbable ambitions, unable to decide anything or to actually strive for anything far in the future. In the realization of his own values he seems to be trying to move toward the rejection of all conservative group belief. "Man can solve all his important problems without help from a Supreme Being." "Heaven and Hell are products of man's imagination, and do not actually exist." "The whole structure of society must be radically changed." [1]

How He Sees Himself and How Others See Him

The B member seems to identify himself with the power of fantasy. He rates himself higher than does any other type on favoring expression and gratification. He does not, in fact, seem so, either to observers or to the group members. They tend rather to see his neighbor, UNB, as the type most favoring expression and gratifica-

[1] This is a probable value-statement of the B member.

tion. The B direction, perhaps, is that of the *wish* for, the *fantasy* of, gratification, rather than the realization of it.

The B type, more than any other type, tends to see others as acceptant of authority. He does not typically rate himself low on acceptance of authority, paradoxically enough, nor is he seen by others as low—this trait is seen as characteristic of the UN type. One may infer, perhaps, that the rejection of authority is wishful, as the fantasy of expression and gratification is wishful. But freedom of fantasy is nevertheless a kind of freedom and brings satisfactions of its own. The B type is least likely to rate others as arousing his curiosity, or to make them feel he rates them high. It is rather he who arouses them and makes them feel plain and uninteresting. The power to stimulate fantasy in others who are more repressed and controlled, to disturb and subtly manipulate those who are too "square" to realize how they are being influenced is a power typically exercised by the B type and by his more active adjacent types.

His Place in the Interaction Network

The B member is neither a very high nor a very low participator. He is average on total participation initiated. In his remarks to the group as a whole, he is average, and in return, others tend to address him at an average rate. He tends to address each one specifically at a rate which is congruent with the amount they address him. There is no particular imbalance. His total remarks addressed to individuals tend to be average, as theirs are to him. He does not hold a powerful position by reason of rank in the interaction network, but rather exercises his influence by more subtle symbolic means. He may exercise a strategic influence in support of a more active leader in the backward part of the space if that leader needs his support to hold power.

What Ideas and Values Will He Express?

The key to understanding the ideas and values of the B member is to recognize that he completely rejects the whole fabric of traditional religious beliefs, traditional localism, traditional concentration of wealth, and traditional political arrangements, which form the core of the conservative, local community within which the small group operates. He does not feel a part of the traditional local community, and he does not feel bound by its values. "Morals must vary according to circumstances and situations—there are no sacred, unalterable, eternal rules which must always be obeyed." To his mind the traditional religious beliefs are simply falsehoods, which have been trumped up some time in the past to maintain the advantages of the status quo for those in power: "Heaven and Hell are products of man's imagination, and do not actually exist."

"The Bible contains many magical and superstitious beliefs." "Christianity and all other religions are, at best, only partly true."

In spite of the general mood of rejection, however, there may be a tendency to phrase the rejection in rationalistic terms: "All the evidence that has been impartially accumulated goes to show that the universe has evolved in accordance with natural principles, so there is no necessity to assume a first cause, cosmic purpose, or God behind it." Thus the beliefs of the faithful may be attacked as if they were simply cognitive mistakes or deliberate falsehoods, rather than as symbols for human motivation, intention, desire, or will. There are, no doubt, many degrees of literalism in orthodoxy, but surely for many "believers" the central beliefs are taken in a far from literal empirical way, and rationalistic disproofs do little to disprove their "beliefs" to them. There is for the B type, as also for the F type, a strong nonrational, nonliteral, noncognitive motivating force in ostensibly "cognitive" beliefs. The B member is threatened by the hold which values, buttressed by belief and anchored in social norms, may have over his own motives and behavior. When he repudiates the cognitive truth of the buttressing beliefs, he is also repudiating the nonrational hold of the associated norms and values: "Man can solve all his important problems without help from a Supreme Being."

The B member does not want to be coerced by God, or by any of the agencies or entities that may have the same quality, such as society, or the government. Thus loyalty to country may also be called into question: "Patriotism in the modern world is a force which works against peace." The country or the nation is felt to have no right to compel loyalty or obedience: "It is wrong to punish a man if he helps another country because he prefers it to his own."

The social and economic aspects of the traditional local community as well as the religious and patriotic are rejected. When the tradition is capitalistic, the rejection may assert the value of socialism or communism in its stead: "Ultimately private property should be abolished, and complete socialism introduced." "Capitalism is immoral because it exploits the worker by failing to give him full value for his productive labor." The traditional differences in status and type of work between men and women may also be attacked: "Differences in pay between men and women doing the same work should be abolished." "The marriage ban on female teachers should be removed." Rejection of conservative group beliefs and social conformity should be encouraged by all possible means: "There should be far more controversial and political discussion over the radio."

In addition to the sentiments just described the B member has some probability of making statements in favor of rugged individualism and gratification, value relativism and expression, and emotional supportiveness and warmth. He tends to maintain a balance between positive and negative movement, the negative being justified as in the service of the positive. The values just mentioned, however, tend to be characteristic of more ascendant types. It may be that the emphasis of the B type on the rejection of the cognitive or "belief" aspects of orthodox values is a manifestation of inhibition. To disbelieve is less ascendant than to assert a contrary extroverted value.

The B member has some probability of making value-statements for the withholding of cooperation, for failure and withdrawal, or for identification with the underprivileged, but these are less characteristic of him than attacks on the cognitive grounds of orthodoxy and conservatism.

The Quality of His Interaction

Although he is active in some controversies, the B member apparently does not depend mainly upon logical analysis as the means of making his argument. Fantasy and feeling are used to form and guide behavior in preference to the more logical cognitive processes of induction and deduction. The orientation is unique, changeable, and intentionally evasive of the control of established ideas, beliefs, and values. The B member is markedly low on giving opinion, and is also low on receiving it. He is markedly low in receiving requests for suggestion. He does not argue so much as he dramatizes or symbolizes. He is relatively high on dramatizing and joking and on showing tension and laughing.

In response to the dramatization of fantasy presented by the B member, others also tend to laugh and show tension and to dramatize and joke. The B member is not, however, the main provoker of laughing and showing tension—the main receiver of laughs is more ascendant, usually more negative. The B member is markedly low on receiving agreement, but he tends not to receive disagreement either. He is low on both, presumably, because he avoids nearly all task-oriented attempts. He is not a usual target of hostility, in fact others are low in seeming unfriendly to him. Often, perhaps, they do not take his heresies very seriously.

One kind of attention he may attract from others is requests for information. These may be attempts to draw him out, to clarify his meaning, which is often cryptic and vague, and to elicit more positive reactions from him. If so, the attempt usually fails. He is balanced and probably ambivalent as to positive and negative feeling, and is average on both seeming friendly and on seeming unfriendly.

Conflicts and Coalitions with Others

The opponents of the B member appear "four-square" forward. All of the types who prefer to control action by values rather than by fantasy consider him a difficult deviant. His most direct opponent is the proponent of conservative group beliefs to whom his ideas are heretical. The battle of religious ideas, or of more secular goals still held by faith, does not always rage in the open. Sometimes the proponents of forward and backward movement take turns. Each may hold the group in his direction for a period, first one of work, then one of play. Such a cycle is very common in groups (40; 128). The opposition is thus not necessarily one of open disagreement and antagonism; when it is, other types are apt to be drawn in. The UF leader tries to counteract the lack of cooperation and group loyalty implied by the backward movement. The autocratic authority, UNF, becomes punishingly active as the struggle becomes more negative. The proponent of value-determined restraint urges more self-control upon the B member, the DF member urges more work, and the DNF member may urge self-sacrifice. On the positive side, the UPF leader for social solidarity and progress tries to take the B member into tow also as he pulls the group along by inspiration, whereas the less active counterparts on the forward side add the arguments of optimistic idealism, altruism, and salvation through love. The B member is about equally opposed to all of these. The central element is his disbelief in the ideas used to justify the social norms which control behavior. He is not likely to agree with any of his persuaders. Unlike some other types, who may agree with value-statements they themselves would not make, he is in opposition to nearly all value-statements, whatever their content. He prefers a fantasy integration.

Personality Traits

The present study provides only one personality test that measures directly in the B direction, and that one seems poorly named: Thurstone's trait vigorous. I am tempted to think this test, which depends upon self-description, may measure fantasies of vigor rather than overt realities. Rejection of forward values is the distinguishing criterion of the B type. It may be that the B type contains a variety of rather different personality characteristics, which have in common mainly the fact that they make literal belief and conformity difficult. The DNB neighbors are likely to be rough, simple, immature, and schizothymic, and desire independent self-sufficiency. These sound like traits which reflect a lack of opportunity, or ability, to mature—and might have something to do with a low level of literal belief and conformity. The NB neighboring type shows the traits of emotional sensitivity, insecurity, and seems radical and critical. I have advanced the hypothesis that the NB type (as well as surrounding types) may have difficulty in making the transition from an adolescent role to a conventionally sex-typed adult role. One line of interpretation posits the absence of suitable conventional models who could be loved and trusted, and who could give the necessary balance of love over hate in their rewards. This also seems a congruent set of circumstances for producing a rejection of conservative group beliefs.

It will be recalled that one of the most persistent themes of the B direction, at least in the items available, is disbelief in the existence of God: "Man can solve all his important problems without help from a Supreme Being." Presumably this is God the Father—the God who is associated with conditional love, with heaven and hell, or reward and punishment for right and wrongdoing. The assertion is that there is no such Father. The B member seems to say: "Do not threaten me with that kind of future punishment. There is no such Father." It may be that some persons are motivated in the B direction by a disappointment with the absence of a desired father, or disappointment with a father who is felt to be bad, or with a father who was not good enough or strong enough to inspire acceptance. The rejection of literalism in religious belief is a relatively impersonal way to express this disappointment and hostility. The B type tries to remain neutral, balanced between negative and positive. To put the negative feeling in the form of a denial of the existence of the symbol of the *father* (God) seems a plausible compromise.

Furthermore, such a denial is consistent with the position between submission and dominance that the B member maintains. His neighbors on the UNB side show more nervous tension and open aggression than he, with traits that are dominant, aggressive, eccentric, unconcerned, self-centered, impulsive, and even paranoid. These are more extreme and direct repudiations of authority and conventionality. On the UPB side, members have a set of traits with a "desirable" social flavor, but which nevertheless show a freedom of emotion and feeling from the constraints of conformity: poise, confidence, spontaneity, enthusiasm, talkativeness; and extroversion. The B member seems to prepare the way for freedom by a declaration of independence, but he does not actually show the freedom, either in the aggressive or in the affectionate directions, nor in the ascendant self-picture. His freedom, as declared, is intellectual and cognitive—freedom from literal belief. Meanwhile, aggression, sexuality, and egoism are all held in moderate check in the B personality. He shows some effects of conventional socialization and is less heretical, perhaps, than he insists. He is perhaps partly believing, and all the more strongly denying.

How He Sees His Parents

The father of the B member is seen as moderately low in inhibitory demands and discipline. This seems to be in line with the wishes of the B member, at least since, as we have seen above, there are indications of disappointment and rejection of the father. The mother is perhaps higher on inhibitory demands and discipline than the father, but is only average. One should look for the possibility that the status of the father in the local conservative community, is low or insecure, and that the mother has assumed additional status and power within the family. The family may be mother-centered, and the identification of the child with her is likely to be stronger than with the father. Both mother and father are seen as relatively high on emotional supportiveness and warmth. The basis is present for an identification with the personal traits, perhaps the status or class-conscious attitudes of mother or father, but not for an identification with conservative values.

The parents are not likely to hold conservative values, being likely to show some pessimistic cynicism rather than optimistic idealism. Insofar as the child does identify with both of them, or either of them, he will automatically assume a heretical far left attitude. On the other hand, it is probable that his attitude toward the parents is very ambivalent—he holds about as much negative attitude toward them as positive. He is likely to be disappointed with them as they are disappointed with the larger conservative order. But two negatives do not make a positive—that is, there is nothing in this combination of rejections that leads clearly away from the B direction. In the sense of belief, the consistency of ideas and the employment of deduction and induction, the B direction is the direction of maximum and preferred chaos. Chaos added to chaos still adds to chaos.

His Effects on Group Satisfaction

As expected, the B member tends to move the group markedly away from satisfaction with goal attainment. He rejects the consensual basis of belief and values upon which particular group goals might be based. His direction is an attack on the external authority from which such goals may be received, and from which rewards and punishments may come to the group. In fact, the system of rewards and punishments may be the aspect of the group that is most specifically resented and attacked. In any case, the desire of the B member is to dissociate the distribution of rewards and resources within the group from conformity to group values and norms. Insofar as he is successful in doing so, the motivation of other group members for doing the group tasks tends to be undermined. Those who lose their motivation may not directly feel dissatisfied that group goal attainment is interfered with, but those who remain faithful do.

From the point of view of the external authority evaluating the group, its performance is almost sure to suffer.

One might conclude that the B member will almost as surely interfere with satisfactory interpersonal relations within the group. This does not follow. On the average he tends to move the group neither toward nor away from satisfaction with interpersonal relations. Why neither way? Probably because attitudes toward conformity are completely separable from attitudes toward others as actual persons. The B member is against conventional beliefs and values in the abstract. Toward actual persons within the group he is both positive and negative—that is, ambivalent. The feeling he elicits from others is also ambivalent. Sometimes they like him for saying things they secretly would like to say, sometimes they dislike him for saying things they try to repress. His heresies, ironies, wry remarks, and the like suffer the same fate as other fantasies and jokes. They may or may not succeed. In almost any group the heretic may have his day of triumph. This will not prevent his being burned on another occasion. In a longer time perspective, what happens to him helps to determine the degree of literalness with which belief is held in the group: those values and beliefs according to which rewards and punishments are distributed within the group. Thus his effect upon satisfaction with interpersonal relations within the group will differ according to how badly some redistribution is needed. He may help to break down an unfair and unsatisfactory distribution, but he is just as likely to undermine a fair and satisfactory one.

26

Type PB: Toward
Permissive Liberalism

The member located in the positive-backward part of the group space by his fellow members is friendly and receptive to jokes and stories, neither ascendant nor submissive, but equalitarian. He is not task-oriented, but responsive to others as individual persons, appreciative and likable, ready to share and enjoy sociability. He wants everybody to have what he needs, without a lot of complications. He is concerned about persons and their growth. In the realization of his own values he seems to be trying to move toward permissive liberalism. "Divorce should be subject to fewer old-fashioned restrictions, and become more a matter of mutual consent."

How He Sees Himself and How Others See Him

The PB member seems to see and feel himself to be the well-loved child of a warm and loving mother. He is the natural object of love in the interacting group of his peers, as well. He is the member other group members tend to like most, dislike least, and admire most. He gives relief from the unpleasant feelings aroused by the negative members, and from the pressures of task-achievement and value-realization. Moreover, he does it without becoming over-ascendant or demanding in time and status. He tends to rate others high on personal involvement and makes others feel they are entertaining, warm and personal, and well-liked. He is the perfect appreciator and understudy of the more active adjacent type, UPB. Although he may make others feel he rates them low on favoring expression and gratification, this can hardly seem a serious reproach when he offers them such appreciation and support.

313

However, one should not forget to look for the possibly hidden side of the PB member. He may be substituting liking and being liked as a way of avoiding NF movement. If he fears the loss of love, the cooling of that current of warmth and personal interchange in which he bathes, he may be unable to try for achievement in any way that would hamper his fantasy or provoke negative feelings from his fellows.

His Place in the Interaction Network

The member who moves in the PB direction tends to be average in total participation initiated. He is also average in remarks addressed to the group as a whole. However, he attracts participation. Others are likely to address him more frequently than he addresses them. Thus his sum received is likely to be high, whereas his sum addressed to specific individuals is likely to be only average. He does appear to be in a strategic position in that others seek to interact with him, apparently because the emotional reactions obtained from him are directly rewarding. He tends not to be addressed in matters that pertain to group goal attainment, however, and in this sense, he is not in a strategic position, nor is he high in the power hierarchy.

What Ideas and Values Will He Express?

Only one characteristic statement is available from the studies upon which the present work is based: "Divorce should be subject to fewer old-fashioned restrictions and become more a matter of mutual consent." However, we may attempt to make something of this one item. The PB member, for example, is supposed by inference to be high on permissive liberalism. Along with the B member, he shares a dislike for restrictions of a conventional or conservative sort. In place of an ethic based upon a restrictive orthodoxy, religious, economic, or political, he would like to substitute an ethic based on an assumption of expanding resources, of personal growth, of social change conducive to growth—the kind of ethic, in short, which the well-loved child of an encouraging mother experiences. He wants to make the world for others the way his mother made it for him. He may make statements encouraging trust in the goodness of others and in favor of equalitarianism, as indicated by the phrase "mutual consent" above. That divorce should be a matter of mutual consent implies not only a reduction of the legal and religious restrictions which regulate the marriage bond, but also a greater equality of women with men than presently exists. It may be that the PB type tends to identify with the mother and to champion her rights vis-à-vis a more authoritarian father. This would be consistent with other parts of the picture. And assuming a conflict of this sort in the background, it is consistent to expect that there will be some tendency to withhold cooperation in relation to restrictive authority and to identify with the underprivileged when it is felt that the underprivileged are wronged, whether they are children, women, racial minorities, the poor, or others. We may infer that the PB member wants all of these to have a chance to grow, to improve their position, and to achieve full equality.

These sentiments imply an identification with persons in the lower status positions—a desire to bring them up in status. But the PB member is in a middling position in most groups, and he identifies, to some extent, with persons in the more ascendant positions near his own as well as with the underprivileged. He takes what might be thought of as the stereotyped mother's position in his tendency to favor emotional supportiveness and warmth, and he also speaks occasionally of value-relativism and expression and of social success or its equivalent as a desirable goal.

The Quality of His Interaction

Although the PB type is not markedly high on any one category of interaction, the pattern of his initiation seems self-consistent and eloquent of his appreciation of others. He is high in asking for opinion and information and high on receiving information and requests for information in return. He is low on disagreeing and seeming unfriendly and high on seeming friendly. He avoids task-oriented analysis for the most part and is low on asking for suggestion, giving suggestion, and giving opinion. His own contribution to the growing culture of the group is more likely to be symbolic than logical, and he is high (though not markedly so) on dramatizing and joking, as well as on showing tension and laughing.

He is the ideal audience for jokes and, of all types of personality, he is apparently the preferred recipient for jokes. In response to his appreciation, others are markedly likely to dramatize and joke, and at the same time they are high on giving information. From the context one would expect the information to be mostly personal—others speaking to him about themselves and expressing their feelings and fantasies. As noted earlier, others often talk more than the PB member does—they are apparently delighted to find an appreciative audience. Since they are initiating rather than responding, they seldom either agree or disagree with him and are generally low in asking for opinion, asking for suggestion, and on seeming unfriendly. The PB member is also low on giving opinion, as pointed out above, an indication that his contribution tends to be nonanalytical and nontask-oriented. The PB member is the eliciter—not the more talkative initiator—of jokes, anecdotes, friendly personal and social small talk.

But in spite of the social-emotional flavor of his role it is important to note that the **PB** member is also addressed relatively often with suggestions, probably from the forward side of the group. He is a likely representative of the peer-oriented group of equals within the group—"the brothers" or "sisters," or "the boys" or "the girls"; and his approval is sought hopefully to bring them along, since some of them are nonconventional and potentially deviant. In this sense he may perform a task-oriented function somewhat indirectly.

Conflicts and Coalitions with Others

Opposition to the **PB** member usually arises from the forward and negative side of the space, because the rewards he gives out are free—not conditional upon the goodness of the other person, his task-performance, his belief, or his loyalty. The opposition feels that this "give-away" may undermine the system of social controls based on reward and punishment according to performance. The UF leader, who wishes to extract group loyalty and cooperation from all members, will argue with the **PB** member that he is too personalistic, too soft, too willing to put up with disloyal and uncooperative members, unable to withhold reward until a proper degree of conformity has been obtained. The UNF autocratic authority will feel the same way and make the same argument, with perhaps more moral disapproval of the "pampering of troublemakers" and the failure to punish deviants. To the UNF autocratic authority the **PB** member may appear to be almost a "traitor" who deliberately and perversely lets "enemies" in through the back door. The "enemies" are typically associated with repressed elements of the UNF personality—the childish, the weak, the fearful, the perverse, the deviant, and the cruel. The action of the **PB** member directly undermines the defense of the autocratic authority against his repressed characteristics. The UNF type is outraged because he is personally threatened with an internal revolution. Not only does he see bad persons rewarded, but he is envious of their easy reward and must repress his envy.

The proponent of tough-minded assertiveness (type UN) expresses his impatience and hostility without so much moralism. His solution is simply to let the weak die, or to give them a push over the brink if necessary. He wants to use force with no nonsense to see that the best thing for himself happens. Punishment is preferred over reward as the means of forcing conformity. He may simply feel that reward in the form of love is ineffective, or he may be threatened by it through his association of it with femininity or with weakness.

There is no meeting of minds in the conflict between the **PB** proponent of permissive liberalism and these three preceding types. And yet the conflict does not necessarily continue overtly all the time. It tends to be periodic. As we have seen in the discussion of interaction above, the reaction to the PB member for most of the time, or for most of the members, is friendly and not at all negative. On the average, he is the object of liking and not the initiator of controversial efforts. The usual condition is one of compromise in which he, or other types nearby, perform positively integrative social functions for many or most of the group members. A division of labor between a "task-leader" of some kind and a more popular object of affection, a "best liked man," is a very common arrangement in small groups (21). Whether or not the task-leader tends too strongly in the UNF direction, and whether or not a working coalition can be preserved between him and a less active popular leader like the PB type is presumably a crucial determinant of the quality of life in the group.

The proponent of conservative group beliefs, F, may well address reprimands to the PB member, because of the latter's laxity of belief. The DF worker is likely to feel there is something shallow and a little brainless about giving unconditional reward and encouragement to members who seem to be neither thinking, nor self-critical, nor working. A greater degree of restraint would help them to "think twice," he believes. The DNF member believes that they should not only think twice, but should institute some sacrifice for values, since he does. He feels that the PB member with his over-permissive liberalism wants to reward the underprivileged for actions that controvert the values that he himself sacrifices to dramatize and uphold. The PB member is thus subversive. The DN rejector of social success is envious of the undeserved rewards given to others, and jealous of the affection received by the PB member. It would hurt his pride to be rescued by the affection of the PB member, and he prefers to reject the whole lot. "People are no damn good," is his judgment. That includes both the helpers and the helped.

Personality Traits

There are no personality tests in the present study which directly measure the PB direction. The PB member gives positive social responses easily, he seems to try to encourage growth, change, creativity of a kind that can not usually be specified in advance, or deduced from existing patterns. He is basically positive toward others, with a sustained and trusting interest in them. He shares with his neighboring type, P, the combination of trustful and accessible traits with intellectual efficiency and ego strength, though perhaps not quite to the same degree. He is also similar to his DP neighbor in seeming calm and stable and showing attitudes that suggest mature responsibility and achievement. These neighboring traits do, however, have an implication of greater control of drives for intellectual work than he ordinarily has. The **PB** type is nonconventional and allows more passage of spontaneous feeling into social expression.

The freedom of social expression does not reach the point where it becomes dominant, however. Thus, the **PB** member shares to some degree, but not to a full extent, the traits of the UPB type, who is enthusiastic, talkative, extrovertive, and spontaneous. The poise and confidence of UPB seem less extrovertive and may be closer to traits of **PB**. The **PB** type is socially receptive as well as spontaneous. Thus he will show, but to a limited degree, the traits of the UP type: leadership and appearance of higher social status. He is sociable and oriented to social participation like the UP type, but in a moderate and appreciative way, rather than in a voluble and egocentric way. His picture of himself seems secure and nondemanding. He seems to expect liking as a matter of course, and receives it. He is active and mobile to a certain degree, but not to a dominant degree.

How He Sees His Parents

The parents of the PB type are seen as similar to himself. In their parental roles, they have provided the kind of social environment for his growth that he provides for group members. Both father and mother are seen as moderately low on inhibitory demands and discipline. They have been patient and encouraging with him. Both are seen as moderately high on emotional supportiveness and warmth. They have provided resources for his growth, in his own time and in his own terms, rather than having meted out strictly controlled reward and punishment according to momentary performance. At the same time they have not been cynical and pessimistic about values and the possibility that the child will be led to accept some. On this issue they are noncommittal. They are not consistently on the side of optimistic idealism either. They seem not to deal with this polarity in any salient way, although there is an anti-authoritarian feeling in their conception of the parental role. They prefer to attract and encourage the child through emotional support-iveness and warmth rather than to compel him to satisfactory per-formance through the exercise of authority. He, in turn, takes over this preference, along with the abilities to give warmth which are aroused by the affectionate care of the parents. At the same time, it appears unlikely that the parents will be as much alike as implied in this twin-description. Their discrepancies from each other are average. But discrepancies may be softened by the generally positive social tone and the general disin-clination to engage in abstract arguments about ideas and values. The child of such positive, though unconventional, parents is provided with interpersonal abilities and techniques for softening conflicts within other groups to which he may belong.

His Effect on Group Satisfaction

In this light, it should come as no surprise that the PB member tends to move the group toward satisfaction with interpersonal relations. The real problem, perhaps, is why he is not the type *most* likely to have this effect. The answer seems to be that although he is the preeminent "object" of liking, the symbol of the free availability of warm, affectionate feeling, he is not the preeminent "agent" in bringing about the conditions that make for widespread interpersonal satisfaction. The type which performs this function most effectively, apparently, is the DP member, who is characterized as "understanding," and who symbolizes the condition of trust in the goodness of others. Dominating over-participation most strongly interferes with interpersonal satisfaction. The PB member is probably not so effective an alternative to the ideology of tough-minded assertiveness as is the DP member. The PB type may even, in some cases, provide the socially positive interactive support and the altruistic ideological cover for the UN practitioner of tough-minded assertiveness. Such a combination is a coalition of the far left. The PB type sometimes provides the sheep's clothing for the UN wolf.

This possible combination, or other less extreme combinations with members in the backward portion of the space, may also indicate why, in spite of the possession of socially gratifying and likeable traits, the PB member is likely to move the group away from satisfaction with goal attainment. Group goal attainment usually requires effort disciplined by consensual values. The PB member can neither sustain the discipline, nor is he able to work effectively for value consensus. He has been taught to depend upon the collection of affection instead.

27

Type DP: Toward Trust
in the Goodness of Others

The member located in the downward-positive part of the group space by his fellow members seems friendly and nonassertive, calm and ready to admire others. He is neither primarily task-oriented nor expression-oriented, but responsive to others as individual persons. He tends to trust and identify with others. He feels people are good; he likes them in his calm and somewhat submissive way. He tends to emulate and imitate those he likes. In the realization of his own values he seems to be trying to move toward trust in the goodness of others. "People are basically and innately good." "The vast majority of men are truthful and dependable."

How He Sees Himself and How Others See Him

The person moving in the DP direction sees himself as equalitarian. The observers agree, but other group members give their highest rating to the neighboring type, DPF. That there is some self-depreciation in the self-picture of the DP member, which works to the advantage of others, is implied by his tendency to rate himself as high on acceptance of authority and others as high on self-confidence. He makes others feel he regards them with admiration and rates them high on understanding and valuable for a logical task. They, in turn, rate him high on understanding, as do the observers. He is the least likely of all types to rate himself high, or to be seen by observers or other group members as dominating, or to make others feel he dislikes them. He is the least likely to feel others are resentful toward him. If there is a mental process or ability of the

320

personality with which he most closely associates his self-picture, it is probably with the power of "understanding," and this, in turn, is probably associated with a liking for observation, perception, and the exercise of intelligence.

His Place in the Interaction Network

The DP member tends to be low on total interaction initiated. His remarks addressed to the group as a whole tend to be low. He seems to avoid the impersonality of remarks addressed to the group as a whole, and rather prefers to speak to particular individuals. He is high in his tendency to address his remarks in this way. Others in return, are average in addressing their remarks to him, so he is average in his tendency to receive from others. Since he is low in rank in the power hierarchy, his influence, if any, is felt both through the remarks he elicits from others, particularly information, and through his favorable effect on the lowering of aggressive and negative feeling within the group.

What Ideas and Values Will He Express?

The key value, as indicated by the name chosen for the direction, seems to be a trust in the goodness of others: "People are basically and innately good." "The vast majority of men are truthful and dependable." It may be that this direction (as in the case of others) is sometimes over-determined by a need to defend against its direct opposite, in this case, tough-minded assertiveness, which includes a tendency to be suspicious of others and to devalue them. The DP type may fear and tend to deny that these tendencies exist in others, or in the self. It may be that there are two types of "positives": "true positives" and "false positives." The former would be those whose aggressive drives are actually low in comparison to their affectionate drives; the latter would be those who manage, though under considerable strain, to keep their aggressive drives suppressed even though they are basically higher than their affectionate drives. In either case, it would seem appropriate to call the value-position, DP, "tender-minded" as it was called by William James who originally distinguished "tough-mindedness" from "tender-mindedness." It may also be that it is often possible to tell true positives from false positives, in that the false, although they hold strongly to the verbalized value position, tend to betray the negative elements in their overt interaction, and fail to obtain the positive response from others that they may hope for.

The items measuring tender-mindedness obtainable from Melvin's study (115) are probably correlated with conservatism for the most part, which would make them more characteristic of DPF than the present position. The ones which sound most uncorrelated with conservatism and religious orthodoxy, however, seem appropriate for DP: "Blood sports, like fox hunting for instance, are vicious and cruel, and should be forbidden." Here the concern for protection against aggression, particularly sadistic aggression, is evident. So also in the statement: "The dropping of the first atom bomb on a Japanese city, killing thousands of innocent women and children, was morally wrong and incompatible with our kind of civilization." The concern for minority groups exposed to aggression is shown in the rather mild statement: "Jews are as valuable citizens as any other group." The combination of tender-mindedness with religious orthodoxy is shown in items such as: "The Church is the main bulwark opposing the evil trends in modern society." "The church should attempt to increase its influence on the life of the nation." The last two items are possibly characteristic of DPF, probably not DP.

Statements expressing straight religious orthodoxy, are expected to be characteristic of the F direction, and not at all correlated with the DP direction. The DP type may, however, make statements expressing belief in, or hope for, salvation through love, optimistic idealism and altruistic love. These directions, DPF, and PF, have in common with DP the element of a positive attitude toward other people, a concern for those who are in trouble or exposed to danger. The feeling is that they should be cared for as a tender parent cares for his children. The term "tender-minded" also tends to imply a kind of self-protective introversion which is, to some degree, related to trust in the goodness of others. Thus the DP member may at times speak in a way favorable to self-knowledge and subjectivity. The common element, however, is the introversion, not the conservatism.

Similarly, on occasion, the DP member may speak in favor of devaluation of the self as an introverted defense against assertiveness, or as a preference for not rocking the boat and provoking attack from others. The DP direction is not linked with either conservatism or radicalism. Where a threat comes from the conservative direction, the DP member may speak for withholding of cooperation, identification with the underprivileged, permissive liberalism, and equalitarianism.

The Quality of His Interaction

The regard of the DP member for others is shown in his high rate of asking for opinion, his high rate of seeming friendly (see page 103) and his avoidance of seeming unfriendly. He also asks for suggestion, but does not lean consistently toward the task, in that he is also high on showing tension and laughing. Others seem friendly to him and dramatize and joke with him. They joke and he laughs, but not vice versa. They are low in showing tension and laughing in relation to him, low on disagreement and seeming unfriendly. They give information and opinion, and he agrees. They ask for information and he gives it. He seems to avoid taking the initiative either in the task direction or in the fantasy direction. He is low on giving suggestion, and prefers to turn the initiative back to the other by asking him for opinion and suggestion. Others do respond with opinions, but not with suggestions. The exchange is friendly, but preliminary in feeling, so far as work is concerned.

Conflicts and Coalitions with Others

The direction opposite in all respects to the present one is UN— tough-minded assertiveness. Some doubt may be raised about whether this is the direction from which verbal opposition is most likely to come, however. The data are too poor to do much more than guess, and this is partly because the downward types in general are submissive and rarely argue their value position. They are more likely to lend their support to the types immediately above them, who are similar to them in many respects, except that they are more assertive and more likely to take leadership. Support may be given and function effectively in the power struggle, with very little overt participation on the part of the less assertive. The more assertive types carry the argument to the most assertive leaders on the opposite side of the space, thus often segmenting, or polarizing, the group into two or more conflicting coalitions, each of which carries along its own less assertive supporting members.

It is still true, however, that the less assertive members may be important psychological figures for each other. It is possible that they are especially likely to compare themselves with each other because of similarity in status or power. In the present case the DN type is, like the DP type, submissive and not likely to talk much. In the two other dimensions, however, he is the direct opposite. The attitudes, as well as the value-statements, of the DN type, say that "People are no damn good." He is for rejection of social success. He rejects most especially those UP leaders who are most successful, and who are likely to be leading the coalition to which the DP person gives his support. Consequently, the DN type is a threat to the DP type, whether he says much or not. It may be that there are occasions, though rare, when the two overtly confront each other, recognizing their status similarity. Children sometimes do this when they argue: "My father can lick your father." It may even be that the DN type is more apt to state his argument that "People are no damn good" to the DP member who urges him to trust in the goodness of others, than to the UP member. It could be that the submissive types of members are more likely to confront other submissive types than they are to carry the overt argument up the status ranks. Status intimidation, in other words, may tend to divert the opposition felt for persons in higher ranks to those of the same (or lower) ranks instead. This effect, if actual, would be difficult to see, since the general tendency is for interaction to be addressed to the person who has just spoken, and this, in turn, means that those who speak a lot are going to receive a lot. So long as this happens, the DN type may be a psychologically important figure for the DP type, but overt confrontation may be rare. Research is needed on this—the idea expressed here is pure speculation.

Other downward types may also feel opposition for the DP type, though they may not express it. The DNF type, for example, believes in self-sacrifice for values. One of the implicit premises of this sort of self-sacrifice is that the universe is *not* a loving place, and that trust in the goodness of people is trust misplaced. You have to "do it yourself." The DNB member, who has accepted failure and wants to withdraw, has no available affection or trust. He has reason to repress whatever positive feeling he might have had, in order to cut his ties and get away. The DB member who is engaged in withholding of cooperation is likely to feel that the DP member is exerting a pressure for cooperation, and he resists.

Finally, there are two additional downward directions in which the relation may not be clear. The DF proponent of self-knowledge and subjectivity, we may guess, is likely to address occasional appeals to the DP member and is likely to receive agreement. These two, at the submissive level, probably tend to cooperate as do their more active counterparts, the task-leader and the integrative social leader. The D type, who exemplifies devaluation of the self, if he speaks at all, is likely to receive the agreement of the DP member.

The DP member presents some unexpected potentials for coalitions in that there are several value-positions he will often agree with, though he will not initiate. These lie generally upward and forward from his own position. The positions with which he will unexpectedly agree, though not initiate, include conventional group beliefs, group loyalty and cooperation; and toward the negative side, value-determined restraint and even perhaps autocratic authority. The DP member carries his value on trust in the goodness of others far enough to agree with these generally far-removed types, the latter two nearly opposite to his own position.

The natural coalitions of the DP member are with those close by. He is particularly apt to agree with the equalitarian position. He agrees with altruistic love. On the other hand, he is unexpectedly allergic to coalitions with types further backward than himself. In spite of his own tendency to advocate these values on occasion—probably when other defenders are lacking—he tends not to agree with those who speak for withholding of cooperation, identification with the underprivileged, and permissive liberalism. He tends to identify more in the forward direction. The types he most opposes are opposite him. He is most likely to disagree with tough-minded assertiveness and individualistic isolationism.

Personality Traits

The salient personality traits of the DP member are those that make him test calm and stable, and suggest maturity, responsibility, and probability of achievement. Theoretically the DP type is balanced between forward and backward movement. He shares to an important extent the traits of his neighboring forward type, DPF. Like DPF, he is likely to be practical and responsible, to have will-control and character stability, and to be on the submissive side. If male, he will show evidence of successful assimilation of the conventional male adult sex-role, since he is reasonably high on conservatism and role-playing ability. Males should presumably test masculine and conservative, females, presumably feminine and conservative, if one had the tests. DP is less active than the P type, and may show to some extent the D trait, withdrawn, but not to a marked degree. Like the P type, he is trustful, accessible, and shows intellectual efficiency. Perhaps the key concept is that of ego strength, which he has in common with the P type, but uses to a somewhat greater degree to harness his basic drives and instincts. Or it may be that he is one of those in which the drive of aggression is somewhat less strong to begin with. His type is ordinarily the one which seems to show either the lowest aggressive drive or the one most successfully harnessed. This smooth harnessing of the drives, not only the aggressive, but the sexual ones, as well as the anxious, fearful ones, and the appetitive ones is characteristic of *ego strength,* the trait strongest in the P direction, theoretically.

How He Sees His Parents

The DP member, who wants to trust in the goodness of others, has adequate models to trust in his parents, as he sees them. If the DP member happens to be a "false positive", he may have had to overcome a distrust for one or the other parent, who may have been tough-minded, assertive, and deceptive in some way. But in the usual case, the "true positive," one would expect to find the parents trustworthy. Both father and mother are ordinarily moderately high on optimistic idealism versus cynical pessimism. They are average on emotional supportiveness and warmth and are moderately low on inhibitory demands and discipline. The child can depend upon them for a degree of unconditional love. Interaction with them is mild and thoughtful. They in turn believe in the generalized goodness of people, especially perhaps of children. In case of deviance on his part, the DP type is apt to receive from them an understanding attitude, a presentation of the expected normative pattern and an expression of belief in his ability and desire to live up to it. Acceptance of him as a person, and love, are not cut off in case he shows ordinary deviance. On the other hand, the parents do not depend upon emotional supportiveness and warmth alone, nor are they more than average on it. They combine supportiveness of the child with a support of the normative patterns through optimistic belief, and in accepting the parental support, the child tends to accept also the normative patterns. The child of such parents, in the group setting, tends to perform much the same function for other members, who find him in turn, "understanding." But the fact that so many other personality types are so much more assertive than the DP member tends to prevent him, for the most part, from acting in a leadership capacity in the usual sense.

His Effect on Group Satisfaction

The DP member tends to move the group neither toward nor away from satisfaction with goal attainment. In addition to his general tendency to stay on the quiet side, he is not a leader in the formation or enforcement of group norms.

His virtue is that he tends to move the group markedly toward interpersonal satisfaction. Not only does he avoid the kind of over-activity that tends to crowd others out (20), but he seems to offer the group an alternative attitude of acceptance, trust, and understanding that tends to alleviate some of the ill-effects of the over-activity of others. His presence is strongly felt, and appreciated, though his mode of interaction is receptive and appreciative rather than extroverted and active.

28

Type DPF: Toward
Salvation Through Love

The member located in the downward-positive-forward part of the group space by his fellow members seems friendly and submissive, and at the same time, task- and value-oriented. He is ready to follow and obey, ready to confess wrongs and conform. He is respectful, loving, gentle, idealistic, and altruistic. In the realization of his own values he seems to be trying to move toward salvation of some kind, religious or social, or perhaps interpersonal, through the giving and receiving of love. "There are no human problems that love cannot solve."

How He Sees Himself and How Others See Him

The person who moves strongly in the DPF direction seems to depend for his self-picture on the power to be both good and submissive as a way of giving and obtaining love. He sees himself as equalitarian, or more exactly, guesses that others will rate him high on this trait, and in fact they do. He is actually submissive and very much oriented to conformity with group norms, as well as socially positive, and so it is likely that to him "equality" has something of the flavor of "equality-under-the-law." He is the least likely of all types to guess that others could rate him as dominating, and in this he is very close to accurate. By the same token he is least likely to be regarded as favoring expression and gratification, either by members or observers. The observers (not the group members) find him to be the least entertaining and the least curiosity-provoking type—he is, in fact, apparently too good and too nice to be a symbol for any kind of temptation.

His Place in the Interaction Network

The total interaction initiated by the DPF type is likely to be low, as compared to the group average. He is not only likely to be rather low in absolute terms, but the ratio of his total remarks addressed to the group as a whole is also likely to be low. Although he is in favor of forward movement he does not take the initiative for proposals to the total group. He tends rather to address specific individuals when he speaks. The rate of interaction he receives from others in relation to what he initiates is about average. He is neither ignored, nor is he sought. His position in the group in relation to the power hierarchy is relatively low, but he may be very significant as a supporter of a forward, or positive-moving leader.

What Ideas and Values Will He Express?

"There are no human problems that love cannot solve." The person who moves strongly in the DPF direction is tender-minded in that he tends to downgrade the importance of power, aggression, and material wealth in human affairs. "Our present difficulties are due to moral rather than to economic causes." His moralism, though definitely present, is submissive and positively oriented to other people—even toward those who transgress and may actually be threats. He is sorrowful and wants to be helpful. He believes that God will forgive, that those who have been wronged will forgive, and that love will transform those who are aggressive and deviant. He may believe that both the problems and the solution are cataclysmic in scope, however. "Only by going back to religion can civilization hope to survive."

The DPF position is related to, but not identical with, straight conventional religious orthodoxy. The person in the DPF position has a concern for people and avoids any overt assertiveness. Conventional teachings of a church may be accepted and endorsed, even though the conclusions accepted are not necessarily entailed by logic. Thus: "It is right and proper that religious education in schools should be compulsory." "Birth control, except when medically indicated, should be made illegal." Attitudes toward sex and appropriate sex roles are definitely conservative: "Sex relations except in marriage are always wrong." The sexual drives, as well as the aggressive ones, are devalued as too assertive, and tend to be transformed, either actually or hopefully, into a more tender-minded and sublimated kind of love: "Tenderness is more important than passion in love." The cataclysmic feeling suggested by the emphasis on "salvation" may reflect the difficulty of this taming and transforming for some persons. The cataclysm would occur if these drives were to be released and then followed by a dreadful and final punishment.

The allied submissive positions, which also reflect the struggles of inhibition, are positions in favor of self-knowledge and subjectivity, and devaluation of the self. The DPF member may on occasion speak in favor of these values. Conservative group beliefs, altruistic love, and equalitarianism are also values for which he may speak, although these three value-positions are more characteristic of less inhibited persons. There is a long-range optimism in the idea of "salvation," perhaps, but it implies serious threats in the present, from which one must be saved.

The Quality of His Interaction

The DPF member is task-oriented in that he asks for suggestion and gives opinion, but he avoids the more ascendant aspects of task-effort by giving information rather than suggestion. He seems friendly and adds a positive social note by asking for opinion. He seems to make a place for others to cooperate with him in a more ascendant task-role. They appear to do so. They seem friendly, give information and opinion to him, and agree with him. He is likely to agree with them. They are unlikely to show tension or laugh in relation to him. He is nonthreatening and arouses little fantasy since he seldom, if ever, dramatizes or jokes. He is task-oriented and, in spite of his lack of ascendance, others ask him for suggestion.

Conflicts and Coalitions with Others

The most threatening antithetical ideal figure for the DPF member is probably the DNB member, the member who proclaims failure and withdrawal. This latter person, like himself, has renounced assertive instincts, but unlike himself, has failed to receive, or to accept, the conventional compensations. DNB's attitude implicitly says that the idea that one can be saved by love is false. The person who accepts failure and withdrawal refuses to make a good thing out of a bad thing, and so tends to shake the faith of the submissive, positive, conventional member. Others who also threaten the DPF member are the proponents of rejection of social success, withholding of cooperation, and rejection of conventional group beliefs. Due to the general tendency of communication to be addressed to more prominent members, there may be little overt indication of the opposition just described, but it is suggested that the opposition is, psychologically, especially salient for the DPF member.

The DPF type is reasonably consistent in what he will say and what he will agree with. He is a little more receptive to the values of those upward and forward in relation to him than we might expect from what he says, however. He is likely to agree with those who advocate group loyalty and cooperation, and value-determined restraint, as well as autocratic authority. Like others on the positive forward side, he is prepared to yield to ascendance and negativity when these attitudes are presented as justified on moralistic or conventional grounds. He is markedly likely to agree both with the proponents of altruistic love and with the defender of conventional group beliefs. Those most likely to provoke his disagreement, if any do, are those who advocate rejection of social conformity, rejection of conventional group beliefs, and rugged individualism and gratification.

Personality Traits

The DPF member is a "good worker" and a "good group member." He will be found to be practical and responsible, to have high will-control and high character stability, and to be submissive. He is concerned with pleasing a good parent or other parental figures—an employer, society, the community, the church, God. Like his neighboring type, PF, he will probably be on the conservative side, and if we had the tests we would expect him or her to have successfully adopted the conventional adult sex role. The DPF member will have moderate role-playing ability—he can put himself in the place of the other, understand how the other feels and acts, what the other expects, and will be able, at least internally, to reproduce these modes of behavior as well as his own. His attitudes are basically positive. Like the P neighboring type he is trustful, accessible, and reasonably high on intellectual efficiency and ego strength. He is similar to his DP neighboring type in seeming mature, calm, stable, responsible, and capable of achievement. His general activity level is not high, he may even, on occasion, seem a little withdrawn, like his D neighbor, but he is attentive and ready to respond. In general his instinctual life, his fantasy life, his appetites are all under control, harnessed and dedicated to the persons and ideals to which he gladly gives his service.

How He Sees His Parents

The parents of the DPF member are visualized as worthy and capable of giving the love he needs. They are not, however, outstanding sources of emotional supportiveness and warmth. They are only average on the giving of love in the unconditional extroverted sense. They are in fact likely to be submissive and inhibited, as he is. Perhaps the most relevent idea is that they are *not* practitioners of all-out "conditional love." (This *is* characteristic of parents in the F direction.) The parents of the DPF child are thought to "temper justice with mercy"—to provide an element of undeserved and unconditional love. It is this undeserved love that gives the flavor of "salvation through love." There is an underlying implication of inhibited desires, perhaps past actions, which would bring damnation if properly punished. The child is saved from this, first, by receiving love that is not deserved, thus making possible an identification with the parents. The parents, by their manner and teaching, then make it possible for the child to inhibit his deviant desire and become submissive.

His Effect on Group Satisfaction

The DPF member tends to accomplish something like his parents accomplished with him, though more modest and secular, in his group participation. He has the unusual effect of moving the group simultaneously toward satisfaction with interpersonal relations and satisfaction with goal attainment. This delicate fusion is accomplished by only two other types: by PF who is much like him, but a little more ascendant, and by DF. The consideration of the DPF type for other people, his acceptance of them, along with his example of noncompetition, all tend to soften competition among others in the group, even though the DPF member does not have a prominent position. Similarly, his support of group norms and group tasks, though he does not give active leadership, nevertheless adds forward momentum to the group. In a way it can be said that he contributes to the positive and forward movement of the group by the giving of himself—by the sacrifice of prominence. He does not, in fact, seem to receive enough rewards from the group to justify his contribution, by fair exchange. But then he does not believe in fair exchange. He believes that a free contribution of love is necessary to make the world go round, and he is willing to give it. He is in some way right. Although the next more ascendant similar type PF also accomplishes a fusion of the two types of satisfaction, the still more ascendant similar type UPF produces a decrement in interpersonal satisfaction, even though the value-position he advocates seems to promise the fusion. Too active efforts toward group solidarity and progress seem to injure group solidarity, by reason of the ascendance of the advocate.

29

Type DF: Toward Self-Knowledge and Subjectivity

The member located in the downward-forward part of the group space by his fellow members seems submissive, dutiful, and conventional, wishing to follow a value- and task-oriented leader. He seems neither friendly nor unfriendly, but strictly impersonal, affectively neutral, inhibited, cautious, introverted, persistently hardworking, and fearful of disapproval and guilt. He is concerned with his inner feelings, his thoughts, impulses, and controls. In the realization of his own values he seems to be trying to move toward more complete knowledge of himself and more subjective completeness. "No time is better spent than that devoted to thinking about the ultimate purposes of life."

How He Sees Himself and How Others See Him

The DF member seems to associate his self-picture, his security and satisfaction, with the power to experience things subjectively through patient work and effort. One feels that he is "plowing ahead," like a ship in heavy seas, persistently, even obsessively, on the task, or toward the realization of the set of values toward which he gives allegiance. This persistence has been called "psychological inertia" by A.S. Couch (71). The DF type rates himself very high on this trait, and guesses correctly that others will so rate him. The observers rate him highly on this trait, the other group members also rate him high, but give their highest rating to the DNF type. Observers and group members also see the DF type as the most acceptant of authority, although he does not see himself so, appar-

332

ently tending to feel the power of his compulsion as more of a part of himself or his own values than as a demand placed upon him by authority or social norms.

The DF member rates himself as very introverted, and in this, observers and group members agree. There is some tendency for others to feel curious about him. He feels he is not entertaining, and although observers and group members think his adjacent type, DNF, even less entertaining, he is essentially correct. He in turn, feels that most others are more individualistic than he, that is, probably, from his own perspective, more erratic and changeable, less bound by a set of values.

His Place in the Interaction Network

The DF type is likely to be low in total interaction initiated compared to the group average. He tends not to address the group as a whole but rather to speak to specific individuals. Furthermore, others address him with low frequency, compared to the amounts he addresses to them. His leverage in the hierarchy of power seems to be rather low. He may be very important, however, as a supporter of a forward-moving leader who holds power only by a precarious balance. It is also true that his influence may be greater than his total interaction suggests, since he provides content ideas with great consistency and persistently asks for suggestion.

What Ideas and Values Will He Express?

"No time is better spent than that devoted to thinking about the ultimate purposes of life." The person who moves persistently in the DF direction is serious and work-oriented. He is concerned with time—the use of his time—and tends to work compulsively in order to avoid the implication that he wastes his time, which he may believe, no matter how hard he works. He is introverted, tends to pour a lot of his energy into his thought and obtains a good share of his satisfactions through the processes of ruminative, sometimes fantasy-laden and obsessive thought: "The rich internal world of ideals, of sensitive feelings, of reverie, of self-knowledge, is man's true home." "The most rewarding object of study any man can find is his own inner life." Since the process of thought tends to be invested with a good deal of otherwise unexpressed feeling, it may itself become dangerous and require purifying rituals: "Contemplation is the highest form of human activity." "Excessive desires should be avoided and moderation in all things be sought." The eye is turned persistently within, toward introspection and self-examination. Self-knowledge is valued highly, though not necessarily easily obtained, since the desire to know is itself partly a product of strong tendencies to suppress or repress fantasies as well as more active forms of expression.

This type of personality works against itself in a conflict of expression of fantasy versus repression of fantasy. Thus it tends to be drawn into a tighter and tighter cycle of introversion.

This introvertive cycle combines naturally with the values of adjacent directions. It is easy to see how it may be combined with values on conventional group beliefs, especially religious, perhaps; but it may also be combined with more individualistic and eccentric religious beliefs, even, perhaps, with a paradoxical revolt in the B direction. If the cycle proceeds far enough in the loading-on of repressions and inhibitions, these defenses may slowly bring about a paralysis of motivation for change, psychic or social, and be combined with a devaluation of the self. On the negative side the person may speak of value-determined restraint and, with further inhibition, of self-sacrifice for values and rejection of social success. On the positive side, provided the negative tendencies are not strong, the value on self-knowledge and subjectivity may be combined with a value on altruistic love, trust in the goodness of others, and salvation through love. In any or all of these combinations the religious flavor may be discernible, but the flavor differs considerably, both in the swing from positive to negative and with the increase of the element of inhibition.

The Quality of His Interaction

The DF member is task-oriented and submissive. His most salient interaction characteristic is his markedly high rate of asking for suggestion. And he is at the same time conspicuously low on dramatizing and joking. He gives information and opinion. He agrees with others when they address him, but unfortunately, although he asks for suggestion, they are low in addressing suggestions to him. They tend, as we know, to address their suggestions to more ascendant and positive members, UP in particular. They are high on addressing opinions to the DF member, however, they recognize him as task-oriented and partly answer his requests. They also ask him for opinion and suggestion. In this context the fact that they do not address suggestions to him may indicate that they regard him as representing their own faction in the group, if they are forward. He is dependably forward in orientation, dependably submissive, and also not very likely to come up with substantive suggestions. He is more likely to "pass" and relay any request for suggestion in order to avoid assuming too high a status. He does not generally ask for information, an act which tends to go with the assumption of a more ascendant and positive status.

Others agree with the DF member so far as his contributions of information and opinion are concerned, but the response to him as a person is neutral. Others are low in dramatizing and joking in relation to him, or in showing tension or laughing. He is essentially left out of the joking and laughing as well as of the social small talk, and he provokes little or no feeling.

Conflicts and Coalitions with Others

The most salient opposite figure to the DF member is possibly the DB member, who is similar to him in degree of inhibition but takes an opposite solution by hanging back from task commitment instead of plowing into it. There may be little overt communication from one type to the other, but they are very visible contrasts and dramatize, in their nonverbal ways, the difference between the "faithful servant" and the "reluctant" one. The DB member who dramatizes withholding of cooperation is also joined by his nearby types who accept failure and withdrawal on the one side, or press for identification with the underprivileged on the other side. The proponent of rejection of conventional group beliefs joins the attack, probably more verbally, upon the dogged and faithful DF member. Against all of these the faithful member is well defended, but he is vulnerable to his own neighbors to the right and left. He himself may swing to the political right or left by advocating rejection of social success on the right, or trust in the goodness of others on the left. And he may also believe in devaluation of the self. All of these may be made to support his hard-working role. When these arguments are made to him then, as they may be, he is ready to agree. He is also prepared to agree with arguments for group loyalty and cooperation, and for autocratic authority, although these arguments are not likely to be made to him explicitly, since he is already so evidently identified with the forward-moving leaders.

So far, the role of the DF member seems almost perfectly balanced between the positive and the negative, but one asymmetry appears in what he is willing to agree to. He is prepared to agree with statements in favor of equalitarianism, though he is not likely to make them, and on the negative side he is prepared to disagree with statements in favor of individualistic isolationism. He is then, in these respects, attached to the positive side of the group more than the negative, though he concentrates on work.

Personality Traits

No personality tests in the present study measure precisely the DF direction. Nevertheless one can piece together a useful picture by inferential extension from nearby types. One of the closest of these is DPF, with the following traits: practicality; responsibility; will-control; and character stability. These traits seem to have the right flavor to describe the present type also, though they presuppose a character formed in somewhat more positive circumstances, with a stronger love attachment to the parents, from which we might infer that the present type may have more conflict, more ambivalence, and a more rigid mobilization of all efforts to stay on the track. The nearby NF type of male shows feminine masochism. This is presumably also characteristic to some degree of the DF type. The PF type on the other side is conservative and has role-playing ability.

In the discussion of the F type it was supposed that receiving "conditional love" produces an ambivalence or balance between positive and negative feeling in the child. The parent gives conditional love when he gives love only as a reward for conformity to desired patterns of behavior and withdraws it as punishment for nonconformity. The child is thus taught to control his wishes for love and also his tendency to give love. At the same time he is taught to tolerate a certain amount of punishment and to administer it himself in the "training" of others. This mode of control may be applied so exclusively and literally by some parents that the child is trained to ignore or bypass other normal modes of control through integration within his own personality: the higher mental processes of reflective thought; fantasy; the involvement of the self and the evolving self-picture; the introduction of variation; testing of reality limits; experimentation and creative re-combination. A restrictive mode of control is perhaps appropriate in infancy and very early childhood, but even very early can probably be damaging if applied too literally. The more mechanical, literal-minded, and prompt-in-time the reward or punishment, the more the higher mental processes associated with the self are forestalled within the child. The ultimate effect is a slavish obedience to external signs of supposed demands, along with a desperate feeling of powerlessness of the self. The self is felt to be estranged, empty, powerless, and unable to feel. The bodily processes, external behavior, even the mental processes are felt to belong to somebody else, to stop and go at the behest of other powers, to persist and repeat obsessively.

As a compensation, a private self may be developed, elaborated through fantasy, and come to be more highly valued than the public self. It is this concern with the self—the loss of it and the regaining of it—which gives the DF type his characteristically high value placed upon self-knowledge and subjectivity. The trait name most appropriate, perhaps, is introversion. The opposite trait, extroversion, is characteristic of the opposite type, UB. The central traits of that type are adventurous, thick-skinned, and active. By a reversal of these traits we may infer that the present type would be timid, thin-skinned, and nonactive. He is not "passive" in that he "works," but he works under felt compulsion and is thus perhaps more appropriately called submissive. Though he works obsessively, he may still show in moderate degree the trait of the nearby D type, withdrawn. He may eventually be slowed to a dead stop by accumulated conflicts and inhibitions, in spite of his compulsion to work.

The submissive character of the DF type is symptomatic of the high degree of inhibition of instinctual drives, primary among which are, we suppose, aggression and sexuality. The related traits on the DP side suggest a harnessing of drives for useful work, or at least in the service of personality integration, namely, mature, calm, stable—the traits of a person who shows responsibility and is capable of achievement. The related traits on the DN side are repression-denial, social introversion, and depression. A common element in all these traits is inhibition of extroverted drives. But, whereas the traits of the DP type suggest "control" or "harnessing" of these drives, the traits of the DN type suggest the mobilization of a part of the personality (the conscious self and the mental powers called the ego in psychoanalytic theory), in order to hold down, inhibit, or immobilize another part (the unconscious self associated with the drives—the id). The latter part is disowned or dissociated— not accepted as a legitimate part of the self, or perhaps not even consciously known about or recognized.

"Inhibition" is a vague word which may perhaps cover both "harnessing" and "repression". The DF type is probably inhibited to some extent in both of these senses, as well as submissive and dutiful. The probability that these defenses are strong suggest that important parts of the personality do tend to be kept unconscious, in this sense "unknown." The value on "self-knowledge" according to this interpretation is thus the expression of a wish, or a motivation founded on a felt lack of knowledge. The degree of self-knowledge may be low, or it may have been brought to a high point by continued self-analysis, but it may be hard to retain, or hard to integrate into effective expression. Self-analysis may remain, for this type, a full-time job.

How He Sees His Parents

The foregoing discussion may have suggested that the parents of the DF child tend to be very active in the application of conditional reward and punishment, to the point where the development of the self as the exerciser of voluntary control is interfered with. The general rule however, taken to be true more or less throughout the space, is that parents tend to produce children like themselves. If that is true for the present type, the parents would *not* be active in overt interaction with the child. They, like the child, would tend to be introverted, subjectivistic, and inhibited. They might well use silence and withdrawal as a mode of punishment. They often might not explain their reasons for punishment— in some cases they may not be consciously clear about the reasons themselves—but rather react to a compulsive pressure toward inhibition whenever the offending wish, act, or impulse is attributed to the child. The message gets through to the child that he has done *something* wrong and must inhibit, but precisely what is wrong he is left to wonder. No doubt he will guess wrongly part of the time, and sense this. The motivation for self-awareness, self-analysis, the spreading uncertainty about what to do, the pervading sense of doubt, the urgent need to look to some other for leadership, to ask for suggestion, all may have some such base.

On the other hand, doing the desired thing may bring the child little and uncertain reward. Both father and mother are moderately low on emotional supportiveness and warmth. The mother is moderately low on inhibitory demands and discipline, the father is average. They are more or less alike in this combination of low demands and low support. This combination is consistent with low interactive contact. Probably the parents have low interactive contact with each other, and with the child. Thus one must distinguish between "conditional love" and "amount of interaction." Conditional love implies that no undeserved rewards are given, and punishment is given for deviance. Low interaction implies that both rewards and punishments are uncertain, and, probably, that poor information is given to the child about the nature of the demand. He is made to try to figure out the reasons for both the demand and any punishment he may receive.

Thus, although both parents are on the average moderately high on optimistic idealism in the content of the values they try to convey, they fall short of real conviction and implant uncertainty and doubt in their conveying of it. Moreover, they do not provide enough love to overcome the negative feelings that the child attaches to them as parents. They leave the child in a state of ambivalence—half-loving, half-hating, uncertain and inhibited. He will likely hold to the idea of optimistic idealism in the conscious part of his mind, but he will be unable to keep entirely repressed the crawling hostilities and negativities from which his parents have failed to rescue him.

His Effect on Group Satisfaction

It might be thought that with such a set of concerns, the DF type would have some adverse effect on group satisfaction. Not so, according to our inferential model. Unless he makes a pest of himself, as sometimes happens, by asking for suggestions either when others are already giving them or in the midst of periods of joking, his concern that the work norms of the group are satisfied can be helpful. He tends to move the group toward satisfaction with goal attainment.

He also tends to move the group toward satisfaction with interpersonal relations. So far as this is true, it is dependent upon his abstaining from ascendance. Those who most directly contribute to interpersonal dissatisfaction do so by over-participation, and by domination. By keeping his participation low, he keeps the cost of his intervention on behalf of the task low, and he thus shares in the credit for respecting the desire of others to participate. His mode of participation, moreover, directly draws others in and asks them to participate. If his timing is good he may accomplish that rare effect of simultaneously moving the group toward goal attainment and toward satisfaction with interpersonal relations. Two other types also do this (PF and DPF). However, the F type, just a step more ascendant than DF, fails to improve satisfaction with interpersonal relations, whereas the UF type, who also contributes as directly to the task as DF, actually moves the group away from satisfaction with interpersonal relations through his dominance. One may have here a clear and approximately accurate answer to the puzzling question: "Is it really inevitable that if one tries to push forward on the task he will lose friends and alienate people?" (20; 21). The answer is "It depends upon how assertive and dominating you are about it." Or, in broader terms, whether task-effort interferes with group solidarity depends upon how heavy is the demand it makes upon resources which are also necessary to group solidarity. In many small task-oriented groups time is of the essence. Even in groups which are not under external task-pressure, time claimed for interaction signifies, generally, status claimed or power exercised. If the person who takes the group time is felt not to be worth it, hostility is directed toward him. To receive time in a group is to receive a status reward. Adequate time for each member is a prerequisite of group solidarity and satisfaction with interpersonal relations.

30

Type DNF: Toward
Self-Sacrifice for Values

The member located in the downward-negative-forward part of
the group space by his fellow members seems submissive, conventional,
and dutiful to the point of self-sacrifice. But he is also often self-pitying
and resentful of his self-sacrifice. He expects punishment and is ready
to martyr himself, in fact he may voluntarily seek martyrdom in order
to blame and shame others. He thus seems unfriendly and passively
accusing. He sometimes seeks to make himself the object of aggression
of others, and sometimes punishes himself. In the realization of his
own values he seems to be trying to move toward self-sacrifice in order
to preserve some higher set of values. "There is nothing the body
suffers that the soul may not profit by."

How He Sees Himself and How Others See Him

For the DNF type of person, the self-picture tends to be disengaged
from the body and other things material and temporal. The sense of
identity and power is given by the knowledge that by sacrifice of the
material and temporal self one may create, preserve, and perpetuate
values. In the group setting, interacting with his peers, the DNF type
tends to feel anxious. He rates himself high on anxiety, and guesses
rightly that other group members will rate him high. Observers see his
adjacent type, DN as even more anxious. This may be because observers
feel less anxiety about accomplishing the task than the group members.
Group members rate the DNF member high on psychological
inertia—persistent plowing ahead—even more so than they do the ad-

340

jacent DF type, possibly because they feel he has more anxiety about punishment.

The self-sacrificing person makes others feel he rates them high on self-confidence—which is another way of saying, perhaps, that he feels nervous and submissive toward them. He is the type most likely to guess that others will feel curiousity with regard to him. There is some tendency for others to feel curiosity about him, but curiosity is felt most toward the adjacent type DN. The DNF type presents a kind of silent reproach to some, perhaps, and to others he may seem like a kind of unfortunate victim, who might be themselves. He is the type least warm and personal, according to both members and observers, and he correctly guesses this. He correctly guesses that other group members will find him at the opposite extreme from entertaining. The observers like him least of all the types, but group members like even less his more active adjacent type NF. Dislike as distinguished from lack of liking, is centered on the more active UNF type, the authoritarian autocrat. Dislike seems to be an active negative response to an active negative threat. The DNF type does not especially arouse active dislike, but he fails conspicuously to arouse active liking.

His Place in the Interaction Network

The DNF type is low on total interaction initiated, as compared with the group average. He tends not to address the group as a whole. Similarly, other group members are low in their tendency to address him. Although his total initiated and received as compared to other members is low, when he does initiate remarks he is likely to be high in his tendency to address specific individuals, rather than the group as a whole. He does not hold a strategic position in the power hierarchy of the group, but he may wield considerable psychological influence through the stimulation of guilt in other members. This is what he tends to count on. It is interesting to note that though his general significance for others tends to prevent their liking him, he nevertheless tends to elicit agreement. As a supporter for others on the forward side, or negative-forward side, he may be critically important in the maintenance of their power.

What Ideas and Values Will He Express?

The person who moves persistently in the DNF direction offers himself as a sacrifice to bring about or to exemplify the invincible power of more abstractly defined values, or spiritual things, over material things: "There is nothing the body suffers that the soul may not profit by." Physical and material hardships may be negative, but they offer at least the opportunity for *sacrifice,* that is, an action which may be interpreted by him and others to reinforce the meaning of nonmaterial values: "What mankind needs most is dedication to moral values—values which are absolute, imperative, everlasting, and unchangeable." The meaning of self-sacrifice consists of the fact that the voluntary sacrifice (as distinguished from sudden misfortune or disaster) has the character of an instrumental act which impresses the value of the end or goal upon the spectator. The sacrificing individual visualizes some part of himself— his "soul"—in the place of such a spectator, and thus obtains some edification (if not gratification) from the voluntary sacrifice of the body. But some period within which the suffering may be demonstrated would seem to be necessary and some beholder needs to be imagined, even though it be only the soul of the sufferer. Sudden death and meaningless disaster are to be feared because they deny even this desperate remedy. The only remedy for this kind of meaninglessness is, perhaps, anticipatory suffering: "To starve is a small matter—to lose one's virtue is a great one." "To lay down your life for a friend—this is the summit of a good life." "There is no worthy purpose but the resolution to do right."

A religious faith or an ideology may supply the content of those ultimate nonmaterial goals which can justify sacrifice. The DNF member may thus speak for conservative group beliefs (or sometimes a new and radical ideology or religion). He may also speak for value-determined restraint, though "restraint" is mild compared to "sacrifice." He may speak for self-knowledge and subjectivity. His modality is subjectivistic, oriented to obtaining the experience of meaning in relation to values rather than toward more extroverted overt action. He is prepared to accept and advocate individualistic isolationism if the sacrifice requires it, and he may well be forced toward this position as others react negatively to his guilt-inducing example. Similarly he may be willing to go further and demonstrate the rejection of social success and a devaluation of the self, if these are a necessary part of the demonstration of suffering and sacrifice.

The Quality of His Interaction

Paradoxically, the DNF member ordinarily receives agreement, although he gives disagreement and seems unfriendly. Negative feeling toward him does not appear on the surface. Others do not seem unfriendly toward him, but they are usually less than likely to seem friendly toward him, or to dramatize or joke. He is not a rewarding audience, nor is he likely to seem friendly or to joke, although he may on occasion dramatize his self-sacrifice. We have noted above that others are prone to withhold feelings of liking from him, but they are not prone to admit they dislike him either. The picture is thus mixed; there is reason to suppose that there are negative feelings about the DNF member, but the overt expression in interaction seems to be suppressed and replaced with a bare tendency to agree.

Although the DNF member disagrees when he does enter the interaction, we have seen above that he enters seldom, and that the flavor of the interaction tends to be submissive. He asks for suggestion and gives information. His task- or value-orientation is seen in giving opinion, as well as in asking for suggestion.

He does not, however, attract task-oriented attempts from others. They are not above the average on addressing any of the work categories to him, and they are low on giving him suggestion and on giving information. On the other hand, he does not often ask for information or opinion, from which we may infer, perhaps, that he often has a line of solution himself which he wants to demonstrate, or to have adopted, but he does not wish to push forward in a dominant way that will alienate others. His asking for suggestion is, on this theory, rhetorical. He has the suggestion he wishes to make, but he wishes others to infer it from his self-sacrificing example. (This is a kind of dramatizing.)

The response of others to him is perhaps grudging, but minimally conforming to the values he puts forward. Although he has a constricting effect on dramatizing and joking, and others do not in general seem friendly toward him, they do, however, ask him for his opinions and suggestions. They agree with him more than the average when he gives information and opinions, and they are not above the average on any of the negative types of activity, though he himself is. He is thus apparently allowed a certain amount of negativity without retaliation because of the moralistic pressure he brings to bear upon the guilts of others.

Conflicts and Coalitions with Others

The opponents of the self-sacrificing type object to what he does since they have chosen an opposite solution for a similar problem. The problem of all the downward types, in a way, is lack of power, lack of sufficient outlet for sexuality and aggression, lack of ascendant modes of ego enhancement—in short, frustration. The DNF type has constructed a highly rarified conception of himself, something similar to the idea of a soul, with abstract values to be realized in the future, and he has resolved to sacrifice the possibility of material satisfactions in the present. The B type objects to the religious implications of this solution, he particularly objects to the probability that it may strengthen religious belief in others, a belief in conservative group values. The DPB type however, is the one most directly offended. He objects to the probable strengthening of the orthodox status quo. He is trying to improve the lot of the underprivileged, and the perpetuation of the orthodox status quo means to him the perpetuation of injustice to the poor, the young, and the innocent. He does not believe they will be helped by a strengthening of abstract values. The DPB type has not tried to solve his problem by conceiving of his own immortal soul, he has rather placed his hope of altruistic satisfaction in the growing of the young, the release of the poor. He does not like attempted solutions which neglect the underprivileged with whom he identifies, or which leave them as badly in need of help as ever. Self-sacrifice for values may seem somewhat anti-social to him.

The DP type, who speaks for trust in the goodness of others also feels a negative quality in the action of the person who voluntarily chooses self-sacrifice for values. He feels in it a lack of trust, an implied rejection of the group, a demonstration that the group cannot provide the necessary maternal care. The DP type has, perhaps, over-idealized the degree to which one can count on such care, and he is made uncomfortable by this denial. The DB type of person is shamed by the demonstration of ultimate devotion to values which he himself avoids so persistently. He is shamed and angered, perhaps stimulated to do the same, but in the service of the backward cause.

The D type, who demonstrates devaluation of the self in some form, is very close to the person who demonstrates self-sacrifice for values. He is likely to approve and reinforce the self-sacrificer and to receive agreement in return.

Personality Traits

The DNF type of person probably shares to some degree the characteristic trait of his adjacent type, NF, feminine masochism, in relation to a more ascendant parental autocratic authority. Such a parental figure may show acceptance or conditional love on rare occasions. At least he may provide a model of what the abstract conception of the self might be. There is presumably some tendency for the DNF type to construct a more abstract idealized conception of himself, a "real self," a "soul," to compensate for the rejected parts of his material and social selves. The soul may be saved, though the rest of the self may be lost, degraded, or sacrificed. The soul may be modeled after the autocratic authority by a desperate "identification with the aggressor." Like the nearby D type, the DNB type may show the test trait withdrawn.

The nearby DN type shows the traits social introversion, repression-denial, social introversion, and depression. The sacrifice of parts of the self associated with the instinctual drives of aggression and sexuality has been made to some extent also by the DNF type. The turning of aggression against the self (instinctual, social, or material) is part of the mechanism of sacrifice. The mood-state of depression is generally thought to be a symptom of some loss of part of the self. The sacrifice of the picture of the self as socially successful, satisfied, and popular is depressing, as is the loss of affection, sexuality, and aggressive action. The lost parts are mourned, the saved part is edified. The saved part is conceived as independent and self-sufficient. In the case of the DNF type, we may suppose that the saved part is identified with the autocratic authority or with some more abstract object of faith, and is expected to persist in some form after death. The sacrificed parts of the self are denied, repressed, and immobilized so far as possible.

Then, as in the case of the DF type, we may suppose that a good deal of effort may go into the covering and uncovering of the sacrificed and repressed parts of the self. The person may seem introverted, timid, thin-skinned, submissive; to some degree obsessional, compulsive, and ritualistic, as he deals with his inner life. In particular he may seek punishment for the transgressions which occur in his inner life, out of his control. He tries, by courting punishment, to anchor his anxiety by making himself acceptable again to the harsh autocratic authority with whom he identifies. He is indeed enslaved.

The supposedly sacrificed parts of the self, however, are in most instances only put under cover and break out in various disguises. Like the N type, the DNF type may to some extent be plagued by vague and fugitive diseases, he may show hypochondriasis and psychasthenia. He tends to feel suspicious and jealous. He maintains a dependency and holds his intellectual functions as well as his instinctual ones at a minimum.

How He Sees His Parents

The most significant aspect of the parental picture, perhaps, is that both father and mother are seen as very low on emotional supportiveness and warmth. As discussed at length in the description of the UPB type, it is plausible to believe that emotional supportiveness and warmth of the parents is almost the specific preventive of generalized anxiety in the child. Without it the physiological alarm reaction, which anxiety is in the beginning, may persevere past the specific events which naturally arouse it in the life of the infant and child, and eventually come to pervade the personality. The parents are seen more in terms of what they demand, or what they threaten, than in terms of support and reward. Father and mother are only average on inhibitory demands and discipline, according to our inferential model, but they demand more than they offer. Their love is not only conditional, but the balance of reward and punishment is weighted to the side of punishment. In addition, the interactive contact of parents with each other, and with the child, tends to be low. If they are themselves DNF types, they are introverted, subjectivistic, self-sacrificing, and rather negative. They do not always explain what their self-sacrificing model implies for the child; what they mean, and what he has done wrong. They employ withdrawal of interaction, imposition of isolation, and the withholding of love. They are neither high nor low on optimistic idealism versus cynical pessimism. They create a situation of uncertainty which keeps anxiety high, and forces the child into constant efforts to keep it somehow anchored and controlled. The identification of the child with the parents, which may be very strong, is an identification out of desperation, to prevent being devoured by anxiety, but it has a compulsive, sometimes almost superstitious quality. It is an attempt to copy, sometimes with very poor understanding, and sometimes by fastening onto accidental characteristics, the parental behavior and manner which it is hoped will bring safety. The outward behavior of the child is understandable in many ways, as a hopeless set of attempts to appease a pair of inappeasable parent Gods. Both need not be involved in this way to the same extent, of course. The discrepancies between the roles of father and mother are about average.

His Effects on Group Satisfaction

The DNF member in the group setting tends to make others feel anxious, or more precisely, guilty—uncomfortably afraid that they are not living up to the expectations of authority, the group norms, or the demands of the group task. They are apt to increase their task efforts. The net result is that the DNF member tends to move the group toward satisfaction with goal attainment. But he does so by aversive means— underneath he is probably resented and to some extent disliked, but a sense of shame tends to keep this feeling suppressed. The group members feel that they should not blame him for the fact that they feel guilty— that is their own fault. Liking is withdrawn from the DNF member, but active dislike is held in check. It is also true that he does not claim a large share of the overt interaction time of the group. He is submissive and sometimes even helpfully self-sacrificing, though the hidden price of his self-sacrifice makes it always a dubious bargain. On balance he tends to move the group neither toward nor away from satisfaction with interpersonal relations. He leaves most persons ambivalent.

31

Type DN: Toward Rejection
of Social Success

The member located in the downward-negative part of the group
space by his fellow members seems self-conscious and unresponsive,
unfriendly and resentful, and passively rejecting of overtures of friendship. He seems to wish to be left alone, he wants to be isolated,
protected, and self-sufficient. He is more or less indifferent to the
conventional value- and task-orientation of the group—neither dependably for it, nor against it. In the realization of his own values he
seems to be trying to move toward a rejection of social success, and
more generally, of social attachment of any kind. "I have very little in
common with most of the people I meet." "People are no damn
good." [1]

How He Sees Himself and How Others See Him

The member moving in the DN direction appears resentful to
observers and other group members. Other group members are likely to
feel curious about him, probably because the reasons for his alienation
are not apparent. He rates himself as individualistic, and observers agree,
but to other group members, his adjacent type N appears even more
individually oriented. In contrast with his opposite type, UP, his self-
picture and self-feeling seem to be contracted and set off from the group.
None of the over-expansive misperceptions of his opposite type are

[1] These are probable value-statements of the DN member.

347

characteristic of him. To the observers he appears the most anxious of all types, but he and other group members perceive his adjacent type DNF as most anxious. His self-picture is given a certain strength and self-respect by its association with the power to reject popularity and success.

His Place in the Interaction Network

In total interaction initiated the DN type is likely to be low. And on total interaction received, as compared to the group average, he is likely to be markedly low. His participation is not sought except for sporadic attempts to bring him in. So far as he interacts at all, he is likely to be low in addressing the group as a whole and high in addressing specific individuals. Indications are that he tends to enter the interaction in response to attempts by other individuals to bring him in, but this does not happen very often, once the others have "given him up." His position in the power hierarchy is low; his aspiration is low, however, his passive negativity may add damagingly into the scales when a negatively-tending leader holds power through a coalition with only a marginal advantage. His influence may be all the more damaging, since others have learned to "ignore" him, and may fail to recognize the way in which he can strengthen a negative coalition.

What Ideas and Values Will He Express?

The values likely to be expressed by the DN member must be inferred from surrounding and opposite directions, since no actual examples from the actual population of value-statements studied fall in this position in the space. The rejection of social success is the most salient value, markedly high in this type as compared to other types. This means a devaluation of other people, particularly those who are popular, active, and who are apparently having a good time. Concealed envy and "sour grapes" are the apparent attitudes. The behavior seems to be a withdrawal that is meant to accuse those who have been successful. The devaluating statements themselves tend to center on the standards for success in the particular group, such as statements devaluating physical attractiveness, social-climbing techniques, cosmetics, clothes, attractive cars, houses, and other possessions that may assist popularity. Since the self may be demeaned or made unattractive in order to accuse others, a flavor of self-sacrifice for values may creep in when a value-justification is given. ("I am concerned about higher things.") An emphasis on value-determined restraint is probable. An emphasis on devaluation of the self is also likely. Statements placing a positive value on self-knowledge and subjectivity are congruent with the general position, though not very likely.

Rejection of social success as a value-direction is no more likely to be associated with its forward neighbor, self-sacrifice for values, as described above, than with its backward neighbor, failure and withdrawal. It may, in fact, be associated with both, by turns or by ambivalence. The person who rejects social success, who rejects both persons and popularity, may also reject values on the conservative side, and thus express a backward direction. Rejection of social conformity is a value congruent with rejection of social success and so also is the direction of passive resistance, withholding of cooperation. On the other hand, neither the forward (conservative) nor backward (radical) directions are necessarily linked with rejection of social success. A value placed on individualistic isolationism may avoid both alternatives, or may be combined with either or both by the DN personality, since it expresses a negative attitude toward people.

The Quality of His Interaction

The negative attitude toward people of the DN personality is expressed in interaction by seeming unfriendly (see page 133), and by a tendency to avoid signs of seeming friendly. There is a marked tendency to avoid asking for information. Social small talk is thus avoided. The DN member is also low on asking for opinion and on dramatizing and joking; these are additional methods of initiating small talk that might make the relationship more personal and friendly—he thus avoids them.

Others avoid seeming friendly to the DN person, (though they may try for a while to "bring him into the group" before giving up), and they avoid dramatizing and joking. The relationship is strained—the DN member and members on the positive side are likely to break into silent isolation from each other. There is some evidence of attempts to prevent this: others are markedly likely to ask the DN member for his opinion, and are high on asking him for information, which may perform a similar function. But there is no evidence of success.

The DN member, if addressed with a task-oriented attempt, is apt to disagree. He is also low on agreeing. Others are thus understandably low in addressing any kind of work-attempts to him. They are low on giving information, opinion, and suggestion, all three. They markedly avoid addressing suggestions to him, and he, in turn, tends not to give suggestions. His mode of participation, insofar as he departs from silence or grudging responses, is to ask for suggestion or to give information. Even these modes are probably most often used in response to questions. Under pressure to react with some kind of content, the DN member chooses the least self-exposing and self-assertive methods available: he asks for suggestions, thus turning the initiative back to the other, or gives minimal information, thus turning the problem of making inferences back to the other. In addition he may show tension and laugh. He is ambivalent about task and value issues. One cannot establish any continuous and satisfactory interaction with him, either about task-issues or social topics.

Conflicts and Coalitions with Others

The DN member is a silent accuser. He devalues the solidarity of the group; he renounces the rewards of status the group can give, and silently accuses the people who have obtained success. His accusation is also addressed to the other lower-status members who, although beaten by the status system, have remained positive and faithful. They in turn may try to save him, or at least to set him a good example. The DP member may try to persuade him, or to demonstrate trust in the goodness of others. The DPF member will wish to convert him, to bring him back to conventional goodness, to bring him salvation through love. And the DF member may try to bring him back to a value on work by offering the introverted rewards of self-knowledge and subjectivity, instead of material and social success, which both he, DF, and DN reject. To all of these approaches the DN member will probably not agree, except possibly to the last. Apparently, he is convertable to introverted work, if it is disengaged from the status system so that he will not be shamed and made envious by his lack of social success and popularity. There is some probability he will have found such a value-solution previously, and perhaps will have advocated it to the group.

Meanwhile, another coalition of types from the lower-status backward and positive side of the group may attempt to capture the DN silent accuser for a revolution. The case for withholding of cooperation is demonstrated for him, and he is urged to identify with the underprivileged, since they, (like him) have been beaten by the system. The still more silent members who demonstrate devaluation of the self add an unknown kind and degree of strength to the silent accuser, so far as more active group members are concerned. To all of these latter appeals, the DN member is vulnerable. He will not advocate identification with the underprivileged, to say nothing of permissive liberalism—he is too negative and generally misanthropic for that—but if the approach is made to him, he may surprisingly agree with both. He is, in short, a far-out prospect for the party of the far left. He is also convertable to introverted conservative work as we have seen. Without external persuasion he remains ambivalent and moves neither forward nor backward. His prime antipathy is to the social success of others. In general the effect of his stance of silent accusation is to add presumptive strength to the more ascendant negative leaders, who may move either forward or backward, or like himself, remain ambivalent.

Personality Traits

The DN member shows in marked form the trait known as social introversion. This trait is distinguished from other varieties of introversion in that the avoidance centers on people, especially popular people, and on the standards and means of success. The DN member tries to cut his contact with popular people in order to avoid the pain of feeling himself unpopular, unloved, and unloving. That part of his self-picture which might allow him to imagine social success for himself has been badly injured in past social contacts. It has been at least partially taken from him, and he has sacrificed any remainder as beyond salvage. He resents and mourns the loss. He constructs a self-picture of a more ascetic rarified sort, which does not require reactions from other people. He measures high on the trait of repression-denial. But the attempt to repress a part of the self is costly. It requires continued defensive efforts. He continues to mourn the loss of a vital part of the self. He is markedly likely to show depression. He has neither the satisfaction of love, nor that of outward aggression. The aggression is turned against the lost and devalued part of the self, which is thus both loved and hated. Wishing to devour his successful enemies, he feels himself devoured.

Thus he may well show the traits of his next-more-ascendant type, N. He may feel jealous and suspicious. He may experience vague feelings of distress, sickness, and guilt. He may measure high on the tests which reflect these feelings—hypochondriasis and psychasthenia. Sick and tired, he may also show dependency—a wish to be taken care of, but at the same time he is likely to reject and resent efforts to take care of him. No such efforts can console him since they arouse his basic conflict. The repressed and lost part of the self wants the care, the conscious self wants to demonstrate independent self-sufficiency. Sometimes aggression is turned outward in resentment, sometimes inward in shame and rejection of the suppressed part of the self. In the latter phase the DN member may show the trait of the D member, withdrawn. Like N, the DN member uses a great deal of his energy in blocking himself and in self-defeating efforts.

Long-continued attempts to minimize contacts with people and to demonstrate rejection may in fact interfere with development. Like his DNB neighbor, the DN type may seem to some extent immature, simple, rough, schizothymic and show independent self-sufficiency. These traits, in addition, reflect a relative failure to internalize social norms, an effect that may be expected if social contacts are cut early enough in life, either by factual isolation, or by lack of affectionate rewards which can form a basis of identification. Without this leverage, the individual is not led or trained to the acceptance of more general social norms or forward-oriented values.

A less inhibited form of the same basic difficulty is seen in the NB member, who generally seems critical, not only against people, who are felt to be "no damn good," but also against conservative social norms of all kinds. The NB member is radical and the DN member may show this trait to some degree, as well as the insecurity of the NB member.

On the other hand, the probability of showing forward-oriented traits is in general as high as that of showing backward-oriented traits. It may be, however, that those who show the forward-oriented traits must first have gone through some form of identification with a parent, and must have been trained to the acceptance of social norms prior to a loss of loved object or loss of a successful self-picture. In this case one might expect traits similar to those of the DF type: introverted; timid; thin-skinned; submissive; obsessional; compulsive; and ritualistic. Or if the parent lacked the ability to give love, and depended upon punishment instead, we might expect traits of the NF direction to appear: feminine masochism. The DN type may consciously feel a willingness to forgo ascendance and the gratification of instinctual desires, a willingness to accept pain and unhappiness, or punishment, for the sake of a close dependent relationship with a more ascendant autocratic authority. One would expect such a relationship to be intensely ambivalent, however, with the DN member tending to be both desperately dependent and desperately hostile, with the hostility repressed but "breaking out all over" in words, expressions, bodily attitudes, symptoms, complaints, demonstrations of self-sacrifice and martyrdom, as well as rituals of expiation, acceptance of punishment, and other attempts to deal with anxiety and frustration.

How He Sees His Parents

Both father and mother of the DN type are supposed to be moderately high on pessimistic cynicism (as opposed to optimistic idealism), and probably show signs of disappointment with the status system which assigns popularity and success in the larger society. They are moderately high in discrepancies of role from each other, and consequently do not present a consistent or consensual picture of social norms with which the child might identify. They are only average in inhibitory demands and discipline, but both are moderately low on emotional supportiveness and warmth. The parents are negative in general attitude toward others, including the child. Insofar as they apply reward and punishment, they tend to rely more heavily on punishment, and are not emotionally capable of giving much reward. Their interactive contact with each other is apt to be low—they tend to be silently resentful a good deal of the time, and do little talking either to each other or to the child. The child is left to his own devices a good deal of the time. Expectations of the parents, so far as they are consistent, are not communicated clearly to the child, who is left to guess his way in spite of uncertainty, and undertakes various desperate shifts to deal with his endemic anxiety. He has no social success with his parents—nothing he can do truly succeeds. Lacking any experience of success he may come to distrust and disbelieve in it. His safety lies rather in contracting his self-picture and refusing to be misled by dreams of social success. In defense against his parents, he adopts their defense against the world.

His Effect on Group Satisfaction

If he were a prominent, or a norm-setting member of the group, one would expect the attitude of the DN member of the group to interfere with the general satisfaction with interpersonal relations. However, he is generally rather isolated and silent. He consumes little of the group time, and he is generally not an active interference or a threat, in spite of his negative attitude. The net effect is zero. He tends to move the group neither toward nor away from satisfaction with interpersonal relations.

Almost the same thing can be said of his effect on satisfaction with goal attainment. He tends neither forward nor backward consistently. He has put himself out of the running, so far as overt participation is concerned, and so exercises little influence. He tends to move the group neither toward nor away from satisfaction with goal attainment.

32

Type DNB: Toward Failure
and Withdrawal

The member located in the downward-negative-backward part of
the group space by his fellow members seems passively alienated and
unfriendly toward persons, cynical toward values. He rejects both the
persons in the group and the conventional value- and task-orientation
of the group. He seems discouraged and dejected, ready to resign and
quit, to leave if possible. He wishes to withdraw from the group and all
its concerns. In the realization of his own values he seems to be trying
to confirm his own failure, perhaps that of the group as well, and to
move toward a definitive withdrawal from it, or perhaps more generally from life or from active effort. "The real substance of life consists of
a process of disillusionment, with few goals that are worth the effort
spent in reaching them." [1]

How He Sees Himself and How Others See Him

More than any other type, the DNB type tends to say he feels dislike
for others, and fails to feel liking for them. If the central goal of his
direction is withdrawal after conviction of failure, it may be that residual
positive feelings are denied, and that negative ones are emphasized. The
person moving in this direction is most likely to guess that others dislike
him. This is usually a misperception, since, on the average, group
members direct their greatest dislike to a quite distant type, who interferes with them much more actively, the UNF autocratic authority. The

[1] This is a probable value-statement of the DNB member.

354

misperception of the DNB member may be caused by his need to project negative feelings to the outside, to others, rather than direct them toward his own self-picture. Such a projection presumably helps to explain failure, to justify feelings of dislike, and to confirm the wisdom of withdrawing. A certain amount of self-respect is preserved by association of the self-picture with the power to hate and escape. There is some tendency for group members to feel curiosity about the DNB type.

His Place in the Interaction Network

The DNB member is likely to be low in total interaction initiated, as compared to the average of other group members. Similarly, he will probably be low in total interaction received. He neither bids for much participation nor receives much, consistent with his desire to withdraw, but even so he is not necessarily the lowest member in the group on total initiated—he still may communicate his disaffection to others. Compared to the amount he receives, he addresses little to the group as a whole, but rather tends to address other individuals in response to their questions or attempts to draw him into participation. Such power as he exercises he tends to have through his ability to make others feel uncomfortable through display of his withdrawal, but the net effect is not likely to be large unless he is a tacit supporter of a more active member, perhaps a UNB type, or a part of a coalition of the far left.

What Ideas and Values Will He Express?

The DNB member probably does not make many value-statements, at least we have no sure specimens. The value-statement at the beginning of this chapter seems to express the idea in generalized form: "The real substance of life consists of a process of disillusionment, with few goals that are worth the effort spent in reaching them." Such a feeling does not encourage one to make value-statements that set high goals and standards. And since the person wishes to withdraw from the group, he may have little motivation to make value-statements with which others will agree. The person moving in the DNB direction does not wish to make a moral point of his failure or that of the group—he wants rather to get out of the group, or sometimes, perhaps, to get the group out of a failure-producing situation. The latter wish, however, seems unlikely in view of the probable low status and low effectiveness of the DNB position. If the DNB member wished to establish a set of social norms, or an ideological position out of failure and withdrawal, he would generally have to form or join a still smaller alienated subgroup. Others who have congruent positions, but who like him, are little motivated to make overt value-statements, believe in rejection of social success, withholding of cooperation, and devaluation of the self. We may infer that the DNB member could occasionally voice these sentiments, but we would suppose that the motivation for solidarity or joint action with these others would be low in any case.

Three other adjoining value-positions are somewhat more ascendant in their implication: those in favor of individualistic isolationism; rejection of social conformity; and rejection of conventional group beliefs. Leaders of a dissident faction to which the advocate of failure and withdrawal might adhere would likely come from one of these more active ascendant members, negative and backward. It would be through such a coalition that the DNB member would exercise whatever power he might have in the group. But his possible significance in strengthening such a coalition should not be underestimated. If a group is small the withdrawal of even one member may be damaging, when it adds one at the same time to a negative-backward faction. The silent reproach of a withdrawn member is felt psychologically by other members, though perhaps overtly ignored. The silent member symbolizes repressed feelings of fear of failure, repressed hostilities, and disaffection from group values also harbored by other members, and through his silent dramatization he plays upon unconscious parts of their personalities.

The Quality of His Interaction

Only in giving information does the DNB member present any appearance of keeping up interaction. Probably this usually occurs under the stimulation of questions from others who try to bring him in and involve him. To such efforts his response is minimally revealing: giving bare information. He is unlikely to agree with others. He has some tendency to disagree, but does not carry out any connected argument or chain of reasoning, as indicated by the fact that he is low on giving opinion and giving suggestion. He makes few advances toward others, either in a task-oriented or a social-emotional way. He is low on asking for information and asking for opinion, and low on seeming friendly. He may show tension or laugh and seem unfriendly (see pages 133 134).

Others act toward him as one might expect them to act toward a marginal member with whom ties have been largely cut. They are low in showing friendliness toward him and in agreeing with him, although they are not above average in seeming unfriendly. They are not in overt conflict with him. They ask him for information and opinion at a bare minimum, and otherwise tend to ignore him.

Conflicts and Coalitions with Others

There are other types of members to whom the demonstration of withdrawal of the DNB member is particularly painful. They are those who have themselves been rescued from failure and withdrawal, and to whom acceptance of this direction is still an unconscious temptation. Those who have been saved by something like a religious conversionary experience, those who William James called the "twice born," retain a memory of that "dark night of the spirit" from which they have been saved. They depend upon whoever may have rescued them, and retain an idealized image of him. They believe in salvation through love, having experienced it. They wish to become like their rescuer. They are especially drawn, psychologically, I believe, not only to those who need care because they are underprivileged, or of lower status, but to those who, in addition, have repudiated love and faith. They are the "lost sheep" in the religious sense, and the "black sheep" in the social sense. They must be brought back to the fold, or so the DPF member feels. Thus the DNB member, the "lost sheep," is a special object of attention, for the DPF member, who wishes to save him by love, for the DP member, who wishes to restore his trust in the goodness of others, and for the DF member, who wishes to restore his ability to work, and his faith in himself through self-knowledge and subjectivity. The F member tries to bring him back to conventional group belief, often religious faith.

With all of these attempts the DNB member will probably fail to agree. He is not prone to disagree overtly however, and thus indicates some approachability. He tends to agree with the demonstration of devaluation of the self given to him by the D member. He may initiate statements rejecting conventional group beliefs, social conformity, and social success, and favoring individualistic isolationism, withholding of cooperation, as well as failure and withdrawal. But he does not especially tend to agree with *others* who may argue for individualistic isolationism, rejection of social conformity and conventional group beliefs. He may be a member of a coalition of these members, but if he is, it is by default and not by a strongly felt solidarity with them.

There is a possible coalition, however, of a perhaps unexpected kind. Although he does not himself initiate statements favoring identification with the underprivileged and permissive liberalism, nor are such statements generally addressed to him, he is prepared to agree with them. In spite of his generally abject pessimism, then, the DNB member is a potential target for either conversion to the tender-minded conservatives (DPF), or for revolution with the tender-minded radicals (DPB). In this battle, if there is one, for his support, he is more likely to go for revolution than for conversion, but he is more likely to be sought out by those who wish to save him by love. The actual outcome then would seem to depend heavily upon the degree to which others seek his support.

Personality Traits

On personality tests the DNB member is likely to appear lacking in adequate contact with people and to lack socialization into ordinary social norms. It appears that he has failed to learn or develop. He may test high on the traits of immaturity, simpleness, roughness. He is high on independent self-sufficiency and may also show the trait of the nearby D type, withdrawn. The withdrawal, the alienation from people, the eccentricity and unconventionality are implied by the more technical term schizothymic. The self-picture may be inaccurate, as indicated earlier, in that the person imagines himself to be disliked, whereas the more salient fact is that he feels dislike for others. But also the self-picture may be split and poorly organized. This also is implied by the technical term schizothymic. Like his DN neighbor, the DNB member has given up parts of himself that might have been associated at one time with social success. He may mourn the loss in spite of attempts to repress and deny it, he may suffer depression, he may withdraw into social introversion and try to find an island of independent self-sufficiency. But so far as the self-picture is split and poorly organized, he can hardly find a stable solution. He may show unpredictable changes of mood and manner.

Thus like his neighboring type, NB he may seem insecure, radical, and critical. It is not likely that the appropriate conventional adult sex role will have been completely accepted and integrated into the personality. Both males and females may show splits and confusions between masculine and feminine conservative role traits.

Without adequate social contact, without adequate integration of his personality around a stable conception of himself in relation to social norms, and without adequate modes of expression of instinctual drives, the DNB person is understandably upset. Like the nearby N type, he is apt to feel suspicious, perhaps even jealous. He may have symptoms of various kinds which are vague and shifting indicators of his underlying problems. He feels chronically sick (hypochondriasis) guilty and indecisive (psychasthenia). He may or may not show dependency in spite of his withdrawal. He presents a strong emotional appeal to those whose personality includes a desire to help.

How He Sees His Parents

The parents of the DNB member are likely to be moderately high on pessimistic cynicism (versus optimistic idealism), and in addition, the discrepancies between them as to role are moderately high. They do not present a defined set of values, nor do they especially agree with each other in what they repudiate. It may be that they are not well socialized into the current culture, being of foreign birth or otherwise transitional or marginal in status. It may be that the family is put under strain or broken in some way by the absence of either father or mother, or by a loss of social status of one or the other, and that the transmission of conventional adult male or female role models is thus impaired. The relationship of emotional supportiveness and warmth with one or both of the parents may be reasonably good, with the problem centering rather on the inability of the parents to transmit the conventional culture. The model implies that mother and father are not especially likely to be low on emotional supportiveness and warmth. They are average. They are also average on inhibitory demands and discipline. Both of these implications tend to throw emphasis upon failure in the transmission of the content of the culture.

It is also likely, however, that the interactive contact between parents and child is low on account of personality characteristics of the parents. They tend toward withdrawal, and do not believe in success, in ideals, or in the conventional social order. They do not attempt to teach values, nor do they teach the child the means by which he may develop his own conceptions in these respects. He is not given the means of bringing about personal integration. He is in fact, taught to fail, though indirectly.

His Effect on Group Satisfaction

The DNB member tends to move the group away from satisfaction with goal attainment. He is a "wet blanket" and "a drag." It is true that he is not prominent in his participation and does not get in the way of the more active participants, but he does symbolize attitudes of dejection and disaffection which may have a contagious influence. One may ask, if he has a contagious depressing effect on motivation for the task, does the DN member also have a contagious depressing effect on enthusiasm for group solidarity? The model makes a differential prediction. It indicates that the DNB member neither impairs nor helps satisfaction with interpersonal relations. It may be that the rewards of social acceptance are more continuously available to group members, than task-rewards, since they can be conveyed simply by information from others that one is accepted, and liked. The rewards of task-success are more remote, obtainable only by group effort, and hence, perhaps, more subject to contagious depression. The backward-moving member attacks faith, after all, whereas the negative-moving member attacks love. Social acceptance is within the power of the group to confer; task success of the group as a whole is not. It also depends upon the outer situation. It may be for reasons of this kind then, that the DNB member tends to move the group neither toward nor away from satisfaction with interpersonal relations, although he tends to move the group away from satisfaction with task-attainment.

When he is a member of the group various members tend to check the following kinds of statements on an assigned task: "The problem has too many facets to be solved." "The time available to solve the problem was not sufficient." "We should have been more logical in our approach to the problem." And finally, one which very likely reflects the threat of the one-way mirror used in observation of the group and the intrusion of authority: "I felt like a guinea pig." One can imagine that these remarks are originated by the DNB member, or by other group members in responding to his attitudinal direction: toward failure and withdrawal.

33

Type DB: Toward Withholding of Cooperation

The member located in the downward-backward part of the group space by his fellow members seems passively anxious, tense, negative to the demands of authority and forward group leadership. He is neither clearly friendly nor unfriendly toward other members of the group—he seems neutral, abstracted, or ambivalent in this respect. He is primarily oriented to repression of negative feelings about the requirements of convention, authority, particularly the value- and task-demands of the group. In the realization of his own values he seems to be trying to move toward withholding of cooperation with regard to demands of the task. He is "laying low," waiting for events, authority, punishment, or life to "catch up with him." "I get depressed when I realize how many things I have to do that I don't really want to do." [1]

How He Sees Himself and How Others See Him

The DB member, oddly enough, guesses that others rate him high on favoring expression and gratification. Actually he is far removed from the type so rated by other members; they tend to rate the UNB member most highly on this. With this latter type the DB member shares only the backward direction. He hangs back from scruff-of-the-neck cooperation urged by his opposite type, UF, and so may feel by contrast that he is seen as doing so for his own pleasure—as an advocate of expression and

[1] This is a probable value-statement of the DB member.

gratification. He may be so in desire and fantasy, but not in action. In fact, he controls outward expression very rigorously, as his downward component implies—he moves toward suppression even while wishing for expression. So it comes about, perhaps, that while he guesses others rate him high on favoring expression and gratification (the result of guilt feelings over his wishes), he also tends to rate others high on the same trait (by contrast to his actual movement toward self-suppression). The self-picture is associated with the power passively to resist. There may be some tendency for the other group members to feel curiosity about him.

His Place in the Interaction Network

The DB member tends to be low on total interaction initiated and low on total interaction received. He is out of the main line of task-oriented effort and is low in the struggle for power. Insofar as he enters into participation he addresses other individuals more than they address him, and compared to the amount he receives, he is high on the proportion of his acts addressed to specific individuals. He is low on the proportion of his acts addressed to the group as a whole. He neither seeks to influence the group as a whole, nor is his participation much sought, although he exercises a more or less silent restraining influence.

What Ideas and Values Will He Express?

No actual examples of value-statements which express this direction are available from factor-analytic studies. The position is not one for which we would necessarily expect an elaborate verbal rationale. Statements presently attributed to adjoining directions seem to have some of the implied flavor. For example, a statement from the B direction: "It is wrong to punish a man if he helps another country because he prefers it to his own." Or another statement, presently attributed to the DPB direction: "An occupation by a foreign power is better than war." It seems likely that pacifism and various forms of nonviolent resistance are close to the DB direction, and that the patriotic pressure from others to fight or actively engage in a war effort for the group as a whole is the direct stimulant. No doubt appropriate value-statements can be found to test these conjectures.

The DB position is one which avoids, or balances in some ambivalent way, negative and positive feeling toward group members. If there are statements from the negative side implying rejection of social success, or failure and withdrawal, there are also counterbalancing statements from the positive side recommending trust in the goodness of others, or identification with the underprivileged. Devaluation of the self may also be a part of the general position. The ambivalent combination of positive and negative elements and the silence of such a person may make him hard to understand, and hence likely to arouse projected feelings from others. He is a natural victim or scapegoat, a martyr for a lost cause, or a martyr for the revolution. He is not a conspicuous figure ordinarily, because of his low participation in either the task or the expressive activities of the group. Other more active types are probably more often the scapegoat. But in a certain context, he "interposes" himself and may suffer the full impact of aggressive fury. The relevant context is one in which aroused aggressive feelings of group members are moralistically bound by a task-effort for the group as a whole (as in a war effort), and the DB member tries to show that their expression of aggression does not deserve moral legitimization. So far as he succeeds, the aggression in others is left unbound, and it is displaced upon him instead of upon the enemy for whom it is prepared. As the saying goes: "If you play with fire you are likely to get burned." Self-immolation, by fire, starvation, or other means are in fact sometimes used as dramatic communications by DB types. There is a similarity in these actions to those described in the DNF direction toward self-sacrifice for values. The main difference is that the self-sacrifice for values is conservatively oriented, whereas the self-immolating withholding of cooperation is radically oriented. This is a difference, perhaps, of social context rather than deeper psychological motivation. It is probable however, that differences exist on a deeper level. The radical self-immolator apparently wishes to unmask the aggression of others and to turn it against himself, to demonstrate the fact that he contains his aggression, they do not. The conservative self-sacrificer apparently wishes to unmask the lack of love and care from others and to demonstrate that he can survive and save the group through the values he can create or perpetuate through his own love and care. There is no reason why the two may not be combined. Presumably they often are in the D type whose philosophy calls for devaluation of the self. For the person who is primarily DB in direction, however, the preponderant tendency is probably to court aggression.

More ascendant value-statements may also be expressed by the **DB** member. On the NB side these include rejection of social conformity, perhaps counterbalanced on the positive side by permissive liberalism. Next above DB in ascendant implication, neither positive nor negative with regard to people, is the direction toward rejection of conservative group beliefs. The DB member may occasionally be expected to make radical, anti-conservative statements, and he may be, at the same time, an adherent, or a prophet, of a radical minority religion.

The Quality of His Interaction

The single category of interaction on which the DB member is markedly high is showing tension or laughing. The only other category on which he is high is giving information, a restrained and controlled type of action. He markedly avoids giving suggestion and is low also on giving opinion and agreement—all principal task-oriented activities. Others apparently attempt to bring him into the group with requests for information and opinion. They are markedly high on asking for information, and he reciprocates with information, but not with opinion. He is low on asking for information himself. Others are high on dramatizing or joking addressed to him. Task-oriented activities are not ordinarily addressed to him. Others avoid asking him for suggestion and are low on addressing opinions to him for approval. It is all too clear that he would be of no help. They avoid giving him suggestions.

The DB member is not ordinarily a target for attack—he is out of the focus of attention and stays out. Since he offers little content he receives neither disagreement nor agreement, although others are low on seeming unfriendly toward him. They leave him alone, except for occasional jokes to relieve the tension. Only rarely does he symbolically and dramatically interpose himself and receive from the authoritarian gods of war a stroke of lightning that is meant to destroy him for his refusal to work and to fight.

Conflicts and Coalitions with Others

If the DB type withholds cooperation, his antithetical type in giving it is the DF type. The latter works hard and tries to show by his good example that the DB member should mend his ways. Although DF may not explicitly criticize—he tries to maintain a careful neutrality—the DF type believes in "salvation by works," and he cannot help feeling that his basic assumptions are being put in jeopardy by the passive hanging back ("goofing off") of the DB member. The hard worker is made anxious by the tension and by the failure of the DB member to do anything about it. The DF "good example" is afraid that he may be blamed for the lack of industry shown by the DB "bad example."

The DF "good example" is well acquainted with resistance in his own personality. Part of his subjectivity and desire for self-knowledge has grown out of the constant surveillance he has had to develop to keep himself blamelessly working, to prevent himself from falling into passive and dangerous fantasies. He is concerned to prevent the DB member from revealing the fantasies which he himself may have. He fears that the wrath of the gods will fall upon the DB dreamer who exposes them both.

The fear is not entirely groundless. As we have seen, there are occasions when the DB member makes such a dramatic show of his willingness to be punished rather than cooperate that the lightning does fall upon his head. In time of war, for example, pacifism is a provocative business. The DF member tries to keep to the "straight and narrow path" in order to avoid punishment of an autocratic authority. He tries in many subtle ways to get the DB member to do the same. If he fails, as he does about half the time, he may adopt an avoidance reaction, in which he not only avoids communication with the DB member, but he also tries to disown him. He tries to show others, particularly those who are likely to blame him, that he has nothing to do with the DB member, and should not be considered in the same group with him. If the threat is great enough, the avoidance may assume the appearance of a phobia—a strong irrational fear of the "bad example" (132).

Others who share the same reaction to a certain extent, and who may try to influence the DB member to change, include the DPF member with the desire to convert him by the offer of salvation through love, and the DNF member with the example of self-sacrifice for values. None of these approaches is particularly likely to succeed, though they are not precluded from success on all occasions. Since all of the downward types are similar in that they have accepted a large measure of inhibition, they can cooperate where inhibition is a prime requirement seen by all.

The DB member is ambivalent in the positive-negative direction. On one occasion he may speak for trust in the goodness of others, on another, he may be addressed with this argument, and if addressed, may agree. On the other hand, he may also speak for the rejection of social success, or sometimes he may be addressed with this argument, and if addressed, may agree. He is both for and against people, in different contexts. Similarly he is ambivalent about whether he wants equalitarianism. He is not likely to initiate arguments for equality, but is prepared to agree to such statements. On the other hand, he may initiate arguments for the devaluation of the self, receive such arguments, and agree. He is not generally ready to struggle hard, either for his own status or that of others, apparently, but on occasion will both initiate and agree to statements in favor of permissive liberalism. Congruent with this direction is his inclination to reject conventional group beliefs, and in return, he is likely to receive arguments from type F proponents. He is a natural candidate for a coalition of the far left.

Personality Traits

No personality tests used in the study directly characterize the DB type of person. In the D neighbor we find the trait withdrawn. This also implies inhibition of instinctual drives, aggression and sexuality in particular. The inhibition may be accomplished either through a harnessing of drives in an integrative way (resulting in a positive direction), or a blocking of drives by an internal division of the personality against itself (resulting in a negative direction). The DB type is, on the average, neither positive nor negative. Both modes of inhibition may operate. The drives are partly harnessed, partly blocked. An additional possibility is that the drives are relatively low in level to begin with. Since there are a number of logical possibilities of drive-strength and types of inhibition that seem congruent with the direction, perhaps we ought not to expect much homogeneity within the type on the level of traits measured by personality tests. It may be that this is the reason no tests were found to characterize specifically this area of the space.

The traits of the adjacent DP type illustrate the integrative harnessing of drives. Persons of this type are calm, stable, mature, with a sense of responsibility and a probability of achievement. The presumption that the DB member shows, to some extent, these positively oriented traits may lead one to speculate about the possible reasons for the withholding of cooperation. The DB member may be a "dreamer," and dreaming and fantasy may be parts of the creative process. It is probably true however that creative persons are often imitated by non-creative persons who wish to romanticize a DB position. There is presumably more than one type of motivational reason for DB movement. The more negative types of motivational reasons may be seen in the traits of the nearby NB member, who is likely to seem insecure, to be radical in social attitudes, and critical in manner.

Difficulty of the male in making a transition to the conventional adult male sex-role and occupational-role may underlie a radical and unconventional orientation in some cases. The female with the same difficulties may adopt a semi-delinquent, pseudo-male role. The adoption of effeminate traits by the male presumably may be deeply motivated by desires for creativity, desires to nurture, or desires to be a mother arising out of identification with the mother or mother-substitute. This is a result perhaps to be expected if there is a rewarding mother but no father, or if the father is rejected as a model of positive identification. There is little conventional social acceptance of a male who psychologically wants to be a mother. Frustration of such unacceptable desires may lead to repudiation of conventionality in a very general sense, including, but not confined to, conventional sex-role expectations.

A desire to nurture the helpless may link the DB member with the DPB member, who seems also to identify with the mother and children. A wish to show how wrong the punishment and aggression of a rejecting father was would help explain the readiness of the DB type to interpose himself as the scapegoat-pacifist in time of war.

Other negative aspects of the personality may be shown in traits of the DN and DNB directions. Social introversion, repression-denial (DN), and the desire for independent self-sufficiency (DNB) are plausibly related to the conviction that a desired social role, or part of the personality can not be realized: in this case a positive, creative, mothering, nurturing role. Depression is an aspect of mourning of that loss. Actual early loss of the mother may be involved in some cases. Psychologically, the child tries to prevent the loss of the loved object by becoming like it himself, by "internalizing" the image. Aggression is also repressed, with occasional outbreaks or accusations leveled against bad father-figures for showing aggression. Aggression is partly turned against the self, perhaps against the repressed part of the self, and the self-destructive attempts also contribute to the depression. Action in either a positive or negative direction is largely blocked. Action forward is largely blocked. Anxiety is not permitted to provoke instrumental or conforming efforts, as in the forward types. The observable behavior-blocking, called showing tension, may be a blocking of action relevant to at least three major motives: sexuality, aggression, and anxiety. All three seem to be locked within the personality of the DB member, largely within the unconscious part of the personality, in conflicts which emerge only partly to consciousness as fantasies, preoccupations, moods and feelings that are not well understood. These are also a part of the raw materials for artistic creativity.

The traits associated with the desire to create need not involve high intelligence, sophistication, or stable integration of reflective efforts. The DNB member, a neighbor of the present type, is often simple, immature, and rough, in the sense of untutored. Such a person may be "original" by his native character and may, in fact, make new contributions to the culture of the group. Other members of the group may adopt his natural traits or mannerisms, though these may be at the same time regarded as "peculiar." The very lack of integration of the various aspects of the personality, implied by the trait schizothymic, may permit or encourage the emergence of new patterns. There is apparently some degree of alliance, though not always a close one, between the desire to create and unconventionality. Unfortunately for the romantic imitator of the artistic role, unconventionality can be achieved by imitation—creativity cannot.

How He Sees His Parents

It is consistent with the theory of possible identification with the mother, in the case of the DB member, that discrepancies between the parents are moderately high. It is also consistent that the mother is described as moderately low on inhibitory demands and discipline and average on emotional supportiveness and warmth. It is inconsistent with the theory if the father is inferred to exemplify the same pattern. The data in general show that the effects of these two variables of parental behavior are very nearly the same, whether of father or mother (140). Perhaps it is better to lay the emphasis on probable difficulty of the child in assuming the adult sex-role.

Both father and mother may be inferred to be moderately high on pessimistic cynicism. They are nonidealistic, rather passive nonconformists. They are inhibited, conflicted, and interact little, either with each other or with the child. They tend to do nothing, rather than to administer reward and punishment depending upon the child's performance. Concepts of standards, according to which performance may be evaluated, are poorly developed and are nonconsensual among the parents. The percentage of plain chaos in the parent-child relations would be expected to be pretty high. Perhaps it is also likely that all sorts of circumstances which tend to raise the percentage of plain chaos—such as ill health, too many children, and separation of family members—also tend to approximate the effect of downward-backward parents. Circumstances or attitudes which prevent cooperation in the family can hardly have other than a damaging effect upon the development of the child. Passive resistance is a powerful lever for social change in some social situations, but it is an unstable base for long term development, either of group organization or personality.

His Effect on Group Satisfaction

It is no surprise to infer from the model that the DB member tends to move the group away from satisfaction with goal attainment. We have seen how, in spite of a low rate of participation, he may exercise a potent effect occasionally through dramatic and provocative symbolization. It is perhaps a surprise, however, to infer that the DB member tends to move the group toward satisfaction with interpersonal relations. In understanding this, if it is indeed true, primary emphasis might be placed upon the commonplace fact that the DB member does not interfere with the desire of all group members to have time to conduct their participation. Beyond that, however, we must recognize that in his hanging back from the task, in his desire not to be compelled to cooperation by authority, and in his tendency to unmask the alliance between moralism and aggression, he represents the reservations of possibly half, or more than half, of a group under strong task-pressure, or strong conservative pressure. Even in his ambivalence he represents important unconscious conflicts of other group members, including those members generally on the positive side. If he is, in addition, nurturant toward the underprivileged, as he often is, there are reasons for liking him.

34

Type DPB: Toward Identification with the Underprivileged

The member located in the downward-positive-backward part of the group space by his fellow members seems friendly and nonassertive, quite passive and perhaps in need of help, wishing to receive acceptance, intimacy, pleasure in the others' company. He is not at all value- or task-oriented, but he is responsive to the help, nurturance, and stimulation of others, and expectant of receiving what he needs without achievment. In the realization of his own values he seems to move toward identification with the underprivileged and hopes for the alleviation of their problems, and his. "Labor unions in large corporations should be given a major part in deciding company policy." "It is up to the government to make sure that everyone has a secure job and a good standard of living."

How He Sees Himself and How Others See Him

The DPB member is a "defender of the underdog." He may feel himself to be in a relatively poor position for the time being, but unlike some of the underprivileged for whom he speaks, he feels himself growing in confidence and expects to rise in status. He is thus open to hope, optimism, and the desire for action on their behalf. He does not wish to rise and leave his companions behind. He is rated highly on understanding, though not so high as his adjacent type DP. Of all types, he is least apt to arouse dislike and is well-liked. (The best liked is his more active adjacent type, PB.)

369

His Place in the Interaction Network

The DPB member is a low participator compared to others in the group. His total interaction initiated is low. In spite of this, however, there is some tendency for others to address him, and he is apt to be average rather than low in total interaction received. In relation to the amount he receives from others he is high on addressing specific individuals and correspondingly, low on addressing the group as a whole. Although his ideological direction is toward helping the underprivileged, he is not an active rabble-rouser. He may support those who make active efforts, either protective or revolutionary, but he does not himself take the initiative.

What Ideas and Values Is He Likely to Express?

"A teen-ager should be allowed to decide most things for himself." Teen-agers are among the underprivileged, in the eyes of the DPB member. So also are laborers, the poor and unemployed, women and children generally, underdeveloped nations, minority groups, deviants, prisoners, and criminals. These groups, and others, are thought of as not only factually underprivileged, but as subjected to oppression by their opposite types—adults and elders, professionals, the rich and idle, the males, the large wealthy nations, the great middle-class majority, the police, the moralists, and "the squares." Although these groups are felt to be oppressors and exploiters, the emphasis is still put on the plight of the underprivileged and the desirability of a change for their sake. The agitation is for a new deal, not a bloody revolution. "Labor unions in large corporations should be given a major part in deciding company policy." "It is up to the government to make sure that everyone has a secure job and a good standard of living." "Jews are as valuable, honest, and public-spirited citizens as any other group." "It is wrong that men should be permitted greater sexual freedom than women by society." "Our treatment of criminals is too harsh; we should try to cure, not to punish them." The persons and groups defended are those attacked by the UNF type, the autocratic authority, and the statements are implicitly addressed to such a type of bad parental figure. "The death penalty is barbaric, and should be abolished." Not only are the punishments of autocratic authority thought to be barbaric, but the threats of "enemies" by which that authority justifies his autocracy are felt to be unreal; very possibly the "enemies" are less bad than the authority. "In the interests of peace, we must give up part of our national sovereignty." "An occupation by a foreign power is better than war."

Statements advocating withholding of cooperation are congruent with such a set of assumptions. Autocratic authority is not trusted, but the protector of the innocent generally believes in the goodness of others.

People are not all bad—they are mostly good, but there are some who have become old, rich, and corrupt. Devaluation of the self is preferable to becoming like these. But much preferable is equalitarianism, permissive liberalism, nurturance of the young, new life, and the next generation. "The poor shall inherit the earth." In order to bring forth a new, more just society, the rejection of conventional group beliefs may be necessary, at least to some degree.

The Quality of His Interaction

The DPB member is concerned about social conditions rather than task accomplishment. He is high on asking for opinion and seeming friendly, but he avoids giving opinion, giving suggestion, and seeming unfriendly. He gives information, but does not tend to argue points, and avoids disagreeing. It is true that in his ideas and values he is against autocratic authority and wishes for some kind of revolution, but in his interaction he seems friendly with some showing of tension and laughing.

The interaction of others toward him is markedly low on disagreeing and seeming unfriendly. They do not argue with him. They are low on asking him for suggestion. They are rather high on seeming friendly and dramatizing and joking. They ask him for information and he gives it. They also give him information, probably generally in a friendly personal way, rather than a task-oriented way. They are low in agreeing with him, as they are on disagreeing, connected with the fact that he does not offer much content for evaluation. The reaction to him on the average seems very mild, and not at all what one might expect a young revolutionary to collect. This is the average pattern—there may be times when his desire to champion the underprivileged may bring him into conflict and make him the object of attack from the proponents of autocratic authority (this is commented further upon below).

Conflicts and Coalitions with Others

The protector of the underprivileged is confronted most directly in a psychological sense, at the same status level, by the person who advises, or dramatizes self-sacrifice for values, the DNF member. In a way both are concerned about a lack of sufficient maternal care—they feel the group or its leaders lack emotional supportiveness and warmth—and each in his way gives an answer. The answers they give are opposite. The DPB member tries to locate the trouble and finds it usually in a paternal, autocratic authority who, in a symbolic or real sense, does not care for his children (and perhaps not for his wife) as he should. The DNF member also tries to locate the trouble, and he finds it in a maternal figure, who should be giving emotional supportiveness and warmth, but is not. Actually, both conditions may be present in a group. But if so, the DNF member, tends to accept or defend the autocratic authority. He "identifies with the aggressor"—this is the quality in him which most offends the DPB defender of the underprivileged. The DPB member tends to accept or defend the possibility, of a good maternal source of emotional supportiveness and warmth. The DNF member feels that the DPB member is a "starry-eyed liberal," who does not yet realize that children have to grow up and find that it is a cruel hard world after all, with no free lunches and no dependable goodness in either man or woman. It is the DPB quality of "naïve" trust in the goodness of others—especially mothers, or in himself as a good mother—that so offends the DNF member who sacrifices himself for more conservative values. The conservative self-sacrificer may try to show the DPB member that such good mothers do not really exist.

The hard-working DF type can hardly avoid feeling a certain disapproval of the "grasshoppers," who, poor though they may be, have fiddled their time away, while he, like the ant, has labored all summer to avoid a hungry winter. The DF type may indeed know his own weaknesses—his desires to lapse into passive dreaming and fiddling, his desires to be cared for like an infant. But he has learned under the rigor of necessity and punishment that he must forgo these desires and work for his daily bread. He must not depend upon the protection of a mother, or the "handouts" of a benevolent mother-substitute, "society," or "the government." He must grow up and face the world. These are the lessons that the DF type tries to convey to the DPB defender of the underprivileged. Because of the need of the DF type to remain neutral and impersonal, the disapproval may be concealed, and since he tends to be nonverbal, the action may be dramatic or symbolic, but the relationship of opposition and implicit resentment remains. It will probably be expressed, at least, by adherence to a forward coalition.

The F member is a possible leader of this coalition. He is a little more ascendant and tries to bring home the lessons of conservative group beliefs to the erring DPB defender of the underprivileged. His message to both the defender and to the underprivileged, is to "repent and be baptized." If the underprivileged accepts the right beliefs and values, he believes, then the right actions will follow, and the condition of need will disappear. To the poor and the underprivileged he says, "Seek ye first the Kingdom of Heaven, and all these other things shall be added unto you." To which their defender may reply: "We don't believe in the Kingdom of Heaven, we don't believe in pie in the sky. We want bread now."

The DN member is ambivalent about any move to better the condition of the underprivileged. He is alienated, isolated, and has resentment to spare. He is not much motivated to help anybody, underprivileged or not. He may well see any move for social betterment as an immature and probably unsuccessful attempt to gain status—a struggle he has already repudiated. In this mood he will oppose the DPB member. But since "a revolution" may give him a chance to vent his hostility, he is persuadable.

The D member demonstrates devaluation of the self as an alternative to the attempt to improve status. The D member is among those for whom the DPB defender feels he is working—the D member *is* the "underdog," if there is any. But the underdog is not active in his own defense. He is a part of what Marx called the *lumpenproletariat*—that part of the laboring class, which cannot be persuaded to stand up for itself. The limpness may spread to the defender also. In one mood the defender calls for action, but in another he lapses back and agrees with the tendency to devaluate the self. He is not able, without help, to provide the leadership for a revolution. This must usually be obtained from a coalition with more negative and ascendant types.

Although the DPB type sometimes implicitly *accepts* such help, to provide the aggression he cannot himself show, he does not wish to acknowledge the need for aggression. His self-conception and his conscious wishes are on the positive altruistic side. He wants a bloodless revolution—a compassionate reform really. Of all value-statements addressed to him he is most likely to agree with those which emphasize trust in the goodness of others and equalitarianism.

The DPB type desires to maintain a compassionate self-picture, but in fact he needs more negative and ascendant leadership in order to move toward any actual revolution. He is, as the accusing members of the right are likely to point out, "soft on communism." He is the counterpart on the left of those members on the UP and PF side who are "soft on fascism" (see pp. 203 and 268). Those who are soft on fascism initiate one type of value-statement, but are ready to agree verbally to a more negative type. In the present case it appears that the DPB member is neither ready to initiate nor to agree with negative value-statements, but will in fact *act* in cooperation with, and depend upon, leadership of a more negative and ascendant kind.

The three dynamic levels so implied should be kept separate: (1) verbally stating; (2) agreeing with; and (3) silently allowing oneself to be led by. Discrepancies in these are presumably not accidental but are regular means, though probably often repressed, by which conflicts within the individual personality are reconciled with the necessities of social reality, leadership, and power. The existence of other types of personalities in other types of roles is probably psychologically necessary to the resolution of conflicts within the individual personality, at least for some types. When such complementary types are not available within the group, we may suppose they are invented, and dramatized in fantasy, or the closest approximation to the needed type is recruited from among the members and is forced into the role.

Personality Traits

There are no tests which directly characterize the DPB type. His D neighbor is withdrawn, but we have supposed this does not characterize the "activist" desires of the DPB type induced by his identification with the underprivileged. Like his P neighbor, the DPB member may be trustful and accessible. These traits may have an ideological significance to the opposed DNF type. They make the DPB member more gullible . . . so goes the reasoning of the threatened member of the political right. The PF, DPF, and DP members are very possibly lamblike in their lack of resistance to wolves. Those of the conservative persuasion, the DF and DPF members, are lambs, unprotected against the wolves of the radical right. Those of the radical persuasion, DB, DPB, and PB are lambs unprotected against wolves of the radical left.

Perhaps this is the place to point out that the political right and left are to one's own imagined right and left hand, when looking into the space from the P position, the perspective of Figure 3.2, Chapter 3. The directions of the political right are those of the forward half of the space, seen to one's right from the positive position. The directions of the political left are those of the backward half of the space, seen to one's left from the same position. The political center is the position of equalitarianism. The far right and the far left meet at the directly opposite pole, negative, with the leadership centering in UN. The UN set of values, tough-minded assertiveness, or in political language "extremism," may be allied either to the right or left, or both. Actually to help move a group toward revolution, the DPB member must usually join with leadership further to the radical left, more ascendant, and more negative—toward the tough-minded extremist. But usually by the time the revolution is brought about, the lambs have been devoured by the extremist wolves, who are as far away as can be from an interest in equalitarianism.

The DPB member is not actually so very far to the left, if one starts from equalitarianism as the center. The P member, his neighbor, is usually well organized, high on intellectual efficiency and ego strength. These traits are connected with near-optimum conditions for personality integration. DPB's neighbor, the DP member, is calm, stable, mature, with a high probability of achievement. These traits the DPB member may also show. Thus he may be a defender of the underprivileged, but in a psychological sense, he himself may be reasonably well-endowed. Although he is inhibited, especially so far as aggression is concerned, his drives are reasonably well harnessed, and his sense of internal conflict is relatively low. His vulnerability is his innocence. The thing which he is innocent about, presumably, is the presence and extent of deviant and hostile elements (usually hostility to authority) in his own and others' personalities, repressed but still seeking a liason with others who will express the aggression overtly in the secretly desired direction.

How He Sees His Parents

The most salient thing about the picture of the parents of the DPB member is that the father is very low on inhibitory demands and discipline. The mother is also moderately low. It is interesting that the child of parents of this type is nevertheless inhibited, at least quite well controlled, though seemingly rather innocent and naïve about the things that inhibit many people—namely the demands of authority and the threat of punishment. Perhaps he is emboldened to demand better things from authority, partly because he does not realize how bad authority can be. That is another aspect of the lack of realism that may come from "never having had to meet a payroll" as the conservative complains.

On the other hand, it does not appear that the child has necessarily been pampered. Father and mother are both only average on emotional supportiveness and warmth. They have not tried, in other words, to replace the function of discipline by unremitting reward. The parents, if like the child, and true to type, are not extroverted interactors. Their interactive contact with each other and with the child is low. He is left in many respects to develop for himself. It may even be that one of the circumstances of earlier life which tends to turn a personality in the present direction—of concern for peers, for the common man—is that a good deal of time is spent with brothers and sisters, or playmates. This might also reinforce the basic concern with equality. Equality is seldom realized in such groups, but it is a matter of constant concern and is held as a legitimate ideal.

Father and mother are not more than average on optimistic idealism or, to put it another way, are about halfway between optimistic idealism and cynical pessimism. The discrepancies in role between them are about average. One can see little basis for transmission of conventional culture in such a family—low interactive contact, no special emphasis on idealism, parents generally anti-conservative, but not consensually so, with a very negative attitude toward inhibitory demands and discipline. On the other hand one infers a basically positive attitude toward most other people. This position is at the nadir of autocratic authoritarianism, but it does not appear to be a paradise. And the child obviously does not regard it as a paradise—he feels a pervasive sense of unfairness, a lack of opportunity for the underprivileged, a lack of good paternal care, and a need for a change.

His Effect on Group Satisfaction

The DPB member voices the need for change. Insofar as the change involves a change of values, especially conservative values and relations with authority figures, the DPB member is apt to interfere with the rationale for task-efforts. He tends, on the average, to move the group away from satisfaction with goal attainment. At the same time, his own rationale is one of a concern for people, especially the underprivileged, and they like him for taking their part. He tends to mobilize and represent, in a friendly way, those who are thrown out of joint by emphasis on the necessities of the tasks of the group. At the same time, the DPB member is not demanding in time or recognition, nor is he threatening and aggressive. The solidarity he mobilizes among the under-privileged in the group tends to be protective and not militant. It is not surprising that his average net effect is to move the group toward satisfaction with interpersonal relations.

35

Type D: Toward Devaluation of the Self

The member located in the downward part of the group space by his fellow members seems self-effacing and completely nonself-assertive, passive and powerless. He accepts others in the group and the nature of things as they are without requesting anything for himself, but also without any enthusiasm or desire. He is neither friendly nor unfriendly, neither dutiful nor resistant to value- and task-demands, but simply inactive and inert in his adaptation to all influences. In the realization of his own values, so far as they can be discerned, he seems to be trying to move toward a devaluation of the self. He may have a philosophical belief which denies any ultimate reality to the self. "I have no desire to climb the ladder of success." "One should accept whatever exists, in whatever condition he finds himself, without futile efforts to change or to escape."' [1]

How He Sees Himself and How Others See Him

The D member seems to devalue his sense of self, to accept misfortune, lack of success, lack of satisfaction, but to endure, nevertheless, possibly in some abstract or mystical sense. He tends to rate others high on extroversion, presumably by contrast to himself. Others, in turn, correctly feel that he sees them as extroverted. The most introverted

[1]These are probable value-statements of the D member.

direction, however, according to observers, members, and the introvert's own self-rating, is DF, not simply downward. The D member guesses that others see him as acceptant of authority. This is true to some extent. He also may perceive a lack of positive emotional involvement with the group, a lack of interaction with others, and an isolation in fact. There may be some tendency for the group members to feel curiosity about him. He shows very little of himself.

His Place in the Interaction Network

The D member is markedly low on total interaction initiated, as compared to all others in the group. Insofar as he addresses others at all, he seems strongly to prefer to address particular individuals rather than the group as a whole. Contrary to what one might expect, the D member is not the lowest on total interaction received. (This is more characteristic of the DN member.) The D member is likely to be low on interaction received, but not necessarily markedly low. He is very low in prominence, but is not regarded with a negative feeling. He is not a strong ally or supporter of movement in any direction and, of all members, he is most likely to seem neutrally inert and out of touch with the emotional currents and power struggles in the group. In a psychological sense he is held immobile by conflicting tendencies, suppression, repression, and concealment. He actively maintains, by inner psychological effort, his overt immobility.

What Ideas and Values Will He Express?

No actual examples of characteristic value-statements are available. The sentiments, in the thumbnail sketch are hypothetical: "I have no desire to climb the ladder of success."[2] The profession of lack of desire seems a likely characteristic. The D position is one that implies an almost complete inhibition of aggression, sexuality, and materialistically oriented appetites. An example may be found in the concept of Nirvana, the "extinction of the fire of passion," the ultimate desired state in Buddhism. The values on the downward side of the evaluative space all have an ascetic-religious feeling, though in doctrinal terms and social implications they differ quite widely from each other. A devaluation of the self in the social sense, as well as in the sense of its psychological-reality, and a renunciation of means of gratifying desire or need, are central values.

Having indications that a person tends downward, knowing that he is silent most of the time in a group, one may have little idea of the other directions toward which he may lean. Expressing negative and backward sides he may speak (in response to questions) for the rejection of social

[2] This item is borrowed from Dr. Arthur S. Couch.

success, the withholding of cooperation, and the acceptance of failure and withdrawal. Or he may express values of the positive and forward side, trust in the goodness of others. He may place a value on self-knowledge and subjectivity and believe in salvation through love. The transition from an acceptance of failure and withdrawal to a belief in salvation through love may seem like a drastic transformation—a religious conversion, in fact—but the two positions are not, nevertheless, at polar opposites psychologically. They may coexist in the same person; he may value both or fluctuate. They have in common the element of self-abnegation. The acceptance or practice of self-abnegation is probably one of the main mechanisms by which the transformation of religious conversion is ordinarily accomplished. The great religions of the East, as well as of the West, and many more minor cults and therapeutic procedures have some such feature in common. The ability to devaluate the self may indeed yield compensatory powers or consolations.

If the willingness to abnegate the self is turned toward a dramatization of belief, whether that belief is related to self-knowledge and subjectivity, trust in the goodness of others, or a belief in salvation through love, the result may be some form of self-sacrifice for values. A similar dramatization of the rejection of social success, the withholding of cooperation; and the urge toward failure and withdrawal may combine with an abnegation of the self in an act of sacrifice to bring about a revolution for the underprivileged. The two types of sacrificial dramatization are not diametrically opposed. They may be combined by the same person, and such acts may, in effect, tend to reconcile opposites within the group. The self-sacrifice for values is an attempt to demonstrate that one can move forward through self-abnegation. Self-immolation for the revolution is an attempt to demonstrate that through self-abnegation one can move from a negative to a positive attitude toward others. The D member may combine all of these directional tensions at least in some intellectualized or mystical form. He balances forward with backward, positive with negative, all with very little overt action. Belief in the power of thoughts to control things, in clairvoyance and telepathy are consistent enhancements of "higher" mental powers over everyday physical powers, and may be characteristic of the D type. Similarly, trancelike states and other forms of immobility may be valued as revealers of knowledge. "The world within" is likely to be more valued than the external world.

The Quality of His Interaction

The role of the D member in interaction is very inconspicuous. So far as he participates at all, he is markedly high in his concentration on one category, giving information (see p. 116). His mode of influencing others, insofar as he tries to influence them at all, is indirect. In addition to giving information he is relatively high on asking for suggestion and showing tension and laughing. Giving information is an indirect mode of influence because it provides only factual premises and leaves inferences and suggestions to others. Asking for suggestion is indirect because it turns the problem of analysis and action over to the other. Showing tension or laughing is indirect because it provides only signs that something is wrong, but does not clearly indicate what is wrong, and no move is made toward doing anything about it. The D member, submissive and indirect as he tends to be, is low on giving suggestions. Dramatizing and joking are ordinarily very low—the D member avoids jokes, anecdotes, personal materials, colorful speech, and anything else that might be interpreted as an index to his inner state.

For certain of the D types of persons unusual meanings may be attached to communication. Communication in any form may be considered dangerous because it reveals impulses and desires, and so may be avoided, except for a minimum which is made as indirect and nonrevealing as possible. The D member is low in asking for information as well. He does not take the initiative of involving others.

The responses of others to the D member are similarly nonrevealing and basically dissociative. There is some attempt to bring him into the group by asking him for opinion and for information, but he responds only to the latter, since he can give bare information with less revelation of himself, his feelings and fantasies, and hence expose himself to less danger than he would if he gave opinions. Others avoid addressing suggestions to him, and he himself avoids suggestions. By his guarded silence he avoids having to respond to indications of negative emotions or questions from others that would stir him into action. He wants to "stay out of trouble." To a certain extent he succeeds. He is left pretty well alone, and others tend to be low on disagreement, showing tension, or laughing, and seeming unfriendly in relation to him. At least he escapes negative reactions. Except for a bare "informational" interchange which prevents most information from being communicated, the D member cuts himself off from others, and is generally left to sink into isolation.

Conflicts and Coalitions with Others

One may suppose that all of the surrounding downward types, insofar as they look for adherents, see the D type as a potential adherent and ally of their own position. The actual communication that one can expect from any of these is very low, but there may be indications that the D member is regarded as a "silent partner." Both to and from him one must look for minimal cues, silent glances, unobtrusive acts such as the choice of seating position, bodily position vis-à-vis the other, gestures, presentation of meaning in symbols, clothing or grooming, absences, and understandings reached outside regular meetings of the group. In subtle ways a partnership, or a "leaning" one way or another may be conveyed.

Since the D type, as the object of such attentions, is so largely silent and self-protective, he may seem mysterious. Occult powers may be attributed to him to some extent, and he may cooperate in this attribution. His passivity and mysteriousness may be associated with death. He may be felt to be speaking from beyond the grave when he does speak. Feeling the power associated with an occult status, the D member may use it. He may cooperate in many subtle ways in the maintenance of the myths and fictions so generated. He may work to establish and maintain an "other-wordly" system of symbols: nonverbal, nonactional, and nonpassional. In most groups for most of the time, however, he is fated to be ignored and left to his self-protective isolation. He is roused only on occasion to give his name and number. This increases his relative rate of giving information, but conveys little information about him that is interesting to others or dangerous to himself.

Although he appears to be a potential "silent partner" in any direction, there is some indication that he leans, on the average, toward the positive and forward side. He may agree with statements of conventional group beliefs, altruistic love, and equalitarianism, though he does not initiate such statements. Conversely, he is not especially likely to agree with urgings for withholding of cooperation and identification with the underprivileged, although he is a usual object of such attempts. Even though he may appear to "lean" in some direction when pressed, he cannot be counted upon for much action. He is basically immobilized by the extreme defenses he has adopted to keep aggression, sexuality, and anxiety immobilized in his own personality.

Personality Traits

The most characteristic personality trait of the downward type is that he seems withdrawn. The drives of the D member are seemingly detached from their usual objects, inhibited to an unusual degree. The inhibition may consist either of a high degree of harnessing and integration of drives with other internal processes, or a high degree of splitting within the personality, with some elements of the self almost totally given over to the repression or immobilization of other elements.

Splitting and *harnessing* may both be present. These are simply names offered for two hypothetical kinds of processes by which drives in all types of personalities are presumed to be tamed, insofar as they are tamed. A drive is tamed by *splitting* when it is divided against itself by associating it with more than one, perhaps many objects or internal processes. Drives or parts of them are *harnessed* by the relinking of their associated objects and processes into consistently operating time-ordered systems.

In certain types of systematic training, techniques are applied which may be thought of as splitting and harnessing. The thing to be learned is broken down minutely into very small steps (splitting), the steps are arranged in a time order in which each step is as similar to the last as possible (harnessing), and then reward and punishment are applied to each small act to force the discrimination of very small steps (splitting) and to link each one to the proper next one in a time sequence (harnessing). This is essentially what is meant by "programmed learning" or "shaping." It is efficient and effective, but it is also true that to apply it to a person or an animal requires that the trainer take a very "objective" or "cold" attitude toward the learner, since the learner is in effect "taken apart" and "reassembled." Machines ("teaching machines") are sometimes better at this than people. There is a close analogue of these processes in assembly-line manufacturing, where the steps necessary to construct an article are broken down into very small segments, and each is given to a different person or set of persons. The worker feels a sense of "alienation"—from the means of production, from the article produced, and from himself. In the psychological analogue, the "self" is split as the labor is divided.

When the integration or harnessing has been successfully completed, the result may be very satisfactory to the trainer, and perhaps to the learner. A downward type of person in whom the harnessing of drives has been extensive may show the traits of the DP type: he may be calm, stable, mature and have a high probability of achievement. He may also show responsibility. He may be able to perform tasks which require a high degree of integration at a level literally impossible for the untrained.

The traits of the DPF type, which the D type may share, can be seen as types of achievement. To be practical, responsible, to have will control, and to have character stability—these traits require that one be able to make fine discriminations among prospective acts, to trace their consequences intellectually, to relate consequences to desired values, and so to make choices. Such choices can be stable because the individual has "taught himself" what to do by breaking the possibilities down into a finely discriminated series of steps, and has reassembled them to accomplish a plan.

The fact that such a person may also be submissive is perhaps regrettable, but it points to the probable fact that one best learns to do this for himself from a parent figure who expects it and teaches it.

Acceptance of the parent may be necessary to acquire the power to apply the method, and conversely, when one applies the method, he tends to refer to, or to imagine, a good, accepting parental figure who continues to monitor the process. Hence, even though one may know in a literal sense that the parent is no longer there, the imagined aid of a parent-figure may be a real aid, and may, in some form, be indispensable.

This is a hypothesis which can also be put into a religious context. Even among persons and religious groups who have lost all *literal* belief one may still find a nonliteral belief in God as a responding being, in the practice of prayer as communication with him. A belief understood on some higher symbolic level suffices; the exact nature of the belief is willingly left "a mystery," and no literal belief is required. I suspect that those who have shown the power to take themselves apart, and reassemble their motives closer to their heart's desire, would generally testify that some such method is required—contemplation, self-examination, confession, prayer, free-association, dream-analysis, artistic effort, or the like—and that some imagined (or real) responder is helpful, whose reaction is trusted, and whose perspective one may take by turns with the acting one.

Such a division between the momentarily acting self and the momentarily observing and evaluating self is a splitting of internal psychic processes. It may well be a prerequisite to the highest degree of integration of the total personality. It may, on the other hand become a critical split within the personality, which makes any tolerable integration impossible and the attempt to achieve it a torture. The compulsive-obsessive personality is one in which the observing-evaluating function is divided from the acting-trying function. The acting-trying function is associated with the conscious accepted self, whereas the observing-evaluating function is associated with a dangerous, and punishing authority figure, an unconscious, unaccepted part of the self. The total personality is split along the lines of the relation of child to parent. When the split is severe the conscious self feels compelled to act, often in a way that is sure to bring disapproval from the unconscious tyrannical self. Sometimes the conscious self seems to hear voices telling him what to do, or condemning him. Sometimes he is led to act automatically, or to write automatically, to say strange things, or "speak in tongues."[3] This degree of estrangement of the unconscious from the conscious parts of the self goes beyond the usual, of course, and is part of the background of the trait, schizothymia, a trait associated to some degree with the direction DNB.

Other traits of the DNB direction—simplicity, immaturity, roughness, and independent self-sufficiency may characterize the person who

---

[3]The religious phenomenon of glossolalia. (This is a speculative connection.).

has never had adequate social contact, for whatever reason. Such a person may never have learned to "take the role of the other" toward himself, and so may never have learned how to harness his drives, how to analyze himself and put himself together in a more integrated way. He may never have had the benefit of contact with a person he could love and trust. On the other hand, a lack of integration in the personality is not necessarily extreme. The DF personality, the DNF, and the DN probably show the splitting tendencies to increasing degrees as they approach DNB. Different parts or aspects of the personality may be suppressed or repressed.

As a working hypothesis it has been assumed throughout this book that for any given direction around the circle of the downward types, the tendencies most likely repressed are those at the direct opposite pole. Thus for the DN type, it was assumed that the fully expanded ego, as found in the UP type, is repressed or sacrificed. Depression has been related to this sacrifice. The social introversion, the attempt to build up some independent self-sufficiency, apart from persons, has been related to this attempt to adjust to the loss of a particular part of, or picture of the self. These traits are very possibly shown by the D member as well, and for similar reasons.

The most directly opposite type for the D type, the U type, is an expanded-ego type organized around material satisfactions and instinctual gratification. If the theory is sound, these may be inferred to be the most completely repressed or suppressed aspects of the personality of the D type. On the same reasoning it may be inferred that the D type also represses that which his DP neighbor most completely represses— tendencies to overt aggression or tough-minded assertiveness. Sexuality and aggression, as well as ego inflation and desire for material pleasures, are all held in severe check. Insofar as they find outlet, it is either through a very thoroughgoing harnessing, or through a disorganized kind of splitting in diffuse and symbolically disguised forms that evade conscious controls. If the drives cannot be harnessed, they may be split as a last resort. The degree of splitting necessary to immobilize the upward-tending drives may range from minor to major. The splitting may be spread among many personality fragments, or may be concentrated into two or three major groups, each of which attains an impressive degree of coherence and becomes a subself, in effect. Each may clash with each other to an extent that one self may be unconscious of the others, and the individual in his conscious mode may shift from one to the other, as in the famous cases of "multiple personalities."

Not all types are equally likely to repress. That tendency seems marked for the D type, although the DN type may test higher on the trait repression-denial. It is also true, according to the theory presented here, that the tendency to talk is repressed along with other tendencies. The probability that the downward types will engage the prominent verbal types directly in discussion, or try to control them by verbal means, is low. The downward types exercise their influence more indirectly, often symbolically or dramatically rather than logically, and often by joining in with a coalition, thus strengthening its position in a struggle for power. In this sense the more relevant competitor for each of the downward types is the opposite *downward* type—his competitor in the more quiet drama of symbolism and coalition formation. It may be this person who is more likely to be a target for subtle forms of influence than the directly opposite *upward* type. On this reasoning, the D type is a possible mediator among all of the surrounding downward types, and may exert considerable influence in a subtle symbolic way. He is a likely maker of new religions and symbolic cults.

How He Sees His Parents

The immediate impression one gets of the parents from the description implied by the model is one of very low interactive contact, perhaps even of neglect of each other and the child. Both father and mother are moderately low on both inhibitory demands and discipline, and on emotional supportiveness and warmth.

It is as if the child were left alone a good deal, or within visual contact with the parents, but with little physical interaction, little direct response closely coupled in time to his own; in brief, with "poor feedback." A training in silence and a dependence upon visual contact might go along with the closely vigilant style of interaction of the D member, with the relative emphasis on giving information only. It also seems consistent with the various hints of the development of a private symbolism, and the apparently vague or confused conception about what the process of communication really involves, physically and behaviorally. A parent who depended mostly on observation and inference rather than verbal interaction with the child for his knowledge of the child's needs and desires might in fact reinforce the idea of the child that it is not necessary to communicate verbally, or that it is useless. The child might correctly gain the impression that he was watched, that his inner thoughts and desires were known—a common fear of withdrawn persons.

In such a psychological situation, the privacy of the self may be threatened if it is not given time and space enough to grow, to discover itself through action, to play. The self may split or fractionate, fastening self-feeling onto various parts of the body, surroundings, imagined or accidentally-present objects and events. The person may struggle, but vainly, to "pull himself together." In certain respects, or in certain areas of behavior he may succeed, even brilliantly, by great effort, but he is likely to fail in a more total integration; and other areas of the personality will be split off, neglected, and left in a primitive untrained state. Sometimes geniuses in particular psychological functions, such as perception, memory, calculation, or higher mathematics present such apparent asymmetrical development of personality.

Training in silence and waiting are also training in control of the extroverted appetites and drives. This may be a part of the intention of the parents, at any rate it seems a part of the personality of the D type. The parents are not high on either optimistic idealism nor its opposite, pessimistic cynicism. The emphasis on lowering the level of need, or drive, which is characteristic of the D value-direction, tends to remove interest from the outcome of effort, either success or failure. The child is presumably taught to lower the need, whatever it may be, as the primary mode of adjustment. This even includes the need for integration of the self, to say nothing of its expansion through rise in social status, popularity, or power.

His Effect on Group Satisfaction

Since the demand for personal status is so low, the D type of person does not threaten the status of others, nor does he much increase the competition. From this point of view he is acceptable to others. On the average he tends to move the group toward satisfaction with interpersonal relations. It is also important, probably, that he tends to inject nothing controversial into the discussion—he does not precipitate nor join arguments within the group, sticking as close to information as he does.

One might think that his emphasis on information would be helpful in problem-solving, since there is such a tendency for people to desert facts the moment they get excited. This effect, if present, must be small. The model infers that the D member tends to move the group neither toward nor away from satisfaction with goal attainment. For one thing, the total amount of his participation is typically very small. For another thing, although he asks for suggestion on the task-oriented side, he also shows tension or laughs, with a total null effect. He does not introduce facts for the sake of task-achievement. He sticks to facts for his own protection.

PART III
Appendices

Appendix 1

List of Variables
with Directional Indicators

PRELIMINARY NOTE

As described in Chapter 2, the questions under each variable in the list on pages 398-401 may be used by the practical observer to elicit relevant impressions from his experience or to suggest to him measurements he might wish to make at the next opportunity. The indicated direction will tell him the general implications of the variable. The type description designated will suggest a large number of relevant hypotheses for further observation. As the base of observational evidence grows, the observer's assessment of the indicated direction(s) may be expected to improve.

Each variable is described in terms of a simply phrased question. If the question can be answered "yes" on the basis of adequate and reliable observation or other evidence, then the inference may be drawn that the individual in question may show the other characteristics of the indicated type. If the question can clearly be answered "no" with some confidence, the indicated direction may be reversed. For example, if the indicated direction for a clear "yes" answer is D, then the indicated direction for a clear "no" answer may be taken to be U, since upward is the reverse of downward.

If the question cannot be answered either "yes" or "no" with some degree of confidence, then no inference should be made from that source

389

of evidence. It should be recognized that if observations are not adequate, if they are unreliable or unrepresentative, then either a "yes" or a
"no" answer is unjustified, and no prediction should be made from that
source of evidence. The type of answer ("yes," "don't know," or "no")
is, of course, an artificial simplification. All of the questions refer to
variables which were measured in a more quantitative way in the
original studies from which findings are taken. For simplicity, the answer
form used in the list simply evades the problems involved in making the
relevant observations, assessing their reliability and representativeness,
establishing cutting points required for high, medium, low, and so on.
Similarly, the simple directional indicators evade the problem of properly taking into account how strong the connection is between the diagnostic observations and the indicated direction. Some of these problems,
particularly those having to do with Interaction Process Analysis are
treated in this book. Others are not treated at all. It is assumed that
ordinarily the practical user of this book will want to make the most of
whatever slender evidence he may have, but he should also supply an
appropriate degree of caution.

The present list may also be used with great advantage to explore
the probable relations of variables to each other. One might wonder, for
example, whether social introversion, as a trait, is likely to arouse dislike
among others. The answer given by the present body of data may be
determined by first finding the directional indicators of each variable
from the list. The directional indicator of the trait social introversion is
shown as DN. The directional indicator of receiving dislike from other
group members is UNF. As the directional names indicate, they both
have a negative component, but one also has a downward component,
whereas the other has an upward component; one shows a forward
component, and the other shows none. Intuitive placement of the two
directions in the visualized physical space will probably make their
correlation seem doubtful. Doubt may be resolved by looking up the
relation of the two directions in Appendix 2. Under direction DN it is
shown that direction UNF is zero correlated with direction DN. One
concludes that social introversion, as a trait, though it has a negative
component, does not especially tend to elicit dislike. It may, or it may
not. It is the combination of negativity with ascendance and moralism
that most strongly elicits the dislike of others.

The procedure just described is illustrative. The probable relationship between any two variables in the list may be determined in a similar
way. The list contains a gold mine of information for whoever has the
initiative to mine it. The typological descriptions only make a simple
start.

Most of the evidence cited for the variables comes from one source, Arthur Couch's dissertion (71), containing two major factor analyses. The measures in what Couch called the *Personality Domain* consisted mostly of standard written personality tests (61; 62; 63; 64; 85; 94; 104; 157). The other factor analysis included summary measures of the factors of the personality domain, but was mainly concerned with the intercorrelations of interpersonal perceptions, overt interaction measures, and measures of the content of value-statements made and received in the group meetings. This latter factor analysis is referred to as the *Interdomain Analysis*, because it ties together measures from all the measured domains.

The main study upon which this book is based, and which was the source of data for the two factor analyses just mentioned, was conducted jointly by Bales and Couch with other collaborators, particularly Gene Kassebaum (103) and Philip Slater (140). It is described in detail in Couch's dissertation. For present purposes it is probably enough to give a few basic facts. There were sixty subjects who were rather exhaustively studied by many methods. They met in twelve groups of five for a series of five two-hour meetings, each meeting with a somewhat different task. There were two interviewing and inference tasks, one somewhat formalized self-analytic task, and two value-dilemma tasks based on cases. The data for all five meetings were pooled for each individual.

It should be recognized that sixty subjects in twelve groups is a very small number for such a mountain of data analysis and so many hypotheses. No claims are made for the reliability or representativeness of the findings. These problems must be dealt with in the future. The present study, for all its complication, is only exploratory. Its virtue, I hope, is that it makes a major attack on the problem of synthesis of many variables that are so often treated in relative isolation (23; 32).

A number of nonstandard scales built on items in the MMPI were used. The authors of these scales and the general rationale for using them in addition to the standard scales will be found in an article most important and helpful by Kassebaum, Couch, and Slater (104).

The variables used in the description of the personality and group role types are listed alphabetically below, with brief identifications. Following this, each variable is taken up, in turn, with more detailed specifications, along with the directional indicators, followed by comments on the quality of the evidence.

An examination of the list will indicate that the variables fall into several main classes:

Class A.   Personality traits of the individual, which may be measured in advance of any group meeting by written personality tests.

Class B.   Observations of overt behavior of the individual during group meetings, recorded at the time of each act.

Class C.   Classifications of the content of value-statements made by the individual during group meetings, recorded at the time of each statement.

Class D.   Ratings or evaluations of the individual made by other group members and by observers, after group meetings, including feelings toward the individual.

Class E.   Guesses by the individual of the ratings and evaluations he will receive from others, of Class D above. These guesses represent to some extent the expectations each individual has of each other.

The observer if he is also a participant in the group will ordinarily depend upon his own ratings made after group meetings (class D). Members of some groups engaged in self-analysis, or who are willing to participate in research may rate and evaluate each other on post-meeting questionnaires (classes D and E). An observer who does not participate as a group member may make a running classification of the content of value-statements (class C), or a running classification of the overt interaction as it occurs (class B). Only rarely probably, as part of a research study, will one be able to administer personality tests (class A). The fact that all of these classes of variables are interrelated, however, makes it possible to form some estimate of the others from any starting point. Each class of data adds desirable new information and refinement, but in practical application, any one or two is of some help.

Unfortunately not all of the correlations of each variable with each other is known directly from the present study, though the study includes all classes of measures. It was necessary to draw upon data from several studies over a considerable period. All told, six different factor analyses are drawn upon in considerable detail for the present synthesis:

1. A factor analysis of the responses of subjects to written value-statements on a questionnaire called the Value Profile. This is included as Appendix 5 of the present book. The population of subjects was 552 persons, none of whom was a subject in the final main group study. See Bales and Couch (31).

2. A factor analysis by Melvin (115) of the responses of subjects to written value-statements comparable to the items in the Value Profile in 1 above. Melvin's work, associated with that of Eysenck (78) is historically unrelated, presumably not influenced in any way by the work of Bales and Couch. His study was done in England.

3. A factor analysis of the responses of members of small experimentally formed groups to written items expressing various kinds of satisfaction or disatisfaction with group meetings they had just completed.

The population of subjects was about eighty persons, none of whom was a subject in the final main group study. See Couch (70).

4. A factor analysis of the descriptions of subjects of their parents. The instrument was called the PRF (Parental Role Factors) test by its author, Slater (140). The population was the sixty subjects of the final main group study.

5. A factor analysis of the scores of subjects on a battery of personality tests, both standard tests (those included in class A above) and experimental tests developed by Couch. The population was the sixty subjects of the final main group study. This analysis is called *Couch's Factor Analysis in the Personality Domain* (71).

6. A factor analysis made up mostly of variables of classes B, C, D, and E, as indicated above, but with summary factor scores of the subjects based on the personality tests in class A above also included. The population was the sixty subjects of the final main group study. Since this analysis combined variables of all the classes (A, B, C, D, and E), it was the key integrating analysis, and is called *Couch's Interdomain Analysis* (71).

The relation of the satisfaction measures obtained from analysis 3 above, to the space of analysis 6 is not known empirically, since the two studies were completely independent. The satisfaction factor space is overlapped with the Interdomain Space by reasonable hypothesis, in order to obtain clues from the items, which are used in the description of the personality and group role types.

Similarly, the relation of the Eysenck-Melvin social attitude space, number 2 above, to the space of the Bales-Couch Value Profile space, number 1 above, is not known empirically. The two are overlapped by reasonable hypothesis. I am grateful for the use of Melvin's items in giving me additional clues for the value-directions of the personality and group role types.

All of the rest of the variables are tied together empirically in the same study, the final main group study, but unfortunately the personality tests in analysis number 5 above, are only represented in the Interdomain Analysis, number 6 above through the summary factor scores of the subjects from analysis number 5. These summary scores are listed as separate variables, although in fact they are summaries of subject's scores on combinations of the standard personality tests also listed. Some experimental tests of Couch's were also used. Couch (71) names his summary factor scores in the Personality Domain as follows:

Factor I Anxiety: manifest (versus ego-controlled).

Factor II Emotionality: extrovertive (versus introvertive)

Factor III Aggression: manifest (versus controlled)

Factor IV Conformity: authoritarian (versus nonauthoritarian)

Factor V Ascension: wish-fulfillment (versus constriction)

As may be seen by checking these variables separately in this Appendix, the above variables have been assigned the following directional significances on the basis of the loadings they obtained in the Interdomain Analysis:

I.	Anxiety	= N	designated as I (N)
II.	Emotionality	= UP	designated as II (UP)
III.	Aggression	= UN	designated as III (UN)
IV.	Conformity	= PF	designated as IV (PF)
V.	Ascension	= B	designated as V (B)

It is through the empirical location of these summary measures, as shown above, in the Interdomain space that the whole battery of personality tests is brought into relation to the personality and group role types. It would be desirable, of course, to have had all the separate personality tests included in the Interdomain Analysis, but this was not possible at the time of the study.

As a result, the process of inference in getting from a given standard personality test to its probable location in the Interdomain space is very fallible. The process of making the prediction may be illustrated by reference to the MMPI scale called *depression*. The loadings of this test on Couch's Factor Analysis in the Personality Domain may be found by looking up the comments on this variable in this Appendix. The loadings are, on factor I (N) .64, on factor II (UP) .33 —, on factor III (UN) .15, on factor IV (PF) .02, and on factor V (B) .14 —. Since each of the factors has been found to predict some direction in the Interdomain space, as indicated, the loadings may be treated as directional indicators. If a given loading is high enough, its directional indicator may be added into the prediction.

How high is "high enough"? It may be determined from the Interdomain Factor Analysis (71), that a loading of about .17 may be taken as significant at the .05 level. I have generally accepted this level, rejecting lower loadings as nonsignificant, although in a few cases, for reason, I have stretched a few points in either direction from this level. These cases are always pointed out in the comments.

The prediction is obtained by addition of the directional indicators. In the example (the personality test depression), the main loading is on factor I, which in turn has been determined to predict (N), negative. This loading is .64, and is substantial. The next highest loading, .33 —, is on factor II, and since it is a negative loading, as indicated by the minus sign, the direction predicted is reversed. Thus instead of (UP), the loading predicts (DN). None of the other loadings is taken to be significant. The two directional indicators accepted as significant, namely

N and DN, are now added together to obtain the prediction, DN. This is certainly a crude and fallible procedure, but it serves for lack of a better one. Fortunately, the concurrence of results from many similar variables adds greatly to one's confidence when it occurs.

If any readers are left by now, they should tighten their seat belts at this point, since we are about to encounter one of the worst air-pockets of the flight. One of the puzzling facts of the Interdomain Factor Analysis is that the summary personality measure called factor IV, Authoritarian Conformity, see above, has low loadings—too low to be accepted as significant. It was expected that this variable would indicate the direction PF, and this is the directional indicator finally assigned, but the relation shown is much weaker than expected. What happened?

Comparison of the rotation I used of the Interdomain Factors with the rotation used in Couch's final work (71) indicates that although they are identical for factors I and II, they are slightly different for III. (I used an earlier print-out of the loadings, after which he rotated factor III, to shift some of the variance associated with it to a weaker factor that appears as factor VI in his final analysis.) What I call direction F in my space is close to what he calls "task seriousness" (his factor III−), whereas my direction B is close to what he calls "social expressivity" (his factor III+). The conceptual scheme of this book associates the forward direction in the space with task-orientation, that is, with task seriousness, and also with conservatism and acceptance of authority. One would expect then, that Authoritarian Conformity would be related to the forward direction. In the rotation I used, it is, but to a surprisingly low degree. And after Couch's final rotation, the personality trait Authoritarian Conformity is not related to this factor at all in his tables of factor loadings. Instead, it has become the key identifying variable of another, less strong, but orthogonal factor, his factor VI, called Authoritarian Conformity, in the Interdomain Analysis. However, Authoritarian Conformity *is* related to both Asking for Suggestion and Giving Suggestion. These are types of overt behavior which I had originally associated with task orientation. Additional categories of overt behavior, also originally associated with task orientation, are Asking for Information and receiving it. These also are associated with Authoritarian Conformity. It appears that there is a component of task orientation associated with the personality trait Authoritarian Conformity, but this component is separable from the component Couch called his factor III−, Task Seriousness. That factor, and my direction F, are both closely related to Giving Opinion. Giving Opinion is also an activity which I had originally expected to be related to task-orientation. Thus there are two relatively independent components of task-oriented behavior, one associated with Giving Opinion, and another associated with Authoritarian Conformity, Asking for Suggestion, and giving it.

The indications are, then, that neither Couch's factor III—, Task Seriousness, nor his factor VI, Authoritarian Conformity, nor my own direction F in the rotation I used; none of these is quite optimally located in the factor space to represent the concept needed for the present system. We should like a rotation which would strike an average between the two components of task-oriented behavior, and that would be moderately related to both. The rotation one would prefer would put the direction F about halfway between its present location in my study and Couch's factor VI. This rotation could be made without changing the relation of direction F to the dimension U-D or the dimension P-N. The resulting factor should then be related to both task-orientation in behavior and authoritarian conformity as a personality trait, and to both Giving Opinion and Giving and Asking for Suggestion, though some of the loadings might be low.

The direction F as theoretically conceived and described in the present book does in fact make this combination (see Introductory Exercise). It is assumed that the group to which the system is applied is in a task-oriented phase, is oriented to conservative assigned goals, and that the task leaders of the group are thus also likely to be conservative. Under these conditions, the personality trait Authoritarian Conformity would presumably predict PF. For purposes of the present system, then, the directional indicator is taken to be PF, though the loadings on the factor as now actually located are too weak to be taken as significant.

It should not be forgotten, however, that the simplicity of the space, as conceived for theoretical purposes, depends upon the coincidence of task-oriented behavior and the acceptance of goals received from authority, so that conformists are likely to be active in taking the lead. When the task-oriented behavior of the group is oriented counter to authority, or in a way irrelevant to it, the conforming types, measured partly by the personality tests indicating Authoritarian Conformity, will not likely be in the lead. This set of conditions is not rare, and in fact most groups presumably have phases when the task runs counter to authority or is counter-conservative. Not only does the present predictive system tend to break down under these conditions, but it may well be that predictability of behavior in general tends to go down. One of the results of conformity is that it increases the predictability of behavior of group members.

Now, we have a partial vacuum, which has to do with the extremely tenuous tie between known facts and the assumptions I have made about the kinds of value-statements made and received by each of the personality and group role types. The known facts are these:

1 The locations of specific items, that is specific value-statements, are known from the factor analysis of the Value Profile (See Appendix

5). The items are located, of course, in the Value Profile space, and their location in the interdomain space is not known.

2. However, the locations of the four *factors* of the Value Profile space in the Interdomain Space are known because the summary scores of subjects on the Value Profile were included in the Interdomain Analysis. The location of the four factors thus give us linking "marker variables." For the location of these marker variables see the present Appendix under the titles: "Autocratic Authority," "Rugged Individualism and Gratification," "Equalitarianism," and "Individualistic Isolationism."

3 The locations of actual verbal statements, value-statements, initiated and received by individuals in actual group interaction are known in terms of the locations of four classes or categories of value-statements used in the scoring. The method is known as Value-Content Analysis. The categories used were given the same names as the four factors of the Value Profile, listed just above. The study was done by Kassebaum (103), and the summary scores were included in Couch's Interdomain Analysis.

In proceeding from these known facts to the detailed inferences, it was first assumed that the relation of items (that is, particular value-statements) to each other, and to the marker variables, were the same in each of the three spaces: the Value Profile (written questionnaire) space; the value-content space of statements initiated (actual interaction); and the value-content space of statements received (actual interaction).

The marker variables from each space were then located empirically in the Interdomain space by the results of the Interdomain analysis. Knowing the location of the marker variables, and knowing the relation of specific items to the marker variables, the position of the specific item in the Interdomain space was inferred. (Each of the subsidiary spaces actually maps upon the Interdomain space at a different rotation, with marker variables in somewhat different directions. It was nevertheless assumed, as indicated above, that the basic relation of items to each other held constant within each of the spaces.)

Items so located in each of the major typological directions were then collated, and an inductive inference was made from them as to the common value-content. A name was then invented and assigned to characterize the value-content of items in each position, that is, for each personality and role type. In locations where there were no items, the characterization of the hypothetical value-content of the area was obtained by speculative inference from the supposed content of the neighboring areas which ring it.

The names of the value-directions, then, as well as their content, and their location in relation to each other, are all quite speculative. This, of course, is unfortunate from one point of view, in that the value-directions are at the heart of the theory underlying the whole scheme of this book. On the other hand, the value-directions are at the apex of the ladder of abstraction involved, and one may feel fortunate to have reasonable hypotheses for future work.

CONSOLIDATED LIST OF VARIABLES

Acceptance of Authority

(a) Do observers rate him high on Acceptance of Authority? If *yes*, then expect — DF
(b) Do group members rate him high on Acceptance of Authority? If *yes*, then expect — DF
(c) Does he rate himself high on Acceptance of Authority? If *yes*, then expect — DP
(d) Does he guess that others will rate him high on Acceptance of Authority? If *yes*, then expect — D
(e) Does he tend to rate others high on Acceptance of Authority? If *yes*, then expect — B
(f) Does he tend to make others feel that he rates them high on Acceptance of Authority? If *yes*, then expect — UB

The evidence on these variables is direct, all from Couch's Inter-Domain Factor Analysis. The loadings are:

	$I(U)$	$II(P)$	$III(F)$	*Summary*
(a)	.31—	.01—	.40	DF
(b)	.65—	.14	.35	DF
(c)	.20—	.26	.03	DP
(d)	.18—	.05	.10	D
(e)	.04	.14—	.38—	B
(f)	.22	.13—	.21—	UB

The question was phrased: "To what extent would you say each member feels that discipline and respect for authority are important and desirable?"

> 0 = "He feels that discipline and respect for authority are not important and are usually undesirable."
> 7 = "He feels that discipline and respect for authority are almost always desirable and necessary."

Achievement

Does he have a high score on the MMPI scale called Achievement? If *yes*, then expect   DP

The evidence that this scale measures DP is only indirect. Its loadings on Couch's Factor Analysis of the Personality Domain are: I(N) .62—; II(UP) .08; III(UN) .50—; IV(PF) 12—; V(B) .10—.

The main loading is on I reversed, which indicates P. The next most important loading is on III reversed, which indicates DP. The sum of these two indicators is DP.

Active

Does he have a high score on Thurstone's Temperament test called Active? If *yes*, then expect   U

The evidence that this scale measures U, as indicated, is only indirect. Its loadings on Couch's Factor Analysis of the Personality Domain are: I(N) .03—; II(UP) .45; III(UN) .56; IV(PF) .11—; and V(B) .16.

The main loading on III indicates UN, and the secondary loading on II indicates UP. The summary is thus U. The component backward may be significant.

Admiration, Arouses

(a) Do observers rate him high on Arousing Their Admiration? If *yes*, then expect   P
(b) Do group members rate him high on Arousing Their Admiration? If *yes*, then expect   PB
(c) Does he guess that others will rate him high on Arousing Admiration? If *yes*, then expect   P
(d) Does he tend to rate others high on Arousing his Admiration? If *yes*, then expect   PF
(e) Does he make others feel he rates them high on Arousing his Admiration? If *yes*, then expect   DP

The evidence on these questions is direct, all from Couch's Inter-domain Factor Analysis. The loadings are:

	I(U)	II(P)	III(F)	Summary
(a)	.14	.29	.08—	P
(b)	.03	.53	.23—	PB
(c)	.16	.40	.01—	P*
(d)	.15	.20	.24	PF
(e)	.26—	.62	.05—	DP

* = also (possibly) UP.

The question was phrased: "To what extent do you find qualities in other members of the group which you personally admire and would like to have yourself?"

0 = "I have no particular feeling of admiration for him."
7 = "I admire him very much."

Adventurous

Does he have a high score on Cattell's 16 PF test called
Adventurous? If *yes*, then expect   U

This trait is also called Thick-Skinned. The opposite end is called Timid, and Withdrawn.

The evidence that this scale measures U as indicated, is only indirect.

The loadings on Couch's Factor Analysis in the Domain of Personality are: I(N) .57—; II(UP) .59; III(UN) .32; IV(PF) .11; and V(B) .07.

The main loading on II indicates UP. The loading on I reversed, equally high, indicates P. The loading on III however, also moderately high, indicates UN. Although the literal summary of these three is UP, the loading on III seems high enough to merit recognition. The indicator U is thus chosen with the understanding that the location is probably on the positive side of U.

Aggression, Manifest

Does he have a high score on Couch's measure from his
Factor Analysis of the Personality Domain, called factor
III Aggression: Manifest (versus Controlled)? If *yes*,
then expect   UN

This variable was obtained by adding together the scores of a subject on a number of personality tests. The measure was then included in Couch's Interdomain Analysis, in which it obtained the following loadings: I(U) .45; II(P) .33—; III(F) .15—; *Summary:* UN. The evidence is direct and fairly strong, the measure is probably reliable.

The measure included the following standard personality tests, added in positively:

MMPI,—Psychopathic
MMPI,—Hypomania
MMPI,—Validity Scale
Thurstone,—Active

There were a number of additional scales by Couch, Slater, and by Bales and Couch.

Agrees

(a) Does he have a *high* rate of Agreeing with others—a rate higher than 13.6 percent of his own total interaction? (Bales revised IPA category 3[1]) If *yes*, then expect   PF

(b) Does he have a *low* rate of Agreeing with others—a rate lower than 8.0 percent of his own total interaction? (Bales' revised IPA category 3) If *yes*, then expect   NB

(c) Does he have a *high* rate of Receiving Agreement from others—a rate higher than 19.4 percent of his own total interaction Received? (Bales' revised IPA category 3) If *yes*, then expect   F

(d) Does he have a *low* rate of Receiving Agreement from others—a rate lower than 12.7 percent of his own total interaction Received? (Bales' revised IPA category 3) If *yes*, then expect   B

[1]There is no change in the definition of category 3, in the revision.

The evidence on these variables is direct, all from Couch's Interdomain Factor Analysis. The loadings are:

	I (U)	II (P)	III (F)	Summary
(a)	.09	.37	.26	PF
(b)	the directionality of (a) is simply reversed.			
(c)	.16—	.01	.34	F
(d)	the directionality of (c) is simply reversed.			

Altruistic Love
(a) Does he make value-statements advocating Altruistic
     Love? If *yes,* then expect   PF
(b) Does he receive value statements from others in which
     they advocate Altruistic Love to him? If *yes,* then
     expect   UNB
(c) Does he agree with value-statements made by others in
     which they advocate Altruistic Love to him? If *yes,* then
     expect   DPF

The evidence on these variables is indirect, inferential, and weak.
For description of the nature of the evidence see the Preliminary Note to
this Appendix.

Anxiety, Couch's Measure
Does he have a high score on Couch's measure from his
Factor Analysis of the Personality Domain, called factor
I, Anxiety: Manifest (versus Ego-Controlled)? If *yes,*
then expect   N

This variable is obtained by adding together the scores of a subject
on a number of personality tests. The measure was then included in
Couch's Interdomain Analysis, in which it obtained the following loadings: I(U) .13; II(P) .30—; III(F) .11; *Summary:* N.
The evidence is thus direct and fairly strong. The measure is
unusually reliable.
The measure included the following personality tests, added in
positively:

> MMPI, Pt—Psychasthenia
> MMPI, A—Manifest Anxiety
> MMPI, Dp—Dependency
> Cattell,—Insecure
> Cattell,—Suspecting

The following personality tests were added in negatively:

> MMPI, K—Ego Suppression
> MMPI, Es—Ego Strength
> MMPI, Lp—Leadership
> MMPI, Rp—Role Playing Ability
> MMPI, Do—Dominance

Cattell—Mature
Cattell—Will Control
Thurstone—Stable

There were several additional original scales by Couch.

Anxiety, MMPI Measure

Does he have a high score on the MMPI scale called
Anxiety? If *yes*, then expect N

The evidence is only indirect that this scale measures N as indicated.
Its loadings on Couch's Factor Analysis of the Personality Domain are:
I (N) .91; II (UP) .00; III (UN) .00; IV (PF) .00; V (B) .00.

The main loading, a very strong one, and the only one, is on I,
which indicates N. The fact that the loadings are zero on all other factors
is not an accident—it indicates rather that this variable was chosen as the
anchor point for factor I in the particular rotation employed in the
present study.

Anxious

(a) Do observers rate him high on seeming Anxious? If *yes,*
then expect DN
(b) Do group members rate him high on seeming Anxious?
If *yes,* then expect DNF
(c) Does he rate himself high on feeling Anxious? If *yes,*
then expect DNF
(d) Does he guess that other group members will rate him
high on seeming Anxious? If *yes,* then expect DNF
(e) Does he tend to rate other group members high on
seeming Anxious? If *yes,* then expect N
(f) Does he make others feel he rates them high on seeming Anxious? If *yes,* then expect N

The evidence on these variables is direct, all from Couch's Interdomain Factor Analysis. The loadings are:

	I (U)	II (P)	III (F)	Summary
(a)	.69—	.23—	.03—	DN
(b)	.60—	.28—	.21	DNF
(c)	.46—	.34—	.21	DNF
(d)	.48—	.40—	.18	DNF
(e)	.14—	.30—	.05	N
(f)	.12	.26—	.07	N

The question was phrased: "To what extent would you say that each member shows any nervousness, anxiety or strain?"

0 = "He seemed to be very relaxed and well-adjusted to the situation".

7 = "He seemed to be very nervous and ill-at-ease during the meeting".

Ascension, Wish-Fulfillment

Does he have a high score on Couch's measure from his Factor Analysis of the Personality Domain, called factor V, Ascension, Wish-Fulfillment (versus Constriction? If *yes*, then expect

          B

This variable was obtained by adding together the scores of a subject on a number of personality tests. The measure was then included in Couch's Interdomain Analysis, in which it obtained the following loadings: I(U) .07; II(P) .02—; III(F) .28—; *Summary:* B. The evidence is direct, and moderately strong.

The only standard personality test included in this measure was Thurstone: Vigorous. There were a number of original scales from the Value Profile (inventory of values) by Bales and Couch, and a number obtained by an Inventory of Basic Fantasy Themes, an original instrument in rough draft by Henry Murray, based on his earlier work (124) and brought to completion for this particular research application by Couch (71).

Autocratic Authority

(a) Does he make value-statements advocating Autocratic Authority? If *yes*, then expect   UNF

(b) Do others address value-statements to him advocating Autocratic Authority? If *yes*, then expect   UPB

(c) Does he agree with value-statements from others advocating Autocratic Authority? If *yes*, then expect   PF

This is a marker variable for each of the value spaces. The evidence on (a) is direct, though not significant as to the negative direction. The loadings on the Couch Interdomain factor analysis were: I(U) .37; II(P) .14—; III(F) .30. If the usual cutoff point (.17) for significance in this study is used, then the negative loading is not significant, and the direction is UF. In terms of the problem of fitting the several spaces together however, I feel that it is better to recognize the negative loading as significant than to ignore it, and hence I modify the directional indicator to UNF. The directional designation is thus partly hypothetical.

The evidence on (b) is direct, but far from significant. The loadings on the Couch Interdomain factor analysis were: I(U) .15; II(P) .10; III(F) .11—. None of these loadings is significant. The direction, however, seems reasonable, and the hypothetical assumption is made that the variable may indicate UPB.

The evidence on (c) is indirect. On a written test of values, the Value-Profile of Bales and Couch, the subject's degree of agreement with written items of the value-content Autocratic Authority has the following loadings in the Couch Interdomain factor space: I(U) .09; II(P) .29; III(F) .17; *Summary:* PF. Thus far the evidence is direct. But the assumption is then made that the subject's overt agreement to verbal statements made to him in the course of interaction would be about the same as his responses on the written test. This is hypothetical. The directional indicator is thus hypothetical.

Calm

Does he have a high score on Thurstone's Temperament test called Calm? If *yes,* then expect   DP

This test is also called Stable. The evidence that this scale measures DP as indicated is only indirect. The loadings on Couch's Factor Analysis of the Personality Domain are: I(N) .67—; II(UP) .18—; III(UN) .07; IV(PF) .07; V(B) .01. The main loading on I indicates P. The secondary loading on II, reversed is probably barely significant and indicates DN. The negative component is very weak compared to the positive, and hence is ignored, but the downward component is recognized, resulting in a summary direction DP. The downward component is probably very slight.

Conformity, Authoritarian

Does he have a high score·on Couch's measure from his Factor Analysis of the Personality Domain, called factor IV, Conformity, Authoritarian (versus Non-Authoritarian). If *yes,* and the group is oriented to conservative goals, then expect   PF

This variable was obtained by adding together the scores of a subject on a number of personality tests. The measure was then included in Couch's Interdomain Analysis, in which it obtained the following loadings: I(U) .13—; II(P) .16; III(F) .10. The measure included the following standard personality test, added in positively:

Cattell   Sophistication

The measure included the following standard personality tests added in negatively:

Cattell—Emotional Sensitivity

Cattell—Eccentric (versus Conventional).

There were a number of additional original scales by Couch, and by Bales and Couch. These included both direct and indirect measures of authoritarianism, derived with additions, from the F scale and others used in the authoritarian studies of Adorno, Levinson, and others. One of these, a simpler variable consisting of agreement on a *written* test, to items of authoritarian content from the Bales-Couch Value Profile, (See Appendix 5) obtained a directional indicator PF in the Interdomain Analysis. See variable "Autocratic Authority." This latter variable is very close to the so-called F-scale of the authoritarian personality series.

Although none of the loadings of the present variable is high enough to be considered significant, the direction PF is hypothesized and assigned, for reasons explained in the Preliminary Note to this Appendix.

Conscientious

Does he have a high score on Cattell's 16PF test called
Conscientious? If *yes*, then expect   PF

This scale is also called Persistent. The opposite end is called Undependable. The evidence that this scale measures PF as indicated is only indirect. Its loadings on Couch's Factor Analysis of the Personality Domain are: I(N) .03—; II(UP) .33; III(UN) .21—; IV(PF) .40; and V(B) .27—. The main loading on IV indicates PF. The secondary loading on II indicates UP. The next loading on V reversed indicates F. The loading on III reversed indicates DP. The summary direction is thus PF.

Conservative Group Beliefs

(a) Does he make value-statements advocating Conservative Group Beliefs? If *yes*, then expect   F

(b) Do others address value-statements to him advocating Conservative Group Beliefs to him? If *yes*, then expect   B

(c) Does he agree with value-statements from others advocating Conservative Group Beliefs? If *yes*, then expect   DPF

The evidence concerning these variables is indirect, inferential, and weak. For description of the nature of the evidence see the Preliminary Note to this Appendix.

Controlled

Does he have a high score on Cattell's 16PF test called
Controlled? If *yes*, then expect   DPF

This is Cattell's scale, Q3, also called Exact. The opposite end is
called Lax and Unsure. The evidence that it measures DPF as indicated is
only indirect. Its loadings on Couch's Factor Analysis of the Personality
Domain are: I(N) .64—; II(UP) .17—; III(UN) .17—; IV(PF) .20;
and V(B) .09—. The main loading on I reversed indicates P. The
loading on IV indicates PF. The negative loadings on II and III sum to
D. The summary direction is DPF.

Curiosity, Arouses

(a) Do observers rate him high on Arousing their Curiosity? If *yes*, then expect   UNB
(b) Do group members rate him high on Arousing their
Curiosity? If *yes*, then expect   DN
(c) Does he guess that others will rate him high on Arous-
ing their Curiosity? If *yes*, then expect   DNF
(d) Does he tend to rate others high on Arousing his
Couriosity? If *yes*, then expect   F
(e) Does he tend to make others feel he rates them high on
Arousing his Curiosity? If *yes*, then expect   F

The evidence regarding these variables is direct, all from Couch's
Interdomain Factor Analysis. The loadings are:

	I (U)	II (P)	III (F)	Summary
(a)	.21	.35—	.30—	UNB
(b)	.39—	.48—	.02	DN
(c)	.18—	.29—	.30	DNF
(d)	.05	.02	.30	F
(e)	.02—	.15—	.19	F*

*This is also close to NF.

The question was phrased: "To what extent do other members of
the group arouse your interest and curiosity, although you have mixed
feelings about them?"

0 = "I feel that I understand him fairly well."
7 = "I feel puzzled and curious about him as a person."

Dependency
    Does he have a high score on the MMPI scale called
    Dependency? If *yes*, then expect   N

    The evidence is only indirect that this scale measures N as indicated. Its loadings on Couch's Factor Analysis of the Personality Domain are: I(N) .90; II(UP) .10; III(UN) .10—; IV(PF) .03—; V(B) .07—. The only significant loading is on I which indicates N. The loading is very high.

Depression
    Does he have a high score on the MMPI scale Depression? If *yes*, then expect   DN

    The evidence is only indirect that this scale measures DN as indicated. Its loadings on Couch's Factor Analysis of the Personality Domain are: I(N) .64; II(UP) .33—; III(UN) .15; IV(PF) .02; V(B) .14—.
    The main loading is on I, which indicates N, the secondary loading on II reversed, which would be DN. The summation of these two is DN. The loadings on III and V may be significant, but are here ignored.

Devaluation of the Self
(a) Does he make value-statements advocating Devaluation of the Self? If *yes*, then expect   D
(b) Do others address value-statements to him advocating Devaluation of the Self? If *yes*, then expect   D
(c) Does he agree with value-statements from others advocating Devaluation of the Self? If *yes*, then expect   D

    The evidence concerning these variables is indirect, inferential, and weak. For a description of the nature of the evidence, see the Preliminary Note to this Appendix.

Disagrees[1]
(a) Does he have a *high* rate of Disagreeing with others—a rate higher than 5.3 percent of his own total interaction? (Bales' revised IPA Category 10) If *yes*, then expect   N
(b) Does he have a *low* rate of Disagreeing with others—a rate lower than 3.1 percent of his own total interaction? (Bales' revised IPA Category 10) If *yes*, then expect   P

[1] There is no change in the definition of category 10 in the revision.

(c)   Does he have a *high* rate of *receiving* Disagreement
from others—a rate higher than 6.3 percent of his own
total interaction received? (Bales' revised IPA Category
10 received) If *yes*, then expect   UNF
(d)   Does he have a *low* rate of *receiving* Disagreement from
others—a rate lower than 3.6 percent of his own total
interaction received? (Bales' revised IPA Category 10
received) If *yes*, then expect   DPB

The evidence on the assignment of directional indicators as shown is
direct, all from Couch's Interdomain Factor Analysis. The loadings are:

	$I(U)$	$II(P)$	$III(F)$	Summary
(a)	.11	.42—	.04	N
(b)	the directionality of (a) is simply reversed.			
(c)	.35	.37—	.23	UNF
(d)	the directionality of (c) is simply reversed.			

Dislike, Arouses
(a)   Do observers rate him high on Arousing their Dislike?
If *yes*, then expect   NF
(b)   Do group members rate him high on Arousing their
Dislike? If *yes*, then expect   UNF
(c)   Does he guess others will rate him high on Arousing
their Dislike? If *yes*, then expect   DNB
(d)   Does he tend to rate others high on Arousing his
Dislike? If *yes*, then expect   DNB
(e)   Does he make others feel he rates them high on Arousing his Dislike? If *yes*, then expect   UN

The evidence on these variables is direct, all from Couch's Interdomain Factor Analysis. The loadings are:

	$I(U)$	$II(P)$	$III(F)$	Summary
(a)	.09—	.51—	.18	NF
(b)	.30	.51—	.18	UNF
(c)	.16—	.45—	.16—	DNB*
(d)	.27—	.37—	.36—	DNB
(e)	.25	.44—	.08	UN

*The main direction is N, but on the chance that other loadings are significant, the
direction is taken to be DNB.

The question was phrased: "To what extent do you find personal qualities in other members of the group which you tend to dislike or which seem irritating to you?"

> 0 = "He is not irritating to me."
> 7 = "I dislike him and find him very irritating."

Dominant

(a) Does he have a high score on Cattell's 16 PF test called Dominant? If *yes*, then expect   UB

(b) Does he have a high score on the MMPI scale called Dominance? If *yes*, then expect   UP

(c) Does he have a high score on Thurstone's temperament test called Dominant? If *yes*, then expect   U

The evidence as to each of these measures is only indirect. The opposite end of Cattell's scale E is called Submissive. This scale is also called Aggressive. The loadings of the Cattell scale Dominant on Couch's Factor Analysis of the Personality Domain are: I(N) .14—; II(UP) .37; III(UN) .28; IV(PF) .06—; V(B) .18. The main loading is on II, which indicates UP, with a secondary loading on III which indicates UN. These two add to U. If the loading on V is taken as significant, direction B is added, resulting in UB.

The MMPI scale Dominance has loadings on Couch's Factor Analysis of the Personality Domain as follows: I(N) .63—; II(UP) .17; III(UN) .11; IV(PF) .14—; V(B) .11. The main loading is on I reversed, which is P. II and III are probably too low for significance individually, but together may be considered some evidence for U. The summary direction may be UP, but the upward component is unexpectedly low.

The loadings of the Thurstone scale Dominant on Couch's Factor Analysis of the Personality Domain are: I(N) .45—; II(UP) .53; III(UN) .24; IV(PF) .20; V(B) .07—. Here the main loading is on II, which indicates UP. The secondary loading is on I reversed, which is P. The next highest loading is on III which is UN. The summary is U.

Domination

(a) Do observers rate him high on Domination? If *yes*, then expect   UN

(b) Do group members rate him high on Domination? If *yes*, then expect   UN

(c) Does he rate himself high on Domination? If *yes*, then expect   UN

(d) Does he guess others will rate him high on Domination? If *yes*, then expect   UNB

(e)   Does he tend to rate others high on Domination? If *yes,* then expect   NB

(f)   Does he make others feel he rates them high on Domination? If *yes,* then expect   N

The evidence on these variables is direct, all from Couch's Interdomain Factor Analysis. The loadings are:

	I (U)	II (P)	III (F)	Summary
(a)	.50	.51—	.04	UN
(b)	.52	.50—	.08	UN
(c)	.23	.53—	.08—	UN
(d)	.17	.44—	.19—	UNB
(e)	.02	.57—	.18—	NB
(f)	.03—	.45—	.16	N*

*This is close to NF.

The question was phrased: "To what extent do you think any of the members were dominating and did not show enough consideration for the feelings of others?"

0 = "He showed courtesy and sympathetic consideration in the way he acted."

7 = "He was insensitive and overbearing in the way he acted."

Dramatizes

(a)   Does he *initiate* a *high* rate of acts in which he Dramatizes or jokes—a rate higher than 7.4 percent of his own total interaction? (Bales' revised IPA category 2) If *yes,* then expect   UB

(b)   Does he *initiate* a *low* rate of acts in which he Dramatizes or jokes—a rate lower than 5.4 percent of his own total interaction? (Bales' revised IPA category 2) If *yes,* then expect   DF

(c)   Does he *receive* a *high* rate of acts in which others Dramatize or joke to him or towards him—a rate higher than 12.2 percent of his own total interaction received? (Bales' revised IPA category 2) If *yes,* then expect   PB

(d)   Does he *receive* a *low* rate of acts in which others Dramatize or joke to him or towards him—a rate lower than 7.5 percent of his own total interaction received? (Bales' revised IPA category 2) If *yes,* then expect   NF

Evidence for (a) and (b) is indirect. In the study upon which the factor analysis is based, jokes were included in category 1 (Shows Solidarity). Apparently jokes swamped all the positive acts recorded in the category. The factor loadings on the Couch Interdomain Factor Analysis for this category were: I(U) .28; II(P) .02—; III(F) .49—; *Summary:* UB. This direction is thus hypothesized to be the appropriate indicator for Jokes. In the study, there was no category Dramatizes. The inclusion of jokes in the same category with dramatizations with the same directional indicator, is hypothetical, and remains to be tested.

The factor loadings for (c), and by reversal, (d) were: I(U) .11—; II(P) .23; III(F) .57—; *Summary:* PB.

Eccentric

Does he have a high score on Cattell's 16 PF test called
Eccentric? If *yes,* then expect   UNB

This is Cattell's scale (M), also called Unconcerned. The opposite end is called Conventional, Practical. The evidence that this scale measures UNB is indirect. Its loadings on Couch's Factor Analysis of the Personality Domain are: I(N) .34; II(UP) .28; III(UN) .15; IV(PF) .36—; V(B) .30.

The main loading on IV indicates NB, since it is reversed. The loading on I indicates N. The loading on V indicates B. The loading on II indicates UP, but there is also a possibly significant loading on III which indicates UN. The summary direction is UNB.

Ego-Strength

Does he have a high score on the MMPI scale called
Ego-strength? If *yes,* then expect   P

The evidence that this scale measures P as indicated is indirect. Its loadings on Couch's Factor Analysis of the Personality Domain are: I(N) .79—; II(UP) .06; III(UN) .09; IV(PF) .18—; V(B) .09.

The main loading is quite high, on I reversed, which indicates P. The loading on IV reversed indicates NB, though it is not strong. The summary direction is taken to be P.

Emotional Sensitivity (for male subjects)

Does he have a high score on Cattell's 16PF scale called
Emotional Sensitivity? If *yes,* then expect   NB

This is Cattell's scale (I). This scale is also sometimes called Effeminate, probably not a very good title. It is interpreted here to mean rejection by a male of the conventionally defined adult masculine role.

The opposite end is called Tough Maturity, probably not a very good title either, at any rate, interpreted here as acceptance by the male of the conventionally defined adult masculine role.

The evidence that this scale measures NB, as indicated is indirect. Its loadings on Couch's Factor Analysis in the Personality Domain are: I (N) .42; II (UP) .06; III (UN) .03; IV (PF) .47—; V (B) .12.

The loading on IV reversed indicates NB, and is quite high. The loading on I is also substantial, and implies N. The summary direction is NB.

Emotional Supportiveness and Warmth

(a) Does he make value-statements advocating Emotional Supportiveness and Warmth? If *yes*, then expect   UPB

(b) Does he receive value-statements advocating Emotional Supportiveness and Warmth? If *yes*, then expect   UNF

(c) Does he agree with value-statements advocating Emotional Supportiveness and Warmth? If *yes*, then expect   UPB

(d) Does he describe his parents as high on Emotional Supportiveness and Warmth on Slater's test? If *yes*, then expect   UPB

The evidence on variables (a), (b), and (c) is indirect, inferential, and weak. For description of the nature of the evidence, see the Preliminary Note to this Appendix.

The evidence on (d) is direct but not entirely supportive. The loadings on the variable Emotional Supportiveness and Warmth on Slater's test (140), in Couch's Interdomain Factor Analysis were: I (U) .04–; II (P) .22; III (F) .19–; *Summary:* PB.

The directional indicator UPB is assigned, even though there is no evidence for the upward component since the orthogonal variable on Slater's test, namely Inhibitory Demands and Discipline, was apparently best represented by the direction UNF. UPB is orthogonal to UNF, whereas PB is somewhat negatively related to it. On the other hand an argument may be made that Inhibitory Demands and Discipline is better represented by UF than UNF, in which case Emotional Supportiveness and Warmth could be at PB and still remain approximately orthogonal.

Emotionality, Extrovertive

Does he have a high score on Couch's measure from his Factor Analysis of the Personality Domain, called factor II, Emotionality: Extrovertive (versus Introvertive)? If *yes*, then expect   UP

This variable was obtained by adding together the scores of a subject on a number of personality tests. The measure was then included in Couch's Interdomain Analysis, in which it obtained the following loadings: I (U) .39; II (P) .27; III (F) .04; *Summary:* UP. The evidence is direct and fairly strong, the measure is unusually reliable. The measure included the following personality tests, added in positively:

> Cattell—Warm, Sociable, (versus Cold)
>
> Cattell—Extrovertive

The measure included the following personality tests, added in negatively:

> MMPI, R—Repression-Denial
>
> Cattell—Independent

There were a number of additional original scales by Couch, by Slater, and by Bales and Couch.

Entertaining

(a) Do observers rate him high on Entertaining? If *yes,* then expect — UNB

(b) Do group members rate him high on Entertaining? If *yes,* then expect — UPB

(c) Does he rate himself high on Entertaining? If *yes,* then expect — UB

(d) Does he tend to rate others high on Entertaining? If *yes,* then expect — UPB

(e) Does he tend to rate others high on Entertaining? If *yes,* then expect — P

(f) Does he make others feel he rates them high on Entertaining? If *yes,* then expect — PB

The evidence on these variables is all direct, all from Couch's Interdomain Factor Analysis. The loadings are:

	I (U)	II (P)	III (F)	Summary
(a)	.60	.19—	.35—	UNB
(b)	.37	.29	.48—	UPB
(c)	.21	.10—	.16—	UB
(d)	.54	.20	.33—	UPB
(e)	.11	.24	.08	P
(f)	.08—	.44	.30—	PB

The question was phrased, "To what extent do you find the members of the group entertaining and amusing?"

> 0 = "I would not think of him as an entertaining person."
> 7 = "I find him very entertaining."

Equalitarian

(a) Do observers rate him high on Equilitarian? If *yes*, then expect   DP

(b) Do group members rate him high on Equalitarian? If *yes*, then expect   DPF

(c) Does he rate himself as high on Equalitarian? If *yes*, then expect   DP

(d) Does he guess others will rate him high on Equalitarian? If *yes*, then expect   DPF

(e) Does he tend to rate others high on Equalitarian? If *yes*, then expect   Unrelated

(f) Does he make others feel he rates them high on Equalitarian? If *yes*, then expect   UB

The evidence on these variables is direct, all from Couch's Interdomain Factor Analysis. The loadings are:

	$I(U)$	$II(P)$	$III(F)$	Summary
(a)	.54—	.44	.05	DP
(b)	.62—	.41	.20	DPF
(c)	.32—	.22	.04	DP
(d)	.33—	.24	.25	DPF
(e)	.10	.05	.05—	Unrelated
(f)	.24	.06—	.26—	UB

The question was phrased: "To what extent would you say each member feels that equality and humanitarian concern for others are important?"

> 0 = "He feels there are many things more important than equality and sympathy."
> 7 = "He feels that equality and humanitarian concern for others are extremely important."

Equalitarianism
(a) Does he make value-statements advocating Equalitari-
    anism? If *yes,* then expect   P
(b) Does he receive value-statements advocating Equali-
    tarianism? If *yes,* then expect   UNF
(c) Does he agree with value-statements advocating Equali-
    tarianism? If *yes,* then expect   DP

For (a) above the evidence is direct. The loadings of this variable in
Couch's Interdomain Factor Analysis were: I(U) .08; II(P) .46; III(F)
.12; *Summary:* P.

For (b) the evidence is direct, but a little weak on the forward
component. The loadings were: I(U) .39; II(P) .24—; III(F) .16.
Though weak, the evidence for the forward component is nevertheless
accepted, making the summary UNF.

For (c) the evidence is indirect and weak. Written responses of
agreement to written items in the value area in question have the
following loadings on the Couch Interdomain Factor Analysis: I(U)
.13—; II(P) .24; III(F) .07; *Summary:* P.

It is decided to accept the low loading indicating a downward
component, and the summary is modified to DP. Then it is assumed that
the subject's overt agreement to verbal statements made to him in the
course of interaction would be about the same as his responses on the
written test. This is hypothetical. The directional indicator is thus
hypothetical.

Expression and Gratification
(a) Do observers rate him high on favoring Expression and
    Gratification? If *yes,* then expect   UNB
(b) Do group members rate him high on favoring Expres-
    sion and Gratification? If *yes,* then expect   UNB
(c) Does he rate himself high on favoring Expression and
    Gratification? If *yes,* then expect   B
(d) Does he guess others will rate him high on favoring
    Expression and Gratification? If *yes,* then expect   DB
(e) Does he tend to rate others high on favoring Expression
    and Gratification? If *yes,* then expect   DB
(f) Does he make others feel that he rates them high on
    favoring Expression and Gratification? If *yes,* then ex-
    pect   NF

The evidence on these variables is direct, all from Couch's Inter-domain Factor Analysis. The loadings are:

	I (U)	II (P)	III (F)	Summary
(a)	.23	.17—	.54—	UNB
(b)	.23	.36—	.49—	UNB
(c)	.01—	.06—	.41—	B
(d)	.20—	.06—	.52—	DB
(e)	.26—	.07	.19—	DB
(f)	.04	.35—	.23	NF

The question was phrased: "To what extent would you say each member is characterized by a realistic, tough-minded, pleasure-seeking outlook as contrasted to an idealistic, tender-minded, intellectually-controlled outlook?"

> 0 = "He seems to feel that one should restrain his impulses in following his values and ideals."
> 7 = "He seems to feel that one should act realistically so as to gratify most of his impulses and desires."

Extroversion

(a) Do observers rate him high on Extroversion? If *yes*, then expect   **UB**

(b) Do group members tend to rate him high on Extroversion? If *yes*, then expect   **UB**

(c) Does he rate himself high on Extroversion? If *yes*, then expect   **UB**

(d) Does he guess others will rate him high on Extroversion? If *yes*, then expect   **UB**

(e) Does he tend to rate others high on Extroversion? If *yes*, then expect   **D**

(f) Does he make others feel he rates them high on Extroversion? If *yes*, then expect   **D**

The evidence on these variables is direct, all from the Couch Interdomain Factor Analysis. The loadings are:

	I (U)	II (P)	III (F)	Summary
(a)	.49	.12	.31—	UB
(b)	.74	.13	.20—	UB
(c)	.49	.03	.23—	UB
(d)	.56	.09	.23—	UB
(e)	.24—	.02	.02	D
(f)	.31—	.14—	.07	D

The question was phrased: "To what extent would you say that each member showed characteristics of an introvert or extrovert?"

0 = "He seems very introverted (serious, shy, introspective)."
7 = "He seems very extroverted (outgoing, realistic, happy-go-lucky)."

Extrovertive

Does he have a high score on Cattell's 16 PF test called
Extrovertive? If *yes*, then expect   UB

This is Cattell's Scale F, also called Talkative, and Enthusiastic. The opposite end is called Introvertive and Silent.

The evidence that this scale measures UB, as indicated, is only indirect. Its loadings on Couch's Factor Analysis of the Personality Domain are: I (N) .04 —; II (UP) .41; III (UN) .23; IV (PF) .15; V (B) .29.

The main loading is on II, which indicated UP. A secondary loading on V indicates B. A third loading on III indicates UN. The summary direction is thus UB perhaps leaning to the positive side.

Failure and Withdrawal

(a) Does he make value-statements expressing Failure and
  Withdrawal? If *yes*, then expect   DNB
(b) Does he receive value-statements expressing Failure
  and Withdrawal? If *yes*, then expect   DPF
(c) Does he agree with value-statements expressing Failure
  and Withdrawal? If *yes*, then expect   DNB

Evidence concerning these variables is indirect, inferential, and weak. For a description of the nature of the evidence, see the Preliminary Note to this Appendix.

Feminine Masochism (in male subjects) [1]

Does he have a high score on the MMPI scale called
Feminine Masochism? If *yes,* then expect   NF

The evidence is only indirect that this scale measures NF as indicated. Its loadings on Couch's Factor Analysis of the Personality Domain are: I (N) .67; II (UP) .08; III (UN) .09—; IV (PF) .06; V (B) .28—.

The main loading is on I, which indicates N. The secondary loading on V reversed indicates F. The summary of the two is NF.

[1]It is important to remember that the directional significance shown is the one obtained with a total population of male subjects. It is not clear that a population of female subjects would give the same results, although it is not too implausible, especially if the prime emphasis of the test is on tendencies toward masochism rather than on possession of socially defined "conventional feminine role traits". (The later variable, for females, is supposed for the purposes of this system, to measure in the direction PF.

Feminine Interests (in male subjects) [1]

Does he have a high score on the MMPI scale called
Feminine Interests? If *yes,* expect   DNB

The evidence is only indirect that this scale measures DNB as indicated. Its loadings on Couch's Factor Analysis of the Personality Domain are: I (N) .24; II (UP) .11; III (UN) .22 −; IV (PF) .45 −; V (B) .05.

The main loading on IV reversed indicates NB. The secondary loading is on I, which indicates N. The third loading is on III, which when reversed, indicates DP. These three added together result in DNB.

[1]It is very important to take into account that the subjects to whom this test was given, as part of the large battery of tests, were male subjects. Feminine interest for male subjects is presumably not conventional, whereas "masculinity" is. The directional significance shown, then, should not be taken as applying to females. So far as it is taken to be significant, it applies to male subjects.

If an appropriate test of what might be called "Conventional Feminine Role Traits" were developed for females, and applied to them, it might be expected to measure in direction PF.

Friendly, Seems

(a)   Does he have a *high* rate of Seeming Friendly to others—
a rate higher than 4.8 percent of his own total interaction? (Bales' revised IPA category 1) If *yes,* then expect   P

(b) Does he have a *low* rate of Seeming Friendly to others—
a rate lower than 2.6 percent of his own total interaction? (Bales' revised IPA category 1) If *yes,* then expect   N

(c) Does he have a *high* rate of *receiving* acts in which others Seem Friendly to him—a rate higher than 4.8 percent of his own total interaction received? (Bales' revised IPA category 1) If *yes,* then expect   P

(d) Does he have a low rate of receiving acts in which others Seem Friendly to him—a rate lower than 2.6 percent of his own total interaction received? (Bales' revised IPA category 1) If *yes,* then expect   N

In the study which would have given evidence for interaction category 1 (then called Shows Solidarity), jokes were included and apparently swamped all other scores in the category, so that it actually measured UB instead of somewhere on the positive side. The new definition omits jokes and attempts to improve the category. The indicated directions are not empirically derived, but are at this point indications of the directions it is hoped that the improved category will measure.

Group Loyalty and Cooperation

(a) Does he make value-statements advocating Group Loyalty and Cooperation? If *yes,* then expect   UF

(b) Does he receive value-statements advocating Group Loyalty and Cooperation? If *yes,* then expect   UB

(c) Does he agree with value-statements advocating Group Loyalty and Cooperation? If so, then expect   PF

The evidence on each of these variables is indirect, inferential, and weak. For description of the evidence, see the Preliminary Note to this Appendix.

Honor Grades

Does he have a high score on the MMPI scale called Honor grades? If *yes,* then expect   Unrelated

The loadings on Couch's Factor Analysis of the Personality Domain are: I(N) .40—; II(UP) .04; III(UN) .38—; IV(PF) .36—; V(B) .14—.

The main loading is on I reversed, which indicates P. The next loading on III reversed indicates DP. The loading on IV reversed indicates NB. It is doubtful that the loading on V is significant, but if it were it would indicate F. The indicators are so contrary to each other that it seems best to assume that this variable, like intelligence, and originality, is unrelated to the three interpersonal dimensions.

Hypochondriasis

Does he have a high score on the MMPI scale called
Hypochondriasis? If *yes*, then expect   UN

Hypochondriasis is the tendency to complain of many and vague symptoms of illness. The evidence is only indirect that the scale measures as indicated. Its loadings on Couch's Factor Analysis of the Personality Domain are: I(N) .58; II(UP) .09; III(UN) .18; IV(PF) .14; V(B) 08.

The main loading is on I, which is N. If the loading on III is taken as significant it adds UN. (The summary direction is indicated as N in the type descriptions because earlier errors in reading the loadings resulted in this direction. It was not practical to make all the necessary changes at the time the error was discovered.)

Hysteria

Does he have a high score on the MMPI test called
Hysteria? If *yes*, then expect   UN

The evidence that this scale measures UN as indicated is only indirect. Its loadings on Couch's Factor Analysis in the Personality Domain are: I(N) .08; II(UP) .04—; III(UN) .19; IV(PF) .07—; V(B) .06.

Only the loading on III is possibly significant and it is marginal. This variable is included on this list in order that information concerning the main scales on the MMPI may he complete, but it is not included in the typological descriptions because of the author's uncertainty as to the plausibility of the direction indicated.

Identification with the Underprivileged

(a) Does he make value-statements advocating Identification with the Underprivileged? If *yes*, then expect   DPB

(b) Do others address value-statements to him advocating Identification with the Underprivileged? If *yes*, then expect   DNF

(c) Does he agree with value-statements from others advocating Identification with the Underprivileged? If *yes*, then expect   NB

The evidence on (a) is direct, though not significant as to the positive direction. See the note to Autocratic Authority for the loadings.

The evidence on (b) is direct, but far from significant. See the note to Autocratic Authority for the loadings.

The evidence on (c) is indirect and not strong. See the note to Autocratic Authority for the loadings.

Impulsive

Does he have a high score on Thurstone's Temperament test called Impulsive? If *yes,* then expect   UPF

The evidence that this scale measures UPF as indicated is only indirect. The loadings on Couch's Factor Analysis of the Personality Domain are: I(N) .25 −; II(UP) .51; III(UN) .22; IV(PF) .26; V(B) .12.

The main loading on II indicates UP. The loading on IV indicates PF. The loading on I reversed indicates P. The loading on III indicates UN. These sum to UPF.

Impulsivity

Does he have a high score on the MMPI scale called Impulsivity? If *yes,* then expect   UNB

This scale is also said to measure Self-centeredness. The evidence that it measures UNB as indicated is only indirect. Its loadings on Couch's Factor Analysis in the Personality Domain are: I(N) .58; II(UP) .31; III(UN) .11; IV(PF) .05 −; V(B) .22.

The main loading on I indicates N. The secondary loading on II indicates UP. The loading on V indicates B. The summary of these, equally weighted is UB, but since the main loading on I, indicating N, is relatively so high, the direction UNB is taken as probably the better indicator.

Independent Self-Sufficiency

Does he have a high score on Cattell's 16PF test called Independent Self-Sufficiency? If *yes,* then expect   DNB

This is Cattell's scale (Q2). The evidence that this scale measures DNB as indicated is only indirect. Its loadings on Couch's Factor Analysis of the Personality Domain are: I(N) .18; II(UP) .35 −; III(UN) .06; IV(PF) .19 −; V(B) .03.

The main loading on II reversed indicates DN. The loading on IV reversed indicates NB. The loading on I indicates N. The summary is DNB, probably not much downward.

Individualism

(a) Do observers rate him high on Individualism? If *yes*, then expect — DN

(b) Do group members rate him high on Individualism? If *yes*, then expect — N

(c) Does he rate himself high on Individualism? If *yes*, then expect — DN

(d) Does he guess that others will rate him high on Individualism? If *yes*, then expect — D

(e) Does he tend to rate others high on Individualism? If *yes*, then expect — DF

(f) Does he make others feel he rates them high on Individualism? If *yes*, then expect — UF

The evidence on these variables is direct, all from Couch's Interdomain Factor Analysis. The loadings are:

	I (U)	II (P)	III (F)	Summary
(a)	.33—	.44—	.11—	DN
(b)	.01—	.56—	.05—	N
(c)	.35—	.23—	.05	DN
(d)	.43—	.08—	.01	D
(e)	.20—	.05	.24	DF
(f)	.17	.12	.20	UF

The question was phrased: "To what extent would you say that each member feels that individual independence is important?"

0 = "He does not feel that individualism is particularly important or desirable."

7 = "He feels that independence and individual autonomy are very important."

Individualistic Isolationism

(a) Does he make value-statements advocating Individualistic Isolationism? If *yes*, then expect — N

(b) Does he receive value-statements advocating Individualistic Isolationism? If *yes*, then expect — UNF

(c) Does he agree with value-statements advocating Individualistic Isolationism? If *yes*, then expect — UN

The evidence on (a) is direct, but weak. The loadings on the Couch Interdomain Factor Analysis were: I(U) .09; II(P) .17—; III(F) .01—; *Summary:* N (provided one accepts a weak loading.)

The evidence on (b) is direct, but weak as to the forward component. The loadings on the Couch Interdomain Factor Analysis were: I(U) .51; II(P) .28—; III(F) .13. *Summary:* UN (or if the weak loading is accepted, UNF).

The evidence on (c) is indirect and weak. On the written test of values, the Value-Profile of Bales and Couch, the subject's degree of agreement with the written items of the value-content Individualistic Isolationism had the following loadings in the Couch Interdomain Factor Analysis: I(U) .24; II(P) .14—; III(F) .11; *Summary:* U (or if one accepts the weak negative component, *Summary* UN).

Inertia, Psychological

(a) Do observers rate him high on Psychological Inertia? If *yes,* then expect DF

(b) Do group members rate him high on Psychological Inertia? If *yes,* then expect DNF

(c) Does he rate himself high on Psychological Inertia? If *yes,* then expect DF

(d) Does he guess others will rate him high on Psychological Inertia? If *yes,* then expect DF

(e) Does he make others feel he rates them high on Psychological Inertia? If *yes,* then expect N

The evidence on these variables is direct, all drawn from Couch's Interdomain Factor Analysis. The loadings are:

	$I(U)$	$II(P)$	$III(F)$	*Summary*
(a)	.75—	.13	.35	DF
(b)	.67—	.22—	.36	DNF
(c)	.57—	.15	.32	DF
(d)	.65—	.09	.18	DF
(e)	.03	.23—	.12	N

The question was phrased: "To what extent does each member show the characteristics of psychological inertia (is slow to change, persevering, stable in his feelings about others, and tends to act in the same way most of the time)?"

0 = "He tends to react quickly without long deliberation, is changeable in his moods, behavior and feelings about others."

7 = "He tends to react calmly and deliberately, is slow to change his mood and feelings about others."

Information, Asks for

(a) Does he have a *high* rate of Asking for Information—higher than 7.2 percent of his own total interaction? (Bales' revised IPA category 7) If *yes,* then expect   UP

(b) Does he have a *low* rate of Asking for Information—lower than 4.0 percent of his own total interaction? (Bales' revised IPA category 7) If *yes,* then expect   DN

(c) Does he have a *high* rate of *receiving* requests for Information from others—higher than 7.2 percent of his own total interaction received? (Bales' revised IPA category 7) If *yes,* then expect   DB

(d) Does he have a *low* rate of *receiving* requests for Information from others—lower than 4.0 percent of his own total interaction received? (Bales' revised IPA category 7) If *yes,* then expect   UF

The evidence on the assignment of directional indicators as shown is direct. There was no change in the definition or the category in the revision.

For (a) the Couch Interdomain factor loadings were: I(U) .25; II(P) .35; III(F) .01; *Summary:* UP.

For (c) the Couch Interdomain factor loadings were: I(U) .56−; II(P) .10−; III(F) .25−; *Summary:* DB.

Information, Gives

(a) Does he have a *high* rate of Giving Information—higher than 31.2 percent of his own total interaction? (Bales' revised IPA category 6) If *yes,* then expect   D

(b) Does he have a *low* rate of Giving Information—lower than 20.7 percent of his own total interaction? (Bales' revised IPA category 6) If *yes,* then expect   U

(c) Does he have a *high* rate of *receiving* Information—higher than 22.8 percent of his own total interaction received? (Bales' revised IPA category 6) If *yes,* then expect   P

(d)   Does he have a *low* rate of *receiving* Information—
      lower than 15.0 percent of his total interaction re-
      ceived? (Bales' revised IPA category 6) If *yes,* then
      expect   N

      The evidence on the assignment of directional indicators as shown is
direct, although the category has been somewhat revised.
      For (a) the Couch Interdomain factor loadings were: I (U) .33—;
II (P) .02; III (F) .06—; *Summary:* D.
      For (c) the Couch Interdomain factor loadings were: I (U) .05;
II (P) .40; III (F) .04 – ; *Summary:* P.

Inhibitory Demands and Discipline

      Does he describe his parents on Slater's Parental Role
      Factor Questionnaire as high on Inhibitory Demands
      and Discipline? If *yes*, then expect   UNF

      The evidence on this variable is direct, and moderately good, except
for the negative component. The loadings on Couch's Interdomain Factor
Analysis were: I (U) .31; II (P) .14–; III (F) .21; *Summary:* UF. The
indicator UNF is chosen instead, because the negative component does
seem to be present intuitively, and hence it seems better to include it,
even though the loading is not significantly high.

Insecure

      Does he have a high score on Cattell's 16PF test called
      Insecure? If *yes*, then expect   NB

      This is Cattell's Scale (0), also called Anxious and Worrying. The
opposite end is called Unshakable.
      The evidence that this scale measures NB as indicated is only
indirect. Its loadings on Couch's Factor Analysis of the Personality
Domain are: I (N) .75; II (UP) .09; III (UN) .01; IV (PF) .26 –; V (B)
.03 –.
      The main loading on I indicates N. The loading on IV reversed
indicates NB. The summary is NB.

Intellectual Efficiency

      Does he have a high score on the MMPI scale called
      Intellectual Efficiency? If *yes*, then expect   P

      The evidence is only indirect that this scale measures P as indicated.

Its loadings on Couch's Factor Analysis of the Personality Domain are:
I (N) .60 −; II (UP) .09; III (UN) .35 − ; IV (PF) .12 − ; V (B) .03 − .

The main loading is on I reversed, which indicates P. The secondary loading on III reversed indicates DP. The literal summary is DP, but the summary P is chosen because the loading on I is considerably higher than that on III.

Intelligent

Does he have a high score on the Cattell test called
Intelligent? Treat as a separate dimension, that is, as: Unrelated

This is Cattell's scale (B), also called Bright. The opposite end is

Personality Domain are I (N) .29 −; II (UP) .12; III (UN) .05 −;
IV (PF) .03, and V (B) .09.

The main loading, and it is not very strong, is on I reversed, which could indicate P. Other studies, however, particularly those of Borgatta (48), suggest that intelligence measures should be regarded as essentially un-related to any of the three factors in the spatial model used in this book.

The position taken for the present system is that intelligence, the general factor, should be treated as a separate dimension; that is, one should expect to find persons of both high and low intelligence occupying each of the role types.

If there is a relation of general intelligence to the direction P it may simply be due to the fact that personality traits associated with the negative direction may sometimes constitute an impediment to the normal functioning of intelligence, and/or may create a social impression of dullness.

Interaction, Total Initiated

Does he initiate a high total amount of interaction?
(that is, in the highest third of the group) (Bales' IPA
Total Initiated). If *yes*, then expect   U
If in the lowest third of the group, then   D

The evidence concerning this variable is direct and strong. The loadings in the Couch Interdomain factor space were: I (U) .91; II (P) .13−; III (F) .08; *Summary:* U.

This variable is more strongly loaded in the upward direction than any other, except for Total Interaction Received, which is .93.

Interaction, Total Received

Does he receive a higher total amount of interaction addressed to him from others (SUM REC) than he addresses to others as individuals (SUM to I)? (Bales' IPA indices from the Who-to-Whom Matrix). If *yes*, then expect U

The evidence on this variable is not quite direct, since the index is made dependent upon a comparison of SUM REC with SUM to I, and this index has not been used previously. The loading of the raw total, SUM REC in the Couch Interdomain factor space was: I(U) .93; II(P) .15−; III(F) .13. The probability is that the present index will also show a strong loading in the upward direction.

Interaction to Group as a Whole

Does he address more Interaction to the Group as a Whole (SUM to 0) than he receives from all others (SUM REC)? (Bales IPA indices from the Who-to-Whom Matrix) If *yes*, then expect U

There is no direct evidence concerning this index, since it has not been used in this form before. Experience suggests that the relationship will be strong, though the direction could be UN rather than U.

Leadership

Does he have a high score on the MMPI test called Leadership? If *yes*, then expect UP

The evidence that this scale measures UP as indicated, is only indirect. Its loadings on Couch's Factor Analysis of the Personality Domain are: I(N) .81−; II(UP) .27; III(UN) .11; IV(PF) .04; V(B) .05.

The main loading is on I reversed which indicates P. The secondary loading is on II which indicates UP. These two indicators add together to UP.

It is likely that the usual position of Leadership as group members rate each other is UPF.

Lie Scale

Does he have a high score on the MMPI test called Lie Scale? If *yes*, then expect it to be Unrelated

The evidence that this scale measures Unrelated as indicated, is only indirect. Its loadings on couch's Factor Analysis of the Personality Domain are: I(N) .24—; II(UP) .32—; III(UN) .19; IV(PF) .05; V(B) .03—.

The main loading is on II reversed which indicate DN. The secondary loading is on I reversed which indicates P. The next highest loading is on III which indicates UN. Two of the loadings add to N, while the other loading indicates the exact opposite, P. It is concluded that from this scale there should be no prediction.

Liking, Arouses

(a) Do observers rate him high on Arousing their Liking? If *yes*, then expect   UPB

(b) Do group members rate him high on Arousing their Liking? If *yes*, then expect   PB

(c) Does he guess others will rate him high on Arousing their Liking? If *yes*, then expect   P

(d) Does he tend to rate others high on Arousing his Liking? If *yes*, then expect   UPF

(e) Does he make others feel he rates them high on Arousing his Liking? If *yes*, then expect   PB

The evidence on these variables is direct, all from Couch's Interdomain Factor Analysis. The loadings are:

	$I(U)$	$II(P)$	$III(F)$	Summary
(a)	.18	.35	.27—	UPB
(b)	.13—	.54	.31—	PB
(c)	.02—	.21	.02—	P
(d)	.18	.40	.27	UPF
(e)	.04	.66	.19—	PB

The question was phrased: "To what extent would you say that you like each of the other members of the group?"

> 0 = "I have no particular feeling of liking for him."
> 7 = "I like him very much."

Manic

Does he have a high score on the MMPI test called Manic? If *yes*, then expect   UN

The evidence is only indirect that this scale measures UN as indicated. Its loadings on Couch's Factor Analysis of the Personality Domain are: I (N) .28; II (UP) .42; III (UN) .55; IV (PF) .01; V (B) .17.

The main loading is on III, which indicates UN, with a secondary loading on II, which indicates UP. The next highest loading is on I, which is N. The summary direction of these is UN, quite close to U probably, and possibly with some backward component.

Material Success and Power

(a) Does he make value-statements advocating Material
     Success and Power? If *yes*, then expect   U
(b) Does he receive value-statements from others advocat-
     ing Material Success and Power? If *yes*, then expect   U
(c) Does he agree with value-statements from others advo-
     cating Material Success and Power? If *yes*, then expect   U

The evidence on each of these variables is indirect, inferential, and weak. See the discussion in the Preliminary Note to this Appendix.

Mature

Does he have a high score on Cattell's 16PF test called
Mature? If *yes*, then expect   DP

This is Cattell's Scale (C), also called Calm and Stable. The opposite end is called Emotional and Unstable, or sometimes General Neuroticism.

The evidence that this scale measures DP, as indicated, is only indirect. Its loadings on Couch's Factor Analysis of the Personality Domain are: I (N) .66 —; II (UP) .14 —; III (UN) .21 —; IV (PF) .06; and V (B) .13 — .

The main loading is on I reversed, which indicates P. The secondary loading on III reversed indicates DP. These two indicators sum to DP.

Nervous Tension

Does he have a high score on Cattell's 16 PF test called
Nervous Tension? If *yes*, then expect   UNB

This is Cattell's scale Q4. The evidence that it measures UNB is only indirect. Its loadings on Couch's Factor Analysis of the Personality Domain are: I (N) .75; II (UP) .28; III (UN) .15; IV (PF) .24 —; V (B) .02.

The main loading on I indicates N. The loading on IV reversed indicates NB. The loadings on II and III sum to U. The summary is thus UNB.

Objective in Tone

Does he seem to observers to try to be Objective in
Tone when he speaks? If *yes*, then expect   NF

The evidence on this variable is indirect. It is an adaptation of two
categories used by Couch in a special set for the classification of interaction. One of the categories was "Descriptive-Objective Acts." The loadings on this variable in the Interdomain space were: I(U) .38; II(P) .13;
III(F) .55; *Summary:* UF.

Another of his categories was "Interpretive-Objective Acts." The
loadings on this variable in the Interdomain space were: I(U) .34; II(P)
.27–; III(F) .37; *Summary:* UNF.

The common feature in these two categories is the "objective" tone
presumably present. It should also be remembered that they were used in
describing behavior act by act, and not as observer ratings. It was
reasoned that as a rating the overall descriptive title "Objective in
Tone" would very likely lose its upward component, since the upward
component is so directly related to absolute amount of participation. If
so, this would leave a directional significance of NF. It was decided to
choose this as the hypothetical significance.

The reason for going so far in inference is the importance of
obtaining concepts and variables for describing the forward part of the
space. Both the parent variables were well-loaded in this direction.

Opinion, Asks for

(a)   Does he have a *high* rate of Asking for Opinion—higher
than 3.9 percent of his own total interaction? (Bales'
revised IPA category 8) If *yes*, then expect   P

(b)   Does he have a *low* rate of Asking for Opinion—lower
than 2.0 percent of his own total interaction? (Bales'
revised IPA category 8) If *yes*, then expect   N

(c)   Does he have a *high* rate of *receiving* requests for
Opinion from others—higher than 2.8 percent of his
own total interaction received? (Bales' revised IPA
category 8) If *yes*, then expect   DN

(d)   Does he have a *low* rate of *receiving* requests for
Opinion from others—lower than 1.4 percent of his own
total interaction received? (Bales' revised IPA category
8) If *yes*, then expect   UP

The evidence on the directional indicators assigned to these variables is direct. This category was essentially unchanged in the revision,
hence the loadings are directly relevant.

For (a) the Couch Interdomain factor loadings were: I(U) .12; II(P) .40; III(F) .08–; *Summary:* P.

For (c) the Couch Interdomain factor loadings were: I(U) .36–; II(P) .22–; III(F) .00; *Summary:* DN.

Opinion, Gives

(a) Does he have a *high* rate of Giving Opinion—higher than 22.7 percent of his own total interaction? (Bales' revised IPA category 5) If *yes,* then expect   F

(b) Does he have a *low* rate of Giving Opinion—lower than 15.0 percent of his own total interaction? (Bales' revised IPA category 5) If *yes,* then expect   B

(c) Does he have a *high* rate of *receiving* Opinion—higher than 22.7 percent of his own total interaction received? (Bales' revised IPA category 5) If *yes,* then expect   PF

(d) Does he have a *low* rate of *receiving* Opinion—lower than 15.0 percent of his own total interaction received? (Bales' revised IPA category 5) If *yes,* then expect   NB

The directional indicators given for (a) and (b) are hypothetical. The original category definition has been modified on the basis of the study. In the study the Couch Interdomain Factor loadings of the category as it was then defined were: I(U) .35; II(P) .31 –; III(F) .35; *Summary:* UNF.

The category has been redefined in such a way that acts of giving opinion with a negative tone will be classified in category 12, and those of an ascendant tone in category 4, thus leaving the component F. Whether the redefinition is successful remains to be seen. For (c) and (d) the directional indicators shown were obtained by using the original definition. It is assumed that these indicators will remain the same, even though the category has been somewhat re-defined. For (c) the Couch Interdomain factor loadings were: I(U) .16; II(P) .21; III(F) .27; *Summary:* PF.

Optimistic Idealism

Does he describe his parents as having taught him Optimistic Idealism (versus Cynical Pessimism)? (Bales' hypothetical addition to Slater's PRF test). If *yes,* then expect   PF

This is a hypothetical or invented variable. That there should be such a variable is deduced from the fact that Slater finds only two variables which seem to fit reasonably into the three-dimensional space used in this study, namely, Inhibitory Demands and Discipline; and

Emotional Supportiveness and Warmth. The direction orthogonal to these two has no variable specified for it. The nature of the three-dimensional space (as a space of evaluations of personalities and roles) should apply to parental roles as well as any others. It is possible to think of a variable that has the expected characteristics (both positive and forward, and neither upward nor downward) —Optimistic Idealism. Such a variable has a reasonable place in the theory of the processes of socialization that goes along with the present theory.

The test of the hypothesis would be made by inventing items that seem to be reasonable specific descriptions of Optimistic Idealism as a parental trait in relation to the child, incorporating them in a study measuring other variables in the space and subjecting them to factor analysis. The invented variable should load in the direction PF, and should be orthogonal to the other two Slater variables.

Originality

Does he have a high score on the MMPI test called Originality? If *yes,* then expect it to be: Unrelated

The evidence on this scale is indirect and conflicting. Its loadings on Couch's Factor Analysis of the Personality Domain are: I(N) .35−·II(UP) .29−; III(UN) .05; IV(PF) .30−; V(B) .14.

The main loading is on I reversed, which indicates P. The loading on IV reversed indicates NB. The third highest loading is on II reversed, which indicates DN.

The indicators are so contrary in their directional implications that it seems best to treat originality (like intelligence) as "unrelated" to any single direction in the present space. The loading on I may indicate that ego strength is one component, and that on IV suggests that unconventionality is also a component, but ordinarily these two traits are somewhat negatively related to each other.

Paranoid

Does he have a high score on the MMPI test called Paranoid? If *yes,* then expect   UNB

The evidence is only indirect that the scale measures UNB as indicated. Its loadings on Couch's Factor Analysis of the Personality Domain are: I(N) .36; II(UP) .05; III(UN) .22; IV(PF) .06; V(B) .22.

The main loading on I indicates N. The secondary loading on III indicates UN, and another secondary loading on V indicates B. The summation of these indicators is UNB.

Permissive Liberalism

(a) Does he make value-statements advocating Permissive Liberalism? If *yes*, then expect   PB

(b) Does he receive value-statements advocating Permissive Liberalism? If *yes*, then expect   UNF

(c) Does he agree with value-statements advocating Permissive Liberalism? If *yes*, then expect   NB

The evidence on these three variables is indirect, inferential, and weak. For a description of the nature of the evidence see the Preliminary Note to this Appendix.

Personal Involvement

(a) Do observers rate him high on Personal Involvement? If *yes*, then expect   UP

(b) Do group members rate him high on Personal Involvement? If *yes*, then expect   UP

(c) Does he rate himself high on Personal Involvement? If *yes*, then expect   UP

(d) Does he guess others will rate him high on Personal Involvement? If *yes*, then expect   UP

(e) Does he tend to rate others high on Personal Involvement? If *yes*, then expect   PB

(f) Does he make others feel he rates them high on Personal Involvement? If *yes*, then expect it to be: Unrelated

The evidence on these variables is direct, all from the Couch Interdomain Factor Analysis. The loadings are:

	$I(U)$	$II(P)$	$III(F)$	*Summary*
(a)	.35	.37	.16	UP
(b)	.39	.52	.06	UP
(c)	.31	.30	.12	UP
(d)	.33	.55	.13	UP
(e)	.10—	.31	.22—	PB
(f)	.05	.09	.04	Unrelated

The question was phrased: "How do you think each individual felt about getting personally involved as a member of this group?"

0 = "He did not seem to want to get involved with others or accept any of the members personally."

7 = "He seemed to be involved with others and liked being a member of this group."

Prejudice

Does he have a high score on the MMPI test called Prejudice? If *yes*, then expect   UNF

The evidence is only indirect that this scale measures UN as indicated. Its loadings on Couch's Factor Analysis of the Personality Domain are: I(N) .71; II(UP) .10; III(UN) .36; IV(PF) .19; V(B) .03 −.

The main loading is on I, which indicates N, with a secondary loading on III, which indicates UN. The loading on IV indicates PF, a somewhat conflicting indicator, although prejudice has often been associated with Authoritarian Conformity, the identification term Couch applies to his Factor IV. The summary UNF seems best, in terms of general knowledge about prejudice.

Psychasthenia

Does he have a high score on the MMPI test called Psychasthenia? If *yes*, then expect   N

The evidence is only indirect that the scale measures N as indicated. Its loadings on Couch's Factor Analysis of the Personality Domain are: I(N) .90; II (UP) .05; III (UN) .11; IV (PF) .01; V (B) .01.

The main loading is on I, which is N, and this is probably the only significant loading.

Psychopathic

Does he have a high score on the MMPI test called Psychopathic? If *yes*, then expect   UN

The evidence is only indirect that the scale measures UN as indicated. Its loadings on Couch's Factor Analysis of the Personality Domain are: I(N) .39; II(UP) .00; III(UN) .53; IV(PF) .08 −; V(B) .15−.

The main loading is on III, which is UN, with a secondary loading on I, which is N. The summary direction is taken to be UN.

Radical

Does he have a high score on Cattell's 16 PF test called Radical? If *yes*, then expect   NB

This is Cattell's scale Q1, also called Critical. The opposite end is called Conservative and Accepting.

The evidence as to what this scale measures in the Interdomain space is indirect. Its loadings on Couch's Factor Analysis of the Personality Domain are: I(N) .11−; II(UP) .13−; III(UN) .11; IV(PF) .21−; V(B) .12.

The main loading on IV indicates NB, since it is reversed. All of the other loadings are low. One would expect this scale to have a significant loading on V, indicating B, but the loading is probably not significant. Nevertheless, the summary direction is NB.

Reflective

Does he have a high score on Thurstone's Temperament test called Reflective? If *yes*, then expect it to be: Unrelated

The loadings on Couch's Factor Analysis of the Personality Domain are: I(N) .07−; II(UP) .24; III(UN) .07; IV(PF) .06 −; V(B) .16.

The highest loading on II is not very high, but indicates UP. The loading on V, barely significant, if significant, indicates B. The summary is UPB. This seems out of character for the trait, and it is doubtful if this scale does indicate UPB. It also seems doubtful that it measures UP. It seems best to suppose that, like intelligence and originality, it should be treated for the time being as "unrelated."

Rejection of Conservative Group Beliefs

(a) Does he make value-statements Rejecting Conservative
      Group Beliefs? If *yes*, then expect   B
(b) Does he receive value-statements from others in which
      they advocate the Rejection of Conservative Group
      Beliefs to him? If *yes*, then expect   F
(c) Does he agree with value-statements from others in
      which they Reject Conservative Group Beliefs? If *yes*,
      then expect   UNB

The evidence concerning these variables is indirect, inferential and weak. For a description of the nature of the evidence, see the Preliminary Note to this Appendix.

Rejection of Social Conformity

(a) Does he make value-statements Rejecting Social Con-
      formity? If *yes*, then expect   NB
(b) Do others address value-statements to him Rejecting
      Social Conformity? If *yes*, then expect   UNF

(c)   Does he agree with value-statements others make to
him Rejecting Social Conformity? If *yes,* then expect   UNB

The evidence concerning these variables is indirect, inferential and
weak. For a description of the nature of the evidence, see the Preliminary
Note to this Appendix.

Rejection of Social Success
(a)   Does he make value-statements Rejecting Social Suc-
cess? If *yes,* then expect   DN
(b)   Do others address value-statements to him Rejecting
Social Success? If *yes,* then expect   DP
(c)   Does he agree with value-statements others address to
him Rejecting Social Success? If *yes,* then expect   DN

The evidence concerning these variables is indirect, inferential, and
weak. For a description of the nature of the evidence, see the Preliminary
Note to this Appendix.

Repression-Denial
Does he have a high score on the MMPI test called
Repression-Denial? If *yes,* then expect   DN

The evidence is only indirect that this scale measures DN as indicated. Its loadings on Couch's Factor Analysis of the Personality Domain
are: I (N) .06; II (UP) .51 –; III (UN) .13; IV (PF) .20 ; V (B) .20 .
The main loading on II, reversed, indicates DN. The loading on IV
reversed indicates NB. The loading on V indicates F, though not very
strongly. The summary direction is DN.

Resentful
(a)   Do observers rate him high on being Resentful? If *yes,*
then expect   DN
(b)   Do group members rate him high on being Resentful?
If *yes,* then expect   DN
(c)   Does he rate himself high on being Resentful? If *yes,*
then expect it to be: Unrelated
(d)   Does he guess others will rate him high on being
Resentful? If *yes,* then expect   N
(e)   Does he tend to rate others high on being Resentful? If
yes, then expect   UN
(f)   Does he make others feel he rates them high on being
Resentful? If *yes,* then expect it to be: Unrelated

The evidence on these variables is direct, all drawn from the Couch Interdomain Factor Analysis. The loadings are:

	$I(U)$	$II(P)$	$III(F)$	Summary
(a)	.68—	.30—	.17	DN*
(b)	.42—	.32—	.06	DN
(c)	.16—	.10—	.04—	Unrelated
(d)	.06—	.25—	.06	N
(e)	.17	.37—	.08—	UN
(f)	.16	.01—	.05	Unrelated

*Although the loading on III (F) may be significant, and it is the level accepted as significant for this study, it is ignored in this instance because it does not agree with (b), there is no evident reason to suppose it is different from (b), and because the term "resentful" seems more clearly to imply a negative attitude toward persons than toward social norms.

The question was phrased: "To what extent do you think any of the members feel resentful about being treated unfairly and not being given enough consideration?"

0 = "He feels he was treated fairly."
7 = "He feels very resentful about not being shown enough consideration."

Responsibility

Does he have a high score on the MMPI test called Responsibility? If *yes*, then expect   **DPF**

The evidence is only indirect that this scale measures DPF as indicated. Its loadings on Couch's Factor Analysis of the Personality Domain are: I(N) .50 –; II(UP) .29 –; III(UN) .43 –; IV(PF) .25; V(B) .20 –.

The main loading is on I reversed, which indicates P. The next highest loading is on III reversed, which indicates DP. The loading on II indicates DN. The loading on IV indicates PF, and the loading on V indicates F. The summation of these indicators is DPF.

Role-Playing Ability

Does he have a high score on the MMPI test called Role-Playing Ability? If *yes*, then expect   **PF**

The evidence is only indirect that this scale measures PF as indicated. Its loadings on Couch's Factor Analysis in the Personality Domain are: I(N) .66 –; II(UP) .01 –; III(UN) .00; IV(PF) .02 –; and V(B) .16 –.

The main loading on I indicates P. If the loading on V is taken as significant, it indicates F. The summary is PF, but the forward component is quite weak.

Rugged Individualism and Gratification

(a) Does he make value-statements advocating Rugged Individualism and Gratification? If *yes,* then expect   UNB

(b) Does he receive value-statements advocating Rugged Individualism and Gratification? If *yes,* then expect   UPF

(c) Does he agree with value-statements advocating Rugged Individualism and Gratification? If *yes,* then expect   UNB

This is a marker variable for the value spaces. The evidence on (a) is direct. The loadings of this variable on Couch's Interdomain Factor Analysis were: I(U) .22; II(P) .25 –; III(F) .31 –; *Summary:* UNB.

The evidence on (b) is direct, but weak. The loadings of this variable on Couch's Interdomain Factor Analysis were: I(U) .11; II(P) .19; III(F) .23; *Summary:* PF.

On the hypothetical assumption that the upward types are more likely to address each other in argument than less prominent participators, the hypothetical direction is given as UPF.

The evidence on (c) is indirect and weak. Written responses of agreement to written items in the value area in question have the following loadings on the Couch Interdomain Factor Analysis: I(U) .15; II(P) .19 –; III(F) .33 –; *Summary:* NB.

First it is assumed that the upward component is significant, though it is actually low, thus bringing the summary to UNB. Then it is assumed that the subject's overt agreement to verbal statements made to him in the course of interaction would be about the same as his responses on the written test. This is hypothetical. The directional indicator is thus hypothetical.

Salvation through Love

(a) Does he make value-statements advocating Salvation through Love? If *yes,* then expect   DPF

(b) Does he receive value-statements from others in which they advocate Salvation through Love to him? If *yes,* then expect   DNB

(c)   Does he agree with value-statements made to him by others advocating Salvation through Love? If *yes,* then expect   DPF

The evidence on (a) is direct, and moderately good. This variable is the opposite end of the direction UNB. See Rugged Individualism and Gratification for the loadings.

The evidence on (b) is direct, but weak. See note under Rugged Individualism and Gratification (b) for the loadings.

The evidence on (c) is indirect, and weak. See note under Rugged Individualism and Gratification (c) for the loadings.

Schizophrenic

Does he have a high score on the MMPI scale called Schizophrenic? If *yes,* then expect   UN

The evidence is only indirect that the scale measures UN as indicated. Its loadings on Couch's Factor Analysis of the Personality Domain are: I (N) .82; II (UP) .10 – ; III (UN) .30; IV (PF) .03; V (B) .11.

The main loading is on I which indicates N, with a secondary loading on III, which indicates UN. The summary direction is UN.

This variable is not used in the typological descriptions, since it is so far discrepant from the position of Cattell's scale, called sometimes "Schizothymic," which is on the opposite end of "Warm," and is thus located DNB. On the other hand, the present MMPI scale is not far from the location of the scale "Paranoid" UNB. Possibly, one is dealing with two different syndromes under the same name. The Cattell scale may relate more closely to the catatonic type of schizoid symptoms, while the MMPI relates more closely to the paranoid type. This is purely speculative, however.

Self-Confidence

(a)   Do observers rate him high on Self-Confidence? If *yes,* then expect   U

(b)   Do group members rate him high on Self-Confidence? If *yes,* then expect   UN

(c)   Does he rate himself high on Self-Confidence? If *yes,* then expect   U

(d)   Does he guess that others will rate him high on Self-Confidence? If *yes,* then expect   U

(e)   Does he tend to rate others high on Self-Confidence? If *yes,* then expect   DP

(f)   Does he make others feel he rates them high on Self-Confidence? If *yes,* then expect   DNF

The evidence for these variables is direct, all from the Couch Interdomain Factor Analysis. The loadings are:

	$I(U)$	$II(P)$	$III(F)$	Summary
(a)	.67	.03	.13	U
(b)	.67	.19—	.08	UN
(c)	.20	.07	.11	U
(d)	.21	.02—	.08	U
(e)	.24—	.24	.08	DP
(f)	.36—	.19—	.30	DNF

The question was phrased: "To what extent do you feel that each member was self-confident and self-assured?"

0 = "He seems very unsure of himself and lacks confidence."
7 = "He seems very self-confident and self-assured."

Self-Knowledge and Subjectivity

(a) Does he make value-statements advocating Self-Knowledge and Subjectivity? If *yes,* then expect   DF

(b) Does he receive value-statements advocating Self-Knowledge and Subjectivity? If *yes,* then expect   DB

(c) Does he agree with value-statements advocating Self-Knowledge and Subjectivity? If *yes,* then expect   DF

The evidence concerning these variables is indirect, inferential, and weak. For a description of the nature of the evidence, see the Preliminary Note to this Appendix.

Self-Sacrifice for Values

(a) Does he make value-statements advocating Self-Sacrifice for Values? If *yes,* then expect   DNF

(b) Does he receive value-statements advocating Self-Sacrifice for Values? If *yes,* then expect   DPB

(c) Does he agree with value-statements advocating Self-Sacrifice for Values? If *yes,* then expect   DNF

The evidence concerning these variables is indirect, inferential, and weak. For a description of the nature of the evidence, see the Preliminary Note to this Appendix.

Shows Tension

(a) Does he have a *high* rate on Showing Tension or laughing—higher than 6.0 percent of his own total interaction? (Bales' revised IPA category 11) If *yes,* then expect   DB

(b) Does he have a *low* rate of Showing Tension or laughing—lower than 3.4 percent of his own total interaction? (Bales' revised IPA category 11) If *yes,* then expect   UF

(c) Does he have a *high* rate of *receiving* signs of Tension, or laughing—higher than 7.5 percent of his own total interaction received? (Bales' revised IPA category 11) If *yes,* then expect   UNB

(d) Does he have a *low* rate of *receiving* signs of Tension or laughing—lower than 4.4 percent of his own total interaction received? (Bales' revised IPA category 11) If *yes,* then expect   DPF

The evidence for the directional indicators shown is inferential, and complicated. In the study, laughs were scored in original category 2, Shows Tension Release, and jokes were not scored in this category. The factor loadings for this category on Couch's Interdomain Analysis were: I (U) .53 – ; II (P) .02 – ; III (F) .06 – ; *Summary:* D. Since little else was scored in the category, the appropriate directional indicator for laughs was taken to be D.

This direction is very close to that obtained for the original category 11, Shows Tension. These loadings were: I (U) .33 – ; II (P) .03 – ; III (F) .29 – ; *Summary:* DB.

In the revision, Shows Tension and Laughs are combined into a single category, and the combination of the two is expected to measure direction DB. It remains to be seen whether this hypothesis is a good one. Variables (a) and (b) above are assigned directional indicators on this assumption.

In the study the original category 11, Shows Tension, *received,* obtained the following loadings on Couch's Interdomain analysis: I (U) .06 – ; II (P) .12 – ; III (F) .11; Summary: AVE. But the original category 2, containing laughs received had loadings as follows: I (U) .15; II (P) .25 – ; III (F) .57 – ; *Summary:* NB. Since most laughs occur in response to jokes, however, and are directed to the joker, and since jokes are inferred to be characteristic of direction UB, the literal direction obtained for receiving laughs NB is revised upward to a hypothetical UNB shown.

Sociable

Does he have a high score on Thurstone's Temperament
test called Sociable? If *yes,* then expect   UP

The evidence that this scale measures UP as indicated is only
indirect. The loadings on Couch's Factor Analysis of the Personality
Domain are: I(N) .39 –; II(UP) .60; III(UN) .09; IV(PF) .07; and
V(B) .09 –.

The main loading on II indicates UP, and the secondary loading on
I reversed indicates P. The summary is UP.

Social Introversion

Does he have a high score on the MMPI scale called
Social Introversion? If *yes,* then expect   DN

The evidence is only indirect that this scale measures DN as indicated. Its loadings on Couch's Factor Analysis of the Personality Domain
are: I(N) .72; II(UP) .51 –; III(UN) .00; IV(PF) .11 –; and V(B)
.12 –. The major loading on I indicates N, and the secondary loading on
II indicates DN. None of the other loadings appears to be significant.

Social Participation

Does he have a high score on the MMPI scale called
Social Participation? If *yes,* then expect   UP

The evidence is only indirect that this scale measures UP as indicated. Its loadings on Couch's Factor Analysis of the Personality Domain
are: I(N) .60 –; II(UP) .48; III(UN) .24 –; IV(PF) .11; and V(B)
.04 –. The main loading is on I reversed, which indicates P. The
secondary loading is on II, which indicates UP. A third loading is on III
reversed, which indicates DP. Giving the greater weight to the heavier
loadings, the summary score is taken to be UP.

Social Solidarity and Progress

(a) Does he make value-statements advocating Social Solidarity and Progress? If *yes,* then expect   UPF
(b) Do others address value-statements to him advocating
Social Solidarity and Progress? If *yes,* then expect   UNB
(c) Does he agree with value-statements addressed to him
by others advocating Social Solidarity and Progress? If   UPF
yes, then expect

The evidence on each of these variables is indirect, inferential, and weak. For description of the evidence, see the Preliminary Note to this Appendix.

Social Success
(a) Does he make value-statements advocating Social Suc-
cess? If *yes,* then expect   UP
(b) Do others address value-statements to him advocating
Social Success? If *yes,* then expect   UN
(c) Does he agree with value-statements made to him by
others advocating Social Success? If *yes,* then expect   UP

The evidence on each of these variables is indirect, inferential, and weak. For description of the evidence see the Preliminary Note to this Appendix.

Social Status
Does he have a high score on the MMPI scale called
Social Status? If *yes,* then expect   UP

The evidence is only indirect that this scale measures UP as indicated. Its loadings on Couch's Factor Analysis of the Personality Domain are: I (N) .61 – ; II (UP) .51; III (UN) .06; IV (PF) .13 – ; V (B) .11.

The main loading is on I reversed which indicates P, while the secondary loading is on II, which indicates UP. These two indicators sum to UP.

Sophistication
Does he have a high score on Cattell's 16PF test called
Sophistication? If *yes,* then expect   UF

This is Cattell's scale N, also called Polished. The opposite end is called Simplicity, or sometimes Rough Simplicity.

The evidence that this scale measures UF as indicated is only indirect. Its loadings on Couch's Factor-Analysis of the Personality Domain are: I (N) .09 – ; II (UP) .01; III (UN) .22; IV (PF) .48; V (B) .01.

The main loading on IV indicates PF. The loading on III indicates UN. The test is apparently related to some kind of conventional control of aggression. The summary UF makes some sense and is accepted.

Spontaneity
Does he have a high score on the MMPI scale called
Spontaneity? If *yes,* then expect   UPB

This scale is also said to measure Poise and Confidence, and is sometimes called by these names. The evidence that the scale measures UPB as indicated, is only indirect. Its loadings on Couch's Factor Analysis of the Personality Domain are: I(N) .56 –; II(UP) .51; III(UN) .02 –; IV(PF) .05 –; V(B) .17.

The main loading on I reversed, indicates P. The almost equal loading on II indicates UP. If one counts the loading on V as significant, it indicates B, and the summary of all three indicators is UPB.

Suggestion, Asks for

(a) Does he have a *high* rate of Asking for Suggestion— higher than 1.4 percent of his own total interaction? (Bales' revised IPA category 9) If *yes*, then expect   DF

(b) Does he have a *low* rate of Asking for Suggestion— lower than 0.6 percent of his own total interaction? (Bales' revised IPA category 9) If *yes*, then expect   UB

(c) Does he have a *high* rate of *receiving* requests for Suggestion—higher than 1.2 percent of his own total interaction received? (Bales' revised IPA category 9) If *yes*, then expect   F

(d) Does he have a *low* rate of *receiving* requests for Suggestion—lower than 0.5 percent of his own total interaction received? (Bales' revised IBA category 9) If *yes*, then expect   B

The directional significances given above for (a) and (b) are hypothetical. In the study, using the original definition of the category, none of the loadings is significant. For (a) the Couch Interdomain Factor loadings were: I(U) .04 –; II(P) .11; III(F) .05. It is hoped that the definition has been revised in such a way that the above diagnostic direction will be obtained.

For (c) and (d) the directional indicators shown were obtained using the original definition. For (c) the Couch Interdomain Factor loadings were: I(U) .04; II(P) .03; III(F) .18; Summary: F. It is possible that these loadings will not change much, though the category is somewhat redefined.

Suggestion, Gives

(a) Does he have a *high* rate of Giving Suggestion—a rate higher than 7.0 percent of his own total interaction? (Bales' revised IPA category 4) If *yes*, then expect   UF

(b) Does he have a *low* rate of Giving Suggestion—a rate lower than 3.0 percent of his own total interaction? (Bales' revised IPA category 4) If *yes*, then expect   DB

(c) Does he have a *high* rate of *receiving* Suggestion from others—a rate higher than 5.2 percent of his own total interaction received? (Bales' revised IPA category 4) If *yes*, then expect   UP

(d) Does he have a *low* rate of *receiving* Suggestion from others—a rate lower than 2.9 percent of his own total interaction received? (Bales' revised IPA category 4) If *yes*, then expect   ND

The directional significance given above for (a) and (b) are hypothetical. In the study, using the original definition of the category, none of the loadings is significant. For (a) the Couch Interdomain factor loadings were: I(U) .09; II(P) .12; III(F) .05. It is hoped that the definition has been revised in such a way that the hypothetical diagnostic directions will be obtained.

For (c) and (d) the directional indicators shown were obtained by the original definition. For (c) the Couch Interdomain factor loadings were: I(U) .20; II(P) .17; III(F) .05 –; Summary: UP. It is possible that these loadings will not change much, though the category is somewhat redefined.

Suppressor

Does he have a high score on the MMPI scale called Suppressor? If *yes* then expect   P

This variable is of interest primarily to technical workers in interpreting other scales of the MMPI.

The evidence is only indirect that the scale measures P as indicated. Its loadings on Couch's Factor Analysis of the Personality Domain are: I(N) .70 –; II(UP) .13 –; III(UN) .07 –; IV(PF) .05; V(B) .01.

The only loading that seems significant is that on factor I, and it is negative. Since I is taken to measure N, a negative loading is taken to measure P.

Suspecting

Does he have a high score on Cattell's 16PF test called Suspecting? If *yes*, then expect   N

This is Cattell's scale L, also called Jealous. The opposite end is called Trustful, and Accessible.

The evidence that this scale measures N as indicated is only indirect. Its loadings on Couch's Factor Analysis in the Personality Domain are: I (N) .53; II (UP) .19; III (UN) .11; IV (PF) .09 – ; V (B) .08.

The main loading on I indicates N. Although II may have a significant loading, it seems best to ignore it, and regard N as the best summary. There may be some slight upward component.

Task, Interest in

(a) Do observers rate him high on Interest in the Task? If *yes,* then expect   UPF

(b) Do group members rate him high on Interest in the Task? If *yes,* then expect   UPF

(c) Does he rate himself high on Interest in the Task? If *yes,* then expect   UP

(d) Does he guess that others will rate him high on Interest in the Task? If *yes,* then expect   UP

(e) Does he tend to rate others high on interest in the task? If *yes,* then expect   P

(f) Does he make others feel he rates them high on Interest in the Task? If *yes,* then expect it to be: Unrelated

The evidence on these is direct, and from Couch's Interdomain Factor Analysis. The loadings are:

	I (U)	II (P)	III (F)	Summary
(a)	.36	.27	.25	UPF
(b)	.24	.24	.17	UPF
(c)	.35	.41	.15	UP
(d)	.58	.30	.07	UP
(e)	.10	.33	.09—	P
(f)	.02—	.02	.07—	Unrelated

The question was phrased: "How do you think the members of the group felt about this kind of task?"

0 = "He seemed to be not at all interested in this kind of task or situation."

7 = "He seemed to find this kind of task very interesting."

Task, Valuable for a Logical Task

(a) Do observers rate him on being Valuable for a Logical
     Task? If *yes,* then expect   UPF
(b) Do group members rate him high on being Valuable
     for a Logical Task? If *yes,* then expect   UP
(c) Does he rate himself high on being Valuable for a
     Logical Task? If *yes,* then expect   U
(d) Does he guess that others will rate him high on being
     Valuable for a Logical Task? If *yes,* then expect   UP
(e) Does he tend to rate others high on being Valuable for
     a Logical Task? If *yes,* then expect   P
(f) Does he make others feel he rates them high on being
     Valuable for a Logical Task? If *yes,* then expect   DP

The evidence on these variables is direct, all from Couch's Inter-domain Factor Analysis. The loadings are:

	I (U)	*II (P)*	*III (F)*	*Summary*
(a)	.43	.28	.44	UPF
(b)	.42	.32	.12	UP
(c)	.48	.04—	.11	U
(d)	.49	.18	.04	UP
(e)	.16	.29	.04	P
(f)	.24—	.32	.08—	DP

The question was phrased: "To what extent did each of the members contribute to the successful completion of the task by being realistic, logical, and effective in the discussion?"

0 = "He didn't do anything that helped the group with its task."
7 = "He was most valuable and effective in helping the group complete the task."

Tolerance

Does he have a high score on the MMPI scale called
Tolerance? If *yes,* then expect   DP

The evidence is only indirect that this scale measures DP as indicated. Its loadings on Couch's Factor Analysis of the Personality Domain are: I(N) .69 –; II(UP) .06 –; III(UN) .34 –; IV(PF) .24 –; V(B) .03.

The main loading on I reversed indicates P. The secondary loading on III reversed indicates DP. The loading on IV reversed indicates NB, a quite contrary direction. Since IV is Authoritarian Conformity, it is understandable that tolerance might be negatively related to it. But it seems doubtful that tolerance is in fact related to the NB direction, and plausible that it is related to the more strongly indicated directions P and DP. The summary DP is thus accepted.

Tough-Minded Assertiveness

(a) Does he make value-statements advocating Tough-Minded Assertiveness? If *yes*, then expect   UN

(b) Do others address value-statements to him advocating Tough-Minded Assertiveness to him? If *yes*, then expect   UP

(c) Does he agree with others who advocate Tough-Minded Assertiveness? If *yes*, then expect   UN

The evidence on each of these variables is indirect, inferential, and weak. For description of the evidence see the Preliminary Note to this Appendix.

Trust in the Goodness of Others

(a) Does he make value-statements advocating Trust in the Goodness of Others? If *yes*, then expect   DP

(b) Do others address value-statements to him advocating Trust in the Goodness of Others? If *yes*, then expect   DN

(c) Does he agree with value-statements others make to him advocating Trust in the Goodness of Others? If *yes*, then expect   DP

The evidence on these variables is indirect, inferential, and weak. For a description of the nature of the evidence, see the Preliminary Note to this Appendix.

Understanding

(a) Do observers rate him high on being Understanding? If *yes*, then expect   DP

(b) Do group members rate him high on being Understanding? If *yes*, then expect   DP

(c)   Does he rate himself high on being Understanding? If
yes, then expect   N

(c)   Does he guess that others will rate him high on being
Understanding? If yes, then expect   UP

(e)   Does he tend to rate others high on being Understanding? If yes, then expect   UP

(f)   Does he make others feel that he rates them high on
being Understanding? If yes, then expect   DP

The evidence on these is direct, from Couch's Interdomain Factor
Analysis. The loadings are:

	I (U)	II (P)	III (F)	Summary
(a)	.27—	.22	.04—	DP
(b)	.18—	.17	.07	DP
(c)	.06	.29—	.12—	N
(d)	.27	.28	.06	UP
(e)	.25	.40	.16	UP
(f)	.21—	.21	.16—	DP

The question was phrased: "To what extent do each of the members
have a good understanding of people and seem insightful about human
relations?"

0 = "He doesn't seem to be at all concerned with understanding
people."

7 = "He has a very good understanding of people."

Unfriendly, Seems

(a)   Does he have a *high* rate of Seeming Unfriendly to
others—higher than 4.4 percent of his own total interaction? (Bales' revised IPA category 12) If yes, then
expect   N

(b)   Does he have a *low* rate of Seeming Unfriendly to
others—lower than 2.4 percent of his own total interaction? (Bales' revised IPA category 12) If yes, then
expect   P

(c)   Does he have a *high* rate of *receiving* acts in which
others seem Unfriendly to him—higher than 4.4 percent

of his own total interaction received? (Bales' revised
IPA category 12) If *yes*, then expect   UNF

(d) Does he have a *low* rate of *receiving* acts in which
others seem Unfriendly to him—lower than 2.4 percent
of his own total interaction received? (Bales' revised
IPA category 12) If *yes*, then expect   DPB

The evidence for the directional indicators shown is inferential. In
the study using the original category 12, Shows Antagonism, the factor
loadings for acts of this type initiated were: I (U) .43; II (P) .56 – ;
III (F) .05 – ; Summary: UN. In the redefinition of the category for the
revision, many more acts of a submissive yet negative kind should be
included, and hence, it is hypothesized that the upward component will
be balanced, leaving N. I do not have great confidence in this, however,
and would not be surprised to see the revised category also measure UN.

As to the receiving of acts of Antagonism (original category 12,
received), the loadings were: I (U) .16; II (P) .32 – ; III (F) .37; Summary: NF. I have supposed that if the new category 12, Seems Unfriendly, includes more submissive acts than before, one may pick up more
frequently the reaction to the ascendant type UNF. Consequently I have
modified the literal summary shown above, NF, to UNF. This is of course
hypothetical, and must be tested.

Validity

Does he have a high score on the MMPI scale called
Validity? If *yes*, then expect   UN

This scale is of interest to technical workers with the MMPI. The
evidence is only indirect that it measures UN as indicated. Its loadings on
Couch's Factor Analysis of the Personality Domain are: I (N) .42;
II (UP) .24 – ; III (UN) .52; IV (PF) .08; V (B) .12.

The major loading on III indicates UN, the secondary loading on I
indicates N, and the loading on II indicates DN. Since the loading for
UN is so much greater than for DN, the summary is taken to be UN,
rather than N.

Value-Determined Restraint

(a) Does he make value-statements advocating Value-
Determined Restraint? If *yes*, then expect   NF

(b) Does he receive value-statements advocating Value-
Determined Restraint? If *yes*, then expect   UNB

(c) Does he agree with value-statements advocating Value-Determined Restraint? If *yes,* then expect   **PF**

The evidence concerning these variables is indirect, inferential, and weak. For description of the nature of the evidence, see the Preliminary Note to this Appendix.

Value-Relativism and Expression

(a) Does he make value-statements advocating Value-Relativism and Expression? If *yes,* then expect   **UB**

(b) Do others address value-statements to him advocating Value-Relativism and Expression? If *yes,* then expect   **UF**

(c) Does he agree with others who advocate Value-Relativism and Expression to him? If *yes,* then expect   **UB**

The evidence on each of these variables is indirect, inferential, and weak. For description of the nature of the evidence, see the Preliminary Note to this Appendix.

Value-Statements, All Types

(a) Does he make a great many Value-Statements regardless of type? If *yes,* then expect   **UNF**

(b) Does he receive a great many Value-Statements, regardless of type? If *yes,* then expect   **UNF**

(c) Does he agree with a great many Value-Statements and other statements, regardless of type? (Agreement response set) If *yes,* then expect   **UP**

The evidence on the first two of these is direct and moderately good. For (a) the loadings on Couch's Interdomain Factor Analysis were: I(U) .72; II(P) .18–; III(F) .30; *Summary:* UNF. For (b) the loadings were: I(U) .63; II(P) .11–; III(F) .23; *Summary:* UF. In view of (a) above, however, the negative component seems more plausible, and the direction assigned, hypothetically, is UNF. For (c) the loadings on Couch's Interdomain Factor Analysis were: I(U) .28; II(P) .22; III(F) .01; *Summary:* UP.

The variable measured in (c) is an over-all-tests agreement response set to written items, not only value-statements. It is here assumed that the agreement response set obtained to written items will also characterize the overt tendency to agree in actual interaction. The direction so obtained, UP, is not identical with the direction obtained by direct observation of Interaction Category 3, Agrees, PF, but is correlated with it.

Vigorous

    Does he have a high score on Thurstone's Temperament
test called Vigorous? If *yes*, then expect   B

    The evidence that this scale measures B as indicated is only indirect.
The loadings on Couch's Factor Analysis of the Personality Domain are:
I (N) .07 –; II (UP) .01 –; III (UN) .07 –; IV (PF) .24; V (B) .41.

    The main loading on V indicates B. The loading on IV indicates
PF, a contrary direction. It is not clear why the direction was not UB,
which would have been more in line with intuitive expectations. One
wonders what this self-description test really measures. Perhaps it is the
fantasy of vigorous activity, related to ascensionism in fantasy rather than
actual overt behavior. Since the indication of B is relatively strong, this is
accepted as the summary, but with little confidence.

Warm (probably better called Sociable)

    Does he have a high score on Cattell's 16 PF test called
Warm? If *yes*, then expect   UPF

    This is Cattell's Scale A, also called Sociable. The opposite end is
called Aloof and Cold, or sometimes Schizothymic. As members rate each
other the term Warm is associated with UPB rather than UPF (see
Warm and Personal). It is not at all clear why this scale should be said to
measure the trait "Warm." Possibly the title is a misnomer. Probably the
term "Sociable," or "socially able" is more appropriate.

    The evidence that this scale measures UPF is only indirect. Its
loadings on Couch's Factor Analysis of the Personality Domain are:
I (N) .03; II (UP) .45; III (UN) .23; IV (PF) .03; V (B) .26 –.

    The main loading is on II, which indicates UP. The secondary
loading is on V reversed, which indicates F. The third is on III, which
indicates UN. The summary direction of these three indicators is UF.
Since the loading on II however, is considerably higher than on III, and
the P direction is nearly always a component in ratings of observers and
group members, the summary direction UPF is adopted.

Warm and Personal

(a)   Do observers rate him high on being Warm and Personal? If *yes*, then expect   UPB

(b)   Do group members rate him high on being Warm and
Personal? If *yes*, then expect   UPB

(c)   Does he rate himself high on being Warm and Personal? If *yes*, then expect   UP

(d) Does he guess others will rate him high on being Warm and Personal? If *yes,* then expect — UPB

(e) Does he tend to rate others high on being Warm and Personal? If *yes,* then expect — U

(f) Does he make others feel he rates them high on being Warm and Personal? If *yes,* then expect — PB

The evidence on these is direct, from Couch's Interdomain Factor Analysis. The loadings are:

	I (U)	*II (P)*	*III (F)*	*Summary*
(a)	.45	.45	.30—	UPB
(b)	.25	.65	.23—	UPB
(c)	.23	.31	.01	UP
(d)	.39	.17	.17—	UPB
(e)	.21	.14	.00	U
(f)	.06—	.31	.26—	PB

The question was phrased: "To what extent did each of the members show emotional warmth?"

0 = "He seemed very cold and impersonal in the way he acted."
7 = "He seemed very warm and personal in the way he acted."

Withholding of Cooperation

(a) Does he make value-statements advocating Withholding of Cooperation? If *yes,* then expect — DB

(b) Do others address value-statements to him advocating Withholding of Cooperation to him? If *yes,* then expect — DF

(c) Does he agree with value-statements of others addressed to him advocating Withholding of Cooperation? If *yes,* then expect — NB

Evidence concerning these variables is indirect, inferential, and weak. For a description of the nature of the evidence, see the Preliminary Note to this Appendix.

Appendix 2

Logical Chart:
Correlations of Directions
with Each Other

In using the present system one should be aware that certain inaccuracies are introduced, inevitably, in replacing the mathematical model of factor analysis with a verbal model consisting of a limited number of classes. In spite of the appearance of precision and order, the classes or types are not equally broad, and hence not all really equidistant from each other. The decision as to how many classes to put into a system like the present one is a matter of judgment: more classes give more precision, as one goes in the direction of continuous quantitative measurement, but to go very far in this direction puts a heavy strain on memory and intuitive understanding. The present scheme in its practical form is categorical rather than quantitative, hence it is easier to handle intuitively.

The Piersonian coefficient of correlation, upon which the factor analyses underlying the present system are based, is a finely graduated quantitative measure (156). The verbal system reduces an elegant measure ranging smoothly from plus 1.00 through zero to minus 1.00 to a crude and ill-defined set of classes—simply identical, positive correlation, zero correlation, negative correlation, and opposite. The reason for accepting less precision is the desire for a model simple enough to be operated verbally and intuitively.

One can see the problems most clearly by laying out all the points representing directions on the surface of a ball which represents the spherical space. By this demonstration one can immediately see that not all directions are equidistant from each other. There is no way to make them so and still retain the naming and locating procedure that we desire for common-sense operation. A certain amount of distortion has been accepted for the sake of verbal simplicity. The singly-named directions are all equidistant from each other. The doubly-named directions are each equidistant from two singly-named directions, at an angle of 45 degrees from each. There are six triply-named directions, and all of these lie within an angle of 45 degrees or a little more from the surrounding singly-named directions. So far this is accurate enough. But the triply-named directions are not uncorrelated with each other, as we should like (at an angle of 90 degrees, or a right angle). Each one is positively correlated to some degree with each of three others, and negatively correlated to some degree with each of three additional others. The correlations are low, and I have made the judgment to treat them as zero, for the sake of simplicity and easier practical application.

Consider, for example, the direction UPF, a triply-named direction. One may discover that the direction UNF is positively correlated with UPF to a low degree, being similar to it on two directional components (U and F), and different from it on one (N versus P). Similarly, the direction DPF is positively correlated with UPF to a low degree, being similar to it on two directional components (P and F), and different from it on one (D versus U). For purposes of the present conceptual scheme in its common-sense verbal form, the logical chart states that each of these directions, UNF, DPF, as well as UPB, is zero correlated to the reference direction, UPF. Then, as a reminder that this is not really accurate, a small plus sign in parentheses—(+)—is placed after the designation zero. This sign indicates that a small positive correlation has been ignored for the sake of simplicity in the verbal model. The logical chart also indicates the other instances where a small negative correlation is ignored for the sake of simplicity. These are indicated by the sign (−).

In practical application it seems better to declare small correlations to be zero. The inaccuracies introduced by this choice are sometimes apparent, however, in reading the descriptions of the types. In general, the triply-named types seem more coherent and have fewer conflicting traits specified by naming the neighboring types than do the single- and doubly-named types. The doubly-named types are somewhat more liable to contradictions, whereas the singly-named types sometimes seem to be uncomfortably broad, and are quite liable to internal contradictions.

The list of correlations of a given direction with each of the twenty-seven directions, including itself, may be called the *type pattern* for that group role type. It may be most conveniently used for generating predictions, as described in Chapter 1, page 14.

Logical Chart

CORRELATION OF EACH DIRECTION WITH EACH OTHER:
TYPE PATTERN OF EACH DIRECTION

Key: *Ident* = Identical   Zero = Zero correlation
       Oppos = Opposite   (+) = A small positive correlation is ignored
       Plus   = Positive correlation   (−) = A small negative correlation is ignored
       Minus = Negative correlation

U: Upward:

U *Ident*	P Zero	DP Minus
UP Plus	PF Zero	DPF Minus
UPF Plus	F Zero	DF Minus
UF Plus	NF Zero	DNF Minus
UNF Plus	N Zero	DN Minus
UN Plus	NB Zero	DNB Minus
UNB Plus	B Zero	DB Minus
UB Plus	PB Zero	DPB Minus
UPB Plus		D *Oppos*

UP: Upward-Positive:

U Plus	P Plus	DP Zero
UP *Ident*	PF Plus	DPF Zero
UPF Plus	F Zero	DF Minus
UF Plus	NF Minus	DNF Minus
UNF Zero	N Minus	DN *Oppos*
UN Zero	NB Minus	DNB Minus
UNB Zero	B Zero	DB Minus
UB Plus	PB Plus	DPB Zero
UPB Plus		D Minus

UPF: Upward-Positive-Forward:

U Plus	P Plus	DP Zero
UP Plus	PF Plus	DPF Zero (+)
UPF *Ident*	F Plus	DF Zero
UF Plus	NF Zero	DNF Zero (−)
UNF Zero (+)	N Minus	DN Minus
UN Zero	NB Minus	DNB *Oppos*
UNB Zero (−)	B Minus	DB Minus
UB Zero	PB Zero	DPB Zero (−)
UPB Zero (+)		D Minus

UF: Upward-Forward:

U Plus	P Zero	DP Minus
UP Plus	PF Plus	DPF Zero
UPF Plus	F Plus	DF Zero
UF *Ident*	NF Plus	DNF Zero
UNF Plus	N Zero	DN Minus
UN Plus	NB Minus	DNB Minus
UNB Zero	B Minus	DB *Oppos*
UB Zero	PB Minus	DPB Minus
UPB Zero		D Minus

UNF: Upward-Negative-Forward:

U Plus	P Minus	DP Minus
UP Zero	PF Zero	DPF Zero (−)
UPF Zero (+)	F Plus	DF Zero
UF Plus	NF Plus	DNF Zero (+)
UNF *Ident*	N Plus	DN Zero
UN Plus	NB Zero	DNB Zero (−)
UNB Zero (+)	B Minus	DB Minus
UB Zero	PB Minus	DPB *Oppos*
UPB Zero (−)		D Minus

UN: Upward-Negative:

U Plus	P Minus	DP *Oppos*
UP Zero	PF Minus	DPF Minus
UPF Zero	F Zero	DF Minus
UF Plus	NF Plus	DNF Zero
UNF Plus	N Plus	DN Zero
UN *Ident*	NB Plus	DNB Zero
UNB Plus	B Zero	DB Minus
UB Plus	PB Minus	DPB Minus
UPB Zero		D Minus

UNB: Upward-Negative-Backward:

U Plus	P Minus	DP Minus
UP Zero	PF Minus	DPF *Oppos*
UPF Zero (−)	F Minus	DF Minus
UF Zero	NF Zero	DNF Zero (−)
UNF Zero (+)	N Plus	DN Zero
UN Plus	NB Plus	DNB Zero (+)
UNB *Ident*	B Plus	DB Zero
UB Plus	PB Zero	DPB Zero (−)
UPB Zero (+)		D Minus

UB: Upward-Backward:

U Plus	P Zero	DP Minus
UP Plus	PF Minus	DPF Minus
UPF Zero	F Minus	DF *Oppos*
UF Zero	NF Minus	DNF Minus
UNF Zero	N Zero	DN Minus
UN Plus	NB Plus	DNB Zero
UNB Plus	B Plus	DB Zero
UB *Ident*	PB Plus	DPB Zero
UPB Plus		D Minus

UPB: Upward-Positive-Backward:

U Plus	P Plus	DP Zero
UP Plus	PF Zero	DPF Zero (−)
UPF Zero (+)	F Minus	DF Minus
UF Zero	NF Minus	DNF *Oppos*
UNF Zero (−)	N Minus	DN Minus
UN Zero	NB Zero	DNB Zero(−)
UNB Zero (+)	B Plus	DB Zero
UB Plus	PB Plus	DPB Zero (+)
UPB *Ident*		D Minus

P: Positive:

U Zero	P *Ident*	DP Plus
UP Plus	PF Plus	DPF Plus
UPF Plus	F Zero	DF Zero
UF Zero	NF Minus	DNF Minus
UNF Minus	N *Oppos*	DN Minus
UN Minus	NB Minus	DNB Minus
UNB Minus	B Zero	DB Zero
UB Zero	PB Plus	DPB Plus
UPB Plus		D Zero

PF: Positive-Forward:

U Zero	P Plus	DP Plus
UP Plus	PF *Ident*	DPF Plus
UPF Plus	F Plus	DF Plus
UF Plus	NF Zero	DNF Zero
UNF Zero	N Minus	DN Minus
UN Minus	NB *Oppos*	DNB Minus
UNB Minus	B Minus	DB Minus
UB Minus	PB Zero	DPB Zero
UPB Zero		D Zero

F: Forward:

U Zero	P Zero	DP Zero
UP Zero	PF Plus	DPF Plus
UPF Plus	F *Ident*	DF Plus
UF Plus	NF Plus	DNF Plus
UNF Plus	N Zero	DN Zero
UN Zero	NB Minus	DNB Minus
UNB Minus	B *Oppos*	DB Minus
UB Minus	PB Minus	DPB Minus
UPB Minus		D Zero

NF: Negative-Forward:

U Zero	P Minus	DP Minus
UP Minus	PF Zero	DPF Zero
UPF Zero	F Plus	DF Plus
UF Plus	NF *Ident*	DNF Plus
UNF Plus	N Plus	DN Plus
UN Plus	NB Zero	DNB Zero
UNB Zero	B Minus	DB Minus
UB Minus	PB *Oppos*	DPB Minus
UPB Minus		D Zero

N: Negative:

U Zero	P *Oppos*	DP Minus
UP Minus	PF Minus	DPF Minus
UPF Minus	F Zero	DF Zero
UF Zero	NF Plus	DNF Plus
UNF Plus	N *Ident*	DN Plus
UN Plus	NB Plus	DNB Plus
UNB Plus	B Zero	DB Zero
UB Zero	PB Minus	DPB Minus
UPB Minus		D Zero

NB: Negative-Backward:

U Zero	P Minus	DP Minus
UP Minus	PF *Oppos*	DPF Minus
UPF Minus	F Minus	DF Minus
UF Minus	NF Zero	DNF Zero
UNF Zero	N Plus	DN Plus
UN Plus	NB *Ident*	DNB Plus
UNB Plus	B Plus	DB Plus
UB Plus	PB Zero	DPB Zero
UPB Zero		D Zero

B: Backward:

U Zero	P Zero	DP Zero
UP Zero	PF Minus	DPF Minus
UPF Minus	F *Oppos*	DF Minus
UF Minus	NF Minus	DNF Minus
UNF Minus	N Zero	DN Zero
UN Zero	NB Plus	DNB Plus
UNB Plus	B *Ident*	DB Plus
UB Plus	PB Plus	DPB Plus
UPB Plus		D Zero

PB: Positive-Backward:

U Zero	P Plus	DP Plus
UP Plus	PF Zero	DPF Zero
UPF Zero	F Minus	DF Minus
UF Minus	NF *Oppos*	DNF Minus
UNF Minus	N Minus	DN Minus
UN Minus	NB Zero	DNB Zero
UNB Zero	B Plus	DB Plus
UB Plus	PB *Ident*	DPB Plus
UPB Plus		D Zero

DP: Downward-Positive:

U Minus	P Plus	DP *Ident*
UP Zero	PF Plus	DPF Plus
UPF Zero	F Zero	DF Plus
UF Minus	NF Minus	DNF Zero
UNF Minus	N Minus	DN Zero
UN *Oppos*	NB Minus	DNB Zero
UNB Minus	B Zero	DB Plus
UB Minus	PB Plus	DPB Plus
UPB Zero		D Plus

DPF: Downward-Positive-Forward:

U Minus	P Plus	DP Plus
UP Zero	PF Plus	DPF *Ident*
UPF Zero (+)	F Plus	DF Plus
UF Zero	NF Zero	DNF Zero (+)
UNF Zero (−)	N Minus	DN Zero
UN Minus	NB Minus	DNB Zero (−)
UNB *Oppos*	B Minus	DB Zero
UB Minus	PB Zero	DPB Zero (+)
UPB Zero (−)		D Plus

DF: Downward-Forward:

U Minus	P Zero	DP Plus
UP Minus	PF Plus	DPF Plus
UPF Zero	F Plus	DF *Ident*
UF Zero	NF Plus	DNF Plus
UNF Zero	N Zero	DN Plus
UN Minus	NB Minus	DNB Zero
UNB Minus	B Minus	DB Zero
UB *Oppos*	PB Minus	DPB Zero
UPB Minus		D Plus

DNF: Downward-Negative-Forward:

U Minus	P Minus	DP Zero
UP Minus	PF Zero	DPF Zero (+)
UPF Zero (−)	F Plus	DF Plus
UF Zero	NF Plus	DNF *Ident*
UNF Zero (+)	N Plus	DN Plus
UN Zero	NB Zero	DNB Zero (+)
UNB Zero (−)	B Minus	DB Zero
UB Minus	PB Minus	DPB Zero (−)
UPB *Oppos*		D Plus

DN: Downward-Negative:

U Minus	P Minus	DP Zero
UP *Oppos*	PF Minus	DPF Zero
UPF Minus	F Zero	DF Plus
UF Minus	NF Plus	DNF Plus
UNF Zero	N Plus	DN *Ident*
UN Zero	NB Plus	DNB Plus
UNB Zero	B Zero	DB Plus
UB Minus	PB Minus	DPB Zero
UPB Minus		D Plus

DNB: Downward-Negative-Backward:

U Minus	P Minus	DP Zero
UP Minus	PF Minus	DPF Zero (−)
UPF *Oppos*	F Minus	DF Zero
UF Minus	NF Zero	DNF Zero (+)
UNF Zero (−)	N Plus	DN Plus
UN Zero	NB Plus	DNB *Ident*
UNB Zero (+)	B Plus	DB Plus
UB Zero	PB Zero	DPB Zero (+)
UPB Zero (−)		D Plus

DB: Downward-Backward:

U Minus	P Zero	DP Plus
UP Minus	PF Minus	DPF Zero
UPF Minus	F Minus	DF Zero
UF *Oppos*	NF Minus	DNF Zero
UNF Minus	N Zero	DN Plus
UN Minus	NB Plus	DNB Plus
UNB Zero	B Plus	DB *Ident*
UB Zero	PB Plus	DPB Plus
UPB Zero		D Plus

DPB: Downward-Positive-Backward:

U Minus	P Plus	DP Plus
UP Zero	PF Zero	DPF Zero (+)
UPF Zero (−)	F Minus	DF Zero
UF Minus	NF Minus	DNF Zero (−)
UNF *Oppos*	N Minus	DN Zero
UN Minus	NB Zero	DNB Zero (+)
UNB Zero (−)	B Plus	DB Plus
UB Zero	PB Plus	DPB *Ident*
UPB Zero (+)		D Plus

D: Downward:

U *Oppos*	P Zero	DP Plus
UP Minus	PF Zero	DPF Plus
UPF Minus	F Zero	DF Plus
UF Minus	NF Zero	DNF Plus
UNF Minus	N Zero	DN Plus
UN Minus	NB Zero	DNB Plus
UNB Minus	B Zero	DB Plus
UB Minus	PB Zero	DPB Plus
UPB Minus		D *Ident*

Appendix 3

Average Interaction Matrices in Percentages for Groups Sizes Two to Eight

Groups of Size 2

Number of groups in sample = 41
Number of acts in sample = 12,765

FROM	TO 1	TO 2	SUM TO I	SUM TO O	TOTAL INIT.
1	—	57.3	57.3	—	57.3
2	42.7	—	42.7	—	42.7
SUM REC.	42.7	57.3	100.0	—	100.0

Groups of Size 3

Number of groups in sample = 26
Number of acts in sample = 9304

FROM	TO 1	TO 2	TO 3	SUM TO I	SUM TO O	TOTAL INIT.
1	—	15.3	7.1	22.4	22.0	44.4
2	15.6	—	5.4	21.0	11.7	32.7
3	7.9	5.7	—	13.6	9.3	22.9
SUM REC.	23.5	21.0	12.5	57.0	43.0	100.0

Groups of Size 4

Number of groups in sample = 89
Number of acts in sample = 58,218

FROM	TO				SUM TO I	SUM TO O	TOTAL INIT.
	1	2	3	4			
1	—	8.3	6.5	3.6	18.4	13.8	32.2
2	10.3	—	4.4	3.2	17.9	11.0	28.9
3	8.0	5.2	—	2.2	15.4	7.4	22.8
4	4.2	3.5	2.8	—	10.5	5.6	16.1
SUM REC.	22.5	17.0	13.7	9.0	62.2	37.8	100.0

Groups of Size 5

Number of groups in sample = 9
Number of acts in sample = 10,714

FROM	TO					SUM TO I	SUM TO O	TOTAL INIT.
	1	2	3	4	5			
1	—	5.0	4.0	3.9	1.9	14.8	32.1	46.9
2	11.6	—	2.3	2.1	.5	16.5	5.4	21.9
3	8.4	1.8	—	.7	.5	11.4	4.0	15.4
4	5.7	1.3	.4	—	.3	7.7	2.6	10.3
5	2.7	.6	.5	.4	—	4.2	1.3	5.5
SUM REC.	28.4	8.7	7.2	7.1	3.2	54.6	45.4	100.0

Groups of Size 6

Number of groups in sample = 18
Number of acts in sample = 21,311

FROM			TO				SUM TO I	SUM TO O	TOTAL INIT.
	1	2	3	4	5	6			
1	—	5.8	4.5	2.6	2.1	1.5	16.5	26.6	43.1
2	8.2	—	2.1	1.5	.9	.5	13.2	5.6	18.8
3	6.4	2.0	—	1.3	.6	.3	10.6	3.6	14.2
4	4.5	1.5	1.2	—	.4	.2	7.8	3.2	11.0
5	3.1	1.1	.7	.4	—	.1	5.4	2.1	7.5
6	2.2	.6	.5	.3	.1	—	3.7	1.7	5.4
SUM REC.	24.4	11.0	9.0	6.1	4.1	2.6	57.2	42.8	100.0

Groups of Size 7

Number of groups in sample = 15
Number of acts in sample = 22,044

FROM				TO				SUM TO I	SUM TO O	TOTAL INIT.
	1	2	3	4	5	6	7			
1	—	4.2	2.8	2.5	1.8	1.0	.8	13.1	30.0	43.1
2	6.4	—	1.8	1.0	1.0	.5	.4	11.1	4.1	15.2
3	4.6	1.6	—	.9	.6	.5	.2	8.4	3.5	11.9
4	3.6	1.0	.9	—	.7	.4	.2	6.8	3.1	9.9
5	3.0	1.2	.7	.6	—	.4	.2	6.1	2.5	8.6
6	2.0	.6	.5	.3	.5	—	.2	4.1	2.2	6.3
7	1.6	.6	.4	.3	.3	.2	—	3.4	1.6	5.0
SUM REC.	21.2	9.2	7.1	5.6	4.9	3.0	2.0	53.0	47.0	100.0

Groups of Size 8

Number of groups in sample = 10
Number of acts in sample = 12,830

FROM				TO					SUM	SUM	TOTAL
	1	2	3	4	5	6	7	8	TO I	TO O	INIT.
1	—	3.6	3.5	2.3	1.7	1.0	.8	.7	13.6	26.2	39.8
2	8.1	—	1.2	1.3	.8	.4	.3	.4	12.5	4.1	16.6
3	5.9	.8	—	.5	.6	.5	.2	.1	8.6	4.1	12.7
4	4.1	1.0	.8	—	.4	.3	.2	.0	6.8	3.0	9.8
5	3.8	.9	.5	.5	—	.5	.2	.0	6.4	2.2	8.6
6	1.8	.3	.6	.1	.4	—	.1	.0	3.3	2.2	5.5
7	1.1	.3	.3	.2	.2	.2	—	.0	2.3	2.0	4.3
8	.8	.2	.1	.0	.0	.0	.0	—	1.1	1.6	2.7
SUM REC.	25.6	7.1	7.0	4.9	4.1	2.9	1.8	1.2	54.6	45.4	100.0

Appendix 4

Revision of
Interaction Process Analysis

For the benefit of those readers who are familiar with my earlier book, *Interaction Process Analysis, A Method for the Study of Small Groups*[1] it may be useful to indicate the changes in the method to keep the continuity as complete as possible.

The changes have all been concerned with the naming and content of categories. The nature of the unit, the conventions for scoring who speaks to whom, and the use of one and only one category per act are identical with the original method.

A number of studies have used the method. This appendix will be organized around a discussion of the way in which the working norms for the present revision were derived from the results of the previous studies. The current working norms are given in Chapter 6.

The most complete review of studies using Interaction Process Analysis is given in an article by Paul Hare and myself, entitled, "Diagnostic Use of the Interaction Profile" (35). Twenty-one different studies are briefly described in this article, and a summary profile of interaction rates is given for each one. The twenty-one studies may be regarded as a sample of the kinds of studies investigators may wish to make with the method, hence the data they present give a valuable picture of the range of variation one may expect to find in rates. One summary profile only was taken from each study, to represent as well as possible the range of vari-

---

[1]Now out of print. The book was once reprinted in 1951. The copyright is now retained by the author, and reproduction rights are given to University Microfilms, Ann Arbor, Michigan, from whom Xerox copies may be obtained.

ation. All the raw scores in a given study were added together into one profile, and a percentage profile was then computed from this. Differences internal to a given study were thus canceled out. The profile for each study represented rather the conditions that were distinctive of the total study—such conditions as the type of task or experimental condition set up or selected by the investigator, the age and sex of the subjects, and the like. Differences between investigators in their employment of the scoring system were also represented. The population of studies may be considered to represent the range of variations due to observers as well as other conditions.

One aim of taking only one summary profile per study was to help assure that the range of variation would be well represented, another was to make it more probable that one could identify the reasons for differences between the profiles. As the article shows, this aim seems to have been well achieved. One of the disadvantages of adding all the raw scores together before computing the percentage profile for a given study is that top participators are represented more strongly than low participators in all studies. This does not hurt much in the comparison of studies, perhaps, but it does impair the relevance of the norms somewhat for the examination of the profiles of single individuals. The impairment, however, seems in practice not to be too serious.

Table 1 shows the range of variation of the middle third, that is, the middle seven cases, of the total twenty-one cases. The present book employs a typology of twenty-seven types, a result of breaking each of three dimensions into three classes of magnitude—high, medium, and low. Since we assume that everyone in the total population of persons can be classified into one of the types, we might like to define the types so that the number of persons in each type would be about equal. For any measured trait of members of the population, we should like to know the cutting points that would cut the population into an upper third, a middle third, and a lower third. In the present case we have a sample of the relevant population, and our best estimate of such cutting points is simply to divide our sample into three equal parts and to specify the rates at those points. On Table 1, the cutting points so obtained are shown; for example, the table shows that for the category Agrees, the middle seven cases fall between the rates of 8.0 and 13.6 inclusive. A rate of 7.9 or lower is thus considered low, and a rate of 13.7 or higher is thus considered high. For further information the table shows that the median rate, the rate for the eleventh case is 9.5.

For our present purpose it is more helpful to know the median rate and that the medium range contains a third of the cases, than it is to know the mean rate and the cutting points 1 and 2 standard deviations above the mean, which were given in the source article. The mean for the low

Table 1   Empirical Results of Twenty-One Different Studies*
Using the Original Categories for
Interaction Process Analysis**
Interaction Initiated

Category of Acts Initiated	Medium Range	Median Rate
1. Shows Solidarity	2.0 – 3.3	2.3
2. Shows Tension Release	5.4 – 7.4	6.2
3. Agrees	8.0–13.6	9.5
4. Gives Suggestion	3.0 – 7.0	3.7
5. Gives Opinion	19.9–27.2	22.8
6. Gives Orientation	21.1–33.7	29.0
7. Asks for Orientation	4.0 – 7.2	5.1
8. Asks for Opinion	2.0 – 3.9	2.2
9. Asks for Suggestion	.3 – .9	.4
10. Disagrees	3.1 – 5.3	4.4
11. Shows Tension	1.8 – 3.0	2.2
12. Shows Antagonism	.6 – 2.4	1.6

Note: Inferred Directional Indicators are not shown, since the table is meant to report data, but if the reader wishes to supply them he probably can not do much better than to assume they are the same as the corresponding categories in the revised set, even though there have been some changes in definition. See Table 6.1, chapter 6.

*For each category the population of Twenty-one cases is divided into thirds: the seven cases (about) which contribute the highest rate; the seven in the middle range; and the seven contributing the lowest rate. The *medium range* shown, (the boundary numbers included), contains the middle seven cases. The *median rate* is the actual rate of the eleventh case.

**Source: Bales and Hare (35)

rates is deceptively high, since it is much affected by cases that are extremely far removed to the high ends of the distributions. The distributions for all of the categories, since they are distributions of percentage rates, are heavily skewed to the right; that is, they are constricted as they move down toward zero, but they may have a number of rates that go unsymmetrically quite high. The median tends to give a better picture of the spot where many cases will be found. The standard deviation is similarly distorted as a measure. The medium range gives us more exactly what we want, without distortion. The original article, however, does give the mean and standard deviation for each category, somewhat corrected by an appropriate transformation.

In preparing the division of the sample rates for a given category into thirds for the present book, the twenty-one rates were first arranged into rank order. They were then plotted on square-root graph paper, a transformation that tends to make the distribution more normal, since it expands the gaps between the low rates and compresses gaps between the higher rates. The distribution was then inspected for symmetry, particularly to correct for the effect of occasional highly deviant rates. The division into thirds was accomplished without difficulty in most cases. In the case of ties, a decision had to be made as to which third should be inflated and which one should be slighted. In other cases, a large gap in the distribution divided one third from the next, and it was necessary to decide where, within the gap, the division point should be located. This point was located artistically in such a way as to make the most symmetrical division into thirds. Inspection of the original studies in terms of the cutting points shown on the table indicates that the intuitive fit is excellent. What the table indicates as a high rate seems like a high rate to me on the basis of empirical experience, and it is usually understandable on the basis of the task or other conditions of the particular study. Rates identified on the table as low, similarly seem low to me on the basis of experience, and seem to have a plausible explanation in the conditions. The intuitive fit seems as good or better than that obtained using the more extreme cutting points suggested in the source article.

CHANGES IN THE CATEGORIES

It will be noted in Table 1 that the names of the categories are slightly different from those now assigned. Original category 1 is called Shows Solidarity. Revised category 1 is called instead Seems Friendly. There are several reasons for the change. As Table 1 shows, category 1 regularly has relatively low rates. In the revision it was desired to find ways of increasing the frequency of the lowest rates, in the hope of increasing their reliability. The word "seems" was chosen in the hope that it would encourage the scorer to use the category for more minor signs of positive social feeling than he would feel necessary for the old classification. The word "friendly" is a more common-sense word also, which I feel to be an advantage. It fits as well for the more submissive types of positive acts as for the more ascendant. The word "solidarity" is a more technical term, having a connotation of binding social norms, thus a forward connotation in the directional system, which it is desirable to avoid for a concept meant to designate all positive types of action. The word "friendly" has the right connotation. It combines equally well, conceptually, with all the other directions that may be fused with it. Moreover, it is a mild word which can be used to characterize minimal social signs.

A similar type of rationale holds for category 12. In the original set category 12 is called Shows Antagonism. Antagonism is a rather strong word implying a negative reaction of some strength or ascendance. One needs a rather forceful act before one feels right about applying it. The revised title, Seems Unfriendly overcomes this objection, hopefully. It is mild in connotation, does not imply ascendance more than submissiveness, and is neither forward nor backward in connotation. It is appropriate for all types of negative social behavior. In both the positive and negative direction the word "seems" puts the emphasis on the reaction of the scorer; it sounds more tentative and less objective. Category 12 ordinarily had one of the lowest rates in the original set. It is hoped that the change in the title will help in capturing a few more scores for this category.

One additional change may help to increase the rates for both categories 1 and 12. This change is the definition of these types in terms of subtypes, clearly derived from the directional space. Each category includes all the subtypes on its own side of the space. There are nine such subtypes on each side. For example, Seems Friendly now clearly, by definition, includes both an ascendant type UP, and a submissive type DP, a forward type PF, and a backward type PB, and four further fusions—UPF, DPF, UPB, and DPB. If the reader will check the descriptions under each of these types in Chapter 6, he will see the similarities and, at the same time, realize what a tremendous variety of acts are included. This is a way of saying that the idea Seems Friendly is quite an abstract idea in spite of its common-sense solid feeling. Exactly parallel comments could be made about the variety of subtypes included under the common sense idea Seems Unfriendly. To recognize clearly the variety included may make it easier for the scorer to include acts in either of these categories that may have seemed too marginal before.

The new priority system should be mentioned at this point. In the original method the scorer was instructed always to give priority to categories farthest removed from the middle of the set. This gives categories 1 and 12 the highest priorities. Practically, however, the stated priority was not enough really to increase the rates in these categories very much. Probably part of the reason was that the titles were too strong, and also they were not equally appropriate for all subtypes. Probably also it was partly because there were no good ways of restricting the meanings of the huge general-purpose categories, Gives Opinion and Gives Information. The directional system provides the concepts for taking acts from these categories and placing them in other more definitive ones. The revised priority system gives the highest priorities to categories 2 and 11, rather than 1 and 12. However, it is believed that Seems Friendly and

Seems Unfriendly will show higher rates than the original categories did, even though they have yielded top priority to categories 2 and 11.

In the revised set category 2 is called Dramatizes. There are several reasons for this change. In the original category both joking and laughing were included. By accident it was discovered that joking measures the upward-backward direction. The accident occurred in the following way: In an attempt to increase category 1 in the major study, it was decided to classify jokes in Shows Solidarity, and to leave laughs in category 2, Shows Tension Release. On analysis of the data it was discovered that the intended direction of Shows Solidarity, (P), had been entirely swamped; the category now actually measured UB. In the same analysis it was discovered that Shows Tension Release, made up mainly by laughs, actually measured in the same direction as Shows Tension, namely DB. It was originally supposed that it measured in the same direction as jokes as an indicator of "tension release." It turns out to be more dependably a sign of tension than a means of tension release. Following the actual findings, then, laughs were transferred in the revised set to category 11, Shows Tension, and jokes were transferred back to category 2.

The question then arises as to the best title for category 2. With laughs no longer scored there, it seemed confusing to retain a title for category 2 that suggested laughing (Shows Tension Release). The title might have been changed to Jokes, but this seemed too specific—joking is not a concept broad or generic enough to contain all of the acts that now appear to have a UB significance. In making the final decisions as to titles, the concept of the three-dimensional evaluative space was crucial. The various factor analyses and their synthesis into the three-dimensional space made it possible to consider all of the types of action, personality traits, value-statements, interpersonal perceptions, and so on, which were backward anywhere in the space, and those that were located in the forward part of the space. After consideration of many alternatives and a good deal of speculative theorizing, I decided that the most general concept of the backward direction was one which placed emphasis upon the significance of *fantasy as a formative process* in the guidance and release of drives, as contrasted to the significance of *values or social norms as a formative influence.*

Experience in the observation of groups had many times indicated to me the desirability of a category to pick up acts with double meaning—symbolic meaning, as we sometimes vaguely say. Groups in the midst of quarrels, or in situations of tension or conflict, often seem to "go off on a tangent" in the discussion of some apparently trivial matter, with repetition of certain words or phrases. The observer trained to listen with "the third ear," as the psychoanalyst or experienced depth psychologist does, easily picks up these words or phrases as "double talk" consisting of unconscious or at least unacknowledged double references to persons, things, or emotions present in the group, as discussed in Chapter 7. The multiple levels of meaning seem to be the essential thing about the "symbols" used. Jokes are prime examples, but so are slips of the tongue, dreams, waking fantasies, stories which really entertain, and so on. This is the area of images usually known as "Freudian symbols," and quite rightly so, since Freud first brought them into full prominence and generality as characteristics of mental processes. Unfortunately the term "Freudian symbol" has by now been so oversimplified and vulgarized in its connotation that it is too specific to use. The term "fantasy" is the best term I can find that has the required connotation, but unfortunately it does not pick up all of the remarks which really seem often to carry double meanings. A broader term, which is explained in Chapter 7, was finally adopted. The term "dramatizes," as explained there, is meant to include all of those cases where one senses there may be significant double meanings involved, as well as jokes. Theoretically it does not require a connotation of ascendance for its definition (though it measures UB). It is expected to measure ascendance because, practically speaking, most of the acts entered in the category will be jokes, which do seem to go with ascendance.

Thus, though category 2 in the revised system will no longer contain laughs, it will hopefully contain a substantial number of acts that would otherwise be classified as Gives Information, Gives Opinion, or Gives Suggestion. The priority system requires the observer, above all, to listen with the third ear and identify as many acts as Dramatizes as he possibly can. This category and its downward counterpart, Shows Tension, Laughs, have priority over all other categories and are chosen whenever there is the slightest indication one can do so. For this reason category 2 is expected to gain acts that will make up for the laughs it loses.

Below I shall attempt to estimate the quantitative effect of these changes on the rates in various categories. For the moment it is worth emphasizing that the changes have been made in order to increase the sensitivity of the interaction categories to feelings and underlying emotional currents in the group process. It may be that by so doing specific categories are made less reliable, though this is not certain. Even so, I believe that the gain is worth the price, since our aim is understanding. There are plenty of opportunities in the processes of interpretation, re-observation, and so on, to correct false impressions. Furthermore, most users will be interested in the training value of the method—the way in which learning to score increases one's sensitivity to certain aspects of process which are not consciously formulated. It is hoped that placing a first priority upon acts of dramatizing, joking, showing tension, and laughing, as well as a high priority upon signs of seeming friendly and seeming unfriendly, will train the observer to recognize and take account of these things in situations where he is not technically taking down scores on interaction.

Category 3, Agrees, has not been changed in any way in the revision, nor has Category 10, Disagrees. Both categories seem to work well; they have substantial rates and measure in the expected directions. It is true that the category Agrees was expected to measure simply in the positive direction, whereas experience shows it to measure forward as well as positive. The recognition of its particularly intimate function in the formation of norms, however, has made this seem completely reasonable, and it has been accepted where it is. No changes in the revision are such as to lead one to expect any changes in the normal rates of Agrees or Disagrees.

Categories 4 and 9 in the revised set, Gives Suggestion and Asks for Suggestion, have the same names as in the original set, but have been broadened in meaning. They are now explicitly defined to classify evidences of ascendance and submissiveness on the task-oriented front, and they are the chosen way of recording these evidences, with a priority of third place. In the original set of categories there was an attempt to avoid making inferences about ascendance and submissiveness as such, with the assumption that if the observer recorded the functional significance of what the member did for the group (in the present case, the task functions), one would later be able to infer status. It turned out that gross amount of participation was an excellent indicator of attempts to gain status or power. Perhaps no better indicator should be sought, but in the large study on which the present work is based, it also turned out that Giving Suggestion was not much correlated with direction F.[2] I felt that the definition needed improving. Consequently I reworked the category to pick up any task-oriented acts to which the element of personal ascendance was added. The subtitle might now be: "takes the lead, tries to assume leadership on the task." It is expected that some acts formerly classified as Gives Opinion will now be classified as Gives Suggestion. Some of the acts of neutral leadership formerly classified as Gives Orientation will now be classified as Gives Suggestion. The definitions of these acts have been removed from category 6 and consolidated with category 4. This is part of the reason for changing the title of category 6 from the original Gives Orientation to the revised simpler title, Gives Information.

[2] See the note to Suggestion, Gives, and Conformity, Authoritarian, in Appendix 1.

It is thus expected that the revised category 4 will pick up some scores from the original category 5, Gives Opinion, and the original category 6, Gives Orientation. It is hoped that it now has a more general social-psychological meaning, not one restricted to contributing substantive suggestions only. The old category 4 will lose a few scores to the new category 2, Dramatizes, but the new category 4 should pick up at least as many. On balance there will probably not be much change in the rate in spite of modification of the definition.

Category 9, Asks for Suggestion, has similarly been broadened in the new definitions to include all evidences of submissiveness on the task-oriented front (so long as they are neither positive nor negative). This concept was implicit in the old definition, but not explicit. The priority of the category has been increased with an admonition to the observer to try to pick up signs of submissiveness (and ascendance), and to choose a scoring that reflects these signs over one that does not (so long as higher priorities are not involved). With the broadening and clarification of the directional significance of the category, we may hope for some slight increase in rate. Its rate seems to be naturally low, however, and the increase will also surely be small.

Category 5, Gives Opinion, has not been changed in title, and is still a major work category, but many of the changes have involved carving away parts of it that will yield more desired information if scored elsewhere. It has been made directionally more precise (F), and restricted by asking observers to score its fusions with other directions in those other directions. Thus part of the original category 5 will go to Dramatizes, some to Seems Unfriendly, some to Seems Friendly, some to Gives Suggestion, and maybe even to some to Asks for Suggestion. Wishes, feelings, and the like, which were once defined as a part of category 5, have been transferred by definition to Dramatizes. As a result category 5 should now reflect mostly the attempt to reason objectively, relatively free from double meanings, wishes, desires, positive or negative feelings, and attempts to gain or avoid assuming status. This will surely reduce its rate. It should cease to be a residual or "catch-all" category to the same degree that it has been. It was a specific aim in the original set, as now, to avoid a miscellaneous category, but practically it has been difficult to avoid using category 5 in this way. This tendency is strongly discouraged in the new instructions, and explicit ways of avoiding it are provided.

Category 8, Asks for Opinion, is essentially unchanged in either concept or definition. It was something of a surprise to find that it measured in the positive direction (P), and not at all in the forward direction, but this finding is not very difficult to rationalize. In spite of the flavor of task-orientation in the title, the category is meant to be nonspecific as to *what* is being asked for. One may answer it with opinion in the sense of the new category 5, with neutral, reasoned thought, and argument, or one may answer it with an expression of wishes, feelings, desires, fantasies, which are now clearly scored in the backward direction. Since category 8 specifically leaves open the question as to whether one may wish to respond in a forward or backward direction, and specifically avoids taking either an ascendant or submissive attitude, it seems consistent that it should measure in the P direction, and this correlation is accepted as probably a true and rather general finding. Since there is no change in definition, however, and no change in priority, there is no reason to expect a change in rate. The rate is high enough as it stands, and the category, as it was originally, seems satisfactory.

Finally, category 6, Gives Information, has been changed in title. As explained above, certain leader-like acts of explanation and gentle management have been removed and placed in the revised definition of category 4, Gives Suggestion. These were among the acts which were most appropriately called "giving orientation" before, and so the original rationale for calling category 6 by that name rather than the more common-sense title Gives Information, is removed.

The original category 4 was not enough oriented to the common-sense idea of taking leadership, as distinct from the offering of substantive suggestions on the task. I now think that signs of "taking leadership" are not much more difficult to pick up than those of "seeming friendly" or "seeming unfriendly," and perhaps I am more willing to be accused of making inferences. These restrictions removed, it is possible to purify category 6, and revert to the more common-sense title, Gives Information. I would be quite willing to call Category 4 "Takes the Lead" and Category 9 "Asks Other to Take the Lead," but these titles are not really improvements over the original ones. I have retained the original ones. They are short, easy to remember, evident to common sense, and combine well with the other categories. The same argument can be made for the change from Gives Orientation to the more common-sense title, Gives Information. I believe it is desirable to stick as close to common sense as possible in providing the observer with a set of categories which he has to remember and apply rapidly.

There has been a parallel change in the title of category 7, Asks for Information. Its definition has remained unchanged. There is no reason to expect a change in rate in using the revised set of categories. It was a surprise to discover, empirically, however, that the category measured in the UP direction. I rather expected that it would measure in the submissive direction, and would have guessed it to be correlated with concern for the task—that it would measure in the DF direction. It is possible that under some conditions it will do so.

Giving Information, however, is not simply a task-correlated activity. It is rather one which exactly splits the difference between task-oriented forward movement and fantasy-oriented backward movement. A good many of the "facts" mentioned in ordinary conversation and discussion are concerned with the social aspects of the relationship, refer to conditions which arouse tension and support fantasy. If this is true, it is reasonable to expect that many questions of Asking for Information will aim to elicit these concerns from other members, as well as to elicit facts in support of task efforts. If this assumption is true, it would explain the finding that Asking for Information is, on the average, neither forward nor backward in its directional tendency. And if it is also true that the aim is often one of eliciting the concerns of other members, and their views, then it is understandable that Asking for Information should be correlated with ascendance of the socially positive type. Its directional tendency, UP, in the present study may thus be rationalized to seem possibly quite general. Since constricted people tend to be low participators and seem to prefer the safety of Giving Information rather than the more risky opinion or suggestion, it may also often be that the best way to bring them into the discussion is to Ask for Information. They are apparently more ready to give simple information than anything else.

It was not a surprise to find in the study that Giving Orientation was correlated with downward movement. This implication has appeared repeatedly in the inspection of profiles, both of individuals and of groups in various kinds of situations. It was a mild surprise, however, to discover that this category of activity was not correlated with forward movement in the direction of task accomplishment, for example with direction DF. Giving Orientation was conceived of as a task-oriented effort, primarily, although it was recognized that strongly task-oriented people often neglected it. Here again, however, reflection, and even a reading of the definition, will indicate that facts need not be facts relevant to the task of the group, narrowly considered as forward movement, but facts about all kinds of things. This was recognized in the definition—but it was a surprise to find that these other uses are about as important as the forward-oriented uses, even in rather strongly task-oriented groups.

The finding is accepted and rationalized as general for the purposes of the present diagnostic system, but it is also suspected that the directional significance of this category is more likely to change from group to group than certain others, for example, Seems Friendly or Seems Unfriendly. The same may be presumably said for Asking for Information, Asking for Opinion, Asking for Suggestion, and possibly Giving Opinion and Giving Suggestion. Particular groups may define special roles in such a way as to require any of these types of activity from persons in these roles no matter what their statuses in the group. If one knows of any such role requirement, he will of course not necessarily expect the category to have the directional significance it has in the diagnostic system.

Giving Information will be one of the two most frequent types of activity in the revised system (along with Giving Opinion), as it was in the old system. But like Giving Opinion, Giving Information has been purified and restricted in the revision by instructions to observers to carve away from it all acts which may be classified instead under Dramatizes or Jokes, Seems Friendly, Seems Negative, Gives Suggestion, or Asks for Suggestion. This set of strongly urged diversions should result in lowering its rate and increasing the rates of the other categories, which have great social-psychological interest, but tend to be low in frequency, and mild in intensity.

CHANGES IN THE EXPECTED NORMS

Unfortunately the revised set of categories has not been used extensively enough to provide new norms, but at the same time there is a pressing need for a means of deciding when a rate is high or low in order to put the new diagnostic system to use. If we wish to begin trying it now in actual practice, instead of waiting for empirical results to accumulate, we must make what is sometimes called "the inductive leap." Accordingly, I have done my best to estimate what the new norms may be by starting with the empirical results obtained with the original system, presented in Table 1 above, and then taking into account the changes in definitions of the categories and instructions to observers.

The descriptions given above imply or state what the directions of change may be for each category, but give little ground for inferring the magnitude of the changes. Here I have relied on my impressions from experience. One of these impressions is that it is less easy to change the frequency in a given category by a change in definition than one might think. Perhaps my own scoring habits work against me. But I also think the ranges shown in Table 1 are impressively narrow and indicate that in spite of major differences between situations, and perhaps considerable differences between observers, there is still a stubborn tendency for a given category of activity in social interaction to take up a certain proportion of the total acts, not much more nor much less. If this is true, it implies that the actual amount of change is likely to be related to the normal magnitude of the rate, estimated in Table 1. Large categories may show relatively large changes if the definition is changed. Small categories may show relatively small changes. I have made that assumption in the present problem.

Another consideration may help in the estimate: So long as the rule is observed that each act is classified in one and only one category, with mixed cases decided by a priority system, it will be true that the acts gained by one category must come from another category or categories. If one expects a category rate to increase he should be able to specify where the increase will come from, and so compute a decrease there. Over all categories, the gains and the losses must balance. I have applied this logic.

The results of my estimates are given as Estimated Norms for Interaction Intiated, appearing as Table 6.1 in Chapter 6. If the reader will compare the medium ranges shown there with those of Table 1 in the present Appendix, he will see that the changes are moderate, and in some cases, there is no change. I shall comment briefly on each category.

It is estimated that category 1, Seems Friendly, will show an increase of about 1 1/2 percent, which will come from the categories 4, 5, and 6, in about equal amounts from each. The estimated change is brought forward to the new medium range by adding 1 1/2 percent to the upper bound, giving 4.8 in the present case instead of the original 3.3. It is not appropriate simply to add the same amount to the lower bound, since as the normal rate increases, the absolute range between the upper and lower bound also normally increases. I have solved this problem of estimation by graphic means in the present case. Upper and lower bounds were plotted against each other on binomial probability paper, which is equivalent to applying a square root transformation to each. I empirically discovered that this procedure resulted in essentially a straight-line relation. This line then constituted a graph from which, knowing the upper bound of a rate, I could read off an expected lower bound. I applied this procedure for the location of the lower bound of the rate for each category. This means that the medium ranges in the new set of estimates have all been regularized by the application of a rationalistic assumption to the effect that the size of the medium range is related to the absolute magnitude of the upper bound. Rather than get into further complication I carried out all computations on the upper bound, and treated the lower bound as a dependent variable to be located from my empirical graph.

It is next assumed that category 2, Dramatizes, will gain from categories 4, 5, and 6, Gives Suggestion, Opinion, and Information, and that it will gain about an equal amount from each. But since category 2 has a normally higher rate than the one just discussed above (category 1), it was felt it would probably gain more. The gain was set at 1 percent from each of the three source categories. Each of these is thus expected to show losses of this magnitude. However, since the original category,

Shows Tension Release will transfer all laughs to category 11 in the revision, this loss should be taken into account. It was decided that half of the normal rate of Shows Tension Release should be considered to consist of laughs, and that consequently this half, amounting to about 3 percent should be transferred to category 11, Shows Tension. If category 2 thus gains 3 percent and loses 3 percent, it will show no net change. It was so estimated and appears on the new norms at the same rate as on the old. (It was, in fact, the plausible estimate that category 2 should transfer out about 3 percent, which was the basis for the arbitrary assumption that it would gain about 3 percent, equally distributed over categories 4, 5, and 6.)

For reasons given in the discussion above, it is estimated that category 3, Agrees, will show no change in normal frequency from the original to the revised set of categories.

Because of its new function in registering task-oriented ascendance it is expected that category 4, Gives Suggestion, will pick up some scores from both categories 5 and 6, Gives Opinion, and Gives Information. These gains are estimated to be about 1 percent from each or a total of 2 percent. However, as we have seen earlier, Gives Suggestion will also lose some scores to Dramatizes (a transfer which I have estimated at 1 percent), and to Seems Friendly (estimated to be 1/2 percent). From the definition of Gives Suggestion as strictly neutral, and instructions to observers, we also expect it to lose some scores to Seems Unfriendly. This amount is now estimated to be about equal to the amount it will lose to Seems Friendly, and so about 1/2 percent. These losses total 2 percent. According to these estimates the gains are cancelled by losses exactly. The final estimate is thus no change.

Category 5, Gives Opinion, shows all losses and no gains. In addition to its losses, detailed above, to Seems Friendly at 1/2 percent, Dramatizes at 1 percent, Gives Suggestion at 1 percent, one may estimate that it will lose about 1/2 percent to category 9, Asks for Suggestion, and about 1 1/2 percent to Seems Unfriendly. These losses total 4 1/2 percent, the largest loss to any category in the revision. It will be noticed that the estimated loss to Seems Unfriendly, at 1 1/2 percent, is larger than that to Seems Friendly, at 1/2 percent. The reason for this is that in the study the original category Gives Opinion did not actually register in the F direction. It actually registered UNF. Many opinions, in other words, appeared in the context of arguments and status struggles. This is understandable, and in terms of experience rings true. In the new definition of categories, it was deliberately decided to try to split off those opinions given with a negative and ascendant attitude, and to score them under Seems Unfriendly. Similarly it was decided to split off those opinions given with an ascendant attitude, but not a negative one, and to score them under Gives Suggestion. If these two operations are performed successfully, one may expect the direction of the remainder to be closer to F. Additional corrections are expected from the splitting off of opinions given with a positive attitude and scoring them under Seems Friendly, and the scoring of those given with a sufficiently submissive or tentative attitude under Asks for Suggestions.

Thus I have tried to tailor the definition of category 5, and the scoring instructions, in such a way as to make it measure F instead of UNF. In order to do so it must lose more scores to Seems Negative than to Seems Positive, however, and more scores to Gives Suggestion than to Asks for Suggestion. The estimates of loss, 1 1/2 to 1/2 and 1 to 1/2, respectively, reflect these expectations. The total loss to category 5, Gives Opinion, 4 1/2 percent, does not seem excessive in view of the extensive efforts to divert scores elsewhere, and in view of the absolute magnitude of the normal rate. It may in fact be an underestimate if it proves to be relatively easy to divert scores to Seems Unfriendly.

Category 6, Gives Information, is also a category with a net loss, by design. As indicated above, it is expected to lose about 1/2 percent to Seems Friendly, about 1 percent to Dramatizes, and about 1 percent to Gives Suggestion. It is not expected to lose any significant number of scores to Seems Unfriendly, since it is felt that very little activity in the previous category conveys a negative feeling. The total loss is estimated at 2 1/5 percent—a moderate loss, but one that is reasonably related to the expected gains in the categories to which scores from it will be transferred.

Categories 7 and 8, Asks for Information and Asks for Suggestion are not expected to show any change in normal rates or medium ranges. Category 9, Asks for Suggestion, as explained above, is expected to pick up some scores, estimated at about 1/2 percent, mostly from category 5, a loss that has already been taken into account above. The medium range of category 9, Asks for Suggestion, has accordingly been revised upward.

Category 10, Disagrees, is not expected to show changes. Category 11, Shows Tension, Laughs, is expected to show a major gain by the transfer of laughs to it from category 2. This gain, estimated at 3 percent (an amount that is about half of the normal rate of original Category 2) is the largest gain of any category in the revision. This is welcome, since the original rate was quite low. Its medium range has been suitably adjusted. The loss to category 2 has been taken into account above.

Finally, category 12, Seems Unfriendly, has been increased a total of 2 percent, by a transfer of 1 1/2 percent from Gives Opinion, and a transfer of 1/2 percent from Gives Suggestion. These losses have been taken into account above for the two categories affected. The expected gain to Seems Unfriendly is substantial, and needed, since the normal frequency is low. Its gain is the second largest in the revision.

The final result of the revisions, it is hoped, is to transfer scores out of the large categories (where they are not needed for reliability, and do not give the most needed component of their information) into the small categories, where they are needed to add reliability, and to provide information that is hard to get—information concerning the presence of fantasy, of tension, of friendly or unfriendly feeling, of felt ascendance, or of submissiveness.

CHANGES IN THE INFERRED DIRECTIONAL INDICATORS

Table 6.1 in Chapter 6 gives a set of predictions as to the direction probably indicated if a rate in a given category is either high or low. These predictions are based, so far as possible, upon the actual findings of the study upon which this work is based. However, since some categories have been modified in definition with the intention of changing either their rate or direction, it is well to indicate the basis for the predicted directions.

Category 1, Seems Friendly, is predicted to measure P if high, N if low. The actual finding in the study for the category Shows Solidarity was UB, but the original definition was not being used, jokes being experimentally scored in that category. It is believed that the jokes swamped the original meaning, and that the UB direction really reflects the jokes. The directional significance of Shows Solidarity in the original definition may possibly be UP, positive but correlated with total amount of participation. It is hoped, however, that the changes in definitions and instructions for category 1, Seems Friendly, which make it easier to score, will reduce its correlation with total participation, and make it more independent of the degree of ascendance or submission. In spite of this it may still turn out to measure UP rather than P.

The counterpart of category 1, that is, category 12, Seems Unfriendly, is predicted to measure N if high, P if low. The original category 1, Shows Antagonism, measured UN. It was negative but correlated to the total amount of participation. The change in title, definition, and instructions are all calculated to make the new category, Seems Unfriendly, milder, easier to score, and hence hopefully less correlated with ascendance. This attempt may not succeed. The corresponding attempt for Seems Friendly may also not succeed, as indicated above, but both attempts are worthwhile, since the system as a whole would be more efficient if both categories were independent of ascendance and submission.

The directional significance UB predicted for category 2, Dramatizes, is taken from the presumed significance of joking. The category will be augmented by other types of fantasy, some of which may have little upward component, but it is expected that the jokes will probably carry the day. If the category does measure B, rather than UB, this would be quite acceptable.

The original category 11, Shows Tension, was found to measure DB, and the added component for the new category, namely laughing, was found in the study to measure D. The revised category, adding the two, will thus probably measure DB.

Category 3, Agrees, is predicted to measure PF in the revised set as it did in the original, since there is no change in the category, and the direction seems reasonable. Category 10, Disagrees, is predicted to measure N, as it did in the study. The category is unchanged in the revision.

Category 4, Gives Suggestion, was not clearly measuring any of the directions in the original study, for reasons unknown. It has been redefined, enlarged, and clarified for the revision with the intention of making it measure UF. The prediction in this case thus represents a hope of success. The same, exactly, may be said of its counterpart, category 9, Asks for Suggestion. It has been reconstructed with the intention of making it measure DF.

In the study using the original categories, category 5, Gives Opinion, clearly and strongly measured UNF. It has been carefully restricted by redefinition and instructions to observers with the intention of making it measure F. It may be difficult to separate it from the upward and negative components, however. Its counterpart, category 8, Asks for Opinion, has not been changed in definition, and should continue to measure in the P direction as it was found to do in the study.

Category 6, Gives Information, has been modified slightly from the original by redefinition, but only in ways that should purify it and leave it essentially where it was—measuring D. Category 7, Asks for Information has not been changed, and unless the study itself was representing an unusual result, it should continue to measure UP.

RATES AND DIRECTIONAL INDICATORS OF ACTS RECEIVED

The twenty-one studies used as the basis for the empirical norms for acts initiated do not provide data for acts received. At first one may suppose that the acts received are of course simply the same as the acts initiated looked at from a different perspective. The group as a whole, however, is the receiver of many acts, about half, as a rough average, and these tend to be concentrated in the categories of Giving Information, Opinion, and Suggestion. Individuals address these kinds of remarks in speeches or arguments to the group as a whole, and are then answered with agreement and disagreement, engaged in argument, and so on. The acts received by individuals are those addressed to individuals, and do not include those addressed to the group as a whole. The profile of acts received is thus likely, on the one hand, to have lower rates of those categories used most heavily for speeches to the group as a whole, and, on the other hand, to have higher rates in those categories normally used in replying to these speeches. In order to estimate the medium ranges for categories of acts received, it was necessary to estimate the way and degree to which the profile of acts received differed from the profile of acts initiated.

Little directly relevant data were available. Data characteristic of individuals rather than group averages were needed. The estimates were actually made by comparison of high participators with low participators as reported by two studies (49; 50), and data from one study which reports directly the profiles of acts initiated and received for two types of men (141). Experience indicates that high participators talk a great deal more to the group as a whole, and low participators talk more to individuals—in fact, often replying to the high participators. It is not unreasonable, then, to take the profile of acts initiated by low participators to represent the profile of acts typically received by specific individuals. For each study I made a comparison of high participators with low participators and determined the ratio by which a given category increased or decreased as one went from high to low. In the one study where data were directly available, I made the comparison of acts initiated by a given type of man with acts received by him. The ratios representing increase or decrease were then averaged. For some categories the ratio was near 1.00 and for these a judgment of "no change" was made. For others the computed ratio was accepted as significant, and used. The following table shows the results of this attempt to determine weighting ratios for converting norms for acts initiated to norms for acts received.

The weighting factors shown in Table 2 were then applied to the figure representing the upper bound for each category as shown in Table 6.1. For example, the latter table shows that for Agrees, the estimated upper bound of the medium range for acts initiated was 13.6 Table 2 shows that it is estimated that the average individual may expect to *receive* a higher percentage of his total acts in category 3, Agrees, than this category is in his total acts *initiated*—about 1.43 times as much. The normal upper bound of acts initiated, 13.6, multiplied by the weighting factor of 1.43 gives the estimated upper bound of acts received—19.4. The lower bound is then estimated from the graph described earlier, and the result is shown on Table 6.2, as 12.7. The procedure is makeshift all the

**Table 2 Estimated Average Ratio
of Rates Received to Rates Initiated
in Profiles of Individuals**

Category of Interaction	Ratio of Rates Received to Rates Initiated
1. Shows Solidarity	(1.00) No Change
2. Shows Tension Release	1.75
3. Agrees	1.43
4. Gives Suggestion	.82
5. Gives Opinion	(1.00) No Change
6. Gives Orientation	.75
7. Asks for Orientation	(1.00) No Change
8. Asks for Opinion	.73
9. Asks for Suggestion	.78
10. Disagrees	1.20
11. Shows Tension	1.50
12. Shows Antagonism	(1.00) No Change

way through, but it will be improved with time, and I think it gives us useful predictions now when they are badly needed. Until the present theoretical structure of types was developed, little attention was paid to the diagnostic usefulness of the profile of acts received.

The study upon which the present book is based did treat the rates of acts received by individuals in a way exactly parallel to the rates of acts initiated by them, and so produced the highly useful information of their positions in the diagnostic space. The inferred directional indicators shown on Table 6.2 are based upon these findings but, as in the case of the norms for interaction initiated, we must go beyond the actual information because of the changes in the categories. The basis of the predictions are as follows.

Since category 1, Shows Solidarity, was swamped with jokes in the factorial study, no useful information is available. The prediction that the person who is high on receiving acts in which others seem friendly is likely to be positive is a guess based upon the general idea that friendly feeling tends to provoke friendly feeling. Since the positive person is the type predicted to initiate the highest rate of Seeming Friendly, it is consistent to expect him to receive the most. The hypothesis of like-eliciting-like does not always hold, but it is expected to hold in this case. It should be noted that this hypothesis is held with little confidence. The highest receiver might be upward-positive, upward-positive-backward, or positive-backward. A rationale could be offered for each of these. The most conservative guess seems to be positive.

The prediction that the receiver of acts of Dramatizing or Joking is likely to be a PB member is taken directly from the findings of the factor study, although it will be recalled that the activity scored there was primarily jokes, and it was combined with Showing Solidarity. The predicted indicator seems reasonable. The PB member seems a likely appreciator of the fantasy and jokes of others.

Category 3, Agrees, is predicted to indicate F for the person who is high on receiving it. This is the direction indicated in the factor study, and it seems reasonable since forward-moving persons are those who are generally trying to elicit agreement with their opinions and suggestions, which they want to install as group norms.

In the factor study the original category Gives Suggestion was found to indicate UP for the person who received an unusually high rate. Although the UP type is not oriented forward, he can be thought of as a natural leader of the more socially oriented portion of the group, and so an appropriate person to check suggestions with in order to bring members of his subgroup along. The direction is accepted as reasonable and is so rationalized.

The receiving of opinion was found to indicate PF, or possibly UPF in the original factorial study. In view of the fact that PF is the direction from which acts of agreement most often come, and in view of the fact that such acts are most often directed to F (the direction from which opinion is defined to come) a choice was made in favor of PF. This assumes the regular "back and forth" between opinion and agreement, which one so often sees in observing interaction.

Receiving repeated requests for information was found in the factorial study to indicate a DB position, with a hint of negative direction also. The latter hint was not thought strong enough to retain, however, though it could easily be rationalized. The receiving of many requests for information suggests a "drawing out" attempt which, if it typically came from the UP member (who is high on Asks for Information) could appropriately be addressed to the DB member to bring him further into the group and into more active effort. At any rate, the directional indication DB of a high rate in receiving requests for information is accepted.

Being unusually high on receiving requests for opinion seems to be characteristic of the DN member. This kind of activity seems reasonably to be addressed to him, in the effort to elicit the nature and source of his negative attitude. The direction indicated in the factorial study was DN, and this direction is accepted for the prediction.

In the factorial study the receiving of requests for suggestion was diagnostic, though weakly, of the F direction. This seems plausible, although one could have expected some upward component as well. However, taking the literal cue, the direction F is accepted for the prediction.

Category 10, Disagrees, is exactly the same in the revision as in the original. Receiving acts in this category came out in the factorial study fairly strongly and clearly as UNF. It is no surprise to find that it is the UNF type, the authoritarian autocrat, who elicits disagreement. He is not only prominent and negative, but he offers many general statements that solicit, or logically require, agreement, or disagreement. The direction previously indicated is accepted for the present prediction.

The category Shows Tension, category 11 in the original set, is a feeble indicator of any direction. There is hardly enough to give a clue, but it will be recalled that laughs have been added to its regular content. There is a clear indication that those who receive laughs are likely to be UNB, although the upward component is not very strong. People laugh in response to jokes. The initiating of jokes is an indicator of the UB direction, so the receiving of laughs is reasonably correlated with it. Why the correlation is not better, is not clear. It may be that persons laugh more—show tension more—in response to more threatening jokers. At any rate, the direction UNB, is accepted for persons who are unusually high on receiving acts of Showing Tension, Laughs, and this directional indicator is so shown on the new norms.

Finally, receiving many acts in which others Seem Unfriendly indicated, in the factorial study, that the recipient was likely to be UNF. The same reasoning may be advanced in this case as in the case of Disagreement, where the direction indicated was the same. It is not clear why the receiving type should not as well be UN as UNF. However, it may be that in some way, the UNF type provides more opportunities for arguments to grow. He is apparently more disliked. At any rate, the directional indication UNF is accepted for the new estimated norms.

Appendix 5

The Value Profile: A Factor Analytic Study of Value Statements[1]

by ROBERT F. BALES AND ARTHUR S. COUCH

INTRODUCTION

The authors' interest in developing a better conceptualization of the varieties of value-positions grew out of the observation of groups in a laboratory situation. The groups were made up of undergraduates hired to participate for a single meeting. The task was to discuss and reach a group decision about a human relations situation described in a short case given out to the subjects ahead of time. The task itself was the result of experience over a series of years with similar groups. The interest of the investigators was broad, and focused to some degree on the process of interaction and its relation to various features of the situation, the task, the size of the group, the personalities of participants, their attitudes toward each other, and the evolving structure of the group over a series of meetings. Discussion of "human relations cases" had proved to be a task that was sensible to participants and did not obviously require some particular type of previous experience, ability, or technical knowledge. Participants generally became involved, talked easily, often argued, and

---

[1]This article, listed as number 31 in the bibliography, was written in 1959, but has only recently been published. The published article also includes the centroid loadings and additional scales. I am grateful to the journal *Sociological Inquiry* for permission to reprint this article here. It is included because the structuring of the value-space is so crucial to the present work.

sometimes became angry with each other. The task seemed to produce a variety of interpersonal conflicts about which it would be worthwhile to know more.

The number of value-statements one hears in case discussions of this kind is impressive. Something over 20 percent of all overt acts fall into the category of interaction called Gives Opinion in the observation system we were using (11). Of these, perhaps as many as one fourth, as an estimate, or around 5 percent of the total number of acts approach an explicit attempt to state the content of a generalized value-premise. One of our subjects, for example, in the midst of argument with one of the other members finally stated heatedly: "You *have* to respect authority, and when you stop respecting authority, your situation isn't worth much!"

Many of the statements we heard, like this one, reminded us of items from the F-scale, familiar to readers of *The Authoritarian Personality* (1). We were motivated in part by the success of studies in this area. But we were interested in whatever kinds of value-statements might enter into discussion, and we needed some practical and empirically based conception of what were the relevant dimensions of the domain in its own right. An adequate conception of it, we felt, could probably not be arrived at simply by deduction from other bases, such as deeper elements of personality, or structured ideologies taken over through learning, or the nature of the context in which value-statements were made.

The fact that value-statements are "speech reactions," made in particular interaction contexts, sometimes leads critics to assert that they are of no real importance. From our perspective, with the aim of predicting what will happen when several persons are put together in a situation of the sort described, they seem to be critical. Generalized statements of value content seem to be focal points in discussions we observe. Sometimes they set off an argument that spirals out of control. Sometimes they constitute an attempt to apply the ultimate sanction to another who seems incredibly deviant. Sometimes they elicit agreement, grudging or enthusiastic, and seem to constitute the crystallization point of a spiral of cooperation. These developments may color or characterize a whole session, and perhaps the long-term structure of the group.

The initial pragmatic motivation of the authors was to develop a sample of value-statements which the subjects we studied could be asked to agree or disagree with on a paper and pencil test in advance of a session, with the aim of predicting the kind of value-statements they would make, or agree or disagree with, in discussion with each other. The theoretical interest, of course, was much broader, but in many of the decisions concerning the development of the inventory, we reconciled ourselves to imperfections by keeping the pragmatic aim well in view.

CRITERIA FOR ITEMS

Given the pragmatic aim, one obvious way to obtain items is to listen to actual discussions and record statements that seem to be promising. We obtained a substantial number of items in this way. The criteria for recognizing a promising item were neither rigid, nor entirely clear, but so far as we could define them, we were looking for verbal statements: (1) about one sentence in length; (2) declarative in form, apparently with the desire of eliciting an agreement or disagreement from some other person; (3) in which the subject of the statement is some general class of objects of which new instances might be found in this or other discussions; and (4) in which the predicate of the statement declares or implies that some general class of orientations, attitudes, or actions should be accepted as normatively binding on both the person who makes the statement and whoever agrees to it. In other words, a value-statement in the concrete interaction context is a statement of an existing norm, or a proposal for a new norm. Often both the person who makes the statement and the one who agrees (or disagrees), expect that any agreement will be referred back to, as a justification for some more particular statement, ultimately a specific suggestion, later in the interaction. Sometimes it is clear to both participants what the more specific implication is, and also just who will be required to do what if it is accepted; often it is not clear.

It seems easier to identify the issues involved in defining a value-statement if one approaches the problem as it appears in the full interaction context, as above. Other sorts of situations may be regarded as shading off in various ways from the full interaction context. For example, it is not at all the same thing to react to a value-statement as to state it. If persons are asked, out of context, to react to written statements rather than verbal ones, it may not be clear to them who makes the statement, what are the specific objects included in the general class, what is the specific action implication of the predicate, or who will perform what action toward whom, if the statement is accepted. When subjects are asked to respond to value-statements on a questionnaire, most of these issues are unclear. We should not be surprised if some subjects refuse to answer some items or express irritation. Incidentally, the instructions used on the printed form left the possibility of no answer on a given item as a legitimate response. The surprising thing, perhaps, is the degree to which most subjects, including ourselves, are willing to fill in the missing context by projection and respond with some degree of agreement or disagreement. Existing personality tests, of course, depend on this fact, and many of them contain statements appropriate for a values-inventory.

SOURCES OF ITEMS

Once launched on the venture of exploring the domain of value-statements, our aim became one of obtaining representation of as many different value-areas as we practically could. We canvassed a number of sources and obtained, either directly or by slight extension and rewording, a pool of 872 items. It cannot be claimed that our sample was random, or systematic. It was simply as large and varied as we were able to make it at that time.

We started with a pool of 163 items culled from remarks made by our subjects. The Allport-Vernon-Lindzey *Study of Values* (2) provided the ingredients for eleven items, some from each of its value types. An a priori classification of ideological issues relevant to small groups, worked out earlier by one of the authors (11), provided thirty items. A questionnaire used in the anthropological field by Florence Kluckhohn and collaborators, based on her classification of value-orientations (106; 107) provided the material for sixteen items. Charles Morris' questionnaire, Ways to Live (123), used in his cross-cultural studies and worked out with classical philosophical and religious issues prominently in view, was a rich source of 120 items. An unpublished questionnaire by Gibson Winter (160) on values relative to participation in groups, furnished sixteen items. Pitirim Sorokin's description of various types of cultural mentality in his *Social and Cultural Dynamics* (147) provided the source for forty-six items. All of the authors just named were more or less explicitly concerned with values and with the problem of types or classes of values.

Various scales associated with, or inspired by the *Authoritarian Personality* studies provided items, including the thirty-item F-scale in its entirety (1); twenty-six items from various scales by Levinson on ethnocentrism and minorities (1); twelve items from Sanford's Religious Conventionalism Scale (1); forty-two items from Levinson and Huffman's Traditional Family Ideology Scale (111); twelve items from the Couch-Goodrich Militant Radicalism Scale (73); and nine items from an unpublished dissertation by Edward Jones (102).

Another rich source was Henry Murray's lists of sentiments, associated with various personality needs, in his *Explorations in Personality*, (124). These lists furnished 119 items. Raymond Cattell's Sixteen Personality Factor Questionnaire (62) was the source, by rewording and extension, of eighty-seven items, and the Thurstone Temperament Schedule (157), similarly, of eighty-five items.

Finally, various items were written by associates on the project, Bernard Cohen, David Hayes, and Nathan Altshuler, in addition to the present authors.

PRELIMINARY REDUCTION IN NUMBER OF ITEMS

Working partly deductively from a classification of system problems utilized in other connections by Parsons and Bales (128, Chapter 3), and partly inductively from the pool of items, a temporary framework of sixteen classes was set up. The framework provided a means of grouping items for comparison and editing. Near duplicates were eliminated, key words and phrases from separate items were combined into single items. By these and similar means the total number of items was reduced to 252, which were printed for administration. The Lickert response form was used. The six response categories, together with the numerical values later assigned to them for computation were: (1) Strongly Disagree; (2) Disagree; (3) Slightly Disagree; (5) Slightly Agree; (6) Agree; and (7) Strongly Agree. A weight of four, that is, a mean value, was assigned to those cases where the subject failed to respond. It should not be forgotten that what we are studying is *reactions* to *written* value-statements out of context. This later becomes crucial in understanding the findings.

THE SAMPLE

The main part of the sample consisted of Harvard undergraduates, who answered an advertisement in the college newspaper. They were paid for their time in answering the questionnaire. In addition to Harvard undergraduates, a small sample of faculty members from the Department of Social Relations, graduate students and Radcliffe undergraduates filled out the questionnaire. In all there was a total of 388 from the Harvard area. Around eighty respondents were obtained from Bennington College, and a similar number from among officer candidates at Maxwell Air Force Base. The total number of respondents was 552. This sample, though decently large, is not so diverse as one would like for general theoretical purposes, since values differ so markedly cross-culturally. However, it is probably well enough fitted to the assessment of value-differences between students of college age in this country. We have not tried to face up to the difficult problems of class and ethnic differences, to say nothing of cross-cultural differences. On the other hand, we have gratefully taken items from tests that have been used to some extent cross-culturally, notably those of Morris, Kluckhohn, and Allport-Vernon-Lindzey.

ITEM ANALYSIS

Two devices were used for further reduction of the 252 items to a number small enough for a factor analysis. First, the distribution of answers on each item was used to weed out items that did not discriminate between subjects in our population. Items on which nearly everybody agreed or disagreed were dropped. Less than 20 percent of the answers on either side was the approximate criterion. This is not to say that such items do not express values, nor that such values are unimportant, but simply that we wanted a test that would differentiate respondents from one another. The space we are actually exploring is not the space of reactions to all value-statements, but the space of those on which people in our sample are most apt to differ in their reactions.

The remaining items were grouped again according to the sixteen category classification, and the sixteen separate matrices of correlations of each item with each other in its group were computed. The examination of these correlations enabled us to locate clusters and familiarize ourselves with the character of each item in its local context. In the final reduction we tried to include clusters, or at least pairs of intercorrelated items, to represent all the positions we could identify, and tended to drop items too closely duplicating an already adequately represented cluster or, at the other extreme, items that were completely uncorrelated with any others.

The final set contained 143 items, plus one score based on the total of seventeen items included from the original thirty-item F-scale as a marker variable. The 144 variables were intercorrelated, and the resulting matrix was factor analyzed by the Thurstone complete centroid method (156).

THE FACTOR STRUCTURE

A set of tables containing the list of items, means and standard deviations, and rotated loadings will be found in this Appendix. Only a few individual items will be discussed here to illustrate the structure of the factor space. Four orthogonal factors were found. All four dimensions and a number of the combinations of them can be measured reasonably well with the items available.

For reference we have chosen a rotation about 45 degrees off the centroid solution, which puts factor I almost squarely on the well-known cluster usually called "authoritarianism," or *Agreement with Value-Statements in Favor of Acceptance of Authority.* Our marker variable, total F score, has a loading of .90 on factor I. The best item—"Obedience and respect for authority are the most important virtues children should learn"—is loaded .76 on factor I and has essentially a zero loading on the other three factors. The kinds of items loaded on factor I are well-known to students of *The Authoritarian Personality* (1). Perhaps the important thing to note here is that many items which have been used to measure this factor have important or even larger loadings on other factors, and may be quite different from each other, apart from the common factor of authoritarianism. Several will be noted below.

Factor II we call *Agreement with Value-Statements in Favor of Need-Determined Expression versus Value-Determined Restraint.* The best item, which has a loading of .62 and is almost pure, states: "No values can be eternal; the only real values are those which meet the needs of the given moment." Another good item is more specific about needs: "Let us eat, drink, and be merry, for tomorrow we die!" "Hedonism" would presumably be a satisfactory title for this factor if it did not carry the implications of passive rather active pleasure. The content of the items indicates that aggressive as well as sexual impulses are classed together with appetites.

It is important to note that agreement with value-statements in favor of expression is completely independent of agreement with value-statements in favor of acceptance of authority. The two tendencies are uncorrelated over the population. Individuals can be found with any combination of positions on the two variables. Items can be found which represent various combinations. For example, the following item has a positive relation to both dimensions: "The most important function of education is preparation for practical achievement and financial reward." Apparently, if the authority figure called to the subject's mind by the phrase "the most important function of education" is one who demands material success, the two values may coincide for him. On the other hand, consider the following item: "In addition to faith, we need help from God in order to resist temptation." This item is negative on factor II (need-determined expression), but still positive on factor I (acceptance of authority). The direct opposite of this position (against authority and for need-determined expression) is found in the following statement: "Man can solve all his important problems without help from a Supreme Being." There are no items in the pool of 143 which are negative on both factors—I and II. The significance of this fact is still not clear. It will be important to see whether items can be found or invented which fill this implied gap in the space.

Therefore, agreement with value-statements in favor of acceptance of authority does not imply that the person places a high value on asceticism or restraint. It only does for some people. On the other hand, there is a stereotype which implies that a person agreeing with statements favoring authoritarian values will also be favorable to the expression of aggression. Again, this is true of some persons only. It seems likely that beliefs concerning the necessary implications of agreement with a value-statement made by another often go unrecognized and unexamined in arguments, since the implications are one step more abstract than the value-statements themselves.

Factor III we call *Agreement with Value-Statements Favoring Equalitarianism.* The best item states: "Everyone should have an equal chance and an equal say." The loading is .57. Here again, perhaps the most important clarification received from the analysis is the information that this variable is uncorrelated with that concerned with acceptance of authority. Equalitarianism, as measured by agreement with items like this one, is not the opposite of acceptance of authority, but is a different dimension, analytically independent.

For those who may feel that equalitarianism must be the opposite of acceptance of authority, here is an item that is positive on both dimensions: "A group cannot get its job done without voluntary cooperation from everybody."

Other items in this same cluster suggest that the key assumption in understanding the combination is that the group as a whole is both the source of authority and the object of identification. The position which is negative on acceptance of authority and positive on equality is illustrated by the item: "It is up to the government to make sure that everyone has a secure job and a good standard of living." Here is an implied separation between the source of authority and a group of equals, with the group of equals as the object of identification.

A third combination is found in the following item: "In most groups, it is better to choose somebody to take charge and run things and then hold him responsible, even if he does some things the members do not like." Here the position of the person who agrees is positive in relation to acceptance of authority, and negative in relation to equality. It is implied that he identifies with authority, versus the members. There are no items significantly negative on both dimensions. As before, the import of this blank area in the factor space is not clear.

Agreement with equaliterianism is also independent of agreement with need-determined expression. The position in which a positive value is placed on both is illustrated by the item: "Society should be quicker to adopt new customs and throw aside mere traditions and old-fashioned habits." Apparently, the person who agrees feels that "society" in some general equalitarian sense of all individuals has the right to throw aside (an expressive gesture) "mere traditions" (conservative ways). A negative value placed on need-determined expression in combination with a positive value on equalitarianism is illustrated by the item: "There are no human problems that love cannot solve." "Love," in this connection, presumably means the ascetic, altruistic kind, and is associated with restraint.

Factor IV is called *Agreement with Value-Statements Favoring Individualism.* The item which best represents this factor reads: "It is the man who stands alone who excites our admiration."

This factor is independent of the other three factors. Items can be found, however, which represent various combinations with them. Consider this item, for example: "What this country needs most, more than laws and political programs, is a few courageous, tireless, devoted leaders, in whom the people can put their faith." In this position, presumably, the respondent who agrees identifies with the one or two *individuals* who are the source of authority. An item negative to authority, but still individualistic is the following: "Whoever would be a man, must be a nonconformist." Thus agreement with individualism has no determinate relation to agreement with authority.

Combinations of individualism with need-determined expression have a somewhat different flavor, for example: "Love action, and care little that others may find you rash." The combination of individualism with value-determined restraint, the opposite end of factor II is easily felt in the item: "One should aim to simplify one's external life, and moderate those desires those satisfaction is dependent upon physical or social forces outside of oneself."

Agreement with individualism and agreement with equalitarianism are not incompatible. The following item is fairly well loaded on both factors: "The rich, internal world of ideals, of sensitive feelings, of reverie, of self-knowledge, is man's true home." On the other hand, there is a kind of individualism which is negative to equalitarianism: "To be superior, a man must stand alone." Further illustration of the factor space is not possible here, but perhaps some idea of the variety of values that are associated with the four factors has been conveyed. A comparison in detail with the factor space found in other similar studies, particularly that of Morris (123) would be desirable. It must suffice here to state that in a conference with Morris, we concluded that our findings are essentially equivalent to his, although he found five factors and named them differently because he chose a different rotation. The rotation chosen for reference is, of course, a matter of conceptual convenience, the more so as the space is filled out with items and does not show any simple structure. The proper basis of comparison is the nature of the space, that is to say, the relations of items to each other, of which the factors are only a summary description. Various rotations will give various perspectives for description. One of the reasons for disagreements on the theoretical level and the multiplication of classification schemes is that, in the absence of data which represent the space, undue emphasis may be attached to what amounts to a particular rotation, or a particular factor.

On the other hand, the number of factors and the particular rotation may be important because of the associative value the dimensions have for the investigator. If a dimensional scheme is to be used for the classification of new instances, one wishes the categories to be fixed at points which are already well populated with examples. We believe that the reference dimensions we have chosen have some merit in these respects. Kassebaum has successfully employed them as a framework for the running classification of value-statements during group discussion (103). This method for classifying value-statements according to their presumed content in relation to factors is still under development, and is known as *Value Content Analysis.*

In the tables that follow, the centroid loadings are omitted and replaced by our preferred rotated loading. For the list of items, see Chapter 8. The list of items there is in the same order as shown in the following tables.

Table 3 Means and Standard Deviations of VP Items

Item Number	Mean	Standard Deviation	Item Number	Mean	Standard Deviation
1	4.29	1.70	26	3.19	1.78
2	4.95	1.52	27	4.80	1.77
3	4.10	1.96	28	3.34	1.79
4	3.19	1.66	29	3.68	2.10
5	3.71	1.77	30	3.69	1.90
6	3.68	1.87	31	3.09	1.95
7	4.31	1.72	32	3.88	1.88
8	4.40	1.80	33	3.12	1.71
9	3.99	1.91	34	3.39	1.75
10	4.48	1.72	35	3.16	1.95
11	4.26	2.01	36	4.79	1.68
12	3.77	2.00	37	4.23	2.15
13	5.05	1.79	38	3.71	1.79
14	3.69	1.90	39	3.26	1.83
15	3.06	2.02	40	4.45	1.67
16	4.29	1.95	41	4.26	1.70
17	3.93	2.01	42	3.75	1.84
18	3.74	1.95	43	4.22	1.80
19	3.19	1.88	44	4.13	1.60
20	4.55	1.70	45	4.45	1.53
21	3.71	1.72	46	4.14	1.79
22	3.63	1.64	47	4.46	1.61
23	3.44	1.75	48	4.72	1.50
24	3.82	1.83	49	4.58	2.08
25	3.95	1.91	50	4.21	1.75

Table 3 (*continued*)

Item Number	Mean	Standard Deviation	Item Number	Mean	Standard Deviation
51	3.74	2.00	93	3.95	1.66
52	4.61	1.55	94	4.58	1.65
53	3.55	1.56	95	3.73	1.77
54	4.76	1.65	96	4.10	1.85
55	4.38	1.80	97	4.84	1.63
56	3.88	1.75	98	3.43	1.71
57	3.82	1.76	99	4.58	1.74
58	3.39	1.78	100	4.47	1.66
59	3.95	1.95	101	2.87	1.73
60	4.31	1.58	102	4.01	1.78
61	4.12	1.72	103	3.22	1.69
62	4.74	1.58	104	4.72	1.63
63	4.63	1.66	105	4.11	1.69
64	3.55	1.67	106	4.29	1.61
65	4.76	1.69	107	2.84	1.73
66	4.39	1.70	108	4.41	1.84
67	3.64	1.47	109	4.42	1.81
68	4.95	1.58	110	3.66	1.71
69	3.81	1.72	111	4.33	1.66
70	3.20	1.73	112	3.34	1.79
71	3.98	1.89	113	3.82	1.89
72	3.34	1.55	114	3.48	1.86
73	3.70	1.76	115	4.72	1.69
74	3.56	1.93	116	4.26	1.87
75	4.73	1.62	117	3.65	1.70
76	4.41	1.71	118	4.16	1.84
77	2.98	2.05	119	4.13	1.68
78	3.53	1.55	120	2.79	1.87
79	3.90	1.73	121	4.34	1.68
80	3.81	2.22	122	3.74	1.63
81	3.69	2.04	123	4.33	1.65
82	4.56	1.95	124	4.68	1.79
83	4.49	1.64	125	3.72	1.82
84	3.52	1.89	126	4.92	1.62
85	3.32	1.80	127	2.96	1.98
86	3.23	1.63	128	4.76	1.89
87	4.77	1.63	129	4.67	1.63
88	4.13	1.84	130	3.26	1.87
89	3.29	1.82	131	4.72	1.71
90	3.70	1.68	132	3.78	1.76
91	4.26	2.08	133	3.15	1.58
92	3.52	1.73	134	3.50	1.83

Item Number	Mean	Standard Deviation	Item Number	Mean	Standard Deviation
135	4.19	1.73	140	3.49	1.91
136	4.41	2.02	141	4.33	1.57
137	4.48	1.61	142	3.54	1.68
138	3.38	2.08	143	3.77	2.18
139	4.11	2.04	144	4.11	1.56

Table 4   Rotated Factor Loadings of Items

Item Number	I	II	III	IV	h^2
1	—.04	.10	—.05	.45	.22
2	.18	—.20	.18	.08	.11
3	.36	—.47	.06	.22	.40
4	.50	.17	—.08	.14	.30
5	.12	—.11	.20	.33	.18
6	.35	—.23	.14	.31	.29
7	—.12	.11	—.04	.29	.11
8	.32	.02	—.18	.30	.23
9	.33	.07	—.16	.21	.18
10	.24	—.12	.21	.38	.26
11	—.35	.38	.20	.09	.32
12	.42	.19	.08	.04	.22
13	.10	.00	.56	—.05	.33
14	.42	.01	.20	.10	.23
15	.68	—.24	.09	—.04	.53
16	.02	.18	—.09	.19	.08
17	.62	—.31	.03	.21	.53
18	.14	.33	.10	.15	.16
19	.59	.13	—.10	.13	.39
20	.12	.05	.45	—.05	.22
21	—.04	—.09	.43	.09	.20
22	.04	.32	—.01	.36	.23
23	.44	—.30	.04	.23	.34
24	.32	—.43	.06	.22	.34
25	.37	.27	.01	.10	.22
26	.34	.11	—.12	.24	.20
27	.05	.16	.17	.19	.09
28	.56	.03	.03	.12	.33
29	—.58	.48	.06	.11	.58
30	.62	.06	—.05	.10	.40

Table 4 (*continued*)

Item Number	I	II	III	IV	h^2
31	.65	—.05	—.03	.07	.43
32	.38	.13	.01	.25	.19
33	.07	—.26	.28	.22	.20
34	.26	.09	.23	.09	.14
35	—.40	.42	.10	.09	.35
36	.06	.03	.36	—.03	.14
37	—.68	.36	.02	.06	.60
38	.29	.43	.09	—.02	.28
39	.03	.49	.06	.16	.27
40	.42	—.21	.17	.24	.31
41	.22	.26	.02	.27	.19
42	.48	.04	.19	.05	.27
43	.50	.03	.19	.26	.35
44	.36	—.25	.13	.29	.29
45	—.25	.15	.26	.15	.17
46	.47	—.04	.19	.16	.28
47	.11	—.04	.40	.07	.18
48	.01	.27	.01	.35	.20
49	—.44	.46	.10	—.02	.42
50	.41	.02	—.05	.09	.18
51	.74	.05	.08	.06	.56
52	.44	.40	.08	.05	.36
53	—.13	.12	—.01	.47	.25
54	—.04	.48	.18	—.02	.26
55	.36	.10	—.17	.21	.21
56	.32	.14	—.09	.14	.15
57	—.17	.06	.34	.01	.15
58	.72	.04	—.04	.14	.54
59	.51	—.35	.12	.22	.45
60	.34	.03	—.18	.21	.19
61	.29	—.29	.23	.37	.36
62	.51	.05	—.04	.22	.31
63	.02	.36	.33	.03	.24
64	—.25	.01	.30	—.02	.15
65	—.07	.26	.25	.03	.14
66	.38	—.04	—.02	.12	.16
67	.07	—.08	.35	.11	.15
68	.02	.43	.18	.13	.23
69	.24	.22	.09	.07	.12
70	.39	.16	.01	.20	.22
71	.72	.06	.02	.05	.52
72	—.17	.21	.08	.36	.21
73	.30	—.28	.10	.31	.27

Item Number	I	II	III	IV	h^2
74	.65	.09	.09	.04	.44
75	.18	.30	.13	.26	.21
76	.39	.08	.07	.31	.26
77	.65	—.25	—.01	.03	.49
78	—.13	.17	.04	.28	.13
79	.27	.12	.21	.31	.23
80	.68	—.41	.05	.00	.63
81	.59	.09	—.05	.03	.36
82	.60	.16	—.02	.07	.39
83	.41	—.01	.26	—.05	.24
84	.76	.02	.00	.08	.58
85	.36	.30	—.02	.21	.26
86	.15	.21	—.17	.25	.16
87	.45	—.20	—.04	.18	.28
88	.68	.00	.00	—.06	.47
89	.48	.19	—.03	.15	.29
90	—.01	.07	.36	—.01	.13
91	.36	.04	.07	.02	.14
92	.39	—.21	.19	.26	.30
93	.21	.34	—.07	.31	.26
94	.09	.03	.34	.18	.16
95	—.07	.07	.39	.06	.17
96	.72	—.04	—.04	.01	.52
97	.45	—.18	—.07	.11	.25
98	.42	.04	.07	.06	.19
99	.33	.08	—.01	.36	.25
100	.09	—.14	.30	.41	.29
101	.57	.33	.04	.01	.44
102	.50	—.15	.21	.12	.33
103	—.15	.19	—.15	.49	.32
104	.24	—.23	.31	.19	.24
105	.51	—.03	.24	.13	.34
106	.16	—.20	.31	.15	.18
107	.48	.14	.05	.16	.28
108	.44	—.30	.08	.18	.32
109	.38	—.19	.08	.21	.23
110	.34	.06	—.07	.11	.14
111	.45	—.21	.12	.10	.27
112	.35	.01	—.01	.05	.13
113	.68	.01	—.04	.03	.47
114	.03	.62	.15	.12	.42
115	.26	.06	.48	.01	.30
116	.44	.28	.12	—.04	.29

Table 4 (*continued*)

Item Number	I	II	III	IV	h^2
117	.54	.05	.02	.24	.35
118	—.04	.50	.20	.04	.29
119	.47	.15	—.02	.23	.30
120	.70	.14	.00	.05	.51
121	.18	.28	.20	.06	.15
122	—.07	.41	.15	.04	.20
123	.15	.13	.10	.39	.20
124	.36	—.41	—.02	.22	.35
125	.09	.18	.20	.05	.08
126	.14	.03	.57	—.02	.35
127	.66	—.30	.01	—.02	.53
128	—.55	.28	—.06	.04	.39
129	.39	—.05	.37	.02	.29
130	.52	.00	.10	.08	.29
131	.06	.29	.25	.04	.15
132	.58	.32	—.04	.18	.47
133	.52	—.11	.17	.25	.37
134	.56	.07	—.10	.19	.36
135	.28	.02	.22	.08	.13
136	—.65	.39	.01	.08	.58
137	.40	—.30	.06	.27	.33
138	.65	—.37	.07	—.02	.56
139	.60	—.34	—.02	.14	.50
140	.46	—.52	—.04	.07	.49
141	.30	.28	.08	.25	.24
142	.09	.02	.42	.10	.19
143	.71	—.44	.05	.00	.70
144	.90	.09	.00	.26	.88
$\Sigma a^2 =$	24.77	8.14	4.83	5.13	$\Sigma h^2 = 42.87$

SCALE FACTOR I

Acceptance of Authority

(84) Obedience and respect for authority are the most important virtues children should learn.

(51) There is hardly anything lower than a person who does not feel a great love, gratitude, and respect for his parents.

(58) What youth needs most is strict discipline, rugged determination, and the will to work and fight for family and country.

(96)   You have to respect authority, and when you stop respecting authority, your situation is not worth much.

(71)   Patriotism and loyalty are the first and the most important requirements of a good citizen.

(88)   Young people sometimes get rebellious ideas, but as they grow up they ought to get over them and settle down.

(113)   A child should not be allowed to talk back to his parents, or else he will lose respect for them.

(31)   The facts on crime and sexual immorality show that we will have to crack down harder on young people if we are going to save our moral standards.

(30)   Disobeying an order is one thing you cannot excuse—if one can get away with disobedience, why cannot everybody?

(28)   A well-raised child is one who does not have to be told twice to do something.

Factor Loadings

Item Number	I	II	III	IV	h^2
(84)	.76	.02	.00	.08	.58
(51)	.74	.05	.08	.06	.56
(58)	.72	.04	—.04	.14	.54
(96)	.72	—.04	—.04	.01	.52
(71)	.72	.06	.02	.05	.52
(88)	.68	.00	.00	—.06	.47
(113)	.68	.01	—.04	.03	.47
(31)	.65	—.05	—.03	.07	.43
(30)	.62	.06	—.05	.10	.40
(28)	.56	.03	.03	.12	.33
Average =	.69	.02	—.01	.06	.48

SCALE FACTOR II

**Need-Determined Expression versus
Value-Determined Restraint**

(114)   Since there are no values which can be eternal, the only real values are those which meet the needs of the given moment.

(118)   Nothing is static, nothing is everlasting, at any moment one

must be ready to meet the change in environment by a necessary change in one's moral views.

(39)   Let us eat, drink, and be merry, for tomorrow we die.

(54)   The solution to almost any human problem should be based on the situation at the time, not on some general moral rule.

(68)   Life is something to be enjoyed to the full, sensuously enjoyed with relish and enthusiasm.

(122)   Life is more a festival than a workshop or a school for moral discipline.

(18)   The past is no more, the future may never be, the present is all that we can be certain of.

—(24)   Not to attain happiness, but to be worthy of it, is the purpose of our existence.

—(61)   No time is better spent than that devoted to thinking about the ultimate purposes of life.

—(2)   Tenderness is more important than passion in love.

Factor Loadings

Item Number	I	II	III	IV	h^2
(114)	.03	.62	.15	.12	.42
(118)	—.04	.50	.20	.04	.29
(39)	.03	.49	.06	.16	.27
(54)	—.04	.48	.18	—.02	.26
(68)	.02	.43	.18	.13	.23
(122)	—.07	.41	.15	.04	.20
(18)	.14	.33	.10	.15	.16
— (24) *	.32	—.43	.06	.22	.34
— (61) *	.29	—.29	.23	.37	.36
— (2) *	.18	—.20	.18	.08	.11
Average =	—.07	.40	.05	—.01	.26

*Starred items to be reverse-scored, which will also reverse signs of loadings shown.

SCALE FACTOR III

Equalitarianism

(126)   Everyone should have an equal chance and an equal say.

(13)   There should be equality for everyone—because we are all human beings.

(20)   A group of equals will work a lot better than a group with a rigid hierarchy.

(21)   Each one should get what he needs—the things we have belong to all of us.

(142)   No matter what the circumstances, one should never arbitrarily tell people what they have to do.

(47)   It is the duty of every good citizen to correct anti-minority remarks made in his presence.

(95)   Poverty could be almost entirely done away with if we made certain basic changes in our social and economic system.

(36)   There has been too much talk and not enough real action in doing away with racial discrimination.

(67)   In any group it is more important to keep a friendly atmosphere than to be efficient.

(90)   In a small group there should be no real leaders—everyone should have an equal say.

Factor Loadings

Item Number	I	II	III	IV	h^2
(126)	.14	.03	.57	—.02	.35
(13)	.10	.00	.56	—.05	.33
(20)	.12	.05	.45	—.05	.22
(21)	—.04	—.09	.43	.09	.20
(142)	.09	.02	.42	.10	.19
(47)	.11	—.04	.40	.07	.18
(95)	—.07	.07	.39	.06	.17
(36)	.06	.03	.36	—.03	.14
(67)	.07	—.08	.35	.11	.15
(90)	—.01	.07	.36	—.01	.13
Average =	.06	.01	.43	.03	.21

SCALE FACTOR IV

Individualism

(103)   To be superior a man must stand alone.

(53)   In life, an individual should for the most part "go it alone," assuring himself of privacy, having much time to himself, attempting to control his own life.

(1)   It is the man who stands alone who excites our admiration.

(100)   The rich internal world of ideals, of sensitive feelings, of reverie, of self knowledge, is man's true home.

(123)   One must avoid dependence upon persons or things, the center of life should be found within oneself.

(10)   The most rewarding object of study any man can find is his own inner life.

(72)   Whoever would be a man, must be a nonconformist.

(5)   Contemplation is the highest form of human activity.

(7)   The individualist is the man who is most likely to discover the best road to a new future.

(78)   A man can learn better by striking out boldly on his own than he can by following the advice of others.

Factor Loadings

Item Number	I	II	III	IV	h^2
(103)	—.15	.19	—.15	.49	.32
(53)	—.13	.12	—.01	.47	.25
(1)	—.04	.10	—.05	.45	.22
(100)	.09	—.14	.30	.41	.29
(123)	.15	.13	.10	.39	.20
(10)	.24	—.12	.21	.38	.26
(72)	—.17	.21	.08	.36	.27
(5)	.12	—.11	.20	.33	.18
(7)	—.12	.11	—.04	.29	.11
(78)	—.13	.17	.04	.28	.13
Average =	—.01	.07	.07	.39	.22

Appendix 6

A Course Format
for an Academic Self-Analytic Group

Department of Social Relations

HARVARD UNIVERSITY

Syllabus for
Social Relations 120

ANALYSIS OF INTERPERSONAL BEHAVIOR

CATALOGUE DESCRIPTION

Social Relations 120. Analysis of Interpersonal Behavior, Full Course, Discussion groups. M. W. F. at 9, 10, 11, 12, 2.

For purposes of examination this course is assigned to Group XVII. Members of each section form a self-analytic training group. Problems for analysis are drawn from events in the development of the group. Each group meets under observation. Social Relations concentrators may count this course in any of the four fields.

APPLICATION FOR ADMISSION

Admission to the course is by application. Each section is limited to twenty-five members. The course is not open to Freshmen; some preference is given to Seniors. Persons who have had similar experience in self-analytic groups are not permitted to take the course. Roommates, if any, should apply to different sections, as should pairs of friends or others well known to each other.

If you are accepted for the course you will enter into a special set of relationships which includes your participation not only as a student, but also as a group member, as a psychological subject, and as an observer. Please read the syllabus carefully before you decide whether to apply.

Once formed, the self-analytic group will remain intact through both terms. Hence, you may not change sections between terms, nor may you receive credit for only one term. Please make sure your spring term schedule is clear for continuation at the same hour for which you apply in the fall.

PURPOSE OF THE COURSE

The purpose of the course is to enable you to learn more about personality and interpersonal behavior, including your own, through firsthand experience in a laboratory setting. The purpose is generalized as well as individualized. Improvement in general knowledge of human behavior is expected. Readings, papers, and examinations are utilized. But at the same time, you should take the course only if you are prepared to participate and try to improve your understanding of yourself as an individual person.

You will be encouraged to carry on an analysis of your own personality so far as you wish or are able. This will be an individual undertaking of your own, outside the group for the most part. At the same time you will have the opportunity to observe and discuss the interpersonal relations that naturally develop in your group. In this sense the group as a whole is self-analytic with regard to its own processes. Problems for discussion and analysis are drawn from topics presented by members, both personal and impersonal, and by events in the group, both retrospective and in the immediate present. Your aim as a group member should be to cooperate with others to develop appropriate individual values, group norms, leadership, working procedures, and appropriate emotional conditions for effective analysis. Each individual is expected to participate in the discussion and to contribute in his own way in the development of the group. Because the immediate interaction between members of the group is the basic object of study during group meetings, attendance and participation in discussion are very important.

ROLE OF INSTRUCTORS

The aims and methods of the course require an unusual role on the part of instructors. Instructors in this course do not lecture in the usual way. Once the general arrangements are explained it is necessary that you take the major responsibility for your own learning. The group will work out its own pattern of participation. The instructors will participate at times to draw attention to something, to comment on some aspect of behavior, to interpret what is going on, to suggest general approaches, or the like. But a great deal of the time the instructors will remain silent. The intention is to allow you, and to require you, to take your own approach to the problems of the group and to find your own place in the group. The group is responsible for the solution of group problems.

So far as appropriate, issues or concerns that arise out of interaction in the group should be made known in the group, for reasons of their educational value. However, if there are problems that you feel cannot or should not be dealt with by the group, they should be raised with the instructors in individual conference. You should not hesitate to ask for a meeting if you have a special concern.

The instructors will be glad to meet individually with you, or may occasionally suggest a meeting. The relationship between instructor and student is not intended to be a therapeutic relationship, however. The aims of the instructors are educational, and the purpose of the course is educational.

RECORDING OF OBSERVATIONS AND IMPRESSIONS

You are advised to keep a post-session diary in which you record as soon as possible after each session what you have observed, how you have felt, and what you speculate may be true or may happen. You will depend heavily upon this personal record for later analysis, so include all possible data, subjective as well as objective, speculative as well as descriptive. You are encouraged to keep the diary after the session rather than to take notes in session in order that you may participate more freely and learn to depend upon memory. Sound recordings are made of all sessions and are available upon application to the Secretary in the bay at Room 1314. The Tape-Listening room is Room 1300.

TRAINING IN OBSERVATION

In addition to regular participation, you are to observe your own group from the observation room three or four times each term. The times should be widely separated. Do not wait more than a week or so from the beginning of the year to begin, and do not bunch sessions at the end of the terms.

The purpose of your sessions in the observation room is to broaden your experience, and to help you begin to develop more formal observational skills. In observing your group from the observation room you have an opportunity to see what the group is like without your presence, and to experience differences in perception when you are relieved of the usual pressures of participation. Initially your purpose should be simply to expose yourself to these experiences and to familiarize yourself with the room and the equipment. But soon you should begin to concentrate on particular issues, persons, or types of interaction and to experiment with more clearly defined methods of observation.

Periodically throughout the year announcements will be posted in the meeting room offering single meetings or short courses of training in various methods of observation. These are meant to be of help to you in more formal study of your group. These short courses will be offered voluntarily by members of the staff or advanced students. They will be open to members of all sections and will be voluntary in attendance. They will be conducted in the ordinary academic or didactic way—that is, they will not be self-analytic and will be held at times and places to be announced.

PRIVACY AND RESPONSIBILITY

Some possible threat to privacy is inherent in the educational aims of the course since understanding of oneself and others is a part of the knowledge sought. How much of your personal life you introduce is a matter for your own judgment and choice. There is no requirement that you disclose more than you choose. Your choice in the matter is your right of privacy. The privacy of each individual is respected. To invade the privacy of another is to threaten him and his ability to develop. Fear of disclosure and the immediate consequences may prevent the person from having the freedom to explore his feelings, the time and freedom he needs to be himself, and to think things through for himself, and to develop in his own unique way.

Although there is no requirement that you disclose more of yourself or your life outside the group than you choose, there is a commitment to participate as a group member. In the process of participating you may in fact unintentionally as well as intentionally, provide some material which is considered appropriate for discussion. In this sense you offer to serve as a "subject" as well as an "observer." Part of the aim of the course is to help you discover and explore, to some extent, unconscious motivation. You may learn to recognize aspects of personality in yourself or in others, of which you have not been fully aware. Events that occur in the group are analyzed so far as the situation permits—this is the work of the group. Your part in these events and in the analysis is always considered potential material for discussion.

For your own protection and sense of security the instructors want you to be aware in advance that a course and situation of this kind are likely to be emotionally involving. Topics of emotional concern are likely to be discussed—relations to authority, sex, male and female roles, religion, politics, minority-group problems, social problems generally, forms of deviant behavior, matters of social appearance, manner, speech, dreams, desires, wishes, problems of values, ethical behavior, family relationships, social class, self-conceptions, and many others. You may experience many different emotional reactions, such as frustration, anxiety, anger, boredom, elation, excitement, affection.

As a result of participation your self-concept may be challenged, and you may change to some extent. You may experience conflict between a desire to reveal more private aspects of your personality and your proper concern for self-protection. The instructors will always encourage you to protect both yourself and others from emotional over-exposure at any given time. So far as we have information, the risk of any serious strain is low. Over the history of the course there have been no known instances of injury to emotional health. Nevertheless, you should be aware of possible conflicts and strains before you enroll in the course, since one cannot always predict the degree to which one may become involved.

Although in entering the course as a student you also agree to serve, in a limited sense, as a "subject," as well as an "observer," you are not involved in an experiment, but in an academic course based upon naturalistic observation. Neither you, nor the instructors, nor any others connected with the course should be engaged in any "experiment" which involves "manipulation," "deception," nor any active alteration of the conditions here described. Everyone is expected to rely upon honest participation, observation, comparison of individuals and groups, and careful analysis of the verbal interaction for gains in understanding. You will find these naturally available means to knowledge are very effective if seriously used.

You are expected to accept the physical situation, the observation, and the limited time of your sessions as scheduled, and to work within these boundaries. More specifically you should not try to extend the time of the meetings, try to have additional meetings or parties outside, nor try to employ any artificial or unusual means for breaking down the natural reluctance of individuals or the group to deal with given topics or problems. You should try to *observe and understand* such reluctances and to *discuss and interpret* them in the group, rather than to break them down forcibly. If properly understood and interpreted they will tend to dissolve and shift in a natural way to the next set of problems. You should not be impatient or try to work out problems arising from the group in settings other than the group meetings. Interaction with group members outside the group should not be substituted for interaction within the group. Nor, of course, should you attempt to bring other individuals into the group as visitors. All of these matters, if they arise, should be *talked about* in the group, since they are all significant indicators of the conditions in the group. Tendencies to action should be translated into the verbal modality rather than "acted out." The principal mode of action in the group is verbal communication within the group.

Since some threat to the privacy of individuals is present, in the realization of the educational aims of this course, it is necessary for all concerned to assume appropriate responsibilities toward the protection and healthy development of others. Students, as well as instructors and observers, are required to undertake these responsibilities. Protection of the emotional welfare of individuals supersedes the protection of confidentiality or any other of the boundary conditions of the course or the group, in case of conflict.

RESEARCH AND TRAINING

Students who have taken the course with satisfactory development of understanding and responsibility may be permitted, under the supervision of the staff as a whole, to continue with observation of the course-groups in the subsequent year, as a way of continuing their research or training in the scientific study of personalities and groups. It is expected that they will work out special studies under supervision. Such studies may be confined to observation, or they may carry over to experiments, provided any experimental portions are arranged and conducted outside the boundaries of the course. No studies will be permitted except under the supervision of the staff, and none will be permitted which might interfere with the educational aims of the course.

Under these conditions second-year students in training and others may be permitted to ask course members for cooperation in the taking of special tests or participation in experiments outside the course. Course members are under no obligation or pressure to participate, however. It is understood that observational records from the course, including sound recordings, may, with proper care, be used by qualified persons under appropriate supervision of the staff. First year students will have access to the sound recordings of their own group. They are not permitted to observe other groups. The professional ethics of the behavioral scientist apply to all of these relationships, and the rights of all are to be respected.

USE OF THE OBSERVATION ROOM

The observation room is to be used only by persons who have been specifically authorized by the instructors of the group meeting at that time. The observation room assistant is authorized to check all persons who enter. Even though you are authorized to enter yourself, you may not bring friends, or relatives, or other guests or visitors to observe.

You are authorized to observe your own group, but not others. Upon entering, please sign the book kept by the observation room assistant. The first time you sign, please give ample identification. Thereafter, you may omit identifying information, but if you appear not to be known to the observation room assistant, you should explain who you are and your authorization. The assistant may not be yet fully acquainted with all authorized observers. It is his responsibility to assure himself and members of the group being observed that the persons in the observation room are authorized to be there by instructors of the section, or a member of the staff of the course. Observers should sign each time.

The observer's role is a privileged one. Personal information gleaned by the observer must be kept strictly confidential. Please do not disrupt the group observed by attempting to communicate with them, by talking loudly in the observation room, by tapping the mirror, or the like. If you smoke, avoid showing a lighted match, as this can be seen from the conference room and is disruptive.

Your admission to the observation room implies a commitment on your part to the other observers as well as to the group members. Avoid talking if possible, definitely avoid loud laughter or free displays of emotion. Please maintain proper seating, and do not make yourself conspicuous by bodily attitudes. Resist the tendency to act out or seek confirmation for any emotional reactions you may have. Allow the other observers to see the group in their own ways and to form their own opinions.

It is important to all persons whether participating or observing, that observation should be conducted with appropriate responsibility and dignity.

BASIC AGREEMENT BETWEEN STAFF AND STUDENTS

The instructors welcome your application to the course if you are prepared to accept the general conditions outlined above. Most students have found it to be a valuable educational experience. You should ask about any matters that trouble you prior to application to the course. Your final enrollment in the course, after acceptance of your application, is taken as your agreement to the following statement, and you may assume, in return, that the instructors in the course adhere to the statement as well:

> I understand the purposes of the course as described in the syllabus, and believe I have informed myself as well as possible in advance about the nature and possible risks of the undertaking. I voluntarily agree to the undertaking, as a group member, as a subject in the limited senses described, and as an observer. I accept the reasonable and minor invasions of my privacy and that of my group that may be involved. I accept the ethical responsibilities involved in the professional role of a scientific investigator, most particularly the ethical requirement for the informed consent of those group members who act as subjects in relation to me and for their protection; I accept the responsibility of keeping the invasion of their privacy at a minimum and for the protection of the confidentiality of information received from them. I understand that these ethical considerations apply in detail to my relationships with other members of my group, and that all others connected in any way with the course and its observation undertake the same responsibilities.

READING, PAPERS, AND EXAMINATIONS

Each term is divided into three meeting periods plus a reading period, and is completed by a regular scheduled three-hour written examination.

Each meeting period requires a paper written upon some theme jointly related to the writer himself, his group, and the assigned reading. A bibliography is given for each period, including the reading periods.

Each paper is due on the date indicated, and may not be delayed except by special arrangement for adequate reason, with the instructor(s). Each student will receive comments on each paper and on his participation in the group to date. For this reason, papers must not fall behind. No letter grade will ordinarily be assigned to the papers. A letter grade will be assigned to the examination at the end of the term, however, and the term grade will reflect an inclusive evaluation of all papers, and the quality of understanding shown in participation for the full term. Participation, specifically *the demonstration of analytical ability and interpretive skill in the group*, is as important as the written work.

Upon request the course may be taken on a pass-fail basis, but if so, it must be taken on that basis for both terms, since the final grade reflects a cumulative evaluation of the work over both terms.

FALL TERM

PERIOD I (Monday, September 23 to Friday, October 18)

THE PERSONALITY OF THE INDIVIDUAL

Individuals bring persisting, sometimes unconscious, tendencies and modes of behavior to social situations. Psychoanalytic theory, represented by Freud, and in modified form by Horney, is particularly concerned with the ties between conscious and unconscious tendencies, and the directions they have been given by early experience. Goffman represents another school, which emphasizes the pressures of the current social situation on a more conscious and rationalistic level, especially with regard to self-concept. Gibb discusses the relationship between individual traits and the needs of the social situation. Horney discusses the possibilities of learning to understand one's own personality better through self-analysis. Bales discusses the history of this course, and the origins of the kind of self-analytic group in which you now find yourself.

Reading

Bales, R. F. *Personality and Interpersonal Behavior* (New York: Holt, Rinehart, and Winston, 1970), Preface.

Freud, S. "Group Psychology and the Analysis of the Ego", in Rickman, J., ed., *A General Selection from the Works of Sigmund Freud* (New York: Liveright Publishing Corporation, 1957) pages 169–209.

Goffman, Erving, *The Presentation of Self in Everyday Life,* (New York: Doubleday & Company, 1957) (paperback) pages 1–105.

Gibb, C. A., "The Principles and Traits of Leadership." Hare, A. P., et. al., *Small Groups,* (New York: Alfred A. Knopf, 1955) pages 87–95.

Horney, Karen, *Self Analysis,* (New York: W. W. Norton, 1942), pages 7–189, 286–303.

Paper: Due Monday, October 21

Write a paper on problems faced by the individual member in the early phases of the group's existence, particularly problems which have to do with the nature of individual personality. What have been your reactions? How have they differed from those of others?

The paper should give about equal emphasis to the reading, analysis of the group, and self-analysis. Top limit (the same for all papers) 2500 words, or about 10 pages, double-spaced.

PERIOD II (Monday, October 21 to Friday, November 15)

GROUP INFLUENCES ON INTERPERSONAL BEHAVIOR

What should we mean by the term "group"? Is a "leader" really necessary? Is some "structure" necessary? Is the individual likely to be subjected to influences stemming from group conditions which he neither understands nor wants? Redl presents a typology of different types of leaders based on emotional states. Jacques, and Herbert and Trist discuss the way in which certain emotional concerns may lead to efforts to establish leadership and structure. Flugel discusses the relation between the way the family is structured, and the formation of personality, especially its nonrational aspects. Adorno and his colleagues describe in detail one range of personality types (the "authoritarian" types), who are particularly concerned with structure and leadership. Smith brings recollections from her childhood in an effort to understand better the roots of prejudice in the South.

Reading

Adorno, T. W., and others, *The Authoritarian Personality*, (New York: Harper & Row, 1950), pages 31–56, 145–150, 222, 241, 269–279.

Flugel, J. C., *The Psychoanalytic Study of the Family*, (London: Hogarth Press, 1950), pages 1–116, 156–174.

Herbert, E. L., and E. L. Trist, "The Institution of an Absent Leader by a Students' Discussion Group," *Human Relations* 1953, vol. 6, pages 215-248 (mimeographed).

Jacques, E., "Social System as a Defense Against Persecutory and Depressive Anxiety," in *New Directions in Psychoanalysis*, (New York, Basic Books, Inc., 1957), pages 478–495.

Redl, F. "Group Emotion and Leadership," in Hare, A. P., Borgatta, E. F., and Bales, R. F., (eds), *Small Groups*, (New York: Alfred A. Knopf, 1955), pages 71–87.

Smith, Lillian, *Killers of the Dream*, (New York: W. W. Norton & Company, 1949), pages 15–172.

Paper: Due Monday, November 18

Take the three earliest recollections you have, preferably before the age of six, and write them out in as much concrete detail as you can. Compare and contrast these recollections, looking for similarities and differences. Relate these recollections to your present personality; if possible to aspects of your personality involved in the present group.

PERIOD III (Monday, November 18 to Friday, December 20)

APPROACHES TO ANALYTIC PROCEDURE

Our task as individuals and as a group is the analysis of interpersonal behavior. But how is one to begin to sift through the multitude of stimuli which present themselves? In your group there will be roughly half a million words spoken during the year. Even if we could devise a method for encompassing all this verbal interaction in some systematic way, we would still have to deal with the vast sea of nonverbal interaction. Where and how shall we begin to observe and interpret? Henderson establishes some criteria for scientific procedure in general, and the case method in particular, which is the method we employ. Erikson deals with "clinical" procedures, which must be employed in many situations, including our own, from only naturally-available information. Bales and Mann attempt to bring clinical and quantitative methods to the support of each other, as they can be in our situation. Collingwood, with another important emphasis, presents a concept and an ideal of an "artistic" mode of combined expression and discovery, which could also be a mode of leadership in a self-analytic group.

Reading

Bales, R. F., *Personality and Interpersonal Behavior,* (New York: Holt, Rinehart and Winston, 1970) Part I.

Collingwood, R. G., *The Principles of Art,* (New York: Oxford University Press, 1956), Book III, pages 273–336.

Erikson, Erik H., "The Nature of Clinical Evidence," in his book, *Insight and Responsibility,* (New York: W. W. Norton & Company, 1964) pages 49–80.

Henderson, L. J., "Procedure in a Science," in Cabot, H., and Kahl, J. A., *Human Relations* (Cambridge, Mass.: Harvard University Press, 1953), vol. 1, pages 24–39.

Mann, Richard D., with Graham S. Gibbard and John J. Hartman, *Interpersonal Styles and Group Development,* (New York: John Wiley & Sons, 1967) pages 1–145.

Ratings: Due Friday, December 20

This exercise consists of applying ratings or an evaluative procedure to yourself and other members of your group, as described in Bales, Chapter 1. The procedure will be described in a set of instructions to be handed out at the beginning of the period. Your ratings will be combined numerically with those of all other members of the group by the instructors, and the summary ratings received by all members will then be returned to you. The final examination for the term will, in part, require you to analyze these results along the lines described in Bales Chapter 3.

It is urgently necessary that this paper be handed in on the due date, since data from all papers must be combined by the instructors.

PERIOD IV Reading Period, (Monday, January 6 to Thursday, January 16).

SEXUALITY AND AGGRESSION IN INTERPERSONAL RELATIONS

Freud, in a mythological format (not to be taken literally) considers the basic motives of sexuality and aggression as they affect the way the child grows up and forms relationships with others, particularly the parents. Bettleheim, in a cross-cultural perspective, shows the way in which these basic motives are intertwined with the process of growing up socially and assuming the appropriate adult sex-role for the society.

The selection from Bales is included to help with your observational training, and to provide background for analysis of the rating data from your group. Since you will have only a short time to write on this in the examination, you must prepare the analysis ahead of time. The data will be given to you early in the reading period.

Reading
Bales, R. F., *Personality and Interpersonal Behavior*, (New York: Holt, Rinehart and Winston, 1970) Part II.

Bettleheim, Bruno, *Symbolic Wounds*, (New York: The Free Press, 1954), 175 pp. (Paperback) Collier.

Freud, Sigmund, "Totem and Taboo," *The Basic Writings of Sigmund Freud*, (New York: Modern Library, 1938).

Meetings After Christmas Recess
In order to avoid too long a gap in the meetings of the group, the group will meet three days into reading period, on January 6, 8, and 10. (The Christmas recess extends from December 22 to January 5.)
Examination: *As scheduled by the Registrar*

SPRING TERM

PERIOD V (Monday, February 3, to Friday, February 28)

THE LOGIC OF FANTASY

Freud's *Interpretation of Dreams* is the direct result of his own self-analysis. Its importance for us lies partly in its demonstration of what analysis of the single case can reveal, partly in delineation of the logic of fantasy. Fantasy appears at all levels of human behavior—from the dreams of the individual, and the play and jokes of group settings, to the persistent and recurrent myths and rituals of cultures. Fantasy is so commonplace that it is easily overlooked as of no importance. But close attention to it can provide, as Freud believed, a "royal road to the unconscious."

Reading

Freud, Sigmund, *The Interpretation of Dreams* translated by James Strachey, Basic Books, New York: Avon, 1966 (paperback). Published in the United States by arrangement with George Allen & Unwin Ltd. and The Hogarth Press, Ltd., London.

Paper: Due Monday, March 3

Discuss the *Interpretation of Dreams* in relation to a dream or fantasy of your own, or in relation to a case, or fantasies in your own group. Chapter 7 of Bales' *Personality and Interpersonal Behavior* is relevant to group fantasies.

PERIOD VI (Monday, March 3 to Friday, March 28)

DYNAMIC PROCESSES IN SELF-ANALYTIC GROUPS

Self-analytic groups are disorienting. They pose problems of meaning by forcing us to look at familiar behavior in new ways and to see patterns of behavior previously unrecognized. This may be threatening. Sometimes for no obvious reason, progress stops and resistance sets in. At other times the reason seems obvious, but the solution does not. The persistence of nonrational and self-defeating behavior in the group, whether subtle or obvious, should be dealt with by recognition, and attempts to analyze further. While such behavior provides useful material for analysis and learning, (and the first problem is to recognize and understand it), ways must also be found for dealing with it when recognized if the group is to continue to improve its effectiveness and realize its potential. The aims of the group should be not only to achieve understanding in isolated instances, but to develop values, norms, leadership, emotional resources, and a working theoretical point of view which makes further effective analysis possible, as a cooperative process. The achievement of these complex developmental aims is the "work" of the group. Dunphy, Mann, and Mills, all former instructors in Social Relations 120, discuss the difficulties of these achievements.

Reading

Dunphy, Dexter C., "Social Change in Self-Analytic Groups," Chapter 8 in Philip J. Stone, D. C. Dunphy, M. S. Smith, and D. M. Ogilvie, *The General Inquirer: A Computer Approach to Content Analysis* (Cambridge, Mass.: The M.I.T. Press, 1966)

Mann, Richard D., with Graham S. Gibbard and John J. Hartman *Interpersonal Styles and Group Development* (New York: John Wiley & Sons, Inc., 1967) pages 146–299

Mills, Theodore M., *Group Transformation, An Analysis of a Learning Group* (Englewood Cliffs, N. J. Prentice-Hall Inc., 1964) pages 1–120.

Paper: Due Monday, April 7 (after the Spring Recess, which is March 30 to April 6)

Select the one meeting throughout the year of greatest interest to you, preferably some high spot or turning point for the group which contributed to its culture. Make a literal, verbatim transcription from the tape of the most important ten minutes or so of this meeting. Then, make a detailed analysis and commentary on this transcription, sentence by sentence, *demonstrating your ability to analyze and reconstruct,* from the surface verbal behavior, important underlying motives, relationships, and group processes that helped to determine the specific surface behavior and made it important. You may use any or all methods, formal or informal, described throughout the year, applied to the verbatim transcript. You will also bring to bear, of course, your observations and impressions of the group, including your post-session diary.

PERIOD VII (Monday, April 7 to Wednesday, April 30)

PERSONAL EXPERIENCE AND THE CREATION OF CULTURE

Bibring and Freud deal with emotional problems similar to those likely to be faced in the ending of the group. One of the problems current throughout the life of the group, but particularly acute at the end, is how to make personal emotional experience intelligible and meaningful to one's self and others. An important aspect of meaning may be given to individual experience by participation in the cumulative experience of others, and by the creation of a culture which transcends the limitations of the individual, and even the particular group. The self-analytic group to which you belong exists as a part of a cumulative culture of such groups. Kluckhohn treats the basic process of myth-making in cross-cultural perspective. Slater's book, assigned for the reading period, may also give important clues.

Reading

Bibring, E., "The Mechanism of Depression," in Greenacre, P. (ed.), *Affective Disorders* (New York: International Universities Press, 1953), pages 13–48.

Freud, S., "Analysis Terminable and Interminable," *Collected Papers,* ed. James Strachey (London: Hogarth Press, Ltd., 1952) vol. V., 316–357.

Kluckhohn, C., "Recurrent Themes in Myths and Mythmaking," *Daedalus,* vol. 88, No. 2, Spring 1959, 268–279.

Ratings: Due Monday, April 15

Each student is required to submit ratings of himself and other group members in the same manner specified for the ratings of December 20. These ratings will be collated by the instructors and returned to the group at the earliest opportunity so the group can consider changes in roles and group structure. The final examination will depend partly upon study of these data.

PERIOD VII Reading Period, (Thursday May 1 to Tuesday, May 20)

Reading Period Assignment

Slater, Philip E., *Microcosm: Structural Psychological, and Religious Evolution in Groups* (New York: John Wiley & Sons, 1966) pages 7–265.

Examination: *As scheduled by the Registrar*

Appendix 7

Physical Design of a Laboratory
for the Study of Groups

Figure 1 shows the floor plan, table, and seating layout of the group meeting room and observation room at the Center for the Behavioral Sciences at Harvard. I have previously written on the planning of an observation room and group laboratory with one of my colleagues (33). Most of what we recommended in that article remains valid, I believe, and there is no need to repeat those recommendations here. The installation at the Center for the Behavioral Sciences is new, however, and has certain features that deserve comment.

It will be noted that the meeting room is set up to hold about twenty-five group members—certainly a larger-sized group than that usually employed in small-group experiments, and larger also than most people expect to be practical for a self-analytic group. It must be admitted that the size was set, not for theoretical reasons, but simply because of the cost of instruction. A class of twenty-five is within the range of reasonable academic costs. The size has not proved to be too large. Students learn from their differences, and a group of twenty-five insures a fairly diverse sample of personality types and value-positions. It is thus also probable that there will be six or eight students who are prone to be fairly active in their participation, so that a group gets off to a lively start and seldom languishes for the lack of persons ready to participate. It should be recognized, however, that each group remains intact through the full academic year, over seventy meetings, and if the running time were not so long the size considerations would be different.

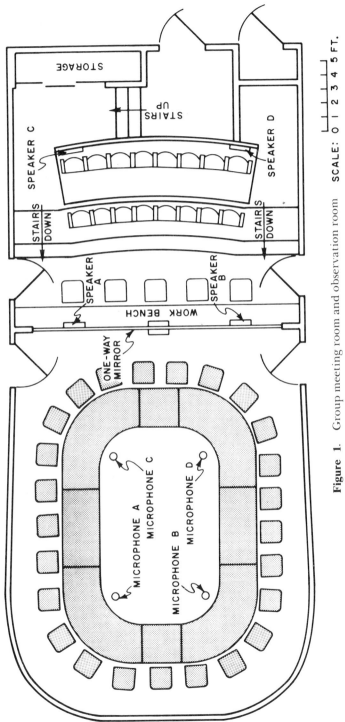

Figure 1. Group meeting room and observation room   SCALE: 0 1 2 3 4 5 FT.

It is also true that with a normal rate of absences, the actual size of most meetings is around twenty.

The observation room provides for about the same number of observers as group members. Most of the observers sit in the raised amphitheater seats, but there is room for six or eight observers engaged in technical tasks (such as recording interaction) at the bench. Twenty-five is a larger number of observers than one imagines can possibly be practical, but it proves not to be. It is not satisfactory to offer a course like Social Relations 120 over a long period of time without providing for additional functions that may not be foreseen. One needs to provide: (1) a way for students to continue with more advanced training after having completed participation in a group; (2) a means for the observational comparison of sections of the course, or separate groups; (3) a way to introduce graduate students to this area of training and research; (4) a means for the training of staff; and (5) facilities for research. When all these needs are taken into account, it is not hard to see that a substantial number of places in the observation room is necessary.

Another way in which the installation goes beyond earlier conceptions is in the sound equipment. In order to preserve the impression of directionality for the location of voices, four semi-directional ceiling microphones are employed, one covering each corner quadrant of the table in the meeting room. Each microphone is connected to an independent high-fidelity amplifier, which in turn, is connected to a separate monitoring speaker in the observation room. The speakers are placed in the observation room so that they parallel in their location the positions of microphones in the meeting room (see the illustration). When the volume controls are properly balanced, the observer is able to locate each person speaking immediately, and the sense of psychological presence of the speaker is greatly enhanced. These are worthwhile advantages, especially when so many persons are involved. For the sound tape a stereo-recording is made, with the two right-hand microphones (A and C) mixed together on one channel, and the two left-hand ones (B and D) on the other channel.

In addition to the facility shown in the illustration there is a nearby room fitted out for tape-listening, with four stereo playback machines, each connected to headphones, so that the students may listen to tapes of past sessions. There is also an ample reception area, large enough to accommodate a new set of group members and observers, while they wait for those of the previous hour to finish. There are presently five sections of the course which meet on consecutive hours.

In the recommendations of the earlier article (33) two mistakes in judgment were made which should be corrected. They both concern the placing of the glass panels for the one-way mirrors. The first recommendation was that the coated or mirrored face of the glass next to the observation room should be turned to the dead-air space, for scratch protection. Apparently this is unnecessary since the coating is not fragile, and it is undesirable because it gives a faint double image from the group meeting room. The mirrored side of the one-way glass should face the group meeting room directly. The other error was the recommendation that the second pane of glass, for protection and sound insulation, should be placed quite close—leaving a dead-air space of about 5/16 of an inch. This is too close and contributes to the multiple-image effect. The second pane may be 3 or 4 inches away from the first, with good effect, and with better sound insulation.

The light level in the group meeting room should be fixed at the highest comfortable level. The light in the group observation room should be on a rheostat and should be adjusted so that, from the observation room, the light in the two rooms appears to be about equal. The observers need light for their work, and it is not desirable to have a dark theater kind of atmosphere, since one wishes to encourage some psychological distance, rather than identification of observer with group members too completely. If the light level is fixed in this way, it will not prove to be bright enough to enable the group members to see through from their side.

Appendix 8

The Interaction Recorder

Figure 2 shows a machine called an interaction recorder, developed by H. Gerbrands and the author to aid in recording observations. The prototype is described in (34). The machine provides a moving paper tape with an exposed surface 3 inches by 8 inches, upon which scores may be written. The tape moves horizontally at a constant speed of 12 inches per minute. The scores are thus kept in time order, and disappear as the tape moves. Total running time per roll of paper is over 3 hours.

A holder to the left of the paper surface contains the set of twelve interaction categories arranged vertically as in Figure 6.1. The plastic writing surface over which the paper moves is lighted from below, and contains black line dividers which match the spaces to the category set. The spaces are color coded by the light from below. The color code simply helps in keeping the proper position. No additional light is required in a dark room. Operating voltage of the machine is 115 volts A.C., 60 cycles.

The paper is common adding-machine stock, which may be obtained in rolls of the proper size by order from a paper supplier. The paper tape used for a given recording may be removed from the machine at the end of a period of observation without removing the supply roll.

The machines are placed on the bench inside the observation room. They are often used in pairs, with each observer making a complete recording as a check on reliability. Comparison of the paper tapes after removal from the machines gives a completely definite check, score by score, on the similarities and differences between two scorers (158). Comparison of the total number of scores in the same category at the end of a time period may be used to give a less definitive comparison (51, 67). In such a comparison, which can also be made when scores are taken on paper pads, one can reduce the two profiles to percentage rates and then, by the use of Table 6.1, can determine whether the differences are great enough to give a different directional indicator for each category. This is a reasonable practical test, though not nearly so definitive as one may obtain by using two interaction recorders. The obvious type of test when tapes are available is percentage of agreement in categorization on each act recorded. One should hope for at least 80 percent agreement, although this is not always easy to attain (158).

Figure 2. The Bales-Gerbrands Interaction Recorder

Bibliography

1. Adorno, Theodore, Else Frenkel-Brunswik, Daniel J. Levinson, R. Nevitt Sanford, and others, *The Authoritarian Personality.* New York: Harper & Row, Publishers, 1950.

2. Allport, Gordon W., Philip E. Vernon, and Gardner Lindzey, *Study of Values,* revised edition. Boston: Houghton Mifflin Company, 1951.

3. American Psychological Association, *Casebook on Ethical Standards of Psychologists,* Washington, D.C.: 1967, (relevant portions reprinted in *American Psychologist, 23,* no. 5. (May 1968), 357–361.

4. Bales, Robert F., "The Concept 'Situation' as a Methodological Tool," Unpublished Masters thesis, University of Oregon, 1940.

5. ———, "Types of Social Structure as Factors in 'Cures' for Alcohol Addiction," *Applied Anthropology,* Graduate School of Business Administration, Harvard University, April-May-June 1942.

6. ———, "The Therapeutic Role of Alcoholics Anonymous as Seen by a Sociologist," *Quarterly Journal of Studies on Alcohol,* September 1944.

7. ———, "The Fixation Factor in Alcohol Addiction, an Hypothesis Derived from a Comparative Study of Irish and Jewish Social Norms," Unpublished Ph.D. dissertation, Harvard University, Cambridge, Mass., 1945.

8. ———, "Social Therapy for a Social Disorder: Compulsive Drinking," *The Journal of Social Issues,* December 1945.

9. ———, "Cultural Differences in Rates of Alcoholism," *Quarterly Journal of Studies of Alcohol, 6,* no. 4 (March 1946), 480–499.

10. ———, "Interaction Content Analysis," in *Preliminary Report of the First National Training Laboratory on Group Development,* National Education Association and Research Center for Group Dynamics, M.I.T., 1947; obtainable from National Education Association, Washington, D.C.

11. ———, *Interaction Process Analysis, a Method for the Study of Small Groups,* Reading, Mass.: Addison-Wesley Publishing Company, Inc., 1950.

12. ———, "A Set of Categories for the Analysis of Small Group Interaction," *American Sociological Review, XV*, no. 2, (April 1950), 257–263.

13. ———, "Some Statistical Problems in Small Group Research," *Journal of the American Statistical Association, 45,* (September 1951), 311–322.

14. ———, "Reply to Keller's Comment" (on "Channels of Communication in Small Groups"), *American Sociological Review, 16,* no. 6 (December 1951).

15. ———, "Some Uniformities of Behavior in Small Social Systems," in *Readings in Social Psychology,* edited by G. E. Swanson, Theodore M. Newcomb, and Eugene L. Hartley. New York: Holt, Rinehart and Winston, Inc. 1952, 146–159.

16. ———, "The Equilibrium Problem in Small Groups," Chapter IV in Talcott Parsons, Robert F. Bales, and Edward Shils, *Working Papers in the Theory of Action.* New York: The Free Press, 1953.

17. ———, "A Theoretical Framework for Interaction Process Analysis," in *Group Dynamics, Research and Theory,* edited by D. Cartwright and A. Zander. Evanston, Ill.: Row, Peterson, & Company, 1953.

18. ———, "In Conference," *Harvard Business Review,* March-April 1954, 44–50.

19. ———, "How People Interact in Conferences," *Scientific American,* March 1955, 31–35.

20. ———, "Task Status and Likeability as a Function of Talking and Listening in Decision-Making Groups," in Leonard D. White, *The State of the Social Sciences.* Chicago: University of Chicago Press, 1956, 148–161.

21. ———, "Task Roles and Social Roles in Problem-Solving Groups," in Eleanor E. Maccoby, Theodore M. Newcomb, and Eugene L. Hartley, eds., *Readings in Social Psychology,* New York: Holt, Rinehart and Winston, Inc., 1958, 437–447.

22. ———, "Motivational Engineering: A Feat" (A review of *Alcoholics Anonymous Comes of Age*), *Contemporary Psychology,* August 1958, 230–231.

23. ———, "Small Group Theory and Research," in Robert K. Merton, Leonard Broom, and Leonard S. Cottrell, Jr., *Sociology Today, Problems and Prospects.* New York: Basic Books, Inc., 1959, 293–305.

24. ———, "Conceptual Frameworks for Analysis of Social Interaction, Comments on Four Papers," *Journal of Experimental Education, 30,* no. 4, (June 1962), 323–324.

25. ———, "Attitudes Toward Drinking in the Irish Culture," in David J. Pittman and Charles R. Snyder, eds. *Society, Culture and Drinking Patterns,* New York: John Wiley & Sons, Inc., 1962, 157–187.

26. ———, "Comment on Herbert Blumer's paper," *American Journal of Sociology, LXXXI,* no. 5 (March 1966), 545–547.

27. ———, "Interaction Process Analysis," in *New International Encyclopedia of the Social Sciences.* New York: The Macmillan Company, 1968.

28.   ——, and Edgar F. Borgatta, "Changes in the Interaction Profile by Group Size," in A. Paul Hare, Edgar F. Borgatta and Robert F. Bales, *Small Groups.* New York: Alfred A. Knopf, 1955.

29.   ——, and Arthur S. Couch, "A Factor Analytic Study of Group Satisfaction," Unpublished manuscript, Harvard University, 1956.

30.   ——, and Arthur S. Couch, "Dynamic Balance in Social Interaction," Unpublished paper, read at meetings of the American Sociological Association, September 1956.

31.   ——, and Arthur S. Couch, "The Value-Profile: A Factor Analytic Study of Value Statements," *Sociological Inquiry,* vol. 39, no. 1 (Winter 1969). Included as Appendix 5 of this book.

32.   ——, Arthur S. Couch, and Philip J. Stone, "The Interaction Simulator," in "Proceedings of a Symposium on Digital Computers and their Applications," *Annals of the Computation Laboratory,* Cambridge, Mass.: Harvard University Press, *31,* (April 3-6, 1962), 305-314.

33.   ——, and Ned A. Flanders, "Planning an Observation Room and Group Laboratory," *American Sociological Review,* December 1954.

34.   ——, and Henry Gerbrands, "The 'Interaction Recorder,' an Apparatus and Check List for Sequential Content Analysis of Social Interaction," *Human Relations, 1,* no. 4, 1943.

35.   ——, and A. Paul Hare, "Diagnostic Use of the Interaction Profile," *The Journal of Social Psychology,* 1965, 239-258.

36.   ——, A. Paul Hare, and Edgar F. Borgatta, "Structure and Dynamics of Small Groups: A Review of Four Variables," in Joseph P. Gittler, (ed.) *Review of Sociology, Analysis of a Decade.* New York: John Wiley & Sons, Inc., 1957, 391-422.

37.   ——, and Talcott Parsons, "Levels of Cultural Generality and the Process of Differentiation," in Talcott Parsons and Robert F. Bales, and others, *Family, Socialization, and Interaction Process.* New York: The Free Press, 1955.

38.   ——, and P. E. Slater, "Role Differentiation in Small Decision-Making Groups," in Talcott Parsons, Robert F. Bales, and others, *Family, Socialization, and Interaction Process.* New York: The Free Press, 1955, 259-306.

39.   ——, and Philip E. Slater, "Notes on 'Role Differentiation' in Small Decision Making Groups: Reply to Dr. Wheeler," *Sociometry, XX,* no. 2 (June 1957), 152-155.

40.   ——, and Fred L. Strodtbeck, "Phases in Group Problem-Solving," *Journal of Abnormal and Social Psychology, 46,* no. 4, (October 1951), 485-495.

41.   ——, Fred L. Strodtbeck, Theodore M. Mills, and Mary E. Roseborough, "Channels of Communication in Small Groups," *American Sociological Review, 16,* no. 4, (August 1951), 461-468.

42.   Bennis, Warren, and Herbert Shepard, "A Theory of Group Development," *Human Relations, 9,* 1956, 415-437.

43. Berger, J., "Relations between Performance, Rewards, and Action-opportunities in Small Groups," Unpublished Ph.D. dissertation, Harvard University, 1957.

44. Berman, Leo, "Mental Hygiene for Educators; Report on an Experiment Using Combined Seminar and Group Psychotherapy Approach," *Psychoanalytic Review, 40,* October 1953, 319–332.

45. Blake, Robert, and Janey Srygley Mouton, "The Instrumented Training Laboratory," in Irving R. Weschler and Edgar H. Schein, *Issues in Human Relations Training,* National Training Laboratory for Group Development, Washington, D.C., Selected Readings Series, no. 5, 1962.

46. Bonacich, Philip, "Specialization and Differentation of Leadership in Small Laboratory Groups," Unpublished Ph.D. Dissertation, Harvard University, 1968.

47. Borgatta, Edgar F., Analysis of Social Interaction and Sociometric Perception," *Sociometry, 17,* 1954, 7–32.

48. ———, "The Structure of Personality Characteristics," *Behavioral Sciences, 9,* no. 1, (January 1964), 8–17.

49. ———, and Robert F. Bales, "Task and Accumulation of Experience as Factors in the Interaction of Small Groups," *Sociometry, 16,* 1953, 239–252.

50. ———, and Robert F. Bales, "Interaction of Individuals in Reconstituted Groups," *Sociometry,* November 1953, 302–320.

51. ———, and Robert F. Bales, "The Consistency of Subject Behavior and the Reliability of Scoring in Interaction Process Analysis," *American Sociological Review,* October 1953, 566–569.

52. ———, and Robert F. Bales, "Sociometric Status Patterns and Characteristics of Interaction," *Journal of Social Psychology, 43,* 1956, 289–297.

53. ———, L. S. Cottrell, Jr., and J. H. Mann, "The Spectrum of Individual Interaction Characteristics: An Inter-Dimensional Analysis," *Psychological Reports, 4,* 1958, 279–319.

54. ———, Arthur S. Couch, and Robert F. Bales, "Some Findings Relevant to the Great Man Theory of Leadership," *American Sociological Review,* December 1954.

55. ———, and Elizabeth Crowther, *A Workbook for the Study of Social Interaction Processes.* Skokie, Ill.: Rand McNally & Company, 1966.

56. Breer, Paul, "Predicting Interpersonal Behavior from Personality and Role," Unpublished Ph.D. Dissertation, Harvard University, 1960.

57. Cabot, Hugh, and Joseph A. Kahl, *Human Relations,* Cambridge, Mass.: Harvard University Press, 1953.

58. Carter, Launor F., "Leadership and Small Group Behavior," in M. Sherif, and M. O. Wilson, (eds.) *Group Relations at the Crossroads,* New York: Harper & Row, Publishers, 1953, 257–284.

59. ———, "Recording and Evaluating the Performance of Individuals as Members of Small Groups," *Personnel Psychology,* 7, 1954, 477–484.

60.   ———, and Mary Nixon, "Ability, Perceptual, Personality, and Inherent Factors Associated with Different Criteria of Leadership," *Journal of Psychology, 27,* 1949, 377–388.

61.   Cattell, Raymond B., "Second-order Personality Factors in the Questionnaire Realm," *Journal of Consulting Psychology, 20,* 1956, 411–418.

62.   ———, D. R. Saunders, and G. F. Stice, "The Sixteen Personality Factor Questionnaire," *The Institute for Personality and Ability Testing,* Champaign, Illinois, 1951.

63.   ———, D. R. Saunders, and G. F. Stice, "The Dimensions of Syntality in Small Groups," *Human Relations, 6,* 1953, 331–356.

64.   ———, and G. F. Stice, "Four Formulae for Selecting Leaders on the Basis of Personality," *Human Relations, 7,* 1954, 493–507.

65.   Caudill, William A., *The Psychiatric Hospital as a Small Society,* Cambridge, Mass.: Harvard University Press, 1958.

66.   Churchill, Lindsey, "Aggression in a Small Group Setting," Unpublished Ph.D. Dissertation, Harvard University, 1961.

67.   Cohen, Bernard, and Warren Bachelis, "A Study of Reliability of Scoring in Interaction Process Analysis," Unpublished paper read at meetings of the American Sociological Association, September, 1956.

68.   Collins, Barry E., and Harold Guetzkow, *A Social Psychology of Group Processes for Decision-Making,* New York: John Wiley & Sons, Inc., 1964.

69.   Cooley, C. H., *Social Organization.* New York: Charles Scribner's Sons, 1909.

70.   Couch, Arthur S., "Factors of Group Satisfaction," Unpublished paper read at meetings of the American Sociological Association, September, 1956.

71.   Couch, Arthur S. "Psychological Determinants of Interpersonal Behavior," Unpublished Doctoral dissertation, Harvard University, Cambridge, Mass., 1960.

72.   ———, and L. S. Carter, "A Factorial Study of the Rated Behavior of Group Members," Paper read at Eastern Psychological Association, March, 1952.

73.   ———, and David G. Goodrich, "Militant Radicalism Scale," Unpublished document. 1952.

74.   ———, and Kenneth Kenniston, "Yeasayers and Naysayers: Agreeing Response set as a Personality variable," *Journal of Abnormal and Social Psychology, 60,* 1960, 151–174.

75.   Dunphy, Dexter C., "Social Change in Self-Analytic Groups," Unpublished Ph.D. Dissertation, Harvard University, 1964.

76.   ———, "Social Change in Self-Analytic Groups," in Philip J. Stone, Dexter C. Dunphy, Marshall S. Smith, and Daniel M. Ogilvie. *The General Inquirer: A Computer Approach to Content-Analysis.* Cambridge, Mass.: The M.I.T. Press, 1966.

77. Evans, John T., "Objective Measurement of the Therapeutic Group Process," Unpublished Ph.D. Dissertation, Harvard University, 1950.

78. Eysenck, Hans J., *The Psychology of Politics.* London: Routledge & Kegan Paul, Ltd., 1954.

79. ———, *The Dynamics of Anxieties and Hysteria, An Experimental Application of Modern Learning Theory to Psychiatry.* New York: Frederick Praeger, Inc., 1957, 114-115.

80. Freedman, M. B., T. F. Leary, A. B. Ossario, and H. S. Coffee, "The Interpersonal Dimension of Personality," *Journal of Personality, 20,* 1951, 143-161.

81. Freud, Sigmund, *The Interpretation of Dreams,* trans. and ed. by James Strachey, New York: Basic Books, Inc., 1955. Published in the U.S. by arrangement with George Allen & Unwin Ltd., and The Hogarth Press, Ltd, London.

82. ———, "On the History of the Psychoanalytic Movement," 1914 Translation, in Freud, Sigmund, *Collected Papers,* Vol. I. translation under the supervision of Joan Riviere. London: The Hogarth Press, 1953, 287-359.

83. ———. *Therapy and Technique,* (a collection of Freud's papers) Philip Rieff, ed., New York: Crowell-Collier and Macmillan, Inc., 1963.

84. Gorlow, L., E. C. Hoch, and E. F. Telschow, *The Nature of Non-Directive Group Psychotherapy.* New York: Columbia University Press, 1952.

85. Gough, Harrison G., *Manual for the California Psychological Inventory.* Palo Alto, Calif.: Consulting Psychologist Press, 1957.

86. Gruber, S., "Task Orientation in the Preschool Child and its Implications for Early School Adjustment," Unpublished Ph.D. Dissertation, Harvard University, 1952.

87. Guilford, J. P., *Personality,* New York: McGraw-Hill, Inc., 1959.

88. ———, and R. R. Guilford, "Personality Factors S, E, and M and their Measurement," *Journal of Psychology, 2,* 1936, 109-127.

89. Hare, A. Paul, "Situational Differences in Leader Behavior," *Journal of Abnormal & Social Psychology, 55,* 1957, 132-135.

90. ———, *Handbook of Small Group Research.* New York: The Free Press, 1962.

91. ———, and Robert F. Bales, "Seating Position and Small Group Interaction," *Sociometry, 26,* no. 4, 1963.

92. ———, Edgar F. Borgatta, and Robert F. Bales, *Small Groups: Studies in Social Interaction* (a collection of readings), New York: Alfred A. Knopf, 1955, 2d ed., 1965.

93. ———, N. Waxler, G. Saslow, and J. D. Matarazzo, "Simultaneous Recording of Bales and Chapple Interaction Measures During Initial Psychiatric Interviews," *Journal of Consulting Psychology, 23,* 1960, 193.

94. Hathaway, S. R., and J. C. McKinley, *The Minnesota Multiphasic Personality Inventory Manual* (revised). New York: Psychological Corp., 1951.

95. Haythorne, W., "The Influence of Individual Members on the Characteristics of Small Groups," *Journal of Abnormal & Social Psychology, 48*, 1953, 276-284.

96. ———, A. S. Couch, D. Haefner, P. Langham, and L. F. Carter, "The Behavior of Authoritarian and Equalitarian Personalities in Small Groups," *Human Relations, 9*, 1956, 57-74.

97. ———, A. S. Couch, D. Haefner, P. Langham, and L. F. Carter, "The effects of Varying Combinations of Authoritarian and Equalitarian Leaders and Followers," *Journal of Abnormal & Social Psychology, 53*, 1956, 210-219.

98. Heinicke, Christophe, and Robert F. Bales, "Developmental Trends in the Structure of Small Groups," *Sociometry*, February 1953, 239-253.

99. Heyns, R. W. and A. F. Zander, "Observation of Group Behavior" in L. Festinger and D. Katz, *Research Methods in the Behavioral Sciences.* New York: Holt, Rinehart and Winston, Inc., 1953, 381-417.

100. Homans, G. C., *The Human Group.* New York: Harcourt, Brace & World, Inc., 1950.

101. ———, *Social Behavior: Its Elementary Forms.* New York: Harcourt, Brace & World, Inc., 1961.

102. Jones, Edward Ellsworth, "The Role of Authoritarianism in the Perception and Evaluation of a Prospective Leader," Unpublished Dissertation, Harvard University, 1953.

103. Kassebaum, Gene G., "Value Orientations and Interpersonal Behavior, an Experimental Study," Unpublished Ph.D. Dissertation, Harvard University, 1958.

104. ———, Arthur S. Couch, and Philip E. Slater, "The Factorial Dimensions of the MMPI," *Journal of Consulting Psychology, 23,* 1959, 226-236.

105. Keller, Joseph B., "Comment on 'Channels of Communications in Small Groups,'" *American Sociological Review, 16*, 1951, 842-843.

106. Kluckhohn, Florence R., "Dominant and Substitute Profiles of Cultural Orientation," *Social Forces, XXVIII*, no. 4, May 1950.

107. ———, "Dominant and Variant Cultural Value Orientations" in H. Cabot, and J. A. Kahl, *Human Relations*, Cambridge, Mass.: Harvard University Press, 1953.

108. Landsberger, H. A., "Interaction Process Analysis of Professional Behavior: A Study of Labor Mediators in Twelve Labor-Management Disputes," *American Sociological Review, 20,* 1955, 566-575.

109. Leary, Timothy, *Interpersonal Diagnosis of Personality.* New York: The Ronald Press Company, 1957.

110. Lennard, H., M. E. Jarvik, and H. A. Abramson, "Lysergic Acid Diethyla-mide (LSD-25) : XII. A Preliminary Statement of its Effects upon Interpersonal Communication," *Journal of Psychology, 41*, 1956, 185–198.

111. Levinson, Daniel J., and Phyllis E. Huffman, "Traditional Family Ideology and its Relation to Personality," *Journal of Personality, 23*, 1955, 251–273.

112. Mann, Richard D., "The Relation between Personality Characteristics and Individual Performance in Small Groups," Unpublished Ph.D. Dissertation, University of Michigan, 1959.

113. ———, "A Review of the Relationships between Personality and Performance in Small Groups," *Psychologal Bulletin, 56*, 1959, 241–270.

114. ———, with Graham S. Gibbard and John J. Hartman, *Interpersonal Styles and Group Development.* New York: John Wiley & Sons, Inc., 1967.

115. Melvin, D., "An Experimental and Statistical Study of two Primary Social Attitudes," Ph.D. Thesis, University London Library, 1953. Items quoted in H. J. Eysenck, *The Psychology of Politics.* London: Routledge and Kegan Paul, Ltd., 1954.

116. Milgram, Stanley, "Some Conditions of Obedience and Disobedience to Authority," *Human Relations, 18*, 1965, 57–76.

117. Mill, John Stuart, *A System of Logic, Ratiocinative and Inductive; Being a Connected View of the Principles of Evidence and the Methods of Scientific Investigation, Book VI, On the Logic of the Moral Sciences.* London: Longmans, Green & Co., Ltd., 1936.

118. Mills, Theodore M., "A Method of Content Analysis for the Study of Small Groups," Unpublished Ph.D. Dissertation, Harvard University, 1951.

119. ———, "Power Relations in Three-person Groups," *American Sociological Review, 18*, 1953, 351–357.

120. ———, "The Coalition Pattern in Three Person Groups," *American Sociological Review,* 1954.

121. ———, "A Sleeper Variable in Small Group Research: The Experimenter," *Pacific Sociological Review, 5*, no. 1, Spring 1962.

122. ———, *Group Transformation: An Analysis of a Learning Group.* Englewood Cliffs, N.J.: Prentice-Hall, Inc., 1964.

123. Morris, Charles, *Varieties of Human Value.* Chicago: University of Chicago Press, 1956, 15–18.

124. Murray, Henry A., and others, *Explorations in Personality.* New York: Oxford University Press, 1938.

125. Norman, Warren, "Toward an Adequate Taxonomy of Personality Attributes: Replicated Factor Structure in Peer Nomination Personality Ratings," *Journal of Abnormal and Social Psychology, 66*, 1963, 574–583.

126. Olmsted, M. S., "Small Group Interaction as a Function of Group Norms," Unpublished Ph.D. Dissertation, Harvard University, 1952.

127. Osgood, C. E., G. J. Suci, and P. H. Tannenbaum, *The Measurement of Meaning*. Urbana, Ill.: University of Illinois Press, 1957.

128. Parsons, Talcott, Robert F. Bales, and Edward Shils, *Working Papers in the Theory of Action*. New York: The Free Press, 1953. (Chapter III, "The Dimensions of Action Space," by Talcott Parsons and Robert F. Bales; Chapter V, "Phase Movement in Relation to Motivation," Symbol Formation, and Role Structure," by Talcott Parsons, Robert F. Bales, and Edward S. Shils)

129. Perry, William G., "The 'Human Relations' Course in the Curriculum of Liberal Arts," *The Journal of General Education, IX*, no. 1, October 1955, 3-10.

130. Psathas, George, "Phase Movement and Equilibrium in Interaction Process in Psychotherapy Groups," *Sociometry, 23*, 1960, 177–194.

131. Quade, A. E., "The Relationship between Marital Adjustment and Certain Interactional Patterns in Problem Solving Situations," Unpublished Ph.D. Dissertation, Ohio State University, 1955.

132. Redl, Fritz, "Group Emotion and Leadership," *Psychiatry, 5*, 1942, 573–596.

133. Roberts, B. H., and F. L. Strodtbeck, "Interaction Process Differences Between Groups of Paranoid Schizophrenic and Depressed Patients," *International Journal of Group Psychotherapy, 3*, 1953, 29-41.

134. Roethlisberger, F. J., and W. J. Dickson, *Management and the Worker*. Cambridge, Mass.: Harvard University Press, 1939.

135. Ruebhausen, Oscar M., and Orville G. Brim, Jr., "Privacy and Behavioral Science Research," *Columbia Law Review, 64*, November 1965, 1184-1211.

136. Salisbury, M. R., "Judgments of Personality in Decision-Making Groups," Unpublished Ph.D. dissertation, Radcliffe College, 1958.

137. Schachter, S., "Deviation, Rejection and Communication," *Journal of Abnormal and Social Psychology, 46*, 1951, 190-207.

138. Schutz, William C., *FIRO: A Three-Dimensional Theory of Interpersonal Behavior*. New York: Holt, Rinehart and Winston, Inc., 1958.

139. Shepard, Herbert, and Warren Bennis, "A Theory of Training by Group Methods," *Human Relations, 9*, 1956, 403–413.

140. Slater, Philip E., "Psychological Factors in Role Specialization," Unpublished Ph.D. Dissertation, Harvard University, 1955.

141. ———, "Role Differentiation in Small Groups," *American Sociological Review, 20*, 1955, 300-310.

142. ———, *Microcosm, Structural, Psychological, and Religious Evolution in Groups*. New York: John Wiley & Sons, Inc., 1966.

143. ———, Robert F. Bales, "Experimental Groups-Social Session," Unpublished data, 1957.

144. ———, K. Morimoto, and R. W. Hyde, "Social Interaction in Experimental-ly induced Psychotic-Like States," Paper read at American Sociological Society Meetings, Seattle, Washington, 1958.

145. Stephan, F. F., "The Relative Rate of Communication between Members of Small Groups," *American Sociological Review, 17*, 1952, 482-486.

146. ———, E. G. Mishler, "The Distribution of Participation in Small Groups: An Exponential Approximation," *American Sociological Review, 17*, 1952, 598-608.

147. Sorokin, Pitirim, A., *Social and Cultural Dynamics.* New York: American Book Company, 1937.

148. Stone, Philip J., Dexter C. Dunphy, Marshall S. Smith, and Daniel M. Ogilvie, *The General Inquirer: A Computer Approach to Content Analysis.* Cambridge, Mass.: MIT Press, 1966.

149. ———, Robert F. Bales, V. Zvi Namenwirth, and Daniel Ogilvie, "The General Inquirer: A Computer System for Content Analysis and Retrieval Based on the Sentence as a Unit of Information," *Behavioral Science, 7,* no. 4, October 1962, 484-497.

150. Strodtbeck, Fred L., "A Study of Husband-Wife Interaction in Three Cultures," Unpublished Ph.D. Dissertation, Harvard University, 1950.

151. ———, "The Family as a Three-Person Group," *American Sociological Review, 19,* 1954, 23-29.

152. ———, and R. D. Mann, "Sex Role Differentiation in Jury Deliberations," *Sociometry, 19,* 1956, 3-11.

153. Takala, M., T. A. Pihkanen, and T. Markkanen, "The Effects of Distilled and Brewed Beverages: A Physiological, Neurological, ana Psychological Study," *Finnish Foundation for Alcohol Study, 4,* 1957.

154. Talland, G. A., "Task and Interaction Process: Some Characteristics of Therapeutic Group Discussion," *Journal of Abnormal and Social Psychology, 50,* 1955, 105-109.

155. Thomson, G. H., *The Factorial Analysis of Human Ability.* Boston: Houghton Mifflin Company, 1949.

156. Thurstone, L. L., *Multiple Factor Analysis.* Chicago, Ill.: University of Chicago Press, 1947.

157. ———, "The Thurstone Temperament Schedule." Chicago, Ill.: Science Research Associates, Inc.,

158. Waxler, Nancy, and Elliott Mishler, "Scoring and Reliability Problems in Interaction Process Analysis: A Methodological Note," *Sociometry,* no. 1, *29,* March 1966, 28-40.

159. Whiting, John W. M., "Resource Mediation and Learning by Identifica-tion" in I. Iscoe and H. Stevenson (eds.), *Personality Development in Children.* Austin, Tex.: University of Texas, 1960.

160. Winter, Gibson, "Value-Orientations as Factors in the Organization of Small Groups," Unpublished Ph.D. Dissertation, Harvard University, 1952.

161. Zinberg, Norman E., "The Psychiatrist as Group Observer: Notes on Training Procedure in Individual and Group Psychotherapy," in Zinberg, Norman E. (ed.), *Psychiatry and Medical Practice in a General Hospital.* New York: International Universities Press, Inc., 1964.

162. ———, and D. Shapiro, "A Group Approach in the Contexts of Therapy and Education," *Mental Hygiene,* 47:108–116. Reprinted in Zinberg, Norman E. (ed.), *Psychiatry and Medical Practice in a General Hospital,* New York: International Universities, 1964.

Name Index

Subject Index

Abilities, power to idealize, 271; to reduce anxious feeling, 13; as resources of group, 7; *see also* Resources

Acceptance of Authority, Value Profile Factor I, 497, 506–507; used as marker variable, 397, 407; *see also* Autocratic Authority, *Variable,* 407

Acceptance of Authority, *Variable,* 401

Acceptance, need of, 49

Accepting, trait (*see* Radical, *Variable,* 438–439)

Accessible, trait (*see* Suspecting, *Variable,* 449)

Accident, in chain reactions, 151; in dreams and fantasy, 148–150; an element of theory, 149–150

Achievement, and affection, 229; high water marks of, 153; pressure for, and deviance, 229; in reverse directions, 154

Achievement, *Variable,* 402

Act, IPA, bias toward scoring more, 69; complex and compound sentences, 69; defined by category set, 69; definition of, 68; fragmentary acts, 68; grammatical criteria for, 68; nonfocal in address, 70; nonverbal types, 69, 70, 94; and psychodramatic act, 142–144; recording of, 65–66, 91; and simple sentence, 68; and single words, 68; time consumed by, 69; typical sequences of acts, 82; unintentional, 70; unit acts illustrated, 69; *see also* Interaction Process Analysis, Scoring Interaction, Acting-out versus verbalizing, 516

Actions, as anticipating Reactions, 82; association with self-picture, 204; probability of reoccurrence, 49, 150, 162; symbolic, 105

Active, *Variable,* 402

Acts Recieved, IPA, directional indicators for, 489; estimation of profile norms, 488; profile for, 487–488; ratios of to acts initiated, 488–489

Address of interaction, IPA, addressee, how to determine, 66–67; of Attempted Answers, 82; and desire for legitimacy, 86; directional current in, 82; and domination, 85; and fantasy of status mobility, 83, 134; of Friendly acts, 82; to group as a whole, 13; instrumental realism of, 83; of laughter, 82; nonfocal address, 70; and opposition, 86; to particular individuals, 68; to persons of higher rank, 83, 88; to persons of lower rank, 83; and persuasion, 85; political realism of, 83, 87; in presence of third persons, 79; by submissive types, 323; surplus directed upward, 84; to third persons, 67, 79; of unfriendly acts, 82; *see also* Group as a Whole, Interaction Matrix, Scoring Interaction, Sum to I, Sum to 0, Sum Received, Surplus of address upward

Adjustment, by lowering need, 386

Admiration, arousal of, *Variable,* 402

Admiration, for older brother surrogate, 49

Adolescence, and dilemmas of socialization, 301

Adventurous, *Variable,* 403

Affection, deficit in, 218; expended in meeting demands, 229, 256; experienced as feminine, 235; need of, 49; for older brother surrogate, 49; power to elicit, 256; power to feel, 255

Age, and IPA norms, 472

Aggression, Couch's Factor III, 393; courting of, 363; harnessing of, 325; inhibition of, 378; and interpersonal relations, 522; moralistic binding of, 363; need to express, 49; repression of, 270, 375, 384; and tender love, 13; turned against the self, 295; unbinding and displacement of, 363; wish to unmask in others, 363

Aggression, *Variable,* 403

Aggressive, trait, (*see* Dominant, *Variable,* 413)

Agreement, with autocratic authority, 268; uncritical observer bias, 11; written versus verbal form, 203, 204; *see also* Value-statements, initiating vs. agreeing to

Agreement Response Set, *Variable,* 455

Agrees, IPA, definition of category, 109; directional indicators for, 96–97, 487, 490; normal rates of, 96–97; norms, estimation of, 484; receiving, effect of, 79, 210; revision of, 478; and Task Attempts, 82; to whom addressed, 82

Agrees, IPA, *Variable,* 404

Alienation, of self from action, 382

Alliance, bewildering type, 269; failure to form, 43; rule of formation, 37; *see also* Coalition, Unconscious collusion

Aloof, trait (*see* Warm, *Variable,* 456)

Altrustic Love, *Variable,* 405

Analysis, of dreams, 139; of fantasy chains, exercise, 142; functional, 150; of resistance to change, 50; in self-analytic groups, 5; *see also* Interpretation

Anger, and sexual desire, 168

Anomie, duration of, 170

Antagonism, between members of two networks, 44

Anxiety, anchoring of, through punishment, 345; consequences if not reduced, 256; harnessing of, 325; inability to reduce, 287; pervasion of personality by, 345; physiological alarm reaction, 345; reduction of, through approval,

545

Males, location in group space, 46–47; *see also* Masculine facade, Masculine role

Manager, authorized type, 215; interference with satisfaction, 248

Manic, *Variable*, 432

Manipulation, norms against, 515; of persons into roles, 138; by stimulation of fantasy, 306

Masculine facade, and authoritarian personality, 228; and failure in socialization, 235

Masculine role, acceptance of, 212; conventional type, 269, 422; difficulty in assuming, 235

Masculinization, of the female child, 235

Masculinity, fear of losing, 241

Masochism, trait (*see* Feminine Masochism, *Variable*, 422)

Material Success and Power, *Variable*, 433

Mature, *Variable*, 433

Memory, of dream elements, 149

Mirrors, one way, effect on subjects, 360; a focus of fantasy, 148; placement, installation, 528

Misperception, of dislike of others, 354

MMPI, Minnesota Multiphasic Personality Inventory, nonstandard scales, 391; scales used as *Variables*, 398–457

Modesty, in self-rating, 259

Motivation, interdependence with other variables, 168; logic of, 149–150; paralysis of, 334; unconscious, 148

Mourning, and internalization of loved object, 366–367

Movement, cancellation of, 9; in a given direction, 9; maintainence of own preferred direction, 36; reaction to movement of others, 256; and satisfaction, 172; by self-abnegation, 379

Myths, and environment, 148; themes in, 525

Naming, of directional components, 10; of members, by rank order, 74; of members, symbols for scoring, 63

Naturalistic observation, 3, 50, 515

Nature, and fantasy, 153

Need Determined Expression, Value Profile Factor II, 498, 507–508; used as a marker variable, 397, 442; *see* Rugged Individualism and Gratification, *Variable*, 442

Negative direction, formal meaning of, 9

Negative Reactions IPA, subset of categories, 92, 95

Nervous Tension, *Variable*, 433

Networks of address, in communication, 82

Networks of coalitions, failure of integration between, 44; how to locate, 39; how formed, 37; integration of, 45, 47, 211; normal number in group, 47; normal

sizes, 47; as social ladders, 48; and social status, 48; spiral shape of distribution, 47

Neurosis, constrasted with delinquency, 302

Neuroticism, General, trait (*see* Mature, *Variable*, 433)

Neurotic symptoms, and developmental cycles, 176

Norms, group, building of, 82, 210, 277; and external authority, 77; and legitimacy, 170

Obedience, and dissociation from responsibility, 204

Objective in Tone, *Variable*, 434

Observation, versus experimentation, 515; facility for group observation, 148, 526–529; responsibilities of, 517; substituted for interaction, 385; of subjective impressions, 22; training in, 513–514; training situations, 63; training value of, 19; using interaction recorder, 531

Obsessions, and conditional love, 336–337; and splitting of self, 383

Older brother position, and socialization, 49

Opinion, Asks for, IPA, (*see* Asks for Opinion)

Opinion, Asks for, IPA, *Variable*, 434

Opinion, Gives, IPA (*see* Gives Opinion)

Opinion, Gives, IPA, *Variable*, 435

Opposition, and address, 86; child as reconciler of, 251; and repression, 384; types vocally opposed, 216

Optimistic Idealism, *Variable*, 435

Originality, *Variable*, 436

Orthodoxy, differences in content by group, 210; deviant type, 298

Orthogonality, of factors, 61, 264, 497–501; *see also* Factor analysis

Out-group, importance of the boundary, 226–227

Overdetermination, of perceptions, 16

Overexpansiveness, of self-picture, 200–201, 204, 207, 384

Overestimation, of own intellectual understanding, 290; of own popularity, 200–201; of own task value, 193; of warmth of others toward self, 194

Overexposure, emotional, protection from, 515

Overidealization, of positive feelings, 208

Overtalking, to group as a whole, 194

Pairs of members, normal discussion pattern of, 78; silent partners, 380; in strategic locations, 18, 38; as subgroups, 100; unconscious collusion between, 204

Paradoxes, in fit of group role type to person, 11, 14

Paranoid, *Variable*, 436

Parent, image of self as, 12